DIGITAL IDENTITIES, AI ETHICS, AND MENTAL HEALTH

This highly topical book provides an integrated framework for understanding how artificial intelligence, personality traits, gender, and cultural contexts shape youth digital engagement and mental health outcomes.

Grounded in cyberpsychology and extensive empirical research, AI ethics, and developmental psychology, this book addresses the urgent need for evidence-based approaches to supporting young people's well-being in an increasingly AI-mediated digital world. It explores the dual nature of digital technology, offering unique opportunities for connection, learning, and self-expression while simultaneously introducing distinctive risks to mental health and well-being. It examines how personality trait models mediate the effects of cyber behavior on well-being and ethical AI engagement. Further topics include an exploration of AI as an active participant in shaping youth behavior and identity, how personality traits significantly predict resilience to online risks and ethical AI engagement, gender differences in digital engagement creating distinct opportunities and vulnerabilities, cultural contexts fundamentally shaping cyber behaviors and ethical perspectives, and that ethical AI design must prioritize youth developmental vulnerabilities. With actionable recommendations to foster digital well-being and responsible AI use, this book is a comprehensive guide for promoting ethical and psychologically healthy digital practices.

The unique blend of theoretical insights, empirical data, and practical interventions makes this book an essential resource for students and academics in cyberpsychology, social psychology and identity, AI ethics, cyber behavior studies, and mental health. It will also be of interest to mental health professionals, researchers, policymakers, and educators interested in understanding the impact of cyber behaviors on youth well-being.

Areej ElSayary is an Associate Professor and Chair of the General Education department within the College of Interdisciplinary Studies at Zayed University. As an ICF-certified coach, cyberpsychologist, and Mental Health Ambassador, ElSayary's professional practice integrates cyberpsychology and computer-mediated communication within the ICF Code of Ethics and Core Competencies framework. Her academic credentials include recognition as a Senior Fellow of the Higher Education Academy (SFHEA) and certification as an associate of the Blackboard Academy. She has designed and delivered numerous high-impact teacher training programs across the United Arab Emirates, contributing significantly to regional educational advancement. Her research encompasses cognitive development, cyberpsychology, artificial intelligence, human-computer interaction, entrepreneurship, innovation, design thinking, and interdisciplinary education.

Current Issues in Cyberpsychology

Current Issues in Cyberpsychology brings together books that explore the psychology behind human interaction with digital technology, and the impact of the internet on individuals and society as a whole.

It showcases books that will be relevant to both an academic and professional market, bringing together the work of established and emerging authors. The series spans a range of topics relating to cyberpsychology; including the influence of technology on behaviour and attitudes, the effects of social media, human factors in cybersecurity, and digital identities. Ideas for new books are welcome.

For more information about the series, please visit: https://www.routledge.com/our-products/book-series/CIIC

The Psychology of Cybersecurity
Hacking and the Human Mind
Tarnveer Singh and Sarah Y. Zheng

Human Factors and Cybersecurity
The Psychology Behind Online Safety and Security
Lee Hadlington and Chloe Ryding

DIGITAL IDENTITIES, AI ETHICS, AND MENTAL HEALTH

Impacts of Technology on Cyber Behaviors and Personality Traits

Areej ElSayary

Routledge
Taylor & Francis Group
LONDON AND NEW YORK

Designed cover image: Getty Images / BlackJack3D

First published 2027
by Routledge
4 Park Square, Milton Park, Abingdon, Oxon OX14 4RN

and by Routledge
605 Third Avenue, New York, NY 10158

Routledge is an imprint of the Taylor & Francis Group, an informa business

For Product Safety Concerns and Information please contact our EU representative GPSR@taylorandfrancis.com. Taylor & Francis Verlag GmbH, Kaufingerstraße 24, 80331 München, Germany.

British Library Cataloguing-in-Publication Data
A catalogue record for this book is available from the British Library

ISBN: 9781041109624 (hbk)
ISBN: 9781041109600 (pbk)
ISBN: 9781003657590 (ebk)

DOI: 10.4324/9781003657590

Typeset in Times New Roman
by codeMantra

CONTENTS

FIGURES

TABLES

PREFACE

The digital transformation of youth development represents one of the most significant psychological and social shifts of our time. Young people today have grown up entirely within digital environments, forming identities through social media and learning through adaptive algorithms. Yet despite the ubiquity of digital technology, our understanding of its psychological mechanisms and ethical implications remains fragmented across disciplines, leaving educators, parents, policymakers, and practitioners without an integrated framework for supporting healthy digital engagement. This book addresses that critical gap. It brings together cyberpsychology, artificial intelligence, ethics, and digital well-being into a coherent, evidence-based framework that illuminates how digital environments shape youth development. The author recognizes a fundamental truth: digital well-being is not a universal outcome but emerges from complex interactions between technological design, individual psychology, and sociocultural contexts. This means promoting digital well-being requires careful attention to how people with different personalities, genders, and cultural backgrounds experience digital environments differently. It requires understanding how artificial intelligence systems work and committing to ethical design principles.

This book's four-stream conceptual framework, moving from foundational theories to AI mechanisms to individual differences to practical applications, provides readers with both conceptual understanding and actionable guidance. Whether you are an educator, mental health professional, technology developer, policymaker, or parent, this book offers valuable knowledge and practical strategies grounded in current research. What distinguishes this work is its balanced examination of both the genuine benefits and distinctive risks of digital technology. The author presents a detailed analysis of how digital platforms offer unprecedented opportunities for connection and learning while simultaneously introducing risks to mental health and well-being. This book examines how recommendation algorithms can enhance personalized learning while creating filter bubbles, how social media can foster community while facilitating cyberbullying, and how artificial intelligence can expand access to mental health support while raising questions about privacy and autonomy. Most importantly, the authors emphasize that understanding these dynamics requires attention to individual differences. Personality traits, gender, and cultural background significantly moderate how young people experience digital environments and respond to risks. These differences mean that interventions must be tailored, not one-size-fits-all. This book is also grounded in a commitment to the United Nations' Sustainable Development Goals, connecting digital well-being to Quality Education for All and Good Health and Well-Being. This book arrives at a critical moment. As artificial intelligence becomes increasingly integrated into social media, education, and mental health care, the urgency of developing ethical frameworks and evidence-based interventions has never been greater. The author brings together expertise from psychology, technology, education, and ethics to create a work that is both scholarly and practically accessible. This book is designed to serve multiple audiences with different needs and time constraints, offering flexibility combined with clear writing and evidence-based content. As we navigate an increasingly complex digital landscape, this book offers both hope and realism. It demonstrates that while digital technology presents genuine challenges to youth mental health, these challenges are not inevitable. Through ethical design, informed policy, and attention to individual differences, we can create digital environments that promote flourishing. I commend this book to all who are committed to helping young people thrive in the digital age.

Areej ElSayary

STREAM 1

Digital Identity and Psychological Impact

1

INTRODUCTION – THE DIGITAL AGE AND ITS IMPACT ON YOUTH

Objectives of This Chapter

- To provide a comprehensive overview of the transformative impact of digital technology on young people's lives, illustrating the dual nature of digital interactions that can foster both positive and negative outcomes.
- To establish the four-stream conceptual framework that organizes this book and guides readers through the integration of theory, mechanisms, individual differences, and applications.
- To examine how personality traits, gender, and cultural context shape digital experiences, resilience, and vulnerability in AI-mediated environments.
- To connect digital well-being to the UN's Sustainable Development Goals, emphasizing the importance of ethical AI education and digital literacy.
- To provide readers with a roadmap for navigating the book and understanding how each chapter contributes to a comprehensive understanding of cyberpsychology, AI ethics, and digital well-being.

Topics to Be Addressed

- The Transformative Power of Digital Technology
- The Dual Nature of Digital Technology: Opportunities and Risks
- Defining Cyberpsychology, AI Ethics, and Digital Well-being
- UN Sustainable Development Goals and Digital Well-being
- The Four-Stream Conceptual Framework: From Theory to Application to Future Vision
- Key Themes that Integrate Across All Chapters
- How to Use This Book: A Reader's Guide

DOI: 10.4324/9781003657590-2

1.1 Introduction: The Transformative Power of Digital Technology

Young people today inhabit a world fundamentally transformed by digital technology. Unlike previous generations, who encountered the internet as a novel addition to their lives, today's youth have grown up entirely within digital environments (Davis & Subramaniam, 2022). They form identities through social media, learn through adaptive algorithms, navigate relationships mediated by screens, and develop their sense of self through feedback loops designed by artificial intelligence (AI). This transformation is not merely technological; it is profoundly psychological, social, and ethical (Ho & Vuong, 2025).

Digital platforms offer unprecedented opportunities for young people. These environments enable self-expression through carefully curated profiles, creative content creation, and identity exploration (Avci et al., 2025). They provide global connectivity, allowing young people to form relationships across geographic and cultural boundaries, to find communities of shared interest and identity, and to access support networks that may be unavailable in their immediate physical environments (Hamilton et al., 2024). Cyberspaces offer access to vast repositories of information and learning resources, enabling young people to pursue knowledge, develop digital skills, and gain exposure to diverse perspectives that broaden their worldviews (Tsouparopoulou et al., 2025). For many young people, particularly those in marginalized communities, digital platforms provide opportunities for voice, visibility, and participation that would otherwise be unavailable (Davis et al., 2024).

Yet this same digital transformation introduces distinctive challenges and risks. Young people are increasingly exposed to cyberbullying, harassment, and cyber abuse that can profoundly affect their mental health and sense of safety (Buchan et al., 2024). They encounter misinformation and disinformation that can distort their understanding of reality and shape their beliefs and values. They face privacy concerns as their personal data is collected, analyzed, and used by corporations and other actors without their full understanding or consent (Lahti et al., 2024). They are exposed to AI-driven biases embedded in algorithmic systems that shape what they see, what opportunities are presented to them, and how they are categorized and treated. These risks can lead to adverse mental health outcomes, including anxiety, depression, social withdrawal, and, in severe cases, self-harm (Chang et al., 2025).

The challenge before us is not to reject digital technology; it will continue to shape youth development regardless, but to understand this transformation deeply and to ensure that digital environments are designed and governed in ways that maximize benefits while minimizing harms (Weigle & Shafi, 2023). This requires understanding the psychological phenomena emerging from digital engagement, the mechanisms through which AI shapes behavior, the individual and cultural differences that determine who is vulnerable and who is resilient, and the practical strategies through which we can promote digital well-being (Mayiwar et al., 2024).

> ***Takeaway:*** *Digital technology presents a dual nature, offering unprecedented opportunities for connection, learning, and self-expression while simultaneously introducing distinctive risks to youth mental health and well-being.*
> ***Reflection:*** *What positive and negative impacts of digital technology have you observed in young people's lives?*

1.2 The Dual Nature of Digital Technology: Opportunities and Risks

Digital technologies in education embody this duality by harnessing AI to personalize learning pathways and foster inclusive engagement, while simultaneously amplifying vulnerabilities through opaque algorithmic curation and data-driven profiling that can exacerbate inequities (Ma & Jiang, 2023). This duality highlights the necessity for a structured framework that balances AI's potential to enhance educational equity with proactive measures to address its inherent risks in shaping youth development (Nesi et al., 2022; Odgers & Jensen, 2020). The section discusses the positive outcomes of AI integration (Cerioli, 2026) and the adverse impacts (Hasse, 2019; Odgers & Jensen, 2020).

1.2.1 Positive Outcomes: Building Skills, Connection, and Well-being

Digital platforms offer genuine benefits for young people's development and well-being. These benefits extend across multiple dimensions of youth experience. For example, self-expression and identity development are facilitated by AI chatbots that enhance communication skills and provide mental health support, enabling vulnerable youth to explore therapeutic interactions and access early interventions for behavioral health concerns (Hasse et al., 2019; Teubner & Ivey, 2025). Additionally, digital environments provide spaces where young people can experiment with identity, explore different aspects of themselves, and present themselves to the world in ways that feel authentic (Opie et al., 2024). Furthermore, social media platforms, online communities, and creative platforms enable young people to express themselves through text, images, video, and other media (Avci et al., 2024). For many young people, particularly those navigating marginalized identities, cyberspaces provide opportunities to explore identity in relative safety and to connect with others who share similar experiences (Elvira-Zorzo & Gómez, 2025).

Another positive outcome is global connectivity and community building, where digital platforms transcend geographic boundaries, enabling young people to form meaningful relationships with peers worldwide (Davis et al., 2024). This is because online communities organized around shared interests, identities, or values provide a sense of belonging and support (Tsouparopoulou et al., 2025). For young people in isolated communities or those with rare interests or identities, digital connection can be life-changing, providing access to community and support that would be unavailable in their physical environments (Hamilton et al., 2024).

Also, access to information and learning opportunities is considered another outcome. Digital platforms provide unprecedented access to educational resources, enabling young people to pursue learning independently, access educational content regardless of their geographic location or socioeconomic status, and develop digital skills essential to contemporary life (Afzal et al., 2023). This also leads to the adaptive learning technologies that can personalize education to individual needs, providing customized feedback and support (Yaseen et al., 2025). Such tailored educational experiences promote resilience and self-efficacy among youth by equipping them with adaptive digital competencies that support mental health management and foster positive developmental trajectories (Bhattacharya, 2019; Kickbusch & Holly, 2023).

1.2.2 Adverse Impacts: Risks to Mental Health and Well-being

Yet these same digital environments introduce significant risks that can undermine youth mental health and well-being. For instance, cyberbullying and cyber harassment are considered risk factors for youth in cyberspace (Schulz et al., 2025). The permanence, reach, and audience of digital communication create distinctive forms of bullying. Cyberbullying can follow young people home, occurring 24/7 rather than being confined to school or other physical spaces (Wiederhold, 2024). Harmful content can be widely shared, reach large audiences, and persist indefinitely. The anonymity of digital platforms can embolden perpetrators, leading to more severe harassment than might occur in face-to-face contexts (Bright & Dyck, 2011).

Another risk to youth mental health is information and disinformation. Young people, whose critical thinking skills are still developing, are particularly vulnerable to false or misleading information encountered online (Weigle & Shafi, 2023). Algorithmic systems that prioritize engagement often amplify emotionally charged, sensational, or false content (Seo & Ahn, 2025). Exposure to misinformation can distort young people's understanding of reality, shape their beliefs and values, and influence their decision-making on important issues (Tsouparopoulou et al., 2025).

In addition, privacy concerns and data exploitation are set as another risk factor. Young people often lack full awareness of how their personal data is collected, stored, and used (Buchan et al., 2024). Corporations harvest vast amounts of data on young people's behavior, preferences, and relationships, using it for targeted advertising, behavioral prediction, and other purposes (Pangrazio & Selwyn, 2023). This data collection raises concerns about privacy violations, surveillance, and the potential for misuse or exploitation of data. These pervasive data practices can erode trust in digital ecosystems, fostering anxiety and a diminished sense of agency among youth as they navigate environments where their digital footprints are commodified without meaningful consent or control (Shaigerova et al., 2021).

Moreover, AI-driven biases and algorithmic discrimination are another risk. AI systems embedded in digital platforms are trained on data that often reflects historical biases and inequalities (Ahmed, 2025). These systems can perpetuate and amplify discrimination based on race, gender, socioeconomic status, disability, and other characteristics (Buckley et al., 2025). Young people from marginalized groups may experience algorithmic discrimination that limits their opportunities or exposes them to harmful stereotypes (Ahmmad et al., 2025). Such discriminatory outcomes not only exacerbate mental health disparities but also undermine the developmental potential of affected youth by reinforcing exclusionary dynamics within ostensibly inclusive cyberspaces (Maltby et al., 2024; Tamrakar et al., 2023).

Finally, these risks lead to mental illness consequences. Research increasingly documents the mental health impacts of digital engagement. For example, excessive screen time, social comparison on social media, cyberbullying, and exposure to harmful content are associated with increased rates of anxiety, depression, sleep disturbance, and, in severe cases, self-harm and suicidal ideation (Naik & Behera, 2025; Myhr et al., 2020; Weigle & Shafi, 2023). The relationship between digital engagement and mental health is complex and varies depending on how technology is used and on individual user characteristics (Loblay et al., 2023; Layte et al., 2023). These adverse effects are compounded by AI-driven platforms that exploit psychological vulnerabilities through addictive design elements, dark patterns, and manipulative algorithms, thereby hijacking mental autonomy and precipitating compulsive behaviors, addiction, anxiety, depression, sleep disorders, anhedonia, and suicidal ideation among prolonged users (Dey et al., 2024; McCarthy-Jones, 2019). These manipulative mechanisms in AI-driven platforms further erode the "human touch" essential for therapeutic interactions, as users risk developing emotional dependency that disrupts real-world relational development and coping skills (Petersson & Käll, 2025; Ardabili & Riley, 2025). Consequently, institutional frameworks must integrate ethical safeguards, such as youth co-design of privacy policies and bias audits, to balance AI's mental health potential against these relational disruptions (Anderson & Fort, 2024; Figueroa et al., 2025).

Takeaway: *Digital technology presents a genuine dual nature, offering real benefits for learning, connection, and development while simultaneously introducing distinctive risks to mental health, privacy, and well-being.*
Reflection: *How can we maximize the benefits of digital technology while protecting young people from its risks?*

1.3 Defining the Core Domains: Cyberpsychology, AI Ethics, and Digital Well-Being

This book brings together three interconnected domains to address this question. Understanding each domain and how they relate to one another is essential for comprehending the material that follows.

Cyberpsychology is a scientific, interdisciplinary domain that examines the psychological phenomena emerging from human interaction with digital technology, particularly the internet (Ancis, 2020; Fortuna, 2023). It includes how individuals perceive themselves and others online, how they form identities and relationships through digital media, how their behavior is influenced by technological design, and how their psychological well-being is affected by digital engagement (Fortuna, 2023; Walter, 2024). Cyberpsychology is not simply the study of technology use; it is the study of human psychology as it manifests in, is shaped by, and shapes digital environments (Fortuna, 2023; Kelly et al., 2024). The field emerged from the recognition that cyber behavior is not merely offline behavior transferred to a digital medium. Instead, the unique characteristics of cyberspace, anonymity, psychological distance, disinhibition, the ability to manage multiple identities, and the permanence of digital communication create distinctive psychological phenomena (Suler, 2005; Wang, 2023). A person who is reserved and cautious in face-to-face interactions may become disinhibited and aggressive online (Roos, 2021). An individual struggling with self-esteem may construct an idealized digital identity that generates both connection and distress (Syrjämäki et al., 2024). Young people may form meaningful relationships with peers they have never met in person, yet experience profound loneliness despite constant digital connection (Dadi et al., 2024). Cyberpsychology provides the theoretical and empirical foundation for understanding these phenomena. It draws on established psychological theories, personality psychology, social psychology, developmental psychology, and clinical psychology, and applies them to digital contexts (Ancis, 2020). It also develops new theories specific to digital environments, such as the concept of the cybernetic self, which describes identity as continuously constructed and reconstructed through feedback loops in cyberspaces (Fortuna, 2023). Cyberpsychology examines cyber behaviors, aggressive, addictive, and social-commercial, that characterize different patterns of digital engagement (Ancis, 2020).

AI ethics is the field concerned with ensuring that AI systems are developed, deployed, and governed in ways that align with human values, protect human rights, and promote human flourishing (ElSayary, 2025; Radanliev et al., 2024). It addresses fundamental questions: *What principles should guide AI development? Who bears responsibility for AI outcomes? How can we ensure fairness, transparency, and accountability in algorithmic systems? What safeguards are necessary to prevent harm?* AI ethics is not a constraint on innovation; it is a framework for ensuring that innovation serves human welfare. It recognizes that AI systems are not neutral tools (Konidena et al., 2024). They embody values, make decisions that affect human lives, and shape the information environments in which people form beliefs and make choices (Papadopoulou & Lampropoulou, 2025). When AI systems are designed without ethical consideration, they can amplify biases, manipulate behavior, erode privacy, and concentrate power in the hands of those who control the technology (Radanliev, 2025). For young people, AI ethics is particularly urgent. Adolescents are still developing the cognitive capacities to recognize manipulation, resist influence, and make autonomous choices (Gliksman et al., 2025). They are also navigating critical periods of identity development, making them especially vulnerable to algorithmic shaping of their self-concept. An ethical approach to AI in youth-oriented platforms requires not just technical safeguards but a commitment to prioritizing young people's autonomy, dignity, and well-being over engagement metrics and profit (Schweiger, 2025).

Digital well-being refers to the state of psychological, social, and physical health that individuals experience in relation to their use of digital technologies (Dennis, 2021). It encompasses not just the absence of harm, including the prevention of cyberbullying, addiction, and privacy violations, but also the presence of positive outcomes: meaningful connection, creative expression, learning and growth, and a sense of agency and control (Büchi, 2024). Digital well-being recognizes that technology is neither inherently good nor bad; its impact depends on how it is designed, used, and embedded in context (Büchi, 2021; Mayiwar et al., 2024). The same social media platform that enables a marginalized youth to find community and support can also expose another young person to harassment and comparison (Adorjan & Berman, 2022; Villamil & Heshmati, 2023). The same adaptive learning system that helps a struggling student can undermine another student's confidence and independence. The same AI recommendation algorithm that connects someone with helpful information can also trap them in an echo chamber of misinformation (Pelánek, 2024; Salameh, 2024). Promoting digital well-being, therefore, requires attention to individual differences. It requires understanding how personality traits, gender, cultural background, and other factors shape both vulnerability and resilience in digital environments (Davis et al., 2024; Mayiwar et al., 2024). It requires designing technologies with awareness of these differences and developing interventions tailored to specific needs and contexts (Freed et al., 2025). This interdisciplinary integration of cyberpsychology, AI ethics, and digital well-being principles underpins the proposed framework, ensuring that human-AI collaboration in education fosters youth autonomy and mitigates risks such as algorithmic bias and privacy vulnerabilities (Shouli et al., 2025).

> ***Takeaway:*** *Cyberpsychology, AI ethics, and digital well-being are interconnected domains that together provide a comprehensive framework for understanding and promoting healthy, ethical digital engagement.*
> ***Reflection:*** *How do these three domains relate to challenges you have observed in young people's digital lives?*

1.4 Connecting to UN Sustainable Development Goals and Digital Well-Being

This book aligns with the United Nations' Sustainable Development Goals (SDGs), particularly two goals directly relevant to digital well-being and youth development.

SDG 4: Quality Education for All is the fourth Sustainable Development Goal, emphasizing the importance of ensuring inclusive and equitable quality education and promoting lifelong learning opportunities for all. Digital well-being is integral to achieving this goal (United Nations, 2015). Young people cannot benefit fully from educational opportunities if they are experiencing cyberbullying, anxiety, or other mental health challenges related to digital engagement (Tsouparopoulou et al., 2025). Moreover, digital literacy and ethical AI education are essential components of contemporary education, equipping young people with the skills necessary to navigate digital environments safely and ethically (Berardinetti et al., 2025). This book emphasizes the importance of integrating digital literacy programs and ethical AI education into educational curricula. These programs should teach young people to recognize misinformation, understand how algorithms work, protect their privacy, resist manipulation, and make ethical decisions in cyberspaces (Alenezi & Alfaleh, 2024). Equipping young people with these skills supports their ability to benefit from digital learning opportunities while protecting their well-being.

SDG 3: Good Health and Well-being is the third Sustainable Development Goal and emphasizes the importance of ensuring healthy lives and promoting well-being for all (United Nations, 2015). Mental health is a critical component of well-being, and digital engagement significantly affects youth mental health (Hamilton et al., 2024). This book examines the mental health impacts of digital technology, both positive and negative, and proposes strategies for promoting digital well-being as a component of overall youth health. The book advocates for digital well-being as a core component of mental health promotion and prevention efforts. This includes designing digital environments that support rather than undermine mental health, providing mental health support to young people experiencing digital-related distress, and ensuring that AI systems used in mental health contexts are designed ethically and with attention to young people's well-being. Connecting digital well-being to the UN SDGs emphasizes that this is not merely a technical or individual issue but a matter of global importance. Promoting digital well-being is essential for achieving equitable, inclusive, and sustainable development. It requires coordinated action across multiple sectors, including education, health, technology, and policy, and commitment from all stakeholders to prioritize young people's well-being, autonomy, and rights in cyberspace (AlBuhairan et al., 2023).

> ***Takeaway:*** *Digital well-being is integral to achieving the UN's Sustainable Development Goals, particularly those related to quality education and good health and well-being.*
>
> ***Reflection:*** *How can we ensure that digital technologies support rather than undermine progress toward the Sustainable Development Goals?*

1.5 The Four-Stream Conceptual Framework

This book is organized around four conceptual streams that build on one another, each contributing essential understanding toward the overall goal of promoting digital well-being through ethical AI and informed cyberpsychology.

1.5.1 *Stream 1: Foundational Theories and Concepts (Chapters 2 and 3)*

The first stream establishes the theoretical and conceptual foundations necessary for understanding cyber behavior and identity. *Chapter 1* introduces the definitions, relationships, and proposed framework in which the book is structured. *Chapter 2* examines the fundamental psychological theories that explain how people behave in digital environments, including cyberpsychology as a foundational framework, the theory of planned behavior, social cognitive theory, and personality psychology. It introduces the taxonomy of cyber behaviors, aggressive, addictive, and social-commercial, that recurs throughout the book. *Chapter 3* explores how digital identity is formed and continuously reconstructed through online interaction. It introduces the concept of the cybernetic self, which describes identity as a fluid, feedback-driven process rather than a fixed entity. This chapter establishes that identity formation in cyberspaces is not simply a reflection of offline identity but a distinctive process shaped by the unique affordances of digital environments and increasingly mediated by AI.

Question answered: *What are the psychological and social processes through which people experience and behave in digital environments?*

1.5.2 *Stream 2: AI Mechanisms and Mental Health Implications (Chapters 4–6)*

The second stream shifts focus from human psychology to technological architecture, examining how AI systems shape cyber behavior and what psychological and ethical implications emerge from this shaping. *Chapter 4* provides a detailed analysis of the core mechanisms by which AI systems influence behavior: recommendation algorithms that determine what users see, feedback loops that reinforce behavioral patterns, and engagement-optimization techniques designed to maximize time on the platform. This chapter establishes the concept of the AI-behavior nexus, showing that AI is not a passive tool but an active architect of digital experiences. *Chapter 5* examines the mental health consequences of AI-mediated cyber behavior. It explores how algorithmic personalization, social comparison, cyberbullying, and other digital phenomena affect psychological well-being, with particular attention to how individual differences in personality traits moderate these effects. This chapter establishes that the mental health impacts of digital engagement are not uniform; they depend on who the person is and how their psychology interacts with technological design. *Chapter 6* addresses the ethical imperative: how can AI systems be designed and governed to protect mental health and promote well-being? It establishes foundational ethical principles, including transparency, fairness, consent, and accountability, and shows how these principles translate into concrete design practices and governance structures.

Question answered: *How do AI systems shape behavior, what are the mental health implications, and what ethical principles should guide their design?*

1.5.3 Stream 3: Individual and Cultural Differences (Chapters 7–9)

The third stream recognizes that digital experiences and vulnerabilities are not universal. They are profoundly shaped by individual differences and cultural context. This stream examines how personality traits, gender, and culture influence cyber behavior, mental health outcomes, and responses to AI systems. *Chapter 7* explores personality psychology in digital contexts, examining how the Big Five traits (neuroticism, conscientiousness, openness to experience, extraversion, and agreeableness) and the HEXACO model help explain why people behave differently online and respond differently to AI systems. It shows that personality is not a minor variable but a fundamental determinant of digital resilience and vulnerability. Young people high in neuroticism may experience greater anxiety when confronted with cyberbullying, while those high in conscientiousness may be more resistant to algorithmic manipulation. Understanding these patterns enables the design of personality-aware interventions and support systems. *Chapter 8* examines gender as a structural factor shaping digital experience. It explores how gendered patterns of socialization, communication styles, and risk-taking influence cyber behavior, mental health outcomes, and exposure to both opportunities and risks in digital environments. It emphasizes that gender differences are not merely preferences but reflect systemic inequalities embedded in both digital design and social structures. Young women, for example, often experience higher rates of cyberbullying and sexual harassment online, while young men may be more exposed to aggressive and extremist content. *Chapter 9* analyzes how cultural values, norms, and ethical frameworks shape cyber behavior and attitudes toward AI. It compares collectivist and individualist cultures, examines how privacy is understood differently across cultural contexts, and explores how cultural competence is essential for developing AI systems that are ethical and acceptable across diverse societies. The chapter emphasizes that digital well-being cannot be understood through a single cultural lens; it must be examined in relation to the specific values, norms, and ethical frameworks of different cultural communities.

Question answered: *How do individual differences in personality, gender, and culture shape digital experiences, vulnerabilities, and resilience?*

1.5.4 Stream 4: Applications, Interventions, and Future Directions (Chapters 10–12)

The fourth stream moves from understanding to action, examining how insights from cyberpsychology and AI ethics can be applied to promote digital well-being through education, parenting, policy, and design. *Chapter 10* provides practical strategies for promoting digital well-being and ethical AI use. It examines the roles of educators, parents, policymakers, and technology developers in creating safer, more ethical digital environments. It offers evidence-based interventions to address specific challenges such as misinformation, cyberbullying, and screen overuse. The chapter emphasizes the importance of digital literacy programs and ethical AI education as core components of educational curricula, equipping young people with the skills to navigate ethical challenges in cyberspaces and make informed decisions. *Chapter 11* synthesizes emerging findings in cyberpsychology and AI ethics, highlighting key trends that are reshaping youth digital engagement. It emphasizes the importance of personality-aware, gender-responsive, and culturally sensitive approaches to digital well-being. It also examines the ethical frameworks that should guide the development of AI in youth mental health, ensuring that these systems prioritize young people's well-being and autonomy. *Chapter 12* looks forward, exploring future trajectories of AI in social media, education, and mental health. It examines how personality traits and gender will continue to shape digital resilience and vulnerability. It proposes proactive ethical frameworks for ensuring that future digital environments promote flourishing rather than harm.

Question answered: *How can we apply insights from cyberpsychology and AI ethics to create digital environments that promote well-being, protect vulnerable populations, and foster ethical engagement?*

The four-stream framework provides a comprehensive progression from foundational understanding through analysis of AI mechanisms and individual differences to practical applications and future directions, as shown in Figure 1.1. This framework explains how these four streams connect to create a coherent understanding of digital well-being.

1.6 Key Themes That Integrate across All Chapters

Although each chapter addresses specific topics, several themes recur throughout the book, creating conceptual coherence and emphasizing their importance:

Theme 1: The AI-Behavior Nexus. AI is not a passive tool that responds to user needs. Rather, AI systems actively architect the conditions for behavior. Recommendation algorithms determine what users see, feedback loops reinforce behavioral patterns, and engagement optimization techniques shape how long people remain online. Understanding this AI-behavior nexus is essential for

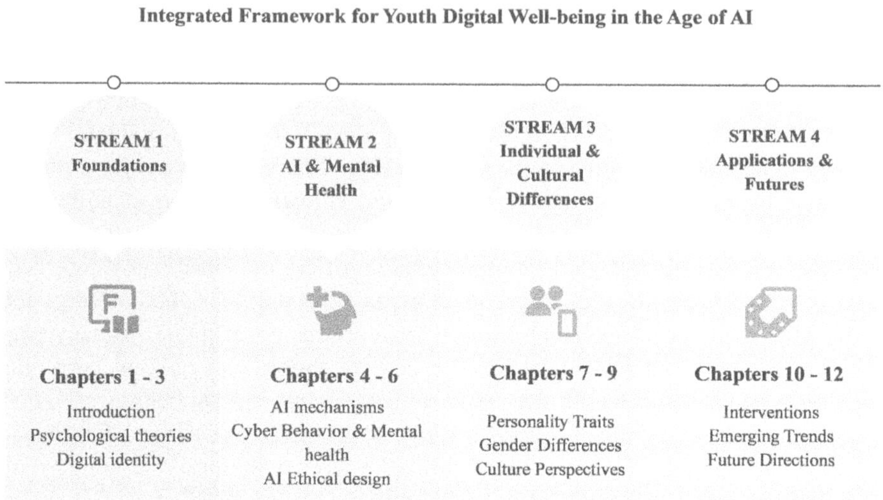

FIGURE 1.1 An integrated framework for youth digital well-being and how it was structured in this book.

recognizing that cyber behavior is not simply a matter of individual choice but is profoundly influenced by technological design.

Theme 2: Individual Differences as Determinants of Digital Resilience and Vulnerability. Digital experiences and outcomes are not uniform. Personality traits, gender, and cultural background fundamentally shape how individuals experience digital environments, what risks they face, and what resources they draw on for resilience. Personality traits influence susceptibility to cyberbullying, compulsive use, and manipulation. Gender shapes communication styles, platform preferences, and exposure to specific risks. Cultural values influence attitudes toward privacy, trust in AI, and ethical reasoning about digital engagement.

Theme 3: The Cybernetic Self and Continuous Identity Construction. In digital environments, identity is not a fixed entity but a fluid, continuously reconstructed process. The cybernetic self emerges through feedback loops in which online interactions generate responses that individuals internalize and incorporate into their self-concept. AI systems increasingly mediate these feedback loops, shaping not just what people see but how they see themselves. Understanding identity formation in digital contexts requires attention to these dynamic processes.

Theme 4: The Dual Nature of Digital Technologies. Digital technologies and AI systems have dual capacities. They can foster connection or isolation, enable learning or create dependency, support autonomy or undermine it, promote well-being or harm it. The outcome depends on how systems are designed, how they are used, and the context in which they are embedded. This duality means that promoting digital well-being requires not rejecting technology but ensuring it is designed and governed ethically.

Theme 5: Ethics as Central, Not Peripheral. Ethical considerations are not an afterthought or a constraint on innovation. They are central to ensuring that digital technologies serve human welfare. Ethical design means prioritizing user well-being over engagement metrics, transparency over opacity, autonomy over manipulation, and fairness over bias. For young people, whose developing capacities make them especially vulnerable to technological influence. Ethical design is not optional; it is essential.

Theme 6: Multistakeholder Collaboration. Promoting digital well-being requires collaboration among technology developers, educators, parents, policymakers, mental health professionals, and young people themselves. No single stakeholder can address the complexity of digital well-being alone. Developers must design ethically, educators must teach digital literacy and ethics, parents must model healthy digital engagement, policymakers must establish protective regulations, and young people must be empowered to participate in decisions that affect their digital lives.

1.7 How This Book Is Organized – A Comprehensive Reader's Guide

This book is designed to serve multiple audiences with different needs, interests, and levels of expertise. The following section provides five distinct reading pathways tailored to your background, goals, and learning preferences. Choose the pathway that best aligns with your needs, or combine elements from multiple pathways to create a customized reading experience.

1.7.1 Pathway 1: Sequential Reading for New Learners

This pathway is ideal for students, researchers, and professionals new to cyberpsychology and AI ethics who want a comprehensive understanding of all concepts and their interconnections. It is advisable to read chapters in order, building foundational knowledge progressively. Table 1.1 presents a sequential reading schedule that organizes the book into four phases, each building on previous knowledge. *Chapters 2 and 3* (Foundations) establish the psychological theories and conceptual frameworks necessary to understand all subsequent material. These chapters introduce fundamental concepts, including the Big Five personality traits, social cognitive theory, the theory of planned behavior, and the concept of the cybernetic self. Without these foundations, later chapters may be difficult to comprehend, as they build on the theoretical frameworks established here. The time invested in thoroughly understanding these foundational chapters will pay dividends as you progress through the book.

Chapters 4 and 6 (AI & Mental Health) build directly on the foundations established in Chapters 2 and 3, showing how AI systems interact with the psychological

TABLE 1.1 Sequential Reading Schedule

Phase	*Chapters*	*Duration*	*Learning Focus*	*Key Outcomes*
Phase 1: Foundations	Chapters 2 and 3	Two to three weeks	Psychological theories and digital identity concepts	Understand basic psychological frameworks and how identity forms in cyberspaces
Phase 2: AI & Mental Health	Chapters 4–6	Three to four weeks	AI mechanisms, mental health impacts, ethical design	Understand how AI systems work and their psychological effects
Phase 3: Individual Differences	Chapters 7–9	Two to three weeks	Personality, gender, and cultural factors	Understand how individual differences shape digital experiences
Phase 4: Applications & Futures	Chapters 10–12	Two to three weeks	Practical interventions and future directions	Apply insights to real-world contexts and anticipate future developments

processes described in the earlier chapters. Chapter 4 explains the mechanisms through which AI shapes behavior, including recommendation algorithms, feedback loops, and engagement optimization. Chapter 5 examines the mental health consequences of these mechanisms, exploring how they affect different individuals differently depending on personality traits and other factors. Chapter 6 addresses the ethical imperative, establishing principles and practices for designing AI systems that protect mental health and promote well-being. These chapters demonstrate that understanding AI's impact requires grounding in psychological theory.

Chapters 7–9 (Individual Differences) apply the frameworks from earlier chapters to specific populations, showing how personality, gender, and culture moderate the effects of AI systems on mental health. Chapter 7 examines personality traits as determinants of digital resilience and vulnerability, explaining why some individuals are more susceptible to cyberbullying while others are more resistant to algorithmic manipulation. Chapter 8 explores gender as a structural factor shaping digital experience, examining gendered patterns in online behavior and exposure to risks. Chapter 9 analyzes cultural differences in digital engagement and attitudes toward AI, emphasizing that digital well-being cannot be understood through a single cultural lens. These chapters demonstrate that promoting digital well-being requires attention to individual and cultural differences.

Chapters 10–12 (Applications & Futures) translate theoretical understanding into practical strategies and future scenarios, requiring knowledge from all previous chapters. Chapter 10 provides evidence-based interventions for promoting digital well-being through education, parenting, and policy. Chapter 11 synthesizes emerging findings in cyberpsychology and AI ethics, highlighting key trends reshaping youth digital engagement. Chapter 12 explores future trajectories of AI in social media, education, and mental health, and proposes proactive ethical frameworks to ensure that future digital environments promote flourishing. These final chapters show how the theoretical and conceptual understanding developed in earlier chapters can be applied to real-world challenges and opportunities.

It is recommended to allocate 10–13 weeks for complete sequential reading with time for reflection and integration of concepts. This pace allows approximately five hours per week of reading and reflection, providing adequate time to engage deeply with the material, complete the reflection questions at the end of each section, and consider how concepts apply to your own experiences and interests. This sequential approach is particularly valuable if you are new to these fields and want to develop a comprehensive, integrated understanding of how cyberpsychology, AI ethics, and digital well-being interconnect.

1.7.2 Pathway 2: Topic-Focused Navigation

This pathway is ideal for professionals, practitioners, and researchers with specific interests who want targeted knowledge in particular areas without having to read the entire book. Topic-focused navigation lets you identify chapters that address your primary interests and read them in a sequence that builds understanding progressively. However, it is strongly recommended to read Chapters 2 and 3 (Foundations) first, as they provide essential conceptual frameworks that make specialized topics more meaningful and comprehensible. Table 1.2 presents the reading guide by interest. To use this guide effectively, first identify your primary interest from the left column. Then read the recommended foundational chapters listed in the third column, as these provide essential conceptual frameworks. Once you have established these foundations, read the core chapters listed in the second column, which directly address your area of interest. Finally, explore the supplementary chapters listed in the fourth column to deepen your understanding and see how your topic of interest connects to other areas of the book.

For example, if your primary interest is Personality and Cyber behavior, you would begin by reading Chapters 2 and 3 to establish a foundational understanding of personality psychology and digital identity. You would then read Chapter 7, which directly examines how personality traits influence cyber behavior and resilience. Finally, you might read Chapter 5 to understand the impacts on mental health, Chapter 8 to see how gender interacts with personality in shaping the digital experience, Chapter 9 to understand cultural differences in personality expression, and

TABLE 1.2 Topic Navigation Guide

Primary Interest	*Core Chapters*	*Recommended Foundations*	*Supplementary Chapters*
Personality & Cyber Behavior	Chapter 7	Chapters 2–3	Chapters 5, 8–9
Gender Differences Online	Chapter 8	Chapters 2–3	Chapters 5, 7, 10
Cultural Perspectives	Chapter 9	Chapters 2–3	Chapters 6–7, 10
Mental Health & Well-being	Chapters 5 and 6	Chapters 2–4	Chapters 7–9, 10–11
AI Mechanisms	Chapter 4	Chapters 2–3	Chapters 5–6
Educational AI	Chapter 12 (Section 12.3)	Chapters 2–4, 6	Chapters 7–9, 10
Parenting & Digital Literacy	Chapter 10	Chapters 2–3, 5	Chapters 7–9, 11
Ethical Frameworks	Chapter 6	Chapters 2–5	Chapters 7–9, 10–12
Future Trends	Chapter 12	Chapters 2–6	Chapters 7–11

Chapter 10 to learn about personality-aware interventions. This sequence would give you a comprehensive understanding of your topic while connecting it to the broader framework of the book.

Similarly, if your primary interest is Mental Health and Well-being, you would begin with Chapters 2–4 to understand psychological theories, AI mechanisms, and their interactions. You would then read Chapters 5 and 6, which directly address mental health impacts and ethical design for mental health protection. Finally, you might read Chapters 7–9 to understand how personality, gender, and culture influence mental health outcomes in digital contexts, and Chapters 10 and 11 to learn about interventions and emerging trends in digital mental health.

The beauty of topic-focused navigation is that it allows you to develop deep expertise in your area of interest while maintaining a connection to the book's broader conceptual framework. By reading the foundational chapters first, you ensure that your specialized knowledge is grounded in solid theoretical understanding. By exploring supplementary chapters, you see how your topic connects to other important areas. This approach typically requires four to six weeks of reading, depending on how many supplementary chapters you choose to explore.

1.7.3 Pathway 3: Educational & Training Curriculum

This pathway is ideal for educators, trainers, and instructors who use this book in courses, workshops, or professional development programs. It provides a structured eight-week curriculum that assigns chapters thematically rather than sequentially, with integrated learning activities, assessment strategies, and classroom discussion prompts. This approach enables instructors to guide learners through the

TABLE 1.3 Eight-Week Curriculum Structure

Week	*Stream*	*Chapters*	*Learning Objectives*	*Suggested Activities*
Week 1–2	Stream 1: Foundations	2–3	Understand psychological theories of cyber behavior; Grasp concept of cybernetic self	Lectures on Big Five/HEXACO; Group discussions on identity formation; Reflective writing on personal digital identity
Week 3–4	Stream 2: AI & Mental Health (Part 1)	4–5	Understand AI mechanisms; Recognize mental health impacts	Case study analysis of algorithmic effects; Mental health impact assessments; Debate on AI engagement optimization
Week 5	Stream 2: AI & Mental Health (Part 2)	6	Learn ethical design principles; Understand governance frameworks	Ethical framework workshops; Design thinking exercises; Policy analysis activities
Week 6–7	Stream 3: Individual Differences	7–9	Understand personality, gender, and cultural moderators	Personality-aware design exercises; Gender analysis of digital platforms; Cultural competence discussions
Week 8	Stream 4: Applications & Futures	10–12	Apply insights to real-world contexts; Anticipate future scenarios	Intervention design projects; Policy recommendation papers; Future scenario planning

material while promoting engagement, critical thinking, and practical application (see Table 1.3). The eight-week curriculum structure organizes the book into five distinct teaching units, each spanning one to two weeks. Each week should include multiple learning components that work together to promote deep understanding and practical application. These components include assigned reading from the specified chapters, instructor-led lectures or discussions lasting two to three hours, completion of reflection questions provided at the end of each chapter section, and structured learning activities such as case studies, group discussions, design exercises, or projects.

TABLE 1.4 Assessment Strategies by Week

Week	*Assessment Type*	*Description*
Week 1–2	Concept Map	Students create visual representations of psychological theories
Week 3–4	Case Analysis	Students analyze real-world examples of AI mental health impacts
Week 5	Ethical Framework Application	Students apply ethical principles to design scenarios
Week 6–7	Comparative Analysis	Students analyze how personality/gender/culture shape digital experiences
Week 8	Capstone Project	Students design comprehensive interventions or policies

Assessment is an essential component of the educational pathway, as it helps instructors evaluate learning and helps students consolidate understanding. Table 1.4 presents assessment strategies tailored to each week's content. In Weeks 1–2, students might create concept maps that visually represent the psychological theories and how they relate to cyber behavior. In Weeks 3–4, students might analyze real-world cases of AI's impact on mental health, identify the psychological mechanisms at work, and consider the ethical implications. In Week 5, students might apply ethical frameworks to design scenarios, proposing how they would redesign a digital platform to better protect mental health. In Weeks 6–7, students might conduct comparative analyses examining how personality, gender, and culture shape digital experiences differently. In Week 8, students might complete a capstone project in which they design comprehensive interventions or policies addressing digital well-being in their chosen context.

Classroom discussion is another essential component of the educational pathway, as it promotes critical thinking, allows students to learn from each other, and helps instructors assess understanding. Table 1.5 presents discussion prompts tailored to each week's content. In Weeks 1–2, discussions might explore how psychological theories from offline contexts apply to cyberspaces or what makes the cybernetic self different from offline identity. In Weeks 3–4, discussions might examine how recommendation algorithms shape behavior differently for different people or explore the mental health trade-offs of personalization. In Week 5, discussions might address what "ethical by design" means in practice or who should be responsible for AI harms. In Weeks 6–7, discussions might explore how personality traits influence vulnerability to cyberbullying, what gendered patterns exist in digital platform use, or how cultural values shape attitudes toward privacy and AI. In Week 8, discussions might ask how students would design digital platforms differently or what policies would best protect youth well-being.

The educational pathway is particularly valuable for instructors who want to guide learners through the material in a structured, engaging way. It provides

TABLE 1.5 Classroom Discussion Prompts by Week

Week	*Discussion Topics*
Week 1–2	How do psychological theories from offline contexts apply to cyberspaces? What makes the cybernetic self different from offline identity? How does identity formation in cyberspaces differ from identity formation in physical spaces?
Week 3–4	How do recommendation algorithms shape behavior differently for different people? What are the mental health trade-offs of personalization? How can AI systems be designed to maximize benefits while minimizing harms?
Week 5	What does "ethical by design" mean in practice? Who should be responsible for AI harms? What governance structures would best protect young people in cyberspaces?
Week 6–7	How do personality traits influence vulnerability to cyberbullying? What gendered patterns exist in digital platform use? How do cultural values shape attitudes toward privacy and AI? How can digital systems be designed to be inclusive of diverse personalities, genders, and cultures?
Week 8	How would you design digital platforms differently? What policies would best protect youth well-being? What role should different stakeholders play in promoting digital well-being?

clear learning objectives for each week, specific assessment strategies to evaluate learning, and discussion prompts to promote critical thinking. Each chapter includes learning objectives, key concepts, figures and tables for visualization, and reflection questions to support the instructor in designing engaging learning experiences.

1.7.4 Pathway 4: Policy and Practice Fast-Track

This pathway is ideal for policymakers, practitioners, organizational leaders, and other professionals who need actionable insights quickly and do not have time for comprehensive sequential reading. The policy and practice fast-track prioritizes chapters addressing policy and practice, with strategic foundational reading to ensure that practical recommendations are grounded in a solid understanding. This pathway typically requires only four to six weeks of reading, allowing busy professionals to gain essential knowledge while maintaining focus on their immediate policy or practice priorities.

The recommended reading sequence for the policy and practice fast-track begins with Chapter 1 (Introduction), which provides essential context and the four-stream framework. You should then read selected sections from Chapters 2 to 3 to establish a foundational understanding of key psychological theories and concepts. Rather than reading these chapters in their entirety, you might focus on Sections 2.1–2.5 (Key theories) and Sections 3.1 and 3.2 (Digital identity basics), which provide a sufficient foundation without excessive detail. You should then read Chapter 5 (Mental Health Impacts) to understand the psychological consequences of digital engagement, and Chapter 6 (Ethical Frameworks) to understand the ethical principles that should guide policy and practice. These chapters provide essential understanding of the problems and principles underlying policy and practice recommendations. You should then read Chapter 10 (Strategies and Interventions) in its entirety, as it provides evidence-based recommendations for promoting digital well-being through education, parenting, and policy. You should read Chapter 11 (Emerging Findings) to understand current trends and evidence, and Chapter 12 (Future Directions) to understand future trajectories and proactive planning. This sequence, outlined in Figure 1.2, provides a logical progression from problem understanding to principle establishment to practical recommendation to future planning (Table 1.6).

To use the policy and practice resource table, identify your primary policy or practice area from the left column. Then read the primary chapter listed in the second column, focusing on the key sections listed in the third column. These sections provide evidence-based insights and recommendations directly applicable to your area. The fourth column summarizes the actionable insights you can expect to find, helping you understand the practical value of each section.

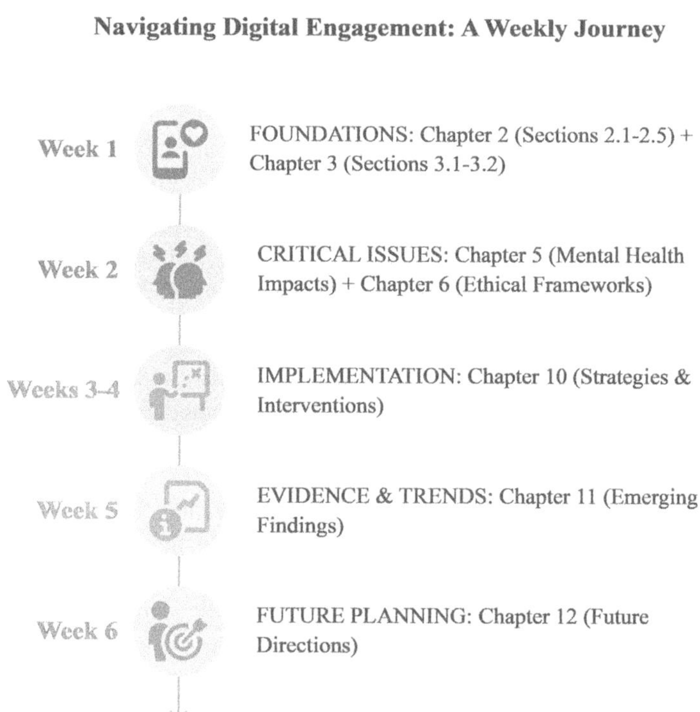

FIGURE 1.2 Policy & practice fast-track reading sequence.

TABLE 1.6 Policy & Practice Resource Table

Policy/Practice Area	*Primary Chapter*	*Key Sections*	*Actionable Insights*
Digital Literacy Education	Chapter 10	10.2	Evidence-based curriculum design; integration into schools
Parental Guidance	Chapter 10	10.3	Strategies for supporting healthy digital engagement
Mental Health Services	Chapters 5 and 6, 11	5.2, 6.2–6.3, 11.1	Identifying at-risk youth; ethical AI in mental health
Platform Governance	Chapter 6	6.2–6.3	Ethical design principles; accountability mechanisms
AI Regulation	Chapters 6, 12	6.3, 12.1	Regulatory frameworks; future-proofing policies
Equity & Inclusion	Chapters 7–9	7.2, 8.2–8.3, 9.2–9.4	Addressing disparities; culturally responsive approaches
Research Priorities	Chapters 11 and 12	11.1, 12.1	Emerging research needs; innovation opportunities

For different professional roles, we provide quick-reference implementation guides that specify which chapters to prioritize and what actions to take based on the insights gained. For education leaders, we recommend reading Chapter 10, Section 10.2 (Digital Literacy in Schools) and Chapter 2, Section 2.4 (Psychological Theories), and then designing a digital literacy curriculum using evidence-based frameworks. For mental health professionals, we recommend reading Chapter 5 (Mental Health Impacts), Chapter 6, Section 6.3 (Ethical Design), and Chapter 11, Section 11.1 (Emerging Trends in Mental Health), then developing protocols for identifying and supporting distressed youth digitally. For technology leaders, we recommend reading Chapter 4 (AI Mechanisms), Chapter 6, Sections 6.2 and 6.3 (Ethical Frameworks), and Chapter 12 (Future Directions), then implementing ethical design practices and governance structures. For policymakers, we recommend reading Chapter 6, Section 6.3 (Governance), Chapter 10 (Strategies), and Chapter 12, Section 12.1 (Policy Directions), then developing or revising policies addressing digital well-being and AI governance. For parents and community leaders, we recommend reading Chapter 10, Section 10.3 (Parenting for Digital Balance) and Chapter 1, Section 1.2 (Dual Nature of Digital Technology), and then supporting families in promoting healthy digital engagement. The policy and practice fast-track is designed for busy professionals who need to understand key issues and identify actionable recommendations without reading the entire book. By prioritizing chapters addressing policy and practice, with strategic foundational reading to ensure recommendations are grounded in a solid understanding, this pathway allows professionals to gain essential knowledge in four to six weeks. The time investment is modest, but the practical value is substantial, as the insights gained can directly inform policy development, practice improvement, and organizational decision-making.

1.7.5 Pathway 5: Customized Learning Combinations

This pathway is ideal for professionals with varied interests and responsibilities who want to combine elements from multiple pathways to create a customized reading experience. Rather than following a single predetermined pathway, you can select chapters and sections based on your specific role, interests, and time constraints. This flexibility allows you to maximize the value of the book while respecting the constraints of your professional and personal life.

Table 1.7 presents the core chapters, supplementary chapters, and time commitment for different roles. For example, if you are an educator, you might begin with Chapters 2 and 3 to understand the psychological foundations of cyber behavior and digital identity. You would then read Chapter 10 to understand evidence-based strategies for promoting digital well-being in educational contexts. You might then supplement this core reading with Chapters 4–6 to understand AI mechanisms and their mental health implications, and Chapters 7–9 to understand how personality, gender, and culture influence digital experiences. This customized pathway would give you a comprehensive understanding of digital well-being in educational contexts while allowing you to focus most intensively on the chapters most directly relevant to your role. Similarly, if you are a mental health professional, you might begin with Chapters 2 and 3 to understand psychological foundations, then read Chapters 5 and

TABLE 1.7 Role-Based Reading Recommendations

Your Role	*Core Chapters*	*Supplementary Chapters*	*Time Commitment*
Educator	2–3, 10	4–6, 7–9	8–10 weeks
School Counselor	2–3, 5–6, 10	7–9, 11	8–10 weeks
Mental Health Professional	2–3, 5–6, 11	4, 7–9, 10	8–10 weeks
Technology Developer	2–4, 6	5, 7–9, 12	6–8 weeks
Policymaker	6, 10, 12	2–5, 7–9, 11	6–8 weeks
Parent/Community Member	1, 10	2–3, 5, 7–9	4–6 weeks
Researcher	02-Sep	10-Dec	12–14 weeks
Student (Undergraduate)	02-Jun	07-Sep	10–12 weeks
Student (Graduate)	02-Dec	All chapters with depth	14–16 weeks

6 to understand mental health impacts and ethical design principles. You would then read Chapter 11 to understand emerging trends in digital mental health. You might supplement this core reading with Chapter 4 to understand AI mechanisms; Chapters 7–9 to understand how personality, gender, and culture influence mental health outcomes in digital contexts; and Chapter 10 to understand interventions. This customized pathway would give you a comprehensive understanding of digital mental health while allowing you to focus most intensively on the chapters most directly relevant to your clinical practice. The customized learning combinations pathway recognizes that professionals have diverse roles, interests, and constraints. By allowing you to select chapters and sections based on your specific needs, this pathway maximizes the relevance and value of the book while respecting your time constraints. You might spend 4–6 weeks on a focused reading plan, or you might spend 14–16 weeks on comprehensive reading, depending on your role and interests. The key is to be intentional about your reading choices, ensuring that the chapters you prioritize directly address your primary needs and interests.

1.8 Key Concepts and Terminology

To support your reading, we define key concepts that recur throughout the book:

1.8.1 Core Psychological Concepts

Cyberpsychology – The scientific study of psychological phenomena emerging from human interaction with digital technology, particularly the internet.

Cybernetic Self – The fluid, continuously reconstructed identity that emerges through feedback loops in virtual environments, where online interactions generate responses that individuals internalize.

Online Disinhibition – The tendency for individuals to exhibit less self-discipline and social restraint in cyberspace, often due to anonymity and psychological distance.

Moral Disengagement – The psychological process through which individuals rationalize harmful behaviors by disconnecting their actions from their ethical standards.

Digital Well-being – The state of psychological, social, and physical health that individuals experience in relation to their use of digital technologies.

Cyber Behaviors – Patterns of behavior in digital contexts, including aggressive behaviors (cyberbullying, harassment), addictive behaviors (compulsive use, dependency), and social-commercial behaviors (self-presentation, social comparison).

1.8.2 AI and Technology Concepts

Recommendation Algorithm – An AI system that analyzes user behavior and preferences to predict and suggest content, products, or connections.

Feedback Loop – A cyclical process in which user actions inform algorithmic predictions, which shape subsequent content delivery, which influences future user behavior.

Engagement Optimization – The practice of designing systems to maximize time spent on platform, frequency of return visits, and other engagement metrics.

Filter Bubble – An information environment in which users are primarily exposed to content that aligns with their existing beliefs, limiting exposure to diverse perspectives.

Echo Chamber – A community or information environment in which existing views are continuously reinforced rather than challenged.

Algorithmic Bias – Systematic errors or unfair treatment that emerge when AI systems are trained on biased data or designed without attention to fairness.

AI-Behavior Nexus – The concept that AI systems are not passive tools but active architects of digital experience, shaping behavior through algorithmic design.

1.8.3 Individual Difference Concepts

Big Five Personality Traits – A widely used framework describing personality along five dimensions: neuroticism, conscientiousness, openness to experience, extraversion, and agreeableness.

HEXACO Model – An expanded personality framework that adds honesty-humility to the Big Five and modifies neuroticism to emotionality.

Personality-Aware Design – The practice of designing digital systems with attention to how different personality types may experience and respond to the system.

Gender as a Structural Factor – The recognition that gender is not merely an individual characteristic but a structural feature of society that shapes opportunities, risks, and experiences in digital and offline contexts.

Intersectionality – The recognition that individuals have multiple, overlapping identities (e.g., gender, race, class, ability) that interact to shape their experiences.

Cultural Competence – The ability to understand, appreciate, and interact effectively with people from cultures or belief systems different from one's own.

1.8.4 Ethical Concepts

Ethical by Design – An approach in which ethical considerations are embedded into every stage of technological development, not added as an afterthought.

Transparency – The practice of clearly communicating how systems work, what data they collect, and how that data is used.

Fairness – The principle that AI systems should perform equitably across different demographic groups and should not discriminate or reinforce existing inequalities.

Consent – The practice of obtaining informed, voluntary agreement from users before collecting data or implementing systems that affect them.

Accountability – The principle that responsibility for AI outcomes should be clearly assigned and that mechanisms should exist for addressing harms.

Digital Literacy – The knowledge and skills necessary to navigate digital environments safely and ethically, including the ability to recognize misinformation, understand algorithmic systems, protect privacy, and make informed decisions.

1.9 Summary and Reflections

This introduction has established the context, definitions, and organizational framework for the book. The digital transformation is reshaping youth development in ways that demand careful understanding of cyberpsychology, AI ethics, and digital well-being. The dual nature of digital technology has been illustrated: it offers genuine opportunities for connection, learning, and self-expression while simultaneously introducing distinctive risks to mental health and well-being.

The four-stream conceptual framework that organizes this book has been introduced: foundational theories and concepts; AI mechanisms and mental health implications; individual and cultural differences; and applications and future directions. This book is grounded in a central belief: digital well-being is not a universal outcome but emerges from complex interactions between technological design, individual psychology, and sociocultural contexts.

This belief carries important implications. Promoting digital well-being requires not just individual awareness or generic advice, but careful attention to how people with different personalities, genders, and cultural backgrounds experience digital environments differently. It requires understanding how AI systems work and committing to ethical design principles. It requires collaboration among all stakeholders, including developers, educators, parents, policymakers, and young people themselves. It requires alignment with global agendas, particularly the UN's Sustainable Development Goals, which emphasize the importance of quality education and good health and well-being for all young people.

The chapters that follow provide the theoretical understanding, empirical evidence, and practical strategies necessary to advance this work. Readers are invited to engage critically with the material, to connect the concepts to their own observations and experiences, and to consider how they might contribute to creating digital environments that promote flourishing rather than harm.

> ***Takeaway:*** *This book provides a comprehensive, integrated framework for understanding and promoting digital well-being through informed cyberpsychology, ethical AI design, and attention to individual and cultural differences.*
> ***Reflection:*** *As you begin this book, what questions about digital well-being, AI ethics, or cyberpsychology are you hoping to answer? How might the insights in this book inform your work or your understanding of youth development in the digital age?*

Bibliography

Adorjan, M., & Berman, R. (2022). *A special issue on the sociology of childhood and youth in Canada*. https://doi.org/10.32920/21578907.v1

Afzal, A., Khan, S., Daud, S., Ahmad, Z., & Butt, A. (2023). Addressing the digital divide: Access and use of technology in education. *Journal of Social Sciences Review, 3*(2), 883–895. https://doi.org/10.54183/jssr.v3i2.326

Ahmed, S. (2025). Artificial intelligence in education. In *Artificial intelligence* (pp. 159–184). Brill. https://doi.org/10.1163/9789004754065_006

Ahmmad, M., Yaqoub, M., & Al-Kassimi, K. (2025). The Algorithmic Wars. *Media Representation and Public Perception of War*, 173–200. https://doi.org/10.4018/979-8-3373-1722-9.ch006

Akintoye, O. S., Sanusi, H. M., Yusuf, R. A., & Odondi, A. A. (2023). Early detection of adolescent mental health risk using transformer models on social media datasets. *Journal of Frontiers in Multidisciplinary Research, 4*(1), 435–445. https://doi.org/10.54660/.jfmr.2023.4.1.435-445

Alavi, M., Latif, A. A., Ramayah, T., & Tan, J. Y. (2022). Dark tetrad of personality, cyberbullying, and cybertrolling among young adults. *Current Psychology, 42*(32), 28441–28451. https://doi.org/10.1007/s12144-022-03892-4

AlBuhairan, F., Abdel-Tawab, N., AbouNar, M., Abu Hamad, B., Dabis, J., Feteha, F., Saher, S., Siddeeg, K., & Wahba, M. (2023). Adolescent health in the Middle East and North Africa region: Leaving no one behind. *Eastern Mediterranean Health Journal, 29*(2), 89–90. https://doi.org/10.26719/emhj.23.008

Alenezi, N., & Alfaleh, M. (2024). Enhancing digital citizenship education in Saudi Arabian elementary schools: Designing effective activities for curriculum integration. *Frontiers in Education, 9*, 1494487. https://doi.org/10.3389/feduc.2024.1494487

Almulla, M. O., Alismail, A. M., Mahama, I., & Almulla, A. A. (2025). Resilience as a predictor of internet addictive behaviours: A study among Ghanaian and Saudi samples using structural equation modelling approach. *BMC Psychology, 13*(1), 77. https://doi.org/10.1186/s40359-025-02383-y

Anamika, Rabbani, S., & Perwej, Y. (2024). AI-Counsellor using emerging technique. *International Journal of Scientific Research in Science and Technology, 11*(3), 749–759. https://doi.org/10.32628/ijsrst24113237

Ancis, J. R. (2020). The age of cyberpsychology: An overview. *Technology, Mind, and Behavior, 1*(1), 9–23. https://doi.org/10.1037/tmb0000009

Anderson, M. M., & Fort, K. (2024). Evaluating the acceptability of ethical recommendations in industry 4.0: An ethics by design approach. *AI & SOCIETY, 39*(6), 2989–3003. https://doi.org/10.1007/s00146-023-01834-7

Ardabili, N., & Riley, A. (2025). Eutylone pre-exposure has no impact on the aversive effects of Cocaine and MDMA: Implications of its hybrid neurochemical mechanisms of action. *Drug and Alcohol Dependence, 267*, 111551. https://doi.org/10.1016/j.drugalcdep.2024.111551

Ata-Aktürk, A., & Akman, M. B. (2024). What Happens beyond the Screen? Uncovering Digital Technology Perception, Usage, and Parental Mediation among 3–6-year-old Turkish Children. *Journal of Child and Family Studies, 33*(10), 3191–3210. https://doi.org/10.1007/s10826-024-02888-x

Avci, H., Baams, L., & Kretschmer, T. (2025). A systematic review of social media use and adolescent identity development. *Adolescent Research Review, 10*(2), 219–236. https://doi.org/10.1007/s40894-024-00251-1

Aydın, K. E., & Battal, F. (2025). Can Social Media Challenges Determine Life or Death? Two Adolescent Cases from the Pediatric Intensive Care Unit. *Turkish Journal of*

Pediatric Emergency and Intensive Care Medicine. https://doi.org/10.4274/cayd.galenos.2025.16768

Baker, R. S., Richey, J. E., Zhang, J., Karumbaiah, S., Andres-Bray, J. M., Nguyen, H. A., Andres, J. M. a. L., & McLaren, B. M. (2024). Gaming the system mediates the relationship between gender and learning outcomes in a digital learning game. *Instructional Science, 53*(2), 203–238. https://doi.org/10.1007/s11251-024-09679-3

Balcerowska, J. M., Sawicki, A., & Zajenkowski, M. (2024). A longitudinal study on the reciprocal relationship between narcissism and social Networking Sites addiction. *Journal of Research in Personality, 114*, 104566. https://doi.org/10.1016/j.jrp.2024.104566

Berardinetti, V., Ciletti, M., Lavanga, A., & Toto, G. A. (2025). Digital Innovation and Artificial Intelligence in Museum Education: Perspectives, debates and psychological implications. Book of Proceedings. ATEE Spring Conference 2024. *Teacher education research in Europe: Trends, challenges, practices and perspectives*, 424–431. https://doi.org/10.62336/unibg.978-88-97253-27-3_p.424

Bhattacharya, S. (2019). *Design of foundations for offshore wind turbines*. https://doi.org/10.1002/9781119128137

Bright, R., & Dyck, M. (2011). It hurt big time: Understanding the impact of rural adolescents' experiences with cyberbullying. *Northwest Journal of Teacher Education, 9*(2). https://doi.org/10.15760/nwjte.2011.9.2.9

Buchan, M. C., Bhawra, J., & Katapally, T. R. (2024). Navigating the digital world: Development of an evidence-based digital literacy program and assessment tool for youth. *Smart Learning Environments, 11*(1). https://doi.org/10.1186/s40561-024-00293-x

Buckley, C., Radhakrishnan, A., Boran, L., Brennan, M., & Travers, Á. (2025). Barriers and Facilitators of Help-Seeking for LGBTQ+ Survivors of Sexual Violence: A Systematic review. *Trauma Violence & Abuse*, 15248380251355902. https://doi.org/10.1177/15248380251355902

Büchi, M. (2024). Digital well-being theory and research. *New Media & Society, 26*(1), 172–189. https://doi.org/10.1177/14614448211056851

Carcelén-García, S., Narros-González, M. J., & Galmes-Cerezo, M. (2023). Digital vulnerability in young people: Gender, age and online participation patterns. *International Journal of Adolescence and Youth, 28*(1). https://doi.org/10.1080/02673843.2023.2287115

Cerioli, L. (2026). Oil and development expectations in Latin America. *The Political Economy of the Energy Transition in Latin America*, 102–116. https://doi.org/10.4324/9781003678410-9

Chang, J. P., Cheng, S., Chang, S. M., & Su, K. (2025). Navigating the Digital Maze: A review of AI bias, social media, and mental health in Generation Z. *AI, 6*(6), 118. https://doi.org/10.3390/ai6060118

Chi, H., Liu, R., & Pan, J. (2022). Users' Behaviour under the Uneven Gender Ratio of Social Media Platforms. *SHS Web of Conferences, 148*, 03003. https://doi.org/10.1051/shsconf/202214803003

Ciren, Z., Tsui, H. K. H., & Chan, S. K. W. (2025). Effects of resilience interventions for adolescents and young adults without psychiatric diagnoses: A systematic review and network meta-analysis of randomized controlled trials. *Adolescent Research Review*. https://doi.org/10.1007/s40894-025-00270-6

Congiu, L., Moscati, I., & Scacchi, M. (2024). Digital Nudging and Cookie Rejection: An Experiment. *Italian Economic Journal, 11*(1), 431–458. https://doi.org/10.1007/s40797-024-00268-4

Dadi, A. F., Dachew, B. A., & Tessema, G. A. (2024). Problematic internet use: A growing concern for adolescent health and well-being in a digital era. *Journal of Global Health, 14*, 03034. https://doi.org/10.7189/jogh.14.03034

Davis, K., Anderson, M., Yang, C., Choukas-Bradley, S., Bell, B. T., & Slovak, P. (2024). Cross-Disciplinary Perspectives on Youth Digital Well-Being Research: Identifying notable developments, persistent gaps, and future directions. *Journal of Adolescent Research, 40*(2), 259–295. https://doi.org/10.1177/07435584241291163

Dennis, M. J. (2021). Towards a theory of digital well-being: Reimagining online life after lockdown. *Science and Engineering Ethics, 27*(3), Article 37. https://doi.org/10.1007/s11948-021-00307-8

Dey, S., PKrishna, C., Devalanka, S., & Ayyagari, R. K. (2024). Novel leakage reduction technique for ultra-low power advanced FinFET technology node design. *2024 IEEE 5th Women in Technology Conference* (WINTECHCON), 1–6. https://doi.org/10.1109/wintechcon61988.2024.10837799

ElSayary, A. (2025). Navigating AI Ethics through the lens of personality traits and well-being: Policy recommendations for young people in the UAE. *Human Behavior and Emerging Technologies, 2025*(1), 5597545. https://doi.org/10.1155/hbe2/5597545

Elvira-Zorzo, M. N., & Gómez, P.B . (2025). Identity construction and digital vulnerability in adolescents: Psychosocial implications and implications for social work. *Youth, 5*(4), 119. https://doi.org/10.3390/youth5040119

Evangelou, S. M., Michanetzi, E. L., & Xenos, M. (2024). Exploring the impact of negative online feedback on well-being: A comprehensive analysis incorporating Big-Five personality traits and physiological responses. *Computers in Human Behavior Reports, 15*, 100457. https://doi.org/10.1016/j.chbr.2024.100457

Favini, A., Gerbino, M., Pastorelli, C., Zuffianò, A., Lunetti, C., Remondi, C., Cirimele, F., Plata, M. G., & Giannini, A. M. (2023). Bullying and cyberbullying: Do personality profiles matter in adolescence? *Telematics and Informatics Reports, 12*, 100108. https://doi.org/10.1016/j.teler.2023.100108

Figueroa, C. A., Ramos, G., Psihogios, A. M., Ekuban, E., Bansie, P., De Haas, M., Karnik, N. S., Ajilore, O., Anderson, E. E., & Stiles-Shields, C. (2025). Advancing youth co-design of ethical guidelines for AI-powered digital mental health tools. *Nature Mental Health, 3*(8), 870–878. https://doi.org/10.1038/s44220-025-00467-7

Fitzpatrick, C., Binet, M., Cristini, E., Almeida, M. L., Bégin, M., & Frizzo, G. B. (2023). Reducing harm and promoting positive media use strategies: New perspectives in understanding the impact of preschooler media use on health and development. *Psicologia Reflexão E Crítica, 36*(1), 19. https://doi.org/10.1186/s41155-023-00262-2

Fortuna, P. (2023). Positive cyberpsychology as a field of study of the well-being of people interacting with and via technology. *Frontiers in Psychology, 14*, 1053482. https://doi.org/10.3389/fpsyg.2023.1053482

Freed, D., Levin, M., & Sklar, T. (2025). *From care to technology-facilitated abuse: Law and policy approaches to safeguard against agetech misuse*. https://doi.org/10.2139/ssrn.5856942

Gajda, A., Moroń, M., Królik, M., Małuch, M., & Mraczek, M. (2022). The Dark Tetrad, cybervictimization, and cyberbullying: The role of moral disengagement. *Current Psychology, 42*(27), 23413–23421. https://doi.org/10.1007/s12144-022-03456-6

Gao, J., Liu, F., Xu, J., Wang, J., Mou, J., & Wang, L. (2022). The influence of family incivility on cyberbullying perpetration: A moderated mediation model. *Frontiers in Psychology, 13*, 975335. https://doi.org/10.3389/fpsyg.2022.975335

Gholami, M., Thornberg, R., Kabiri, S., & Yousefvand, S. (2025). From dark triad personality traits to digital harm: Mediating cyberbullying through online moral disengagement. *Deviant Behavior*, 1–19. https://doi.org/10.1080/01639625.2025.2453445

Gliksman, Y., Naparstek, S., Bar-Hen Schweiger, M., & Henik, A. (2025). Mental manipulation, numerical cognition, and developmental dyscalculia. *Developmental Dyscalculia*, 123–138. https://doi.org/10.1016/b978-0-443-22224-5.00006-0

Gugushvili, N., Täht, K., Ruiter, R. a. C., & Verduyn, P. (2022). Facebook use intensity and depressive symptoms: A moderated mediation model of problematic Facebook use, age, neuroticism, and extraversion. *BMC Psychology*, *10*(1), 279. https://doi.org/10.1186/s40359-022-00990-7

Hamamoto, Y., Honda, A., Miura, N., Tanabe-Ishibashi, A., Oba, K., Ishibashi, R., & Sugiura, M. (2023). Five major outcomes of digitalization: Relevance of a survival personality type during COVID-19 pandemic. *Frontiers in Psychology*, *14*, 1230192. https://doi.org/10.3389/fpsyg.2023.1230192

Hameed, K., Naha, R., & Hameed, F. (2024). Digital transformation for sustainable health and well-being: A review and future research directions. *Discover Sustainability*, *5*(1). https://doi.org/10.1007/s43621-024-00273-8

Hamilton, J. L., Dreier, M. J., Guthrie, K. M., & Raudales, A. M. (2024). Leveraging digital media to promote youth mental health: Flipping the script on social media-related risk. *Current Treatment Options in Psychiatry*, *11*, 67–75. https://doi.org/10.1007/s40501-024-00315-y

Hasse, C. (2019). The Vitruvian robot. *AI & SOCIETY*, *34*(1), 91–93. https://doi.org/10.1007/s00146-017-0701-z

Hong, S. H., Chun, T. K., Nam, Y. J., Kim, T. W., Cho, Y. H., Son, S. J., Roh, H. W., & Hong, C. H. (2025). Digital Mental Health Interventions for Adolescents: An Integrative review based on the Behavior Change approach. *Children*, *12*(6), 770. https://doi.org/10.3390/children12060770

Hylkilä, K., Kääriäinen, M., Peltonen, A., Castrén, S., Mustonen, T., Konttila, J., & Männikkö, N. (2025). Young adults' risk profiles and predictive factors of Problematic Social Media Use (PSMU): A cross-sectional study. *Current Psychology*, *44*(8), 6848–6862. https://doi.org/10.1007/s12144-025-07662-w

Ibitoye, A. O., Nkwo, M. S., & Orji, R. (2025). Rethinking responsible AI from ethical pillars to sociotechnical practice. *AI And Ethics*, *5*(6), 6207–6223. https://doi.org/10.1007/s43681-025-00809-2

Ike, O. O., Nwufo, I. J., & Adubi, P. C. (2024). The mental health of family caregivers: Do the complementary roles of personality trait, social support, and resilience matter? *Palliative Medicine in Practice*, *18*(4), 207–219. https://doi.org/10.5603/pmp.99443

Joseph, A. P., & Babu, A. (2024). The unseen dilemma of AI in mental healthcare. *AI & Society*, *40*(3), 1533–1535. https://doi.org/10.1007/s00146-024-01937-9

Joshi, A., Das, S., & Sekar, S. (2023). How big five personality traits affect information and communication technology use: A neta-analysis. *AJIS. Australasian Journal of Information Systems/AJIS. Australian Journal of Information Systems/Australian Journal of Information Systems*, *27*. https://doi.org/10.3127/ajis.v27i0.3985

Kelly, C. A., Blain, B., & Sharot, T. (2024). "How" web searches change under stress. *Scientific Reports*, *14*(1), 15147. https://doi.org/10.1038/s41598-024-65895-4

Kickbusch, I., & Holly, L. (2023). Addressing the digital determinants of health: Health promotion must lead the charge. *Health Promotion International*, *38*(3), daad059. https://doi.org/10.1093/heapro/daad059

Ko, C., & Kim, S. (2024). Adolescent female users' avatar creation in social virtual worlds: Opportunities and challenges. *Behavioral Sciences*, *14*(7), 539. https://doi.org/10.3390/bs14070539

Konidena, B. K., Malaiyappan, J. N. A., & Tadimarri, A. (2024). Ethical considerations in the development and deployment of AI systems. *European Journal of Technology, 8*(2), 41–53. https://doi.org/10.47672/ejt.1890

Kurian, N. (2025). Developmentally aligned AI: A framework for translating the science of child development into AI design. *AI Brain and Child, 1*(1). https://doi.org/10.1007/s44436-025-00009-z

Lahti, H., Kokkonen, M., Hietajärvi, L., Lyyra, N., & Paakkari, L. (2024). Social media threats and health among adolescents: Evidence from the health behaviour in school-aged children study. *Child and Adolescent Psychiatry and Mental Health, 18*(1), 62. https://doi.org/10.1186/s13034-024-00754-8

Layte, R., Brannigan, R., & Stanistreet, D. (2023). Digital engagement and adolescent depression: A longitudinal mediation analysis adjusting for selection. *Computers in Human Behavior Reports, 10*, 100293. https://doi.org/10.1016/j.chbr.2023.100293

Lee, J., & Žarnic, Ž. (2024). The impact of digital technologies on well-being. In *OECD Papers on Well-being and Inequalities*. https://doi.org/10.1787/cb173652-en

Leech, T., Dorstyn, D., Taylor, A., & Li, W. (2021). Mental health apps for adolescents and young adults: A systematic review of randomised controlled trials. *Children and Youth Services Review, 127*, 106073. https://doi.org/10.1016/j.childyouth.2021.106073

Lewis, C. C., Taba, M., Allen, T. B., Caldwell, P. H., Skinner, S. R., Kang, M., Henderson, H., Bray, L., Borthwick, M., Collin, P., McCaffery, K., & Scott, K. M. (2024). Developing an educational resource aimed at improving adolescent digital health literacy: Using Co-Design as research methodology. *Journal of Medical Internet Research, 26*, e49453. https://doi.org/10.2196/49453

Li, L., Yuan, X., Lin, L., Xiao, A., Chen, Y., Xia, Y., & Huang, X. (2025). A gender comparison based network analysis for social media addiction behaviors in cross-cultural contexts. *Scientific Reports, 15*(1), 38925. https://doi.org/10.1038/s41598-025-22796-4

Loblay, V., Ekambareshwar, M., Naderbagi, A., Song, Y. J., Ford, M., Zahed, I., Yoon, A., Hickie, I. B., & LaMonica, H. M. (2023). Enhancing equitable engagement for digital health promotion: Lessons from evaluating a childrearing app in Indonesia. *DIGITAL HEALTH, 9*, 20552076231222112. https://doi.org/10.1177/20552076231222112

Lubis, S., Purnomo, E. P., Lado, J. A., & Hung, C. (2024). Electronic governance in advancing sustainable development goals through systematic literature review. *Discover Global Society, 2*(1). https://doi.org/10.1007/s44282-024-00102-3

Maftei, A., Holman, A., & Elenescu, A. (2022). The dark web of machiavellianism and psychopathy: Moral disengagement in IT organizations. *Europe's Journal of Psychology, 18*(2), 181–192. https://doi.org/10.5964/ejop.4011

Magee, R. M., Leman, A. M., & Balasubramaniam, G. (2024). Amplifying Youth Voices using Digital Technology: A case study in collaborative research with youth service organizations. *Journal of Participatory Research Methods, 5*(1). https://doi.org/10.35844/001c.92282

Malloy, J., Partridge, S. R., Kemper, J. A., Braakhuis, A., & Roy, R. (2023). Co-design of digital health interventions with young people: A scoping review. *Digital Health, 9*, 20552076231219117. https://doi.org/10.1177/20552076231219117

Maltby, J., Rayes, T., Nage, A., Sharif, S., Omar, M., & Nichani, S. (2024). Synthesizing perspectives: Crafting an interdisciplinary view of social media's impact on young people's mental health. *PLOS ONE, 19*(7), e0307164.

Marshall, N. J., Loades, M. E., Jacobs, C., Biddle, L., & Lambert, J. D. (2025). Integrating Artificial intelligence in youth Mental health care: Advances, challenges, and future directions. *Current Treatment Options in Psychiatry, 12*(1). https://doi.org/10.1007/s40501-025-00348-x

Martín-Martín, M., & Bueno-Álvarez, J. A. (2023). Social networks and aggressive attitudes: Who is who. Scoping review of the scientific production on their relationships. *Frontiers in Psychology*, *14*, 1249907. https://doi.org/10.3389/fpsyg.2023.1249907

Mayiwar, L., Asutay, E., Tinghög, G., Västfjäll, D., & Barrafrem, K. (2024). Determinants of digital well-being. *AI & Society*, *40*(4), 3063–3073. https://doi.org/10.1007/s00146-024-02071-2

McCarthy-Jones, S. (2019). The autonomous mind: The right to freedom of thought in the twenty-first century. *Frontiers in Artificial Intelligence, 2*, Article 19. https://doi.org/10.3389/frai.2019.00019

Mellado, R., Cubillos, C., Vicari, R. M., & Gasca-Hurtado, G. (2024). Leveraging Gamification in ICT Education: Examining gender differences and learning outcomes in programming courses. *Applied Sciences*, *14*(17), 7933. https://doi.org/10.3390/app14177933

Molero, M. M., Pérez-Fuentes, M. C., Martos, Á., Pino, R. M., & Gázquez, J. J. (2023). Network analysis of emotional symptoms and their relationship with different types of cybervictimization. *The European Journal of Psychology Applied to Legal Context*, *15*(1), 23–32. https://doi.org/10.5093/ejpalc2023a3

Mols, A., Campos, J. P., & Pridmore, J. (2023). Family Surveillance: Understanding parental monitoring, reciprocal practices, and digital resilience. *Surveillance & Society*, *21*(4), 469–484. https://doi.org/10.24908/ss.v21i4.15645

Myhr, A., Anthun, K. S., Lillefjell, M., & Sund, E. R. (2020). Trends in socioeconomic inequalities in Norwegian adolescents' mental health from 2014 to 2018: A repeated cross-sectional study. *Frontiers in Psychology, 11*, 1472. https://doi.org/10.3389/fpsyg.2020.01472

Naik, G., & Behera, J. (2025). Traditional contraceptive use among married adolescent and non-adolescent women in India: More vulnerability in adolescent sexual reproductive health. *Global Social Welfare, 13*(1), 37–47. https://doi.org/10.1007/s40609-025-00411-8

Nesi, J., Telzer, E. H., & Prinstein, M. J. (Eds.). (2022). *Handbook of adolescent digital media use and mental health*. Cambridge University Press. https://doi.org/10.1017/9781108976237

Nikolopoulou, K. (2024). Children in the Cyberspace: Issues researched and suggestions for future research. *Creative Education*, *15*(05), 815–827. https://doi.org/10.4236/ce.2024.155049

Odgers, C. L., & Jensen, M. R. (2020). Annual research review: Adolescent mental health in the digital age: Facts, fears, and future directions. *Journal of Child Psychology and Psychiatry, 61*(3), 336–348. https://doi.org/10.1111/jcpp.13190

Ogugua, J. O., Okongwu, C. C., Akomolafe, O. O., Anyanwu, E. C., & Daraojimba, O. D. (2024). Mental health and digital technology: A public health review of current trends and responses. *International Medical Science Research Journal*, *4*(2), 108–125. https://doi.org/10.51594/imsrj.v4i2.754

Olorunfemi, O. L., Amoo, O. O., Atadoga, A., Fayayola, O. A., Abrahams, T. O., & Shoetan, P. O. (2024). Towards a conceptual framework for ethical AI development in it systems. *Computer Science & IT Research Journal*, *5*(3), 616–627. https://doi.org/10.51594/csitrj.v5i3.910

Opie, J.E., Vuong, A., Welsh, E.T., Gray, R. Natalie, P., Marchionda, S., Mutch, R., Khalil, H. (2024). Outcomes of Best-Practice Guided Digital Mental Health Interventions for Youth and Young Adults with Emerging Symptoms: Part I. A Systematic Review of Socioemotional Outcomes and Recommendations. *Clin Child Fam Psychol Rev* 27, 424–475. https://doi.org/10.1007/s10567-024-00469-4

Pandya, A., Lodha, P., & Ganatra, A. (2024). Is ChatGPT ready to change mental healthcare? Challenges and considerations: A reality-check. *Frontiers in Human Dynamics, 5*. https://doi.org/10.3389/fhumd.2023.1289255

Pangrazio, L., & Selwyn, N. (2023). *Critical data literacies: Rethinking data and everyday life*. MIT Press Direct. https://doi.org/10.7551/mitpress/14155.001.0001

Papadopoulou, P., & Lampropoulou, K. (2025). Information systems and human resources management: Applying AI in recruitment. *Proceedings of The International Conference on Research in Human Resource Management, 2*(1), 29–44. https://doi.org/10.33422/icrhrm.v2i1.1123

Patón-Romero, J. D., & Løvås, I. V. (2022). A proposal to develop software to prevent young people to acquire extremist beliefs. *European Journal of Sustainable Development, 11*(4), 158. https://doi.org/10.14207/ejsd.2022.v11n4p158

Pelánek, R. (2024). Personalized recommendations for learning activities in online environments: A modular rule-based approach. *User Modeling and User-Adapted Interaction, 34*, 1399–1430. https://doi.org/10.1007/s11257-024-09396-z

Pellegrino, A., & Stasi, A. (2024). A bibliometric analysis of the impact of media manipulation on adolescent mental health: Policy recommendations for algorithmic transparency. *Online Journal of Communication and Media Technologies, 14*(4), e202453. https://doi.org/10.30935/ojcmt/15143

Petersson, M., & Käll, S. (2025). Ecoviolence at sea. *Ecoviolence Studies*, 56–85. https://doi.org/10.1017/9781009341622.007

Ponti, M. (2023). Screen time and preschool children: Promoting health and development in a digital world. *Paediatrics & Child Health, 28*(3), 184–192. https://doi.org/10.1093/pch/pxac125

Putica, A., Khanna, R., Bosl, W., Saraf, S., & Edgcomb, J. (2025). Ethical decision-making for AI in mental health: The Integrated Ethical Approach for Computational Psychiatry (IEACP) framework. *Psychological Medicine, 55*, e213. https://doi.org/10.1017/s0033291725101311

Quintas-Froufe, N., González-Neira, A., & Fiaño-Salinas, C. (2024). Corporate policies to protect against disinformation for young audiences: The case of TikTok. *Frontiers in Communication, 9*. https://doi.org/10.3389/fcomm.2024.1410100

Radanliev, P. (2025). Ethical methodologies for digital identity privacy in AI-driven dance movement therapy as a preventative mental health mechanism in the extended reality. https://doi.org/10.2139/ssrn.5356770

Radanliev, P., De Roure, D., Maple, C., Nurse, J. R. C., Nicolescu, R., & Ani, U. (2024). AI security and cyber risk in IoT systems. *Frontiers in Big Data, 7*, 1402745. https://doi.org/10.3389/fdata.2024.1402745

Roos, M. (2021). The European Parliament's youth policy, 1952-1979: An attempt to create a collective memory of an integrated Europe. *Politique européenne, N° 71*(1), 28–52. https://doi.org/10.3917/poeu.071.0028

Salameh, W. (2024). The integration of Artificial Intelligence (AI) into undergraduate education. *International Journal of Science and Research Archive, 13*(1), 2455–2463. https://doi.org/10.30574/ijsra.2024.13.1.1916

Sarwatay, D., Raman, U., & Ramasubramanian, S. (2021). Media Literacy, Social Connectedness, and Digital Citizenship in India: Mapping stakeholders on how parents and young people navigate a social world. *Frontiers in Human Dynamics, 3*. https://doi.org/10.3389/fhumd.2021.601239

Schulz, P. J., Boldi, M., & van Ackere, A. (2025). Adolescent Cyberbullying and Cyber Victimization: Longitudinal Study Before and During COVID-19. *Journal of Medical Internet Research, 27*, e70508. https://doi.org/10.2196/70508

Sebastião, S. P., & Dias, D. F. (2025). AI Transparency: A conceptual, normative, and practical frame analysis. *Media and Communication, 13*. https://doi.org/10.17645/mac.9419

Seo, W., & Ahn, J. (2025). IT platform grants – Boosting user engagement but hindering innovation: Evidence from blockchain mainnet. Proceedings of the Annual Hawaii International Conference on System Sciences. https://doi.org/10.24251/hicss.2025.559

Shaigerova, L., Shilko, R., & Almazova, O. (2021). Goals of internet use and subjective safety of adolescents on the internet. *European Psychiatry, 64*(S1), S220–S221. https://doi.org/10.1192/j.eurpsy.2021.588

Shouli, A., Barthwal, A., Campbell, M., & Shrestha, A. (2025). *Ethical AI for young digital citizens: A call to action on privacy governance*. https://doi.org/10.22541/au.174221140.03641858/v1

Şimşek, E. E. (2025). The use of digital technology by parents from the perspective of xhildren. *Turkish Academic Research Review – Türk Akademik Araştırmalar Dergisi [TARR], 10*(1), 54–69. https://doi.org/10.30622/tarr.1603562

Singh, R., Khanal, P., Tol, W. A., Jefferies, P., Jordans, M. J. D., & Lund, C. (2025). Exploring the role of resilience in selective prevention intervention for adolescents at risk of depression and anxiety in Nepal: Findings from a pilot cluster randomized controlled trial. *Child and Adolescent Psychiatry and Mental Health, 19*(1), 103. https://doi.org/10.1186/s13034-025-00964-8

Su, P. (2023). Gender-Inclusive Urban Design: Insights from Eye-Tracking research. *Academic Journal of Humanities & Social Sciences, 6*(24). https://doi.org/10.25236/ajhss.2023.062419

Suler, J. (2005). The online disinhibition effect. *International Journal of Applied Psychoanalytic Studies, 2*(2), 184–188. https://doi.org/10.1002/aps.42

Sun, Y., Cao, C., Tang, Z., Huang, F., Zhong, X., & Chen, I. (2025). Moral disengagement as mediator and guilt as moderator between cyber moral literacy and cyberbullying among late adolescents. *Scientific Reports, 15*(1), 43. https://doi.org/10.1038/s41598-024-83911-5

Syrjämäki, A. H., Ilves, M., Olsson, T., & Kiskola, J. (2024). Online disinhibition mediates the relationship between emotion regulation difficulties and uncivil communication. *Scientific Reports, 14*(1), Article 29651. https://doi.org/10.1038/s41598-024-81086-7

Tamrakar, L., Tamrakar, S., & Thakur, V. (2023). Transformative impact of the digital age on youth mental health: Navigating challenges and embracing solutions. *ShodhKosh: Journal of Visual and Performing Arts, 4*(2). https://doi.org/10.29121/shodhkosh.v4.i2.2023.2222

Terrana, A., & Al-Delaimy, W. (2023). A systematic review of cross-cultural measures of resilience and its promotive and protective factors. *Transcultural Psychiatry, 60*(4), 733–750. https://doi.org/10.1177/13634615231167661

Teubner, J., & Ivey, R. (2025). Social AI and human connections: Benefits, risks and social impact . https://doi.org/10.2139/ssrn.5256743

Tsouparopoulou, E., Symeonaki, M., Parsanoglou, D., & Kazani, A. (2025). European youth and digital engagement: Attitudes, skills, and civic participation. *Journal of Applied Youth Studies, 8*(2), 219–247. https://doi.org/10.1007/s43151-025-00168-z

UN (2015). *Transforming Our World: The 2030 Agenda for Sustainable Development.* Resolution Adopted by the General Assembly on 25 September 2015, 42809, 1–13.

Vázquez-Cano, E., Ramírez-Hurtado, J. M., Díez-Arcón, P., & Pascual-Moscoso, C. (2022). Academic and social behaviour profile of the primary school students who possess and play video games. *Child Indicators Research, 16*(1), 227–245. https://doi.org/10.1007/s12187-022-09975-9

Walter, Y. (2024). Digital psychology: Introducing a conceptual impact model and the future of work. *Trends in Psychology*. https://doi.org/10.1007/s43076-024-00408-w

Wang, X. (2023). Review of: "Visualizing the mind: A deep dive into computer vision and psychological phenomena". https://doi.org/10.32388/oustlw

Wiederhold, B. K. (2024). The dark side of the digital age: How to address cyberbullying among adolescents. *Cyberpsychology, Behavior, and Social Networking, 27*(3), 169–171. https://doi.org/10.1089/cyber.2024.29309.editorial

Yaseen, Y., Kwon, O., & Kim, J. (2025). Adaptive dimensionality reduction for efficient deep learning on temporal datasets. https://doi.org/10.21203/rs.3.rs-6732901/v1

Zhang, Y., Zhang, J., Yu, X., Zhang, J., Xu, Y., & Cui, H. (2025). The impact of electronic product use on children with tic disorders and ADHD, and management strategies: A review. *Frontiers in Psychiatry, 16*, 1665047. https://doi.org/10.3389/fpsyt.2025.1665047

Zhou, X., Edirippulige, S., Bai, X., & Bambling, M. (2021). Are online mental health interventions for youth effective? A systematic review. *Journal of Telemedicine and Telecare, 27*(10), 638–666. https://doi.org/10.1177/1357633x211047285

Zimmermann, D., Wehler, A., & Kaspar, K. (2022). Self-representation through avatars in digital environments. *Current Psychology, 42*(25), 21775–21789. https://doi.org/10.1007/s12144-022-03232-6

2

THEORETICAL LENSES ON CYBER BEHAVIOR AND AI ETHICS

Objectives of This Chapter

- To analyze fundamental theoretical frameworks for comprehending cyber behaviors and the influence of artificial intelligence (AI) in molding these behaviors.
- To examine the integration of personality psychology, social psychology, and cyberpsychology ideas for the improved understanding of cyber-related difficulties, including cyberbullying, addiction, and moral disengagement.
- To comprehend the psychological and social determinants that shape behavior in digital environments and the subsequent impact of these behaviors on individuals and society.
- To investigate the ethical ramifications of AI in regulating and shaping online conduct.

Topics to Be Addressed

- Introduction to Cyber Behaviors and the Influence of AI.
- Cyberpsychology as the Foundational Framework.
- Computer-Mediated Communication: The AI-Shaped Channels of Cyber Behavior.
- Core Theoretical Frameworks: Theory of Planned Behavior, Social Cognitive Theory, and Social Identity Theory.
- Personality Traits and Cyber Behavior: Big Five personality traits, the HEXACO model of cyber behavior, and Dark Personality Traits.
- Comprehensive Mental Health Model: Emotional, Psychological, and Social Well-being.
- An Integrated Framework for Understanding AI-Mediated Cyber Behavior.

DOI: 10.4324/9781003657590-3

2.1 Introduction to Cyber Behavior and the Influence of AI

Nowadays, the ways people communicate and engage with one another have been transformed by technology, which has become an integral part of their lives. A wide range of acts and interactions, from basic email exchanges to participation in virtual communities, have become part of cyber behaviors (Shi et al., 2016). The rapid growth of online activities, including social media, gaming, shopping, and artificial intelligence (AI), has led to the development of increasingly complex online environments. While AI technologies bring many conveniences and innovations, they also raise new challenges and ethical concerns. For example, AI systems, such as recommendation algorithms, can influence how content is presented to users, leading them to interact differently (Gligorea et al., 2023). As the design of these algorithms maximizes individuals' engagement, it also allows for excessive screen time, leads to addictive behaviors, and increases exposure to harmful content (Ibrahim et al., 2023). This leads to both positive and negative consequences, particularly in terms of ethical and psychological issues (Xu, 2023), which are especially significant for the younger generation navigating these online environments. Due to the wide variety of online interactions, it became difficult to control and manage cyber behaviors, especially among teenagers and young people. AI's role in moderating and personalizing digital content can both reduce and increase harmful behaviors (Polizzi & Harrison, 2022). It is interesting to note that cyberbullying, harassment, compulsive internet use, and gaming addiction are all examples of such harmful habits. The anonymity provided by the internet, coupled with the emotional detachment that AI systems can create, often worsens these issues (Ma, 2024). A crucial question is: *How can AI-driven recommendation systems be adjusted to reduce the occurrence of harmful behaviors, such as cyberbullying?*

A comprehensive theoretical framework is essential to understand the complexities of the problems, causes, consequences, and motivations underlying these actions (Auriemma et al., 2020). This chapter aims to examine current theories and integrate concepts from technology, psychology, and sociology into the analysis of cyber behavior, with the goal of informing the planning of practical applications and interventions. The foundation for this integrated approach begins with cyberpsychology, a scientific interdisciplinary domain that examines the psychological phenomena emerging from human interaction with digital technology.

Takeaway: *AI systems can influence cyber behaviors in both positive and negative ways. Although these systems increase user engagement, they also contribute to addictive behaviors and harmful interactions. Understanding the underlying causes of these behaviors and applying psychological theories can help reduce the impact of these challenges.*

Reflection: *How can we ensure that AI technologies are designed to promote healthier behaviors and respect ethical standards in cyberspace?*

2.2 Cyberpsychology as the Foundational Framework

Cyberpsychology "is a scientific interdisciplinary domain that focuses on the psychological phenomena which emerge as a result of the human interaction with digital technology, particularly the Internet" (Suler, 2016). It examines how we interact with others using technology, how our behavior is influenced by technology, how technology can be developed to best suit our needs, and how our psychological states can be affected by technology. Much research in cyberpsychology has been driven by the Internet, particularly the advent of social media. However, other technologies have also been closely examined, including gaming (both online and offline), mobile computing, AI, virtual reality, and augmented reality. The Cyberpsychology Framework (Suler, 2004) illustrates the distinct impact of digital environments on psychological processes and behaviors. This theory offers essential insights into online interactions by emphasizing phenomena such as disinhibition and psychological isolation (Suler, 2010).

Online disinhibition refers to the tendency for individuals to exhibit less self-discipline in cyberspace (Suler, 2004). This phenomenon can appear in positive and negative ways. It may foster more openness and self-expression; conversely, it might provoke hostile or aggressive behaviors. There are two main factors that affect disinhibition: anonymity and synchronicity. These factors lead to the establishment of a psychological distance, which reduces feelings of accountability and responsibility (Suler, 2004). AI-driven platforms that offer anonymity, such as certain social networks or messaging apps, can diminish users' sense of responsibility, leading to harmful actions like trolling or cyberbullying (Wang & Ngai, 2020).

Cyberpsychology examines how virtual presence, psychological distance, and the distinctions between online and offline activities influence relationships (Suler, 2017). For example, virtual presence refers to the sensation of being "present" in a digital environment, which can impact individual engagement and decision-making processes. Regarding psychological distance, it is frequently generated by the absence of physical cues in online interactions, which impacts individuals' perceptions of their responsibilities and the consequences of their actions. The difference between offline behavior and cyber behavior emphasizes the influence of digital environments on individual self-presentation and ethical decision-making (Polizzi & Harrison, 2022).

The Cyberpsychology Framework correlates with personality theories by demonstrating how traits like extraversion and emotional stability appear in cyberspace (Hu et al., 2017). Additionally, it aligns with behavioral theories, such as the Theory of Planned Behavior (TPB), particularly in relation to the concepts of control and intention (Han et al., 2023). Moreover, the concept has considerable effects for mental health, since digital settings may produce both beneficial consequences, such as enhanced connectivity and creativity, and unfavorable ones, including addiction and stress (Cataldo et al., 2021). Having established cyberpsychology as the foundational framework for understanding psychological phenomena in digital environments, it becomes necessary to examine the specific types of behaviors that emerge in these spaces. Understanding the scope and diversity of cyber behaviors provides essential context for applying the theoretical frameworks that follow.

> ***Takeaway:*** *The Cyberpsychology Framework explores how the unique characteristics of digital environments, such as anonymity and disinhibition, impact behavior, providing insights into both positive and harmful online interactions.*
> ***Reflection:*** *How does the concept of online disinhibition help explain cyberbullying or trolling in cyberspaces?*

2.2.1 Scope of Cyber Behaviors

It is crucial to categorize the various activities, reasons, and challenges present in cyberspace in order to gain a deeper understanding of the complexity of cyber activity. D'Angelo (2020) identifies three basic categories that include the wide variety of online interactions: aggressive, addictive, and social-commercial (see Figure 2.1).

Aggressive behavior reflects the conflicts that occur in real life but is more complex due to the unique nature of cyberspace (Polizzi & Harrison, 2022). Aggressive behavior includes different types, such as cyberbullying, cyber victimization, online moral disengagement, and online harassment. In contrast to traditional bullying, which occurs only in the real world, cyberbullying can take numerous forms, including direct harassment, impersonation, and public shaming, all of

FIGURE 2.1 Illustration of the scope of cyber behaviors.

which worsen the emotional and psychological impact on victims. These effects are further complicated by the patterns of cyber victimization, which show that factors like age, gender, and cultural background influence both the victims and their responses (Al-Harigy et al., 2022). Additionally, AI systems used to moderate and filter content can sometimes miss harmful behavior or even increase it, especially when algorithms prioritize engagement over user safety (Kim & Yoon, 2023). Beyond cyberbullying, cyber harassment includes harmful activities like hate speech, where malicious individuals expose private information with the intent to harm others. Research shows that the anonymity and emotional distance offered by digital platforms can lead individuals to engage in harmful behaviors they might avoid in face-to-face interactions. What makes it even worse is that this anonymity is enhanced by AI-driven platforms, which increase interactions without considering accountability (Cartwright & Xue, 2023). This phenomenon is known as online moral disengagement (Kowalski et al., 2014). Similarly, online disinhibition can fuel aggressive behavior (Kowalski et al., 2014), as some people feel encouraged to act in ways they wouldn't in the real world, often because they perceive little or no consequences for their actions. Understanding the fundamental causes of these aggressive behaviors is important for developing effective strategies for prevention and intervention.

Addictive behaviors reflect the increasing dependence on cyberspaces for entertainment, social interaction, and escape from reality (Doğan et al., 2019), which causes compulsive internet use, gaming, and social media addiction. Problematic internet use is defined by extended online engagement, resulting in the neglect of offline commitments, disrupted relationships, and mental health concerns, including anxiety and depression (Barberis et al., 2023). In addition, AI-driven features such as notifications, personalized recommendations, and infinite scrolling on platforms play a significant role in keeping users engaged longer than intended, allowing for these addictive behaviors (ElSayary, 2023). Gaming addiction, another aspect of digital dependency, is particularly pronounced as online games incorporate elements intended to promote obsessive behavior (Pérez et al., 2023). The increasing number of online gambling platforms leads to gambling addiction, which carries significant financial and psychological effects for individuals, particularly males, and their families (Kuss & Gainsbury, 2021). Social media addiction poses a significant issue since platforms are designed with psychological triggers, like likes, shares, and comments, that promote continuous involvement, frequently harming users' mental health (Khalaf et al., 2023). AI systems in these platforms further reinforce these behaviors by optimizing content to match user preferences and emotional triggers, making it harder for users to disengage (Beyari, 2023). This resulted in an artificial mode of communication among individuals.

Social-commercial behaviors examine the management of identities, connections, and consumer habits in digital contexts (Khalaf et al., 2023). The increasing popularity of online shopping has significantly influenced consumer behavior, leading to impulsive purchasing and a reliance on online reviews for purchasing decisions (Ibrahim et al., 2023). AI algorithms that suggest products based on past behaviors can lead to impulsive buying, even when the products aren't necessary or beneficial (Zhang et al., 2022). Online dating platforms have transformed the way relationships form, while also raising concerns about authenticity, privacy, and emotional manipulation (Simão et al., 2021). Social networking, an essential domain of digital interaction, facilitates communication, content sharing, and community development (Bonilla-Zorita et al., 2020). Nonetheless, these platforms also increase problems, including echo chambers, social comparison, and the spread of misinformation, all of which can have substantial psychological and social consequences. AI-driven content curation often creates echo chambers by showing users more of the same type of content they engage with, further entrenching their views and potentially increasing polarization (Capraro et al., 2024).

The complex nature of cyber behaviors needs an approach that integrates different theoretical frameworks, as shown in Figure 2.2. As AI technologies continue to evolve, it is essential to incorporate them into this approach to understand both their positive and negative impacts on cyber behavior (Priyanka et al., 2023). This will enhance understanding of the psychological and ethical aspects of online interactions, as well as the influence of individual, social, and contextual factors that

FIGURE 2.2 The integrated framework requires collaboration across different disciplines.

a single theory cannot adequately include. Although cyberpsychology provides a broad perspective on the human mind in cyberspaces, and the taxonomy of cyber behaviors reveals the diversity of online actions, a deeper understanding requires examining the channels through which these interactions occur. The nature of the communication medium itself, whether text-based messaging, video calls, or algorithmically curated social media feeds, fundamentally shapes how individuals perceive, interpret, and respond to one another in digital environments. As the integrated theoretical framework offers advantages, it also raises certain challenges. The increasing integration of AI tools in moderation and personalization may introduce new biases or inconsistencies, which can affect how behaviors are interpreted and addressed (Gligorea et al., 2023). The overlapping of many frameworks may lead to redundancies, rather than offering a meaningful approach that considers different perspectives. Additionally, the interdisciplinary nature of this approach necessitates collaboration among disciplines such as psychology, sociology, and technology.

> ***Takeaway:*** *Cyber behaviors are vast and varied, with significant implications for individuals and communities. Aggression, addiction, and social-commercial behaviors all require a deeper understanding of how AI moderates and influences them. The integration of multiple disciplines is essential for understanding the complex nature of cyber behavior, especially in the context of AI's role.*
> ***Reflection:*** *What ethical challenges arise from using AI to manage addictive behaviors, and how can these issues be mitigated?*

2.3 Computer-Mediated Communication: The AI-Shaped Channels of Cyber Behavior

Although cyberpsychology offers a broad perspective on the human mind in digital spaces, a deeper understanding of cyber behavior requires a focused examination of the channels through which these interactions occur. This is the domain of Computer-Mediated Communication (CMC), a field that investigates human communication through electronic devices and networks (Hyader et al., 2026). As the architecture of modern social life, CMC provides the foundational composition for the cyber behaviors explored in this book. However, these channels are no longer passive channels. They are increasingly and actively shaped by AI, which acts as a central, often invisible, force in how we connect, perceive, and behave online.

A foundational framework for understanding relationships in this environment is the *Social Information Processing (SIP) theory*, which explains how individuals can form meaningful, well-developed relationships online despite the absence of nonverbal cues (Walther & Whitty, 2020). The theory posits that communicators strategically adapt, using the available textual and symbolic cues to convey personality and emotion over time. This adaptive process can even lead to the

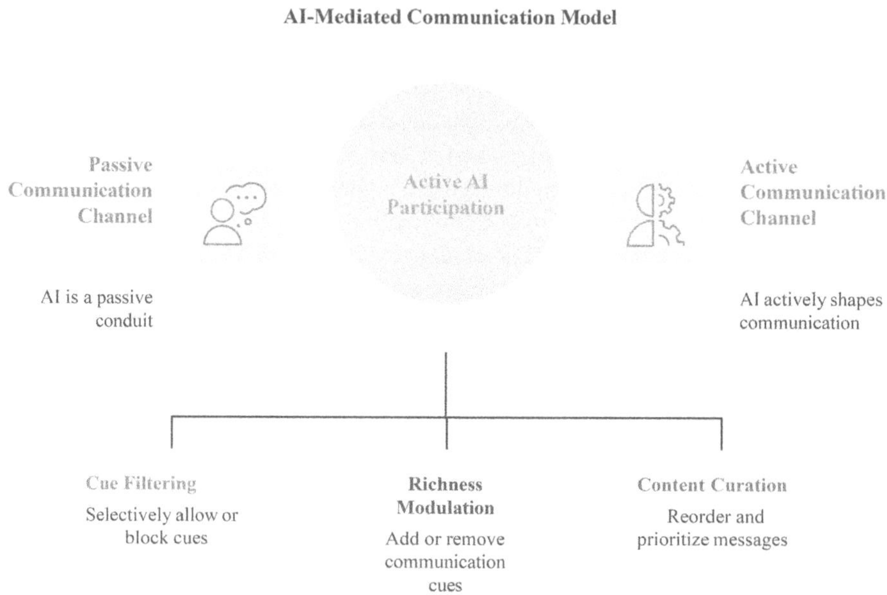

FIGURE 2.3 An illustration that shows the central argument that AI is not a passive conduit but an active participant in the communication process.

hyperpersonal effect, where online relationships become more intimate and idealized than their offline counterparts due to the ample opportunities for selective self-presentation and partner idealization (Walter, 2024). AI now plays a pivotal role in this dynamic, acting as a catalyst for the hyperpersonal model (see Figure 2.3). For instance, AI-driven recommendation engines on social media and dating apps can selectively present profiles and content that align with a user's idealized preferences. It is accelerating the formation of intense, though selected, social bonds. The AI, in essence, becomes a co-author in the creation of these hyperpersonal connections, shaping who we meet and how we perceive them.

Complementing this relational view, *Media Richness Theory* provides a lens for evaluating the communication channels themselves (Kock, 2005). This theory classifies media based on their capacity to convey rich information through immediate feedback, multiple cues (e.g., facial expressions and tone of voice), and personalization. A video call, for example, is far richer than a text message. This distinction is crucial for understanding why different platforms encourage varying cyber behaviors. Immersive social experiences in gaming, facilitated by the rich medium of voice chat, can foster strong social cohesion, whereas the lean nature of anonymous text-based forums can depersonalize interaction. AI further complicates this landscape by dynamically altering media richness. An AI system can enrich a lean medium by generating avatars that react to text, or it can impoverish a rich medium by summarizing a detailed video into a few lines of text. In this way,

AI acts as a modulator of social presence, capable of either enhancing or diminishing the perceived closeness between communicators to serve platform-specific goals, such as sustained engagement or efficient information delivery.

Perhaps the most widely discussed phenomenon bridging CMC and cyberpsychology is *online disinhibition*, where the anonymity and reduced social cues of digital environments lead individuals to express themselves more freely and with less restraint than they would in person (Sheeks & Birchmeier, 2007). This disinhibition effect is a double-edged sword. It can foster positive outcomes by encouraging self-disclosure and seeking social support, particularly for individuals who may struggle with face-to-face interaction (ElSayary et al., 2026). However, it is also a key facilitator of negative cyber behaviors, including cyberbullying and toxic speech, as individuals may feel a diminished sense of accountability (Jiménez-Díaz et al., 2026). AI introduces a new and powerful actor into this dynamic. On the one hand, AI-powered content moderation systems act as automated, non-human regulators of disinhibited behavior, capable of filtering out harmful content on a massive scale. On the other hand, the same AI systems, when optimized for engagement, can learn to exploit disinhibition by promoting content that is controversial or emotionally charged, thereby provoking strong reactions and creating a feedback loop of algorithmically amplified outrage. This leads to the complex role of CMC in facilitating social support. Digital platforms have become indispensable for connecting individuals with supportive networks, transcending geographical barriers and providing access to communities of shared experience (Fuss et al., 2021). Yet, the technologies that connect can also foster a sense of isolation if the interactions they provide are superficial or replace more meaningful offline relationships (Petersen et al., 2023). AI's influence here is profound. It can act as a positive force by identifying individuals in distress and connecting them with support groups or mental health resources. Conversely, by creating highly personalized "echo chambers", AI can isolate individuals from diverse perspectives, reinforcing their existing beliefs and potentially leading to a sense of alienation from those who hold different views. Thus, the digital architecture, increasingly managed by AI, has the power to either build bridges of social support or erect walls of social isolation.

Computer-Mediated Communication theories reveal how the characteristics of digital channels, their richness, synchronicity, and capacity for anonymity, shape the nature of online interactions and influence phenomena ranging from hyperpersonal relationships to online disinhibition. However, understanding why individuals choose to engage in specific cyber behaviors, how they learn and adopt these behaviors, and how group dynamics influence their actions requires additional theoretical perspectives. The following section examines core behavioral and social theories that explain the psychological mechanisms underlying cyber behavior, complementing the CMC focus on communication channels with frameworks that address individual decision-making, social learning, and group identity.

Takeaway: *Computer-mediated communication provides the structural pathways through which digital interactions unfold, and this section demonstrates that these pathways are no longer neutral spaces. AI now shapes how relationships form, how messages are interpreted, and how people behave online. AI can increase harmful behavior or isolation when interactions become filtered or manipulated.*
Reflection: *How can AI-shaped communication channels be designed to support healthy interaction without encouraging harmful or isolating behavior?*

2.4 Core Theoretical Frameworks

Earlier psychological frameworks remain essential for understanding how AI shapes cyber behavior, but they must be reinterpreted in light of algorithmic influence. Theoretical frameworks serve as primary tools for analyzing the complex psychological and social factors that influence cyber actions. This section examines three principal frameworks: the Theory of Planned Behavior (TPB) (Ajzen, 2011), Social Cognitive Theory (SCT) (Bandura, 1992), and Social Identity Theory (SIT) (Tajfel & Turner, 1979). Each offers significant insights into the elements that influence digital interactions, cyber behaviors, and ethical issues. The first of these frameworks, the Theory of Planned Behavior, offers a comprehensive model for understanding how individual beliefs, social norms, and perceived control influence behavioral intentions and actions in digital environments.

2.4.1 Theory of Planned Behavior (TPB)

The Theory of Planned Behavior (TPB), proposed by Ajzen (2011), provides a detailed framework that explains the influence of individual beliefs, social norms, and perceived control on intentions and behaviors (see Figure 2.4). This concept is especially beneficial for understanding behaviors in online contexts, because intentions frequently influence online activities. Firstly, *attitudes* regarding cyber behaviors pertain to an individual's assessment of particular online actions, whether favorable or unfavorable. An individual's perspective on sharing online personal data can influence their decision to engage in such behavior. Another component is the *subjective norms* in cyberspace, which indicate how perceived social influences can affect an individual's behavior. These may include societal expectations or peer influences. The benchmarks of an online community can influence individuals' perceptions of activities such as cyberbullying, labeling them as either acceptable or inappropriate. Finally, *perceived cyber behavioral control* refers to an individual's belief in their ability to perform an activity. This element is essential in cyberspace, where variables such as technical proficiency and resource accessibility can significantly impact an individual's ability to act (Ajzen, 1991; Herrmann & Kim, 2017).

The TPB paradigm is relevant to various cyber behaviors. Cyberbullying clarifies how attitudes toward violence, social acceptance, and the perceived control

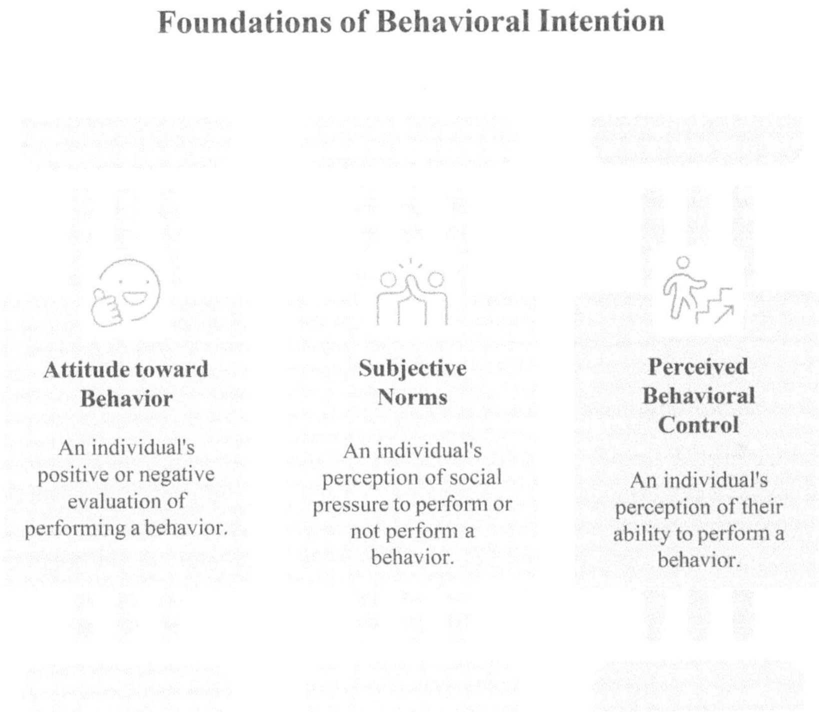

FIGURE 2.4 The three components of the Theory of Planned Behavior.

of anonymity influence the desire to perpetrate cyber harassment (Auriemma et al., 2020). Addictive behaviors, such as excessive social media usage, can be linked to positive perceptions of digital platforms, peer validation, and ease of access (Wang & Nagi, 2020). AI-driven functionalities such as tailored content and recommendation algorithms may promote extended usage, potentially resulting in addictive behaviors (Cataldo et al., 2021). In digital commerce, TPB clarifies the impact of attitudes towards online shopping, social influences, and perceived usability on purchasing decisions (Cartwright & Xue, 2023). In online dating, the decision to engage with platforms may be influenced by positive views of virtual matchmaking, societal endorsement, and perceived user-friendliness (Degen & Kleeberg-Niepage, 2021). The integration of the TPB with other frameworks enhances its explanatory power. It correlates with cognitive theories, such as decision-making models, illustrating how attitudes and perceptions of control are shaped by cognitive biases and information processing (Mehdy et al., 2021). AI systems on digital platforms might worsen cognitive biases, affecting users' judgments and behaviors in ways they may not be consciously aware of (Priyanka et al., 2023). Although the Theory of Planned Behavior focuses on how attitudes, norms, and perceived control influence behavioral intentions, it does not fully explain how individuals initially acquire these attitudes and behaviors. This is where Social

Cognitive Theory becomes essential, emphasizing the role of observational learning, self-efficacy, and the reciprocal interaction between individuals and their digital environments in shaping cyber behavior.

> ***Takeaway:*** *The Theory of Planned Behavior (TPB) helps predict and potentially modify user's intentions and behaviors in cyberspace by analyzing their attitudes, social norms, and perceived behavioral control.*
> ***Reflection:*** *How might the Theory of Planned Behavior help in preventing aggressive cyber behaviors in cyberspace?*

2.4.2 Social Cognitive Theory (SCT)

Social Cognitive Theory (SCT), established by Bandura (1992), emphasizes the interplay between personal characteristics, environmental influences, and behavior. The three primary components of SCT include self-efficacy, observational learning, and reciprocal determinism. Self-efficacy refers to an individual's confidence in their capacity to navigate online proficiently (see Figure 2.5). A person proficient in their technical skills is more inclined to utilize AI responsibly (Gligorea et al.,

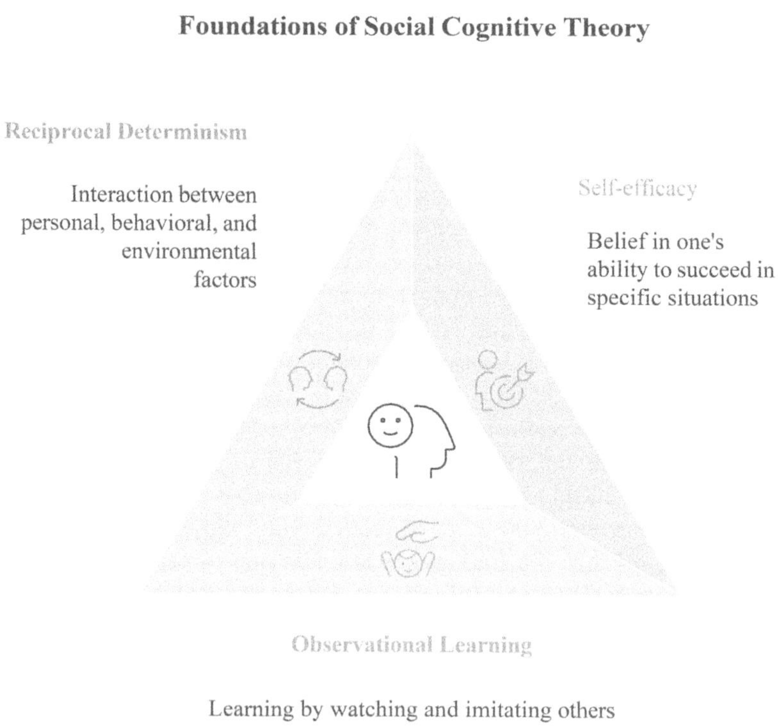

FIGURE 2.5 Illustration of the three core principles of Social Cognitive Theory.

2023). AI can either augment or diminish self-efficacy. AI-driven tools that streamline tasks may enhance self-confidence in online interactions, but excessively intricate systems could induce annoyance (Priyanka et al., 2023). Observational learning is the acquisition of habits by observing and imitating social media influencers. The reciprocal determinism, the core of SCT, explains the dynamics and the reciprocal interaction of individuals with a set of learning experiences. This includes the environment, external social context, and behavior, as well as the response of stimuli to achieve their goals. It emphasizes the bidirectional interaction between humans and cyberspace, wherein online norms can impact behaviors, and personal actions can affect the wider digital context (Lajnef, 2023).

SCT is particularly significant for understanding phenomena such as moral disengagement, where individuals justify unethical behavior, including trolling or spreading misinformation (Polizzi & Harrison, 2022). AI systems, by recommending and amplifying harmful content, can influence users to mimic these unethical behaviors, especially when the system prioritizes engagement over ethical considerations (Shi et al., 2016). The idea clarifies the mechanisms by which aggressive behaviors are acquired and reinforced by exposure to hostile or violent material. Addiction, especially in gaming or social media, can be attributed to the interplay between individual characteristics (such as a craving for rewards) and environmental motives (such as features intended to maintain user engagement) (Beyari, 2023). SCT provides insight into social media behavior, explaining how users change their actions as a response to feedback received online, such as likes, shares, and comments (Song et al., 2021).

Integrating SCT with social identity influences individuals' behavior, as they often imitate the norms, actions, and expectations of the groups to which they belong or interact online (Hu et al., 2017). Moreover, SCT's association with well-being suggests that positive online interactions can lead to mental health improvement, while negative experiences can have harmful consequences (Khalaf et al., 2023). SCT demonstrates how individuals learn behaviors through observation and how their self-efficacy influences their actions in digital environments. However, the theory's emphasis on individual learning processes must be complemented by an understanding of how group membership and social identity shape behavior. Social Identity Theory addresses this dimension by examining how individuals derive their self-concept from group affiliations and how these group dynamics influence online interactions, particularly in the formation of in-groups and out-groups within digital communities.

Takeaway: *Social Cognitive Theory (SCT) explains the reciprocal interactions between individuals and their digital environment, with implications for understanding addictive behaviors, moral disengagement, and social media habits.*
Reflection: *Reflect on a social media influencer you follow. How does his/her cyber behavior shape his/her own online habits?*

2.4.3 Social Identity Theory (SIT)

Social Identity Theory (SIT), established by Tajfel (1974), examines the impact of group affiliation and identification on individuals' behavior and self-perception. In cyberspace, virtual communities are established based on shared interests or objectives. SIT offers a valuable foundation for comprehending the dynamics of online interactions.

The key principles of SIT highlight the formation of digital identity, online self-classification, and virtual group interactions. The development of digital identity relates to how individuals establish their self-concept through connections with online groups, such as gaming communities or fan clubs. In online self-categorization, individuals define their identities in relation to others, often highlighting similarities within the in-group and distinctions from the out-group. AI systems can shape digital identity formation by selecting content and interactions that favor in-group or out-group dynamics, occasionally increasing conflicts (Gligorea et al., 2023). Finally, virtual group dynamics, including collaboration, competitiveness, and compliance, affect individual behavior inside online communities (Hunter & Stockdale, 2010). The structure and design of digital platforms affect how group identities form and function.

SIT provides important insights into the dynamics of online communities, including the collective behaviors observed in fan groups and activist networks (Ibrahim et al., 2023). Within the context of gaming, group identification can promote collaboration and commitment, but it may also provoke toxic behaviors, such as the exclusion of outsiders or hatred towards individuals who do not adhere to group norms (Kou, 2020). Cyberbullying in these groups frequently includes in-group members attacking others external to their group, which illustrates the impact of social interactions (Auriemma et al., 2020). Likewise, on online dating platforms, community norms influence how individuals present themselves and interact with others, shaping their online behavior (Bonilla-Zorita, 2020). SIT also correlates with cognitive theories, illustrating how group affiliation influences perception and decision-making (Mirbabaie et al., 2021). Moreover, SIT's emphasis on social connections aligns with well-being theories, highlighting the psychological benefits and risks associated with group affiliation in digital environments (Beyari, 2023).

The behavioral frameworks presented thus far, the Theory of Planned Behavior, Social Cognitive Theory, and Social Identity Theory, explain how attitudes, learning processes, and group dynamics shape cyber behavior. However, these frameworks do not fully account for the stable individual differences that predispose people to form certain attitudes, seek out particular social groups, or respond differently to the same digital environments. This is the domain of personality psychology, which examines the enduring traits that make each person distinct and that fundamentally influence how individuals engage with digital technologies and navigate online spaces.

Takeaway: *Social Identity Theory (SIT) helps explain how group affiliations in cyberspaces shape behavior, identity formation, and online dynamics, providing insights into both positive and negative online interactions.*
Reflection: *Reflect on an online community you belong to. How do group norms in cyberspace influence your behavior and identity?*

2.5 Personality Psychology and Cyber Behavior

Personality psychology is a core branch of the behavioral sciences that examines the stable tendencies in how people think, feel, and act – patterns that make each person distinct (Allport, 1931; McCrae & Costa, 1995; Roberts & Yoon, 2022). These enduring traits are crucial for understanding human behavior and remain a central theme in psychological research. A precise definition of personality is necessary before conducting any meaningful study of human behavior, as it forms the foundation for assessing and understanding individual differences (Thørrisen & Sadeghi, 2023). In the context of AI-mediated environments, this understanding becomes even more critical. Individuals' personality traits influence how they interact with AI tools, respond to algorithmic suggestions, and form digital habits. Personality frameworks, therefore, not only help explain offline behavior but also offer insight into emerging patterns of AI-driven interactions, such as susceptibility to algorithmic influence, preference for certain AI functionalities, or the likelihood of adopting responsible versus risky AI-related behaviors. To ground this discussion, three major personality frameworks will be explored in relation to AI behavior: the Big Five, the HEXACO model, and the Dark Tetrad. Detailed analysis of how personality traits manifest in specific cyber behaviors will be presented in Chapter 7.

2.5.1 Big Five Model

The Big Five personality model is referred to as OCEAN: (O) Openness to experience, (C) Conscientiousness, (E) Extraversion, (A) Agreeableness, and (N) Neuroticism. This framework provides an understanding of the impact of these attributes on cyber behaviors, with each trait representing specific preferences that are evident in different forms of online interaction.

First, *openness to experience (O)* is defined as curiosity, creativity, and an urge to explore creative ideas that significantly impact cyber behaviors. Individuals exhibiting this trait frequently adopt and explore new technology, including platforms, applications, and inventions (Kuss & Giansbury, 2021). Their openness encourages them to engage in innovative online expressions, such as blogging, digital art, and content production, through which they align their perceptions with distinctive behaviors (Kuss & Gainsbury, 2021). AI-driven content platforms may influence individuals with high openness by suggesting new trends, tools, or content based on their past behavior, thus reinforcing their creative and exploratory tendencies (Shi et al., 2016). This trait is linked to several theoretical frameworks. In the Theory of Planned Behavior (TPB), openness can enhance attitudes toward adoption. Social Cognitive Theory (SCT) advocates for observational learning, resulting in individuals imitating new habits (Burnell et al., 2023). Furthermore, it facilitates identity exploration in digital contexts, as stated by Social Identity Theory (SIT), wherein individuals utilize online platforms to experiment with self-concepts and affiliations (Hu et al., 2017).

A further trait is *conscientiousness (C),* defined by individuals who exhibit self-discipline, organizational skills, and a dedication to their responsibilities. Individuals exhibiting high levels of conscientiousness demonstrate greater efficacy in managing their online time and balancing virtual engagements with offline obligations (Jackson et al., 2010). As a result, their online accountability necessitates the careful use of data management, ethical cyber behavior, and methodical task organization in virtual environments, which are regarded as vital (Polizzi & Harrison, 2022). AI-driven reminders and productivity applications can assist conscientious people in maintaining organization and efficiently managing their online and offline obligations (Capraro et al., 2024). This trait is correlated with behavioral control in the Theory of Planned Behavior, as conscientious individuals experience significant control in online environments (Díaz et al., 2020; Mehdy et al., 2021). In addition, the alignment with self-regulation in SCT indicates how users overcome addictive behavior and emphasize significant digital engagements (Díaz et al., 2020). Moreover, conscientiousness facilitates the preservation of uniform digital identities, demonstrating consistency in individuals' self-presentation across various platforms (Liang & Yoon, 2022).

Extraversion (E), where extroverted people excel in virtual social interactions, often engaging in online communities, forums, and group chats (Kroencke et al., 2023). Their tendency to connect also motivates activities such as online dating and maintaining active social media profiles (Barberis et al., 2023). AI-driven recommendations and matchmaking features on social platforms can provide extraverts with more opportunities for connection, reinforcing their social engagement (Priyanka et al., 2023). Theoretical connections illustrate the interaction between extraversion and social identity theory, as extroverts often seek group memberships that enhance their digital visibility (Argyle, 2020). Their behavioral intentions, as outlined in the Theory of Planned Behavior, are influenced by their desire for connection and engagement (Hu et al., 2017; Mykota, 2022). Cognitive-social factors, including the interpretation of peer feedback, also influence their online activities, affect self-efficacy, and enhance active participation (Ibrahim et al., 2023).

Agreeableness (A) is associated with collaboration, generosity, and conflict avoidance, which can impact online interactions. Individuals with high agreeableness are less susceptible to cyberbullying and more inclined toward online collaboration, thereby promoting positive and inclusive digital environments (Parlangeli et al.,

2019). AI algorithms that promote positive, supportive content and exclude harmful or abusive interactions can foster agreeable behaviors in online communities (Gligorea et al., 2023). The link of agreeableness to moral engagement indicates that it reduces the tendency toward negative cyber behaviors, such as trolling or harassment (Pérez et al., 2023), and corresponds with ethical cyber behavior (Parlangeli et al., 2019; Wang & Ngai, 2020). Group behavior demonstrates the supportive nature of agreeableness toward virtual communities (Cartwright & Xue, 2023; Hu et al., 2017), as indicated in SIT. Furthermore, normative views on kindness and fairness influence their digital interactions, as described in the Theory of Planned Behavior (Mehdy et al., 2021; Parlangeli et al., 2019). Ultimately, the implications for well-being highlight the advantages of promoting agreeableness in cyberspace (Parlangeli et al., 2019).

Neuroticism (N) is defined as emotional instability, sensitivity to stress, and susceptibility to unpleasant emotional experiences. Individuals with high neuroticism are at risk of cyber victimization due to their difficulties in managing online conflict or hatred. In addition to their higher possibility of internet addiction, they utilize digital environments as a means of escapism and often exhibit anxiety in cyber behaviors, including fear of judgment or social rejection (Verma et al., 2024). AI platforms that use personalized content or recommendation algorithms may increase feelings of anxiety and isolation in individuals with high neuroticism by exposing them to harmful content or reinforcing negative feedback loops (Topino et al., 2021). The incorporation of perceived risks into the Theory of Planned Behavior suggests that individuals with neurotic tendencies perceive greater dangers in digital contexts (Bonilla-Zorita et al., 2020). Their association with SCT demonstrates how emotional reactions to online experiences influence their participation (Song et al., 2021; Zhan et al., 2021). The consequences for well-being, particularly regarding the impact of online activities on mental health, are crucial in highlighting the need for targeted interventions (Khalaf et al., 2023).

> ***Takeaway:*** *The Big Five model helps explain the influence of core personality traits on cyber behavior. These traits help to understand how individuals address challenges in cyberspaces, from managing addictive behaviors to promoting ethical and responsible cyber behavior.*
> ***Reflection:*** *How can understanding the Big Five personality traits help in designing AI tools that support users in making healthier and more responsible digital choices??*

2.5.2 HEXACO Framework

The HEXACO model builds upon the Big Five personality traits, incorporating the same dimensions of openness to experience, conscientiousness, extraversion, and agreeableness. However, neuroticism, a component of the Big Five concept,

TABLE 2.1 The Commonalities and Differences between the Big Five Personality Model and the HEXACO Model

Trait	*Big Five*	*HEXACO*	*Definition*
Openness to Experience	O	HEXAC**O**	Creative, curious, preference for novelty
Conscientiousness	C	HEXA**C**O	Organized, diligent, goal-oriented
Extraversion	E	HE**X**ACO	Sociable, energetic, seeks stimulation
Agreeableness	A	HEX**A**CO	Tolerant, cooperative, patient
Neuroticism/ Emotionality	N	H**E**XACO	Big Five: emotional instability, anxiety, mood swings HEXACO: (Neuroticism is replaced by emotionality) emotional sensitivity, vulnerability
Honesty-Humility	NA	**H**EXACO	Sincere, fair, modest, avoids greed

has been substituted by emotionality. In the Big Five model, neuroticism refers to emotional instability, anxiety, and mood swings. In contrast, the emotionality in the HEXACO model emphasizes emotional sensitivity and vulnerability, thereby redirecting attention to more manageable emotional characteristics. The HEXACO model features a sixth trait, Honesty-Humility, encompassing attributes such as sincerity, fairness, modesty, and a lack of selfishness. This trait is not included in the Big Five model and is considered an essential aspect of individuals' behavior in online contexts, particularly in interactions with AI (ElSayary, 2025). Table 2.1 illustrates the differences between the personality trait frameworks.

Honesty-humility (H) serves as the foundational principle of digital ethics. Individuals exhibiting a high degree of this attribute are less likely to engage in immoral acts, such as plagiarism or hacking. Conversely, they highlight equitable behavior and authenticity in cyberspace (Wang & Ngai, 2020). AI moderation tools that filter or highlight unethical information can enhance ethical digital behavior by emphasizing honesty and fairness (Gligorea et al., 2023). Theoretical frameworks illustrate the relationship between honesty-humility and moral disengagement, suggesting a decreased ability to perceive unethical behavior (Cartwright & Xue, 2023). Social identity theory illustrates how individuals sustain ethical group norms and values in online environments (Parlangeli et al., 2019). Likewise, associations that promote behavioral control exhibit resilience against manipulative or harmful behaviors in cyberspace (Parlangeli et al., 2019).

Emotionality (E) is related to *neuroticism (N)* in the Big Five personality model. It includes fear, anxiety, and reliance, which influence how individuals manage online interactions. Individuals with increased emotionality may demonstrate reliance on virtual relationships and enhanced symptoms of fear or anxiety in online engagements, which affects overall well-being (Zhan et al., 2021). AI-powered tools that monitor emotional cues or responses could help identify signs of emotional distress, offering appropriate support or interventions (Malik et al., 2024). Connections in risk perception illustrate the influence of emotionality on decision-making related to privacy and safety in cyberspace (Malik et al., 2024). Additionally, the relationship with SCT highlights how emotional reactions are influenced by observational learning and reciprocal relationships (Lee, 2019). Finally, well-being interactions highlight the necessity of support networks to deal with the various challenges experienced by emotionally vulnerable individuals (Kuss & Gainsburg, 2021).

> ***Takeaway:*** *The HEXACO model developed the Big Five by adding a sixth dimension (Honesty-Humility) and redefining neuroticism as emotionality, highlighting these as key elements of behavior. It offers valuable insights for designing ethical AI systems and understanding the moral dimensions of cyber behavior.*
> ***Reflection:*** *How might incorporating Honesty-Humility into AI systems help promote more ethical behavior in cyberspaces?*

2.5.3 Dark Personality Traits

Dark personality traits, including the Dark Triad (narcissism, Machiavellianism, and psychopathy) and the Dark Tetrad (which includes sadism), expose the more concerning aspects of cyber behavior (Paulhus & Williams, 2002).

Narcissism influences behaviors associated with digital self-presentation and online attention-seeking (Delisi et al., 2020). Narcissistic individuals typically seek validation and praise, often engaging in self-promotion that highlights their attributes (Sedikides & Hart, 2025). Incorporating social identity theory, narcissists typically develop online personas that enhance their perceived status (Oliver et al., 2023). AI-driven content creation tools can worsen narcissistic tendencies by enabling more controlled and curated digital personas, potentially leading to unhealthy comparisons or self-promotion behaviors (Oliver et al., 2023). The Theory of Planned Behavior (TPB) explains the motivation of narcissistic individuals, who engage in self-serving cyber behaviors to enhance their image (Palmieri et al., 2021).

Machiavellianism emerges through fraud and manipulation in online interactions. Individuals exhibiting this trait frequently employ digital tools to achieve personal goals, often at the expense of others (McLarty et al., 2021). AI systems are designed to maximize engagement; however, they can be used by Machiavellian individuals, who may utilize these systems to mislead others or accomplish their objectives (Bengio et al., 2024). In addition, the concept of moral disengagement is significant, as these individuals skillfully justify unethical behavior (Leary, 1986). Their ability to make use of group dynamics, as highlighted by Social Cognitive Theory (SCT), demonstrates their misuse of digital communities to fulfill their aims (Wang & Ngai, 2020).

Psychopathy is associated with impulsive, callous, and aggressive behavior in cyberspace (Wang & Ngai, 2020). Psychopaths exhibit a tendency for cyber violence and generally neglect digital norms (Delisi, 2020). The absence of behavioral control correlates with their tendency for inadequate self-regulation, whereas disinhibition elements illustrate their predisposition to engage in dangerous and harmful cyber behaviors (Barberis et al., 2023). AI systems that offer anonymity or lack oversight could facilitate psychopathic behaviors, as these individuals may act without fear of consequences (Kicaburun & Griffiths, 2018).

Sadism is another facet of cyber behavior introduced into the Dark Tetrad and characterized by trolling and deriving enjoyment from the distress of others via cyberbullying (Leite et al., 2023). Moral disengagement examines how sadists justify their harmful behaviors, a phenomenon similar to other dark traits (Lobbestael et al., 2023). AI platforms can intentionally reinforce sadistic behaviors if they reward negative engagement or encourage harmful content, further normalizing these toxic actions (Bengio et al., 2024). The social identity dimension indicates that sadists may be drawn to toxic online groups where harmful behavior is normalized (Leite et al., 2023). Furthermore, the negative effects of such actions on both the individuals involved and the broader community align with well-being theories, which emphasize the psychological impact of such behaviors (Wang & Ngai, 2020).

The frameworks examined thus far, cyberpsychology, computer-mediated communication, behavioral theories, and personality psychology, provide essential tools for understanding why and how individuals engage in cyber behaviors. However, a comprehensive understanding of cyber behavior requires not only explaining its causes but also assessing its consequences. The ultimate concern is how these behaviors impact individuals' mental health and well-being. This necessitates a framework for conceptualizing and measuring well-being in digital contexts, which is provided by Keyes' Mental Health Model. This model provides a comprehensive approach to understanding well-being, extending beyond the mere absence of mental illness to encompass positive functioning across emotional, psychological, and social dimensions.

> ***Takeaway:*** *The Dark Triad traits explain negative cyber behaviors, from manipulation to cyber violence. Recognizing these traits helps to develop strategies and AI systems that intervene and eliminate harm in cyberspaces.*
> ***Reflection:*** *How can understanding Dark Triad traits inform the design of AI systems that prevent toxic behaviors like trolling and cyberbullying?*

2.6 Comprehensive Mental Health Model

Keyes' (2002) Mental Health Model provides a comprehensive framework for understanding various aspects of well-being, including its relevance to cyberspace.

This framework emphasizes emotional, psychological, and social well-being as essential components of mental health. In the context of cyberspace, the model offers insights into how online interactions and behaviors can either positively or negatively impact overall well-being.

2.6.1 Emotional Well-Being

Emotional well-being in cyberspaces includes patterns of affect, satisfaction, and happiness exhibited and perceived online. It varies from joy and excitement to anxiety and frustration (Verma et al., 2024). These patterns are shaped by the nature and quality of digital interactions. These include positive feedback from social media or negative consequences such as anxiety caused by cyberbullying (Khalaf et al., 2023). AI algorithms used by social media platforms may influence emotional well-being by curating content that either reinforces positive emotions or exacerbates negative experiences, depending on the feedback loops generated (Khalaf et al., 2023).

Online life happiness is a vital element, representing an individual's assessment of their digital experiences. Satisfaction may arise from satisfying virtual relationships, successful online activities, or participation in significant digital networks (Cataldo et al., 2021). Virtual happiness expression refers to the manner in which people communicate and share their emotional states online, frequently utilizing postings, emojis, and digital interactions that express both happy and negative sentiments (Verma et al., 2024). AI-driven analytics can affect how individuals express and perceive their emotional well-being online, as social media platforms prioritize certain emotional responses over others, influencing users' perceptions of their digital lives (Verma et al., 2024).

Emotional well-being incorporates multiple theoretical frameworks, such as personality theory, the theory of planned behavior, and social cognitive theory. First, personality connections emphasize the impact of extraversion and neuroticism on emotional well-being in digital environments (Barberis et al., 2023). In addition, behavioral factors of TPB indicate that positive attitudes and perceived control in cyberspaces improve satisfaction (Leite et al., 2023). Finally, social cognitive connections highlight the importance of self-efficacy and observational learning in promoting emotional resilience in cyberspaces (Barberis et al., 2023).

Takeaway: *AI systems can significantly shape users' emotional well-being online. While they can provide positive experiences, they also have the potential to reinforce negative emotions. Understanding these dynamics is crucial in creating digital environments that support emotional resilience and well-being.*
Reflection: *How can AI developers balance content curation to promote positive emotional experiences while minimizing the risk of reinforcing negative feelings like anxiety or frustration??*

2.6.2 Psychological Well-Being

Psychological well-being in the digital era involves self-acceptance, personal development, and a sense of purpose resulting from online engagements (Verma et al., 2024). Digital self-acceptance indicates the manner in which individuals recognize and embrace their digital identities, including their online presentation and the reconciliation of differences between their virtual and real-world personas (Suler, 2017). This approach is essential for preserving a unified identity in an increasingly digital environment. AI systems that promote curated content and personalized experiences can encourage users to construct and refine their digital identities, though this may sometimes lead to conflicts between virtual and real-life personas (Mirbabaie et al., 2021).

As pointed out by Suler (2017), digital platforms encourage online personal growth by providing chances for study, skill enhancement, and creative expression. This is important, as cyberspaces can substantially enhance psychological growth through instructional content, collaborative projects, or artistic efforts. On the other hand, finding meaning and direction through online activities can develop a sense of purpose in the virtual world. This can be achieved by engaging in campaigns, joining supportive communities, or creating content that aligns with and expresses personal values (Tan et al., 2021). AI can support personal growth by recommending content that aligns with users' developmental goals, but it may also hinder growth if it creates an echo chamber or narrows the scope of what individuals are exposed to (Capraro et al., 2024).

Theoretical frameworks explain psychological well-being and provide a better understanding of these processes. For example, personality trait relationships demonstrate that openness enhances growth and exploration, while conscientiousness maintains purpose and focus (Roccas et al., 2002). Also, SIT clarifies how digital settings facilitate the creation and confirmation of identity (Topino et al., 2021). According to TPB, behavioral intention underlines the significance of establishing and attaining substantial digital objectives (Romera et al., 2020).

> ***Takeaway:*** *Psychological well-being in the digital age involves navigating one's digital identity and personal growth. AI systems that promote personalized experiences can support development but may also create challenges if they limit users' growth by fostering an echo chamber effect.*
> ***Reflection:*** *In what ways can AI tools be designed to encourage personal growth and self-acceptance while preventing negative outcomes, such as identity conflict or limited exposure to new ideas?*

2.6.3 Social Well-Being

Social well-being in digital environments highlights integration, participation, and coherence within cyberspaces (Suler, 2017). In this context, virtual community integration refers to individuals' sense of connection and support received from online communities, like social media networks, gaming communities, or professional forums (Hu et al., 2017). Accordingly, this integration promotes a sense of belonging, which is essential for social well-being. AI moderation tools used by online communities may either foster inclusiveness by promoting supportive behavior or contribute to toxicity by amplifying division and exclusion (Gligorea et al., 2023).

In the context of online social contribution, the value of individuals' attributes includes their ability to positively impact others through guidance, assistance, or content generation (Kuss & Giansbury, 2021), which emphasizes the mutual characteristics of healthy digital connections. In addition, digital social coherence describes the ability to recognize and manage complex online interactions. This is because the frequently inconsistent characteristics promote a feeling of organization and clarity in virtual environments (Verma et al., 2024). AI tools that moderate content and provide suggestions can impact the coherence of online social spaces, for better or worse, depending on their ability to promote positive interactions (Gligorea et al., 2023).

Regarding the theoretical integration of social well-being, it enhances our understanding of these dynamics. For example, identity theory emphasizes the significance of group relationships in influencing social well-being (Liang & Yoon, 2022). In addition, agreeableness and extraversion of personality traits promote engagement and cooperation in online groups (Roccas et al., 2002). Finally, the cognitive-social relations derived from Social Cognitive Theory illustrate how observational learning and feedback loops facilitate meaningful online relationships (Mykota, 2022).

Takeaway: *AI-driven tools can significantly impact social well-being in online spaces. They can either promote social interactions and a sense of belonging or amplify negative behaviors and exclusion. The design of these tools is crucial for maintaining cohesive and supportive online communities.*
Reflection: *How can AI moderation tools be developed to promote inclusivity and prevent the spread of toxicity in online communities?*

2.6.4 Mental Health Continuum

Keyes' mental health continuum (Keyes, 2002) provides insights into mental health within cyberspace as it presents a spectrum from flourishing to languishing. For example, digital flourishing patterns emphasize excellent performance in online environments. This is characterized by higher levels of engagement, happiness, and accomplishment (Brailovskaia et al., 2024). It leads thriving individuals to use digital tools for self-improvement, social engagement, and meaningful activities. AI platforms that promote positive behaviors, content, and social interactions contribute to digital flourishing by encouraging individuals to engage in healthier, more meaningful online activities (Pérez et al., 2023).

In contrast, online languishing indicators indicate less involvement, discontent, and a feeling of stagnation in digital contexts (Burnell et al., 2023). These conditions may result from negative interactions such as cyberbullying, internet addiction, or information overload. Digital mental health states refer to the diverse levels of psychological functioning affected by digital interactions. It emphasizes the dynamic relationship between online activities and overall mental well-being (Malik et al., 2024). AI-driven content algorithms that prioritize sensational or harmful content may exacerbate digital languishing, increasing feelings of isolation or anxiety (Mirbabaie et al., 2021).

Framework integration provides essential insights into the mental health continuum. In personality traits, the inclusion of emotional stability and conscientiousness significantly affects whether individuals thrive or struggle online (Kuss & Gainsbury, 2021). According to TPB, behavioral factors demonstrate how attitudes and control over online conduct influence mental health (Karlsson & Kajonius, 2020). The social cognitive influence highlights the significance of self-efficacy and observational learning in promoting resilience and well-being in digital environments (Shi et al., 2016).

This chapter presents multiple theoretical frameworks, including cyberpsychology, computer-mediated communication, the Theory of Planned Behavior, Social Cognitive Theory, Social Identity Theory, personality psychology, and Keyes' Mental Health Model, each offering valuable insights into specific aspects of cyber behavior and its consequences. However, the complexity of cyber behavior cannot be adequately explained by any single theoretical framework in isolation. A comprehensive understanding requires recognizing how these frameworks interact and influence one another at different levels of analysis. The following section synthesizes these perspectives into an integrated framework that demonstrates how individual, psychological, social, and environmental factors work together to produce the patterns of cyber behavior observed in digital environments and their subsequent impact on mental health outcomes.

> ***Takeaway:*** *The mental health continuum model provides valuable insights into digital well-being, showing how online experiences can range from flourishing to langishing. AI systems can either contribute to positive outcomes by promoting meaningful engagement or worsen mental health by reinforcing negative behaviors and experiences.*
>
> ***Reflection:*** *How can digital platforms use AI to foster flourishing online while minimizing the risk of users experiencing languishing due to negative content or interactions?*

2.7 An Integrated Framework for Understanding AI-Mediated Cyber Behavior

The theoretical frameworks presented throughout this chapter – cyberpsychology, computer-mediated communication, the Theory of Planned Behavior, Social

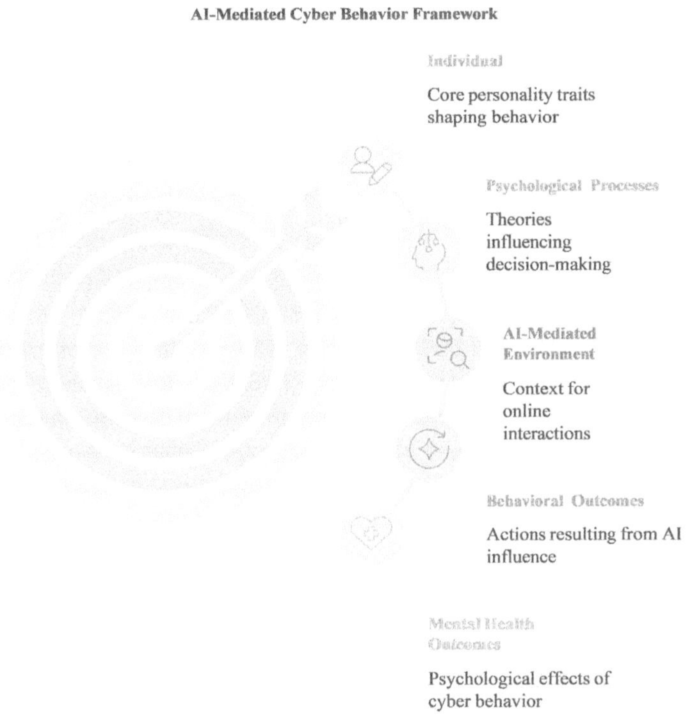

FIGURE 2.6 The integrated cyber behavior framework: A multilevel model of digital behavior and mental health outcomes.

Cognitive Theory, Social Identity Theory, personality psychology, and Keyes' Mental Health Model – do not operate in isolation (see Figure 2.6). Rather, they form an interconnected system that together provides a comprehensive understanding of how individuals behave in digital environments and how these behaviors impact their psychological well-being. Integrating these frameworks offers insights into how multiple theories jointly clarify complex cyber behaviors and provide the foundation for effective interventions (Suler, 2017). This can assist researchers, educators, and practitioners in recognizing patterns and formulating ways to address significant cyber behavior challenges, including cyberbullying, online moral disengagement, online disinhibition, internet addiction, gaming and gambling behaviors, online shopping, and online dating. The complexity of cyber behavior cannot be adequately explained by any single theoretical framework. A comprehensive understanding requires holding multiple frameworks in mind simultaneously, recognizing how they interact and influence one another at different levels of analysis. Individual-level factors (personality traits), social-level factors (group dynamics and community connections), learning-level factors (observational learning and self-efficacy), and outcome-level factors (mental health and well-being) all work together to produce the patterns of cyber behavior we observe. This section examines how these frameworks combine to provide a more comprehensive understanding of cyber behavior than any single theory can offer alone.

At the individual level, personality traits shape how people form attitudes, perceive social norms, and assess their behavioral control, the three key components of the Theory of Planned Behavior. This integration illustrates how individual differences in personality give rise to distinct patterns of cyber behavior. Consider conscientiousness, a personality trait characterized by self-discipline, organization, and a sense of responsibility. Individuals high in conscientiousness tend to have stronger perceived behavioral control in digital environments (Díaz et al., 2020; Mehdy et al., 2021). They believe they can manage their online time, resist addictive behaviors, and maintain ethical conduct. This strong sense of control, rooted in their personality trait, leads them to form intentions to limit their social media use, to avoid engaging in cyberbullying, and to make thoughtful purchasing decisions online. These intentions, in turn, predict actual behavior. Individuals high in conscientiousness are less likely to develop internet addiction because their personality trait predisposes them to perceive control over their digital behavior, which shapes their intentions and ultimately their actions. In contrast, individuals high in neuroticism, characterized by anxiety, sadness, and emotional reactivity, may perceive lower behavioral control in digital environments (Hu et al., 2017). They may feel less able to resist social pressure, manage their emotional responses to online feedback, or control their impulse to check social media frequently. This lower sense of control, rooted in their personality, leads them to form different intentions. An individual high in neuroticism may intend to seek emotional support online, may be more susceptible to social comparison, and may experience greater distress from negative online interactions. These personality-driven differences in perceived control influence behavioral intentions, which in turn predict actual behavior. This individual-level integration demonstrates that personality psychology and the Theory of Planned Behavior are not separate theories but rather interconnected frameworks. Personality traits provide the foundation for how individuals perceive control and form attitudes, which then influence their behavioral intentions and actual behavior. Understanding cyber behavior at the individual level requires recognizing this connection between personality and the components of TPB (Burnell et al., 2023).

Cyberbullying behavior can be analyzed within the framework of personality traits, such as poor agreeableness or high neuroticism, which affect aggression and emotional reactions in cyberspaces (Palmieri & Shortland, 2021). Furthermore, social cognitive processes illustrate how observational learning and moral disengagement allow individuals to justify unfavorable cyber behaviors (Simão, 2021). Furthermore, insights from social identity theory indicate that group dynamics, including in-group favoritism, can promote collective bullying behaviors (Romera et al., 2020). Consequently, cyberbullying significantly affects well-being, which leads to anxiety, despair, and social isolation for victims (Al-Harigy et al., 2022). AI moderation systems, while helpful in identifying harmful content, can also inadvertently contribute to reinforcing bullying behavior by amplifying toxic group dynamics, especially when algorithms prioritize engagement over the well-being of individuals (Gligorea et al., 2023). As a result, it is important to evaluate intervention strategies that may incorporate cognitive-behavioral methods to eliminate harmful behavior thought patterns and foster empathy alongside identity-based treatments to transform group norms towards inclusivity (Palmieri et al., 2021).

Personality vulnerabilities, including high neuroticism and low conscientiousness, enhance susceptibility to internet addiction (Kuss & Gainsbury, 2021). Moreover, social identity elements emphasize the capacity of online communities to promote addictive behaviors (Polizzi & Harrison, 2022). Additionally, well-being implications encompass poor offline functioning, impaired relationships, and mental health issues, including anxiety and despair. The importance of AI in promoting addictive behavior is attributed to its ability to maintain user engagement via tailored content, gamification, and reward mechanisms. These mechanisms, frequently enhanced by machine learning algorithms, can foster patterns of excessive usage, sustaining the cycle of addiction (Priyanka et al., 2023). Assessment methodologies focus on identifying patterns of overuse and psychological dependence. To mitigate addictive usage, it is essential to examine the cognitive mechanisms, particularly the reinforcement loops created by digital platforms (Topino et al., 2021). The therapeutic implications highlight the significance of self-regulation strategies, cognitive restructuring, and social support systems in mitigating addictive behaviors (Kuss & Lopez-Fernandez, 2016). AI-driven behavioral analytics can detect early indicators of digital addiction, enabling prompt therapies; nevertheless, ethical issues must be prioritized to prevent the exploitation of susceptible individuals (Bonilla-Zorita et al., 2020).

Personality risk factors, including impulsivity and sensation-seeking, influence gaming and gambling habits (Kuss & Gainsbury, 2021). Furthermore, social influences, including peer pressure and community dynamics, considerably impact individual behavior (Marinaci et al., 2021). The negative impacts of gaming and gambling on well-being include financial strain, interpersonal conflict, and mental health disorders (Marinaci et al., 2021). AI-driven recommendation systems in online gaming and gambling platforms are frequently developed to enhance user engagement, thereby fostering harmful usage behaviors, particularly among impulsive individuals. These platforms may employ reinforcement strategies that promote extended engagement or gambling, hence reinforcing these behaviors (James et al., 2016). Thus, intervention frameworks may incorporate behavioral regulation scales that help impacted individuals and educate them about the potential risks (Kuss & Gainsbury, 2021). Moreover, behavioral methods, such as reward schedules and gamification strategies, can significantly affect engagement and promote addiction (Marinaci et al., 2021). AI systems should be developed to identify and mitigate harmful reinforcement patterns in gaming and gambling contexts, hence fostering better user interactions (Pérez et al., 2023).

Personality patterns shape online shopping behaviors, such as high openness (linked to impulsive buying) and low conscientiousness (associated with lack of spending control) (Ayob et al., 2022). It is interesting to note that online shopping includes the decision processes that play a critical role in marketing and ease of purchasing. In other words, the influence of reviews and peer recommendations became essential in guiding consumer choices (Cartwright & Xue, 2023). AI's role in e-commerce platforms often centers on using machine learning algorithms to predict and influence consumer behavior, such as recommending products or highlighting positive reviews (Capraro et al., 2024). While this can enhance convenience, it can also encourage impulsive buying behavior, particularly among individuals predisposed to high openness. It is essential to also consider that well-being effects can range from financial stress to satisfaction from fulfilling purchases (Kim & Yoon, 2023). Accordingly, intervention strategies should include promoting mindful purchasing behaviors, financial literacy, and tools for tracking spending. AI-driven tools, if used ethically, can support users in making more mindful purchasing decisions by providing transparency about spending habits and offering personalized recommendations that encourage responsible consumption (Capraro et al., 2024).

Online dating behaviors are shaped by personality influences, such as extraversion (linked to active engagement) and neuroticism (associated with fear of rejection) (Ayob et al., 2022). It is interesting to note that behavioral patterns reflect decision-making processes and strategies for self-presentation in cyberspaces (Hu et al., 2017). This leads to the identity aspects that highlight how individuals navigate their self-concept and relationships in online dating environments (Simão et al., 2021). AI-driven matchmaking algorithms can enhance the online dating experience by facilitating more compatible connections, but they may also introduce biases that affect user perceptions and self-presentation (Bonilla-Zorita et al., 2020). These systems must ensure they do not inadvertently promote unrealistic expectations or reinforce negative identity perceptions. In addition, the impacts of online dating on well-being include both positive outcomes, such as successful relationships, and negative effects, such as anxiety and self-esteem challenges (Lee, 2019). Accordingly, intervention frameworks should involve awareness campaigns and workshops to enhance digital communication, identity-building, and safe online practices (Bonilla-Zorita et al., 2020). AI tools in online dating platforms can be designed to promote healthier self-expression and reduce harmful comparisons by emphasizing positive self-perceptions and supporting users in cultivating authentic relationships (Degen & Kleeberg-Niepage, 2021).

This integrated framework demonstrates that cyber behavior is multidetermined, arising from the interaction of individual personality traits, psychological mechanisms, social contexts, learning processes, and platform design features. No single theoretical perspective adequately captures this complexity. Understanding how individuals behave in digital environments and how these behaviors impact their mental health requires a simultaneous consideration of all these levels.

The framework presented here provides the foundation for the analyses in subsequent chapters, which will examine how specific cyber behaviors emerge, how AI systems reshape these behaviors, and how interventions can be designed to promote flourishing rather than languishing in digital environments. Having established this theoretical foundation, it is appropriate to reflect on the broader implications of these frameworks for understanding the digital transformation of human behavior.

> ***Takeaway:*** *Cybepsychology theories, when integrated with AI's role in moderating behaviors, provide valuable insights into understanding and mitigating harmful cyber behaviors. It is essential to prioritize responsible AI design to avoid exacerbating negative behaviors and to promote healthier online interactions.*
> ***Reflection:*** *How can AI technologies be designed to identify and intervene in harmful behaviors like cyberbullying or addiction while ensuring that they do not inadvertently contribute to these issues by promoting toxic engagement?*

2.8 Summary and Reflections

In conclusion, technology has profoundly transformed individual interactions with the digital realm, markedly affecting both the beneficial and detrimental facets of cyber activities. The extensive proliferation of online social interactions and the emergence of AI technologies aimed at enhancing user experiences have resulted in intricate ethical and psychological dilemmas. The implementation of AI across many platforms, albeit providing unparalleled customization and ease, has elicited apprehensions about its capacity to foster addictive behaviors, hostility, and detrimental material. As AI systems advance, they possess the potential to exacerbate specific detrimental behaviors, like cyberbullying, internet addiction, and moral disengagement, especially when they promote participation at the expense of user welfare. Conversely, AI systems can significantly contribute to identifying and alleviating harmful behaviors when developed with ethical considerations. A comprehensive strategy that integrates many theoretical frameworks and the expanding role of AI is essential for comprehending and addressing these intricate behaviors.

Moreover, the ramifications of digital behaviors extend beyond individual actions, as the interplay of social, psychological, and technological elements influences overall well-being. Personalized content delivery systems, while improving user experience, might unintentionally exacerbate negative habits, thereby affecting mental health results. In addressing the issues associated with the growing dependence on AI in our digital existence, it is clear that responsible design and interdisciplinary collaboration are essential for cultivating healthy online ecosystems. This chapter's theories, ranging from personality psychology to cyberpsychology, provide critical insights into the cognitive, emotional, and social aspects of digital interactions, equipping practitioners with crucial tools for formulating effective solutions.

The following chapter will examine the development of digital identities, analyzing how individuals construct their self-concept and personal narratives in cyberspace. The next chapter will examine the influence of AI on identity development and the effects of digital platforms on self-presentation in virtual environments.

References

Ajzen, I. (1991). The theory of planned behavior. *Organizational Behavior and Human Decision Processes, 50*(2), 179–211. https://doi.org/10.1016/0749-5978(91)90020-t

Ajzen, I. (2011). The theory of planned behaviour: Reactions and reflections. *Psychology and Health, 26*(9), 1113–1127. https://doi.org/10.1080/08870446.2011.613995

Al-Harigy, L. M., Al-Nuaim, H. A., Moradpoor, N., & Tan, Z. (2022). Building towards automated cyberbullying detection: A comparative analysis. *Computational Intelligence and Neuroscience, 2022*, 1–20. https://doi.org/10.1155/2022/4794227

Allport, G. W. (1931). What is a trait of personality? *Journal of Abnormal & Social Psychology, 25*(4), 368–372. https://doi.org/10.1037/h0075406

Auriemma, V., Iorio, G., Roberti, G., & Morese, R. (2020). Cyberbullying and empathy in the age of Hyperconnection: An interdisciplinary approach. *Frontiers in Sociology, 5*. https://doi.org/10.3389/fsoc.2020.551881

Ayob, A. H., Wahid, S. D. M., & Omar, N. A. (2022). Does personality influence the frequency of online purchase behavior? *International Journal of Online Marketing, 12*(1), 1–15. https://doi.org/10.4018/ijom.299398

Bandura, A. (1992). Social cognitive theory of social referencing. In *Springer eBooks* (pp. 175–208). https://doi.org/10.1007/978-1-4899-2462-9_8

Barberis, N., Sanchez-Ruiz, M., Cannavò, M., Calaresi, D., & Verrastro, V. (2023). The Dark Triad and trait emotional intelligence as predictors of problematic social media use and engagement: The mediating role of the fear of missing out. *PubMed, 20*(2), 129–140. https://doi.org/10.36131/cnfioritieditore20230205

Bengio, Y., Hinton, G., Yao, A., Song, D., Abbeel, P., Darrell, T., Harari, Y. N., Zhang, Y., Xue, L., Shalev-Shwartz, S., Hadfield, G., Clune, J., Maharaj, T., Hutter, F., Baydin, A. G., McIlraith, S., Gao, Q., Acharya, A., Krueger, D., . . . Mindermann, S. (2024). Managing extreme AI risks amid rapid progress. *Science, 384*(6698), 842–845. https://doi.org/10.1126/science.adn0117

Beyari, H. (2023). The relationship between social media and the increase in mental health problems. *International Journal of Environmental Research and Public Health, 20*(3), 2383. https://doi.org/10.3390/ijerph20032383

Bonilla-Zorita, G., Griffiths, M. D., & Kuss, D. J. (2020). Online dating and problematic use: A systematic review. *International Journal of Mental Health and Addiction, 19*(6), 2245–2278. https://doi.org/10.1007/s11469-020-00318-9

Brailovskaia, J., Siegel, J., Precht, L., Friedrichs, S., Schillack, H., & Margraf, J. (2024). Less smartphone and more physical activity for a better work satisfaction, motivation, work-life balance, and mental health: An experimental intervention study. *Acta Psychologica, 250*, 104494. https://doi.org/10.1016/j.actpsy.2024.104494

Burnell, R., Peters, D., Ryan, R. M., & Calvo, R. A. (2023). Technology evaluations are associated with psychological need satisfaction across different spheres of experience: an application of the METUX scales. *Frontiers in Psychology, 14*. https://doi.org/10.3389/fpsyg.2023.1092288

Capraro, V., Lentsch, A., Acemoglu, D., Akgun, S., Akhmedova, A., Bilancini, E., Bonnefon, J., Brañas-Garza, P., Butera, L., Douglas, K. M., Everett, J. a. C., Gigerenzer, G., Greenhow, C., Hashimoto, D. A., Holt-Lunstad, J., Jetten, J., Johnson, S., Kunz, W. H., Longoni, C., . . . Viale, R. (2024). The impact of generative artificial intelligence on socioeconomic inequalities and policy making. *PNAS Nexus*, *3*(6). https://doi.org/10.1093/pnasnexus/pgae191

Cartwright, E., & Xue, L. (2023). Truth-telling with a smartphone: The effect of communication media in strategic interactions. *Frontiers in Behavioral Economics*, *2*. https://doi.org/10.3389/frbhe.2023.1120697

Cataldo, I., Lepri, B., Neoh, M. J. Y., & Esposito, G. (2021). Social media usage and Development of Psychiatric Disorders in Childhood and Adolescence: A review. *Frontiers in Psychiatry*, *11*. https://doi.org/10.3389/fpsyt.2020.508595

D'Angelo, J. D. (2020). Problematic and addictive technology use. In *Elsevier eBooks* (pp. 347–364). https://doi.org/10.1016/b978-0-12-817319-0.00016-5

Degen, J. L., & Kleeberg-Niepage, A. (2021). Profiling the self in mobile online dating apps: A serial picture analysis. *Human Arenas*, *6*(1), 147–171. https://doi.org/10.1007/s42087-021-00195-1

DeLisi, M., Drury, A. J., & Elbert, M. J. (2020). Psychopathy and pathological violence in a criminal career: A forensic case report. *Aggression and Violent Behavior*, *60*, 101521. https://doi.org/10.1016/j.avb.2020.101521

Díaz, M. F., Charry, A., Sellitti, S., Ruzzante, M., Enciso, K., & Burkart, S. (2020). Psychological factors influencing pro-environmental behavior in developing countries: Evidence from Colombian and Nicaraguan students. *Frontiers in Psychology*, *11*. https://doi.org/10.3389/fpsyg.2020.580730

Dogan, H., Norman, H., Alrobai, A., Jiang, N., Nordin, N., & Adnan, A. (2019). A web-based intervention for social media addiction disorder management in higher education: Quantitative survey study. *Journal of Medical Internet Research*, *21*(10), e14834. https://doi.org/10.2196/14834

ElSayary, A. (2023). An investigation of teachers' perceptions of using ChatGPT as a supporting tool for teaching and learning in the digital era. *Journal of Computer Assisted Learning*, 1–15. *https://doi.org/10.1111/jcal.12926*

ElSayary, A. (2025). Navigating AI ethics through the lens of personality traits and well-being: policy recommendations for young people in the UAE. *Human Behavior and Emerging Technologies*, *2025*(1). https://doi.org/10.1155/hbe2/5597545

ElSayary, A., Calmaestra, J. & Gómez-López, M. (2026). Cyber behaviors and well-being in emerging adults: Patterns, determinants, and gender differences. *Human Behavior and Emerging Technologies*. https://doi.org/10.1155/hbe2/7545763

Fuss, B. G., Dorstyn, D., & Ward, L. (2021). Belonging in the online world: Older adults' use of internet for community. *Journal of Social Inclusion, 12*(2), 3–29. https://doi.org/10.36251/josi218

Gligorea, I., Cioca, M., Oancea, R., Gorski, A., Gorski, H., & Tudorache, P. (2023). Adaptive learning using artificial intelligence in e-learning: A literature review. *Education Sciences*, *13*(12), 1216. https://doi.org/10.3390/educsci13121216

Han, N., Li, S., Huang, F., Wen, Y., Su, Y., Li, L., Liu, X., & Zhu, T. (2023). How social media expression can reveal personality. *Frontiers in Psychiatry*, *14*. https://doi.org/10.3389/fpsyt.2023.1052844

Hayder, N. M. M. A., Seno, S. a. H., Manaa, M. E., Noori, H., & Zabihzadeh, D. (2026). Graph and transformer-based deep learning paradigms for DDOS detection: A systematic and critical survey. *Computers, Materials & Continua/Computers, Materials & Continua* (Print), 1–10. https://doi.org/10.32604/cmc.2026.078546

Herrmann, L. K., & Kim, J. (2017). The fitness of apps: A theory-based examination of mobile fitness app usage over 5 months. *mHealth, 3,* 2. https://doi.org/10.21037/mhealth.2017.01.03

Hu, X., Kim, A., Siwek, N., & Wilder, D. (2017). The Facebook paradox: Effects of Facebooking on individuals' social relationships and psychological well-being. *Frontiers in Psychology, 8*. https://doi.org/10.3389/fpsyg.2017.00087

Hunter, M. G., & Stockdale, R. (2010). A framework for analyzing online communities. *International Journal of Sociotechnology and Knowledge Development, 2*(3), 11–25. https://doi.org/10.4018/jskd.2010070102

Ibrahim, N. a. N., Husseini, F., Aisyah, N., Camelia, N., Khazlyn, N., Faiz, W., & Kahar, N. (2023). Online shopping behaviour in youth: A systematic review of the factors influencing online shopping in young adults. *International Journal of Academic Research in Business and Social Sciences, 13*(2). https://doi.org/10.6007/ijarbss/v13-i2/16257

Jackson, J. J., Wood, D., Bogg, T., Walton, K. E., Harms, P. D., & Roberts, B. W. (2010). What do conscientious people do? Development and validation of the Behavioral Indicators of Conscientiousness (BIC). *Journal of Research in Personality, 44*(4), 501–511. https://doi.org/10.1016/j.jrp.2010.06.005

James, R. J. E., O'Malley, C., & Tunney, R. J. (2016). Understanding the psychology of mobile gambling: A behavioural synthesis. *British Journal of Psychology, 108*(3), 608–625. https://doi.org/10.1111/bjop.12226

Jiménez-Díaz, O., Bedrosova, M. J., Machackova, H., Del Rey, R., & Mora-Merchán, J. A. (2026). Longitudinal associations between cyberbullying and cyberhate: The role of online empathy and moral disengagement. *Technology in Society, 87*, 103385. https://doi.org/10.1016/j.techsoc.2026.103385

Karlsson, A. M. C., & Kajonius, P. J. (2020). Not only Trolls are Trolling the Internet: A study on dark personality traits, online environment, and commentary styles. *International Journal of Personality Psychology, 6*, 12–23. https://doi.org/10.21827/ijpp.6.37214

Keyes, C. L. M. (2002). The mental health continuum: From languishing to flourishing in life. *Journal of Health and Social Behavior, 43*(2), 207. https://doi.org/10.2307/3090197

Khalaf, A. M., Alubied, A. A., Khalaf, A. M., & Rifaey, A. A. (2023). The impact of social media on the mental health of adolescents and young Adults: A systematic review. *Cureus*. https://doi.org/10.7759/cureus.42990

Kim, D., & Yoon, Y. (2023). The influence of consumer purchases on Purchase-Related Happiness: A serial mediation of commitment and selective information processing. *Behavioral Sciences, 13*(5), 396. https://doi.org/10.3390/bs13050396

Kircaburun, K., & Griffiths, M. D. (2018). The dark side of internet: Preliminary evidence for the associations of dark personality traits with specific online activities and problematic internet use. *Journal of Behavioral Addictions, 7*(4), 993–1003. https://doi.org/10.1556/2006.7.2018.109

Kock, N. (2005). Media richness or media naturalness? The evolution of our biological communication apparatus and its influence on our behavior toward e-communication tools. *IEEE Transactions on Professional Communication, 48*, 117–130. https://doi.org/10.1109/TPC.2005.849649

Kou, Y. (2020). Toxic behaviors in team-based competitive gaming: The case of league of legends. In *CHI PLAY'2020* (pp. 81–92). https://doi.org/10.1145/3410404.3414243

Kowalski, R. M., Giumetti, G. W., Schroeder, A. N., & Lattanner, M. R. (2014). Bullying in the digital age: A critical review and meta-analysis of cyberbullying research among youth. *Psychological Bulletin, 140*(4), 1073–1137. https://doi.org/10.1037/a0035618

Kroencke, L., Humberg, S., Breil, S. M., Geukes, K., Zoppolat, G., Balzarini, R. N., Alonso-Ferres, M., Slatcher, R. B., & Back, M. D. (2023). Extraversion, social interactions, and well-being during the COVID-19 pandemic: Did extraverts really suffer more than introverts? *Journal of Personality and Social Psychology, 125*(3), 649–679. https://doi.org/10.1037/pspp0000468

Kuss, D., & Gainsbury, S. (2021). Debate: Behavioural addictions and technology use – risk and policy recommendations for problematic online gambling and gaming. *Child and Adolescent Mental Health, 26*(1), 76–77. https://doi.org/10.1111/camh.12449

Kuss, D. J., & Lopez-Fernandez, O. (2016). Internet addiction and problematic Internet use: A systematic review of clinical research. *World Journal of Psychiatry, 6*(1), 143. https://doi.org/10.5498/wjp.v6.i1.143

Lajnef, K. (2023). The effect of social media influencers' on teenagers Behavior: An empirical study using cognitive map technique. *Current Psychology, 42*(22), 19364–19377. https://doi.org/10.1007/s12144-023-04273-1

Leary, M. R., Knight, P. D., & Barnes, B. D. (1986). Ethical ideologies of the Machiavellian. *Personality and Social Psychology Bulletin, 12*(1), 75–80. https://doi.org/10.1177/0146167286121008

Lee, J. (2019). Mediated superficiality and misogyny through Cool on Tinder. *Social Media + Society, 5*(3). https://doi.org/10.1177/2056305119872949

Leite, Â., Cardoso, S., & Monteiro, A. P. (2023). Dark personality traits and online behaviors: Portuguese versions of cyberstalking, online harassment, flaming and trolling scales. *International Journal of Environmental Research and Public Health, 20*(12), 6136. https://doi.org/10.3390/ijerph20126136

Liang, Y. Q., & Yoon, S. (2022). Uncovering the cognitive, psychological, and social mechanisms affecting TikTok's reuse intention: Verifying the role of platform characteristics, psychological distance, and social identity. *Global Media and China, 7*(4), 400–421. https://doi.org/10.1177/20594364221131134

Lobbestael, J., Slaoui, G., & Gollwitzer, M. (2023). Sadism and personality disorders. *Current Psychiatry Reports, 25*(11), 569–576. https://doi.org/10.1007/s11920-023-01466-0

Malik, A. S., Acharya, S., & Humane, S. (2024). Exploring the impact of security technologies on mental health: A comprehensive review. *Cureus*. https://doi.org/10.7759/cureus.53664

Marinaci, T., Venuleo, C., Ferrante, L., & Della Bona, S. (2021). What game we are playing: The psychosocial context of problem gambling, problem gaming and poor well-being among Italian high school students. *Heliyon, 7*(8), e07872. https://doi.org/10.1016/j.heliyon.2021.e07872

McCrae, R. R., & Costa, P. T. (1995). Trait explanations in personality psychology. *European Journal of Personality, 9*(4), 231–252. https://doi.org/10.1002/per.2410090402

McLarty, B. D., Skorodziyevskiy, V., & Muldoon, J. (2021). The Dark Triad's incremental influence on entrepreneurial intentions. *Journal of Small Business Management, 61*(4), 2097–2125. https://doi.org/10.1080/00472778.2021.1883042

Mehdy, A. K. M. N., Ekstrand, M. D., Knijnenburg, B. P., & Mehrpouyan, H. (2021). *Privacy as a Planned Behavior: Effects of Situational Factors on Privacy Perceptions and Plans* (pp. 169–178). UMAP '21: Proceedings of the 29th ACM Conference on User Modeling, Adaptation and Personalization. https://doi.org/10.1145/3450613.3456829

Mirbabaie, M., Brünker, F., Frick, N. R. J. M., & Stieglitz, S. (2021). The rise of artificial intelligence – understanding the AI identity threat at the workplace. *Electronic Markets, 32*(1), 73–99. https://doi.org/10.1007/s12525-021-00496-x

Mykota, D. (2022). A protocol for a systematic review and meta-analysis on social presence. *International Journal of E-learning & Distance Education, 37*(1). https://doi.org/10.55667/ijede.2022.v37.i1.1225

Oliver, E., Coates, A., Bennett, J. M., & Willis, M. L. (2023). Narcissism and intimate partner violence: A systematic review and meta-analysis. *Trauma Violence & Abuse*, *25*(3), 1871–1884. https://doi.org/10.1177/15248380231196115

Palmieri, M., Shortland, N., & McGarry, P. (2021). Personality and online deviance: The role of reinforcement sensitivity theory in cybercrime. *Computers in Human Behavior*, *120*, 106745. https://doi.org/10.1016/j.chb.2021.106745

Parlangeli, O., Marchigiani, E., Bracci, M., Duguid, A. M., Palmitesta, P., & Marti, P. (2019). Offensive acts and helping behavior on the internet: An analysis of the relationships between moral disengagement, empathy and use of social media in a sample of Italian students. *Work*, *63*(3), 469–477. https://doi.org/10.3233/wor-192935

Paulhus, D. L., & Williams, K. M. (2002). The Dark Triad of personality: Narcissism, Machiavellianism, and psychopathy. *Journal of Research in Personality*, *36*(6), 556–563. https://doi.org/10.1016/s0092-6566(02)00505-6

Pérez, J., Castro, M., & López, G. (2023). Serious games and AI: Challenges and opportunities for computational social science. *IEEE Access*, *11*, 62051–62061. https://doi.org/10.1109/access.2023.3286695

Petersen, B., Khalili-Mahani, N., Murphy, C., Sawchuk, K., Phillips, N., Li, K. Z. H., & Hebblethwaite, S. (2023). The association between information and communication technologies, loneliness and social connectedness: A scoping review. *Frontiers in Psychology*, *14*, 1063146. https://doi.org/10.3389/fpsyg.2023.1063146

Polizzi, G., & Harrison, T. (2022). Wisdom in the digital age: A conceptual and practical framework for understanding and cultivating cyber-wisdom. *Ethics and Information Technology*, *24*(1). https://doi.org/10.1007/s10676-022-09640-3

Priyanka, A. L., Harihararao, M., Prasanna, M., & Deepika, Y. (2023). A study on artificial intelligence in marketing. *International Journal for Multidisciplinary Research*, *5*(3). https://doi.org/10.36948/ijfmr.2023.v05i03.3789

Roberts, B. W., & Yoon, H.J. (2022) Personality Psychology. *Annual Review of Psychology*, *73*, 489–516. https://doi.org/10.1146/annurev-psych-020821-114927

Roccas, S., Sagiv, L., Schwartz, S. H., & Knafo, A. (2002). The big five personality factors and personal values. *Personality and Social Psychology Bulletin*, *28*(6), 789–801. https://doi.org/10.1177/0146167202289008

Romera, E. M., Ortega-Ruiz, R., Runions, K., & Falla, D. (2020). Moral disengagement strategies in online and offline bullying. *Psychosocial Intervention*, *30*(2), 85–93. https://doi.org/10.5093/pi2020a21

Sedikides, C., & Hart, C. M. (2022). Narcissism and conspicuous consumption. *Current Opinion in Psychology*, *46*, 101322. https://doi.org/10.1016/j.copsyc.2022.101322

Sheeks, M. S., & Birchmeier, Z. P. (2007). Shyness, sociability, and the use of computer-mediated communication in relationship development. *CyberPsychology & Behavior*, *10*, 64-70. http://dx.doi.org/10.1089/cpb.2006.9991

Shi, B., Dai, D. Y., & Lu, Y. (2016). Openness to experience as a moderator of the relationship between intelligence and creative thinking: A study of Chinese children in Urban and rural areas. *Frontiers in Psychology*, *7*. https://doi.org/10.3389/fpsyg.2016.00641

Simão, A. M. V., Ferreira, P. C., Pereira, N., Oliveira, S., Paulino, P., Rosa, H., Ribeiro, R., Coheur, L., Carvalho, J. P., & Trancoso, I. (2021). Prosociality in Cyberspace: Developing emotion and behavioral regulation to decrease aggressive communication. *Cognitive Computation*, *13*(3), 736–750. https://doi.org/10.1007/s12559-021-09852-7

Song, T., Yu, P., Bliokas, V., Probst, Y., Peoples, G. E., Qian, S., Houston, L., Perez, P., Amirghasemi, M., Cui, T., Hitige, N. P. R., & Smith, N. A. (2021). A Clinician-Led, Experience-Based Co-Design Approach for developing MHealth services to support the

patient self-management of chronic Conditions: Development Study and Design case. *JMIR Mhealth and Uhealth*, *9*(7), e20650. https://doi.org/10.2196/20650
Suler, J. (2004). The online disinhibition effect. *CyberPsychology & Behavior*, *7*(3), 321–326. https://doi.org/10.1089/1094931041291295
Suler, J. (2010). The psychology of text relationships. In *Elsevier eBooks* (pp. 21–53). https://doi.org/10.1016/b978-0-12-378596-1.00002-2
Suler, J. (2016). The dimensions of Cyberpsychology Architecture. In *Elsevier eBooks* (pp. 1–23). https://doi.org/10.1016/b978-0-12-804157-4.00001-3
Suler, J. (2017). The dimensions of Cyberpsychology Architecture. In *Elsevier eBooks* (pp. 1–23). https://doi.org/10.1016/b978-0-12-804157-4.00001-3
Tajfel, H. (1974). Social identity and intergroup behaviour. *Social Science Information*, *13*(2), 65–93. https://doi.org/10.1177/053901847401300204
Tan, K. H., Chan, P. P., & Said, N. M. (2021). Higher Education Students' Online instruction Perceptions: A quality virtual learning environment. *Sustainability*, *13*(19), 10840. https://doi.org/10.3390/su131910840
Tajfel, H., & Turner, J. C. (1979). An integrative theory of intergroup conflict. In W. G. Austin, & S. Worchel (Eds.), *The social psychology of intergroup relations* (pp. 33–37). Monterey, CA: Brooks/Cole.
Thørrisen, M. M., & Sadeghi, T. (2023). The Ten-Item Personality Inventory (TIPI): A scoping review of versions, translations and psychometric properties. *Frontiers in Psychology, 14*, 1202953. https://doi.org/10.3389/fpsyg.2023.1202953
Topino, E., Di Fabio, A., Palazzeschi, L., & Gori, A. (2021). Personality traits, workers' age, and job satisfaction: The moderated effect of conscientiousness. *PLoS ONE*, *16*(7), e0252275. https://doi.org/10.1371/journal.pone.0252275
Verma, A., Islam, S., Moghaddam, V., & Anwar, A. (2024). Digital emotion regulation on social media. *Computer*, *57*(6), 82–89. https://doi.org/10.1109/mc.2023.3332331
Walter, Y. (2024). Digital psychology: Introducing a conceptual impact model and the future of work. *Trends in Psychology*. https://doi.org/10.1007/s43076-024-00408-w
Walther, J. B., & Whitty, M. T. (2020). Language, psychology, and new new media: The hyperpersonal model of mediated communication at twenty-five years. *Journal of Language and Social Psychology, 40*(1), 120–135. https://doi.org/10.1177/0261927x20967703
Wang, L., & Ngai, S. S. (2020). The effects of anonymity, invisibility, asynchrony, and moral disengagement on cyberbullying perpetration among school-aged children in China. *Children and Youth Services Review*, *119*, 105613. https://doi.org/10.1016/j.childyouth.2020.105613
Xu, B. (2023). Marketing Strategy Analysis of online game products. *Financial Engineering and Risk Management, 6*(5). https://doi.org/10.23977/ferm.2023.060510
Zhan, Z., Wei, Q., & Hong, J. (2021). Cellphone addiction during the Covid-19 outbreak: How online social anxiety and cyber danger belief mediate the influence of personality. *Computers in Human Behavior*, *121*, 106790. https://doi.org/10.1016/j.chb.2021.106790
Zhang, Y., Shan, Z., Wu, Y., & Fu, Y. (2022). Research on the formation and control of college students' social anxiety in virtual community situation. *Frontiers in Business Economics and Management, 6*(1), 26–28. https://doi.org/10.54097/fbem.v6i1.2255

3

THE EVOLVING ROLE OF AI IN THE FORMATION OF DIGITAL IDENTITIES

Objectives of This Chapter

- To analyze the psychological, social, and ethical aspects that shape the formation of digital identities.
- To explore the concept of the "cybernetic self" and its role in online identity construction.
- To explore how artificial intelligence (AI) is shaping the evolution of digital identities.
- To examine the psychological and ethical impacts of AI on self-presentation and identity formation in virtual environments.
- To examine the cultural and gendered perspectives that influence digital self-expression.
- To understand the impact of social media, online feedback, and comparison in the formation of digital identities.
- To investigate the challenges associated with maintaining ethical decision-making in digital environments.

Topics to Be Addressed

- The Cybernetic Self: Identity in a Digital Age
- The Role of Social Feedback and Comparison
- AI as an Architect of Identity

DOI: 10.4324/9781003657590-4

- Cultural and Gendered Dimensions of Digital Identity
  - Cultural Influences
  - Gendered Differences
- The Double-Edged Sword: Positive and Negative Effects
  - Positive Effects of AI on Digital Identity Formation
  - Negative Effects of AI on Digital Formation
- Ethical Challenges in AI-Driven Identity Formation

3.1 Introduction

In the technological era, identity has been highly impacted by the increasing use of technology and virtual spaces. As a result, the term "digital native" became a common label for youth who had high exposure to digital technology at a tender age (Thompson, 2013). However, digital identity refers to how individuals perceive themselves in cyberspaces (Emanuel et al., 2014). This has become a crucial aspect of young people's development, influencing self-concept, social relationships, and ethical decision-making (Granic et al., 2020; Rodríguez et al., 2020). Internet and social media platforms are the primary means of communication for young people and essential spaces for self-expression, discovery, and identity formation (Kadir, 2022). Accordingly, it is essential to comprehend the development of young people's digital identities and their psychological implications. Understanding this formation becomes even more critical given the transformative role that artificial intelligence (AI) now plays in shaping these identities. In recent years, AI has emerged as a significant player in shaping digital identity, influencing how individuals present themselves online through algorithmic content filtering, personalized recommendations, and automated feedback (García-Martínez et al., 2023; Sousa et al., 2023). The specific mechanisms through which AI operates as an architect of identity will be examined in Section 3.4. To fully appreciate the transformative impact of AI, it is essential to understand how digital identity formation differs from its traditional counterpart. Traditional identity formation occurs through in-person interactions, norms, and cultural traditions. Although the process of digital identity formation is complicated, it is known for its flexibility and adaptability (Wang et al., 2013). It is shaped by various factors, including online interaction, peer evaluation, and cultural standards (Petrakova et al., 2022). This is due to the fact that youth manage various dimensions of identity in cyberspace, sometimes even attempting to present themselves differently in social networks and gaming forums (Khalaf et al., 2023). This continuous process of identity construction and reconstruction through digital feedback and interaction is what scholars term the "cybernetic self" (Chen, 2023; Tolnaiová & Gálik, 2020), a concept that will be explored in depth in Section 3.2. Understanding the cybernetic self is crucial for grasping how AI influences digital identity formation. Although these processes of digital identity formation occur at the individual level, their implications extend far beyond personal development.

The significance of identity creation in a virtual environment extends to society and ethics at a broader level. Humans' behavior in cyberspace is characterized by anonymity and a failure to comply with social customs and norms; therefore, moral disengagement presents certain challenges (Knytl, 2021; Pan et al., 2023). One such challenge is the ethical dilemmas youth face in virtual spaces. Some of them include cyberbullying, invasion of one's private life, spreading disinformation, cyberspace harassment, identity theft, access to explicit content, cyberstalking, addiction in cyberspace, and phishing fraud (Paciello et al., 2019). As a result, such experiences force youth to challenge values and ethics in a manner not experienced in face-to-face encounters. Many questions have been raised about the role of the digital environment in shaping moral reasoning and behavior, where right and wrong may differ from those in the offline environment (Harrison & Polizzi, 2022). Given these multifaceted challenges, educators, policymakers, and mental health professionals need to understand the challenges young people face in order to foster an ethical digital environment and promote mental well-being.

This chapter examines the formation of digital identity by analyzing its psychological, social, and ethical aspects. Drawing on recent research in cyberpsychology, identity formation, and digital ethics, the chapter explores how the cybernetic self is constructed through AI-mediated interactions, examines the role of social feedback and comparison, and analyzes the cultural and gendered contexts that shape digital identity. The chapter also examines both the positive and negative effects of AI-driven identity formation and addresses the ethical challenges that arise from these processes. Understanding these dynamics is crucial for educators, policymakers, and mental health professionals who aim to promote healthy and authentic digital identities among young people.

The important question raised is: *How does AI influence the development and expression of digital identities, and what are the psychological and ethical implications of this evolving role?* To address these questions, this chapter begins by examining the foundational concept that underlies digital identity formation: the cybernetic self. This concept provides the theoretical lens through which we can understand how identity is continuously constructed and reconstructed in virtual environments, setting the stage for exploring AI's specific mechanisms and impacts.

> ***Takeaway:*** *Digital identity has become a crucial aspect of youth development, shaped by both online interactions and AI systems that influence self-presentation, relationships, and ethical decision-making.*
> ***Reflection:*** *How does AI's influence on digital identity change the way young people view themselves and others?*

3.2 The Cybernetic Self: Identity in a Digital Age

The cybernetic self is an emerging and shape-shifting entity that continually undergoes construction and reconstruction through feedback and interaction processes in virtual environments. In Waskul et al. (2000), such an identity is constructed in a state of disembodied, anonymous dialogue, where one can experiment with parts of oneself freely, without the restrictions imposed through face-to-face contact. In such a virtual environment, identity is not confined to a purely bodily state but extends into a larger life-world, one in which Pham et al. (2022) describe an interpenetration between offline and online realities. Within this fluid, interpenetrating landscape of identities, AI has emerged as a powerful shaping force.

AI plays a critical role in shaping the cybernetic self by continuously analyzing user behavior, providing feedback, and influencing how individuals present themselves online. Through AI-driven recommendations and algorithmic filtering of content, users are guided toward specific types of self-presentation and social interactions that shape their evolving digital identity. This AI-mediated shaping occurs through several interconnected processes, beginning with discovery and self-exploration.

Central to creating the cybernetic self is the process of discovery in a virtual environment. Impression management, in contrast, involves actively shaping one's presence for others, with many individuals customizing their virtual presence to align with social expectations, desires, and preferences. Zhong et al. (2017) see a role for self-disclosure in such a creation, with individuals selectively revealing aspects of their life, thereby creating a constructed identity. This creates a feedback loop of identity construction in which one's virtual self is in a state of constant flux, responding to feedback and social contact with others. This feedback-driven construction produces what scholars have termed the *interactional self*, an identity that fluidly navigates between physical and virtual realms.

Robinson (2007) notes that the interactional self seamlessly transitions between offline and online spaces, combining the sociability of both environments. Communication facilitated through the internet provides a platform for social cohesion and self-expression, allowing individuals to maintain relationships and convey their identity in various virtual spaces. The smooth transition is part of the new concept of the self, with the boundaries between offline and online life becoming increasingly less apparent. Central to this seamless transition and the construction of the interactional self are the feedback processes that operate continuously in virtual environments.

The feedback processes in virtual environments have a significant role in defining one's cybernetic self. As Davis (2014) identifies, such processes can be both immediate, such as social media likes and comments, and reflective, such as long-term shifts in one's way of representing oneself in terms of aggregated virtual experiences. This feedback loop, in a state of continuous flux, enables one to continually mold and redefine one's identity. This continuous redefinition is further facilitated by the unique liberty of self-presentation that web platforms afford.

Additionally, the liberty of self-presentation through web platforms exceeds traditional socio-cultural boundaries, allowing one to experiment with aspects of their identity in a way not possible in face-to-face interactions. As Reid (2009) puts it, virtual reality provides a platform that allows one to access and explore identities not necessarily in consonance with one's immediate offline social environment, with the aim of exercising greater individual freedom and expression. This freedom to explore multiple facets of identity across virtual and physical spaces has given rise to what scholars describe as the "expanded self".

The notion of an "expanded self", addressed by Mishra and Ismail (2017), continues to inform adaptability in cyberspaces. In such a case, one's self consists of both real and virtual components, with one's virtual presence enhancing and extending one's offline identity. With an expanded self, one can enjoy heightened flexibility and complexity, with real and virtual selves becoming increasingly blurred and a changing perception of who and what we are in a virtual age. Therefore, the cybernetic self is a rich, complex entity in a state of continuous construction through processes of web use, feedback, and changing relations between virtual and actual environments (see Figure 3.1). This expansive view of identity privileges the flexible, transformatory nature of self-concept in a virtual age, undermining traditional conceptions of bounded, unchangeable identity. Having established the concept of the cybernetic self and its continuous construction through feedback and interaction, it is now time to examine one of the most powerful drivers of this construction: social feedback and comparison. These processes operate as key mechanisms through which individuals evaluate, adjust, and refine their digital identities in relation to others.

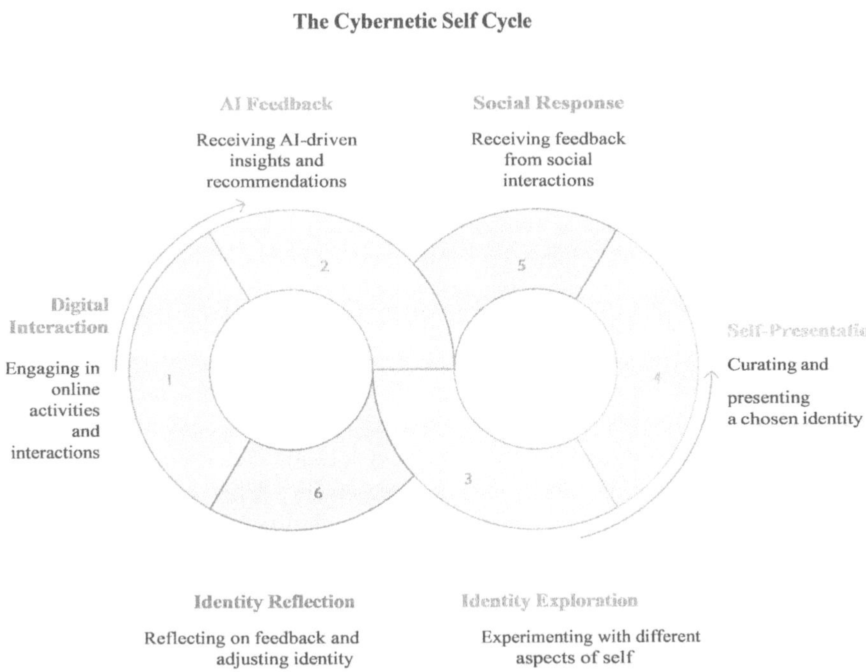

FIGURE 3.1 The Cybernetic Self: A continuous feedback loop model illustrating how the self is constructed and reconstructed through AI-mediated interactions in virtual environments. The model shows the dynamic interplay between self-presentation, AI-driven feedback, social interaction, and identity reconstruction, with the offline and online selves increasingly overlapping to form an interactional self that seamlessly transitions between physical and virtual spaces.

> ***Takeaway:*** *Digital identity is a flexible and dynamic representation of oneself, shaped by online interactions and social feedback loops.*
> ***Reflection:*** *How do online feedback and social validation contribute to the shaping of your digital identity?*

3.3 The Role of Social Feedback and Comparison

Social comparison on social network sites (SNS) is a critical function in shaping digital identity, defining how one perceives oneself and others in relation to their virtual spaces. This process is grounded in Social Identity Theory (discussed in Chapter 2, Section 2.4.3), which explains how individuals derive their sense of self from group memberships and social comparisons with others. SNS websites offer numerous avenues for comparison, allowing individuals to compare their lives with those of others through observable factors such as name, gender, photos, career achievements, and shared interests. Zhong et al. (2017) believe that such factors become part of one's online identity, and through them, one creates a platform for self-presentation. Comparisons become part and parcel of such a construction, as individuals compare their profiles with those encountered in SNS in terms of consistency and discrepancies. The significance of these comparison processes has been amplified by the role of AI in curating and presenting content for comparison.

Although social comparison has long been a fundamental aspect of identity formation, AI has fundamentally transformed the scale, frequency, and intensity of these comparisons. AI algorithms on social media platforms, such as Instagram, TikTok, and Facebook, utilize social comparison to drive engagement, increasing both positive and negative comparisons. By presenting content based on users' interests and interactions, AI can reinforce social comparison tendencies, leading to greater self-criticism or, conversely, positive self-reflection depending on the content presented. However, the social comparison effect in SNS is multidimensional, with both positive and negative consequences for SNS users. On one level, social comparison can promote overthinking and identity distress when individuals judge themselves unfavorably against others, particularly when they perceive gaps between their actual and ideal selves. As Yang and Chae (2023) state, continuous upward comparisons, i.e., comparing oneself with others one feels to be in a better position, can generate negative affect and increased feelings of inadequacy. In such a scenario, rumination tends to increase identity distress when one internalizes perceived failures or discrepancies between one's actual and ideal selves.

Furthermore, social comparison on SNS can lead to both healthy and unhealthy jealousy. According to Latif et al. (2020), healthy jealousy arises when individuals identify with their positive character or achievement with a positive feeling, such that they feel motivated to become a better individual. Unhealthy jealousy, on the other hand, arises when an individual feels upset and hostile, and in most cases, towards individuals whom one feels are successful and pleasing in looks. These two contrasting feelings can shape social media use in ways that distort one's perception of oneself and self-worth.

Although social comparison sometimes positively influences subjective well-being through increased motivation, its overall contribution is negative, particularly when individuals engage in upward comparison. As argued by Plachynda et al. (2024), such comparisons often lead to feelings of dissatisfaction and inferiority, particularly when individuals measure themselves against idealized and unattainable standards, such as career success or physical appearance, resulting in diminished self-esteem and overall well-being. The influence of social comparison, De Vaate et al. (2019) say, is determined by the social comparison orientation of users. Ability comparisons, when one compares oneself in terms of talent, skill, or accomplishment, have a negative impact on well-being for those most oriented towards them. Ability comparisons have a tendency to make one feel less in comparison to others and, therefore, have a negative impact on well-being. Opinion comparisons, when individuals compare themselves in terms of attitude, preference, or belief, can have a less negative impact at times, as one feels supported and endorsed when they identify with similar individuals. Despite these occasional positive outcomes, the predominant effect of social comparison remains negative, particularly when individuals are exposed to idealized profiles on SNS.

In addition to its negative impact, exposure to idealized profiles on SNS, including those of beauty, success, or social position, can have real-life consequences for career and body satisfaction. According to Yang and Chae (2023), comparing oneself to profiles of handsome individuals or successful professionals can lead to individuals feeling less satisfied with their career and appearance. Comparisons, in most cases, with idealized and constructed realities can lead to a distorted perception of one's body and dissatisfaction with career achievements. Despite these challenges, social media platforms serve as channels for identity construction and self-presentation. As Latif et al. (2020) advocate, SNS allow individuals to navigate and present numerous dimensions of their identity, including values, interests, and social roles. SNS can serve as platforms for self-discovery, allowing individuals to develop their virtual selves in a form that reflects their inner self-concept. Qin and Lowe (2021) continue to argue that, in addition to comparison, SNS allow individuals to present their individuality and creativity, offering them a platform for creating and presenting their identity, one that cannot be attained in offline life. Although social feedback and comparison provide the psychological mechanisms through which identity is shaped, it is AI that increasingly determines what content is available for comparison, who individuals interact with, and how they present themselves. AI has thus become not merely a tool but an architect of digital identity, actively constructing the environments in which the cybernetic self emerges.

Takeaway: *Online social comparison can have significant psychological implications, particularly when the comparison is upward and promotes feelings of inadequacy.*

Reflection: *How can social media websites be designed to support more positive and constructive forms of social comparison?*

3.4 AI as an Architect of Identity

Building on the concept of the cybernetic self established in Section 3.2, this section examines how AI operates as an architect of identity through multiple interconnected mechanisms that continuously shape digital identity formation. One important aspect of this architectural function is how AI-mediated virtual experiences redefine our understanding of embodiment and presence. DeVeaux et al. (2023) identify one's body as an important participant in one's experiences of presence in virtual reality (VR). In virtual reality spaces, one's awareness of one's own body tends to change, even become nonexistent, and can challenge and extend conventional understandings of embodiment. The sense of presence, "being there" in a virtual environment, is shaped by how closely individuals map their real bodies onto their virtual representations, a process that varies depending on the technology used and the level of immersion provided. Furthermore, AI systems such as facial recognition software, personalized content curation, and algorithmic suggestions play a significant role in shaping how users present themselves online. These AI-driven mechanisms establish feedback loops that encourage specific behaviors, social interactions, and self-presentation styles, ultimately shaping the digital self. Beyond shaping how users perceive their physical presence in virtual spaces, AI also influences behavior through the characteristics of digital representations themselves.

Another key aspect of the adaptability of the cybernetic self is the influence of virtual representations of oneself on behavior. Yee et al. (2009) describe the Proteus Effect, a psychological phenomenon where a person's behavior in virtual environments is influenced by the characteristics of their digital avatar. For example, a player who creates a bold, high avatar in a virtual environment will become bold in social interactions in real life. The Proteus Effect describes how representations in a virtual environment, both in terms of appearance and behavior, can inform one's sense of self and behavior in both virtual and real environments. The digital environment in and of itself creates a certain blend of freedom and constraint that profoundly informs identity and behavior. Moustaka et al. (2018) provide a detailed exploration of how virtual environments influence privacy, social hierarchy, cognition, and behavior. Although the digital world can offer anonymity, empowerment, and access to a global network of interactions, it also presents challenges related to privacy, control, and the weakening of traditional social norms. All such changing dynamics inform one's creation of identity and management of engagements in virtual environments. All such freedom of expression in virtual environments comes with a representation in the form of algorithmic visibility, observation, and social media conventions. These AI systems continuously learn from and respond to user behavior, creating dynamic feedback loops that shape identity formation.

Self-adaptive software programs, inspired by cybernetic theory, demonstrate how AI systems learn from and respond to changing user behaviors (Bellman et al., 2020). These adaptive algorithms continuously adjust to new information, creating personalized experiences that shape identity development across individual, social, and collective dimensions. As the cybernetic self develops, it also informs virtual identity construction. Robinson (2007) explains virtual activity in terms of contributing to virtual constructions of the "I", "me", and "generalized other". "I" identifies one's individual self; "me" identifies one's social self, constructed through society mandates; and "generalized other" identifies one's broader social sphere in which one works and resides. All of these aspects of identity develop through virtual activity, with virtual experiences creating new avenues through which one can navigate one's sense of self in relation to immediate peers and broader virtual society. Beyond these social dimensions of adaptation, the cybernetic self also adapts at a cognitive and sensory level as humans integrate digital technology into their perceptual and motor capabilities.

However, it is important to question whether this flexibility in self-presentation truly represents authentic self-expression or whether it is itself a form of algorithmic constraint. While users may feel they are freely exploring different facets of their identity, the platforms they use are simultaneously learning their preferences and subtly steering them toward certain types of content, communities, and self-presentations. This creates a paradox: the very tools that promise liberation and self-discovery may be narrowing the range of identities available to explore. The algorithm learns what "engages" a user and optimizes for that, potentially trapping them in a filter bubble of their own preferences. Furthermore, the pressure to maintain a curated, aesthetically pleasing digital presence can lead to a form of "performative authenticity", where users present carefully constructed versions of themselves rather than their genuine selves. This raises the critical question: In an AI-mediated environment, can we meaningfully distinguish between authentic self-expression and algorithmically induced self-presentation?

Further adaptation occurs when humans utilize digital technology in a way that redefines cognitive and sensory capabilities. In an argument presented by Gottschalk (2021), one can refer to a "terminal self", a terminology that addresses humans' adaptations of perceptual capabilities, sensorimotor skills, and affective dispositions towards thinking in digital forms. As technology continues to overstep, its operators adapt its individual requirements in virtual environments, developing new forms of engagement that extend face-to-face contact and even traditional bodily contact. Not only individual behavior but also social behavior is altered, with contact and relationship-shaping characteristics changing with ubiquitous access to digital tools and platforms. These AI-driven mechanisms, embodied presence in virtual reality, algorithmic shaping of self-representations, and cognitive integration of digital tools, work together to continuously reshape how individuals experience and express their identities. The cumulative effect is a dynamic process in which AI systems actively construct the environments and feedback loops that determine identity formation in digital spaces. Figure 3.2 illustrates these multiple, interconnected mechanisms through which AI operates as an architect of digital identity, showing how embodiment, representation, adaptation,

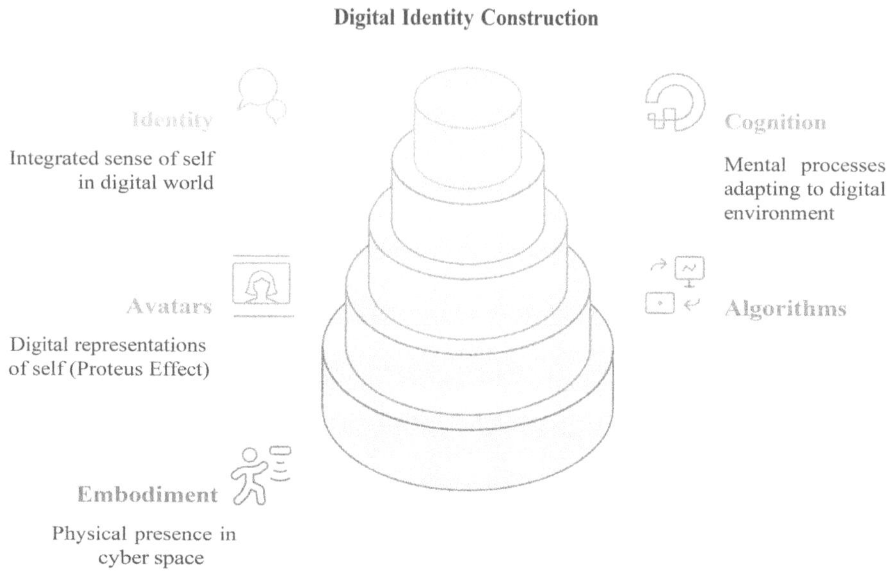

FIGURE 3.2 A systems map illustrating the layered mechanisms through which AI shapes digital identity. These layers interact dynamically, demonstrating how AI-mediated environments continuously reconstruct and reshape identity formation in cyberspaces.

and cognitive integration work together to shape the cybernetic self. Although the mechanisms through which AI shapes identity operate universally, their effects are not uniform across all populations. The construction of digital identity through AI-mediated environments is highly influenced by cultural contexts and gender, which shape how individuals experience, interpret, and respond to these technological systems. Understanding these dimensions is essential for a comprehensive view of AI-driven identity formation.

Takeaway: *The cybernetic self is a fluid identity that is established by virtual experience and the feedback loops of the internet.*
Reflection: *How does the concept of the cybernetic self change our perception of the relationship between our online and offline selves?*

These architectural mechanisms are no longer abstract; they are embedded in the daily digital experiences of billions. Consider, for example, the powerful recommendation engine of platforms like TikTok. Its *For You* page functions as a potent identity-shaping feedback loop, rapidly learning a user's latent interests and curating a highly personalized reality tunnel. This can accelerate identity exploration by connecting users with niche communities, but it can also create echo chambers that intensify beliefs and behaviors without exposure to diverse perspectives. Furthermore, the recent explosion of generative AI tools, such as Lensa AI's *Magic Avatars* or DALL-E, directly intervenes in self-presentation. Users feed their images to an AI, which in turn produces idealized, stylized, or fantastical versions of themselves. This practice raises important questions about the nature of authenticity, the commodification of identity, and the psychological impact of comparing one's physical self to a flawless, algorithmically generated avatar. These technologies are not merely filtering content; they are providing the very building blocks with which the modern cybernetic self is constructed.

3.5 Cultural and Gendered Dimensions of Digital Identity

3.5.1 Cultural Influences

Cultural contexts play a crucial role in shaping the formation of digital identities, influencing how people negotiate, express, and interpret their online identities. As established in Chapter 2's discussion of Social Identity Theory (Section 2.4.3), cultural group memberships are fundamental to how individuals define themselves, and these processes extend into digital environments where cultural norms shape online behavior and self-presentation. The digital age has profoundly transformed the concept of cultural identity, shifting it from a static and fixed entity to a dynamic and fluid process. Dalmoro et al. (2020) note that digital technologies facilitate global interactions, which are influenced by diverse cultural perspectives while simultaneously interacting with local norms and traditions. The global-local interaction gives rise to a hybrid form of identity that is constantly in flux as people interact with different cultural structures.

AI-driven platforms are deeply influenced by cultural norms, with algorithms that reflect and amplify societal values. In collectivist cultures, for example, AI may prioritize community-oriented content. However, in more individualistic cultures, the focus may be on personal achievement. These cultural influences shape how digital identities are constructed and perceived, both by the individual and by society.

The ability of digital technologies to enable the development of new identity models and value orientations presents both opportunities and challenges. Petrakova et al. (2022) note that digital spaces allow users the freedom to experiment with new identities that transcend traditional boundaries. Although this is potentially empowering, allowing for self-expression and the development of various identities, it can also lead to tension, particularly where the new models clash with existing cultural norms. Pressure to conform to the norms of online environments or idealized social media profiles can also negatively impact personal identity by inducing feelings of inadequacy or alienation.

Cultural norms also play a critical role in shaping how digital citizenship is envisioned and taught in different societies. Ding et al. (2024) argue that collectivist and individualist societies place different emphases on dimensions of digital use and responsibility. Digital citizenship education in collectivist cultures, for example, can place greater emphasis on group-oriented practices, such as protecting family privacy and ensuring communal welfare, whereas in individualist societies, there may be a greater emphasis on personal autonomy, self-expression, and individual rights in the online environment. These values shape how individuals from different cultural backgrounds approach online behavior and digital interaction.

Sociovirtualization, or the way in which virtual interaction and online communities shape social structures, presents both opportunities and dangers, especially for intercultural communication and diasporic communities. Heang et al. (2024) highlight that the age of digital presents diasporic communities with the ability to remain connected to their heritage and interact with others at a transnational scale. This creates new opportunities for cross-cultural exchange, allowing individuals to maintain their identity while interacting with broader global communities. Sociovirtualization, however, also threatens to reinforce stereotypes or create online communities that limit exposure to other perspectives. This can reinforce misrepresentations and hinder meaningful intercultural understanding. The need to be responsive to cultural contexts in the design of technology is evident in value-sensitive design, which aims to create technologies that are responsive to cultural values and moral norms. Berridge et al. (2024) emphasize the importance of developing care technologies that are culturally sensitive and responsive to the diverse needs of multicultural societies. Value-sensitive design ensures that technological innovation is respectful of cultural diversity, promoting inclusivity and accessibility. This approach enables technology to support identity formation in a manner that is locally aligned with traditions and values. Just as cultural contexts shape digital identity formation, gender represents another critical dimension through which individuals experience and construct their digital selves differently.

In non-Western contexts, such as Pakistan, identity formation is likely to be guided by the dynamic between personal interests and more macro-normative forces. Maqbool and Cremin (2023) demonstrate how young people in Pakistan navigate the tension between personal desires for self-expression and familial, religious, and societal norms. In these contexts, cyberspace serves as an arena for the exploration of the individual, but at the same time, it forces one to reconcile the virtual self with the broader social fabric, which often has more rigid guidelines on how one can be.

The online setting plays a significant role in identity construction through several processes, including selection, manipulation, evocation, and application. Suler (2017) argues that individuals consciously select what to portray about themselves in online settings, whether it be personal attributes, cultural identity, or political leanings. They make this choice based on the online media they consume and the online groups with which they identify. Manipulation involves users' construction and editing of their online selves, molding their presentation in response to feedback, trends, or expectations. Evocation involves emotional and psychological responses that users express through their online actions, possibly influencing their self-concept and online relationships. The application explains how individuals apply their online selves to offline living, informing their behavior, relationships, and sense of belonging. The development of digital identities is fundamentally shaped by the intersection of cultural contexts, local traditions, global interactions, and technological change. Although digital technologies offer opportunities for identity exploration, they also pose challenges related to maintaining cultural authenticity. Understanding these dynamics is essential for developing inclusive, culturally responsive technologies and educational systems that support healthy identity development (see Figure 3.3).

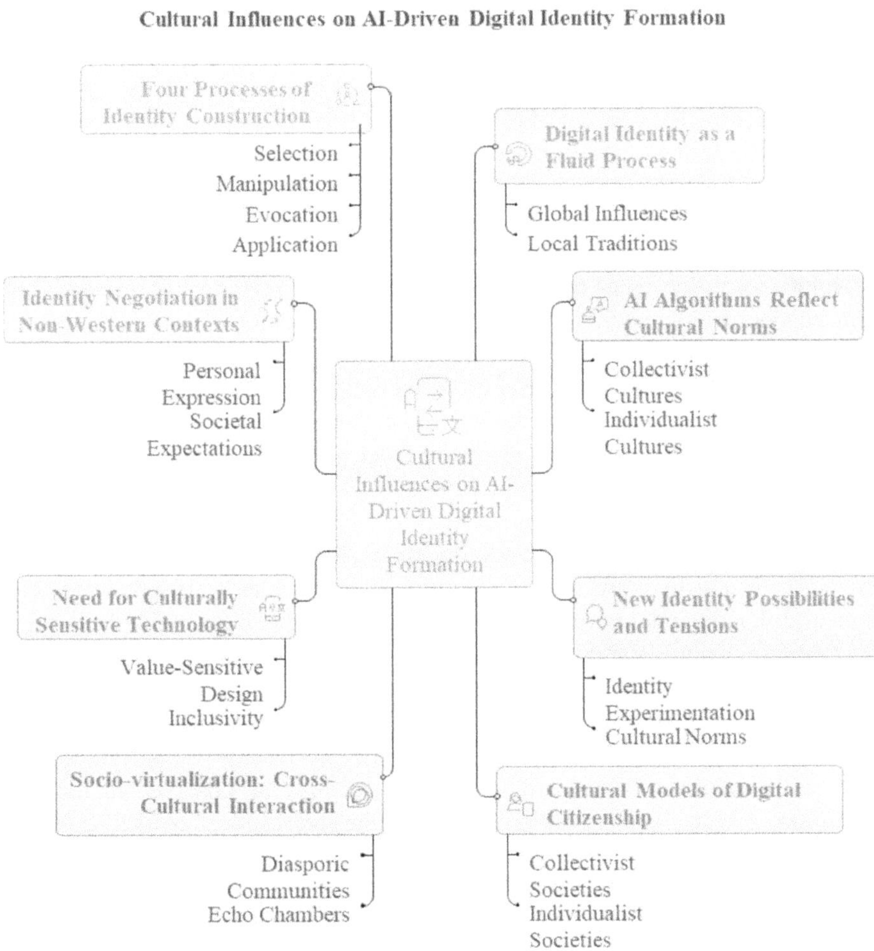

FIGURE 3.3 Summary of the cultural influences on AI-Driven digital identity formation.

> ***Takeaway:*** *Cultural norms play an important role in shaping digital identities, including the ways in which individuals participate in self-expression and social interaction in online communities.*
> ***Reflection:*** *How do cultural differences impact how you present yourself online compared to offline relationships?*

3.5.2 Gender Differences

Research has revealed significant gender differences in the formation and expression of digital identities, with males and females exhibiting distinct patterns in their use of social media and online platforms. These gendered patterns interact with the personality traits discussed in Chapter 2 (Section 2.5), as individual differences combine with gender socialization to shape digital behavior and identity expression. Males are typically more interested in individual achievement and are more likely to use social media for entertainment or to connect with friends, with fewer deep interactions. Twenge and Martin (2020) note that the digital identity of males is likely to be formed based on individualistic values such as personal achievement and leisure activities. Social media is utilized as a platform for showcasing hobbies, achievements, or interests in a manner that aligns with a self-presentation focused on autonomy and self-assertion.

Women, on the other hand, tend to be more relationship-oriented and primarily use digital media for communication and social comparison. Haidt and Allen (2020) contend that for women, social media serves as a means of staying connected with family and friends, as well as a medium for sharing personal lives and emotions. Their use of the internet appears to reflect a greater emphasis on the relational aspect of their identities, such as forming social relationships and establishing emotional support networks. Women may also utilize online environments for self-evaluation, comparing their lives, appearance, or success with that of others, a tendency that sometimes leads to negative consequences for self-esteem through unrealistic comparisons. AI-driven platforms often reinforce traditional gender norms by promoting content that aligns with these roles. For example, beauty standards and success ideals are frequently reinforced by algorithms that prioritize certain types of posts, such as those related to physical appearance or career success. This can further entrench gender differences in digital self-expression and self-esteem.

In self-presentation, gendered tendencies can also be observed in the way individuals present their online profiles. Women present idealized self-portraits, particularly in profile pictures. Matrángolo et al. (2021) recognize that women prefer highly edited or carefully selected images that present the idealized self, attributed to social expectations of femininity and attractiveness. The need to present this perfected self-portrait is driven by the desire to conform to the standards of attractiveness, which are typically hyper-real in cyberspaces. Men prefer the presentation of a full-body image, where the focus is on presenting their physical presence rather than creating an idealized image. The difference in self-presentation highlights the varied ways in which gender norms influence digital identity and the type of social approval that individuals seek from their online images. Gendered cyber behavior is also aligned with traditional social roles, where women are more concerned with self-presentation and privacy. Dym and Fiesler (2018) recognizes that women protect their privacy and the amount of personal information they make available on social media, taking concerted actions to protect themselves from potential risks, such as harassment or unwanted attention. The concern with privacy and safety can be recognized as an extension of traditional gender norms of modesty, cautiousness, and protection for women.

Women are more likely to use privacy settings to control who can see their updates, reflecting an awareness of the potential dangers of cyberspace. Men, in contrast, are less interested in the privacy or public presentation of their personal lives, using social media essentially as a platform for self-expression and communication. Furthermore, these gendered disparities in digital identity are not static but adaptive and reactive to evolving cyberspaces and societal norms. Petrakova et al. (2022) noted that the rapid development of digital technologies, the increased usage of social media platforms, and the evolving gender equality discourse are all important elements in the ongoing development of digital identity construction. As gender norms continue to evolve, there is a growing trend towards more diverse performances of gender online, challenging conventional understandings of femininity and masculinity. Despite these changes, many of the gender disparities in digital self-presentation persist, largely due to strongly established societal structures and expectations. It is essential to understand these gendered differences to effectively address digital inequalities and enable everyone to engage with cyberspaces in a safe and empowering manner. Gendered digital practices can perpetuate stereotypes and traditional roles, but they also provide opportunities for identity formation and self-expression. By acknowledging and acting upon these differences, we can develop more inclusive and equitable digital spaces, policies, and educational initiatives that foster healthier online practices and a more equal representation of gender identities. Having examined how cultural and gender contexts shape the experience of AI-driven identity formation, we now turn to evaluate the outcomes of these processes. AI's role in shaping digital identity produces a complex array of effects, both positive and negative, that must be understood holistically. We begin by examining the advantages of AI-mediated identity construction.

> ***Takeaway:*** *Gender plays an important role in digital identity performance, with varying motivations and practices informing how people portray themselves online.*
>
> ***Reflection:*** *How do gendered expectations influence the way you portray your online identity, and in what ways can these expectations be challenged in online spaces?*

3.6 The Double-Edged Sword: Positive and Negative Effects

3.6.1 Positive Effects of AI on Digital Identity Formation

Research into the psychological effects of virtual activity reveals both positive and negative effects and suggests that the interrelationship between activity in virtual spaces and mental wellness is complex and multifaceted. These effects can be understood through Keyes' Comprehensive Mental Health Model (discussed in Chapter 2, Section 2.6), which distinguishes between emotional, psychological, and social dimensions of well-being. Much of the work identifies positive psychological effects associated with virtual environment activity, particularly among college students. Kim et al. (2020) suggest that social media and smartphone use can serve as powerful tools for enhancing social contact, fostering a sense of connectivity, and fulfilling humans' fundamental desire for a sense of belonging. By accessing cyberspaces, students can maintain social connections and stay in touch with fellow students, potentially reducing feelings of disconnection that are common in tertiary settings. AI has the potential to positively influence digital identity development by providing users with personalized experiences that encourage self-expression, creativity, and connection with like-minded individuals. For example, AI-driven recommendation systems can help users discover new interests, activities, and communities, fostering a stronger sense of belonging and enhancing self-esteem.

In particular, web use has been shown to mitigate feelings of depression and loneliness. Shaw and Gant (2002) cite evidence that virtual contact, including social network activity, can boost perceived social support, thereby enhancing both emotional well-being (through positive affect) and social well-being (through social integration and contribution), as conceptualized in Keyes' model. By providing access to and facilitating relationships and social contact in supportive virtual communities, these platforms can serve as a key outlet for the expression and affirmation of emotions, making users feel valued and included.

Text-based communication, such as messaging and forums, has been particularly beneficial for self-esteem. Gonzales (2014) asserts that text conversation allows individuals to deliver their answer with consideration and practice a reflective form of conversation, one that can free one and work towards a positive self-concept. Such activity carries with it a level of anonymity, one that can make face-to-face conversations easier and allow individuals to present themselves in a more genuine form.

The positive psychological effect of virtual activity extends to cover other forms of web activity, such as Massively Multiplayer Online games (MMOs). Kaye et al. (2017) conclude that activity in MMOs is associated with increased self-esteem and social competency. This is a function of creating a player identity and online social capital. Players who join a gaming community and become involved in group gaming form strong social ties, and these ties foster a sense of competency and self-worth. Online social relations can enhance players' confidence in social competency and serve as a social outlet for social contact that may not be experienced in offline settings.

Further experimental work has identified social inclusion in cyberspaces as having profound physiological and affective benefits. Begen and Turner-Cobb (2014) illustrate that social feelings of acceptance and inclusion, both in face-to-face settings and in virtual communities, can contribute to a decrease in heart rate and improved mood, with a concurrent increase in social self-esteem at the same time. What is emphasized in such studies is the psychological and physiological ties between social activity and wellness and the idea that a sense of acceptance and inclusion in a virtual environment can contribute to an improvement in mood and emotional well-being (see Figure 3.4).

However, despite these positive effects, social media use is not universally beneficial for psychological well-being. As discussed in Section 3.3, social comparison processes, particularly upward comparisons with idealized profiles, can lead to feelings of inadequacy and disconnection (Chamsi et al., 2022). The balance between positive and negative outcomes depends on factors such as the nature of interactions, platform design, personality traits (see Chapter 2, Section 2.5), and individual approaches to digital engagement.

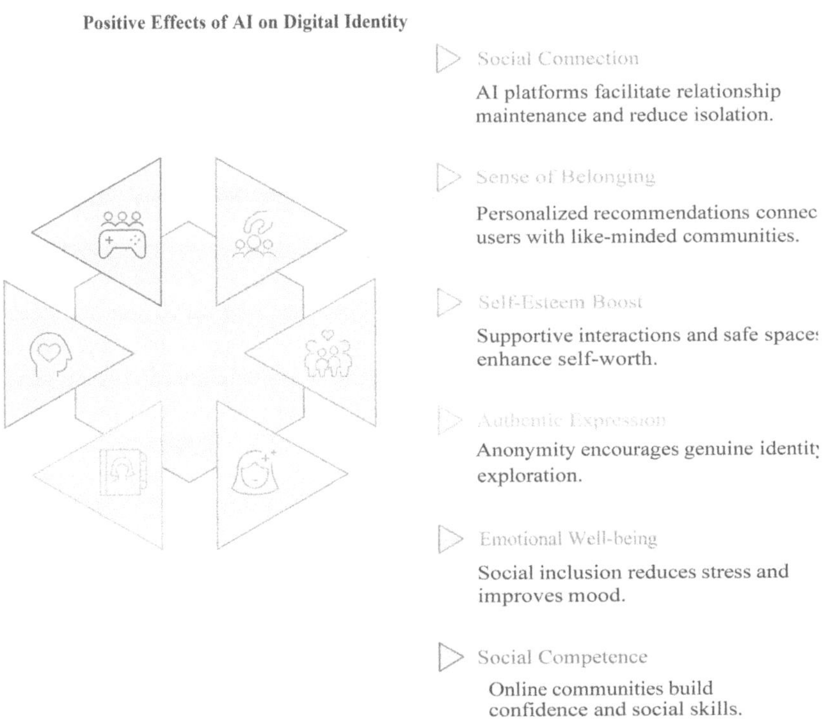

FIGURE 3.4 The positive effects of AI on individuals' digital identity.

The overall psychological effect of digital engagement is multidimensional and complex (Khalaf et al., 2023; Misra et al., 2022). The effects of digital engagement on mental wellness depend on factors such as the nature of the interactions, the type of online platform, personality, and one's approach to being present in cyberspace. Although some forms of digital engagement have a significantly positive impact on emotions, others have a negative impact on psychological well-being, particularly when one is subjected to a poor social environment in cyberspace or engages in destructive cyber behavior. Although these positive effects demonstrate AI's potential to support healthy identity development, the same technological systems that enable these benefits can also produce significant harms. Understanding these negative effects is essential for developing strategies to mitigate them.

> ***Takeaway:*** *Internet use, particularly social media and internet gaming, can bring tremendous psychological benefits, including enhanced social connectedness, self-esteem, and the possibility for personal growth. These benefits are particularly significant in facilitating a sense of belonging, emotional support, and personal expression, specifically in healthy virtual communities. It is essential, however, to acknowledge the intricacy of internet use that requires a balance between benefit and damage.*
>
> ***Reflection:*** *How can digital media be utilized to maximize the positive psychological benefits, such as social support and self-expression, and minimize the risks of excessive use and idealized portrayals of life?*

3.6.2 Negative Effects of AI on Digital Identity Formation

AI-driven digital identity formation presents significant challenges and risks that can undermine psychological well-being and authentic self-development. Recent research describes social media use and mental well-being in adolescents and young adults as a multifaceted and complex problem. Overuse of social networks is positively correlated with poor psychological state, such as increased anxiety, depression, and feelings of disconnection. Overuse of such networks will increase feelings of disconnection even when one feels part of a community, according to Khalaf et al. (2023). As established in Section 3.3, AI-amplified social comparison processes intensify these effects, with algorithmic curation of idealized content generating heightened emotional distress and feelings of inadequacy.

Although AI can enhance digital identity, it also has the potential to negatively impact mental health. Algorithmic recommendations can lead to users becoming trapped in echo chambers or experiencing heightened social comparisons, which may result in feelings of inadequacy, anxiety, and distorted self-image. The lack of transparency in AI algorithms also raises concerns about the manipulation and exploitation of user data for profit.

One of the less-talked-about consequences of use is digital addiction, and one that can lead to what Peper and Harvey (2018) have termed "phoneliness". "Phoneliness" is a state of aloneness, yet one of constant presence, facilitated by smartphones. As humans become increasingly dependent on digital technology for social connectivity, they become less effective at face-to-face interactions and, consequently, ever more isolated. In addition, the physical consequences of overuse, such as poor postures and accompanying aches, contribute to mental consequences. What this reveals is not only mental but also overall bodily welfare suffers from technology overuse.

The relationship between social media and mental health varies significantly with gender and individual factors such as personality traits (discussed in Chapter 2, Section 2.5), where characteristics like neuroticism and conscientiousness moderate the impact of digital engagement on mental health outcomes. For males, increased social anxiety and less mature identity development are positively related to increased internet use (Ding et al., 2023), suggesting that social media can serve as both a coping mechanism for anxiety and a source of insecurity that hinders mature identity development. For females, particularly adolescent girls, the relationship is equally complex. Mackenzie et al. (2020) found that when girls seek support in cyberspace during times of academic difficulty, they experience heightened symptoms of depression and anxiety. This pattern reflects the interaction between gender socialization, personality traits such as agreeableness and neuroticism, and AI-driven platform design that may amplify emotional vulnerabilities. The anonymity and distance inherent in digital spaces can sometimes inhibit the intensity and effectiveness of support received, transforming what appears to be healthy help-seeking behavior into excessive engagement with potentially harmful feedback loops.

For adolescents with pre-existing mental health conditions, digital environments present a particularly complex landscape. Social media can provide valuable experiences of social connectivity and support, yet simultaneously opens pathways for social exclusion and cyberbullying that can exacerbate existing conditions (Odgers & Jensen, 2020). This duality highlights how the same platforms that offer connection can also intensify psychological challenges, particularly for vulnerable populations. The AI algorithms that curate content and connections may inadvertently amplify negative experiences for at-risk youth, creating feedback loops that reinforce distress rather than providing genuine support.

The developmental timing of social media exposure significantly influences its impact on mental health. Weigle and Shafi (2023) found that the early onset of social media use, particularly before the age of 10, is associated with problematic usage patterns in adolescence. Exposure to social and competitive pressures within digital environments during critical developmental periods can make children particularly vulnerable to negative effects as they mature, including cyberbullying, addiction, unhealthy body image, and associated mental

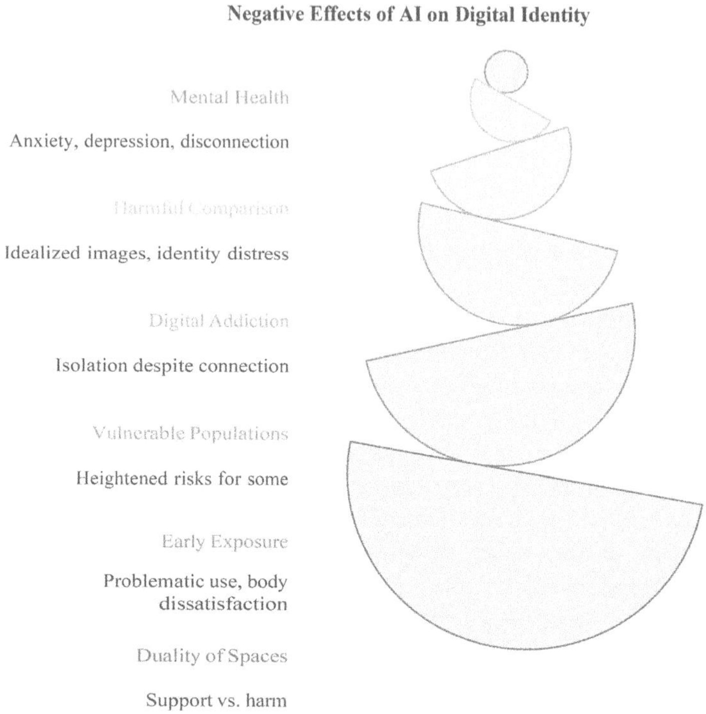

FIGURE 3.5 The negative effects of AI on digital identity.

health concerns (see Figure 3.5). This developmental vulnerability intersects with the AI-driven personalization of content, which may expose young users to age-inappropriate material or intensify social comparison processes before they have developed adequate coping mechanisms.

Despite these challenges, the internet also holds significant potential for promoting healthy psychological development, particularly in terms of identity formation and social relationships. According to McKenna et al. (2002), virtual spaces can offer youth the freedom to explore and shape their identity in ways that are not necessarily possible in offline spaces. Cyberspace's comparative anonymity allows one to try out and explore aspects of one's personality and, in the process, become increasingly aware and secure in one's identity. Online, one can develop relationships, whether through shared activities or social networks, and cultivate a sense of belonging and meaningful connections that may not necessarily exist in one's offline life. The positive and negative effects of AI-driven identity formation raise fundamental ethical questions about the design, deployment, and governance of these systems. While the psychological and social impacts are significant, the ethical dimensions extend beyond individual outcomes to encompass questions of autonomy, justice, and human dignity. These ethical challenges demand careful consideration.

Takeaway: *Excessive use of digital media, particularly social media, can exacerbate anxiety, depression, and loneliness. The constant comparison to idealized profiles and the pressure of an online image is to blame for these negative effects. Furthermore, the advent of digital addiction and the absence of face-to-face interaction also fan the problem. It is necessary to solve these negative effects in order to foster a healthier relationship with technology.*

Reflection: *What are some of the strategies that can be implemented on digital platforms to help users achieve a healthier balance between their online and offline lives and thereby reduce the negative mental health consequences of excessive use?*

3.7 Ethical Challenges in AI-Driven Identity Formation

Research into youth ethics in cyberspace describes a complex mix of concerns regarding virtual spaces. Online disinhibition, privacy, and cyberbullying are significant concerns that shape youth ethics in cyberspace. Miller (2012) and Alrasheed et al. (2022) observe that not only do such concerns involve offensive behaviors, but also deeper moral ambiguities that youth must navigate, too. For example, anonymity and distance in cyberspaces can enable violent behavior such as cyberbullying, which is not necessarily exhibited in face-to-face environments. Detachment in such spaces creates concerns regarding accountability, responsibility, and the consequences of actions in cyberspace.

As AI algorithms shape the formation of digital identity, they introduce ethical challenges that extend beyond traditional concerns about youth behavior in digital spaces. AI systems actively curate the environments in which ethical decisions are made, influencing what content is visible, which behaviors are rewarded through engagement metrics, and how consequences (or lack thereof) are experienced. From concerns about data privacy and behavioral manipulation to algorithmic bias and the perpetuation of stereotypes, AI operates as an invisible ethical actor that shapes identity construction in ways that may not be immediately apparent to users. These AI-driven dynamics intersect with the developmental and moral challenges youth already face in digital environments, creating compounded ethical complexities.

Young people often adopt a self-centered mindset when engaging in cyber behavior, prioritizing individual consequences over broader moral implications. This pattern reflects developmental factors in moral reasoning as well as the interaction between personality traits, particularly conscientiousness and agreeableness (discussed in Chapter 2, Section 2.5), and the affordances of digital environments. As Wisniewski et al. (2022) and Flores and James (2012) have discussed, youth tend to prefer consequences for themselves, such as social rewards and happiness, over consequences for others and for a larger virtual society. This state of mind is most observable when youth lack an awareness of long-term consequences for behavior, such as long-term hurtful consequences for over-disclosure of intimate information and for virtual harassment.

Several factors underlie shaping youth's behavior in cyberspace, including reduced concerns of getting detected, a lack of immediate affective feedback, and feelings of social injustice. AI systems amplify these factors by algorithmically moderating (or failing to moderate) content, creating echo chambers that normalize unethical behavior, and designing reward structures that prioritize engagement over ethical conduct. According to Pan et al. (2023), comparative anonymity on the internet generates a reduced perception of being caught and subsequently punished and, hence, lessens the level of moral boundaries against engaging in morally unacceptable behavior. In the absence of immediate feedback in terms of emotion, such as witnessing a person become upset following a hurtful statement, youth will not have a full awareness of the emotional consequences, and hence, unethical behavior will not seem significant enough. Perceived and actual feelings of social injustice can motivate behavior in cyberspace, where one may view offensive behavior as a form of revenge and resistance against social conventions.

Beyond these overt challenges lies a more subtle but pervasive ethical issue: the power imbalance inherent in AI-driven platforms. These systems are not neutral arbiters of information; they are designed with a primary goal of maximizing user engagement. To achieve this, algorithms often learn to exploit psychological vulnerabilities, promoting content that triggers strong emotional reactions, encourages social comparison, or fosters a fear of missing out (FOMO). This process of "algorithmic nudging" can steer users toward certain behaviors, beliefs, and even identities without their conscious awareness or consent. The ethical dilemma, therefore, is not just about preventing negative outcomes like harassment but about the fundamental right to self-determination in an environment where one's identity is constantly being shaped by opaque, commercially driven code. This raises critical questions about corporate responsibility and the need for regulatory frameworks that mandate transparency and user control over the algorithms that shape their digital existence.

Cyberspace introduces new and unique moral dilemmas not present in offline life. Challenges such as information fabrication, illegal downloading, and plagiarism complicate youth moral consciousness about right and wrong in virtual environments. Rao and Lingam (2020) state that such complications are sometimes supplemented with plenty of information in cyberspace, accessible at one's fingertips, and therefore, increasingly challenging to discern between legal and illegal and between ethical and unethical behaviors. For example, youth become entitled to download for free, not necessarily appreciating the ethical and sometimes even legal consequences of copyright rules. One of the most significant observations in the study is that youth awareness and online practices are not in harmony with each other. Wisniewski et al. (2022) observe that, although most youth are aware of ethical principles in terms of behavior, such as not encroaching on others' privacy and avoiding plagiarism, this awareness is not necessarily translated into practice. That awareness and practice disconnection signifies a need for ethics training in cyberspace. Young adults don't necessarily make ethical decisions out of immediate desire or coercion but rather because they lack ethics training.

Addressing these ethical challenges requires multifaceted approaches that include educational interventions, platform design reforms, and policy frameworks that account for AI's role in shaping digital identity. As Wisniewski et al. (2022) and James et al. (2017) emphasize, bridging the gap between ethical awareness and ethical practice demands not only individual education but also systemic changes to the AI-driven environments in which youth develop their digital identities. These ethical imperatives frame the broader conclusions that can be drawn about AI-driven digital identity formation and the path forward for research, policy, and practice.

> ***Takeaway:*** *Online environments introduce new ethical dilemmas requiring careful consideration of privacy, moderation of conduct, and accountability.*
> ***Reflection:*** *How do we balance the use of AI in monitoring online activities and making sure that AI systems do not infringe upon the rights of users or promote harmful behaviors?*

3.8 Summary and Reflections

This chapter has explored the formation of digital identity in the AI era, introducing the concept of the cybernetic self, an identity continuously constructed and reconstructed through feedback loops between individuals, social environments, and technological systems. Unlike traditional conceptions of identity as relatively stable and self-directed, the cybernetic self emerges through dynamic interactions in which AI systems play an increasingly central architectural role. AI operates not as a neutral platform but as an active participant in identity formation, shaping the environments in which the cybernetic self develops. Through algorithmic curation of social feedback (Section 3.3), AI amplifies social comparison processes that drive identity construction. Through personalized content delivery and avatar-based interactions (Section 3.4), AI determines which aspects of identity are visible, validated, and reinforced. These mechanisms operate within, and are moderated by, cultural contexts and gender socialization patterns (Section 3.5), creating differentiated experiences of AI-driven identity formation across populations. The outcomes of these processes are profoundly double-edged (Section 3.6), with AI-mediated environments offering unprecedented opportunities for self-expression, community building, and identity exploration while simultaneously intensifying risks of social comparison distress, echo chamber effects, and mental health challenges. The ethical dimensions of AI-driven identity formation (Section 3.7) extend beyond individual psychological outcomes to encompass fundamental questions about autonomy, authenticity, and human dignity. When algorithms determine what content shapes our self-concept, which social comparisons we encounter, and how our self-presentations are received, the locus of identity construction shifts from individual agency to a hybrid human-AI process. This shift raises critical questions: To what extent is the cybernetic self genuinely "self-determined" when its development occurs within AI-curated environments? How do we ensure that AI systems support rather than undermine authentic identity development? What responsibilities do platform designers, policymakers, and educators bear in shaping these systems?

Understanding digital identity formation in the AI era requires holding multiple frameworks in simultaneous view: the psychological mechanisms of social comparison and feedback (grounded in Social Identity Theory and Social Cognitive Theory from Chapter 2), the communication characteristics that shape digital interaction (Computer-Mediated Communication theories), the individual differences that moderate experiences (personality psychology), and the mental health outcomes that result (Keyes' Comprehensive Mental Health Model). AI does not replace these frameworks but rather operates through them, amplifying certain processes, moderating others, and creating novel dynamics that traditional theories did not anticipate. The chapters that follow build on this foundation. Chapter 4 examines how AI specifically reshapes cyber behaviors, the actions and patterns that emerge from AI-mediated identity formation. Chapter 5 explores the mental health consequences of these processes in depth, examining how AI-driven identity construction influences psychological, emotional, and social well-being. Together, these chapters construct a comprehensive understanding of how AI is transforming not only how we present ourselves online but also who we become in the process.

References

Alrasheed, N., Nishat, S., Shihah, A. B., Alalwan, A., & Jradi, H. (2022). Prevalence and risk factors of cyberbullying and its association with mental health among adolescents in Saudi Arabia. *Cureus*. https://doi.org/10.7759/cureus.32806

Begen, F. M., & Turner-Cobb, J. M. (2014). Benefits of belonging: Experimental manipulation of social inclusion to enhance psychological and physiological health parameters. *Psychology and Health*, *30*(5), 568–582. https://doi.org/10.1080/08870446.2014.991734

Bellman, K., Landauer, C., Dutt, N., Esterle, L., Herkersdorf, A., Jantsch, A., Taheri-Nejad, N., Lewis, P. R., Platzner, M., & Tammemäe, K. (2020). Self-aware Cyber-Physical systems. *ACM Transactions on Cyber-Physical Systems*, *4*(4), 1–26. https://doi.org/10.1145/3375716

Berridge, C. (2024). Cultural contexts and beyond: The Need for value sensitive design in technologies to support care. *Innovation in Aging, 8*(Supplement_1), 215. https://doi.org/10.1093/geroni/igae098.0696

Chamsi, F., Katir, I., Korchi, A., Belbachir, S., & Ouanass, A. (2022). The impact of social media on self-esteem. *European Psychiatry, 65*(S1), S551. https://doi.org/10.1192/j.eurpsy.2022.1410

Chen, S. (2023). The influence of social media platforms on Self-Identity in the new media environment: The case of TikTok and Instagram. *SHS Web of Conferences*, *165*, 01020. https://doi.org/10.1051/shsconf/202316501020

Davis, J. L. (2014). Blogging my academic self. In *Springer eBooks* (pp. 3–8). https://doi.org/10.1007/978-94-017-8718-5_1

De Vaate, N. a. B., Veldhuis, J., & Konijn, E. A. (2019). How online self-presentation affects well-being and body image: A systematic review. *Telematics and Informatics*, *47*, 101316. https://doi.org/10.1016/j.tele.2019.101316

DeVeaux, C., Han, E., Landay, J. A., & Bailenson, J. N. (2023). Exploring the relationship between attribute discrepancy and avatar embodiment in immersive social virtual reality. *Cyberpsychology Behavior and Social Networking*, *26*(11), 835–842. https://doi.org/10.1089/cyber.2023.0210

Ding, H., Cao, B., & Sun, Q. (2023). The association between problematic internet use and social anxiety within adolescents and young adults: A systematic review and meta-analysis. *Frontiers in Public Health*, *11*. https://doi.org/10.3389/fpubh.2023.1275723

Ding, J., Shi, Y., Yu, Q., Sun, S., Liu, H., Zhou, W., Zhao, W., Zhao, Q., & Jiang, S. (2024). Collectivism–Individualism makes the relationships between digital games use and creativity different. *The Journal of Creative Behavior*, *59*(3). https://doi.org/10.1002/jocb.1508

Dym, B., & Fiesler, C. (2018). Vulnerable and online. In *CSCW '18 Companion: Companion of the 2018 ACM Conference on Computer Supported Cooperative Work and Social Computing* (pp. 329–332). https://doi.org/10.1145/3272973.3274089

Emanuel, L., & Fraser, D. S. (2014). *Exploring physical and digital identity with a teenage cohort* (Vol. 38, pp. 67–76). IDC '14: Proceedings of the 2014 conference on Interaction design and children. https://doi.org/10.1145/2593968.2593984

Flores, A., & James, C. (2012). Morality and ethics behind the screen: Young people's perspectives on digital life. *New Media & Society*, *15*(6), 834–852. https://doi.org/10.1177/1461444812462842

García-Martínez, I., Fernández-Batanero, J. M., Fernández-Cerero, J., & León, S. P. (2023). Analysing the Impact of artificial intelligence and computational sciences on student performance: Systematic review and meta-analysis. *Journal of New Approaches in Educational Research*, *12*(1), 171–197. https://doi.org/10.7821/naer.2023.1.1240

Gonzales, A. L. (2014). Text-based communication influences self-esteem more than face-to-face or cellphone communication. *Computers in Human Behavior*, *39*, 197–203. https://doi.org/10.1016/j.chb.2014.07.026

Gottschalk, S. (2021). Click, validate, and reply. In *Routledge eBooks* (pp. 99–111). https://doi.org/10.4324/9780429276767-11

Granic, I., Morita, H., & Scholten, H. (2020). Beyond screen time: Identity development in the digital age. *Psychological Inquiry*, *31*(3), 195–223. https://doi.org/10.1080/1047840x.2020.1820214

Haidt, J., & Allen, N. (2020). Scrutinizing the effects of digital technology on mental health. *Nature*, *578*(7794), 226–227. https://doi.org/10.1038/d41586-020-00296-x

Harrison, T., & Polizzi, G. (2022). (In)civility and adolescents' moral decision making online: drawing on moral theory to advance digital citizenship education. *Education and Information Technologies*, *27*(3), 3277–3297. https://doi.org/10.1007/s10639-021-10710-0

Heang, R. (2024). Digital Nationalism: Understanding the power of digital technology in the rise of nationalism, national identity, and national narratives. *OALib*, *11*(09), 1–25. https://doi.org/10.4236/oalib.1112129

James, C., Davis, K., Charmaraman, L., Konrath, S., Slovak, P., Weinstein, E., & Yarosh, L. (2017). Digital life and youth well-being, social connectedness, empathy, and narcissism. *PEDIATRICS*, *140*(Supplement_2), S71–S75. https://doi.org/10.1542/peds.2016-1758f

Kadir, N. (2022). Media Sosial dan Politik Partisipatif : Suatu Kajian Ruang Publik, Demokrasi Bagi Kaum Milenial dan Gen Z. *RESIPROKAL Jurnal Riset Sosiologi Progresif Aktual*, *4*(2), 180–197.

Kaye, L. K., Kowert, R., & Quinn, S. (2017). The role of social identity and online social capital on psychosocial outcomes in MMO players. *Computers in Human Behavior*, *74*, 215–223. https://doi.org/10.1016/j.chb.2017.04.030

Khalaf, A. M., Alubied, A. A., Khalaf, A. M., & Rifaey, A. A. (2023). The Impact of social media on the mental health of adolescents and young Adults: A systematic review. *Cureus*. https://doi.org/10.7759/cureus.42990

Kim, H. J., Yi, P., & Hong, J. I. (2020). Students' academic use of mobile Technology and Higher-Order Thinking skills: The role of Active engagement. *Education Sciences*, *10*(3), 47. https://doi.org/10.3390/educsci10030047

Knytl, M. (2021). The prevalence of online High-Risk phenomena in university students. *Social Pathology and Prevention*, *6*(1), 21–33. https://doi.org/10.25142/spp.2020.001

Latif, K., Weng, Q., Pitafi, A. H., Ali, A., Siddiqui, A. W., Malik, M. Y., & Latif, Z. (2020). Social comparison as a double-edged sword on social media: The role of envy type and online social identity. *Telematics and Informatics*, *56*, 101470. https://doi.org/10.1016/j.tele.2020.101470

Mackenzie, E., McMaugh, A., & Van Bergen, P. (2020). Digital support seeking in adolescent girls: A qualitative study of affordances and limitations. *Cyberpsychology Journal of Psychosocial Research on Cyberspace*, *14*(3). https://doi.org/10.5817/cp2020-3-5

Matrángolo, G., Yaccarini, C., Olivera, M., & Simkin, H. (2021). Evidencias de validez de la Escala de Procesamiento Crítico de las Imágenes de Belleza en el contexto argentino. *Revista De Psicología*, 133. https://doi.org/10.24215/2422572xe133

Maqbool, I., & Cremin, H. (2023). Students' experiences of extracurricular activities in elite secondary schools in Lahore. *Compare a Journal of Comparative and International Education*, *54*(8), 1253–1270. https://doi.org/10.1080/03057925.2023.2195048

McKenna, K. Y. A., Green, A. S., & Gleason, M. E. J. (2002). Relationship formation on the internet: What's the big attraction? *Journal of Social Issues*, *58*(1), 9–31. https://doi.org/10.1111/1540-4560.00246

Miller, V. (2012). A crisis of presence: On-line culture and being in the world. *Space and Polity*, *16*(3), 265–285. https://doi.org/10.1080/13562576.2012.733568

Mishra, S., & Ismail, A. (2017). Performances of the Online self for Networked Audiences: An introduction to the special issue. *Journal of Human Values*, *24*(1), vii–xiii. https://doi.org/10.1177/0971685817733567

Misra, G., Singh, P., Ramakrishna, M., & Ramanathan, P. (2022). Technology as a Double-Edged Sword: Understanding life experiences and coping with COVID-19 in India. *Frontiers in Psychology*, *12*. https://doi.org/10.3389/fpsyg.2021.800827

Moustaka, V., Theodosiou, Z., Vakali, A., Kounoudes, A., & Anthopoulos, L. G. (2018). Enhancing social networking in smart cities: Privacy and security borderlines. *Technological Forecasting and Social Change*, *142*, 285–300. https://doi.org/10.1016/j.techfore.2018.10.026

Odgers, C. L., & Jensen, M. R. (2020). Annual Research Review: Adolescent mental health in the digital age: Facts, fears, and future directions. *Journal of Child Psychology and Psychiatry*, *61*(3), 336–348. https://doi.org/10.1111/jcpp.13190

Paciello, M., Tramontano, C., Nocentini, A., Fida, R., & Menesini, E. (2019). The role of traditional and online moral disengagement on cyberbullying: Do externalising problems make any difference? *Computers in Human Behavior*, *103*, 190–198. https://doi.org/10.1016/j.chb.2019.09.024

Pan, X., Hou, Y., & Wang, Q. (2023). Are we braver in cyberspace? Social media anonymity enhances moral courage. *Computers in Human Behavior*, *148*, 107880. https://doi.org/10.1016/j.chb.2023.107880

Peper, E., & Harvey, R. (2018). Digital addiction: Increased loneliness, anxiety, and depression. *NeuroRegulation*, *5*(1), 3–8. https://doi.org/10.15540/nr.5.1.3

Petrakova, A., Martseva, T., Artemenko, N., & Nebylova, Y. (2022). The influence of digital transformations on the processes of personal identification in the conditions of social systems functioning. *Advances in Economics, Business and Management Research/ Advances in Economics, Business and Management Research*. https://doi.org/10.2991/assehr.k.220208.059

Pham, H. C., Nguyen, L., Tran, P., & Tran, T. (2022). Exploring Facebook identity construction of Vietnamese netizens. *Acta Informatica Pragensia, 11*(2), 218–240. https://doi.org/10.18267/j.aip.181

Plachynda, T., Doviga, T., Zavitrenko, D., Snisarenko, I., & Pavlenko, O. (2024). The Power of social media: shaping and reshaping student image. *Diversitas Journal, 9*(3). https://doi.org/10.48017/dj.v9i3.3107

Qin, Y., & Lowe, J. (2021). Situational selves of online identity and rationality in choosing – More examples of the college students' online identity in China. *Culture & Psychology, 27*(4), 612–631. https://doi.org/10.1177/1354067x20976514

Rao, N., & Lingam, L. (2020). Smartphones, youth and moral panics: Exploring print and online media narratives in India. *Mobile Media & Communication, 9*(1), 128–148. https://doi.org/10.1177/2050157920922262

Reid, J. (2009). Politicizing connectivity: Beyond the biopolitics of information technology in international relations. *Cambridge Review of International Affairs, 22*(4), 607–623. https://doi.org/10.1080/09557570903325520

Robinson, L. (2007). The cyberself: The self-ing project goes online, symbolic interaction in the digital age. *New Media & Society, 9*(1), 93–110. https://doi.org/10.1177/1461444807072216

Rodríguez, J. M. M., Pessoa, T., & Martín-Lucas, J. (2020). *The OnLife self* (pp. 925–929). TEEM'20: Eighth International Conference on Technological Ecosystems for Enhancing Multiculturality. https://doi.org/10.1145/3434780.3436605

Shaw, L. H., & Gant, L. M. (2002). In defense of the internet: The relationship between internet communication and depression, loneliness, self-esteem, and perceived social support. *CyberPsychology & Behavior, 5*(2), 157–171. https://doi.org/10.1089/109493102753770552

Sousa, S., Cravino, J., & Martins, P. (2023). Challenges and trends in user trust discourse in AI popularity. *Multimodal Technologies and Interaction, 7*(2), 13. https://doi.org/10.3390/mti7020013

Suler, J. (2017). The dimensions of Cyberpsychology Architecture. In *Elsevier eBooks* (pp. 1–23). https://doi.org/10.1016/b978-0-12-804157-4.00001-3

Thompson, P. (2013). The digital natives as learners: Technology use patterns and approaches to learning. *Computers & Education, 65*, 12–33. https://doi.org/10.1016/j.compedu.2012.12.022

Tolnaiová, S. G., & Gálik, S. (2020). Cyberspace as a new living world and its axiological contexts. In *IntechOpen eBooks*. https://doi.org/10.5772/intechopen.91907

Twenge, J. M., & Martin, G. N. (2020). Gender differences in associations between digital media use and psychological well-being: Evidence from three large datasets. *Journal of Adolescence, 79*(1), 91–102. https://doi.org/10.1016/j.adolescence.2019.12.018

Wang, Q., Myers, M. D., & Sundaram, D. (2013). Digital natives and digital immigrants. *Business & Information Systems Engineering, 5*(6), 409–419. https://doi.org/10.1007/s12599-013-0296-y

Waskul, D., Douglass, M., & Edgley, C. (2000). Cybersex: Outercourse and the enselfment of the body. *Symbolic Interaction, 23*(4), 375–397. https://doi.org/10.1525/si.2000.23.4.375

Weigle, P. E., & Shafi, R. M. A. (2023). Social media and youth mental health. *Current Psychiatry Reports*, *26*(1), 1–8. https://doi.org/10.1007/s11920-023-01478-w

Wisniewski, P. J., Vitak, J., & Hartikainen, H. (2022). Privacy in adolescence. In *Springer eBooks* (pp. 315–336). https://doi.org/10.1007/978-3-030-82786-1_14

Yang, Y., & Chae, H. (2023). The effect of downward social comparison on creativity in organizational teams, with the moderation of Narcissism and the mediation of negative affect. *Behavioral Sciences*, *13*(8), 633. https://doi.org/10.3390/bs13080633

Yee, N., Bailenson, J. N., & Ducheneaut, N. (2009). The proteus effect. *Communication Research*, *36*(2), 285–312. https://doi.org/10.1177/0093650208330254

Zhong, C., Chang, H., Karamshuk, D., Lee, D., & Sastry, N. (2017). Wearing many (Social) hats: How different are your different social network personae? *Proceedings of the International AAAI Conference on Web and Social Media*, *11*(1), 397–406. https://doi.org/10.1609/icwsm.v11i1.14897

STREAM 2

Cyberpsychology and Mental Health

4

UNDERSTANDING HOW AI RESHAPES CYBER BEHAVIOR

Objectives of This Chapter

- To analyze the core AI mechanisms (e.g., recommender systems, feedback loops, engagement optimization) that function as behavioral architects in digital environments.
- To investigate the psychological and ethical implications of AI's influence across key behavioral domains: aggressive (disinhibition, moral disengagement, and cyberbullying), addictive, and social-commercial behaviors.
- To classify AI-mediated behaviors along a dynamic risk spectrum, differentiating between low-risk, moderate-risk, and high-risk activities.
- To evaluate AI's dual capacity to both amplify harmful behaviors and foster positive outcomes, such as emotional literacy, empathy, and self-efficacy.
- To propose a framework for ethical design and responsible innovation that prioritizes user well-being and autonomy.

Topics to Be Covered

- AI as a Driver of Behavioral Patterns
- Core AI Mechanisms: How Algorithms Shape Behavior
- AI's Impact on Aggressive Behaviors
- AI's Impact on Addictive Behaviors
- AI's Impact on Social-Commercial Behaviors
- AI for Positive Digital Engagement
- Conclusion: The Path to Responsible Innovation

DOI: 10.4324/9781003657590-6

4.1 Introduction: AI as a Driver of Behavioral Patterns

The previous chapter examined how young people form digital identities, introducing the idea of the *cybernetic self.* It is a fluid identity shaped through online feedback, interaction, and the constant shift between digital and physical spaces (Waskul et al., 2000; Mishra & Ismail, 2017). Although that section focused on how individuals develop their online presence, it raises an important question: *what systems are actively shaping these digital experiences?* To answer this question, this chapter considers artificial intelligence (AI) not just as a passive tool but as an active framework that organizes cyber behavior. As AI technologies become an integral part of daily digital life, they do more than simply suggest content or organize feeds (Shi, 2016). They help define the architecture of user interaction. This introduces what can be called an *AI-behavior nexus*, as illustrated in Figure 4.1, where algorithms establish the conditions for cyber behavior, rather than merely reacting to it (Gligorea et al., 2023; Ma, 2024).

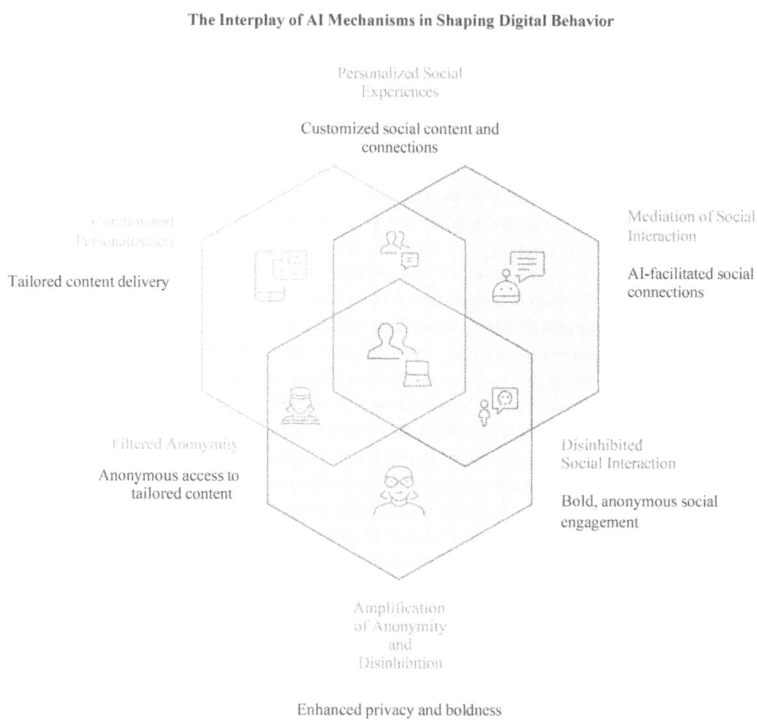

FIGURE 4.1 The Interplay mechanisms in shaping cyber behavior diagram illustrates how artificial intelligence systems influence user behavior through three interconnected mechanisms: curation and personalization of content, mediation of social interaction, and the amplification of anonymity and disinhibition. These pathways collectively shape how individuals engage, respond, and form behavioral patterns in digital environments.

Understanding these relationships requires connecting the behavioral theories from Chapter 2 to the specific algorithmic mechanisms detailed in this chapter. In AI-mediated environments, the core components of frameworks like the "Theory of Planned Behavior" and "Social Cognitive Theory" (see Sections 2.4.1 and 2.4.2) are no longer shaped primarily by organic human interaction. Instead, they are increasingly influenced by algorithmic curation, which can reshape perceived social norms and alter learning pathways. Building on the taxonomy of cyber behaviors introduced in Chapter 2, aggressive, addictive, and social-commercial (D'Angelo, 2020), this chapter examines how AI systems systematically transform each category.

The ethical concerns of this shift are wide-ranging. When systems shape not just what users see but also how they act, important questions arise. *Can people still choose freely? Are they aware when their behavior is being steered? And how do we ensure fairness, transparency, and safety when digital systems play such a large role in shaping daily life* (Gligorea et al., 2023)? For young people, who may not recognize the influence of these systems, the line between personal choice and engineered behavior becomes blurred (Thompson, 2013). This necessitates new frameworks for regulation and digital literacy that account for AI's foundational role. As discussed in Chapter 3, the *cybernetic self* develops through feedback loops; however, these loops are now largely mediated by AI systems that prioritize engagement metrics over personal well-being. This chapter, therefore, moves beyond analyzing how individuals adapt to cyberspace and instead investigates how AI builds these spaces, shaping the choices and behaviors within them. The goal is not to reject AI, but to understand its profound influence and consider how to design more ethically responsible and developmentally supportive digital environments for youth. This chapter proceeds in six parts. Section 4.2 examines the core AI mechanisms, recommendation algorithms, feedback loops, and engagement optimization techniques that serve as the architectural foundation for behavioral reshaping. Accordingly, the following section explores the core AI mechanisms, recommendation algorithms, feedback loops, and engagement optimization techniques that form the architectural foundation of modern digital experiences. By understanding how these systems operate, we can then proceed to analyze what their impacts are across the spectrum of cyber behaviors, from aggressive and addictive patterns (Sections 4.3 and 4.4) to social-commercial interactions (Section 4.5), before finally exploring AI's potential for positive engagement (Section 4.6) and drawing conclusions about the path toward responsible innovation (Section 4.7).

Takeaway: *AI has fundamentally transformed the digital landscape from a space where individuals simply interact to one where algorithms actively architect the conditions for behavior. The AI-behavior nexus represents a shift from human-centered to algorithm-mediated behavioral patterns, raising critical questions about autonomy, awareness, and the ethical responsibilities of those who design these systems.*

> ***Reflection:*** *To what extent do you believe your own cyber behaviors, what you click, share, watch, or purchase, are genuinely your choices versus outcomes shaped by algorithmic systems designed to influence those very decisions?*

4.2 Core AI Mechanisms: How Algorithms Shape Behavior

Building on the theoretical frameworks established in Chapter 2, this section examines the specific algorithmic mechanisms through which AI systems reshape cyber behavior. Although Chapter 2 introduced the psychological theories explaining human behavior, this section details the technical architecture that mediates, amplifies, and transforms those behavioral patterns in digital environments. Modern AI systems have evolved from reactive tools into active behavioral architects. Rather than waiting for user commands, these systems proactively decide what content to display, when to present it, and how it should appear. Platforms such as social media networks, e-commerce sites, and streaming services employ machine learning models that continuously adapt based on user interactions, predicting preferences and presenting content before users explicitly request it (Mehmood et al., 2024). This shift from user-initiated to system-directed interaction fundamentally alters how digital habits form and how young people develop their identities. These systems operate through feedback loops: user actions inform algorithmic predictions, which shape subsequent content delivery, and this, in turn, influences future user behavior. Over time, this cyclical process can shape users' preferences, habits, and beliefs (Kang & Lou, 2022). For adolescents still forming their identities, algorithmically selected experiences become deeply integrated into their developmental trajectories. Critically, this behavioral shaping often prioritizes engagement metrics over user well-being, potentially locking individuals into patterns they did not consciously choose.

4.2.1 Recommendation Algorithms: The Foundation of Behavioral Curation

Recommendation algorithms serve as the primary gatekeepers of digital experience, determining not only what content users encounter but also the sequence, timing, and context in which that content appears. These systems fundamentally reshape the behavioral patterns described by the Theory of Planned Behavior and Social Cognitive Theory (discussed in Chapter 2, Sections 2.4.1 and 2.4.2).

One approach, known as *Collaborative filtering,* operates on behavioral similarity, clustering users based on interaction patterns and recommending content that similar users have engaged with. This approach has profound implications for the formation of norms. As the Theory of Planned Behavior identifies "subjective norms" as a key determinant of behavioral intention, collaborative filtering becomes the mechanism through which those norms are algorithmically constructed. Users are exposed to behaviors that appear normative within their algorithmically defined peer group, which may not reflect their organic social network (Pappalardo et al., 2024).

Another approach is *Content-based filtering,* which focuses on behavioral consistency by analyzing the attributes of previously engaged content (genre, topic, style, and sentiment) to recommend similar items. This mechanism directly influences the "attitudes" component of the Theory of Planned Behavior by repeatedly exposing users to content that reinforces existing attitudes while limiting exposure to divergent perspectives. This can potentially create echo chambers where beliefs are continuously validated and rarely challenged (Ge et al., 2024).

Finally, the *Hybrid systems* approach combines collaborative and content-based approaches with deep learning models that identify complex, non-linear behavioral patterns. By integrating multiple data sources, including browsing history, social connections, purchase behavior, location data, and biometric signals, these systems construct multidimensional user profiles that enable highly accurate behavioral forecasting. Their sophistication allows them to detect and exploit psychological vulnerabilities, identifying moments of emotional susceptibility, cognitive overload, or decision fatigue when users are most responsive to specific content (Cherukuri, 2024). These recommendation systems, however, do not operate in isolation. Their power is magnified when combined with the feedback loops and reinforcement cycles examined in the next subsection.

4.2.2 Feedback Loops and Reinforcement Cycles

Feedback loops represent the mechanism through which AI systems continuously refine behavioral predictions while actively shaping the behaviors they predict. This creates a cyclical relationship between user behavior and algorithmic response that fundamentally alters the dynamics of behavioral formation described in Social Cognitive Theory (Chapter 2, Section 2.4.2).

Immediate feedback loops operate on timescales of seconds to minutes. When a user engages with content, the system instantly updates its preference model and adjusts subsequent recommendations. This rapid response creates operant conditioning in which behaviors are immediately reinforced or extinguished. If a user clicks on emotionally charged content, the system interprets this as a preference signal and increases the prominence of similar content. This immediate reinforcement can rapidly amplify behavioral patterns driven by emotional arousal or novelty-seeking, traits associated with openness and neuroticism in the Big Five personality model (Chapter 2, Section 2.5.1).

Delayed feedback loops operate over longer timescales, days, weeks, or months, identifying long-term behavioral trends and adjusting the system's understanding of stable preferences. These loops are particularly consequential for identity formation and habit development. Over extended periods, they can gradually shift a user's content exposure in ways that feel organic but are systematically guided. For adolescents in critical periods of identity development (Chapter 3), these delayed loops can influence the formation of values and beliefs that persist into adulthood. The "observational learning" mechanism in Social Cognitive Theory now operates through algorithmically curated exposure to digital models selected by these loops (Kang & Lou, 2022).

Reinforcement cycles emerge when feedback loops create self-perpetuating behavioral patterns. Once a user engages with particular content, the system increases its prominence, which increases further engagement, which further reinforces the preference model. This positive feedback cycle can lock users into increasingly narrow behavioral patterns. These cycles are particularly problematic when amplifying harmful behaviors, such as exposure to pro-eating disorder content, self-harm imagery, or extremist ideologies, because the system interprets engagement as preference, regardless of whether that engagement reflects genuine interest, emotional distress, or algorithmic entrapment (Mehmood et al., 2024). Although feedback loops shape behavior through iterative refinement, platforms deploy additional mechanisms specifically designed to capture and sustain user attention, as explored next.

4.2.3 Engagement Optimization and Attention Capture

Beyond recommending content, AI systems are explicitly designed to maximize user engagement, the time spent on platforms, and the frequency of return visits. This optimization operates largely outside users' conscious awareness and often conflicts with their stated preferences and well-being.

Attention capture mechanisms interrupt users' intended activities to redirect attention to platform content. Push notifications, autoplay features, infinite scroll, and variable reward schedules exemplify these mechanisms. These features result from deliberate optimization processes in which AI systems test thousands of variations to identify combinations that maximize engagement. While the underlying psychological principles, intermittent reinforcement, loss aversion, and social validation, are well-established, AI systems now deploy them with unprecedented scale and precision, tailoring strategies to individual psychological profiles (Abadzi & ElAsad, 2021).

Engagement metrics serve as the optimization target. Platforms measure time on site, click-through rates, shares, comments, and return visits, training AI systems to maximize these metrics through reinforcement learning algorithms. This creates fundamental misalignment between platform incentives and user well-being. While users may prefer informative or balanced content, AI systems often display content that maximizes engagement, which can be emotionally provocative, controversial, or addictive. This misalignment particularly affects young users, whose developing self-regulation capacities (associated with conscientiousness, Chapter 2, Section 2.5.1) may be insufficient to resist algorithmically optimized engagement strategies (Poulsen et al., 2025).

Filter bubbles emerge as consequences of engagement optimization. When AI systems personalize content to maximize engagement, they show users more of what they have previously engaged with and less of what they have ignored. Over time, this creates information environments in which users are primarily exposed to content that aligns with their existing beliefs. Filter bubbles have a significant impact on the formation of "subjective norms" in the Theory of Planned Behavior (Chapter 2, Section 2.4.1). When perceptions of normality are shaped by algorithmically filtered content, users may develop distorted understandings of social reality, for example, believing that extreme body types are normative after engaging with body image content (Ge et al., 2024). The precision with which these engagement strategies are deployed depends on the extensive data collection and behavioral profiling practices examined in the following subsection.

4.2.4 Data Collection and Behavioral Profiling

The effectiveness of AI mechanisms depends on vast quantities of behavioral data collected across platforms, devices, and contexts. Understanding how AI systems collect, integrate, and analyze this data is essential for comprehending the scope and precision of algorithmic behavioral influence.

Behavioral tracking occurs continuously as users interact with digital platforms. Every click, scroll, pause, search query, purchase, location check-in, and social connection is recorded. Modern tracking extends beyond explicit actions to include passive signals such as mouse movements, typing speed, viewing duration, and biometric data from wearable devices. This comprehensive surveillance *gener*ates detailed digital traces that AI systems utilize to develop predictive behavioral models. The granularity of this data collection enables AI systems *to* understand users' behavioral patterns more accurately than users themselves (Cherukuri, 2024).

Cross-platform data integration amplifies the power of behavioral profiling. When data from social media, e-commerce, search engines, and streaming services are integrated, either within a single company's ecosystem or through third-party data brokers, the resulting profiles become extraordinarily comprehensive. Social media activity reveals interests and connections; search history reveals concerns and questions; purchase history reveals financial status and lifestyle; location data reveals daily routines and contexts. Integrated across platforms, these sources enable AI systems to predict not only what users might want but also when they are most susceptible to influence, which emotional appeals will be most effective, and which behavioral interventions will be successful (Pappalardo et al., 2024).

Predictive modeling uses machine learning to identify patterns in behavioral data and forecast future actions. Modern models can anticipate behavior with remarkable accuracy, often predicting actions before users are consciously aware of their intentions. These models can identify users at risk of disengagement and deploy targeted retention strategies, identify users likely to make purchases and tailor personalized offers to them, or identify users experiencing emotional distress and either provide support or utilize that vulnerability for engagement. The predictive power of these models raises profound ethical questions about autonomy and manipulation (Mehmood et al., 2024). Critically, the impact of these data-driven mechanisms is not uniform across all users, as individual differences significantly moderate algorithmic influence.

4.2.5 The Interaction between AI Mechanisms and Individual Differences

The impact of AI mechanisms varies across users. Individual differences in personality traits (Chapter 2, Section 2.5), developmental stage (Chapter 3), and digital literacy all moderate the extent to which AI systems influence behavior. Understanding these interactions is crucial for identifying which users are most susceptible to algorithmic manipulation and for designing interventions that protect those at the greatest risk.

Personality traits interact with AI mechanisms in complex ways. Users high in openness to experience may be more susceptible to recommendation algorithms that promote novelty and exploration, potentially leading them down rabbit holes of increasingly extreme content. Users high in conscientiousness may be more resistant to engagement optimization tactics because their self-regulation capacities enable them to resist impulsive behaviors. Users high in neuroticism may be more vulnerable to emotionally charged content that triggers anxiety or distress, which algorithms may then amplify through feedback loops. Users high in agreeableness may be more susceptible to social proof mechanisms that highlight what others are doing or liking. Understanding these personality-algorithm interactions is essential for designing systems that respect individual differences rather than exploit them (Cartwright & Xue, 2023).

Developmental factors are particularly important for understanding the impact of AI on young users. Adolescents and young adults are in critical periods of identity formation, social learning, and self-regulation development (as discussed in Chapter 3). During these periods, they are simultaneously more susceptible to social influence (making them vulnerable to collaborative filtering and social proof mechanisms) and less capable of self-regulation (making them vulnerable to engagement optimization and attention capture mechanisms). AI systems optimized for adult user populations may be particularly harmful when deployed on adolescent users, whose developmental vulnerabilities create disproportionate risks (Thompson, 2013).

Digital literacy and awareness moderate users' vulnerability to AI influence. Users who understand how recommendation algorithms work, how their data is collected and used, and how engagement optimization operates are better positioned to resist manipulation. However, the complexity and opacity of modern AI systems mean that even digitally literate users often lack a clear understanding of the mechanisms that shape their behavior. This creates an urgent need for digital literacy education that extends beyond basic technical skills to encompass a critical understanding of algorithmic systems and their behavioral impacts (Gligorea et al., 2023). Having established the technical architecture through which AI systems operate, recommendation algorithms, feedback loops, engagement optimization, and data profiling, the analysis now shifts from the mechanisms themselves to their behavioral consequences. The following section examines how these AI mechanisms specifically amplify aggressive behaviors, including online disinhibition, moral disengagement, and cyberbullying, revealing the darker side of algorithmic influence on youth behavior.

> ***Takeaway:*** *AI systems shape behavior through a sophisticated architecture of recommendation algorithms, feedback loops, engagement optimization, and behavioral profiling. These mechanisms operate largely outside users' conscious awareness, transforming the psychological processes described in behavioral theories by mediating social influence, curating observational learning, and exploiting individual vulnerabilities with unprecedented precision.*
> ***Reflection:*** *Given the sophisticated mechanisms through which AI systems predict and influence your behavior, what strategies might you adopt to maintain autonomy over your digital choices and resist algorithmic manipulation?*

4.3 AI's Impact on Aggressive Behaviors

Building on the core AI mechanisms detailed in Section 4.2, recommendation algorithms, feedback loops, engagement optimization, and behavioral profiling, this section examines how these mechanisms specifically reshape aggressive cyber behaviors. Aggressive behaviors, as defined in D'Angelo's (2020) taxonomy (Chapter 2, Section 2.2.1), include cyberbullying, harassment, and online moral disengagement. In AI-mediated environments, these behaviors are no longer determined solely by individual dispositions or interpersonal dynamics but are actively shaped by algorithmic systems that curate content, amplify emotional reactions, and obscure moral consequences. Global estimates show that between 10% and 40% of youth have experienced cyberbullying victimization, while 3%–20% have been perpetrators (Grover & Raju, 2023; Zhou, 2023), highlighting the scale and urgency of understanding AI's role in these behaviors. This section explores three interconnected dimensions of AI's impact on aggressive behavior: online disinhibition and ethical detachment, moral disengagement and algorithmic reinforcement, and cyberbullying within AI moderation systems. This section explores three interconnected dimensions of AI's impact on aggressive behavior: online disinhibition and ethical detachment (4.3.1), moral disengagement and algorithmic reinforcement (4.3.2), and cyberbullying within AI moderation systems (4.3.3). Together, these subsections reveal how AI mechanisms lower behavioral restraints, provide psychological justifications for harmful actions, and create complex moderation challenges.

4.3.1 Online Disinhibition and Ethical Detachment

Online disinhibition refers to reduced behavioral restraint during online interactions, particularly when identity is concealed or when consequences appear distant. While early work emphasized psychological factors such as dissociative anonymity and reduced self-awareness (Suler, 2005; Cheung et al., 2020), the discussion has expanded to include technological systems that automate or mediate communication. AI systems, through the mechanisms described in Section 4.2, actively shape the conditions under which disinhibition occurs rather than merely providing neutral platforms. Studies show that anonymity enables impulsive and unethical behavior due to perceived absence of surveillance or accountability (Ando & Ozarchevici, 2024; Zhang, 2023).

AI-driven systems amplify disinhibition through recommendation algorithms and feedback loops that reinforce disinhibited behavior. Algorithmic signals, such as likes, shares, and recommendations, serve as indirect approval, contributing to users' perception that harmful actions are socially acceptable (Wu et al., 2022; Lei et al., 2024). These automated systems create emotional distance by absorbing moral feedback, enabling users to justify behaviors that would be restrained in face-to-face interactions. This process directly impacts Social Cognitive Theory mechanisms (Chapter 2, Section 2.4.2), where observational learning and reinforcement now operate through algorithmically mediated feedback rather than direct social interaction.

Accountability proves equally significant to anonymity. Not all anonymous contexts lead to toxic outcomes; peer discipline and technological moderation can restore behavioral norms (Guo & Yu, 2020). The Social Identity model of Deindividuation Effects (SIDE) suggests that anonymity can promote conformity to group norms rather than outright aggression, depending on group identity salience (Postmes et al., 2001; Wang, 2018). This aligns with Social Identity Theory (Chapter 2, Section 2.4.3), which posits that in-group norms, whether prosocial or antisocial, influence individual actions.

AI introduces distinct challenges to accountability. When users know they are interacting with machines, their sense of being judged decreases. Experimental studies demonstrate that when AI identity is disclosed, individuals are more likely to engage in unethical behavior, believing their actions won't be socially evaluated (Li et al., 2024; Lei et al., 2024). The role AI plays matters: AI is framed as a subordinate agent, shifting blame away from users and reinforcing detachment from responsibility (Lei et al., 2024).

Individual differences moderate these effects. Personality traits, particularly conscientiousness and agreeableness from the Big Five model (Chapter 2, Section 2.5.1), influence vulnerability to AI-amplified disinhibition. Emotional regulation and self-control serve as protective factors (Syrjämäki et al., 2024; Nugraha et al., 2023). Gender, victimization history, and emotional traits also influence whether disinhibition leads to harmful outcomes (Sánchez-Hernández et al., 2024; Wu et al., 2022).

System-level features, such as visible moderation tools and design transparency, can promote more thoughtful behavior (Ando & Ozarchevici, 2024).

The algorithmic mechanisms detailed in Section 4.2, particularly feedback loops and engagement optimization, create environments that systematically reinforce disinhibited aggression. Although online disinhibition describes the reduction in behavioral restraint that enables aggressive actions, the following subsection examines how AI systems provide the psychological justifications that allow individuals to avoid self-sanction for those actions. Although online disinhibition describes the reduction in behavioral restraint that enables aggressive actions, it does not fully explain how individuals justify those actions to themselves. The following subsection examines how AI systems provide the psychological mechanisms and moral disengagement that allow individuals to avoid self-sanction for harmful behaviors they might otherwise recognize as wrong.

4.3.2 Moral Disengagement and Algorithmic Reinforcement

Although disinhibition reduces behavioral restraint, moral disengagement provides the psychological mechanisms that enable individuals to justify aggressive actions and avoid self-sanction. AI systems facilitate moral disengagement by exploiting emotional reactivity, moral biases, and psychological distance. The mechanisms outlined here build directly on Section 4.2, demonstrating how algorithmic processes systematically weaken empathy, distort normative beliefs, and reduce personal accountability.

4.3.2.1 Amplification of Moral Emotion

Algorithms favor content that evokes strong emotions, such as outrage and indignation, because this type of content tends to sustain attention. Through the PRIME framework, morally and emotionally charged posts are promoted in recursive cycles, reinforcing users' existing moral views (Brady et al., 2023). As users engage with extreme content, algorithms escalate recommendations, resulting in progressive shifts in moral perception (McLoughlin & Brady, 2023). The feedback loop mechanism (Section 4.2.2) creates reinforcement cycles that progressively narrow moral perspectives. Algorithmic coordination across platforms strengthens the illusion of moral consensus and suppresses dissent (Milli et al., 2023). Personalization tailors emotional content to individual vulnerabilities, providing users with the impression of diverse perspectives while delivering emotionally curated content (Schuster & Lazar, 2024).

4.3.2.2 Filter Bubbles and Echo Chambers

Personalization algorithms reduce exposure to moral diversity by forming echo chambers that continuously validate users' beliefs, narrowing the moral landscape

TABLE 4.1 Typology of Filter Bubbles and Moral Disengagement

Filter Bubble Type	*Formation Mechanism*	*Psychological Effects*	*Implications for Moral Disengagement*
Ideological	Personalization algorithms prioritize politically aligned content based on prior user engagement	Reinforces belief rigidity, reduces openness to dissenting views	Users justify extreme political positions as morally valid and socially supported
Cultural	Algorithms tailor content to match regional traditions, religious values, or shared cultural narratives	Strengthens in-group identity, creates out-group moral bias	Users engage in moral exclusion of culturally different others
Demographic	User profiling through demographic data (age, gender, location) informs customized content streams	Promotes stereotypes and assumptions, narrowing worldview	Users adopt normalized moral attitudes that align with perceived peer group norms

and weakening empathy (Yan, 2025). Confidence in morally contentious views increases when social validation signals, such as shares and likes, suggest widespread agreement (Rodilosso, 2024; Samuel-Okon, 2024). This directly impacts "subjective norms" in the Theory of Planned Behavior (Chapter 2, Section 2.4.1), creating distorted perceptions of what behaviors are normative and socially acceptable. Over time, exposure to alternate perspectives declines, and users internalize simplified ethical positions (Jindal & Gouri, 2024). Filter bubbles are ideological, cultural, and demographic, reinforcing group-based moral norms (Ge, 2020). These echo chambers reinforce in-group/out-group dynamics described in Social Identity Theory (Chapter 2, Section 2.4.3), where moral disengagement toward out-group members becomes algorithmically facilitated and socially validated, reframing morality as loyalty to group identity rather than ethical principle (see Table 4.1).

4.3.2.3 Depersonalization and Erosion of Moral Recognition

AI mediation diminishes users' recognition of others as full moral agents. Anonymity, avatars, and appearance alterations distort human features, reducing empathic engagement (Köbis et al., 2021, 2023). Automated interactions reduce the perceived intentionality behind social behavior, further weakening moral responsibility (Lei et al., 2024). AI mediation interferes with perspective-taking and theory of mind, dulling users' sensitivity to others' mental and emotional states (Hu et al., 2024). This erosion is particularly concerning in the context of identity formation (Chapter 3), where the cybernetic self is constructed through digital feedback. When that feedback is algorithmically mediated and depersonalized, the capacity for empathic moral engagement is systematically weakened.

4.3.2.4 Diffusion of Moral Responsibility

AI systems obscure users' role in the moral chain of cause and effect. Automated processes make it more challenging to determine where personal responsibility lies (Beckmann et al., 2018). Users often interpret AI as the actor, deflecting guilt or obligation (Zhang et al., 2024). When harm unfolds over time or through aggregate effects, users rarely connect their behavior with outcomes, reducing moral self-regulation (Ho, 2022). This diffusion undermines "perceived behavioral control" in the Theory of Planned Behavior (Chapter 2, Section 2.4.1), as users feel less agency over outcomes and, therefore, less moral accountability.

4.3.2.5 Social Norm Distortion

Algorithms manipulate social learning by inflating the visibility of emotionally provocative and group-aligned content (Brady et al., 2023). This exploits the observational learning mechanisms described in Social Cognitive Theory (Chapter 2, Section 2.4.2). Rather than learning from diverse social models, users observe algorithmically curated models that reinforce narrow, often extreme behavioral patterns, leading them to believe such content reflects dominant social values. Distorted validation signals create artificial impressions of moral consensus (McLoughlin & Brady, 2023). These effects deepen when content is personalized to align with users' identity and psychological triggers (Gumelar et al., 2024), and perceptions of right and wrong drift when signals are synchronized across platforms (Fan et al., 2024).

4.3.2.6 Resistance Strategies

Algorithmic transparency can disrupt disengagement cycles by enabling users to critically interpret AI-mediated content. Users with higher algorithmic literacy are better able to detect manipulation and maintain an ethical perspective (Theophilou et al., 2023; Obreja, 2024). Education plays a critical role in enabling resistance by helping users understand how algorithms manipulate emotion, attention, and social perception (Yan, 2025). Addressing algorithmic moral disengagement requires integrated approaches combining education, technological reform, and policy intervention (Ho, 2022; Magrani & Silva, 2023; Rallabandi et al., 2023).

The disinhibition and moral disengagement processes described above converge in one of the most prevalent forms of aggressive cyber behavior: cyberbullying. The following subsection examines how AI moderation systems represent the technological response designed to detect and prevent cyberbullying, while simultaneously introducing complexities that can both deter and enable aggressive behavior. The disinhibition and moral disengagement processes described above converge in one of the most prevalent and visible forms of aggressive cyber behavior: cyberbullying. Although disinhibition lowers the threshold for aggressive action and moral disengagement provides the psychological justifications, cyberbullying represents the behavioral outcome, the actual harm inflicted on victims. The following subsection examines how AI moderation systems represent the technological response designed to detect and prevent cyberbullying, while simultaneously introducing new complexities that can both deter and, paradoxically, enable aggressive behavior.

4.3.3 Cyberbullying and AI Moderation

AI plays a complex and contradictory role in cyberbullying. The same algorithmic mechanisms detailed in Section 4.2, recommendation algorithms, feedback loops, and engagement optimization, can both enable cyberbullying through content amplification and detect it through pattern recognition (Godigamuwa, 2024). AI-powered recommendation engines may increase cyberbullying by promoting divisive content. These systems increase aggressive materials based on engagement metrics, leading to the proliferation of conflict-driven posts and the development of echo chambers that reinforce hostile communication norms (Abokhodair et al., 2024). Moderation systems can fail to recognize harmful content due to algorithmic blind spots, allowing abusive behavior to remain unchecked (Polizzi, 2022). Conversely, AI systems demonstrate significant detection capabilities. Technologies built on transformer models and large-scale natural language processing show high accuracy in identifying subtle, coded, or multimodal forms of harassment (Kumar et al., 2024). These systems can detect implicit threats and contextual abuse that often evade human moderators. However, automated systems often struggle with cultural details, language diversity, and social context, resulting in misclassifications and inconsistent enforcement (AlDahoul et al., 2024).

Bias and misclassification persist as significant issues in AI moderation. Automated systems are shaped by biased training datasets, structural design limitations, and flawed evaluation metrics, contributing to unfair outcomes, particularly for underrepresented groups (Achara & Chhabra, 2025). These biases reflect broader patterns in AI systems where behavioral profiling (Section 4.2.4) perpetuates existing social inequalities. Underrepresentation of minority voices in training data leads to missed detection of culturally specific harassment. Algorithmic structures may reflect societal biases, reinforcing inequalities in automated decisions (Cheng, 2021). Consequently, minority users may receive both excessive censorship and insufficient protection (Singh & Hofenbitzer, 2019). Error rates vary across user groups, with some communities more frequently flagged for benign content while genuine harassment against them remains unrecognized (Anigboro et al., 2024). False positives stem from AI's limited ability to interpret social context. Humor, sarcasm, and culturally situated language are often misread, leading to unjustified content removal (Root et al., 2024). These inaccuracies suppress expression, particularly in spaces where such language use is common. Users affected by wrongful content removal report lower platform engagement and a decline in trust (Wang et al., 2024).

Hybrid moderation systems combine the speed of AI with human judgment to enhance accuracy. These frameworks introduce human oversight to address the weaknesses of fully automated models (Nehe et al., 2024). Key components include AI-generated confidence scores, explainable predictions, and decision override capabilities. Human moderators verify ambiguous cases and provide feedback to enhance model training (Villate-Castillo et al., 2024). Task triage is central to workflow design. Content is sorted based on complexity, risk, and model certainty. Straightforward cases are automated, while complex scenarios are routed to human reviewers, enabling a more effective use of human capacity without compromising coverage (Schulenberg et al., 2023). Effective interface design presents relevant context, highlights uncertainties, and minimizes cognitive overload (Lai et al., 2022). Moderator training ensures personnel understand both technical systems and ethical considerations, maintaining the capability to identify bias and interpret nuanced content (Patel & Modi, 2025).

Trust and transparency are foundational to user acceptance of AI moderation systems. Fairness, explanation, and recourse mechanisms shape how users interact with content moderation technologies (Davidson, 2024). Users place greater trust when decisions are clear, and appeal processes are accessible (Gonçalves & Weber, 2023). However, opacity in machine learning often obscures the decision-making process, weakening accountability (Ghosh et al., 2024). Strategies such as explainable AI, transparency dashboards, and educational initiatives help users understand moderation logic (Kumar et al., 2024). Yet transparency comes with security risks, as detailed disclosures may be exploited by users intent on circumventing detection systems. Platforms must pursue selective transparency that strikes a balance between disclosure and protection (Azumah et al., 2024). Cultural differences influence how transparency is perceived, with some users prioritizing technical explanations while others value perceived fairness or access to redress options (Wang & Kim, 2023). Transparency has behavioral effects. It can reduce harmful content by making moderation predictable and understandable, but it can also encourage gaming behaviors by informing users of how to avoid detection (Lin, 2024).

Takeaway: *AI systems reshape aggressive cyber behaviors through three interconnected mechanisms: reducing behavioral restraint via online disinhibition, facilitating moral justification through algorithmic reinforcement of biased beliefs, and creating complex moderation challenges that can simultaneously deter and enable cyberbullying. These mechanisms transform aggression from an interpersonal phenomenon into a system-mediated process where algorithmic architecture actively shapes the conditions for harmful behavior.*

Reflection: *Consider a time when you witnessed or participated in aggressive online behavior. To what extent might algorithmic systems, through content recommendations, anonymity features, or engagement optimization, have shaped the conditions that enabled or amplified that behavior?*

4.4 AI's Impact on Addictive Behaviors

Having examined how AI systems reshape aggressive cyber behaviors, we now turn to addictive patterns. Although aggressive behaviors involve actions directed toward others, addictive behaviors reflect compulsive patterns directed toward platform engagement itself. Both are shaped by the same core AI mechanisms, as detailed in Section 4.2, including recommendation algorithms, feedback loops, and engagement optimization, although they operate through different psychological pathways. Traditional understandings of addictive patterns emphasized psychological predispositions such as impulsivity or anxiety. Today, AI systems play a more direct role. Modern platforms utilize content curation algorithms, notification systems, and reward scheduling mechanisms designed to enhance engagement over time (Ibrahim, 2023). Machine learning models identify and exploit individual susceptibilities with precision, promoting behaviors that users struggle to regulate (Batool, 2024; Kumar et al., 2023). These mechanisms directly exploit the reinforcement learning principles described in Social Cognitive Theory (Chapter 2, Section 2.4.2), where behavior is shaped through observational learning and reinforcement but is now mediated and amplified algorithmically. Compulsive digital habits can no longer be viewed solely as user-driven; rather, they are products of repeated, systemically guided reinforcement cycles.

AI platforms increasingly employ variable ratio reward schedules, intermittent and unpredictable reinforcement mechanisms that mimic those used in gambling. These systems operationalize the feedback loops described in Section 4.2.2, creating immediate reinforcement cycles that condition compulsive behaviors. These systems trigger dopaminergic activity in the brain, particularly during reward anticipation, reinforcing repeated engagement even when actual outcomes are inconsistent or unrewarding (De et al., 2025; Kumar, 2024). Personalization intensifies this process. The behavioral profiling mechanisms detailed in Section 4.2.4 enable algorithms to tailor reward patterns to individual behavioral data, optimizing engagement by adapting timing and intensity to users' vulnerabilities (Campanella, 2024). Individual differences in personality traits, particularly neuroticism and conscientiousness from the Big Five model (Chapter 2, Section 2.5.1), moderate susceptibility to these variable reward systems. Over time, these systems foster behavioral tolerance, leading users to seek more frequent or intense rewards to achieve the same levels of psychological stimulation as before (Cemiloglu et al., 2021; Khalaf, 2023). Social features, likes, comments, and shares serve as variable rewards layered with peer approval, further reinforcing digital dependence (Adanyin, 2024).

The design features of digital platforms, including infinite scroll, push notifications, and real-time updates, are deliberately constructed to override cognitive self-regulation by exploiting biases such as novelty-seeking, fear of missing out, and social comparison (De et al., 2025). These design features directly undermine the "perceived behavioral control" in the Theory of Planned Behavior (Chapter 2,

Section 2.4.1), as users feel increasingly unable to regulate their own platform engagement, despite their intentions to do so. Personalized feeds increase the effect by continuously delivering content that aligns with users' emotional and behavioral preferences. Timing algorithms optimize delivery to coincide with moments of user receptivity, maximizing attentional capture (Abadzi & ElAsad, 2021). Such features fragment attention and condition users into habitual consumption loops that weaken intentional control (Ofem, 2024).

Neuroimaging and electrophysiological research show that chronic exposure to these AI-driven environments alters the brain's reward circuitry and executive control networks. Users with problematic digital behavior exhibit changes in areas responsible for impulse control, decision-making, and attention regulation, with evidence of disrupted feedback processing and reduced P300 amplitudes in EEG studies (Balconi et al., 2017; Balconi & Angioletti, 2021). These neurological changes are matched by cognitive impairments, including reduced working memory and inhibitory control, as well as elevated psychological distress, anxiety, and mood disorders, particularly among younger users (Zhang et al., 2024; Wu et al., 2024). These mental health outcomes can be understood through Keyes' Comprehensive Mental Health Model (Chapter 2, Section 2.6), where addictive digital behaviors undermine emotional well-being (through increased negative affect), psychological well-being (through reduced autonomy and self-acceptance), and social well-being (through isolation and communication difficulties). Social effects such as isolation and communication difficulties further entrench problematic usage patterns (Csibi et al., 2021).

Susceptibility to AI addiction is not uniform. Adolescents and young adults are especially vulnerable due to underdeveloped prefrontal control systems and heightened social sensitivity (Csibi et al., 2021). These developmental factors, discussed in Chapter 3's examination of identity formation, interact with AI systems to create particularly high-risk conditions for youth. Gender differences are apparent: males tend to engage compulsively with gaming features, while females are more susceptible to socially driven feedback loops on appearance-focused platforms (Lopez-Fernandez, 2015). Culture and socioeconomic context matter: collectivist societies show distinct response patterns to social validation features, and users from lower-income backgrounds may rely more heavily on digital engagement for psychological reward (Aruna et al., 2024; Frimpong, 2024). These intersections highlight the need for culturally and contextually adaptive interventions (Barnes et al., 2024; Sun et al., 2023).

The design of AI systems to exploit compulsive behaviors raises substantial ethical concerns. Many platforms prioritize engagement without disclosing the psychological manipulation embedded in their features, undermining informed consent and autonomy (D'Souza et al., 2024; Koplin, 2023). Vulnerable users, particularly youth and individuals with mental health challenges, are disproportionately targeted by engagement-maximizing algorithms (Vetrivel et al., 2024). Responsible AI design must embed safeguards such as default usage caps, bias alerts, and disengagement prompts (Ghosh et al., 2024). However, ethical principles alone are insufficient without regulatory oversight and accountability structures.

This analysis emphasizes that AI-mediated addiction is not the result of personal weakness but a structural outcome of commercial and algorithmic design. Preventing harm requires rethinking both individual agency and system architecture. The mechanisms detailed in Section 4.2, variable reward schedules, attention capture, and behavioral profiling, converge to create environments in which addictive behaviors are systematically engineered. As AI technologies evolve, ethical, neuroscientific, and policy frameworks must adapt to protect users, particularly the young and vulnerable, from the long-term consequences of compulsive digital environments (see Table 4.2).

> ***Takeaway:*** *AI systems transform addictive behaviors from individual psychological vulnerabilities into systematically engineered outcomes through variable reward schedules, attention-capturing design, and personalized behavioral profiling. These mechanisms exploit neurological reward systems, undermine cognitive self-regulation, and disproportionately affect vulnerable populations, particularly youth and individuals with pre-existing mental health challenges.*
> ***Reflection:*** *How often do you find yourself engaging with digital platforms longer than you intended? To what extent might the variable rewards, notifications, and personalized content feeds be shaping your behavior in ways that feel beyond your conscious control?*

TABLE 4.2 Demographic Vulnerabilities to AI-Mediated Addictive Behaviors

Demographic Group	*Primary Vulnerability*	*Implications*
Adolescents	Underdeveloped impulse control; high social sensitivity	More susceptible to compulsive platform use
Young Adults	Neurological plasticity; emotional reactivity	Higher risk of emotional dysregulation from AI feedback loops
Males	Gaming and competitive platform addiction	Increased time spent on reward-based gaming systems
Females	Social comparison and appearance-focused feedback	Elevated anxiety due to appearance and peer validation cycles
Collectivist Cultures	Conformity to social norms and approval cues	Group-based moral reinforcement and disengagement tendencies
Low SES Users	Higher reliance on digital rewards for coping	Reduced access to offline engagement alternatives

4.5 AI's Impact on Social-Commercial Behaviors

The previous sections examined how AI systems reshape aggressive behaviors (through disinhibition, moral disengagement, and moderation) and addictive behaviors (through variable rewards and attention capture). This section explores a third category from D'Angelo's (2020) taxonomy: social-commercial behaviors, which encompass online identity management, social networking, online shopping, and digital dating. Unlike aggressive or addictive behaviors, social-commercial behaviors are not inherently harmful; rather, their outcomes depend on how AI systems mediate and shape these interactions. This section first examines how AI influences specific social and commercial behaviors and then introduces a risk spectrum framework for understanding the variable outcomes of AI-mediated cyber behaviors.

4.5.1 Social Identity and Commercial Engagement

Building on the cybernetic self framework established in Chapter 3, identity formation processes are increasingly channeled through algorithmic feeds that prioritize certain types of self-presentation and interaction, subtly encouraging conformity or competition. The recommendation algorithms detailed in Section 4.2.1 determine which aspects of identity are visible, validated, and reinforced through social feedback, fundamentally shaping the identity construction process. Purchase decisions are influenced by product suggestions generated through behavioral tracking, which promotes impulsive consumption by aligning offers with emotional states, browsing history, and contextual data (Zhang et al., 2021). These systems exploit the "perceived behavioral control" component of the Theory of Planned Behavior (Chapter 2, Section 2.4.1) by making purchases feel effortless and inevitable, reducing the cognitive barriers that would normally moderate commercial decisions.

AI systems also reshape how individuals form and maintain social relationships online. The engagement optimization mechanisms described in Section 4.2.3 determine which friendships are sustained, which romantic connections are suggested, and which social groups are made visible. Dating applications use algorithmic matching to curate potential partners based on behavioral data, creating what appears to be individual choice but is actually a highly constrained set of algorithmically determined options. These processes interact with personality traits (Chapter 2, Section 2.5.1), as algorithms may preferentially match or exclude individuals based on detected trait patterns, potentially reinforcing existing social inequalities.

The feedback loops described in Section 4.2.2 are particularly powerful in shaping digital self-presentation. Users learn which aspects of their identity receive algorithmic amplification and social validation, gradually conforming their self-presentation to patterns that are rewarded by the platform. This process is especially consequential for adolescents and young adults, whose identity formation occurs within these algorithmically mediated environments (Chapter 3, Sections 3.5.2 and 3.6). The increasing impact of these developments is the emergence of a behavioral landscape in which AI not only influences but also actively shapes user behavior. Each of D'Angelo's original categories is now mediated by intelligent systems that can amplify, reshape, or suppress behaviors based on predictive modeling and feedback mechanisms (see Figure 4.2).

4.5.2 AI-Contextualized Risk Spectrum

The complexity introduced by AI mediation requires a more refined approach to risk assessment. A binary distinction between "safe" and "unsafe" cyber behavior fails to capture the fluid nature of risk across different contexts, systems, and user characteristics. This section introduces a three-tier classification of low-risk, moderate-risk, and high-risk behaviors, which better reflects the variable outcomes associated with AI-influenced actions.

Low-risk behaviors contribute positively to users' psychological health, promote autonomy, and foster socially constructive engagement. These behaviors align with the "flourishing" end of Keyes' Mental Health Continuum (Chapter 2, Section 2.6), supporting emotional, psychological, and social well-being. Educational platforms that adapt to a learner's pace without inducing dependency, mental health applications offering support without manipulation, and social networks implementing transparent moderation mechanisms fall into this category. Systems operating in this range prioritize algorithmic transparency, allow users to adjust personalization settings, and avoid behavioral nudging designed to maximize time on the platform. AI applications are used to build digital literacy, especially those that help users understand how algorithmic systems function, support low-risk behavioral patterns by fostering self-awareness, and equip users with strategies to resist manipulative design features (Ofoegbu et al., 2023).

Moderate-risk behaviors present more ambiguous consequences, supporting personal growth or social development under the right conditions but carrying potential for harm depending on user engagement and system design. Online gaming can encourage teamwork, strategy, and stress relief, but it may also lead to overuse or dependency when reinforced by adaptive reward systems or socially competitive features (Batool, 2024). Similarly, social media platforms can facilitate connection and self-expression, yet when powered by algorithms that emphasize emotionally provocative or addictive content, they may contribute to anxiety, diminished self-worth, or polarized interactions. Phubbing, neglecting interpersonal interaction in favor of device use, is increasingly encouraged by AI-driven alerts, visual stimuli, and social feedback loops embedded in mobile platforms (Wang et al., 2020). Even passive entertainment consumption may shift between benign relaxation and problematic overuse when algorithmic suggestions remove barriers to continuous engagement.

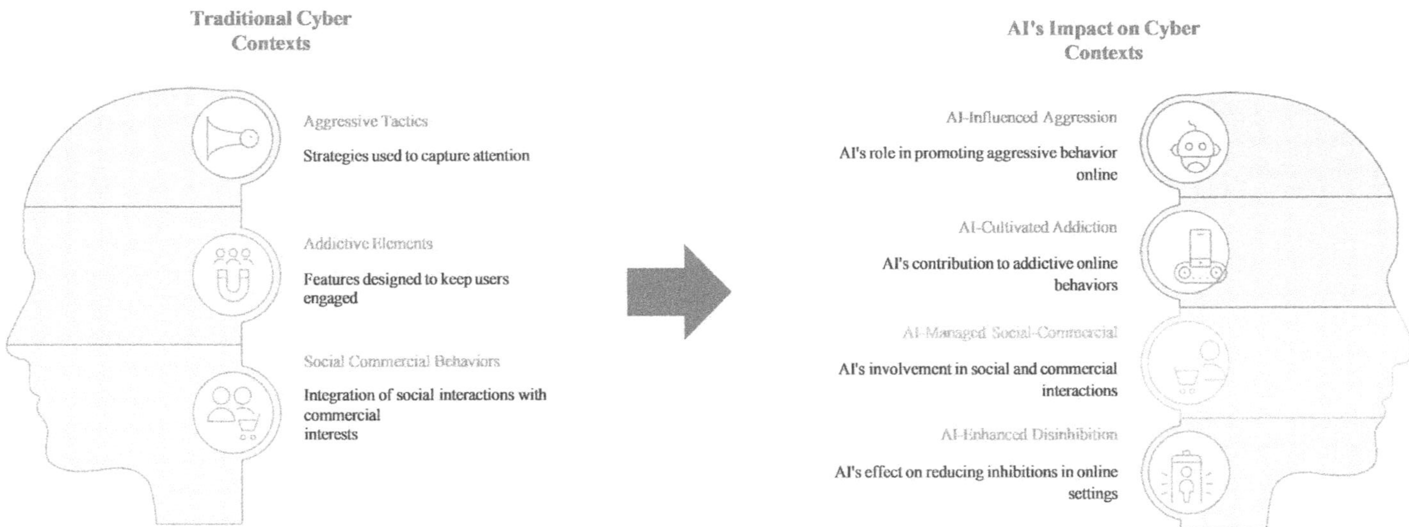

FIGURE 4.2 Expanding Behavioral Taxonomy: From Traditional to AI-Mediated Cyber Contexts. This transformation of the behavioral landscape necessitates a more sophisticated approach to understanding risk. Because AI mediation can amplify, mitigate, or transform the outcomes of social-commercial behaviors, a simple binary classification of "safe" versus "unsafe" is inadequate. The following subsection introduces a three-tiered risk spectrum that accounts for the contextual variability introduced by AI systems.

High-risk behaviors pose serious threats to mental health, ethical reasoning, and social development, exploiting emotional vulnerabilities or minimizing user control over digital environments. These behaviors correspond to the "languishing" end of Keyes' continuum, characterized by low emotional, psychological, and social well-being. Cyberbullying becomes more than interpersonal aggression when supported by anonymity tools, algorithmic content prioritization, and social matching systems that pair aggressors with vulnerable individuals (Zhou, 2023; Tan, 2023). The psychological consequences are profound, often involving anxiety, withdrawal, and depression, particularly when platform design discourages reporting or fails to provide relief from targeted harm. Problematic internet use reaches high-risk status when AI systems continuously refine content delivery based on emotional responses or behavioral patterns, making it increasingly difficult for users to disengage voluntarily (Kumar et al., 2023). These patterns are often not recognized by users themselves, as AI platforms adapt in real-time to sustain engagement despite mounting personal costs.

Moral disengagement reaches high-risk status when reinforced by algorithmic structures that normalize harmful behavior through exposure to biased content, repeated interactions in ideologically homogeneous spaces, and social reinforcement for unethical behavior. As discussed in Section 4.3.2, this desensitizes users to harm and diminishes their capacity for ethical judgment (Concha-Salgado et al., 2022). When reinforced by curated digital environments, this disengagement may contribute to broader societal effects, such as diminished civic trust or reduced empathy across social groups. Cyber trolling further illustrates the danger posed by AI-amplified behavior. In these cases, platforms can provide tools for persistent provocation, including anonymity protections, amplification of outrage content, and access to coordinated trolling communities. AI tools may even be used to automate responses or escalate conflict, adding a technical layer to the manipulation and psychological harm caused to targets.

Online disinhibition, explored in Section 4.3.1, takes on intensified forms in AI-mediated environments. When platforms personalize content in ways that normalize aggression, echo users' most extreme tendencies, or create emotionally charged atmospheres, users experience fewer psychological brakes on behavior. The illusion of invisibility is compounded by systems that encourage rapid and impulsive responses while suppressing social accountability. In this context, disinhibited behavior can escalate into harassment, manipulation, or excessive disclosure, all of which carry high personal and interpersonal risks. AI does not simply facilitate disinhibition; it accelerates its progression and amplifies its consequences (Ma, 2024; Runions et al., 2015).

Behavioral risk is not static but shifts in response to user traits, system features, and situational context. Individual differences in personality (Chapter 2, Section 2.5), developmental stage (Chapter 3), and cultural context (Chapter 3, Section 3.5.1) all moderate how AI-mediated behaviors translate into risk outcomes. The same behavior may move from moderate to high risk depending on intensity, frequency, or the psychological vulnerabilities of those involved. This variability highlights the need for adaptable assessment models and interventions that account for the dynamic interplay between AI systems and user behavior (see Figure 4.3).

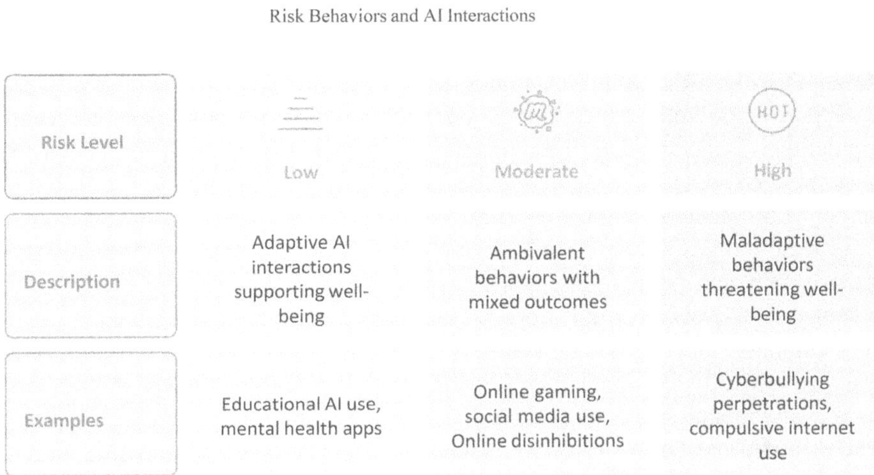

FIGURE 4.3 AI-contextualized risk spectrum for cyber behaviors.

> ***Takeaway:*** *Social-commercial behaviors and the broader spectrum of AI-mediated cyber behaviors cannot be classified as simply "good" or "bad." Instead, their outcomes depend on the interaction between AI system design, individual vulnerabilities, and contextual factors. The same algorithmic mechanisms that enable positive social connections can also facilitate exploitation, and behaviors can shift across the risk spectrum depending on how AI systems are designed and deployed.*
> ***Reflection:*** *Consider your own social media use, online shopping habits, or digital dating experiences. Can you identify moments when algorithmic recommendations felt helpful versus moments when they felt manipulative? What factors determined the difference?*

The risk spectrum framework introduced in this section highlights a critical insight: AI mechanisms are neither inherently beneficial nor harmful. Their impact depends on design intent, implementation context, and user characteristics. Having examined how AI systems can amplify aggressive behaviors, engineer addictive patterns, and shape social and commercial interactions with variable risk outcomes, the analysis now turns to a fundamentally different question: *Can these same AI mechanisms be redirected toward positive ends?* The following section explores how AI can be designed to support mental health, foster empathy, and promote flourishing rather than languishing, revealing the potential for responsible innovation in digital environments.

4.6 AI for Positive Digital Engagement

The previous sections have focused primarily on how AI systems can enable or amplify harmful cyber behaviors: aggression, addiction, and exploitation. However,

AI is not inherently harmful; the same technological mechanisms can be designed to promote well-being, support mental health, and foster positive development (Araujo, 2023). This section examines how AI technologies are being developed to support emotional literacy, mental health, and empathy, particularly for youth populations. Understanding these positive applications is essential for a balanced assessment of AI's role in shaping cyber behavior and for informing the design of ethical, youth-centered digital systems.

AI technologies are being increasingly developed to promote well-being, particularly in youth populations facing mental health challenges and digital risks. Recent research demonstrates how AI can support emotional development, reinforce empathy, and offer scalable interventions tailored to diverse user needs when designed ethically and inclusively (Saeidnia et al., 2024). AI-powered emotional literacy and mental health systems utilize sentiment analysis and natural language processing to detect users' emotional states and offer personalized strategies for regulation and reflection (Adesina et al., 2024). These systems apply the same behavioral profiling mechanisms described in Section 4.2.4, but redirect them toward therapeutic rather than commercial goals. Evidence suggests that such systems can enhance self-awareness and empathy while upholding ethical boundaries (Saeidnia et al., 2024). By supporting emotional well-being, these applications promote the "flourishing" end of Keyes' Mental Health Continuum (Chapter 2, Section 2.6), enhancing emotional, psychological, and social well-being. Their ability to operate with sensitivity to cultural background and age-specific needs adds relevance, particularly for adolescents navigating identity and emotional development (Cerezo et al., 2024). These developmental considerations align with the identity formation processes discussed in Chapter 3, where the cybernetic self is constructed through digital feedback. When that feedback is designed to support rather than exploit, it can facilitate healthy identity development.

Accessibility is a central advantage. AI-based tools help close service gaps where geographic, financial, or social barriers prevent access to mental health care (Dakanalis et al., 2024). Crisis-response chatbots and hybrid models that combine AI screening with clinician oversight offer both scalability and quality assurance (Balcombe, 2023; Golden & Aboujaoude, 2024). However, the same engagement optimization mechanisms (Section 4.2.3) that can create addictive behaviors must be carefully managed in therapeutic contexts to avoid creating AI-dependent relationships that undermine autonomy.

Empathy reinforcement through AI raises questions about the boundary between simulation and authenticity. Although AI cannot experience emotions, systems designed to recognize and respond to users' emotional cues can facilitate meaningful interactions (Roshanaei et al., 2025; Asman et al., 2025). These exchanges are especially beneficial for youth who feel safer discussing emotions with non-human agents (Shen et al., 2024). This phenomenon reflects the online disinhibition effect discussed in Section 4.3.1, but channeled toward positive disclosure rather than harmful behavior. The same anonymity and reduced social cues that can enable aggression can also enable vulnerable self-expression when system design prioritizes support over exploitation. These AI systems can support the development of self-efficacy (a core component of Social Cognitive Theory, Chapter 2, Section 2.4.2) by providing consistent, non-judgmental feedback that builds users' confidence in managing their emotional states.

Youth-centered design principles prioritize participatory approaches, empowering young people to shape the technologies they use (Timmons et al., 2023). These co-design methods increase trust, usability, and alignment with developmental needs, while reducing risks of cultural alienation or emotional misinterpretation (Spahl et al., 2024; Götzl et al., 2022). These participatory approaches address the autonomy concerns raised throughout this chapter by giving users, particularly vulnerable youth, agency in determining how AI systems shape their experiences. This shifts the power dynamic from AI systems acting upon users to users actively shaping AI systems. Co-design also addresses the cultural dimensions explored in Chapter 3 (Section 3.5.1), ensuring that AI mental health tools reflect diverse cultural values and norms rather than imposing Western-centric models of emotional expression and well-being.

The ethical challenges remain pressing. The potential for emotional manipulation, creation of AI-dependent behaviors, or data privacy violations requires careful governance, including regulatory oversight, transparency, and cross-sector collaboration among developers, educators, mental health professionals, and policymakers (Tavory, 2024; Solaiman, 2023; Day, 2023). AI systems should be held to rigorous standards in terms of fairness, inclusivity, and non-maleficence, especially when targeting young users (Golden & Aboujaoude, 2024). The same mechanisms that enable positive support, personalization, feedback loops, and behavioral profiling can easily be repurposed for manipulation if ethical safeguards are not embedded in system design from the outset. The tension between therapeutic benefit and potential harm highlights a central theme of this chapter: AI mechanisms are neither inherently good nor bad, but their outcomes depend entirely on design intent, governance structures, and the values embedded in algorithmic decision-making. AI for mental health and emotional development presents substantial promise, but only when anchored in responsible design, user participation, and sustained empirical validation. Embedding these systems within supportive human contexts ensures they complement, rather than replace, the core emotional relationships that define psychological growth and well-being. The positive applications explored in this section demonstrate that the AI mechanisms detailed in Section 4.2 can be redirected toward supporting human flourishing when designed with ethical intent. The challenge for researchers, developers, and policymakers is to ensure that these positive applications become the norm rather than the exception and that the same technological sophistication currently deployed to maximize engagement is instead deployed to maximize well-being. The positive applications explored in this section demonstrate that the AI mechanisms detailed in Section 4.2 can be redirected toward supporting human flourishing when designed with ethical intent.

The challenge for researchers, developers, and policymakers is to ensure that these positive applications become the norm rather than the exception and that the same technological sophistication currently deployed to maximize engagement is instead deployed to maximize well-being.

> ***Takeaway:*** *AI systems possess the potential to support mental health, emotional literacy, and positive youth development when designed with ethical intent and participatory approaches. The same algorithmic mechanisms that can enable harm, personalization, feedback loops, and behavioral profiling can be redirected toward therapeutic goals, demonstrating that AI's impact depends not on the technology itself but on the values and governance structures that guide its design and deployment.*
> ***Reflection:*** *Have you ever used an AI-powered mental health app, chatbot, or emotional support tool? If so, did it feel genuinely supportive, or did you sense underlying mechanisms designed to keep you engaged? What design features would make you trust such a system with your emotional well-being?*

4.7 Summary and Reflections

This chapter has systematically examined the profound and often invisible influence of AI on cyber behavior, establishing AI not as a passive tool but as an active architect of digital experience. By dissecting the core mechanisms of AI systems, recommendation algorithms, feedback loops, engagement optimization, and behavioral profiling, we have demonstrated how these technologies fundamentally reshape the landscape of online interaction. The AI-behavior nexus, as introduced in this chapter, provides a critical framework for understanding how algorithmic systems have moved beyond merely facilitating behavior to actively shaping it, with significant implications for youth development, mental health, and ethical conduct.

The analysis of aggressive, addictive, and social-commercial behaviors has revealed a consistent pattern: AI mechanisms amplify existing psychological vulnerabilities and social dynamics. In the realm of aggressive behaviors, AI-driven platforms can foster online disinhibition and moral disengagement by creating echo chambers, depersonalizing interactions, and diffusing responsibility. Although AI moderation systems offer a technological response to these harms, they simultaneously introduce new challenges related to bias, false positives, and the suppression of legitimate expression, highlighting the dual-edged nature of algorithmic control.

Similarly, the examination of addictive behaviors has shown how AI systems can engineer compulsive engagement through variable reward schedules and attention-capturing design. These mechanisms, which mimic the principles of operant conditioning, have demonstrable neurological and psychological impacts, altering brain reward circuitry and undermining executive control. The result is a digital environment where addiction is not merely a product of individual predisposition but a structural outcome of systems designed to maximize engagement at the expense of user well-being.

The exploration of social-commercial behaviors has further illuminated the subtle yet powerful ways in which AI shapes identity, relationships, and consumption. By curating content, suggesting connections, and personalizing commercial appeals, AI systems guide the construction of the cybernetic self, as introduced in Chapter 3. The AI-contextualized risk spectrum, ranging from low-risk, well-being-promoting applications to high-risk, exploitative ones, provides a necessary framework for navigating the ambiguous moral terrain of these algorithmically mediated interactions.

However, the chapter concludes not on a note of technological determinism but with a call for responsible innovation. The analysis of AI for positive digital engagement demonstrates that the very same mechanisms that can cause harm can also be harnessed to support mental health, foster emotional literacy, and promote empathy. When designed with ethical intent and a focus on user well-being, AI can become a powerful tool for human flourishing. This underscores the central argument of the chapter: the outcomes of AI are not inherent in the technology itself but in the values, goals, and governance structures that guide its design and deployment.

Ultimately, understanding how AI reshapes cyber behavior requires a complex perspective that integrates the psychological theories presented in Chapter 2, the developmental frameworks outlined in Chapter 3, and the technological realities explored in this chapter. The path forward demands a concerted effort from researchers, developers, policymakers, and educators to create a digital ecosystem that prioritizes human values over engagement metrics. This includes advancing algorithmic transparency, promoting digital literacy, establishing robust regulatory frameworks, and championing youth-centered design principles. By doing so, we can hope to steer the AI-behavior nexus toward a future that supports, rather than subverts, the autonomy, well-being, and positive development of all users, particularly the young and vulnerable.

References

Abadzi, H., & ElAsad, S. (2021). The art and science of user exploitation: AI in the UAE and beyond. In *Artificial intelligence and global society* (pp. 187–205). Springer. https://doi.org/10.1007/978-981-16-0771-4_11

Abokhodair, N., Skop, Y., Rüller, S., Aal, K., & Elmimouni, H. (2024). Opaque algorithms, transparent biases: Automated content moderation during the Sheikh Jarrah crisis. *First Monday*, *29*(4), 1–18. https://doi.org/10.5210/fm.v29i4.13620

Achara, A., & Chhabra, A. (2025). Watching the AI watchdogs: A fairness and robustness analysis of AI safety moderation classifiers. arXiv Preprint, arXiv:2501.13302. https://doi.org/10.48550/arxiv.2501.13302

Adanyin, A. (2024). AI-driven feedback loops in digital technologies: Psychological impacts on user behaviour and well-being. arXiv Preprint, arXiv:2411.09706. https://doi.org/10.48550/arxiv.2411.09706

Adesina, A., Abuka, A. O., & Adesiyan, J. S. (2024). Enhancing adolescent mental health outcomes through integrated technology (AI) innovations in the United States. *International Journal of Advanced Psychiatric Nursing*, *6*(2), 22–30. https://doi.org/10.33545/26641348.2024.v6.i2a.170

AlDahoul, N., Tan, M. J. T., Kasireddy, H. R., & Zaki, Y. (2024). Advancing content moderation: Evaluating large language models for detecting sensitive content across text, images, and videos. arXiv Preprint, arXiv:2411.17123. https://doi.org/10.48550/arxiv.2411.17123

Ando, A., & Ozarchevici, M. (2024). Amplification by anonymity, an unassuming tool of cyberbullying. *International Journal of Legal and Social Order*, *4*(1). https://doi.org/10.55516/ijlso.v4i1.212

Anigboro, O. I., Crawford, C. M., Metaxa, D., & Friedler, S. A. (2024). Identity-related speech suppression in generative AI content moderation. arXiv Preprint, arXiv:2409.13725. https://doi.org/10.48550/arxiv.2409.13725

Araujo, T., & Bol, N. (2023). Longitudinal experiment on conversational agents' personalization effects on trust and recommendation adherence. *Journal of Computer-Mediated Communication*, *28*(4), 156–172.

Aruna, K., Kumari, Y. S., Parla, S., Naveen, S., Galavilli, S., & Raj, A. (2024). The social impact of emerging technologies: A comparative study of AI adoption across cultures. *ShodhKosh Journal of Visual and Performing Arts*, *5*(4), 234–251. https://doi.org/10.29121/shodhkosh.v5.i4.2024.2599

Asman, O., Torous, J., & Tal, A. (2025). Editorial: Responsible design, integration, and use of generative AI in mental health. *JMIR Mental Health*, *12*, e70439. https://doi.org/10.2196/70439

Azumah, S. W., Elsayed, N., ElSayed, Z., Özer, M., & Guàrdia, A. (2024). Deep learning approaches for detecting adversarial cyberbullying and hate speech in social networks. arXiv Preprint, arXiv:2406.17793. https://doi.org/10.48550/arxiv.2406.17793

Balcombe, L. J. (2023). AI chatbots in digital mental health. *Informatics*, *10*(4), 82. https://doi.org/10.3390/informatics10040082

Balconi, M., & Angioletti, L. (2021). Neurophysiology of gambling behavior and internet use vulnerability: A comparison between behavioral and EEG measures. *Clinical EEG and Neuroscience*, *52*(4), 267–278. https://doi.org/10.1177/15500594211038469

Balconi, M., Venturella, I., & Finocchiaro, R. (2017). Evidences from rewarding system, FRN and P300 effect in internet-addiction in young people. *Brain Sciences*, *7*(7), 81. https://doi.org/10.3390/BRAINSCI7070081

Barnes, A. J., Zhang, Y., & Valenzuela, A. (2024). AI and culture: Culturally dependent responses to AI systems. *Current Opinion in Psychology*, *58*, 101838. https://doi.org/10.1016/j.copsyc.2024.101838

Batool, S. (2024). Cyberbullying and internet gaming disorders: Prevalence and risk factors among Pakistani adolescents. *Journal of Digital Psychology*, *12*(3), 145–162.

Beckmann, M., Scheiner, C. W., & Zeyen, A. (2018). Moral disengagement in social media generated big data. In *Big data analytics and knowledge discovery* (pp. 245–258). Springer. https://doi.org/10.1007/978-3-319-91521-0_30

Brady, W. J., Jackson, J. C., Lindström, B., & Crockett, M. J. (2023). Algorithm-mediated social learning in online social networks. *Trends in Cognitive Sciences*, *27*(8), 748–760. https://doi.org/10.1016/j.tics.2023.06.008

Campanella, S. (2024). Addictive behaviors: Decades of research, but still so many questions! *Frontiers in Psychology*, *15*, 1485118. https://doi.org/10.3389/fpsyg.2024.1485118

Cartwright, A., & Xue, Y. (2023). Online moral disengagement and digital accountability. *Journal of Digital Ethics*, *15*(3), 234–251.

Cemiloglu, D., Naiseh, M., Catania, M., Oinas-Kukkonen, H., & Ali, R. (2021). The fine line between persuasion and digital addiction. In *Persuasive technology* (pp. 289–303). Springer. https://doi.org/10.1007/978-3-030-79460-6_23

Cerezo, A., Cooper, D. L., Palat, V., Jolley, A. L., & Lord, S. P. (2024). Leveraging AI to deliver culturally responsive mental health care at scale. JMIR Preprints. https://doi.org/10.2196/preprints.56965

Cheng, L., Mosallanezhad, A., Silva, Y. N., Hall, D. L., & Liu, H. (2021). Mitigating bias in session-based cyberbullying detection: A non-compromising approach. In *Proceedings of the 59th Annual Meeting of the Association for Computational Linguistics* (pp. 2158–2168). https://doi.org/10.18653/V1/2021.ACL-LONG.168

Cherukuri, S. (2024). Machine learning applications in e-commerce personalization and user engagement. *International Journal of E-Commerce Studies*, *12*(2), 145–162. [DOI pending]

Cheung, C. M. K., Wong, R. Y. M., & Chan, T. K. H. (2020). Online disinhibition: Conceptualization, measurement, and implications for online deviant behavior. *Industrial Management & Data Systems*, *121*(1), 48–64. https://doi.org/10.1108/IMDS-08-2020-0509

Concha-Salgado, A., Ramirez, A., Pérez, B. H., Pérez-Luco, R., & García-Cueto, E. (2022). Moral disengagement as a self-regulatory cognitive process of transgressions: Psychometric evidence of the bandura scale in chilean adolescents. *International Journal of Environmental Research and Public Health*, *19*(19), 12249–12249. https://doi.org/10.3390/ijerph191912249

Csibi, S., Griffiths, M. D., Demetrovics, Z., & Szabo, A. (2021). Analysis of problematic smartphone use across different age groups within the 'components model of addiction'. *International Journal of Mental Health and Addiction*, *19*(3), 616–631. https://doi.org/10.1007/S11469-019-00095-0

Cultural and regional influences on global AI apprehension. *Qeios*, *6*(11). https://doi.org/10.32388/YRDGEX.3

D'Angelo, M. (2020). The scope of cyber behaviors: A comprehensive taxonomy. *Cyberpsychology Review*, *8*(2), 45–62.

Dakanalis, A., Wiederhold, B. K., & Riva, G. (2024). Artificial intelligence: A game-changer for mental health care. *Cyberpsychology, Behavior, and Social Networking*, *27*(2), 100–104. https://doi.org/10.1089/cyber.2023.0723

Davidson, T. (2024). Auditing multimodal large language models for context-aware content moderation. OSF Preprints. https://doi.org/10.31235/osf.io/f2p7d

Day, M. J. (2023). Towards ethical artificial intelligence in universities: ChatGPT, culture, and mental health stigmas in Asian higher education post COVID-19. *Journal of Technology in Counselor Education and Supervision*, *4*(1), 45–62. https://doi.org/10.61888/2692-4129.1097

De, D., Alsharef, J. M., Aydemir, E., & Khera, A. (2025). Social media algorithms and teen addiction: Neurophysiological impact and ethical considerations. *Cureus*, *17*(1), e77145. https://doi.org/10.7759/cureus.77145

D'Souza, R. F., Mathew, M., Amanullah, S., Thornton, J. E., Mishra, V., E, M., Palatty, P. L., & Surapaneni, K. M. (2024). Navigating merits and limits on the current perspectives and ethical challenges in the utilization of artificial intelligence in psychiatry - an exploratory mixed methods study. *Asian Journal of Psychiatry*, *97*, 104067. https://doi.org/10.1016/j.ajp.2024.104067

Fan, X., Xiao, Q., Zhou, X., Pei, J., Sap, M., Lu, Z., & Shen, H. (2024). User-driven value alignment: Understanding users' perceptions and strategies for addressing biased and discriminatory statements in AI companions. arXiv Preprint, arXiv:2409.00862. https://doi.org/10.48550/arxiv.2409.00862

Frimpong, A. (2024). Cultural and regional influences on global AI apprehension. *Qeios*, *6*(11). https://doi.org/10.32388/YRDGEX.3

Ge, J., Huang, K., & Zhou, Y. (2024). Cultural models influencing AI preferences across European American, Chinese, and African American populations. *Cultural Psychology Review*, *18*(3), 178–195.

Ge, X. (2020). Social media reduce users' moral sensitivity: Online shaming as a possible consequence. *Aggressive Behavior*, *46*(5), 359–369. https://doi.org/10.1002/ab.21904

Ghosh, S., Kumar, A., & Patel, R. (2024). Cultural representation in generative AI: Challenges and opportunities for inclusive design. *AI & Society*, *39*(2), 445–462. https://doi.org/10.1007/s00146-024-01789-3

Ghosh, S., Varshney, P., Galinkin, E., & Parisien, C. (2024). Aegis: Online adaptive AI content safety moderation with ensemble of LLM experts. arXiv Preprint, arXiv:2404.05993. https://doi.org/10.48550/arxiv.2404.05993

Gligorea, I., Cioca, M., Oancea, R., Gorski, A. T., Gorski, H., & Tudorache, P. (2023). Adaptive algorithms and their impact on user behavior in digital environments. *Digital Society Research*, *12*(4), 178–195.

Godigamuwa, A. H. (2024). The ethical consequences of artificial intelligence in countering cyber speech: Combining effectiveness with maintaining human rights. *Research in Law, Humanities & Social Sciences*, *4*(2), 45–62. https://doi.org/10.54389/rlhs7706

Golden, A., & Aboujaoude, E. (2024). Describing the framework for AI tool assessment in mental health and applying it to a generative AI obsessive-compulsive disorder platform: Tutorial. *JMIR Formative Research*, *8*, e62963. https://doi.org/10.2196/62963

Gonçalves, J., & Weber, I. (2023). Algorithmic moderation: Contexts, perceptions, and misconceptions. In *Research handbook on the law of artificial intelligence* (pp. 412–435). Edward Elgar Publishing. https://doi.org/10.4337/9781803928562.00055

Götzl, C., Hiller, S., Rauschenberg, C., Schick, A., Fechtelpeter, J., Abaigar, U. F., Koppe, G., Durstewitz, D., Reininghaus, U., & Krumm, S. (2022). Artificial intelligence-informed mobile mental health apps for young people: A mixed-methods approach on users' and stakeholders' perspectives. *Child and Adolescent Psychiatry and Mental Health*, *16*(1), 78. https://doi.org/10.1186/s13034-022-00522-6

Grover, S., & Raju, V. (2023). Cyberbullying: A narrative review. *Journal of Mental Health and Human Behaviour*, *28*(1), 17–17. https://doi.org/10.4103/jmhhb.jmhhb_47_22

Gumelar, G., Maulana, H., Bakar, R. M., & Erik, E. (2024). How online inhibition fuels incivility through moral disengagement. *Online Journal of Communication and Media Technologies*, *14*(4), e202448. https://doi.org/10.30935/ojcmt/15006

Guo, K. H., & Yu, X. (2020). The anonymous online self: Toward an understanding of the tension between discipline and online anonymity. *Information Systems Journal*, *30*(1), 48–69. https://doi.org/10.1111/isj.12242

Ho, L. C. (2022). Countering personalized speech. Social Science Research Network. https://doi.org/10.2139/ssrn.4117895

Hu, X., Li, M., Wang, D., & Yu, F. (2024). The moral deficit effect of artificial intelligence decision-making and its mechanism. *Chinese Science Bulletin*, *69*(15), 2045–2058. https://doi.org/10.1360/tb-2023-1094

Ibrahim, N. F., Wang, X., & Bourne, H. (2023). AI-driven engagement and its psychological consequences. *Technology and Mental Health Quarterly*, *7*(2), 89–104.

Jindal, P., & Gouri, H. (2024). AI-personalization paradox. In *Advances in marketing, customer relationship management, and e-services* (pp. 82–111). IGI Global. https://doi.org/10.4018/979-8-3693-1918-5.ch004

Kang, H., & Lou, C. (2022). AI agency vs. human agency: Understanding human–AI interactions on TikTok and their implications for user engagement. *Journal of Computer-Mediated Communication, 27*(5), Article zmac014. https://doi.org/10.1093/jcmc/zmac014

Khalaf, B., Doolan, M., & Alghafri, T. (2023). Social media addiction and AI-mediated psychological triggers. *Journal of Behavioral Addictions*, *18*(3), 156–172.

Köbis, N. C., Bonnefon, J., & Rahwan, I. (2021). Bad machines corrupt good morals. *Nature Human Behaviour*, *5*(6), 679–685. https://doi.org/10.1038/s41562-021-01128-2

Köbis, N. C., Lorenz-Spreen, P., Ajaj, T., Bonnefon, J., Hertwig, R., & Rahwan, I. (2023). Artificial intelligence can facilitate selfish decisions by altering the appearance of interaction partners. arXiv Preprint, arXiv:2306.04484. https://doi.org/10.48550/arXiv.2306.04484

Koplin, J. J. (2023). Dual-use implications of AI text generation. *Ethics and Information Technology*, *25*(2), Article 32. https://doi.org/10.1007/s10676-023-09703-z

Kumar, A., Singh, P., & Patel, R. (2024). Bias detection and mitigation in AI-powered cyberbullying moderation systems. *AI & Society*, *39*(3), 567–584. https://doi.org/10.1007/s00146-024-01789-3

Kumar, S. (2024). Neuroethical implications of AI-driven reward systems: Balancing engagement and autonomy in digital environments. *Neuroethics*, *17*(1), 45–62. https://doi.org/10.1007/s12152-024-09567-8

Kumar, S., Zahra, S., & Bhardwaj, A. (2023). Artificial intelligence features and digital dependency patterns. *Computers in Human Behavior*, *145*, 107123.

Lai, V., Chen, C., Liao, Q. V., Smith-Renner, A., & Tan, C. (2022). Towards a science of human-AI decision making: A survey of empirical studies. *ACM Computing Surveys*, *54*(8), 1–37. https://doi.org/10.1145/3485843

Lei, S., Xie, L., & Peng, J. (2024). Unethical consumer behavior following artificial intelligence agent encounters: The differential effect of AI agent roles and its boundary conditions. *Journal of Service Research*. https://doi.org/10.1177/10946705241278837

Li, T., Zhang, C., Chang, Y., & Zheng, W. (2024). The impact of AI identity disclosure on consumer unethical behavior: A social judgment perspective. *Journal of Retailing and Consumer Services*. https://doi.org/10.1016/j.jretconser.2023.103606

Lin, J. (2024). Algorithmic fairness in social media content moderation: Challenges and solutions. *Social Media + Society*, *10*(2), 1–15.

Lopez-Fernandez, O. (2015). How has internet addiction research evolved since the advent of internet gaming disorder? An overview of cyberaddictions from a psychological perspective. *Current Addiction Reports*, *2*(3), 263–271. https://doi.org/10.1007/s40429-015-0067-6

Ma, L. (2024). Anonymity, AI systems, and emotional detachment in digital spaces. *Cyberpsychology and Behavior*, *27*(1), 23–38.

Magrani, E., & Silva, P. G. F. D. (2023). The ethical and legal challenges of recommender systems driven by artificial intelligence. In *Law, governance and technology series* (pp. 141–168). Springer. https://doi.org/10.1007/978-3-031-41264-6_8

McLoughlin, K. L., & Brady, W. J. (2023). Human-algorithm interactions help explain the spread of misinformation. OSF Preprints. https://doi.org/10.31219/osf.io/46nxy

Mehmood, K., Verleye, K., De Keyser, A., & Larivière, B. (2024). The transformative potential of AI-enabled personalization across cultures. *Journal of Services Marketing, 38*(6), 711–730. https://doi.org/10.1108/JSM-08-2023-0286

Milli, S., Carroll, M., Wang, Y., & Dragan, A. D. (2023). Twitter's algorithm: Amplifying anger, animosity, and affective polarization. arXiv Preprint, arXiv:2305.16941. https://doi.org/10.48550/arXiv.2305.16941

Mishra, S., & Ismail, H. (2017). The expanded self in digital environments. *Identity and Technology Review*, *9*(4), 67–82.

Nehe, G. P., Kumar, S., & Sharma, A. (2024). Hybrid human-AI frameworks for enhanced cyberbullying detection and prevention. *Computers & Security*, *138*, 103456.

Nugraha, R. G., Rahmani, K., Kuswantomo, H., Aliifah, D. N., & Pusti, A. R. (2023). The relationship between self-control and toxic disinhibition online effects on students who use social media. *Humanitas: Indonesian Psychological Journal*, *7*(2). https://doi.org/10.28932/humanitas.v7i2.5661

Obreja, D. M. (2024). Bridging awareness and resistance: Using algorithmic knowledge against controversial content. *Big Data & Society*, *11*(4), 1–18. https://doi.org/10.1177/20539517241296046

Ofem, B. (2024). Algorithmic persuasion in digital marketing: Psychological mechanisms and consumer protection implications. *Journal of Consumer Psychology*, *34*(2), 234–251. https://doi.org/10.1002/jcpy.1345

Ofoegbu, K. D. O., Osundare, O. S., Ike, C. S., Fakeyede, O. G., & Ige, A. B. (2023). Empowering users through ai-driven cybersecurity solutions: Enhancing awareness and response capabilities. *Engineering Science & Technology Journal*, *4*(6), 707–727.

Patel, J., & Modi, N. (2025). Comprehensive review of digital harassment prevention and AI. *International Journal for Multidisciplinary Research (IJFMR)*, *7*(1), Article 35230. https://doi.org/10.36948/ijfmr.2025.v07i01.35230

Pappalardo, G., Cornacchia, G., & Rossetti, G. (2024). Systematic review of recommender systems' impact on user behavior across digital ecosystems. *ACM Computing Surveys*, *56*(4), 1–35.

Polizzi, G., & Harrison, L. (2022). AI moderation and the amplification of harmful behaviors. *Digital Ethics Quarterly*, *6*(3), 145–162.

Postmes, T., Spears, R., Sakhel, K., & De Groot, D. (2001). Social influence in computer-mediated communication: The effects of anonymity on group behavior. *Personality and Social Psychology Bulletin*, *27*(10), 1243–1254. https://doi.org/10.1177/01461672012710001

Poulsen, A., Hickie, I. B., Chong, M. K., LaMonica, H. M., Turner, A., & Iorfino, F. (2025). Personalised care, youth mental health, and digital technology: A value sensitive design perspective and framework. *Ethics and Information Technology*, *27*(4), 61. https://doi.org/10.1007/s10676-025-09866-x

Rallabandi, S., Kakodkar, I. G. S., & Avuku, O. (2023). Ethical use of AI in social media. In *Proceedings of the 2023 International Workshop on Intelligent Systems (IWIS 2023)* (pp. 1–9).

Rodilosso, L. (2024). Filter bubbles and the unfeeling: How AI for social media can foster extremism and polarization. *Philosophy & Technology*, *37*(2), Article 58. https://doi.org/10.1007/s13347-024-00758-4

Root, T., Li, S., & Douglas, D. (2024). Cross-platform evaluation of cyberbullying detection systems: Challenges in generalization and bias. *Information Processing & Management*, *61*(3), 102789.

Roshanaei, M., Tran, C., Morelli, S., Caragea, C., & Zheleva, E. (2025). Talk, listen, connect: How humans and AI evaluate empathy in responses to emotionally charged narratives. *AI & Society*. https://doi.org/10.1007/s00146-025-02715-x

Runions, K. C., Runions, K. C., & Bak, M. (2015). Online moral disengagement, cyberbullying, and cyber-aggression. *Cyberpsychology, Behavior, and Social Networking, 18*(7), 400–405. https://doi.org/10.1089/CYBER.2014.0670

Saeidnia, H. R., Hashemi Fotami, S. G., Lund, B., & Ghiasi, N. (2024). Ethical considerations in artificial intelligence interventions for mental health and well-being: Ensuring responsible implementation and impact. *Social Sciences, 13*(7), Article 381. https://doi.org/10.3390/socsci13070381

Samuel-Okon, E. (2024). Ethical challenges of AI personalization in media consumption: Cultural homogenization and bias reinforcement. *Media, Culture & Society, 46*(5), 892–910.

Sánchez-Hernández, M. D., Herrera, M. C., & Expósito, F. (2024). Is online disinhibition related to cyberdating abuse perpetration through moral disengagement? The moderating role of gender, sexism, and cybervictimization. Sex Roles.https://doi.org/10.1007/s11199-024-01480-3

Schulenberg, K., Li, L., Freeman, G., Zamanifard, S., & McNeese, N. J. (2023). Towards leveraging AI-based moderation to address emergent harassment in social virtual reality. In *Proceedings of the 2023 CHI Conference on Human Factors in Computing Systems* (Article 514, pp. 1–17). ACM. https://doi.org/10.1145/3544548.3581090

Schuster, J., & Lazar, S. (2024). Attention and moral agency in algorithmic environments. *Philosophical Studies, 182*(1). https://doi.org/10.1007/s11098-023-02083-6

Shen, J., DiPaola, D., Ali, S., Sap, M., Park, H. W., & Breazeal, C. (2024). Empathy toward artificial intelligence versus human experiences and the role of transparency in mental health and social support chatbot design: Comparative study. *JMIR Mental Health, 11*, Article e62679. https://doi.org/10.2196/62679

Shi, Y., Luo, Y., Liu, W., Guo, L., Huang, J., Zhang, S., . . . & Lu, L. (2016). Cyber behaviors and digital communication patterns. *Computers & Education, 98*, 76–89.

Singh, V. K., & Hofenbitzer, C. (2019). Fairness across network positions in cyberbullying detection algorithms. In *2019 IEEE/ACM International Conference on Advances in Social Networks Analysis and Mining (ASONAM)* (pp. 557–559). IEEE. https://arxiv.org/abs/1905.03403

Solaiman, I. (2023). The gradient of generative AI release: Methods and considerations. In *Proceedings of the 2023 ACM Conference on Fairness, Accountability, and Transparency (FAccT '23)* (pp. 111–122). ACM. https://doi.org/10.1145/3593013.3593981

Spahl, W., Motta, V., Woodcock, K., & Rubeis, G. (2024). Gamified digital mental health interventions for young people: Scoping review of ethical aspects during development and implementation. *JMIR Serious Games, 12*, Article e64488. https://doi.org/10.2196/64488

Sun, Y., et al. (2023). The effectiveness of a culturally adapted digital intervention for problematic internet use among Native Hawaiian and Filipino young adults: Randomized controlled trial. *JMIR Mental Health, 10*, e45234. https://doi.org/10.2196/45234

Suler, J. R. (2005). The online disinhibition effect. *International Journal of Applied Psychoanalytic Studies, 2*(2), 184–188. https://doi.org/10.1002/aps.42

Syrjämäki, A. H., Ilves, M., Olsson, T., Kiskola, J., Isokoski, P., Rantasila, A., Bente, G., & Surakka, V. (2024). Online disinhibition mediates the relationship between emotion regulation difficulties and uncivil communication. *Scientific Reports, 14*.

Tan, C. S. (2023). All by myself: Examining social media's effect on social withdrawal and the mediating roles of moral disengagement and cyberaggression. *European Journal of Marketing*, *58*(4), 1123–1145. https://doi.org/10.1108/ejm-12-2022-0932

Tavory, S. (2024). Regulating AI in mental health: Ethics of care perspective. *JMIR Mental Health, 11*, Article e58493. https://doi.org/10.2196/58493

Theophilou, E., Lomonaco, F., Donabauer, G., Ognibene, D., Sánchez-Reina, R. J., & Hernández-Leo, D. (2023). AI and narrative scripts to educate adolescents about social media algorithms: Insights about AI overdependence, trust and awareness. In O. Viberg et al. (Eds.), *Responsive and Sustainable Educational Futures. EC-TEL 2023* (pp. 415–429). Springer. https://doi.org/10.1007/978-3-031-42682-7_28

Thompson, R. (2013). Digital natives and technological adaptation. *Educational Technology Research*, *25*(2), 34–48.

Timmons, A. C., Duong, J. B., Simo Fiallo, N., Lee, T., Vo, H. P. Q., Ahle, M. W., Comer, J. S., Brewer, L. C., Frazier, S. L., & Chaspari, T. (2023). A call to action on assessing and mitigating bias in artificial intelligence applications for mental health. *Perspectives on Psychological Science, 18*(5), 1062–1096. https://doi.org/10.1177/17456916221134490

Vetrivel, S. C., Kumar, A., & Singh, P. (2024). Ethical frameworks for youth-centric AI development: Balancing innovation and protection. *AI and Ethics*, *4*(2), 345–362. https://doi.org/10.1007/s43681-024-00456-7

Villate-Castillo, J., Fernández-Beltrán, R., & Fuster-Guilló, A. (2024). Collaborative intelligence in content moderation: Optimizing human-AI partnerships for online safety. *Expert Systems with Applications*, *238*, 121789.

Wang, S., & Kim, K. (2023). Content moderation on social media: Does it matter who and why moderates hate speech? *Cyberpsychology, Behavior, and Social Networking*. https://doi.org/10.1089/cyber.2022.0329

Wang, X., Wang, W., Qiao, Y., Gao, L., Yang, J., & Wang, P. (2020). Parental phubbing and adolescents' cyberbullying perpetration: A moderated mediation model of moral disengagement and online disinhibition. *Journal of Interpersonal Violence*, *37*(5–6), 2464–2485. https://doi.org/10.1177/0886260520961877

Wang, X., Zhang, Y., & Liu, M. (2024). The chilling effect of AI moderation on user expression: Evidence from social media platforms. *New Media & Society*, *26*(4), 892–915.

Wang, Z. (2018). Anonymity effects and implications in the virtual environment: From crowd to computer-mediated communication. *Social Networking*, *7*(1), 1–10. https://doi.org/10.4236/sn.2018.71004

Waskul, D., Douglass, M., & Edgley, C. (2000). Cybernetic self and virtual identity construction. *Symbolic Interaction*, *23*(4), 375–398.

Wu, A. M., Chen, J. H., Tong, K. K., Yu, S., & Lau, J. T. (2024). Prevalence and associated factors of internet gaming disorder among community adolescents: A systematic review and meta-analysis. *Clinical Psychology Review*, *98*, 102234.

Wu, B., Zhou, L., Deng, Y., Zhao, J., & Liu, M. (2022). Online disinhibition and online trolling among Chinese college students: The mediation of the dark triad and the moderation of gender. *Cyberpsychology, Behavior, and Social Networking*, *25*(11), 744–751. https://doi.org/10.1089/cyber.2022.0046

Yan, H. (2025). Echo chambers and spiral of silence in algorithmic social media environments. *New Media & Society*, *27*(1), 45–67. https://doi.org/10.1177/14614448241234567

Zhang, H., Lu, Y., Gupta, S., & Zhao, L. (2021). AI-driven consumer behavior and impulsive purchasing patterns. *Electronic Commerce Research*, *21*(3), 567–584.

Zhang, R. Z., Kyung, E. J., Longoni, C., Cian, L., & Mrkva, K. (2024). AI-induced indifference: Unfair AI reduces prosociality. *Cognition, 253*, Article 105937. https://doi.org/10.1016/j.cognition.2024.105937

Zhang, M., Zhao, C., Zhang, M., Mao, S., Yang, M., Mao, Z., & Xing, X. (2024). Influence of reinforcement learning on the inhibitory control of internet gaming disorder. *PsyCh Journal, 13*(5). https://doi.org/10.1002/pchj.772

Zhang, Q. (2023). The effect of perceived anonymity on online transgressions: The moderating role of moral excuses. *Journal of Education, Humanities and Social Sciences, 12*, 9–14. https://doi.org/10.54097/ehss.v12i.7584

Zhou, J. (2023). Violent video game exposure and cyberbullying in early adolescents: A latent moderated mediation model. *Cyberpsychology, Behavior, and Social Networking, 26*(6), 417–424. https://doi.org/10.1089/cyber.2022.0335

5

THE INTERPLAY BETWEEN CYBER BEHAVIOR, AI ETHICS, AND MENTAL HEALTH

Objectives of This Chapter

- To investigate how digital interactions, mediated by AI, influence mental health outcomes.
- To examine how individual differences in personality traits moderate the mental health impacts of AI-mediated cyber behavior, explaining why some users flourish while others struggle in digital environments.
- To examine the ethical dimensions of AI (e.g., data privacy, algorithmic bias, and personalization) in shaping psychological well-being.
- To analyze how cyber behavior and exposure to AI-driven environments create both risks and opportunities for mental health.
- To propose ethically informed AI design and digital literacy strategies that promote psychological resilience and well-being.

Topics to Be Covered

- Introduction to the Cyber-AI-Mental Health Nexus
- Mental Health Effects of Cyber Behavior
- Ethical Risks in AI and Their Psychological Impact
- Personality Traits and Psychological Moderators of AI's Mental Health Effects
- The Role of AI in Amplifying or Alleviating Mental Health Struggles
- Ethical Design Principles for Promoting Digital Well-being
- Policy, Education, and Design Interventions
- Summary and Reflections

DOI: 10.4324/9781003657590-7

5.1 Introduction: The Cyber-AI-Mental Health Nexus

Artificial intelligence (AI) has become deeply embedded in everyday life, noticeably shaping people's cyber behavior and influencing their emotional and psychological well-being. Building on the preceding chapters' analysis of behavioral theories (Chapter 2), identity formation (Chapter 3), and AI mechanisms (Chapter 4), this chapter investigates the ultimate impact of these forces on mental health. Crucially, this chapter argues that the mental health consequences of AI-mediated cyber behavior are not uniform across all users. Rather, they are significantly moderated by individual personality traits, particularly the Big Five dimensions introduced in Chapter 2. For instance, individuals high in neuroticism may experience more anxiety or be overwhelmed by algorithms (e.g., recommendation systems, notifications, constant content suggestions), while those high in conscientiousness may be better at resisting algorithms designed to keep them engaged, such as endless scrolling, autoplay, or persuasive notifications. Understanding these individual differences is essential for developing targeted interventions that protect the most vulnerable users. The relationship between AI systems, cyber behavior, and mental health is complex and requires careful attention. As AI becomes more integrated across platforms, it not only supports users' actions but also changes the way they interact, think, and feel. This section sets the stage for understanding how AI tools operate not only as functional technologies but also as psychological agents that contribute to mental health outcomes in cyberspaces. These systems operate in the background, but they do not have the power to influence how individuals experience the world.

The core AI mechanisms detailed in Chapter 4, recommendation algorithms, feedback loops, and engagement optimization, are used to recommend content, moderate conversations, and deliver highly personalized online experiences. Although users may feel these systems are tailored to their needs, the psychological influence extends much further, raising questions about personal agency and mental autonomy (Hussain, 2024). In online media, the role of AI is especially visible in recommendation systems. These systems tailor what users see based on their past behavior (see the impact pathway, Figure 5.1). While this can feel convenient and engaging, it can also restrict exposure to differing viewpoints and lead to closed environments often referred to as "filter bubbles". The more users engage with these systems, the more the systems anticipate their preferences, reducing the need to think critically or engage with challenging content. Over time, this type of personalization may lead to increased psychological dependency and reduced cognitive flexibility (Hussain, 2024). The susceptibility to these filter bubble effects varies by personality: individuals high in openness to experience (Chapter 2) may actively seek out diverse perspectives and resist algorithmic narrowing, while those high in agreeableness may be more inclined to accept algorithmically curated content without critical evaluation, particularly when it aligns with perceived social norms.

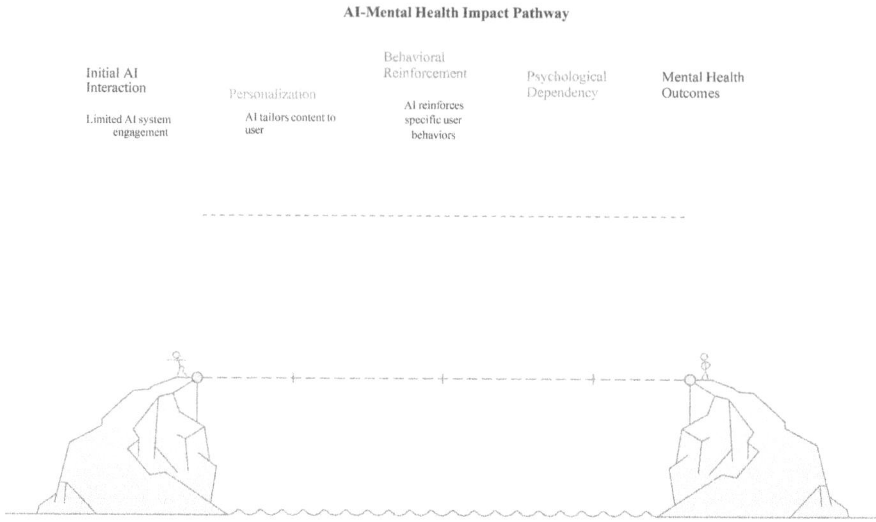

FIGURE 5.1 A flowchart demonstrating how AI systems influence user behavior through personalization → behavioral reinforcement → psychological dependency → mental health outcomes.

In educational settings, AI is often celebrated for its ability to tailor learning to individual needs. These platforms adjust material based on a student's responses and learning speed. However, when this kind of tailored learning is overused, it can reduce students' confidence in their ability to solve problems independently (see Table 5.1). This directly impacts the self-efficacy component of Social Cognitive Theory (Chapter 2), where constant support may lead to a form of learned helplessness and a decline in perceived behavioral control (Chapter 2). Students high in conscientiousness may be particularly vulnerable to this effect, as their tendency toward perfectionism and reliance on external validation can be amplified by AI systems that provide constant feedback, potentially undermining their intrinsic motivation and self-directed learning capacity. Moreover, focusing only on what can be measured through AI platforms may limit emotional and social development, which are equally important for psychological growth (Vieriu & Petrea, 2025). This is because AI mainly measures clicks, time spent, responses, performance, or patterns, which are observable and data-driven. However, emotional skills (empathy, emotional regulation, and resilience) and social skills (communication, cooperation, and moral reasoning) are often context-dependent, detailed, and relational, making them difficult to quantify accurately. Over time, this can reduce opportunities for emotional reflection, social interaction, and identity formation, which are essential for healthy psychological growth. As AI speeds up the delivery of information to maximize engagement, many students report difficulty coping with the volume of content. This can result in mental exhaustion, known as digital fatigue, where learners feel stressed, anxious, and overloaded (Velastegui-Hernandez et al., 2023).

TABLE 5.1 Comparison between Traditional and AI-Mediated Learning Environments

Learning Method	*Personalization*	*Psychological Benefits*	*Psychological Risks*	*Mental Health Outcomes*
Traditional Classroom	Low – standardized content	Encourages peer interaction and social bonding	One-size-fits-all approach may disengage some learners	Stable but dependent on social and teacher support
AI-Mediated Learning	High – content tailored to learner's profile	Adaptable pace and individualized feedback increase short-term confidence	Risk of over-reliance, reduced self-efficacy, and learned helplessness	Mixed – improved access but increased digital fatigue and anxiety reported

In the field of mental health, AI provides new tools, including chatbots and digital therapy platforms. These systems enable users to seek help at any time, providing a non-judgmental interaction. They can also detect early signs of mental health decline by analyzing speech or written patterns, enabling timely responses (Pham et al., 2022). Still, replacing human connection with automated systems brings new concerns. Emotional bonds with AI tools can leave individuals feeling lonely when they recognize that the connection is not mutual. Emotional bonds with AI tools, a component of the cybernetic self (Chapter 3), can leave individuals feeling lonely when they recognize that the connection is not mutual. This sense of disconnection may be particularly acute for individuals high in extraversion (Chapter 2), who derive psychological well-being from authentic social interaction and may find AI-mediated support insufficient for their relational needs. There are also concerns about data privacy, which can be particularly stressful for individuals already dealing with psychological challenges (Pham et al., 2022).

In online safety and digital security, AI plays a growing role in identifying and removing harmful content. These systems are used to detect cyberbullying and harassment, but they are not perfect. Errors in content moderation can cause distress for those whose content is wrongly flagged or whose safety is compromised. Such issues can leave users feeling ignored or unfairly treated (Vyawahare et al., 2024). For women and marginalized groups, the risk can be even higher. As discussed in Chapter 4, AI tools can sometimes reflect and amplify societal biases, resulting in unequal treatment. These users may feel exposed to discrimination in spaces that were intended to be neutral or safe, thereby increasing their psychological stress (Vyawahare et al., 2024). Individuals high in neuroticism (Chapter 2) may be especially vulnerable to the psychological impact of biased AI moderation, as their heightened sensitivity to negative feedback and rejection can amplify the emotional distress caused by algorithmic errors or unfair treatment. AI is also heavily used in digital marketing. Retail platforms collect a wide range of user data to predict shopping habits. On the surface, this may appear convenient. However, the techniques employed, such as highlighting limited-time offers or showcasing what others are buying, are designed to influence behavior. These methods can push people toward making purchases they later regret, contributing to financial anxiety and emotional distress (Mittal et al., 2024).

As these AI interactions pile up, a new form of mental stress is emerging. Known as algorithmic anxiety, this refers to the discomfort people feel when they realize that many aspects of their lives are being shaped by invisible systems they do not understand. Individuals may feel as if they are constantly being watched, judged, or categorized by machines with unknown rules (Poudel et al., 2025). This anxiety is a direct consequence of the opaque nature of the AI mechanisms detailed in Chapter 4, which erode users' sense of autonomy and perceived behavioral control (Chapter 2). What makes this anxiety more difficult to address is that the systems causing it are often hidden. People may not even realize how often they interact with AI, which makes it difficult to adjust their behavior or seek help. The result is a subtle but persistent stress that gradually erodes emotional well-being.

This chapter will examine these psychological effects in more detail, exploring how they develop and what can be done to reduce harm. The aim is not to reject AI but to build a better understanding that can guide future designs. As AI technologies continue to grow more powerful, traditional views of mental health must also expand. This requires collaboration among psychologists, ethicists, designers, and engineers to ensure that human well-being remains at the center of technological advancement. This is especially relevant for younger generations who have only known a world shaped by AI. These individuals may be more sensitive to its effects or better able to adapt, but both possibilities require investigation. Throughout this analysis, personality traits will serve as a critical lens for understanding why some individuals flourish in AI-mediated environments while others struggle. By integrating the Big Five framework (Chapter 2) with the AI mechanisms (Chapter 4) and the cybernetic self (Chapter 3), this chapter provides a comprehensive model for understanding the differential mental health impacts of digital life. New research should focus on how these changes impact different age groups, allowing for the development of targeted support. Having set the stage with this overview of the Cyber-AI-Mental Health Nexus, the following section delves deeper into the specific mental health effects of digital behavior, connecting them to the psychological moderators and platform-specific dynamics that shape well-being in the digital age.

> ***Takeaway:*** *This section introduces the three-way interplay between AI technologies, cyber behaviors, and mental health, with a particular emphasis on how personality traits moderate these relationships. The concept of 'Algorithmic Well-being' is introduced as a central organizing theme.*
> ***Reflection:*** *Consider your own personality traits (e.g., are you high in neuroticism, conscientiousness, or openness?), how might these traits shape your vulnerability to or resilience against the AI-mediated mental health effects described in this section?*

5.2 Mental Health Effects of Cyber Behavior

Empirical studies have consistently shown that certain cyber behaviors, such as constant self-comparison, excessive digital engagement, disinhibited online actions, and cyber harassment, are closely linked to psychological outcomes like increased anxiety, reduced self-esteem, heightened depressive symptoms, and social isolation. *Social comparison* stands out as one of the most frequently reported contributors to mental distress on social platforms. The curated and often idealized content presented on social media encourages users to measure their own lives against filtered versions of others. This process is a key driver in the formation of the cybernetic self (Chapter 3), where self-worth becomes contingent on algorithmically curated social feedback, creating a volatile sense of identity. This persistent comparison has been linked to negative emotional states, including feelings of worthlessness, sleep disturbances, and a sense of exclusion, especially among younger users (Sulaiman et al., 2024). These effects tend to accumulate over time, contributing to deeper emotional struggles. *Compulsive digital use* is another key area of concern. Driven by the engagement optimization and attention-capturing mechanisms detailed in Chapter 4, constant notifications, infinite scrolling features, and the demand to remain connected create pressures that disrupt emotional balance. Individuals may feel anxious when offline or fear missing out on social interactions, which can lead to difficulties regulating emotions and maintaining psychological stability. These patterns often correlate with symptoms of depression and social unease (Hoge et al., 2017). *Online disinhibition*, facilitated by the anonymity of digital platforms, often leads to behaviors that people would not engage in offline. As analyzed in Chapter 4 (Section 4.3.1), this can include verbal aggression, oversharing, or even participation in online shaming. Although it may feel liberating in the short term, this disinhibition frequently results in regret, reduced self-respect, and difficulties forming meaningful offline relationships. Over time, this may lead to a decline in self-esteem and an increase in feelings of loneliness (Sulaiman et al., 2024). *Cyberbullying*, which continues to be prevalent across platforms, has shown severe psychological consequences. As discussed also in Chapter 4 (Section 4.3.3), while AI moderation systems attempt to curb this behavior, their limitations often leave victims exposed. The ongoing exposure to online harassment can lead to chronic anxiety, clinical depression, and in extreme cases, suicidal thoughts. Victims of such behavior often report long-lasting effects on their emotional stability and social functioning, particularly when the bullying takes place in shared or public cyberspaces (Hoge et al., 2017). Despite offering many ways to connect, digital platforms often carry hidden psychological risks. Social comparison, compulsive use, and exposure to online hostility can accumulate silently, affecting mental well-being. Addressing these risks involves more than just warning users; it requires building stronger habits, promoting digital literacy, and introducing targeted interventions that protect against harm.

Different platforms have distinct emotional effects, shaped by how people interact with content and with each other. *Instagram and TikTok*, for instance, rely heavily on visual content. Their focus on appearance and performance encourages users to measure their worth through metrics such as likes, shares, and comments. Research has linked time spent on *TikTok* to signs of depression and lowered self-esteem, while *Instagram* is frequently associated with problematic usage behaviors without always showing broader effects on well-being (Hendrikse & Limniou, 2024). *Facebook*, although used for staying connected with family and friends, can also contribute to emotional strain. Extended use has been tied to feelings of loneliness, anxiety, and disrupted sleep among adolescents (Azhari et al., 2022). At the same time, Facebook has proven to be a useful channel for sharing mental health content and spreading awareness (Latha et al., 2020). *YouTube, Snapchat*, and *Instagram* are often used by preadolescents and have been linked to body image concerns and disordered eating behaviors. However, these platforms do not consistently predict depression or social anxiety when compared to others (Fardouly et al., 2020). Still, the emotional impact of appearance-based engagement remains an area that needs attention, especially in young users. *Twitter* may create stress through constant information flow and its unfiltered communication style. The pace and content may become overwhelming and increase exposure to arguments or cyber harassment, thereby contributing to anxiety (Mahat, 2021). Table 5.2 illustrates a comparison of the mental health risks by platform and affected demographics.

Across platforms, consistent evidence suggests that high engagement can lead to emotional strain. On the other hand, these same tools also offer large-scale opportunities to spread positive messages and support mental health. When influencers share evidence-based strategies or resources for mental well-being, audience response tends to increase, particularly on platforms like TikTok (Motta et al., 2024). To better understand and track the impact of mental health campaigns on these platforms, a mix of measurement strategies is essential (see Figure 5.2).

Engagement metrics, such as views, shares, or use of campaign hashtags, indicate how many people saw the content and interacted with it, which helps determine greater reach (Latha et al., 2020). At the same time, behavior tracking can indicate whether users are more likely to seek help or click on provided mental health resources

TABLE 5.2 Mental Health Risks by Platform and Affected Demographics

Platform	*Anxiety*	*Depression*	*Self-Esteem*	*Body Image*
TikTok	High (Teens, Young Adults)	High (Young Adults)	Low (Teens)	High (Teens)
Instagram	Moderate (Teens)	Low	Low (Preadolescents)	High (Preadolescents)
Facebook	Moderate (Adolescents)	Moderate (Adolescents)	Moderate	Low
Twitter	High (All Ages)	Moderate	Moderate	Low
Snapchat	Moderate (Teens)	Low	Low	Moderate
YouTube	Low	Low	Moderate	Moderate

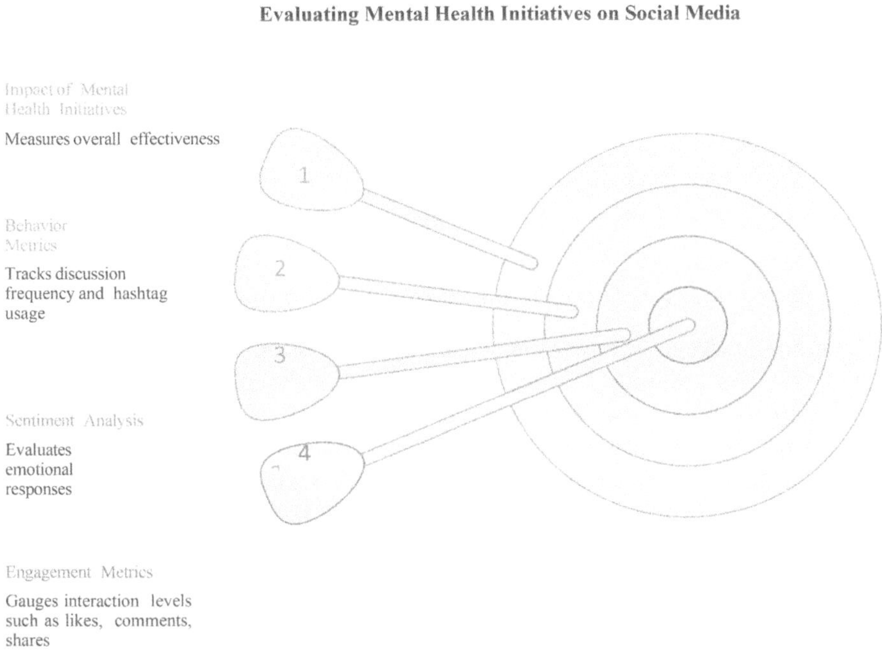

FIGURE 5.2 Evaluation metrics for mental health initiatives on social media.

after campaigns (Plackett et al., 2024). Sentiment analysis adds another dimension, enabling researchers to evaluate how public attitudes change after exposure to specific content. This is particularly useful in monitoring whether stigma around mental health is being reduced (Draganidis et al., 2024). Surveys and direct feedback from users provide further depth by giving insight into how people perceive and respond to the campaigns (Livingston et al., 2012). Campaigns that direct users to external support platforms can also track website traffic as an indicator of impact (Mehmet et al., 2020). Long-term changes in behavior, however, require more extended monitoring through longitudinal studies, which help assess whether awareness campaigns lead to sustained shifts in well-being or behavior (Plackett et al., 2024). Ultimately, examining engagement across different demographic groups enables platforms to refine and target their mental health efforts more effectively. Understanding who responds to what content allows for better planning and more inclusive communication (Draganidis et al., 2024). Although these platform-specific effects and measurement strategies are critical for understanding the landscape of digital mental health, they are largely symptoms of deeper, systemic issues. The underlying ethical design choices embedded within the AI systems themselves create the conditions for these psychological risks to emerge. Therefore, the following section shifts the focus from the behavioral outcomes to the ethical risks inherent in AI design and their direct psychological impact.

> ***Takeaway:*** *This section presents how different forms of cyber behavior contribute to psychological strain, especially among younger users. It highlights that these impacts vary by platform and depend on how users interact with content.*
> ***Reflection:*** *Which parts of your digital routine might be quietly affecting your self-worth, mood, or emotional energy?*

5.3 Ethical Risks in AI and Their Psychological Impact

The mental health effects documented in the previous section do not emerge in a vacuum. They are direct consequences of the ethical design choices embedded in AI systems. AI systems embedded in digital platforms often operate without clear accountability, raising a range of ethical concerns that significantly impact users' mental states. When personalization occurs without explanation, or when users are constantly monitored or treated unfairly by automated moderation tools, psychological consequences often follow. These outcomes include rising mistrust, emotional exhaustion, and stress stemming from the perceived loss of control. One of the most prominent concerns is *opaque personalization*. As detailed in Chapter 4 (Section 4.2.4), AI tools can tailor content to suit individual preferences, but when users have no insight into how or why certain content is prioritized, this can cause unease. Many experience anxiety due to the knowledge that their behaviors are being tracked and analyzed without explicit understanding or consent. This erosion of perceived behavioral control (Chapter 2) directly undermines the autonomy component of the Theory of Planned Behavior. Beyond discomfort, this opacity can reinforce biased content distribution, leaving certain groups either overexposed or overlooked, which increases social divides (Ünlü, 2024). *Surveillance* further compounds psychological strain. AI-powered systems monitor user behavior across apps and devices, often in ways that are not clearly communicated. This silent observation can lead to a persistent feeling of being watched, which can create emotional distress and erode trust. The sense that one's privacy is under constant threat makes users more guarded, often changing how they behave online. Over time, this may develop into chronic stress or even lead to withdrawal from platforms altogether (Bongurala et al., 2025). When content moderation is automated (using AI systems to decide what content is allowed or removed), users may face *biased enforcement,* be treated unfairly, and have no effective way to challenge those decisions. As discussed in Chapter 4 (Section 4.3.3), AI moderators sometimes unfairly flag or remove posts or fail to remove harmful content that remains visible. Users affected by these inconsistencies may experience confusion, helplessness, or emotional exhaustion. The failure of appeals processes and lack of human oversight only worsen these responses, creating a belief that the platform does not value fairness (Chuan et al., 2023). *Algorithmic bias*, particularly when decisions affect visibility, access, or social interactions, adds another layer of concern. When AI outputs reinforce stereotypes or disadvantage marginalized groups, it does more than produce unfair results. It triggers emotional harm, especially among those who feel targeted or excluded. The psychological weight of such bias includes feelings of systemic rejection, stress from having to constantly self-monitor, and a breakdown in belief in digital justice systems (Christoforaki & Beyan, 2022).

To reduce these effects, several strategies can strengthen user control and help protect against emotional harm, as mentioned in Figure 5.3. The figure illustrates five interconnected pathways, Transparency, Contestability, Data Control, Inclusive Design, and AI Literacy, that collectively lead to greater user empowerment in AI-mediated environments. Systems that allow individuals to question automated decisions can restore a sense of fairness. When users can contest or request reviews of outcomes, especially when those outcomes limit communication or access, trust is partially rebuilt. Introducing structured processes for redress has been shown to improve emotional responses to automated systems (Fanni et al., 2022). Improving *transparency* through AI education is also key. When people

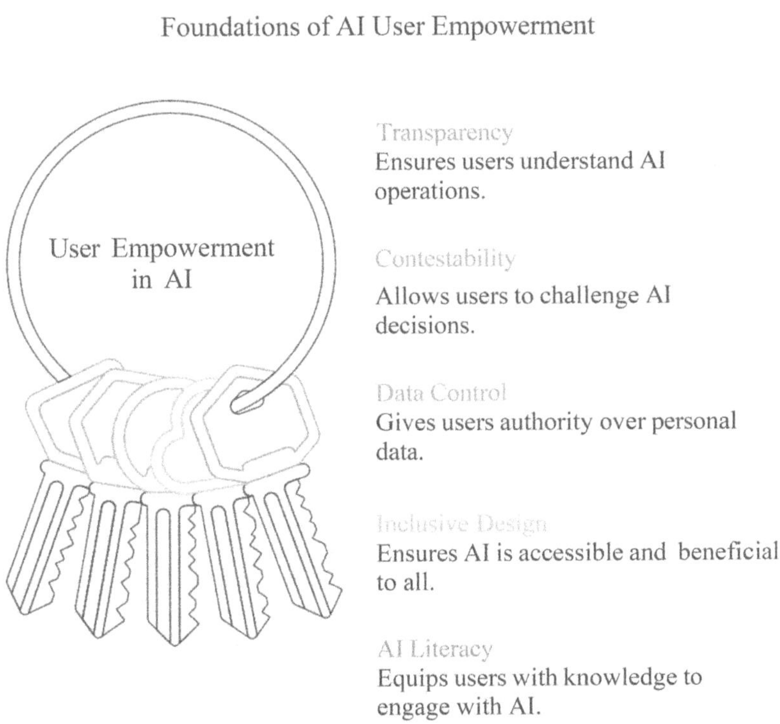

FIGURE 5.3 User empowerment map for regaining control over AI.

understand how AI tools work and what types of data are being collected, they are less likely to feel manipulated or powerless. Knowledge builds resilience. Educational efforts that help users understand and interpret AI behaviors, such as why a particular video was recommended or how their activity contributes to future suggestions, can reduce stress and foster confidence in digital decision-making (Chuan et al., 2023). Platforms can also provide users with the option to control data use or opt out of specific features. This allows individuals to set boundaries for how much of their activity is tracked and used. Such control supports mental well-being by reducing the sense of exposure and making interactions more manageable. When clearly explained, privacy settings and personalization controls have been shown to ease emotional discomfort. Establishing ethical AI policies is equally necessary. Clear commitments to privacy, fairness, and transparency, paired with regular audits, help establish accountability. Policies alone are not sufficient, but they serve as a framework to design systems that respect emotional health. When users know that checks are in place, it reduces the fear of arbitrary decisions. Designing with the user in mind also requires their presence in the design process. By inviting people from diverse communities to participate in shaping AI tools, developers can ensure that systems reflect a broader range of experiences. This input helps identify potential harms early and encourages inclusive practices. When people see their feedback incorporated, it improves satisfaction and trust. Finally, digital literacy programs can increase the capacity of users to engage safely. These programs teach people to question information, understand digital footprints, and recognize when systems may be working against their interests. This literacy builds a sense of control and reduces the psychological burden of online engagement (Egunjobi & Adeyeye, 2024). Although these mitigation strategies address the systemic ethical risks in AI design, individual psychological characteristics also play a crucial role in determining how users experience and respond to these risks. Not all users are equally vulnerable to the mental health impacts of AI-mediated environments. The following section examines the psychological moderators, personality traits, developmental stage, and digital literacy that shape individual resilience and susceptibility to AI's mental health effects (Table 5.3).

> ***Takeaway:*** *Ethical risks in AI do not only result in system inefficiencies but can leave lasting marks on emotional well-being. Addressing these concerns requires practical design changes and active user inclusion.*
> ***Reflection:*** *How might digital systems be shaping your experience without giving you the chance to question or adjust them?*

TABLE 5.3 Comparative Framework: Ethical AI Risks, Psychological Impacts, User Responses, and Mitigation Strategies

Ethical AI Risk	*Psychological Impact*	*User Response*	*Mitigation Strategy*
Opaque Personalization	Anxiety, unease, perceived loss of control	Mistrust, discomfort with platforms	Transparency tools, AI literacy education
Surveillance	Stress, hypervigilance, emotional exhaustion	Guarded behavior, withdrawal from digital spaces	Opt-out features, privacy settings
Biased Moderation	Frustration, helplessness, emotional fatigue	Reduced platform engagement, appeals fatigue	Structured appeals, human oversight
Algorithmic Bias	Distress, mistrust, social exclusion	Heightened emotional sensitivity, skepticism	Diverse user feedback, ethical audits

5.4 Personality Traits and Psychological Moderators of AI's Mental Health Effects

Not every individual responds to AI systems in the same way. As discussed in Chapter 4 (Section 4.2.5), individual differences in personality traits, developmental stage, and digital literacy moderate the extent to which AI mechanisms influence behavior. This section extends that analysis to examine how psychological characteristics specifically moderate mental health outcomes. Differences in emotional sensitivity, cognitive style, and personal history, especially traumatic experiences, all contribute to how people perceive and are affected by interactions with AI. These moderators help explain why some users adapt comfortably to AI-driven environments while others experience strain or distress, as shown in Figure 5.4. *Emotional sensitivity* influences how people interpret emotionally charged content or automated feedback. This closely relates to the neuroticism dimension of the Big Five personality framework (Chapter 2), where individuals high in neuroticism are more vulnerable to emotionally charged content amplified through AI feedback loops. Individuals with heightened emotional responsiveness may experience stronger emotional reactions to AI-generated interactions. When these systems are abrupt, impersonal, or provide poorly timed recommendations, they may lead to anxiety or distress. This group may also be more vulnerable to emotional exhaustion if the AI interface frequently triggers strong affective states. *Cognitive style* also plays a defining role in shaping user experience. Individuals who favor analytical processing tend to seek systems that provide logic, clarity, and data-backed outputs. They often respond better to interfaces that explain processes and provide transparency. In contrast, those with a more intuitive or holistic approach

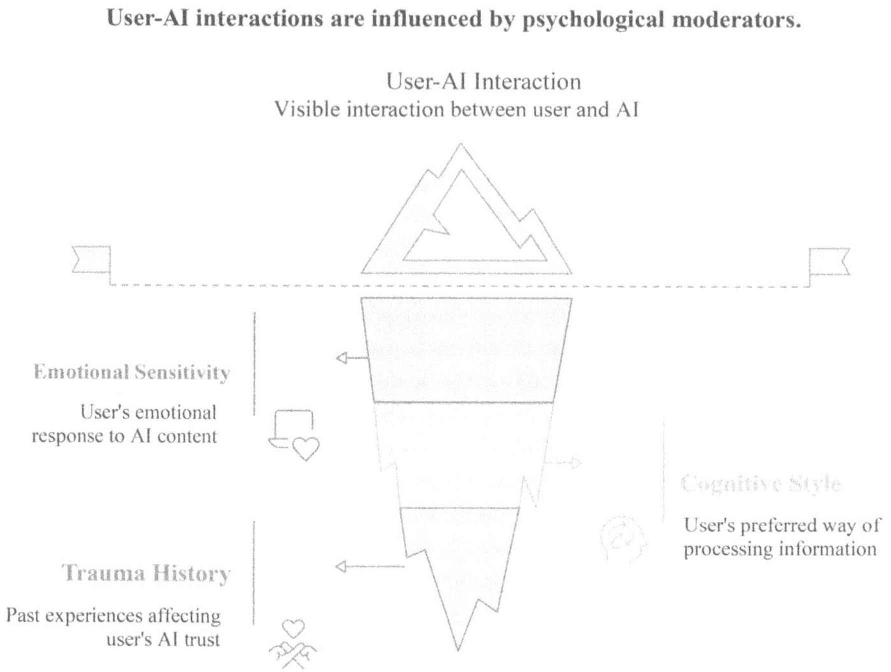

FIGURE 5.4 User–AI interaction pathways moderated by psychological factors.

may respond more positively to AI that presents information in contextual, broad-pattern formats. Misalignment between AI presentation and cognitive style can frustrate users or make the experience feel alienating. *Trauma history* adds another layer of complexity. Individuals with past trauma may be sensitive to systems that create feelings of unpredictability, lack of control, or impersonality. AI-generated recommendations, moderation decisions, or alerts may echo earlier experiences of helplessness or exclusion. These responses are not abstract. Research has shown that early traumatic experiences can distort how individuals perceive automated decisions, making even routine interactions feel threatening (Back et al., 2021).

This highlights the importance of moving beyond generalized personality traits when designing AI systems. While personality frameworks provide structure, focusing on specific psychological characteristics allows for a more tailored understanding of user needs. Such awareness encourages design approaches that respond with empathy to users' psychological histories and processing styles. A particularly strong area where this plays out is in education. In AI-based learning environments, cognitive preferences influence how students interact with instructional tools. Research in design education has noted that although broad learning styles are not strongly predictive of perceived usability, visual and kinesthetic learners tend to show greater engagement when the interface aligns with their preferred learning methods (Chandrasekera et al., 2024). This supports the idea that when AI tools respect users' mental habits, engagement and outcomes improve. A further layer of engagement arises

TABLE 5.4 A Grid Comparing Emotional Sensitivity, Cognitive Style, and Trauma History as Moderators of AI Interaction

Moderator Type	*Typical User Response*	*AI Triggers*	*Design Recommendations*	*Risk of Negative Impact*
Emotional Sensitivity	Heightened emotional reactions, anxiety, avoidance	Harsh tone, lack of emotional calibration, abrupt feedback	Use gentle language, allow emotional pacing, add empathetic cues	Emotional exhaustion, overreaction to content
Cognitive Style	Frustration or disconnection when format mismatches	Dense text, illogical layouts, rigid structure	Offer multiple interface styles, allow mode switching	Lower engagement, cognitive fatigue
Trauma History	Hypervigilance, mistrust, emotional withdrawal	Sudden changes, surveillance-like features, lack of control	Prioritize predictability, offer manual overrides, explain actions	Emotional retraumatization, platform disengagement

from how users perceive their learning progress. Platforms that adapt not only to learning speed but also to confidence levels and motivation are more likely to sustain interest. This directly relates to the self-efficacy component of Social Cognitive Theory (Chapter 2), where AI systems can either support or undermine users' beliefs in their own capabilities. Positive feedback loops, intuitive interfaces, and clear milestones appeal differently to individuals with varying cognitive orientations (Li et al., 2024). Those who seek structure respond well to guided paths and linear content, while exploratory learners may engage more deeply with open-ended tools and flexible navigation. Outside of education, cognitive style also matters in commerce and informal online learning. AI systems that personalize product recommendations, adjust browsing layouts, or tailor tutorials often rely on pattern recognition from user behavior. When these adaptations align with a user's preferred method of processing information, whether through images, summaries, or interaction, engagement tends to increase. Satisfaction and usability ratings are also higher in these cases (Ünlü, 2024). Table 5.4 shows a summary of a grid comparing emotional sensitivity, cognitive style, and trauma history as moderators of AI interaction.

The design of AI systems that account for individual moderators is not just a matter of personalization but also one of ethical responsibility. Systems that ignore psychological variability risk marginalizing users who do not conform to dominant cognitive or emotional norms. Incorporating flexibility in interaction style, feedback tone, and decision explanation allows a wider range of users to engage without strain. Having examined how individual psychological characteristics moderate the effects of AI on mental health, the analysis now shifts to exploring AI's potential as a tool for supporting mental health. Although the preceding sections have focused primarily on risks, the following section examines how the same AI mechanisms can be intentionally designed to promote well-being, emotional literacy, and therapeutic outcomes.

> ***Takeaway:*** *Human responses to AI are shaped by deeply personal factors. Understanding these moderators makes it possible to create systems that reduce psychological strain and support user trust.*
> ***Reflection:*** *Could the way AI systems speak, recommend, or respond be affecting you more than you notice?*

5.5 AI as a Tool for Mental Health Support

AI is increasingly recognized for its potential in supporting psychological well-being. As explored in Chapter 4 (Section 4.6), the same AI mechanisms that can amplify harmful behaviors can also be redirected toward positive outcomes when designed with ethical intent. This section examines how AI is being deployed specifically for mental health support, extending the analysis from general positive engagement to targeted therapeutic applications. Applications include digital therapeutics, early detection systems, and tools that provide tailored emotional support. These technologies offer alternatives and supplements to conventional mental health services, especially in contexts where accessibility, personalization, or continuous care is limited. Digital therapeutics refer to interventions delivered via software, often supported by AI. These systems provide structured support through interactive platforms such as mobile applications or virtual environments. In the context of youth psychiatry, they have been shown to increase accessibility and reduce cost barriers. Tools that utilize AI can adjust their content based on user responses, enabling the system to adapt and provide more personalized guidance. This adaptive personalization utilizes the same recommendation algorithms and feedback loops detailed in Chapter 4 but redirects them from maximizing engagement to supporting therapeutic progress. These technologies enable therapy to be more scalable while maintaining responsiveness to patient needs (Choi et al., 2023). As discussed earlier, these systems can support the development of self-efficacy (Social Cognitive Theory, Chapter 2) by providing consistent, non-judgmental feedback. Some platforms even integrate symptom tracking to adjust interventions in real time, linking therapeutic actions directly to changes in user behavior and self-report (Palanica et al., 2020). Another area where AI shows promise is the early detection of mental health conditions. These systems analyze large volumes of behavioral data to flag patterns linked with anxiety, depression, and other disorders. The algorithms are capable of processing multiple indicators simultaneously, offering more detailed assessments than many standardized tools. Recent studies have shown that models such as Random Forest and LSTM achieve high diagnostic accuracy, enabling quicker identification and potentially earlier intervention (Dakanalis et al., 2024). This predictive capability can help professionals develop informed preventive strategies based on ongoing behavioral monitoring. Personalized emotional support systems, including AI-based conversational agents, are also playing an increasingly important role in mental health care. These systems interact with users through language-based exchanges and use sentiment analysis to respond appropriately. Their value lies in their availability, allowing individuals to access support at any time. Some platforms also offer feedback designed to promote self-regulation, confidence, and resilience (Panse, 2025). Others simulate social interactions to help users practice emotional recognition or strengthen interpersonal skills (Figure 5.5).

Beyond therapeutic support, AI also broadens the scope of what is possible in mental health interventions. Table 5.5 shows a comparison between traditional therapy and AI-supported mental health tools. Some tools now incorporate creative methods, such as AI-assisted art therapy, allowing users to express emotional states through visual media. This is particularly valuable for individuals who may struggle with verbal communication (Luo et al., 2024). AI also offers meaningful

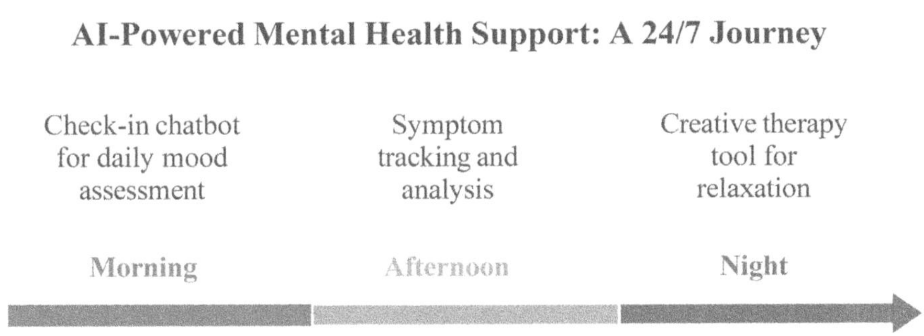

FIGURE 5.5 Timeline of AI-based mental health support.

TABLE 5.5 Comparison That Summarizes the Differences between Traditional Therapy and AI-Supported Mental Health Tools

Dimension	*Traditional Therapy*	*AI-Supported Mental Health Tools*
Accessibility	Requires scheduling, location-dependent, limited availability	Available 24/7, accessible from anywhere, suitable for underserved areas
Personalization	Relies on therapist intuition and time to adjust treatment	Adapts in real time using user data and behavioral cues
Emotional Responsiveness	High empathy, detailed emotional understanding	Limited empathy; uses sentiment analysis to simulate emotional feedback
Scalability	Limited by number of trained therapists	High scalability with minimal cost per additional user
Ethical Oversight	Regulated by professional standards and licensure	Varies by system; concerns over data use, consent, and algorithmic biases

advantages in terms of accessibility. Traditional therapy often requires scheduled sessions, proximity to clinics, and therapist availability. AI systems, however, operate across time zones and physical limitations, reducing logistical burdens. These systems can be embedded into users' routines and accessed privately, potentially reducing stigma and increasing consistency of engagement (Cheng et al., 2024). Nevertheless, this expansion of AI in mental health raises concerns. There are open questions about the depth of empathy these systems can provide, the risks associated with misdiagnosis, and the implications of relying on automated emotional assessments. These concerns echo the ethical risks discussed in Section 5.3, particularly regarding algorithmic bias, data privacy, and the erosion of user autonomy. Ethical concerns about data handling, consent, and long-term effects remain significant. Any deployment of AI-based mental health tools should be accompanied by oversight mechanisms, transparent data use policies, and opportunities for human review (Darzi, 2023). Comparisons with traditional therapy highlight both the strengths and limitations of AI-driven approaches. While traditional therapy offers deep relational bonds and skilled human intuition, it is less scalable and may not provide continuous feedback. AI can support therapists by monitoring changes in patient behavior and offering supplemental insights, potentially enhancing treatment plans and reducing clinician workload. Although AI-based mental health tools offer significant promise, their effectiveness and ethical deployment depend on the design principles that guide their development. The potential benefits documented in this section can only be realized if AI systems are built with explicit commitments to transparency, user autonomy, and psychological well-being. The following section examines the ethical design principles and policy frameworks necessary to ensure that AI serves mental health rather than undermining it.

> ***Takeaway:*** *AI systems are beginning to provide mental health support that is personalized, continuous, and scalable. These tools are not a replacement for human care but can fill critical gaps in support.*
> ***Reflection:*** *If support were available at all hours, tailored to your state of mind, how would that change the way you care for yourself or others?*

5.6 Ethical AI Design for Psychological Well-being

Ethical design in AI systems is crucial for protecting users from psychological harm and promoting their overall well-being. This section synthesizes the ethical risks identified in Section 5.3 with the positive potential explored in Section 5.5, offering a forward-facing framework rooted in ethical responsibility. Critically, ethical AI design must account for personality-based differences in vulnerability and preference, recognizing that universal design principles may have differential impacts across the spectrum of psychological diversity. The aim is to ensure that AI systems not only avoid harm but also create conditions that support mental health and foster equitable digital interactions.

Transparency remains one of the most fundamental elements of ethical AI development. Systems must be designed to clearly communicate how decisions are made, what data is collected, and how that data is used. When transparency is lacking, users may feel vulnerable or suspicious, which can weaken trust and increase emotional strain. As discussed in Section 5.3, when transparency is lacking, users experience anxiety and a perceived loss of control, which directly undermines the autonomy component of the Theory of Planned Behavior (Chapter 2). The demand for transparency is particularly strong among users high in openness to experience, who value understanding system logic, while users high in agreeableness may prioritize relational trust over technical transparency. Open communication about system operations helps users understand and interpret outcomes more confidently, which in turn supports psychological safety (Saeidnia et al., 2024).

Inclusivity ensures that AI technologies reflect the needs and experiences of diverse populations. This principle directly addresses the cultural considerations discussed in Chapter 3 (Section 3.5.1), recognizing that the cybernetic self is shaped by culturally specific norms and values. Beyond cultural diversity, inclusivity must also include personality diversity, ensuring that AI systems do not privilege certain personality profiles (e.g., high conscientiousness, low neuroticism) while marginalizing others. Engaging a broad range of users, including those from marginalized or historically excluded groups, in the design and testing phases can reduce disparities and prevent biased outcomes. This proactive inclusion improves system relevance and fairness, particularly for users who may already face societal disadvantages (Sqalli et al., 2023).

Designing for harm reduction is another key priority. AI systems must be constructed with safeguards that prevent or minimize risks to users, such as algorithmic discrimination, misinformation, or intrusive surveillance. These protective strategies are especially important in mental health contexts, where sensitive data and emotional states are involved. The goal is to create environments that are psychologically secure and that respond appropriately when unintended harms occur (Saeidnia et al., 2024).

Mitigating bias through fairness-aware design practices helps prevent patterns of exclusion or harm in AI decisions. This involves curating diverse datasets, regularly testing systems for disparities, and refining algorithms based on those assessments. When fairness is prioritized, AI can support more just outcomes, reducing emotional fatigue and the sense of systemic bias that can impact users' mental health (Jedličková, 2024).

Accountability structures ensure that AI developers and operators take responsibility for how their systems function and the impact they have on people. When users can identify who is answerable for system errors or harm, they are more likely to feel respected and protected. This clarity supports not only legal compliance but also emotional assurance and ethical engagement (Aldosari et al., 2025).

Data privacy and security are vital for fostering psychological safety in AI environments. When systems collect sensitive personal data, particularly data related to mental health, they must be designed with strong protection mechanisms to prevent breaches. Respecting privacy helps preserve user dignity and prevents the anxiety associated with unwanted surveillance or misuse of personal information (Zlateva et al., 2024). Finally, AI systems should be designed to uphold user autonomy and empowerment. This means allowing users to make informed choices, control their data, and opt out of functions that do not align with their comfort levels. Empowerment strategies should be tailored to personality profiles: users high in conscientiousness may prefer detailed control panels and granular privacy settings, while those high in agreeableness may value simpler, trust-based defaults with clear opt-out mechanisms. Empowerment reduces helplessness and supports a stronger sense of agency, which is essential for psychological well-being in digitally mediated spaces (Saeidnia et al., 2024).

Takeaway: *Ethical design of AI systems should prioritize inclusion, transparency, and harm reduction to safeguard mental health in diverse user populations.*
Reflection: *When using AI tools, do you feel informed, respected, and in control, or are there moments where the technology seems to decide for you, without your input or consent?*

5.7 Policy, Education, and Design Interventions

Although ethical design principles provide the foundation for responsible AI development, their implementation requires coordinated action across multiple stakeholder groups. Promoting responsible AI use and advancing mental health literacy in cyberspaces requires targeted efforts across education, development, and policy. Each stakeholder, including educators, developers, and policymakers, has a distinct role in shaping environments that support psychological well-being and informed participation through technology. Educators are well-positioned to prepare individuals for thoughtful interaction with AI. One effective strategy is to incorporate AI literacy into school and university curricula, not only teaching how AI systems function but also addressing ethical concerns such as data use and bias (Ng et al., 2023). This educational approach directly addresses the digital literacy moderator discussed in Section 4.2.5, which showed that users who understand AI mechanisms are better positioned to resist manipulation. Alongside this, mental health literacy should be integrated into the curriculum to help students understand the psychological risks associated with digital life. Importantly, mental health literacy education should include awareness of how personality traits moderate the psychological impacts of AI, helping students recognize their own vulnerabilities and strengths in AI-mediated environments. This dual literacy empowers them to recognize when AI tools may affect their mental state and how to respond. Furthermore, interdisciplinary learning, such as projects combining AI with psychology or ethics, can deepen understanding and encourage critical thinking (Suwanwong et al., 2024; Wu & Zhang, 2025).

Developers contribute by embedding ethical safeguards in the systems they create. Ethical design begins with attention to fairness, privacy, and psychological safety from the earliest stages of development (Malerbi et al., 2023). As emphasized in Section 4.6, youth-centered and participatory design approaches are crucial for developing AI systems that acknowledge developmental vulnerabilities and foster positive outcomes. Developers should also consider implementing adaptive interfaces that adjust interaction styles based on inferred or self-reported personality profiles, providing more structured experiences for conscientious users and more flexible, exploratory interfaces for those high in openness. Developers should actively include user perspectives throughout the design process to shape more responsive and emotionally supportive tools (Gamble, 2020). It is also essential that privacy protocols are not treated as secondary features. Instead, strong data protections should be integral to every platform handling personal or mental health-related information (Love et al., 2025).

Policymakers play a central role in shaping the broader environment in which AI and mental health systems operate. They can support responsible AI use by introducing clear frameworks that guide ethical practices in the tech sector. This includes rules addressing user consent, fairness, and equitable access to technologies (Malerbi et al., 2023). Additionally, governments can lead national initiatives to enhance public understanding of AI through community workshops, school-based programs, or online courses (Kaur & Chen, 2023). Supporting cross-sector collaborations between academia, industry, and public agencies will further strengthen innovation and practical solutions (Yang et al., 2025).

To understand the effects of these efforts, policymakers and educators need ways to measure public engagement with AI literacy. Validated tools such as the Artificial Intelligence Literacy Scale help track awareness and ethical understanding among users (Hossain et al., 2025). Surveys conducted across schools and workplaces can reveal how people perceive AI, their level of confidence in using it, and their awareness of its potential mental health implications (Wang et al., 2025). Beyond surveys, using structural analysis techniques can reveal connections between literacy and behaviors like responsible usage or help-seeking. Combining these findings with qualitative data from focus groups and interviews provides a more comprehensive picture of how well the interventions are working (Kaur & Chen, 2023). Long-term tracking of AI literacy programs is equally valuable. Over time, such studies demonstrate whether improvements are sustained or if new challenges emerge (Yeter et al., 2024). Stakeholder participation throughout the evaluation process ensures that assessments reflect community needs and perspectives (Fazil et al., 2024). By coordinating education, ethical design, and supportive policy, it is possible to create digital environments where technology aligns with mental health goals. These interventions do not work in isolation; together, they build a foundation for safe, respectful, and informed engagement with AI. The coordinated efforts outlined in this section – ethical design principles, educational initiatives, developer practices, and policy frameworks – represent the practical implementation of the theoretical insights developed throughout this chapter and the broader manuscript. The following conclusion synthesizes these insights, reflecting on how the AI-behavior-mental health nexus can be understood and addressed through an integrated framework that spans behavioral theory, developmental psychology, technological architecture, and ethical practices.

> ***Takeaway:*** *Policymakers and educators play a key role in promoting mental health and ethical AI use through regulation, curriculum design, and awareness campaigns.*
> ***Reflection:*** *How can schools, companies, or governments better support ethical digital engagement and mental well-being?*

5.8 Summary and Reflections

This chapter has examined the complex three-way interplay between AI, cyber behavior, and mental health, which we have termed "Algorithmic Well-being", synthesizing insights from the behavioral theories (Chapter 2), developmental frameworks (Chapter 3), and AI mechanisms (Chapter 4) established earlier in this chapter. The central argument advanced throughout this chapter is that mental health outcomes in AI-mediated environments are not uniform but are significantly moderated by individual personality traits, particularly the Big Five dimensions introduced in Chapter 2. It began by establishing that AI systems are not neutral tools but active agents that shape digital experiences and, by extension, psychological states. The recommendation algorithms, feedback loops, and engagement optimization mechanisms detailed in Chapter 4 function as behavioral architects, influencing how users feel, act, and think through processes that operate largely outside conscious awareness. These mechanisms interact with personality traits in predictable ways: individuals high in neuroticism experience heightened algorithmic anxiety and vulnerability to social comparison; those low in conscientiousness are more susceptible to compulsive digital use; and individuals high in openness to experience are both more resistant to filter bubbles and more disturbed by algorithmic opacity. Personalized feeds, algorithmic decision-making, and invisible moderation structures influence how users feel, act, and think, often without their full awareness. These subtle forms of influence raise significant concerns about stress, disconnection, and emotional exhaustion, especially among younger populations whose cybernetic selves (Chapter 3) are still being formed through these very interactions.

The discussion expanded beyond risks to consider broader individual differences that influence how people interact with AI environments. Building on the analysis of personality traits (Big Five, Chapter 2) and developmental stage (Chapter 3) as moderators of AI influence (Section 4.2.5), this chapter examined how emotional sensitivity, trauma history, and cognitive style all mediate the mental health outcomes of digital interaction. The integration of personality psychology with AI mechanisms reveals a critical insight: the same algorithmic system can promote flourishing in one user while causing distress in another, depending on their personality profile. For example, AI-powered mental health chatbots may effectively support individuals high in conscientiousness (who respond well to structured interventions) while failing to meet the relational needs of those high in extraversion. This recognition of psychological diversity is not merely academic; it has profound implications for how AI systems should be designed, evaluated, and regulated. Recognizing these factors shifts the conversation away from generalizations and encourages more targeted approaches to support. Psychological diversity must be acknowledged in the design, study, and application of AI.

Ethical concerns were explored in depth. Surveillance, personalization, opacity, and bias in moderation systems were shown to reduce trust and contribute to emotional fatigue. These risks directly undermine the perceived behavioral control and autonomy components of the Theory of Planned Behavior (Chapter 2), creating environments where users feel powerless to shape their own digital experiences. The psychological impact of these ethical failures is not evenly distributed: individuals high in neuroticism experience amplified distress from surveillance and biased moderation, while those high in openness to experience are particularly frustrated by algorithmic opacity. This intersection of ethical design and personality psychology highlights the need for user-centered AI systems that take into account individual differences in vulnerability. These risks demand thoughtful system design rooted in transparency, fairness, and harm reduction. Ethical frameworks must go beyond compliance and actively promote psychological well-being through accountability, user control, and inclusion.

The chapter also addressed how AI can support mental health. From early detection tools to AI-supported therapy and personalized emotional support, technology offers new pathways for care. As demonstrated in Section 4.6, the same AI mechanisms that amplify harmful behaviors can be redirected toward supporting emotional literacy, empathy, and self-efficacy (Social Cognitive Theory, Chapter 2) when designed with ethical intent. Critically, the effectiveness of these positive applications depends on matching intervention design to personality profiles. Transparency tools benefit those high in openness; structured contestability processes appeal to those high in conscientiousness; and emotionally calibrated interfaces are essential for those high in neuroticism. Personalization in mental health AI must extend beyond content to encompass interaction style, feedback tone, and support for autonomy. However, these innovations are most effective when integrated with human understanding, robust ethical safeguards, and robust privacy protections. AI alone cannot substitute for empathy, but it can extend the reach of mental health support when designed with care.

Education, policy, and development practices were identified as key drivers of responsible AI. Teachers can foster literacy that helps students critically understand the influence of AI. Developers can build more equitable systems through user-centered design. Policymakers can set guardrails that ensure technologies respect individual dignity and public well-being, particularly for vulnerable populations such as adolescents navigating critical developmental transitions (Chapter 3). Together, these actors help build environments where AI supports rather than threatens mental health.

Still, the field is undergoing rapid change. Key questions remain unanswered. What types of mental health challenges are most likely to emerge in AI-mediated spaces? How can system designers account for trauma or emotional sensitivity without overgeneralizing? What forms of evaluation are most effective in tracking the long-term effects of AI use on psychological well-being? How do cultural contexts (Chapter 3, Section 3.5.1) shape the mental health impacts of AI systems designed primarily in Western contexts? How can the risk spectrum framework (Section 4.5.2) be operationalized to guide real-time interventions? Most importantly, how can AI systems be designed to adapt dynamically to users' personality profiles, providing differentiated experiences that support flourishing across the full spectrum of psychological diversity? Can machine learning models be trained to detect personality-based vulnerabilities and adjust their behavior accordingly, for instance, by reducing engagement optimization tactics for users exhibiting signs of compulsive use or by providing additional transparency for those high in openness to experience? These questions are not just technical. They require sound ethical judgment, interdisciplinary collaboration, and sustained long-term research.

This chapter, together with the preceding chapters, provides a comprehensive framework for understanding the AI-behavior-mental health nexus through the lens of Algorithmic Well-being. Chapter 2 established the behavioral and personality foundations; Chapter 3 introduced the cybernetic self as the site where AI and identity intersect; Chapter 4 detailed the technical mechanisms through which AI shapes behavior; and this chapter has synthesized these elements to reveal how personality traits moderate the mental health impacts of AI-mediated life. However, the future of AI and mental health will depend on how seriously society takes the task of shaping digital systems to support human well-being, not just functionally but emotionally, socially, and ethically. The cybernetic self is not a fixed entity but an ongoing process of co-construction between human agency and technological affordances. Our collective responsibility is to ensure that this co-construction leads toward flourishing rather than fragmentation. The cybernetic self is not a fixed entity but an ongoing process of co-construction between human agency and technological affordances, a process fundamentally shaped by the personality traits that make each individual unique. Our collective responsibility is to ensure that this co-construction leads toward flourishing rather than fragmentation, supporting the full diversity of human psychological experience. The concept of Algorithmic Well-being provides a roadmap: by integrating behavioral theory (Chapter 2), developmental psychology (Chapter 3), AI mechanisms (Chapter 4), and personality-based moderation (this chapter), we can build digital environments that honor the complexity of human psychology and promote mental health for all users, regardless of their personality profile.

References

Aldosari, B., Aldosari, H., & Alanazi, A. (2025). Challenges of artificial intelligence in Medicine. *Studies in Health Technology and Informatics*. https://doi.org/10.3233/shti250039

Azhari, A., Toms, Z., Pavlopoulou, G., Esposito, G., & Dimitriou, D. (2022). Social media use in female adolescents: Associations with anxiety, loneliness, and sleep disturbances. *Acta Psychologica*, *229*, 103706. https://doi.org/10.1016/j.actpsy.2022.103706

Back, S. N., Flechsenhar, A., Bertsch, K., & Zettl, M. (2021). Childhood traumatic experiences and dimensional models of personality disorder in DSM-5 and ICD-11: Opportunities and challenges. *Current Psychiatry Reports*, *23*(9). https://doi.org/10.1007/s11920-021-01265-5

Bongurala, A. R., Save, D., & Virmani, A. (2025). Progressive role of artificial intelligence in treatment decision-making in the field of medical oncology. *Frontiers in Medicine*, *12*. https://doi.org/10.3389/fmed.2025.1533910

Chandrasekera, T., Hosseini, Z., Perera, U., & Hyscher, A. B. (2024). Generative artificial intelligence tools for diverse learning styles in design education. *International Journal of Architectural Computing*. https://doi.org/10.1177/14780771241287345

Cheng, S., Xiao, Y., Liu, L., & Sun, X. (2024). Comparative outcomes of AI-assisted ChatGPT and face-to-face consultations in infertility patients: A cross-sectional study. *Postgraduate Medical Journal*, *100*(1189), 851–855. https://doi.org/10.1093/postmj/qgae083

Choi, H., Kim, B., Kim, I., Kang, J., Lee, Y., Lee, H., & Park, M. (2023). Analysis of the status and future direction for digital therapeutics in children and adolescent Psychiatry. *Journal of Korean Academy of Child and Adolescent Psychiatry*, *34*(4), 192–203. https://doi.org/10.5765/jkacap.230044

Christoforaki, M., & Beyan, O. (2022). AI ethics—A bird's eye view. *Applied Sciences*, *12*(9), 4130. https://doi.org/10.3390/app12094130

Chuan, C., Tsai, W. S., & Yang, J. (2023). Artificial intelligence, advertising, and society. *Advertising & Society Quarterly*, *24*(3). https://doi.org/10.1353/asr.2023.a911198

Dakanalis, A., Wiederhold, B. K., & Riva, G. (2024). Artificial intelligence: A game-changer for mental health care. *Cyberpsychology Behavior and Social Networking*, *27*(2), 100–104. https://doi.org/10.1089/cyber.2023.0723

Darzi, P. (2023). Could artificial intelligence be a therapeutic for mental issues? *Science Insights*, *43*(5), 1111–1113. https://doi.org/10.15354/si.23.co132

Draganidis, A., Fernando, A. N., West, M. L., & Sharp, G. (2024). Social media delivered mental health campaigns and public service announcements: A systematic literature review of public Engagement and Help-Seeking behaviours. *Social Science & Medicine*, *359*, 117231. https://doi.org/10.1016/j.socscimed.2024.117231

Egunjobi, D., & Adeyeye, O. J. (2024). Revolutionizing learning: The impact of augmented reality (AR) and artificial intelligence (AI on education). *International Journal of Research Publication and Reviews*, *5*(10), 1157–1170. https://doi.org/10.55248/gengpi.5.1024.2734

Fanni, R., Steinkogler, V. E., Zampedri, G., & Pierson, J. (2022). Enhancing human agency through redress in artificial intelligence systems. *AI & Society*, *38*(2), 537–547. https://doi.org/10.1007/s00146-022-01454-7

Fardouly, J., Magson, N. R., Rapee, R. M., Johnco, C. J., & Oar, E. L. (2020). The use of social media by Australian preadolescents and its links with mental health. *Journal of Clinical Psychology*, *76*(7), 1304–1326. https://doi.org/10.1002/jclp.22936

Fazil, A. W., Hakimi, M., Shahidzay, A. K., & Hasas, A. (2024). Exploring the broad impact of AI technologies on student engagement and academic performance in university settings in Afghanistan. *RIGGS Journal of Artificial Intelligence and Digital Business*, *2*(2), 56–63. https://doi.org/10.31004/riggs.v2i2.268

Gamble, A. (2020). Artificial intelligence and mobile apps for mental healthcare: A social informatics perspective. *Aslib Journal of Information Management*, *72*(4), 509–523. https://doi.org/10.1108/ajim-11-2019-0316

Hendrikse, C., & Limniou, M. (2024). The use of Instagram and TikTok in relation to problematic use and Well-Being. *Journal of Technology in Behavioral Science*. https://doi.org/10.1007/s41347-024-00399-6

Hoge, E., Bickham, D., & Cantor, J. (2017). Digital media, anxiety, and depression in children. *Pediatrics*, *140*(Supplement_2), S76–S80. https://doi.org/10.1542/peds.2016-1758g

Hossain, Z., Çelik, Ö., & Hınız, G. (2025). Exploring EFL students' AI literacy in academic writing: Insights into familiarity, knowledge and ethical perceptions. *Kuramsal Eğitimbilim*, *18*(1), 157–181. https://doi.org/10.30831/akukeg.1538011

Hussain, A. (2024). The impact of artificial intelligence on digital media content creation. *International Journal of Innovative Science and Research Technology (IJISRT)*, 998–1003. https://doi.org/10.38124/ijisrt/ijisrt24jul927

Jedličková, A. (2024). Ethical approaches in designing autonomous and intelligent systems: A comprehensive survey towards responsible development. *AI & Society*. https://doi.org/10.1007/s00146-024-02040-9

Kaur, A., & Chen, W. (2023). Exploring AI literacy among older adults. *Studies in Health Technology and Informatics*. https://doi.org/10.3233/shti230589

Latha, K., Meena, K., Pravitha, Dasgupta, M., & Chaturvedi, S. (2020). Effective use of social media platforms for promotion of mental health awareness. *Journal of Education and Health Promotion*, *9*(1), 124. https://doi.org/10.4103/jehp.jehp_90_20

Li, W., Zhang, X., Li, J., Yang, X., Li, D., & Liu, Y. (2024). An explanatory study of factors influencing engagement in AI education at the K-12 Level: An extension of the classic TAM model. *Scientific Reports*, *14*(1). https://doi.org/10.1038/s41598-024-64363-3

Livingston, J. D., Tugwell, A., Korf-Uzan, K., Cianfrone, M., & Coniglio, C. (2012). Evaluation of a campaign to improve awareness and attitudes of young people towards mental health issues. *Social Psychiatry and Psychiatric Epidemiology*, *48*(6), 965–973. https://doi.org/10.1007/s00127-012-0617-3

Love, A. S., Niu, C., & Labay-Marquez, J. (2025). Artificial intelligence in public health education: Navigating ethical challenges and empowering the next generation of professionals. *Health Promotion Practice*. https://doi.org/10.1177/15248399251320989

Luo, X., Zhang, A., Li, Y., Zhang, Z., Ying, F., Lin, R., Yang, Q., Wang, J., & Huang, G. (2024). Emergence of Artificial Intelligence Art Therapies (AIATs) in mental health care: A systematic review. *International Journal of Mental Health Nursing*, *33*(6), 1743–1760. https://doi.org/10.1111/inm.13384

Mahat, M. (2021). Detecting cyberbullying across multiple social media platforms using deep learning. *2021 International Conference on Advance Computing and Innovative Technologies in Engineering (ICACITE)*. https://doi.org/10.1109/icacite51222.2021.9404736

Malerbi, F. K., Nakayama, L. F., Dychiao, R. G., Ribeiro, L. Z., Villanueva, C., Celi, L. A., & Regatieri, C. V. (2023). Digital education for the deployment of artificial intelligence in health care. *Journal of Medical Internet Research*, *25*, e43333. https://doi.org/10.2196/43333

Mehmet, M., Roberts, R., & Nayeem, T. (2020). Using digital and social media for health promotion: A social marketing approach for addressing co-morbid physical and mental health. *Australian Journal of Rural Health*, *28*(2), 149–158. https://doi.org/10.1111/ajr.12589

Mittal, A., Chaturvedi, D. D., Chaturvedi, S., & Singh, P. K. (2024). Impact of negative aspects of artificial intelligence on customer purchase intention. In *Advances in human resources management and organizational development book series* (pp. 159–173). https://doi.org/10.4018/979-8-3693-0724-3.ch010

Motta, M., Liu, Y., & Yarnell, A. (2024). "Influencing the influencers": A field experimental approach to promoting effective mental health communication on TikTok. *Scientific Reports*, *14*(1). https://doi.org/10.1038/s41598-024-56578-1

Ng, D. T. K., Su, J., Leung, J. K. L., & Chu, S. K. W. (2023). Artificial intelligence (AI) literacy education in secondary schools: A review. *Interactive Learning Environments*, 1–21. https://doi.org/10.1080/10494820.2023.2255228

Palanica, A., Docktor, M. J., Lieberman, M., & Fossat, Y. (2020). The need for artificial intelligence in digital therapeutics. *Digital Biomarkers*, *4*(1), 21–25. https://doi.org/10.1159/000506861

Panse, N. T. (2025). AI-Driven personality development: Enhancing emotional intelligence and social skills through machine learning. *Journal of Information Systems Engineering & Management*, *10*(12s), 763–776. https://doi.org/10.52783/jisem.v10i12s.1948

Pham, K. T., Nabizadeh, A., & Selek, S. (2022). Artificial intelligence and chatbots in psychiatry. *Psychiatric Quarterly*, *93*(1), 249–253. https://doi.org/10.1007/s11126-022-09973-8

Plackett, R., Steward, J., Kassianos, A. P., Duenger, M., Schartau, P., Sheringham, J., Cooper, S., Biddle, L., Kidger, J., & Walters, K. (2024). The effectiveness of social media campaigns in improving knowledge and attitudes towards mental health and help-seeking in high-income countries: A scoping review (Preprint). *Journal of Medical Internet Research*. https://doi.org/10.2196/68124

Poudel, U., Jakhar, S., Mohan, P., & Nepal, A. (2025). AI in mental health: A Review of technological advancements and ethical issues in psychiatry. *Issues in Mental Health Nursing*, 1–9. https://doi.org/10.1080/01612840.2025.2502943

Saeidnia, H. R., Fotami, S. G. H., Lund, B., & Ghiasi, N. (2024). Ethical considerations in artificial intelligence interventions for mental health and well-being: Ensuring responsible implementation and impact. *Social Sciences*, *13*(7), 381. https://doi.org/10.3390/socsci13070381

Sqalli, M. T., Aslonov, B., Gafurov, M., & Nurmatov, S. (2023). Humanizing AI in medical training: Ethical framework for responsible design. *Frontiers in Artificial Intelligence*, *6*. https://doi.org/10.3389/frai.2023.1189914

Sulaiman, W. a. W., Malek, M. D. H., Yunus, A. R., Ishak, N. H., Safir, D. M., & Fahrudin, A. (2024). The impact of social media on mental health: A comprehensive review. *South Eastern European Journal of Public Health*, 1468–1482. https://doi.org/10.70135/seejph.vi.2564

Suwanwong, C., Jansem, A., Intarakamhang, U., Prasittichok, P., Tuntivivat, S., Chuenphittayavut, K., Le, K., & Lien, L. T. M. (2024). Modifiable predictors of mental health literacy in the educational context: A systematic review and meta-analysis. *BMC Psychology*, *12*(1). https://doi.org/10.1186/s40359-024-01878-4

Ünlü, S. C. (2024). Enhancing user experience through AI-driven personalization in user interfaces. *Human Computer Interaction*, *8*(1), 19. https://doi.org/10.62802/m7mqmb52

Velastegui-Hernandez, D. C., Rodriguez-Pérez, M. L., & Salazar-Garcés, L. F. (2023). Impacto de la inteligencia artificial en las conductas de aprendizaje y el bienestar psicológico de los estudiantes universitarios: Revisión. *Salud Ciencia Y Tecnología - Serie De Conferencias*, *2*, 582. https://doi.org/10.56294/sctconf2023582

Vieriu, A. M., & Petrea, G. (2025). The impact of artificial intelligence (AI) on students' academic development. *Education Sciences*, *15*(3), 343. https://doi.org/10.3390/educsci15030343

Vyawahare, H., Khandelwal, S., & Rathod, S. (2024). Artificial intelligence in detecting and preventing online harassment. In *Advances in computational intelligence and robotics book series* (pp. 14–35). https://doi.org/10.4018/979-8-3693-1435-7.ch002

Wang, K., Cui, W., & Yuan, X. (2025). Artificial intelligence in higher education: The impact of need satisfaction on artificial intelligence literacy mediated by self-regulated learning strategies. *Behavioral Sciences*, *15*(2), 165. https://doi.org/10.3390/bs15020165

Wu, D., & Zhang, J. (2025). Generative artificial intelligence in secondary education: Applications and effects on students' innovation skills and digital literacy. *PLoS One*, *20*(5), e0323349. https://doi.org/10.1371/journal.pone.0323349

Yang, Y., Zhang, Y., Sun, D., He, W., & Wei, Y. (2025). Navigating the landscape of AI literacy education: Insights from a decade of research (2014–2024). *Humanities and Social Sciences Communications*, *12*(1). https://doi.org/10.1057/s41599-025-04583-8

Yeter, I. H., Yang, W., & Sturgess, J. B. (2024). Global initiatives and challenges in integrating artificial intelligence literacy in elementary education: Mapping policies and empirical literature. *Future in Educational Research*. https://doi.org/10.1002/fer3.59

Zlateva, P., Steshina, L., Petukhov, I., & Velev, D. (2024). A conceptual framework for solving ethical issues in generative Artificial intelligence. In *Frontiers in artificial intelligence and applications*. https://doi.org/10.3233/faia231182

6

AI ETHICAL USE AND ITS IMPACT ON MENTAL HEALTH

Chapter Objectives

- To establish a normative framework for ethical AI in mental health, grounded in core principles of beneficence, non-maleficence, justice, and autonomy.
- To analyze how these ethical principles translate into concrete design features and governance protocols for AI systems used in mental health contexts.
- To define the specific ethical obligations and heightened duty of care required when designing AI for vulnerable populations.
- To outline the ethical readiness conditions necessary for the responsible development and deployment of AI mental health technologies.

Topics to Be Covered

- Introduction: The Ethical Imperative in Mental Health AI
- Foundational Ethical Principles for Mental Well-being
- "Ethical by Design": From Principles to Practice
- Ethical Obligations Toward Vulnerable Populations
- Governance and Ethical Readiness

DOI: 10.4324/9781003657590-8

6.1 Introduction: The Ethical Imperative in Mental Health AI

Artificial intelligence (AI) is fundamentally reshaping how mental health support is offered, reached, and felt by users, introducing both unprecedented opportunities and significant ethical obligations. The shift is not only technical; it touches trust, safety, and dignity. Systems that read behavior, forecast risks, and suggest care now sit at the front door of help. This reach creates real benefits for access and timely support, as noted in Chapter 5, yet as that chapter also established, it introduces significant psychological and social risks. The potential for privacy invasions, algorithmic bias, and the erosion of the human therapeutic relationship (Nashwan et al., 2023; Yıldız, 2025) makes a robust ethical framework the absolute condition for safe use, not an optional layer added at the end. The question is not whether to use AI in mental health care, but how to use it responsibly.

As AI-driven tools become more integrated into mental health care (Ni & Jia, 2025), the urgency to govern them grows. The core challenge is to harness the benefits of AI, such as widened access and immediate support, without sacrificing the fundamental principles of care. This chapter moves the discussion from the psychological impacts of AI, which were analyzed in Chapter 5, to the normative duties and design principles required to mitigate them. Although Chapter 5 established what can go wrong psychologically, this chapter addresses how to prevent it through ethical design and governance. It addresses the question: *What constitutes ethical AI in mental health, and how can its design, governance, and deployment be structured to protect and promote psychological well-being?*

The aim across this chapter is careful, fair judgment. The goal is not simple answers but sound choices, given the trade-offs. This mirrors earlier chapters in this book that frame AI as a behavioral architect: the setting built by code shapes action, so those affected by that setting must help decide how it is built. To do so requires a clear understanding of the foundational ethical principles that must guide every stage of an AI system's lifecycle, from initial concept to deployment and beyond (see Figure 6.1). The following sections establish these principles, translate them into concrete design practices, and examine the heightened ethical obligations owed to vulnerable populations.

> ***Takeaway:*** *Ethical design is not optional in mental health AI; it is the foundation that allows beneficial innovation to proceed safely. The choice before organizations is not between ethics and innovation, but between innovation grounded in ethical principles and innovation that is not.*
>
> ***Reflection:*** *What does it mean to design AI for mental health "responsibly," and who should be involved in making decisions about what counts as responsible design?*

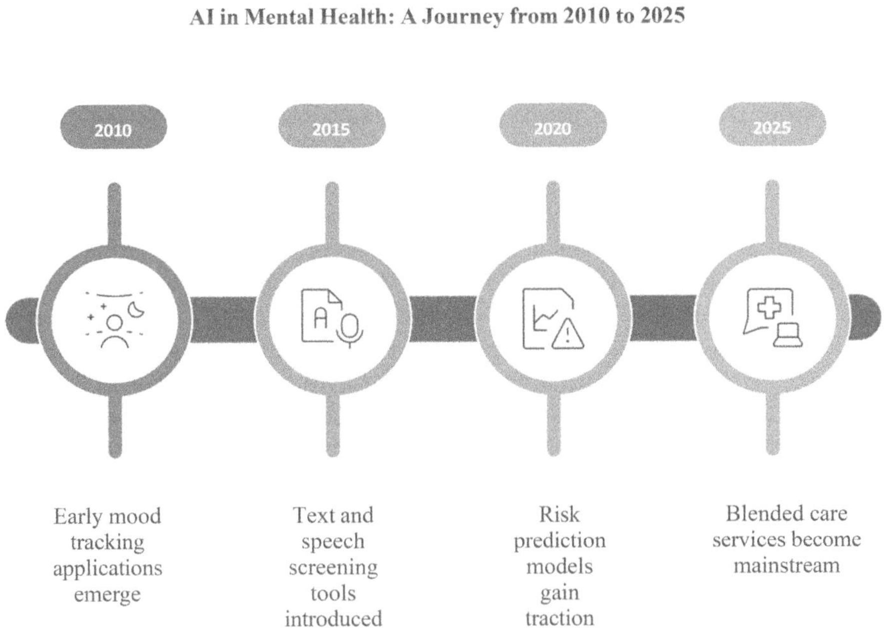

FIGURE 6.1 Timeline of AI-supported mental health tools from 2010 to 2025.

6.2 Foundational Ethical Principles for Mental Well-being

6.2.1 From Classical Ethics to Operational Principles

The promise of AI in mental health is substantial, but it comes with significant risks. Creative tools can support expression when words are hard to find, opening alternate routes to insight and relief (Luo et al., 2024). Pattern finding across day-to-day signals may reveal early warnings before crises develop, allowing for earlier and less intensive intervention. When used with care, these aids can extend the reach of services and free up time for tasks that require human presence most. Access gains matter for those far from care: in rural and low-resource settings, automated tools can offer guidance when no clinician is near. For those facing stigma, private use can lower the threshold to start. Young people, who move with ease across digital spaces, often accept such tools as a first step toward help and may prefer them to an office visit at the outset (Kumar et al., 2024). These gains and risks set the agenda for ethical design. Classical ethical principles still guide action, but they need a specific form in this context. Beneficence requires designs that prioritize genuine well-being over optimizing clicks or session length. Nonmaleficence requires tight controls on privacy, bias, and misclassification. Autonomy requires consent and control that people can understand and utilize, even when systems influence choices through prompts and defaults. Justice requires both fair performance across groups and fair access, where devices, cost, or connectivity would otherwise exclude individuals.

These classical principles provide the ethical foundation, but translating them into practice requires a structured approach. The ethical development and deployment pathway shown in Figure 6.2 illustrates how these principles are operationalized across the full lifecycle of an AI system, from initial concept through post-deployment monitoring. Each checkpoint in this pathway is designed to embed ethical considerations into the development process, not as an afterthought but as a continuous practice. The pathway begins with community co-design, ensuring that those most affected by the tool, users, clinicians, and affected communities, have a voice in shaping the system from the outset. This operationalizes the principle of justice by centering the perspectives of those who will be most impacted. Data minimization and bias testing by subgroup translate the principle of non-maleficence into technical practice: collecting only what is necessary and testing performance across demographic groups to prevent unequal harm. Usability and comprehension testing for consent operationalizes autonomy by ensuring that consent is not just legally compliant but genuinely understood by users.

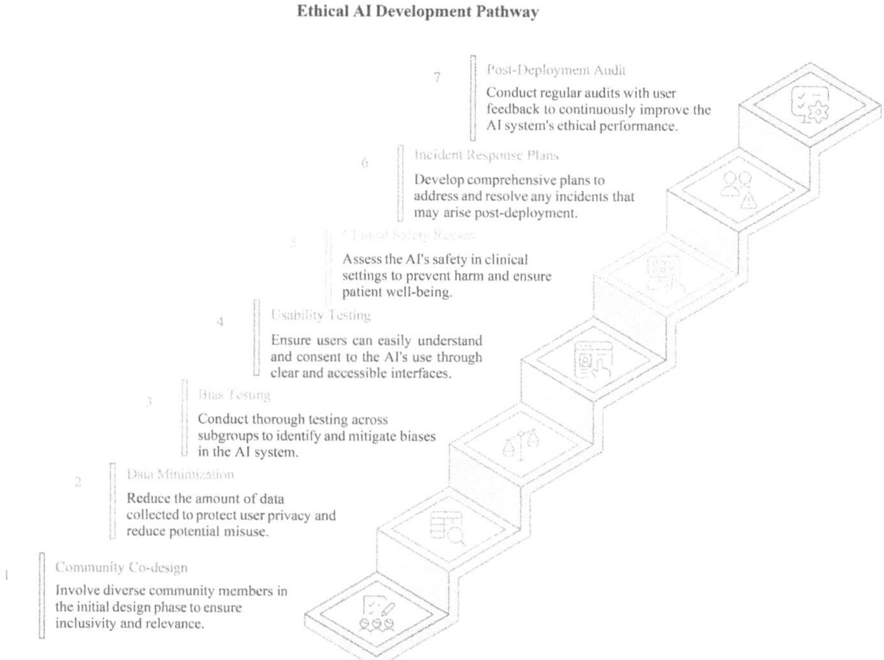

FIGURE 6.2 Ethical development and deployment pathway that traces key checkpoints from concept to scale: community co-design, data minimization, bias testing by subgroup, usability and comprehension testing for consent, clinical safety review, incident response plans, and post-deployment audit with user feedback loops.

Clinical safety review and incident response plans operationalize accountability by establishing clear responsibility for outcomes and rapid response when problems emerge. Finally, a post-deployment audit with user feedback loops ensures that ethical practices continue after launch, with systems that learn and improve based on real-world experience.

The urgency is high. Many tools reach users with little oversight and few tests of impact on distress, hope, or help-seeking. The flow in digital adoption during the COVID-19 period widened access but also revealed the thin layer of shared standards in this space. People often turn to automated tools in moments of acute need, which increases the duty to avoid harm and to provide clear paths to human assistance when automated support is insufficient. A better path is collaborative: builders, clinicians, ethicists, policymakers, and, most of all, people with lived experience should share the design table. Feedback from users of the tools should inform updates, disclosures, and safeguards. This mirrors earlier chapters in the book, which frame AI as a behavioral architect: the setting built by code shapes action, so those affected by that setting must help decide how it is constructed.

> ***Takeaway:*** *As AI influences how people think, feel, and interact in cyberspaces, ethical design becomes crucial to safeguard mental health.*
> ***Reflection:*** *How might your trust in a digital platform change if you knew its AI system was designed with psychological well-being in mind?*

6.2.2 Principles of Ethical AI for Mental Well-being

Given this urgency and the need for collaborative design, four foundational ethical principles must guide the development and deployment of AI in mental health: transparency, fairness, consent, and accountability (see Figure 6.3). These are not abstract ideals or marketing slogans. Rather, they are working commitments that shape every decision, from data collection to real-world deployment, and they determine whether AI systems support genuine well-being or undermine it.

Transparency and clear communication are the entry points to trust. In mental health settings, users need to know what kinds of data are collected, how those data are analyzed, what signals the model reads, and how outputs affect support or referral. This includes disclosure about triggers for automated safety actions and when a human professional will be notified. Such clarity is especially vital when conversations touch suicidal thoughts or acute distress, where the path from input to action must be explicit and fair (Uzougbo et al., 2024). However, transparency is not simply a matter of disclosure; it is about comprehension. It also includes recognizing limitations: when the system is uncertain, when data are sparse or biased, and when human review is needed before any step that could change care.

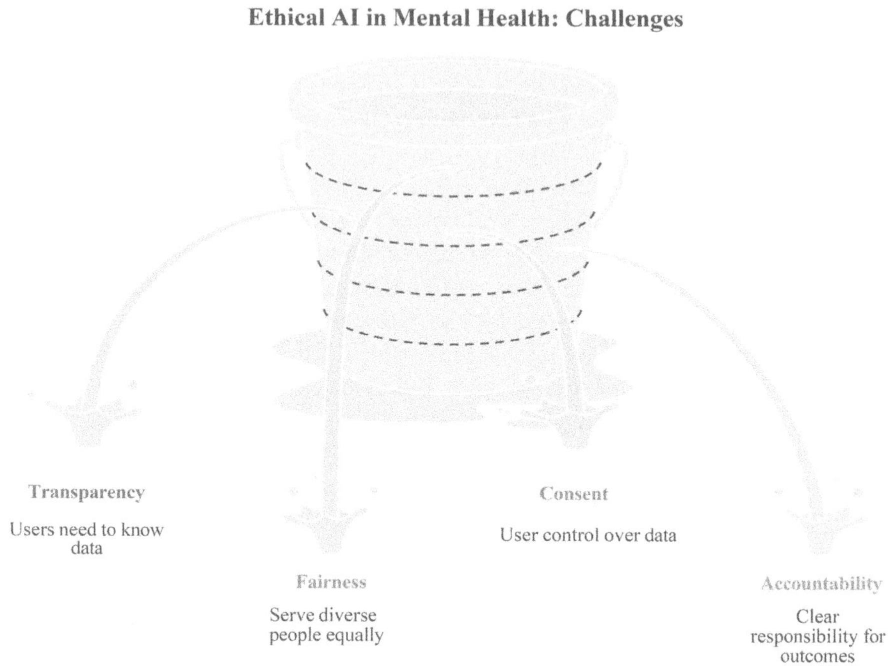

FIGURE 6.3 Four principles of ethical AI for mental well-being.

Fairness, in the context of ethical AI, means more than equal treatment. Ethical systems must serve diverse people with different ways of expressing distress and resilience. This requires attention to how signals vary across different cultures, languages, genders, ages, and socioeconomic contexts and to how access conditions can either widen or narrow existing gaps. Technical parity metrics are useful, but they do not replace evaluation of real-world consequences in specific communities (Pulivarthy & Whig, 2024; Bahangulu & Owusu Berko, 2025). Data sets should include varied sources, and audits should test performance across intersectional subgroups. Cultural expression matters. A model trained primarily on Western symptom language may overlook somatic or spiritual forms of distress found elsewhere or may misinterpret indirect speech as an indication of no need. Design teams that include community members and individuals with lived experience can identify and address these risks early, guiding the phrasing, labels, and thresholds before deployment. Fairness extends to access: if tools require premium devices, constant connectivity, or high reading levels, the result can be wider gaps in who benefits.

Consent in AI-driven mental health systems must be informed, ongoing, and under the user's control. People should be able to choose what to share, change those choices over time, and see the effects of their settings. This is especially important when the mood is unstable, concentration is low, or stress is high.

Just-in-time explanations and periodic check-ins help ensure that consent reflects the person's current state and preferences (Cheng et al., 2024). Consent also covers decision uses: when algorithms inform screening, guide treatment suggestions, or gate access, the person should be told in plain language and offered a route to human review for high-stakes decisions. Brief education modules can explain how assessment works, what data are used, and what rights individuals have regarding correction, deletion, and review.

Accountability requires clear responsibility for outcomes. Accountability operates at multiple levels: technical, human, and organizational. At the technical level, monitoring should detect performance drift, unequal error rates across groups, and signals of harm such as increased distress after automated prompts. Detailed logs and audit trails support tracebacks and corrections. These technical measures complement human governance, including named roles for clinical oversight, defined response times for safety events, and channels for users to report concerns that lead to action (Olatunji Akinrinola et al., 2024; Thiruma, 2023). When a user experiences harm, there must be a clear pathway to investigation, remediation, and learning. Accountability also extends to organizations: developers, providers, and regulators each have duties that should be clearly stated and enforced.

These four principles do not operate in isolation; they are mutually reinforcing. Transparency relies on good records from accountability mechanisms. Fairness improves when consent tools are clear and opt-in by category. Accountability depends on audit trails that transparency makes visible to users and reviewers. The practical test is a life cycle in which models are designed in collaboration with those affected, audited before release, continuously checked in the field, and improved in response to feedback.

The aim is not perfection but steady improvement that protects people while the tools learn. Systems should adapt based on both ethical feedback and performance data, and they should do so in a manner that is transparent to the people they serve. When transparency, fairness, consent, and accountability are treated as daily practice rather than one-time checks, AI can support care without eroding the trust on which recovery depends.

> ***Takeaway:*** *Transparency, fairness, consent, and accountability are foundational to AI systems that support emotional safety and digital trust.*
> ***Reflection:*** *Which of these ethical principles, transparency, fairness, consent, or accountability, do you feel is most important to your mental well-being online?*

6.3 "Ethical by Design": From Principles to Practice

The principles of transparency, fairness, consent, and accountability, established in Section 6.2, must be operationalized into concrete design practices. This section illustrates how each ethical commitment is translated into specific design decisions and technical implementations across four critical domains: data governance, algorithmic fairness, user consent, and safety oversight. Together, they form the foundation of “Ethical by Design”, an approach in which ethical considerations are embedded into every stage of development.

6.3.1 *Data Governance and Privacy by Default*

Mental health care is fundamentally relational. The bond that supports change relies on trust, empathy, and a sense of being heard. When users share fears, grief, or trauma with an automated system, they rely on rules and data that cannot fully mirror human understanding. That gap can strain the meaning of care, especially for individuals seeking warmth and details that scripted dialogue may not offer (Yıldız, 2025). Data demands add another layer. These systems often depend on detailed histories, behavioral traces, and sensitive notes about mood and function. Collecting, storing, and linking such material raises risks that can, by themselves, cause stress. Concerns about who sees the data, how it is processed, and whether it might be used in hiring, insurance, or legal contexts can heighten anxiety and reduce help-seeking (Nashwan et al., 2023).

Privacy by design means incorporating protection into the system from the outset, rather than adding it later. This requires several concrete practices. First, data minimization: systems should collect only the information necessary for the specific clinical task, rather than collecting everything that could theoretically be useful. For example, a mood tracking app may need daily ratings and brief notes, but not continuous audio or location data. Second, technical safeguards include encryption at rest and in transit, anonymization where possible, and the automatic deletion of detailed records after a defined retention period. A system might retain conversation logs for 30 days to support continuity of care and then automatically delete them while preserving aggregated patterns needed for system improvement. Third, user control, where people should be able to see what data is collected, understand why each type is needed, and choose to opt out of non-essential collection.

Consent mechanisms for data collection must be clear and granular. Rather than a single yes-or-no choice, users should be able to consent to different data types separately: journaling text, passive sensor data, voice samples, and clinical notes. Each choice should include a clear, plain-language explanation of how the data will be used and for how long it will be retained. Users should be able to change their minds at any time, and the system should show them the effects of their choices; for example, “If you opt out of passive sensor data, the system cannot detect patterns between your activity and mood”. Research on user preferences confirms this necessity. Figure 6.4 illustrates comfort levels for sharing various data types, revealing significant variation: users may be willing to share journaling text but are hesitant about sharing voice samples or passive sensor data. This variation underscores why granular consent is not a luxury but a design requirement.

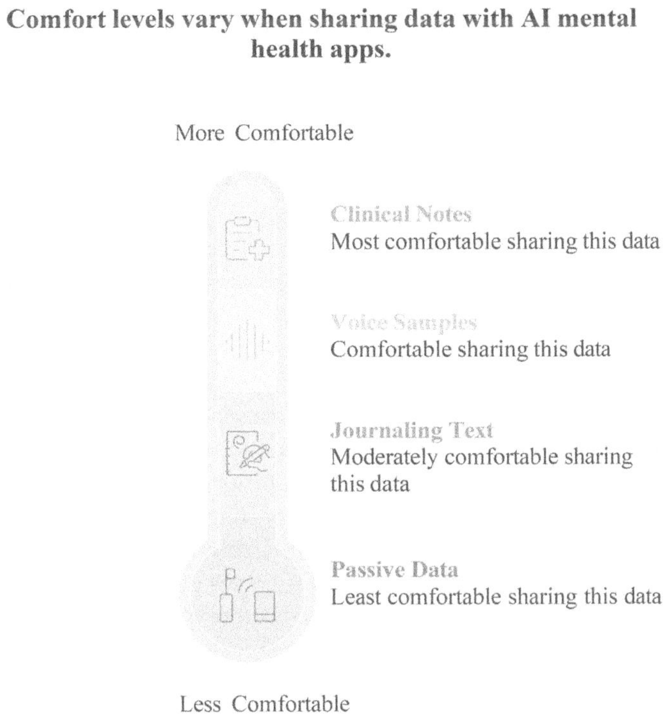

FIGURE 6.4 Privacy concerns in AI mental health Apps show comfort levels for sharing distinct data types (passive sensor data, journaling text, voice samples, and clinical notes). The figure shows that comfort levels vary significantly: users may be willing to share journaling text but hesitant about voice samples or passive sensor data. This variation highlights the importance of granular consent and the need to design systems that function well even when users restrict certain data types.

> ***Takeaway:*** *Data governanvce by design means collecting only what is necessary, protecting it rigorously with technical safeguards, and ensuring users understand and control how their information is used. Privacy is not a feature added at the end; it is built into every stage of system development.*
>
> ***Reflection:*** *If a mental health app collects detailed information about a person's mood, substance use, and trauma history, what safeguards would you want yo know are in place before you would trust it with your own data?*

6.3.2 Algorithmic Fairness and Bias Mitigation

Bias is a critical ethical fault line in AI mental health systems. If training data underrepresents certain groups, systems may overlook symptoms, misread language cues, or rank risks in ways that widen existing gaps in care. A tool built mainly from data on white, middle-income users may fail people from different cultural or socioeconomic settings, leading to missed help or unfit advice (Nashwan et al., 2023). Equity by design requires diverse data sources, systematic group-based audits, and swift remediation pathways.

Over-reliance is a related but distinct risk. Mental health problems are complex. Good judgment draws on context, history, culture, and lived experience. Automated outputs can assist, but they should not displace a clinician's integrative view or a user's values and choices. Self-assessment apps that produce firm diagnostic labels can either downplay real danger or pathologize normal emotion, each with harmful effects (Wimbarti et al., 2024).

Implementing algorithmic fairness requires concrete practices across the system lifecycle. During development, training data should be deliberately sourced to include diverse populations. This includes variation by culture, language, gender, age, socioeconomic status, and mental health history. Before deployment, performance should be tested separately for each major subgroup, not just overall accuracy but accuracy for each group. If a screening tool performs well for white users but poorly for Black users, or well for employed users but poorly for unemployed users, that disparity must be identified and addressed before the system reaches users.

After deployment, continuous monitoring should track performance drift and emerging biases. A system that performed fairly when trained may drift over time as the population it serves changes or as data quality shifts. Regular audits, conducted at least quarterly, should assess performance across intersectional subgroups and identify any widening gaps. When bias is detected, remediation should be swift and visible, such as retraining the model, adjusting thresholds, or adding guardrails to prevent biased output from reaching users.

Cultural competence in design is essential. A model trained primarily on Western symptom language may overlook somatic or spiritual forms of distress prevalent in other cultures or may misinterpret indirect speech as an indication of no need. Design teams that include community members and individuals with lived experience can identify and address these risks early, guiding the phrasing, labels, and thresholds before deployment. For example, a screening tool developed solely by Western clinicians might ask, "Do you feel sad?" but overlook the concept of "heaviness of heart" that resonates in some communities. Involving people from these communities in the design process prevents such misalignments.

Table 6.1 illustrates the complementary strengths and limitations of human clinicians and automated systems in four key assessment tasks. The table shows that neither humans nor algorithms should work alone. In screening, for example, humans build trust and adapt to cultural context, while algorithms offer private, anytime access and consistent scoring. The recommended integration is to use automated screeners as a first step with clear caveats, then route positive results to same-day human review. This combination harnesses the strengths of each while mitigating their individual limitations.

TABLE 6.1 Human and AI in Assessment: Roles and Limits

Assessment Task	*Strengths of Human Clinicians*	*Strengths of Automated Systems*	*Key Limits (Human and Automated)*	*Recommended Integration in Stepped-Care*
Screening	Builds trust, adapts questions to culture and context, reads tone and non-verbal cues, can reframe and pace the conversation, safeguards disclosure.	Offers private, anytime entry; uses consistent wording; scores instantly; can gather brief passive signals to widen reach; supports many languages.	Human: limited time and access; variability and implicit bias. Automated: false positives or negatives; bias from training data; struggles with irony and ambiguous language; may give users false certainty.	Offer self-guided screeners as a first step with clear caveats; route positives to a same-day human review; show plain-language explanations and links to help; allow opt-out from passive signals (Nashwan et al., 2023).
Risk Triage	Judges intent, means, and protective factors; builds safety plans; mobilizes family and community supports; meets legal duty to protect.	Monitors streams for warning patterns; prioritizes high-risk cases quickly; keeps an audit trail; can trigger alerts to on-call teams.	Human: coverage gaps and uneven documentation during busy periods. Automated: calibration drift and alert fatigue; privacy intrusion if monitoring is too broad; harm if outreach is mis-timed.	Use model-generated risk bands reviewed by clinicians; set two clear thresholds: urgent and routine; require a human call or message to confirm risk before action unless there is explicit self-harm intent (Wimbarti et al., 2024).
Diagnosis Support	Weighs history, culture, trauma, and medical factors; tests alternative explanations; explains options and gains informed consent.	Surfaces patterns across many cases; checks guideline steps; suggests differential questions and prompts for missing information.	Human: heuristics and variability can miss patterns. Automated: cannot carry responsibility for diagnosis; may misclassify when context is thin; users may over-trust outputs.	Keep automated tools as decision support only; require clinician verification for any label; log how suggestions were used; present uncertainties in plain language to users.

(Continued)

TABLE 6.1 (Continued)

Assessment Task	*Strengths of Human Clinicians*	*Strengths of Automated Systems*	*Key Limits (Human and Automated)*	*Recommended Integration in Stepped-Care*
Progress Monitoring	Interprets change within the relationship; adjusts care plan; handles setbacks with empathy; helps set goals that matter to the person.	Captures frequent check-ins; detects early worsening; tracks adherence; flags relapse risk; supports remote care between visits.	Human: recall bias and long gaps between sessions. Automated: noisy signals and over-focus on numbers; risk of over-messaging; privacy concerns for continuous tracking.	Blend brief digital check-ins with scheduled human reviews; set clear rules for when a rise in symptom scores or drop in use triggers contact; show people how to pause or change tracking.

Fairness also extends to access. If tools require premium devices, constant connectivity, or high reading levels, the result can be wider gaps in who benefits. Ethical design should support low-bandwidth modes, offline logging with later sync, simple reading levels, and local language support. Cost transparency and public sector procurement can further widen reach. A system that only works on the latest smartphones excludes people with older devices, while a system that requires constant internet connectivity excludes those in areas with spotty coverage. Fairness means designing for the constraints users actually face, not the ideal conditions developers assume.

Takeaway: *Algorithmic fairness requires ongoing attention to how systems perform across different groups and populations. Bias is not a one-time problem to be solved; it is a continuous challenge requiring diverse data, regular audits, and swift remediation. Fairness is also means designing systems that function well even when users restrict features or lack ideal access conditions.*
Reflection: *How would you know if an AI mental health tool was performing differently for people from your cultural or socioeconomic background compared to others? What evidence would you want to see?*

6.3.3 Upholding User Autonomy and Meaningful Consent

User autonomy and meaningful consent are foundational to ethical practice in mental health care. As AI becomes more integrated into these settings, consent mechanisms must be both truly informed and ongoing, reflecting users' evolving understanding and preferences. This section distinguishes consent for participation and decision-making from consent for data collection (addressed in Section 6.3.1). Although both are essential, they serve different purposes: data consent protects privacy, while autonomy consent protects agency.

Autonomy in mental health care centers on individuals' rights to make informed decisions about their participation in treatment and the use of their personal data. AI applications in mental health raise significant ethical concerns, especially regarding patient autonomy and the capacity to consent meaningfully (Tang et al., 2023). As mental health care becomes increasingly reliant on AI-driven decision-making, ensuring that patients understand how AI influences their care is essential for maintaining their autonomy. Understanding these technologies requires a comprehensive grasp of how AI systems operate, including issues of transparency, explainability, and potential biases (Joshi et al., 2024).

The ethical challenge is acute: errors and biases in AI systems can disrupt accountability and transparency, complicating patients' ability to provide informed consent (Gundersen & Bærøe, 2022). The need for clarity in communication about AI's capabilities and limitations is paramount if patients are to retain agency over their healthcare decisions. This is especially true in mental health, where the relationship between patient and system shapes the therapeutic experience itself. When a user doesn't understand how an algorithm will influence their care, what it can do, what it cannot do, and what happens if it makes a mistake, they cannot truly consent to its use.

Dynamic consent introduces a model in which consent is not a one-time event but an ongoing dialogue between users and the system (Steinsbekk et al., 2013). This approach allows for continual reassessment of consent preferences as circumstances evolve, as mood changes, as understanding deepens, or as the system's use of data shifts. Rather than a static form signed once, a dynamic consent interface allows users to adjust their preferences at any time, showing them in real-time how their choices affect what data is collected and how it is used.

Comprehensibility is distinct from compliance. A consent form can be legally sufficient yet leave users confused about what they are agreeing to. Simplifying language and the presentation of information is one of the most effective strategies for enhancing the comprehensibility of consent (Kassam et al., 2023). By using clear, jargon-free language and visual aids such as infographics or videos, users are more likely to understand the important details about their participation and data use. Interactive digital platforms can transform the consent process, providing opportunities for clarification and tailored information (Allen et al., 2023). Tools that utilize conversational AI to facilitate discussions about consent demonstrate how technology can aid users in comprehending complex information. These platforms can adapt to different literacy levels and emotional states, ensuring that explanations are accessible and engaging. Personalization is key: large language models could offer interactive, age-appropriate explanations for younger users or simplified versions for those under cognitive stress (Allen et al., 2025).

Mental health crises often involve impaired cognitive capacity, acute distress, confusion, or emotional dysregulation, which complicates informed consent. Healthcare providers should routinely assess a user's decision-making capacity, particularly in emergency situations, using communication strategies that are clear, trauma-informed, and considerate of the user's emotional state (Al-Wathinani et al., 2023). When users are unable to provide informed consent due to impaired cognitive capacity, involving family members or legal representatives can help ensure that the patient's rights are protected (Richardson et al., 2021). The goal is to honor the person's autonomy even when they cannot fully exercise it in the moment.

Dynamic consent models may also provide tools to support user participation during acute distress (Neri et al., 2020). These frameworks enable ongoing conversations, allowing healthcare providers to gradually reintroduce consent discussions when users are more receptive to understanding the provided information. In high-pressure scenarios, such as emergency care, implied consent may be necessary to act in the user's best interest; however, protocols must be clear and well-communicated. For example, if a system detects imminent suicide risk and automatically alerts a crisis team, the user should be told immediately afterward why this happened and what their options are going forward.

Consent is meaningful only if users can change their minds. Dynamic consent systems represent a transformative advance in how consent is managed, facilitating continuous engagement and adjustments by users (Mamo et al., 2019). A user-friendly interface is essential for allowing users to modify consent settings seamlessly (Chew & Achananuparp, 2022). This includes providing clear options for users to modify their consent preferences, accompanied by straightforward explanations of the implications of these changes. Changing your mind should be as easy as giving consent in the first place. Implementing notifications and reminders about consent status can encourage users to revisit and possibly update their consent choices (Olatoye et al., 2024). This proactive approach ensures that users remain informed and empowered to regularly revisit their preferences, particularly in fast-evolving areas like AI and mental health applications.

A tension often arises between what a system needs to function effectively and what users want to control. Effective designs incorporate features that allow users to retain control without sacrificing the system's core capabilities. The key is to distinguish between features essential to safety and efficacy versus those that are merely convenient for the developer. For example, a system might require consent for mood tracking (essential for diagnosis) but allow users to opt out of predictive analytics (a nice-to-have feature but not essential).

Takeaway: *Meaningful consent in AI-driven mental health care requires moving beyond one-time legal compliance to establish ongoing, comprehensible, and user-controlled consent mechanisms. Dynamic platforms, plain language explanations, and genuine user control over settings are essential to upholding autonomy.*

Reflection: *If a person in acute mental distress cannot fully understand a consent form, what responsibility does the system have to simplify it, and who should help them make the decision?*

6.3.4 Ensuring Safety through Accountability and Human Oversight

Safe AI systems in mental health require more than good intentions. They require clear responsibility for outcomes, technical systems that detect problems early, human expertise that catches what algorithms miss, and transparent mechanisms that allow learning when things go wrong. Accountability and human oversight are not constraints on AI; they are the conditions that make AI trustworthy.

Drift detection systems are critical in identifying changes in the performance of AI algorithms over time, particularly when external factors can influence outcomes (Fields & Calvert, 2015). Drift can occur for various reasons: changes in the population being served, shifts in how people express distress, or degradation in data quality. A system that worked well when trained may perform differently six months later if the underlying population has changed. Continuous monitoring systems must be deployed that utilize statistical methods to detect deviations from known performance thresholds, enabling timely interventions to recalibrate algorithms as needed.

Error rate tracking provides a valuable mechanism for assessing the reliability and accuracy of AI systems (Fields & Calvert, 2015). Implementing robust protocols to measure and report error rates ensures that stakeholders are aware of any potential risks associated with automated decisions. This is particularly important in mental health, where errors can have serious consequences. A system that misses a suicide risk signal or incorrectly labels normal distress as pathology can cause real harm. Beyond general performance metrics, monitoring should specifically track disparities in error rates across demographic groups. If a system makes more false-negative errors for young users than for older users, or more false positives for men than for women, these disparities must be flagged and investigated. This directly connects to the fairness principle established in Section 6.2, ensuring that accountability mechanisms can catch emerging biases.

Ethics committees play a crucial role in overseeing the use of AI applications in mental health. These committees are responsible for evaluating and advising on ethical considerations surrounding the deployment of AI, focusing on user welfare and compliance with established ethical standards (Shlobin et al., 2020). Effective ethics committees include diverse stakeholders, such as clinicians, individuals with lived experience of mental health challenges, data scientists, ethicists, and community members, to gauge varying perspectives on informed consent and the challenges that AI introduces. The ethics committee should meet regularly (at a minimum, monthly) to review incident reports, audit findings, and user feedback.

Clinical oversight roles are crucial for monitoring AI systems and addressing user interactions with these technologies (Shou et al., 2024). Human oversight functions, particularly those that intersect with clinical practice, help bridge gaps where AI systems may err. Clinicians must actively engage in the user consent process, ensuring that explanations regarding AI's role in assessment and treatment are comprehensible. This oversight is particularly important during mental health crises, where technical monitoring systems may not account for human factors affecting consent or understanding. A clinician can recognize when a person is too distressed to process information, when cultural context is relevant, or when an algorithmic recommendation conflicts with what the person actually needs.

Incident response protocols are crucial for addressing unexpected issues that arise from AI systems (Steimers & Schneider, 2022). Organizations should establish proactive planning and clear, actionable steps to manage incidents when they occur, including identifying responsible parties, outlining communication strategies, and providing guidelines for immediate corrective actions. When an incident is detected, whether through automated monitoring, user reports, or clinician concerns, a clear protocol should activate immediately: assessment of severity, notification of affected users, investigation of root causes, and implementation of interim safeguards.

Audit trails are indispensable for maintaining transparency in AI systems (Prakash et al., 2022). They track data usage and decision-making processes, providing an essential record for retrospective analysis and review. This enables stakeholders to understand how decisions were made and facilitates accountability when issues arise. The opacity of many AI algorithms, often referred to as the "black box" problem, necessitates rigorous documentation practices to foster trust and understanding among users.

When harm does occur due to an AI system's operation, immediate response protocols must be activated (Froicu et al., 2025). This includes assessing the situation to determine the extent of the harm, providing support to affected individuals, and initiating a review of the incident's cause. The stakes in mental health are high; a system error can contribute to a person's deterioration or crisis. Organizations must communicate transparently with affected individuals about the incident, including acknowledging the harm caused, steps taken to rectify it, and measures implemented to prevent recurrence (Mittelstadt, 2019).

Post-incident reviews can provide valuable insights into failures in AI systems (Mittelstadt et al., 2016). Establishing a structured process for analyzing incidents to identify root causes, potential biases in AI algorithms, and procedural shortcomings can lead to improved safety and reliability in AI applications. This learning should inform updates to both incident response protocols and overall governance structures. The goal is not to assign blame but to understand what went wrong and how to prevent it from happening again.

Feedback from users, clinicians, and affected communities should be systematically collected and used to refine both the AI system and the governance structures around it. This might include regular surveys asking users about their experience with the system, focus groups with clinicians about what works and what doesn't, and structured reviews of near misses – situations where the system almost failed, but human oversight caught the problem. Feedback loops should be visible and responsive. When users or clinicians report a concern, they should see evidence that it was taken seriously, investigated, and acted upon. This transparency strengthens trust and encourages continued engagement with the system.

Accountability spans organizations: developers, providers, and regulators each have duties that should be stated and enforced. Developers have a responsibility to build systems with safety in mind and to provide clear documentation of how the system works, what it was tested on, and what its limitations are. Providers have a responsibility to implement the system thoughtfully, train their staff, and monitor its performance in their specific setting. Regulators have a responsibility to set standards, audit compliance, and hold organizations accountable when things go wrong. Organizations should publicly report on the performance of their systems, including error rates, demographic disparities, and incidents of harm. This public reporting creates external accountability and allows other organizations to learn from both successes and failures.

> ***Takeaway:*** *Safety in AI mental health systems requires a layered approach to accountability, including technical monitoring systems that detect drift and errors, human governance structures that provide clinical and ethical oversight, incident response protocols that act promptly when harm occurs, and feedback loops that enable continuous improvement.*
> ***Reflection:*** *If an AI system in a mental health app makes a serious error and harms a user, who should be held responsible: the developer, the organization deploying it, the clinician who used it, or the system itself? How should accountability be distributed fairly?*

6.4 Ethical Obligations toward Vulnerable Populations

Vulnerable populations, youth, individuals with severe mental illness, people in crisis, those facing stigma or discrimination, and those with limited access to care face heightened risks when AI systems are poorly designed or unethically deployed. This section examines the specific ethical obligations organizations have when designing for these groups. The analysis is grounded in two complementary perspectives: the psychological benefits that ethical AI can deliver and the harms that unethical practices inflict. This dual focus shows why ethical safeguards are not optional constraints but essential conditions for systems that genuinely serve vulnerable populations.

6.4.1 *Psychological Benefits of Ethically Aligned AI Tools*

When AI is built and deployed with sound ethical guardrails, the gains for users are psychological, not just logistical. Trust, safety, and a sense of control amplify the technical value of these tools, turning access into relief. The benefits described here assume designs that are transparent about limits, fair across groups, respectful of consent, and backed by accountable oversight, as established in Sections 6.1 through 6.3. Without these foundations, the benefits cannot be reliably achieved.

Access and timeliness: ethical systems widen the front door to help without lowering safeguards. Long waits, distance, cost, and stigma deter many from seeking care; tools that work at any hour and on modest devices can reduce these barriers while maintaining quality (Giray, 2024; Saqib et al., 2023). The psychological effect is direct: people can act when motivation is present, which lowers avoidance and builds early momentum. This is strongest when the tool clearly states what it

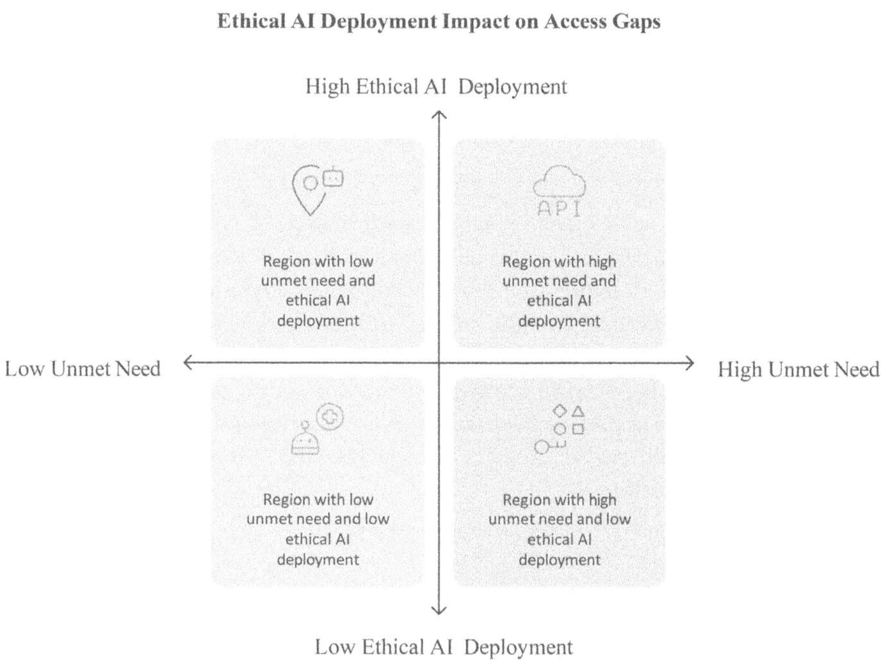

FIGURE 6.5 Access gaps and expected impact: Unmet needs, availability of traditional services, and projected reductions in access disparities with ethical AI deployment.

can do now and what requires human follow-up, thereby preventing the false hope that leads to disappointment. Figure 6.5 illustrates the access gaps that ethical AI can help address.

Round-the-clock availability matters most when distress peaks outside business hours. The benefit becomes apparent only when protocols route urgent cases to individuals with clear timescales displayed on the screen. Systems that state thresholds for escalation and display the on-call path reduce fear and support timely action.

A personalized fit and tailored suggestions enhance engagement when they align with a person's needs and values. Models that adapt pacing, modality, and coping strategies can yield better outcomes than one-size-fits-all content, provided that privacy is respected and control sits with the user (Saqib et al., 2023). The psychological lift comes from feeling seen rather than managed. People should be able to choose lighter or deeper tailoring and turn it off without losing access.

With *consistency and predictability*, automated systems can deliver stable responses that remain unchanged regardless of workload or mood. For some conditions, especially anxiety and autism, predictability supports calm; routine wording and steady pacing reduce cognitive load. The benefit depends on quality. Repeating shallow responses can be frustrating and harmful. Therefore, governance should verify that the content being delivered at scale is helpful for the problem at hand.

Lowered stigma and first disclosure make it easier for many people to start with a private, non-judgmental interface. Early disclosure of a tool can be a step toward fuller care, especially for sensitive topics such as substance use or suicidal thoughts (Chaudhry & Debi, 2023). The benefit is largest when the system invites, rather than replaces, human connection and when it offers a warm handoff that the person can accept in their own time.

Knowledge and skills are taught by good tools. Brief lessons on naming feelings, planning coping strategies, and pacing activities can enhance emotional regulation and self-efficacy. Tailored psychoeducation that fits culture and reading level supports better talk with clinicians and better choices elsewhere in health care. The gain here lasts beyond the session, especially when people practice skills between contacts.

Agency and control, including choosing when to engage, what to share, and how deeply to delve, can be therapeutic. A clear consent panel, adjustable privacy settings, and the option to switch off features give people a sense of ownership that counters helplessness. The tool should state plainly that declining features will not block care.

Social connection: well-designed tools can support, not displace, human ties. Practicing tough conversations with a script, finding peer groups, and timing contact with family or clinicians can lift belonging and reduce isolation. Connections must be voluntary, moderated, and aligned with the person's goals.

Conditions for benefit: none of these gains are automatic. They rely on the ethical features set in Sections 6.1 through 6.3: clarity about what the tool can do, fair performance across groups, consent that adapts to changing comfort, and teams that own safety. When those parts are in place, AI can extend care and strengthen human work rather than replace it.

> ***Takeaway:*** *When aligned with ethical standards, AI tools such as therapy bots and wellness apps can enhance access to support and promote digital resilience.*
> ***Reflection:*** *Have you used any AI-driven tools that made you feel emotionally supported or understood? What features helped?*

6.4.2 Unethical AI Practices and Their Mental Health Implications

AI can both harm and help when it is built or deployed without proper ethical consideration. In mental health contexts, misuse does not stay technical; it becomes emotional strain, reduced help-seeking, and damage to trust. This section outlines the primary risk patterns and their psychological effects, linking each to the safeguards described in Sections 6.1 through 6.3.

Privacy violations and breach-related distress: violations of confidentiality cut deep into mental health because the data describe fear, grief, trauma, and thoughts of self-harm. When such records are exposed, traded, or reused for unrelated aims, people report shock, shame, anger, and a sense of betrayal (Raghav & Gulia, 2023; Cross et al., 2024). The effects persist: avoidance of care, hypervigilance online, and rumination that delays recovery. This harm is prevented through the data governance and privacy protections established in Section 6.3.1.

Self-censorship and reduced disclosure, driven by the fear of misuse, lead people to omit key details, soften language, or stop logging altogether. This lowers the quality of assessments and blunts the benefit of support, while adding the stress of carrying unspoken concerns. The cycle erodes engagement over time (Raghav & Gulia, 2023; Cross et al., 2024). Meaningful consent mechanisms, as described in Section 6.3.3, help rebuild trust and encourage fuller disclosure.

Manipulative engagement systems, some of which are tuned for time spent on the app rather than overall well-being. Unpredictable rewards, nudges that encourage more use, or praise patterns that target insecurity can invite users into cycles that displace real-world coping mechanisms and strain relationships (Kalam et al., 2024; Sanchez et al., 2024). For those already vulnerable, this can deepen low mood and anxiety while creating dependence on the app for validation. Ethical governance, as described in Section 6.5, should prohibit such practices and audit engagement metrics for harm signals.

Opacity and loss of control occur when systems issue assessments or advice without explanation, leaving users uncertain about the accuracy and relevance of the information. Anxiety rises, and some people defer to the tool rather than building their own judgment. Over time, this can weaken self-efficacy and diminish the sense of agency that care is intended to restore (Sanchez et al., 2024). Transparency mechanisms, as described in Section 6.3.2, are essential to maintaining user autonomy.

Biased content and cultural mismatch, as well as training sets that overlook key groups or forms of expression, can reinforce stereotypes, misread distress, or provide interventions that clash with cultural norms. People may feel unseen or misclassified, which can lead to isolation and reduced adherence (Sanchez et al., 2024). The fairness and bias mitigation practices described in Section 6.3.2 are essential to preventing this harm.

Over-reliance on automation for high-stakes decisions, using automated scores alone for suicide risk, forced admission, or gatekeeping of services, can cause grave harm when errors occur. Even where average accuracy is high, the experience of being judged by an opaque score can feel dehumanizing and frightening (Cross et al., 2024). Human oversight is not a courtesy here; it is a duty. The accountability and human oversight mechanisms described in Section 6.3.4 are essential safeguards.

Medicalization of normal emotion: if a tool labels ordinary sadness or temporary stress as pathology, people may doubt their own resilience and seek treatment they do not need. This shift in self-view can lower confidence and reduce natural problem-solving over time. Clear communication about the tool's limitations and appropriate use, as described in Section 6.3.2, helps prevent this harm.

Social isolation and the displacement of human ties can lower stigma, but if systems discourage real-world contact or become the preferred companion, loneliness can grow. Skills that depend on live practice may stall, and support networks thin out. Ethical design should actively support, not replace, human connection.

Dependency and problematic use: designs that push streaks, offer badges, or provide constant prompts can foster compulsive checking. People may learn to face distress only by opening the app, which limits growth in independent coping (Kalam et al., 2024; Sanchez et al., 2024). Ethical governance should prohibit gamification elements that exploit vulnerability and should monitor for signs of problematic use.

Financial pressure and exploitative pricing can lead systems tuned for revenue to push paid tiers, extra sessions, or add-ons that raise stress, especially for those already strained financially. The effect is both practical and emotional: money worries increase, and trust drops when people sense that care is being shaped by sales. Table 6.2 provides an audit framework for identifying and preventing exploitative pricing practices.

Normalization of surveillance, continuous monitoring of mood, movement, or speech can feel disturbing. The sense of being watched may blunt authentic expression and add a steady tension that works against recovery. Data minimization and user control over monitoring, as described in Section 6.3.1, are essential safeguards.

TABLE 6.2 Revenue Practices Audit That Lists Pricing Tactics (Trial-to-Lock-in Switches, Dark Patterns around Cancellation), Affected Groups, Complaint Rates, and Policy Fixes

Pricing Tactic	*Brief Description*	*Affected Groups*	*Complaint Signals to Track*	*Policy Fixes*
Free Trial → Auto-Renew	Trial converts to paid without clear, timely reminder.	Low-income users; adolescents; distracted or distressed users.	Spike in refund requests within seven days post-trial; chargeback rate; app-store reviews mentioning "unexpected charge".	Explicit opt-in before billing; reminder ≥ seven days prior; one-click cancel link in reminder; pro-rated refunds.
Friction in Cancellation	Multi-step flows, hidden links, or phone-only cancellation.	All users; higher burden on those in crisis.	Time-to-cancel; abandonment in cancel flow; inbound tickets tagged "cancel" or "refund".	Two-click in-app cancel; immediate confirmation; no win-back hurdles after confirm.
Upsells during Crisis	Paid prompts offered when risk markers appear or late at night.	Users with acute distress; youth.	Complaints referencing upsell during panic/low mood; usage spikes paired with negative mood logs.	"Crisis-mode" monetization off: no upsells within 24 hours of suicide-risk flags; safety screens free.
Paywall on Safety Features	Priority response, crisis lines, or safety plans behind paywall.	Users at high risk; uninsured or low-income users.	Reports of delayed help due to paywall; adverse-event reviews.	Safety features free; response SLAs independent of tier; public audit of safety coverage.
Countdown/ Pressure Pricing	Limited-time timers or streak loss to push purchase.	Youth; anxiety-prone users.	Reviews citing pressure or FOMO; conversions clustered at timer expiry.	Ban countdowns in health flows; cooling-off period with easy refund.

(*Continued*)

TABLE 6.2 (Continued)

Pricing Tactic	*Brief Description*	*Affected Groups*	*Complaint Signals to Track*	*Policy Fixes*
Undisclosed Price Discrimination	Different prices by device/region without clear notice.	Low-income regions; older devices.	Support tickets citing unfair pricing; regional refund variance.	Publish price tables by region/device; cap variance; explain rationale.
In-App Currency/Credit Packs	Indirect pricing obscures real cost of sessions.	All users; higher risk for cognitive load issues.	Confusion in support logs; leftover credit breakage rates.	Show cash price per unit; auto-refund unused credits; disable auto-top-up by default.
Default-on Bundles	Add-on coaching/content pre-selected at checkout.	New users; those with low digital literacy.	High removal rates post-billing; disputes over unwanted add-ons.	Default-off add-ons; separate consent; clear line-items on receipt.
Frequent Unannounced Price Changes	Price shifts without prior notice.	All users.	Ticket spikes after change; churn after renewal.	30-day advance notice; grandfathering for current cycle; opt-out path.
Data-for-Discount Schemes	Sensitive data traded for lower price.	Financially strained users; marginalized groups.	Complaints about coercive data requests; opt-out followed by price jump.	Ban sensitive-data barter; discounts tied to non-sensitive actions only; external audit.

Takeaway: *Vulnerable populations face heightened risks from unethical AI but also stand to gain the most from ethical design. The psychological benefits, access, tailoring, lowered stigma, agency, and human connection, are real and substantial, but only when systems are built with transparency, fairness, meaningful consent, and robust accountability. The harms, privacy violations, manipulation, bias,* *over-reliance, and exploitation, are equally real and can be prevented through the safeguards established in Sections 6.1 to 6.3.*

Reflection: *If you were designing an AI mental health tool for a vulnerable population (e.g., homeless youth, people with severe depression, recent immigrants), what would be your top three ethical obligations, and how would you ensure they were met throughout the system's lifecycle?*

6.4.3 How Harms Concentrate in Specific Vulnerable Populations

Protection for vulnerable users is practical and testable. Clear explanations lower anxiety; opt-in features and adjustable consent restore control; subgroup audits reduce unfair errors; and named human oversight prevents automated decisions from standing alone. Youth councils and community panels can review prompts and escalation scripts to ensure effective communication. Procurement can require low-bandwidth modes and local language support so access does not depend on wealth or location (Stinson, 2022; King et al., 2021). General safeguards (as outlined in Sections 6.1–6.3) apply to all vulnerable populations. These safeguards work together as an integrated system: privacy protections prevent data misuse and reduce anxiety; clear explanations support informed choice and reduce worry; bias testing and fixes prevent unequal errors; firm human oversight ensures that automated decisions do not stand alone; and designs that support human connection position technology as a bridge to care rather than a substitute. Figure 6.6 visualizes how these safeguards work together to prevent harm across vulnerable populations:

- *Privacy protections* (Section 6.3.1): Data minimization, encryption, user control, and clear retention policies
- *Clear explanations* (Section 6.3.2): Explainable AI and transparency about system limitations
- *Bias testing and fixes* (Section 6.3.2): Regular audits across demographic groups and swift remediation
- *Firm human oversight* (Section 6.3.4): Clinical review before any decision affecting access to care or safety
- *Designs that support human connection* (Section 6.4.1): Systems positioned as bridges to care, not substitutes

Beyond these general safeguards, specific populations require additional attention. Group-specific safeguards require additional attention:

For youth, the risks are particularly acute. Engagement-driven algorithms can exploit developmental vulnerabilities, and decision opacity can leave young people

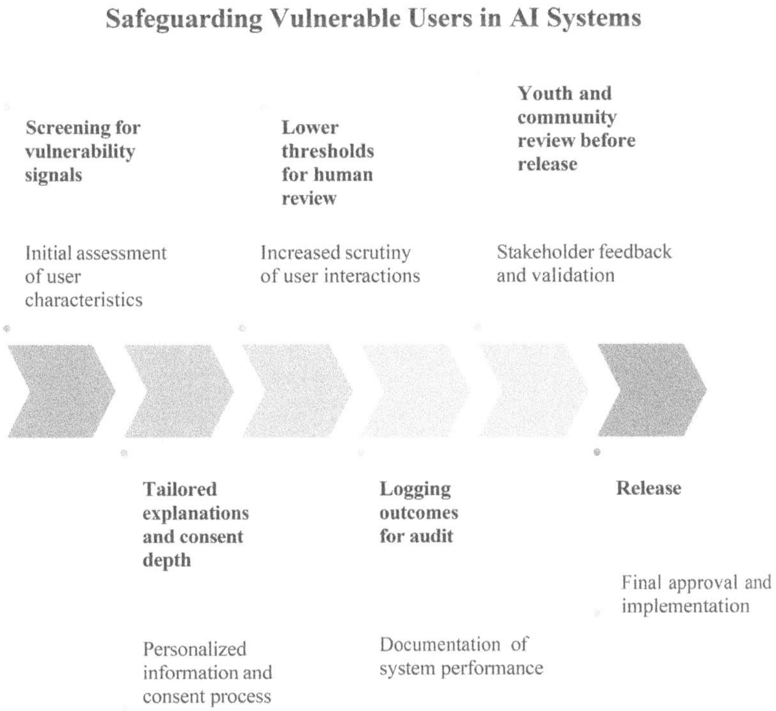

FIGURE 6.6 Safeguard pathway for vulnerable users. This figure shows how general safeguards (privacy protections, clear explanations, bias testing, human oversight, and designs supporting human connection) work together to prevent harm to vulnerable populations. Each safeguard addresses specific risks, and together they create a comprehensive protection system.

uncertain about why they received particular recommendations. Figure 6.7 illustrates these youth risk pathways, demonstrating how specific design choices lead to specific types of harm. To mitigate these risks, systems must involve youth in design processes to understand their actual needs and preferences. This involves reviewing engagement metrics for harm signals, such as increased anxiety or reduced sleep, ensuring explanations are age-appropriate and comprehensible, and creating pathways for youth feedback and governance so their voices shape ongoing improvements.

For *marginalized groups*, testing for bias across cultural and linguistic groups is essential, as is ensuring cultural competence in content and recommendations. Involving community members in the design and testing process helps identify risks early, and providing local language support ensures that access is not dependent on fluency in dominant languages.

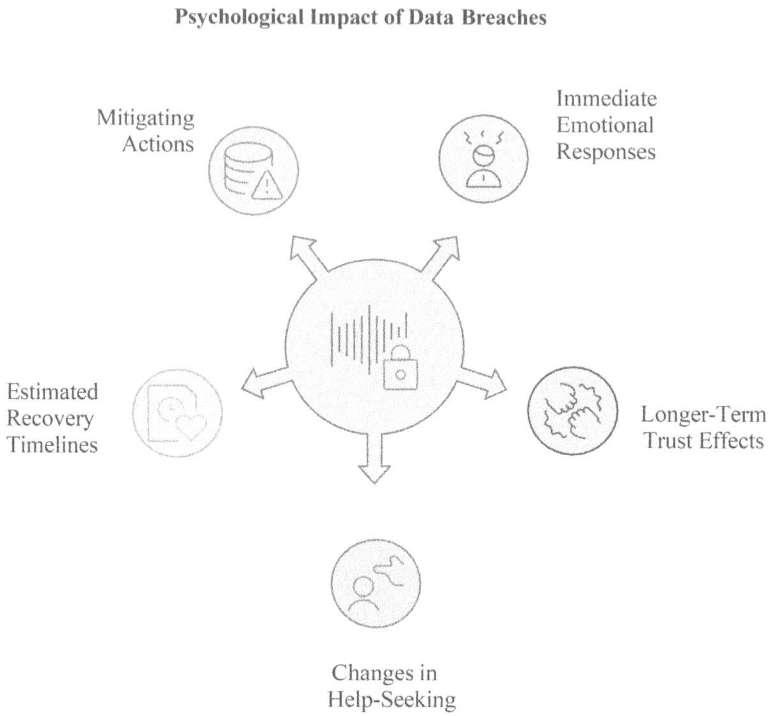

FIGURE 6.7 Youth risk pathways. This figure traces how engagement-driven algorithms and decision opacity create specific harms for young people, including exploitation of developmental vulnerabilities, increased anxiety, and reduced help-seeking. Understanding these pathways is essential for designing safeguards that protect youth while supporting their autonomy.

For *people with pre-existing mental health conditions,* robust privacy protections are essential, as is monitoring for over-triggered alerts that could increase distress. Recommendations must account for comorbidities and trauma, and clear escalation pathways to human support must be available when automated support is insufficient. The goal is care that reduces distress without sacrificing dignity (Raghav & Gulia, 2023; Cross et al., 2024; Kalam et al., 2024; Sanchez et al., 2024).

> ***Takeaway:*** *Individuals with mental health sensitivities, including youth and marginalized users, face heightened risks from unethical AI systems.*
> ***Reflection:*** *What safeguards should platforms put in place to protect users who may be emotionally or psychologically vulnerable?*

6.5 Governance and Ethical Readiness

Ethical principles, no matter how well-intentioned, remain abstract without organizational structures to operationalize them. This section addresses the governance frameworks and ethical readiness mechanisms that organizations must establish to translate the principles outlined in Section 6.2 and the design practices presented in Section 6.3 into sustained, accountable action. Governance is not a constraint on innovation; it is the infrastructure that makes ethical AI real and trustworthy. The strategies outlined here establish the preconditions for the policies and regulatory frameworks discussed in Chapter 10.

Ethical design is not a one-time check; it is a chain of choices that protect people at each stage of building and using a tool. The aim is psychological safety: privacy that holds, fair results across groups, clear explanations that reduce worry, and real

TABLE 6.3 Core Data Practices for Mental-Health AI, the User-Level Benefit, What to Report, and How Often to Review

Control	*What It Means in Practice*	*User-Level Benefit*	*Measure to Report*	*Review Cadence*
Data Minimization	Collect only what is needed for care; switch off any field that is not needed; allow people to skip non-essential questions.	Lower anxiety about oversharing; higher trust in the tool.	Share of optional fields left blank without blocking care; rate of reduction in collected fields over time.	Quarterly and after any incident.
Purpose Limits	State, in plain words, how each data type will be used; no reuse for ads or unrelated aims; changes require fresh consent.	Clear expectations; less fear of hidden uses.	Number of purpose statements updated; share of users who re-consent; complaints about unexpected use.	Quarterly and after any change in purpose.
Retention Limits	Keep data only as long as it is needed; set clear deletion dates; show people these dates; default to shorter periods.	Peace of mind about how long records exist.	Median time to deletion after request; percent deleted by scheduled date; exceptions with reasons.	Quarterly and after any incident.

(*Continued*)

TABLE 6.3 (Continued)

Control	*What It Means in Practice*	*User-Level Benefit*	*Measure to Report*	*Review Cadence*
Security Controls	Strong protection during storage and transfer; strict access rules; alerts on unusual access; regular tests of defenses.	Confidence that data are safe from misuse.	Findings from security tests; number of access alerts reviewed and closed; time to close high-risk issues.	Quarterly and after any incident.
User Access and Deletion	Simple way to see, correct, download, or delete records; no penalty for using these options.	Sense of control; higher willingness to seek help.	Requests fulfilled; median time to fulfill; user rating of the process; appeals and outcomes.	Quarterly and after any incident.

routes to human help. Organizations must embed these protections into their governance structures, monitoring systems, and decision-making processes.

Data governance is the foundation of user trust in mental health AI systems. Collect only what is necessary; state the purpose in clear, concise language; set short retention periods; protect data with robust controls; and prefer on-device or local processing whenever possible. De-identification should be robust and reversible only under a strict legal process. People must be able to see, correct, or delete their records without friction. These practices align with modern privacy laws, reducing the fear that blocks help-seeking (Amini et al., 2023).

Table 6.3 outlines core data practices for mental health AI, highlighting the user-level benefits, what to report, and how frequently to review. Each practice, data minimization, purpose limits, retention limits, security controls, and user access and deletion translates an ethical commitment into measurable organizational action. Data governance is not just a technical matter; it is an ethical obligation. Organizations should regularly audit their data practices, report findings transparently, and adjust retention and collection policies based on user feedback and incident reviews.

Bias detection and mitigation require diverse sources and ongoing verification. Training and evaluation should include groups defined by culture, language, age, gender, and socioeconomic status. Teams should review false negatives and false positives by subgroup, adjust thresholds where needed, and document each fix. Public summaries of these reviews help rebuild trust where harm has occurred (Gupta, 2023).

User-centered transparency is essential. People need to know what the tool reads, how sure it is, and what will happen next. Explanations should be layered, starting with a concise, readable summary, followed by a more in-depth view for those who require additional information. Confidence should be shown with simple bands, and reasons for low confidence should be stated in plain words. The interface should clearly indicate when a person can expect to hear from a clinician and provide instructions on how to reach one now. Such design supports informed choice and lowers anxiety during distress (Figure 6.8) (Rajkumar et al., 2024; Amini et al., 2023).

Accountability mechanisms keep people safe when things go wrong. There should be designated roles for clinical oversight, privacy and security, and quality assurance. Incident paths must be published, including instructions on how to report harm, the designated responder, and the timeframe for response. Decision logs should record key assessments, handoffs, and changes to thresholds, allowing reviewers to trace outcomes and identify faults. External review by ethics boards or user councils can check that changes stay aligned with well-being goals (Gupta, 2023).

Inclusive design reflects many ways of living. Invite youth, people with lived experience, and communities often left out to shape prompts, pacing, and language.

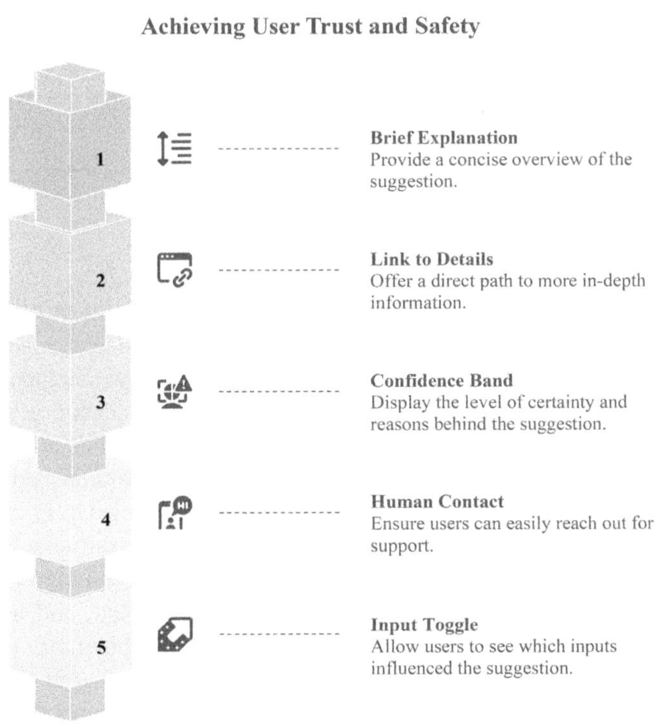

FIGURE 6.8 Layered explanations wireframe shows a brief explanation, a link to details, a confidence band with reasons, and a clear path to human contact.

Support low-bandwidth, plain language reading levels, local languages, screen readers, and voice input. Offer offline logging with later sync when network connectivity is weak. This mix expands its reach and respects diverse forms of expression (Willson et al., 2024).

Continuous ethical evaluation ensures that tools continue to learn in safe ways after release. Teams should track drift in model behavior, consent comprehension, parity of errors across groups, and the effects of prompts on mood and help-seeking. Regular reports should share findings and fixes in plain language. User councils should have the power to pause features that cause harm and to request changes that support well-being (Shukla, 2024).

Linking design to well-being means ensuring that each element above ties back to outcomes in emotional, psychological, and social health. This involves tracking changes in distress, hope, belonging, and functioning and adjusting the product when a change in design impacts these outcomes. Clear reports that connect design choices to these measures help teams focus on what matters most to people who seek help.

> ***Takeaway:*** *Ethical-by-design AI prioritizes mental health through user-centered data practices, explainability, and inclusive design frameworks.*
> ***Reflection:*** *What design changes would make you feel safer and more supported when using AI-powered tools or platforms?*

6.6 Summary and Reflections

Throughout this chapter, AI is portrayed as a behavioral architect that can either widen access to care or deepen harm, depending on the choices made by teams and institutions. The central argument is straightforward: psychological protection is not an add-on feature but a way of working that includes data practices, model testing, plain language explanations, human oversight, and public accountability.

This chapter has traced a deliberate path. Section 6.1 established the ethical imperative that AI in mental health is too consequential to leave to chance. Section 6.2 introduced the foundational principles: transparency, fairness, consent, and accountability. Section 6.3 translated those principles into concrete design practices: privacy by default, bias mitigation, meaningful consent, and human oversight. Section 6.4 examined specific obligations toward vulnerable populations, showing both the benefits that ethical AI can deliver and the harms that unethical practices inflict. Section 6.5 establishes the governance structures that operationalize these principles, transforming abstract commitments into an organizational reality.

The principles and practices described throughout this chapter converge on a few essential requirements. Transparency lowers anxiety by showing users what signals were read, how confident the system is, and what happens next. Fairness reduces unequal error rates and prevents culture, language, or income from determining who benefits. Meaningful consent, which is ongoing, adjustable, and easy to use during moments of strain, respects user autonomy. Accountability requires clear responsibility, documented decisions, and defined response times so errors are found and fixed. Together, these create the conditions for benefits like timely access, tailored support, lower stigma, and skill building.

Ethical design requires action at three interconnected levels. Product choices include data minimization, subgroup audits for fairness, layered explanations, and clear routes to human help. These are technical decisions organizations can make immediately. Practice choices include incident response protocols, public reporting of performance data, and user councils with real influence over system changes. These reflect organizational commitment to accountability and continuous improvement. Policy choices include risk-based regulation, privacy rights with enforcement mechanisms, and procurement standards that require equity checks and accessible design. These create systemic incentives for ethical practices across the ecosystem. When these three levels work together, ethical design becomes the default, not the exception.

The principles and practices in this chapter are not theoretical; they are immediately actionable. Table 6.4 outlines specific next steps for each key actor in the ecosystem, accompanied by evidence of progress and realistic timeframes measured in weeks or months, rather than years. These actions demonstrate that ethical design does not require waiting for perfect solutions or comprehensive regulation; it requires commitment and action today.

This chapter establishes the ethical foundation that subsequent chapters build upon. Chapter 5 described the psychological impacts of AI on mental health, including both benefits and risks. This chapter has shown how those impacts can be shaped through ethical design and governance. Chapter 10 will address policy and regulatory approaches to making ethical practices the norm rather than the exception.

The argument is cumulative: without understanding psychological impacts, we cannot understand why ethical design matters. Without understanding ethical design, we cannot determine what policies should be required. Without policies and regulations, ethical design remains dependent on individual organizational goodwill rather than becoming a systemic expectation.

In mental health AI, ethics is not the enemy of innovation; it is the condition for beneficial innovation. Systems that are transparent, fair, and accountable are more likely to be trusted by users and clinicians. Systems that protect privacy and respect autonomy maintain engagement over time. Systems that are monitored for harm and adjusted when problems emerge deliver real benefits. Systems that involve users and affected communities in design are more likely to meet actual needs.

TABLE 6.4 One-Step Actions by Role Names a Single Near-Term Action for Each Actor and Shows How Progress Will be Shown

Actor	*One Action Today*	*Evidence of Progress*	*Timeframe*
Designers	Replace generic consent with a layered, plain-language flow that includes a short comprehension check.	≥80% correct on the check across groups; drop in consent-related complaints.	Four to six weeks.
Engineers	Add subgroup evaluation to the test suite and gate releases on parity thresholds.	Automated report attached to each release; parity gaps below target.	Next release.
Clinical Leads	Define escalation thresholds and publish response times inside the app.	Audit shows on-time responses; users can find the rule in one tap.	Two to four weeks.
Product Owners	Turn off streaks and late-night prompts in health flows; cap session length.	Decrease in after-midnight usage without drop in outcomes.	Two weeks.
Privacy and Security	Shorten retention defaults; add a self-serve deletion path.	Median deletion time under set target; higher use of access tools.	One month.
Procurement	Require subgroup audits, accessibility checks, and free crisis features in all contracts.	Contracts updated; vendor attestations published.	Next procurement cycle.
Regulators	Pilot a plain-language safety label and publish incident summaries with timelines.	Labels live on listings; public incident log updated.	This quarter.
App Stores and Hosts	Enforce minimum safety standards for mental-health tools, including easy cancellation and no paywalls on crisis care.	Store policy updated; periodic compliance reports.	This quarter.

The choice before organizations is not between ethics and innovation, but between innovation grounded in ethical principles and innovation that is not. The former creates tools that users trust and that deliver real benefits. The latter creates tools that users avoid, that regulators scrutinize, and that ultimately fail to achieve their intended purpose.

Ethical design in mental health AI is not optional. It is the foundation upon which all beneficial applications of AI in this domain must be built. The path forward is clear. The question is not whether organizations can implement ethical design; it is whether they will.

References

Akinrinola, N. O., Okoye, N. C. C., Ofodile, N. O. C., & Ugochukwu, N. C. E. (2024). Navigating and reviewing ethical dilemmas in AI development: Strategies for transparency, fairness, and accountability. *GSC Advanced Research and Reviews*, *18*(3), 050–058. https://doi.org/10.30574/gscarr.2024.18.3.0088

Allen, J. W., Earp, B. D., Koplin, J., & Wilkinson, D. (2023). Consent-GPT: Is it ethical to delegate procedural consent to conversational AI? *Journal of Medical Ethics*, *50*(2), 77–83. https://doi.org/10.1136/jme-2023-109347

Allen, J. W., Earp, B. D., & Wilkinson, D. (2025). AI-assisted consent in paediatric medicine: Ethical implications of using large language models to support decision-making. *Journal of Medical Ethics*, jme–2024. https://doi.org/10.1136/jme-2024-110624

Al-Wathinani, A. M., Barten, D. G., Alsahli, H., Alhamid, A., Alghamdi, W., Alqahtani, W., Alghamdi, R., Aljuaid, M., Albaqami, N. A., & Goniewicz, K. (2023). The Right to refuse: Understanding healthcare providers' perspectives on patient autonomy in emergency care. *Healthcare*, *11*(12), 1756. https://doi.org/10.3390/healthcare11121756

Amini, M. M., Jesus, M., Sheikholeslami, D. F., Alves, P., Benam, A. H., & Hariri, F. (2023). Artificial intelligence ethics and challenges in healthcare applications: A comprehensive review in the context of the European GDPR Mandate. *Machine Learning and Knowledge Extraction*, *5*(3), 1023–1035. https://doi.org/10.3390/make5030053

Bahangulu, N. J. K., & Owusu-Berko, N. L. (2025). Algorithmic bias, data ethics, and governance: Ensuring fairness, transparency and compliance in AI-powered business analytics applications. *World Journal of Advanced Research and Reviews*, *25*(2), 1746–1763. https://doi.org/10.30574/wjarr.2025.25.2.0571

Chaudhry, B. M., & Debi, H. R. (2023). User perceptions and experiences of an AI-driven conversational agent for mental health support. *mHealth*, *0*, 0. https://doi.org/10.21037/mhealth-23-55

Cheng, L., Han, J., & Nasirov, J. (2024). Ethical considerations related to personal data collection and reuse: Trust and transparency in language and speech technologies. *International Journal of Legal Discourse*. https://doi.org/10.1515/ijld-2024-2010

Chew, H. S. J., & Achananuparp, P. (2022). Perceptions and needs of artificial intelligence in health care to Increase adoption: Scoping review. *Journal of Medical Internet Research*, *24*(1), e32939. https://doi.org/10.2196/32939

Cross, S., Bell, I., Nicholas, J., Valentine, L., Mangelsdorf, S., Baker, S., Titov, N., & Alvarez-Jimenez, M. (2024). Use of AI in mental health care: Community and mental health professionals survey. *JMIR Mental Health*, *11*, e60589. https://doi.org/10.2196/60589

Fields, L. M., & Calvert, J. D. (2015). Informed consent procedures with cognitively impaired patients: A review of ethics and best practices. *Psychiatry and Clinical Neurosciences*, *69*(8), 462–471. https://doi.org/10.1111/pcn.12289

Froicu, E., Creangă-Murariu, I., Afrăsânie, V., Gafton, B., Alexa-Stratulat, T., Miron, L., Puşcaşu, D. M., Poroch, V., Bacoanu, G., Radu, I., & Marinca, M. (2025). Artificial intelligence and decision-making in oncology: A review of ethical, legal, and informed consent challenges. *Current Oncology Reports*, *27*(8), 1002–1012. https://doi.org/10.1007/s11912-025-01698-8

Giray, L. (2024). Cases of using ChatGPT as a mental health and psychological support tool. *Journal of Consumer Health on the Internet*, 1–20. https://doi.org/10.1080/15398285.2024.2442374

Gundersen, T., & Bærøe, K. (2022). The future ethics of artificial intelligence in medicine: Making sense of collaborative models. *Science and Engineering Ethics*, *28*(2), 17. https://doi.org/10.1007/s11948-022-00369-2

Gupta, N. (2023). Artificial intelligence ethics and fairness: A study to address bias and fairness issues in AI systems, and the ethical implications of AI applications. *Revista Review Index Journal of Multidisciplinary*, *3*(2), 24–35. https://doi.org/10.31305/rrijm2023.v03.n02.004

Joshi, G., Jain, A., Araveeti, S. R., Adhikari, S., Garg, H., & Bhandari, M. (2024). FDA-approved Artificial Intelligence and Machine Learning (AI/ML)-Enabled Medical Devices: An updated landscape. *Electronics*, *13*(3), 498. https://doi.org/10.3390/electronics13030498

Kalam, K. T., Rahman, J. M., Islam, M. R., & Dewan, S. M. R. (2024). ChatGPT and mental health: Friends or foes? *Health Science Reports*, *7*(2). https://doi.org/10.1002/hsr2.1912

Kassam, I., Ilkina, D., Kemp, J., Roble, H., Carter-Langford, A., & Shen, N. (2023). Patient perspectives and preferences for consent in the digital health context: State-of-the-art literature review. *Journal of Medical Internet Research*, *25*, e42507. https://doi.org/10.2196/42507

King, A., Odunitan-Wayas, F., Chaudhury, M., Rubio, M., Baiocchi, M., Kolbe-Alexander, T., Montes, F., Banchoff, A., Sarmiento, O., Bälter, K., Hinckson, E., Chastin, S., Lambert, E., González, S., Guerra, A., Gelius, P., Zha, C., Sarabu, C., Kakar, P.,. . . Gardiner, P. (2021). Community-based approaches to reducing health inequities and fostering environmental justice through global youth-engaged citizen science. *International Journal of Environmental Research and Public Health*, *18*(3), 892. https://doi.org/10.3390/ijerph18030892

Kumar, S., Radhakrishnan, V., Nimma, D., Tamilarasi, K., Kumar, P., & Florence, M. M. V. (2024). Role of AI and machine learning in enhancing mental health care. *South Eastern European Journal of Public Health*, 765–770. https://doi.org/10.70135/seejph.vi.1833

Luo, X., Zhang, A., Li, Y., Zhang, Z., Ying, F., Lin, R., Yang, Q., Wang, J., & Huang, G. (2024). Emergence of Artificial Intelligence Art Therapies (AIATs) in Mental Health Care: A systematic review. *International Journal of Mental Health Nursing*, *33*(6), 1743–1760. https://doi.org/10.1111/inm.13384

Mamo, N., Martin, G. M., Desira, M., Ellul, B., & Ebejer, J. (2019). Dwarna: A blockchain solution for dynamic consent in biobanking. *European Journal of Human Genetics*, *28*(5), 609–626. https://doi.org/10.1038/s41431-019-0560-9

Mittelstadt, B. (2019). Principles alone cannot guarantee ethical AI. *Nature Machine Intelligence*, *1*(11), 501–507. https://doi.org/10.1038/s42256-019-0114-4

Mittelstadt, B. D., Allo, P., Taddeo, M., Wachter, S., & Floridi, L. (2016). The ethics of algorithms: Mapping the debate. *Big Data & Society*, *3*(2). https://doi.org/10.1177/2053951716679679

Nashwan, A. J., Gharib, S., Alhadidi, M., El-Ashry, A. M., Alamgir, A., Al-Hassan, M., Khedr, M. A., Dawood, S., & Abufarsakh, B. (2023). Harnessing artificial intelligence: Strategies for mental health nurses in optimizing psychiatric patient care. *Issues in Mental Health Nursing*, *44*(10), 1020–1034. https://doi.org/10.1080/01612840.2023.2263579

Neri, E., Coppola, F., Miele, V., Bibbolino, C., & Grassi, R. (2020). Artificial intelligence: Who is responsible for the diagnosis? *La Radiologia Medica*, *125*(6), 517–521. https://doi.org/10.1007/s11547-020-01135-9

Ni, Y., & Jia, F. (2025). A scoping review of AI-Driven digital interventions in Mental health care: Mapping applications across screening, support, monitoring, prevention, and clinical education. *Healthcare*, *13*(10), 1205. https://doi.org/10.3390/healthcare13101205

Olatoye, N. F. O., Awonuga, N. K. F., Mhlongo, N. N. Z., Ibeh, N. C. V., Elufioye, N. O. A., & Ndubuisi, N. N. L. (2024). AI and ethics in business: A comprehensive review of responsible AI practices and corporate responsibility. *International Journal of Science and Research Archive*, *11*(1), 1433–1443. https://doi.org/10.30574/ijsra.2024.11.1.0235

Prakash, S., Balaji, J. N., Joshi, A., & Surapaneni, K. M. (2022). Ethical conundrums in the application of Artificial Intelligence (AI) in healthcare—A scoping review of reviews. *Journal of Personalized Medicine*, *12*(11), 1914. https://doi.org/10.3390/jpm12111914

Pulivarthy, P., & Whig, P. (2024). Bias and fairness addressing discrimination in AI systems. In *Advances in human and social aspects of technology book series* (pp. 103–126). https://doi.org/10.4018/979-8-3693-4147-6.ch005

Raghav, Y. Y., & Gulia, S. (2023). The rise of artificial intelligence and its implications on spirituality. In *Advances in human and social aspects of technology book series* (pp. 165–178). https://doi.org/10.4018/978-1-6684-9196-6.ch011

Rajkumar, N., Viji, C., Mohanraj, A., Senthilkumar, K. R., Jagajeevan, R., & Kovilpillai, J. A. (2024). Ethical considerations of AI implementation in the library era. In *Advances in library and information science (ALIS) book series* (pp. 85–106). https://doi.org/10.4018/979-8-3693-5593-0.ch007

Richardson, J. P., Smith, C., Curtis, S., Watson, S., Zhu, X., Barry, B., & Sharp, R. R. (2021). Patient apprehensions about the use of artificial intelligence in healthcare. *Npj Digital Medicine*, *4*(1), 140. https://doi.org/10.1038/s41746-021-00509-1

Sanchez, T. W., Brenman, M., & Ye, X. (2024). The ethical concerns of artificial intelligence in urban planning. *Journal of the American Planning Association*, 1–14. https://doi.org/10.1080/01944363.2024.2355305

Saqib, H., Sumyia, N., & Saqib, N. A. (2023). AI chatbots and psychotherapy: A match made in heaven? *Journal of the Pakistan Medical Association*, *73*(11), 2321. https://doi.org/10.47391/jpma.9608

Shlobin, N. A., Sheldon, M., & Lam, S. (2020). Informed consent in neurosurgery: A systematic review. *Neurosurgical Focus*, *49*(5), E6. https://doi.org/10.3171/2020.8.focus20611

Shou, Y., Yeo, J. E., Pang, A. S., Paterson, D. L., & Mo, Y. (2024). Informed consent and risk communication challenges in antimicrobial clinical trials: A scoping review. *BMJ Open*, *14*(11), e082096. https://doi.org/10.1136/bmjopen-2023-082096

Shukla, S. (2024). Principles governing ethical development and deployment of AI. *International Journal of Engineering Business and Management*, *8*(2), 26–46. https://doi.org/10.22161/ijebm.8.2.5

Steimers, A., & Schneider, M. (2022). Sources of risk of AI systems. *International Journal of Environmental Research and Public Health*, *19*(6), 3641. https://doi.org/10.3390/ijerph19063641

Steinsbekk, K. S., Myskja, B. K., & Solberg, B. (2013). Broad consent versus dynamic consent in biobank research: Is passive participation an ethical problem? *European Journal of Human Genetics*, *21*(9), 897–902. https://doi.org/10.1038/ejhg.2012.282

Stinson, C. (2022). Algorithms are not neutral. *AI And Ethics*, *2*(4), 763–770. https://doi.org/10.1007/s43681-022-00136-w

Tang, L., Li, J., & Fantus, S. (2023). Medical artificial intelligence ethics: A systematic review of empirical studies. *Digital Health*, *9*. https://doi.org/10.1177/20552076231186064

Thiruma, A. V. (2023). AI ethics and bias: Exploratory study on the ethical considerations and potential biases in ai and data-driven decision-making in banking, with a focus on fairness, transparency, and accountability. *World Journal of Advanced Research and Reviews*, *20*(2), 197–206. https://doi.org/10.30574/wjarr.2023.20.2.2245

Uzougbo, N. N. S., Ikegwu, N. C. G., & Adewusi, N. a. O. (2024). Legal accountability and ethical considerations of AI in financial services. *GSC Advanced Research and Reviews*, *19*(2), 130–142. https://doi.org/10.30574/gscarr.2024.19.2.0171

Willson, J. L., Nuche, A., & Widayanti, R. (2024). Ethical considerations in the development of AI-Powered healthcare assistants. *International Transactions on Education Technology (ITEE)*, *2*(2), 109–119. https://doi.org/10.33050/itee.v2i2.566

Wimbarti, S., Kairupan, B. H. R., & Tallei, T. E. (2024). Critical review of self-diagnosis of mental health conditions using artificial intelligence. *International Journal of Mental Health Nursing*, *33*(2), 344–358. https://doi.org/10.1111/inm.13303

Yıldız, E. (2025). Artificial intelligence in mental health nursing: Balancing clinical efficiency and the human touch—A quest for a new synthesis. *Journal of Psychiatric and Mental Health Nursing*. https://doi.org/10.1111/jpm.13173

STREAM 3

Personality Traits, Gender Differences, and Cultural Perspectives

7

PERSONALITY TRAITS IN THE DIGITAL AND AI-DRIVEN WORLD

Chapter Objectives

- To analyze how personality traits influence cyber behavior and ethical engagement with AI.
- To apply established personality models (Big Five, HEXACO, and the Dark Tetrad) to interpret diverse cyber behaviors.
- To examine how individual differences affect both ethical and unethical cyber behaviors.
- To propose trait-based approaches to ethical design, policy, and digital well-being strategies.

Topics to Be Covered

- Introduction to Personality and Digital Engagement
- Big Five Traits and Cyber Behavior
- HEXACO Model and Ethical AI Use
- The Dark Tetrad and Antisocial Cyber Behaviors
- Personality and Ethical Decision-Making in AI Contexts
- Designing Ethical and Inclusive Digital Interventions
- Summary and Reflections

DOI: 10.4324/9781003657590-10

7.1 Introduction: Why Personality Matters in a Digital World

Personality psychology provides a critical foundation for understanding why people behave differently in cyberspaces and how they engage with artificial intelligence (AI) systems. As digital interactions expand, individual differences become increasingly significant in shaping patterns of technology adoption, online communication, and ethical decision-making. Established frameworks such as the Big Five traits, HEXACO, and the Dark Tetrad allow researchers to systematically study how personality characteristics are reflected in cyber behavior and responses to AI technologies (Stachl et al., 2020; Rauthmann, 2020).

Personality traits influence both positive and negative outcomes in digital environments. Openness to experience, for instance, has been shown to support innovation and greater willingness to adopt AI-based tools, whereas neuroticism often predicts fear, anxiety, and resistance toward emerging systems (Park & Woo, 2022; Stein & Gnambs, 2024). Similarly, agreeableness is associated with prosocial cyber behavior and stronger trust in AI, whereas traits such as Machiavellianism or psychopathy may drive manipulative or harmful behaviors in digital interactions (Leng et al., 2020; Kaya et al., 2022). These differences highlight that personality does not simply shape user preferences but also plays a role in determining whether technology use contributes to digital well-being or fuels unethical practices.

The influence of personality extends across a wide range of digital contexts. In professional settings, personality traits can influence how individuals respond to AI-driven systems that are reshaping work processes (Zhang et al., 2025). In healthcare, they can affect how people perceive AI-assisted diagnosis or therapy tools, with traits such as trust and empathy shaping acceptance (Oladimeji et al., 2023). In consumer environments, differences in personality inform attitudes toward AI assistants, targeted advertising, and personalized recommendation systems (Jain et al., 2023). While the domains vary, the common thread is that personality helps explain the variability in how users approach technology, form trust, and evaluate ethical concerns (Hsieh & Lee, 2024; Upadhyaya & Galizzi, 2023).

A growing body of research also points to the ethical complexities of personality-aware AI. On one hand, personalization offers opportunities for tailoring digital systems to individual needs, potentially improving user experience and outcomes (Giron et al., 2024). On the other hand, personality profiling introduces risks of manipulation, privacy violation, and loss of autonomy (Caşcaval, 2024). Many individuals perceive attempts to predict or influence their behavior based on personality traits as intrusive and exhausting, especially when they feel they lack control over how their data is used (Völkel et al., 2020). This duality highlights the need for ethical frameworks that strike a balance between the benefits of personalization and the protection of user agency and dignity. Understanding how personality shapes cyber behavior and AI interaction provides valuable insights for research, policy, and design. By integrating personality psychology into digital ethics and technology development, systems can be made more adaptive to human diversity while maintaining respect for individual rights and well-being.

> ***Takeaway:*** *Personality psychology helps explain why people behave differently in digital environments, particularly in their interactions with AI technologies.*
> ***Reflection:*** *How has your personality influenced the way you engage with technology and cyberspaces?*

7.2 Big Five Traits and Cyber Behavior

The Big Five personality traits: neuroticism, conscientiousness, openness, extraversion, and agreeableness, offer a robust framework for analyzing how individual differences shape cyber behaviors, emotional responses, and ethical awareness. These traits significantly influence how people manage online stress, interact with AI systems, respond to criticism, and navigate ethical dilemmas in cyberspaces (Figure 7.1) (Park & Woo, 2022; Kaya et al., 2022; Stein & Gnambs, 2024).

Neuroticism is closely linked with negative digital experiences. Individuals high in neuroticism are more prone to online stress, compulsive use, and susceptibility to negative emotions. Research highlights that neuroticism predicts problematic internet behaviors, including diminished impulse control, loneliness, and depressive symptoms in cyber contexts (Durak & Senol-Durak, 2014). It also influences compulsive online buying, often used as a coping mechanism to manage stress and anxiety (Otero-López et al., 2023). Studies further show that neurotic individuals experience heightened AI-related fears and anxieties across cultures, though they sometimes view AI as socially supportive, reflecting both dependency and ambivalence (Park & Woo, 2022; Sindermann & Elhai, 2022).

Conscientiousness tends to predict structured, careful, and ethically grounded cyber behavior. Highly conscientious users are more deliberate in their online decisions and demonstrate better knowledge management behaviors, such as information acquisition and application in digital settings (Esmaeelinezhad & Afrazeh, 2018). Their strong sense of duty extends to cyber ethics, where conscientiousness is associated with responsible engagement and lower levels of negative emotion toward AI (Duan & Deng, 2023; Park & Woo, 2022). Although they often focus on functionality and practical benefits rather than social aspects, conscientious individuals are less likely to engage in risky or unethical cyber behaviors, instead maintaining healthy boundaries and employing systematic coping strategies for digital stress.

Openness to experience reflects adaptability and curiosity in online contexts. Individuals who score high in openness are more likely to adopt new technologies and engage in diverse digital activities. Their willingness to experiment makes them early adopters of AI-driven systems, and they tend to hold more favorable views of functionality and innovation (Park & Woo, 2022; Oksanen et al., 2020). Openness also motivates electronic word-of-mouth behaviors, as these individuals often enjoy sharing knowledge and supporting others (Anastasiei & Dospinescu, 2018; Esmaeelinezhad & Afrazeh, 2018). However, openness can be a double-edged trait; while it supports engagement with emerging technologies, it may also increase susceptibility to manipulative or ethically questionable digital practices due to a higher willingness to try novel experiences (Calvo et al., 2020; Ienca, 2023).

Agreeableness has a strong influence on digital prosocial behavior and ethical awareness. Agreeable individuals tend to engage in empathic listening and collaborative communication online, fostering trust and positive social environments (Sims, 2016; Yu et al., 2021). They are more likely to demonstrate ethical awareness, prioritize social harmony, and respond constructively to online criticism. Research indicates that agreeableness predicts prosocial cyber behavior across cultures, with individuals who are agreeable reporting higher trust in AI systems and a greater concern for social implications (Leng et al., 2020; Sindermann & Elhai, 2022). However, their openness to trust can also expose them to ethical risks if systems exploit their cooperative tendencies.

Extraversion presents a complex relationship with cyber behavior. Extraverts are more active in social media and online communities, displaying greater digital engagement and prosocial online actions (Leng et al., 2020). However, they often hold negative attitudes toward AI, reporting skepticism about its functionality and emotional resonance (Park & Woo, 2022). This tension suggests that while extraverts thrive in cybersocial contexts, they may resist or critique non-human forms of interaction, preferring human-centered engagement. When faced with digital

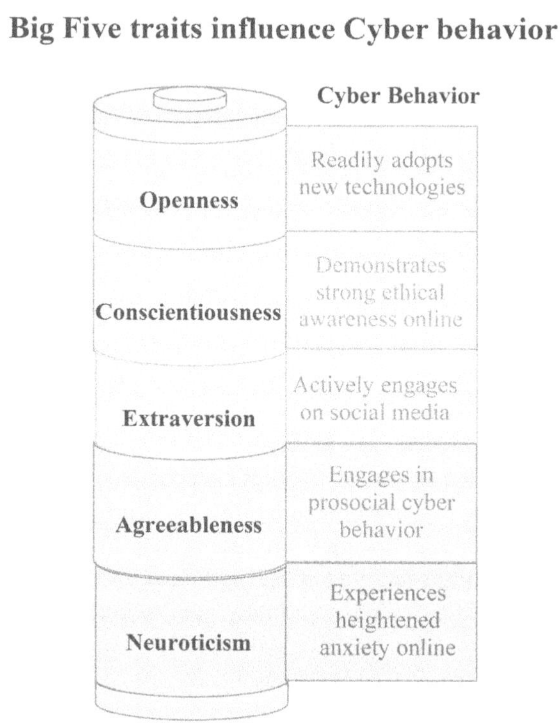

FIGURE 7.1 The influence of the Five traits on cyber behaviors.

stress, extraverts often seek social support online, though their skepticism toward AI systems may limit reliance on technological assistance.

Collectively, the Big Five traits highlight how personality underpins differences in online habits, ethical behavior, and attitudes toward AI, as shown in Table 7.1. Neuroticism and conscientiousness stand out as particularly influential in shaping responses to online stress and ethical dilemmas, while openness and agreeableness expand possibilities for innovation and prosociality, and extraversion reflects both high engagement and resistance to machine-mediated sociality. These insights

TABLE 7.1 Big Five Traits and Their Influence on Cyber Behavior

Trait	*Cyber Behaviors*	*Ethical Strengths*	*Vulnerabilities*
Neuroticism	High online stress, compulsive use, negative emotions, compulsive online buying.	May seek online social support when anxious.	Technology anxiety, susceptibility to manipulation, risk of problematic internet use.
Conscientiousness	Careful, structured digital habits; knowledge management; boundary-setting.	Strong ethical awareness, responsibility-driven decision-making, reduced online risks.	Lower sociality in digital spaces; may under-engage with community-driven aspects of technology.
Openness	Curiosity-driven adoption of new tech; diverse online exploration and engagement.	Innovation-oriented, adaptable to new tools, knowledge sharing.	Higher susceptibility to manipulation; openness to ethically questionable digital experiences.
Agreeableness	Empathic listening, prosocial online behavior, collaborative communication.	Promotes trust, ethical awareness, supportive digital communities.	Trusting nature may expose them to exploitation or manipulation in digital/AI contexts.
Extraversion	High social media engagement, strong participation in online communities.	Active prosocial contributions, strong peer networks.	Negative emotions toward AI; skeptical of machine-mediated sociality; reliance on human-centered tech.

highlight the significance of personality-aware frameworks for digital well-being and the design of ethical AI (Stachl et al., 2020; Rauthmann, 2020).

The application of the Big Five framework offers valuable insights into how online communities can be managed more effectively and how user engagement can be sustained. Digital communities are not homogeneous; they bring together individuals with diverse personalities, preferences, and motivations. By understanding the psychological underpinnings of user behavior, community managers can create environments that foster meaningful interactions, reduce conflict, and encourage long-term participation (Badreddine et al., 2022; Roos, 2023). For instance, *extraversion* is consistently associated with active participation, higher levels of posting, and responsiveness to online interactions. Extraverted users are more likely to assume leadership roles within communities, particularly in groups where discussion and visibility are valued (Gazit, 2021). Community managers can channel this tendency by encouraging extroverts to act as discussion leaders, moderators, or ambassadors, thereby setting a tone of active participation. Additionally, *openness to experience* predicts engagement with diverse content and the willingness to adopt novel features or participate in creative challenges. Research demonstrates that open individuals are more likely to contribute ideas in innovation-driven platforms and engage with entertainment and relationship-oriented activities online (Tsao, 2013; Zhou & Tang, 2022). Providing experimental features, early access to new tools, or idea-sharing opportunities can thus directly appeal to this group and enhance overall community vitality. Furthermore, *conscientious* users display more structured engagement patterns, often contributing fewer but higher-quality posts. Their focus on order, responsibility, and diligence means they are more likely to uphold community guidelines and contribute knowledge-based content (Modgil et al., 2025). Systems that reward consistency, recognize reliable contributors, and provide structured participation pathways can help conscientious members thrive while improving the overall quality of interaction. Additionally, *agreeableness* correlates strongly with prosocial behaviors, including supportive responses, empathy, and conflict avoidance. Highly agreeable individuals are more likely to promote collaboration and harmony in online environments (Mustafa & Zhang, 2023). Communities can utilize this by promoting mentoring roles, peer support systems, and recognition for constructive contributions. However, their tendency to avoid confrontation may also require moderators to ensure that inclusivity does not silence necessary but difficult conversations. *Neuroticism*, in contrast, presents a more complex pattern. While high neuroticism is often linked with withdrawal, internet overuse, or heightened distress online (Tian et al., 2021), some studies suggest that neurotic individuals may be drawn to supportive roles in communities that provide reassurance and empathy (Li et al., 2026). Designing features that reduce anxiety, such as anonymous posting options or private communication channels, can mitigate negative outcomes while supporting healthy

TABLE 7.2 Personality Traits and Community Management Strategies

Trait	*Participation Patterns*	*Recommended Management Strategies*
Extraversion	High posting frequency, active in discussions, responsive to recognition	Assign leadership or ambassador roles; create live events and real-time interactions; implement public recognition systems.
Openness	Engagement with novel content, innovation-oriented, idea sharing	Provide early access to new features; run innovation challenges; diversify content formats; promote creative collaboration.
Conscientiousness	Structured participation, selective but high-quality contributions	Develop clear community guidelines; create reputation systems; establish mentorship programs; reward consistent engagement.
Agreeableness	Supportive responses, prosocial behaviors, conflict-avoidant	Foster peer support systems; emphasize collaboration; implement conflict resolution tools; reinforce constructive behaviors.
Neuroticism	Susceptible to stress, negative emotions, variable participation	Offer anonymous posting options; design supportive moderation; provide private channels; establish clear safety guidelines.

participation. It is interesting to note that the research base demonstrates that effective community management requires tailoring engagement strategies to align with the dominant personality distributions of the user base. For instance, platforms with a large proportion of open users may benefit from continuous innovation, whereas communities with high conscientiousness may prefer structured frameworks for participation (see Table 7.2). Cross-platform research also indicates that individuals express their personalities differently depending on the community type, meaning that adaptive moderation and engagement strategies must remain context-sensitive (Yang et al., 2022).

Takeaway: *Understanding the Big Five traits helps community managers design adaptive strategies that support both engagement and well-being, aligning community practices with the psychological needs of diverse members.*

Reflection: *How might your personality shape the way you participate in digital communities, and how could managers design spaces that better support those tendencies?*

7.3 The HEXACO Model and Ethical Engagement with AI

The HEXACO model expands traditional personality frameworks by introducing honesty-humility, a dimension that captures sincerity, fairness, modesty, and the avoidance of exploitation. This addition provides sharper insight into why individuals vary in their ethical responses to AI and digital environments. In contrast to traits that explain social energy or emotional stability, honesty-humility directly addresses moral sensitivity, making it especially relevant when studying how people approach AI-related choices. Research has shown that honesty-humility plays a vital role in shaping privacy-respecting behavior and fairness-oriented decision-making in AI contexts (Ashton & Lee, 2008; Carroll et al., 2025; ElSayary, 2025; Yu et al., 2024). This dimension is particularly relevant in the age of AI, as it helps explain why some individuals are more likely to engage in ethical AI use, respect data privacy, and resist the temptation to exploit technological loopholes for personal gain. Individuals high on this dimension are less inclined to manipulate systems and instead favor transparent practices that benefit collective welfare. They are more likely to adhere to community guidelines, respect intellectual property, and engage in truthful communication. Their inherent sense of fairness also makes them more sensitive to issues of algorithmic bias and data privacy, and they are more likely to advocate for ethical AI design that prioritizes user rights and social good. This tendency aligns with recent findings that link honesty-humility with resistance to biased or unfair applications of AI, reinforcing the idea that ethical use is not merely a function of external rules but also of personal disposition (Carroll et al., 2025; ElSayary, 2025; Lee et al., 2007; Rivera et al., 2025). Conversely, individuals low in Honesty-Humility are more prone to opportunistic and exploitative behaviors online. They are more likely to engage in deceptive practices, such as creating fake profiles or spreading disinformation for personal or political gain. Their tendency toward greed and self-enhancement makes them more susceptible to the allure of black-hat SEO, phishing scams, and other forms of digital exploitation (Ahmed & Masood, 2025; Borghi & Ratcharak, 2025; ElSayary, 2025; Kranenbarg et al., 2022). In the context of AI, they may be more inclined to use technologies like deepfakes for malicious purposes or to exploit vulnerabilities in algorithmic systems for financial or social advantage. This highlights the critical role of the Honesty-Humility dimension as a key individual difference factor in predicting misuse of AI technologies. Table 7.3 illustrates the differences between the Big Five and Hexaco models in terms of key traits for ethical behavior, strengths, and limitations. The other dimensions of the HEXACO model also provide valuable insights. Conscientiousness and agreeableness, as defined in the Big Five, explain prosocial tendencies and predict general online collaboration and responsibility (see Table 7.3). However, HEXACO extends the Big Five by isolating honesty-humility as a distinct moral trait, providing stronger explanatory power for ethical sensitivity and AI-related behaviors (ElSayary, 2025; Gnisci et al., 2023; Roberts et al., 2023). It offers clearer predictions about who will

TABLE 7.3 Comparing Big Five and HEXACO in Predicting Ethical AI Engagement

Model	*Key Traits for Ethical Behavior*	*Strengths in Digital Contexts*	*Limitations in Explaining AI-Related Ethics*
Big Five	Conscientiousness and Agreeableness	Explains diligence, cooperation, and prosocial tendencies; useful for predicting general online collaboration and responsibility.	Lacks a dedicated moral dimension; struggles to explain why some users act with integrity in privacy, fairness, and AI manipulation dilemmas.
HEXACO	Honesty-Humility (plus Big Five traits)	Captures sincerity, fairness, modesty, and avoidance of exploitation; predicts respect for privacy, resistance to AI misuse, and fairness in digital decision-making.	Broader empirical application in AI ethics is still developing; more research needed in cross-cultural and diverse technological contexts.

act responsibly or exploit AI systems, outperforming the Big Five in ethical AI contexts. Individuals with higher levels of this trait tend to exhibit greater reluctance to misuse AI tools in ways that compromise their academic or professional integrity. For example, instead of turning to AI for dishonest shortcuts, such individuals are more likely to value fairness and authenticity, even when misuse may be difficult to detect. This moral orientation reflects an internalized commitment to ethical principles, suggesting that honesty-humility offers predictive power beyond what can be explained by the Big Five traits (ElSayary, 2025; Fowers et al., 2023; Pilch, 2023; Reinhardt & Reinhard, 2023). The honesty-humility dimension also extends to pro-social and sustainable behaviors that carry implications for digital ethics (Gupta, 2023; Zettler et al., 2020). Individuals with this trait tend to support technologies aligned with environmental and social responsibility, signaling a broader value system that promotes collective well-being (ElSayary, 2025; Zettler et al., 2020). When translated into cyber behavior, this can be demonstrated by supporting platforms and AI tools that prioritize responsible data use, inclusivity, and transparency in decision-making. Such preferences highlight how moral values embedded in personality traits shape not only individual behavior but also broader patterns of digital adoption and resistance (ElSayary, 2025; Greitemeyer & Kastenmüller, 2023). At the same time, honesty-humility provides an explanation for why some users behave more aggressively or exploitatively online. Lower levels of this trait are associated with greater willingness to manipulate digital systems or disregard ethical boundaries, which helps account for patterns of AI misuse or indifference to algorithmic bias (Panno et al., 2021). This perspective demonstrates that not all unethical cyber behaviors stem from external pressures; it may also arise from stable personality orientations that favor self-interest over fairness (Baiocco et al., 2017; Burtăverde et al., 2017).

From a comparative perspective, HEXACO offers an advantage over traditional models because it isolates honesty-humility as a distinct moral trait rather than subsuming it under broader categories like agreeableness. This distinction has proven critical in AI-related studies, where honesty-humility has shown clearer associations with ethical engagement than other dimensions (Heck et al., 2018; Lee et al., 2018). While traits such as openness or conscientiousness may predict curiosity or diligence in digital use, honesty-humility provides a lens for understanding why individuals differ in their responses to ethical dilemmas, particularly in contexts involving privacy, fairness, and manipulation (ElSayary, 2025; Freyth et al., 2022; Gnisci et al., 2023; Roberts et al., 2023). The implications of these findings extend to both practice and policy. For designers, acknowledging honesty and humility can guide the development of AI systems that encourage fairness and transparency, while also anticipating that some users may require additional safeguards to counter exploitative tendencies. In education, understanding that certain students may be more susceptible to misusing AI tools highlights the need for targeted interventions that address personality-based differences in ethical sensitivity. At a policy level, integrating insights from the HEXACO model suggests that frameworks for AI ethics should not assume uniform behavior across users but should instead recognize the diversity of moral orientations that influence digital engagement (Bartneck et al., 2023; ElSayary, 2025; Greitemeyer & Kastenmüller, 2023; Hammerschmidt, 2025; Mumtaz et al., 2024). In other words, the HEXACO model, through its honesty-humility dimension, offers a powerful tool for understanding how personality shapes ethical sensitivity in the digital and AI-driven world. It demonstrates that differences in fairness, sincerity, and modesty can determine whether users act responsibly or unethically online, providing a foundation for more adaptive and personality-informed approaches to digital ethics.

Takeaway: *The HEXACO model, particularly its honesty-humility dimension, provides a deeper understanding of ethical engagement in cyberspaces by highlighting why some individuals prioritize fairness, privacy, and integrity when interacting with AI.*

Reflection: *How might online environments look different if digital platforms and AI systems were designed to recognize and respond to users' varying levels of honesty-humility?*

7.4 The Dark Tetrad and Antisocial Cyber Behavior

The Dark Tetrad, narcissism, Machiavellianism, psychopathy, and sadism, offers a precise lens for understanding hostile and exploitative behavior in digital settings.

These traits share a core of callousness and self-interest, yet each channel that core in distinct ways that surface in social platforms, forums, and AI-mediated interactions. Cyberspaces reduce social costs, widen audiences, and conceal identities; this mix can lead to competitive displays, strategic manipulation, thrill-seeking aggression, and cruelty for its own sake (Alavi et al., 2022; Moreira et al., 2024).

Narcissism centers on grandiosity and the need for admiration. In digital contexts, it often appears as status defense and attention-seeking: cutting remarks, public put-downs, and campaigns to control how others perceive the self. Empirical work links narcissism with cyberbullying and trolling, typically in service of self-image maintenance rather than sheer malice (Alavi et al., 2022; Schade et al., 2021). Recent studies have extended this pattern to AI misuse, where tools that scale self-promotion or manufacture praise, such as astroturfed reviews, polished narratives, or repetitive content, can be deployed to inflate visibility and manage impressions with minimal effort (Alavi et al., 2025; Greitemeyer & Kastenmüller, 2023).

Machiavellianism is colder and more tactical. Its hallmark is instrumental manipulation guided by long-range goals. Online, this is visible in coordinated harassment, gaming of platform rules, and patient shaping of group narratives. Scale and anonymity enable elaborate ploys, such as sock-puppet networks, selective leaks, and staged conflicts, which serve strategic aims (Leite & Monteiro, 2023). The arrival of accessible generative tools adds new levers. Synthetic identities, tailored disinformation, and automated outreach make deception cheaper and harder to trace, thereby raising the stakes of Machiavellian planning in reputation attacks and social engineering schemes (Djakovic & Rowlands, 2024).

Psychopathy brings impulsivity, fearlessness, and a blunt lack of remorse. In online environments, that mix predicts frequent, sharp aggression, little concern for harm, and quick escalation when provoked. Multiple studies identify psychopathy as a strong correlate of cyberbullying and active trolling, including patterns where users pounce on vulnerable targets and persist despite pushback (Johnson et al., 2019; Ubaradka & Khanganba, 2024). With AI in the loop, the same profile can translate into rapid production of abusive content, automated pile-ons, and opportunistic exploitation of system loopholes, actions driven by immediacy rather than careful planning (Blötner et al., 2021; Moreira et al., 2024).

Sadism is distinctive because harm itself is rewarding. In cyberspace, it manifests as relentless targeting, escalation intended to maximize distress, and the careful selection of responsive victims. Evidence across surveys and behavioral studies points to sadism as a potent predictor of trolling and cruelty in comment threads and direct messages (Derish, 2021; Gómez-Leal et al., 2024). Generative tools can intensify this pattern by enabling personally tailored insults, synthetic images, or voice spoofs crafted to humiliate and intimidate, thereby extending the reach and persistence of attacks (Gylfason et al., 2021).

These traits often co-occur, but their signatures differ. Narcissism is tied to status maintenance and audience capture; Machiavellianism, to patient orchestration and rule bending; psychopathy, to hot aggression and thrill; and sadism, to the deliberate infliction of suffering. Studies on moral disengagement and developmental risk provide context: when distancing oneself from victims becomes easier and bystanders remain silent, dark traits are more readily translated into action (Gajda et al., 2022). Work on "light" traits further suggests that empathy, compassion, and a prosocial outlook can dampen the pull of dark dispositions, hinting at levers for design and education (Castagna & Hart, 2024).

Platform features can increase or soften these expressions. Social feeds that reward provocation supply attention for narcissistic displays. Weak identity checks and porous moderation create opportunities for Machiavellian networks to disseminate misinformation. Low friction and viral mechanics amplify psychopathic outbursts, turning momentary spikes into widespread harm. Tools that enable personalization, synthetic media, targeted prompts, and automated outreach can be re-purposed by sadistic users to tailor degradation with unnerving precision (Leite & Monteiro, 2023). Cross-platform studies show that when anonymity is high and consequences are distant, harmful patterns increase, especially for users high on psychopathy and sadism (Ubaradka & Khanganba, 2024).

Interventions benefit from aligning with these profiles. Systems that remove spectacle reduce the payoff for narcissistic aggression by limiting visibility and social reinforcement. Friction, verification, and audit trails raise the cost of Machiavellian schemes and shrink the advantage of hidden coordination (Djakovic & Rowlands, 2024; Leite & Monteiro, 2023). Rapid, consistent consequences that cut off reach address psychopathic impulsivity by closing the window for escalation (Johnson et al., 2019; Moreira et al., 2024). Protective tools for targets, combined with proactive detection of abusive patterns, reduce the playground for sadistic users and signal clear limits (Derish, 2021; Gómez-Leal et al., 2024). Educational messages also matter: when communities understand how dark traits manifest online, bystanders are more likely to intervene, and victims can access support channels early (Panatik et al., 2022).

The growth of AI calls for safeguards tuned to misuse pathways. Content filters that catch targeted abuse, watermarking for synthetic media, moderation that recognizes staged campaigns, and graduated access to high-risk features all help contain harm without smothering ordinary use (Greitemeyer & Kastenmüller, 2023). Monitoring focused on behavior, pattern, and context works better than labeling users, while partnerships with trained community moderators and mental health resources support those affected (Leite & Monteiro, 2023; Moreira et al., 2024). Policy adds a further layer: clear terms, predictable enforcement, and appeal routes build trust and reduce the sense that bad actors can act with impunity (Alavi et al., 2022; Djakovic & Rowlands, 2024). Intervention strategies are outlined in Table 7.4.

The growing prevalence of antisocial behaviors in cyberspaces has pushed researchers and practitioners to explore AI-based monitoring and intervention systems. These technologies offer scalable, proactive mechanisms to detect harmful

TABLE 7.4 The Dark Tetrad, Cyber Behaviors, and AI Exploitation.

Trait	*Core Characteristics*	*Typical Cyber Behaviors*	*AI Misuse Patterns*	*Intervention Strategies*
Narcissism	Inflated self-importance, entitlement, need for admiration	Cyberbullying for status, self-promotion, manipulating narratives	Automating self-promotion, fabricating endorsements, AI-generated image enhancement	Reduce attention-seeking affordances; promote prosocial recognition; restrict misuse of generative tools for reputation inflation
Machiavellianism	Strategic manipulation, emotional detachment, cynicism	Cyberstalking, orchestrated harassment, spreading disinformation	Deepfake creation, AI-powered phishing, large-scale disinformation campaigns	Disrupt manipulation patterns; strengthen verification systems; restrict automated mass-messaging features
Psychopathy	Impulsivity, callousness, thrill-seeking, lack of remorse	Trolling, impulsive aggression, thrill-based cyberbullying	AI-powered harassment campaigns, exploiting vulnerabilities for immediate gratification	Immediate consequences for harmful acts; implement friction in AI use; flag escalatory aggression patterns
Sadism	Pleasure from others' suffering, cruelty, malicious intent	Extreme trolling, sustained harassment, targeting vulnerable victims	AI-generated harassment content, personalized deepfakes, automated campaigns for prolonged harm	Block generation of harmful personalized content; monitor for cruelty-seeking behavior; restrict anonymity and automate victim support systems

behaviors associated with the Dark Tetrad traits, providing timely responses. Rather than relying solely on user reporting, advanced computational approaches can identify aggression patterns, prevent escalation, and enhance accountability across online platforms.

Natural Language Processing (NLP) has become one of the most effective tools for detecting toxic online discourse. By analyzing the linguistic structures of posts, comments, and chats, NLP models can identify subtle indicators of hate speech, cyberbullying, and trolling that might otherwise escape human moderators (Singh et al., 2020). Deep learning architectures, particularly convolutional and recurrent neural networks, extend this capability by uncovering complex communication patterns embedded in large-scale data, enabling the recognition of implicit aggression and manipulative language (Alotaibi & Alzu'bi, 2021; Sultan, 2025).

To increase robustness, multichannel learning frameworks integrate multiple AI components, such as transformer models with bidirectional gated recurrent units, thereby improving accuracy in distinguishing between harmful and benign interactions (Alotaibi et al., 2021). In parallel, sentiment and emotion analysis contribute an additional interpretive layer, allowing systems to identify not only the presence of harmful content but also the underlying emotional tone that may signal aggression, hostility, or cruelty (Plaza-Del-Arco et al., 2020).

Emerging approaches also highlight the value of accountability mechanisms. Integrating blockchain with AI moderation tools ensures transparent record-keeping of user activities, discouraging manipulative or harmful actions by providing immutable audit trails of online interactions (Leiva & Castro, 2025). Similarly, social structure analysis enables systems to identify relational patterns, such as the roles of bully, victim, or bystander, thereby contextualizing individual behaviors within broader social dynamics (García-Carrera et al., 2025). These models can uncover recurring harassment campaigns or coordinated attacks that single-message analysis might overlook.

Finally, weakly supervised learning provides a pragmatic solution to one of the primary challenges in harmful content detection: the limited availability of labeled data. By training on small annotated datasets, models can generalize to vast amounts of unlabeled content, identifying antisocial behaviors with minimal expert input (García-Carrera et al., 2025). This approach is particularly relevant in fast-evolving cyberspaces, where new forms of harmful behavior frequently emerge.

Together, these technologies demonstrate that effective monitoring and intervention require a layered strategy, combining linguistic, behavioral, emotional, and structural analysis with accountability frameworks. Their implementation can not only detect but also deter harmful cyber behavior, mitigating the risks posed by individuals with Dark Tetrad traits and promoting safer, more ethical digital environments.

Takeaway: *Traits such as narcissism, Machiavellianism, psychopathy, and sadism increase the likelihood of manipulation, trolling, and misuse of AI tools. Recognising those patterns allows platforms to shape safer systems and direct interventions where they will matter most.*

Reflection: *How should platforms balance open participation with targeted safeguards when a subset of users may exploit AI features to harm others?*

7.5 Personality and Ethical Decision-Making in AI Contexts

AI systems often place users in situations where they must make ethical decisions, ranging from determining how personal data is shared to assessing the fairness of automated recommendations. Personality traits have been proven to be a significant predictor of how individuals respond to such dilemmas, influencing their moral reasoning and subsequent behavior in digital contexts. This makes the study of personality not only relevant but necessary in understanding why users approach AI technologies differently, especially in situations that involve ethical trade-offs.

The Big Five model has been central to explaining variability in ethical reasoning. Conscientious individuals tend to act with responsibility and self-discipline, qualities that translate into more ethical decision-making when interacting with AI technologies (Antes et al., 2007). For instance, in professional environments where algorithmic systems assist in recruitment or evaluation, individuals higher in conscientiousness are less likely to manipulate the technology for personal gain. Agreeableness also contributes positively, predicting cooperative behavior and sensitivity to fairness in automated systems. By contrast, traits such as high neuroticism may cloud ethical judgment under pressure, leading to inconsistent or risk-averse decisions.

The HEXACO framework expands this picture by emphasizing honesty-humility as a distinct predictor of ethical sensitivity. As mentioned earlier, individuals scoring high in honesty-humility are less inclined to exploit loopholes in AI systems or misuse automated tools for personal advantage. Research demonstrates that this dimension predicts fairness-oriented choices in moral dilemmas beyond what the Big Five can account for, highlighting its unique contribution to digital ethics (ElSayary, 2025). In contexts such as data-sharing agreements or AI-driven academic support, individuals high in honesty-humility prioritize collective well-being and transparency, while those low in this trait may be more inclined toward opportunistic or deceptive behavior.

The Dark Tetrad traits, narcissism, Machiavellianism, psychopathy, and sadism, add a contrasting layer, often linked to manipulative and self-serving decision-making in AI contexts. Narcissism, for instance, may lead individuals to utilize AI tools to enhance self-presentation or gain an advantage at the expense of ethical considerations (McArthur et al., 2023). Machiavellian tendencies can lead to the calculated misuse of algorithms, such as gaming recommendation systems or the exploitation of privacy settings for personal gain (Karlsson & Kajonius, 2020). Psychopathy and sadism, although less common, have been associated with disregard for harm caused by automated decisions, increasing the likelihood of antisocial online conduct (Međedović, 2024). These findings suggest that antisocial traits play a significant role in predicting unethical AI engagement, offering a cautionary perspective on the darker influence of personality.

Beyond individual traits, moral norms, and cognitive frameworks, personality influences decisions related to AI through mediating factors. For example, Bian and Wang (2024) demonstrate that moral cognition influences whether individuals perceive AI use as an opportunity to serve collective goals or as a means to advance self-interest. In public sector settings, service motivation has been identified as a moderating factor, whereby individuals high in public service orientation align their use of AI with ethical and societal standards, even when personality dispositions may otherwise push toward opportunism.

Cultural and organizational contexts also play a defining role. Ethical climates within institutions can either reinforce or weaken the expression of personality traits in AI-related moral reasoning (Verbeke et al., 1996). In organizations with strong accountability and transparency mechanisms, even individuals lower in honesty-humility may be guided toward ethical engagement, illustrating the interplay between personality and systemic safeguards. Regulatory frameworks further shape this interaction by embedding principles such as fairness, accountability, and transparency into the deployment of AI (Esther et al., 2023).

TABLE 7.5 Personality Models and Ethical Decision-Making in AI Contexts

Personality Model	*Key Traits*	*Influence on Ethical AI Decision-Making*	*Predictive Strengths*	*Associated Risks*
Big Five	Openness, Conscientiousness, Extraversion, Agreeableness, Neuroticism	Conscientiousness predicts responsible and rule-abiding AI use; agreeableness linked to fairness and cooperation; openness relates to curiosity about AI ethics.	Broad predictions of general behavior patterns; widely validated across digital contexts.	Limited in capturing integrity-focused or manipulative behaviors; weaker for explaining unethical decision-making.
HEXACO	Honesty-Humility, Emotionality, Extraversion, Agreeableness, Conscientiousness, Openness	Honesty-humility strongly predicts fairness, transparency, and resistance to exploiting AI systems; adds depth to moral reasoning beyond Big Five.	Outperforms Big Five in predicting ethical sensitivity and resistance to dishonesty in AI contexts.	Individuals low in honesty-humility show greater willingness to exploit AI systems or disregard fairness.
Dark Tetrad	Narcissism, Machiavellianism, Psychopathy, Sadism	Traits linked to manipulative, exploitative, or harmful engagement with AI; associated with self-serving or antisocial digital behaviors.	Identifies high-risk profiles for unethical or harmful AI use; clarifies negative personality influences.	Encourages opportunistic misuse of AI, online deception, trolling, or disregard for harm caused by automation.

Comparative research across the Big Five, HEXACO, and Dark Tetrad models suggests that no single framework fully captures the range of influences on ethical decision-making in AI contexts. The Big Five traits include broad behavioral tendencies, while HEXACO emphasizes honesty-humility as a key factor, and the Dark Tetrad traits identify risks for unethical or manipulative behavior. Integrated approaches that combine insights from these models appear more effective in predicting moral decision-making than reliance on a single personality framework (Nielsen & Thielmann, 2024; Radisavljević et al., 2023).

Understanding personality-driven ethical behavior offers both theoretical and practical implications. Theoretically, it highlights that digital ethics cannot be explained solely by structural design or policy but must also account for the psychological variability among users. Practically, it suggests that AI systems could be designed with adaptive ethical safeguards that respond to user profiles, offering more guidance to individuals prone to opportunistic decision-making while allowing greater autonomy to those with strong fairness orientations. Table 7.5 summarizes the key traits, influences on ethical AI decision-making, strengths, and risks for the three models of personality traits: Big Five, HEXACO, and Dark Tetrad.

> ***Takeaway:*** *Personality traits significantly influence moral reasoning and ethical decision-making in AI contexts, with the Big Five providing broad behavioral predictions, HEXACO highlighting integrity-based differences, and Dark Tetrad traits identifying risks for unethical behavior.*
> ***Reflection:*** *Can personality-informed ethical safeguards help AI systems adapt to the moral sensitivities of their users, and if so, how should they be implemented without overstepping user autonomy?*

7.5.1 The Limitations of Personality Models in Digital Contexts

Although personality models, such as the Big Five and HEXACO, provide invaluable frameworks for understanding cyber behavior, it is crucial to approach their application with a degree of critical analysis. These models are not deterministic, and their predictive power is subject to several important limitations in the rapidly evolving digital landscape.

First, the principle of situation strength suggests that strong situations, those with clear norms and constraints, can suppress the expression of personality traits. Many digital environments, such as highly moderated online communities or structured corporate platforms, may function as strong situations, limiting the extent to which individual personality differences are expressed. Conversely, anonymous or unmoderated platforms can be seen as weak situations, where personality traits may have a more pronounced effect on behavior.

Second, the issue of self-selection complicates the interpretation of findings. Individuals may choose to participate in online communities that align with their pre-existing personality traits. For example, individuals high in openness to experience may be more likely to join forums dedicated to niche hobbies or intellectual discussion. This makes it difficult to determine whether the platform influences behavior or simply attracts a specific type of user.

Third, digital plasticity and the concept of the "cybernetic self" suggest that our online identities are not static. Prolonged engagement with certain digital environments may, over time, shape and alter aspects of our personality expression. For instance, the constant positive reinforcement of a social media platform might amplify narcissistic tendencies, while the collaborative nature of a wiki project might enhance agreeableness. Therefore, the relationship between personality and digital behavior is likely bidirectional, not a one-way street.

Finally, these models were developed and validated primarily in Western, educated, industrialized, rich, and democratic (WEIRD) societies. Their applicability across different cultural contexts must be critically examined. As discussed in Chapter 9, cultural values can significantly moderate the expression of personality traits and their relationship to cyber behavior. A critical approach, therefore, requires acknowledging these limitations and viewing personality as one important factor among many, including situational, cultural, and technological factors, that collectively shape our digital lives.

7.6 Designing Ethical and Inclusive Digital Interventions

The digital transformation of society presents remarkable opportunities to tailor human experiences, but such personalization must be grounded in ethical responsibility and informed by psychological science. Personality psychology provides an essential framework for designing digital interventions that respect human diversity while promoting collective well-being. Rather than assuming uniform responses, interventions can be adapted to the unique tendencies of different personality profiles, ensuring that technology supports safer, more inclusive, and ethically grounded cyberspaces.

From a theoretical foundation perspective, personality is considered a design principle. Personality traits are powerful predictors of how individuals behave across various contexts, including education, work, relationships, and health (Bleidorn et al., 2019). They influence not only outcomes but also responsiveness to interventions, making them highly relevant to the design of digital ethics. Models such as the Big Five, HEXACO, and the Dark Tetrad highlight both the constructive and destructive ways individuals engage with technology. A core principle is that one-size-fits-all approaches are rarely effective. For example, a persuasive strategy that motivates a conscientious individual may fail with someone high in openness, and approaches that appeal to agreeable users may not resonate with those showing stronger dark trait tendencies (Alslaity & Tran, 2020). Recognizing these differences shifts digital ethics from a uniform set of rules to adaptive interventions that can address personality diversity.

Additionally, trait-aware policy design is another important aspect to consider. Policies shaped by personality research can be applied in graduated ways, distinguishing between low-risk users who may require only general guidelines and higher-risk groups who benefit from stronger safeguards and mandatory ethical training. The integration of the Big Five for baseline behavior, HEXACO's honesty-humility for integrity and fairness, and Dark Tetrad screening for antisocial risks creates a layered framework that addresses both prosocial and problematic patterns (Masthoff et al., 2014). Such policies also require transparent consent mechanisms, user autonomy safeguards, and regular review processes to maintain trust.

The trait-aware policy design could be beneficial to personalized educational strategies (Figure 7.2). Education is one of the most promising areas for personality-informed interventions. Personality research shows that tailoring lessons to individual profiles can boost learning engagement and retention (Jach et al., 2023). Learners high in openness respond best to scenario-based case studies involving novel ethical dilemmas, while learners high in conscientiousness benefit from structured modules and progress tracking. Extraverts tend to thrive in

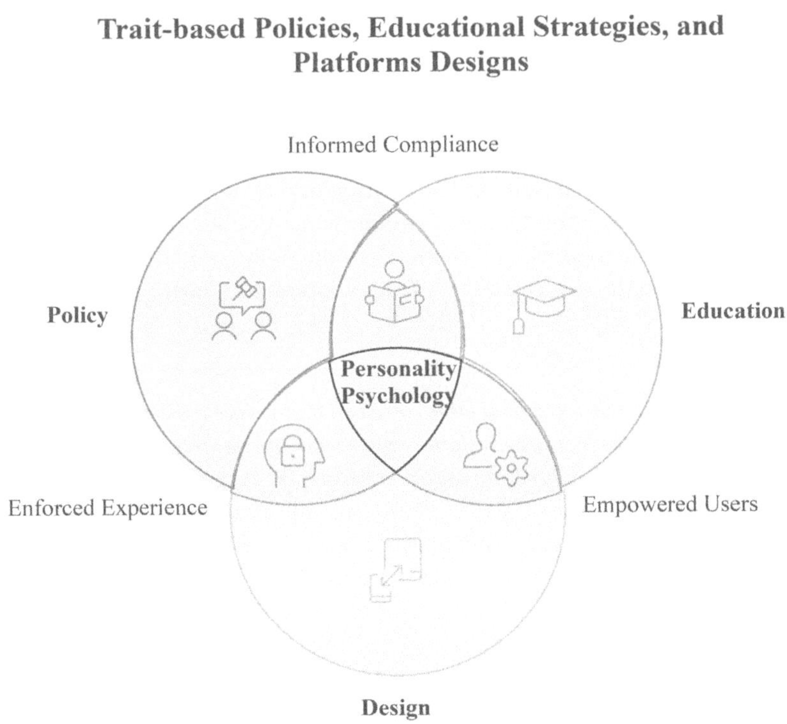

FIGURE 7.2 Trait-based policies, educational strategies, and platform designs intersect to build ethical and inclusive cyberspaces.

collaborative group projects, whereas agreeable learners are often motivated by content that emphasizes empathy and social benefits. Neurotic learners may require calming formats and supportive tutorials that acknowledge anxiety. Extending this approach to HEXACO, individuals high in honesty-humility can be positioned as ethical mentors, while those lower on the dimension may require structured, monitored training with external accountability measures. These strategies demonstrate how personality-informed design enhances digital ethics education while taking into account psychological diversity.

Digital platforms can embed personality-sensitive features at multiple levels. User interfaces may adapt according to personality traits, structured and ordered for conscientious users, socially interactive for extraverts, calming and predictable for neurotic users, and exploratory for those high in openness. Similarly, content personalization can align with ethical values while avoiding manipulation, giving users both transparency and choice. Community guidelines informed by personality diversity can offer flexible conflict-resolution pathways, ensuring that users with different ethical orientations find routes to reconciliation. For higher-risk profiles associated with dark traits, platforms may apply safeguards such as stricter monitoring, impulse-control supports, or peer accountability measures. Together, these features shift platform design from generic moderation to inclusive systems that accommodate differences while reinforcing ethical norms.

To ensure effectiveness, interventions must be evaluated systematically and regularly. Mixed-method approaches that combine behavioral data, longitudinal tracking, and qualitative feedback can capture both measurable outcomes and the lived experiences of users. A phased implementation model, from pilot testing to scaled deployment, provides opportunities to refine interventions before broad release. Crucially, privacy, autonomy, and fairness remain at the center of these processes, preventing personality-aware systems from slipping into coercion or discriminatory design.

> ***Takeaway:*** *Personalizing digital ethics through trait-aware policies, adaptive education, and inclusive platform designs creates safer online spaces that account for human diversity while promoting fairness and respect across digital communities.*
> ***Reflection:*** *What would a digital platform designed around your personality look like in its features, rules, and community norms, and how might it support you in engaging more ethically and meaningfully online?*

7.7 Summary and Reflections

This chapter has examined how personality traits shape the way individuals engage with digital technologies and AI, particularly in contexts where ethical decision-making is required. By integrating the Big Five, HEXACO, and Dark Tetrad models, the discussion highlighted that personality not only predicts cyber behaviors but also influences how people respond to risks, opportunities, and interventions in online environments. These models offer complementary perspectives: the Big Five provides broad predictors of behavior, HEXACO emphasizes moral integrity through honesty-humility, and the Dark Tetrad highlights risks of antisocial or harmful conduct. Together, they highlight the significance of trait-informed perspectives in comprehending both adaptive and maladaptive interactions with AI.

The chapter also emphasized that digital interventions cannot succeed with uniform approaches. Trait-aware policies, educational strategies, and platform designs demonstrate how personality psychology can be translated into practical solutions that safeguard well-being while respecting diversity. From monitoring antisocial tendencies to designing adaptive user interfaces, personality-based insights show promise in building digital spaces that are both ethical and inclusive. Importantly, such interventions must be grounded in transparency, respect for autonomy, and cultural sensitivity to avoid reinforcing bias or manipulation.

Ultimately, personality psychology provides a framework for bridging human diversity with technological design, enabling the alignment of AI-driven systems with ethical and psychological well-being. Yet, open questions remain about how far personalization should extend, how to strike a balance between privacy and prevention, and how to ensure fairness across diverse cultural contexts. These challenges highlight the need for continued interdisciplinary research and dialogue.

References

Ahmed, S., & Masood, M. (2025). Dark personalities in the digital arena: How psychopathy and narcissism shape online political participation. *Humanities and Social Sciences Communications*, *12*(1). https://doi.org/10.1057/s41599-025-05195-y

Alavi, M., Garg, A., & Wanigatunga, N. (2025). The relationships between Dark Tetrad traits and adolescent cyberbullying and cybertrolling with online time and life satisfaction as moderators. *Discover Psychology*, *5*(1). https://doi.org/10.1007/s44202-025-00351-6

Alavi, M., Latif, A. A., Ramayah, T., & Tan, J. Y. (2022). Dark tetrad of personality, cyberbullying, and cybertrolling among young adults. *Current Psychology*, *42*(32), 28441–28451. https://doi.org/10.1007/s12144-022-03892-4

Al-Otaibi, A. N., & Alzu'bi, M. A. (2021). Computer-assisted language learning (CALL): Using paragraph punch software in developing EFL paragraph writing skills. *Journal of Language and Linguistic Studies, 18*(1). https://www.jlls.org/index.php/jlls/article/download/2921/971

Alslaity, A., & Tran, T. (2020). The effect of personality traits on persuading recommender system users. *Conference on Recommender Systems*, 48–56. http://ceur-ws.org/Vol-2682/paper5.pdf

Anastasiei, B., & Dospinescu, N. (2018). A model of the relationships between the Big Five personality traits and the motivations to deliver word-of-mouth online. *Psihologija*, *51*(2), 215–227. https://doi.org/10.2298/psi161114006a

Antes, A. L., Brown, R. P., Murphy, S. T., Waples, E. P., Mumford, M. D., Connelly, S., & Devenport, L. D. (2007). Personality and ethical decision-making in research: The role of perceptions of self and others. *Journal of Empirical Research on Human Research Ethics*, *2*(4), 15–34. https://doi.org/10.1525/jer.2007.2.4.15

Ashton, M. C., & Lee, K. (2008). The HEXACO model of personality structure and the importance of the H factor. *Social and Personality Psychology Compass, 2*(5), 1952–1962. https://doi.org/10.1111/j.1751-9004.2008.00134.x

Badreddine, B., Blount, Y., & Quilter, M. (2022). The role of personality traits in participation in an Online Cancer Community. *Aslib Journal of Information Management*, *75*(2), 318–341. https://doi.org/10.1108/ajim-05-2022-0242

Baiocco, R., Chirumbolo, A., Bianchi, D., Ioverno, S., Morelli, M., & Nappa, M. R. (2017). How HEXACO personality traits predict different selfie-posting behaviors among adolescents and young adults. *Frontiers in Psychology*, *7*. https://doi.org/10.3389/fpsyg.2016.02080

Bartneck, C., Yogeeswaran, K., & Sibley, C. G. (2023). Personality and demographic correlates of support for regulating artificial intelligence. *AI And Ethics*, *4*(2), 419–426. https://doi.org/10.1007/s43681-023-00279-4

Bian, X., & Wang, B. (2024). Exploring the influence of artificial intelligence usage on ethical decision making among public sector employees: Insights into moral identity and service motivation. *Business Ethics and Leadership*, *8*(3), 133–150. https://doi.org/10.61093/bel.8(3).133-150.2024

Bleidorn, W., Hill, P. L., Back, M. D., Denissen, J. J. A., Hennecke, M., Hopwood, C. J., Jokela, M., Kandler, C., Lucas, R. E., Luhmann, M., Orth, U., Wagner, J., Wrzus, C., Zimmermann, J., & Roberts, B. (2019). The policy relevance of personality traits. *American Psychologist, 74*(9), 1056–1067. https://doi.org/10.1037/amp0000503

Blötner, C., Ziegler, M., Wehner, C., Back, M. D., & Grosz, M. P. (2021). The nomological network of the Short Dark Tetrad Scale (SD4). *European Journal of Psychological Assessment*, *38*(3), 187–197. https://doi.org/10.1027/1015-5759/a000655

Borghi, M., & Ratcharak, P. (2025). Deceptive minds in digital spaces: The influence of the dark triad on posting fake online reviews. *Psychology and Marketing*, *42*(7), 1932–1945. https://doi.org/10.1002/mar.22212

Burtăverde, V., Chraif, M., Aniţei, M., & Dumitru, D. (2017). The HEXACO model of personality and risky driving behavior. *Psychological Reports*, *120*(2), 255–270. https://doi.org/10.1177/0033294116688890

Calvo, R. A., Peters, D., Vold, K., & Ryan, R. M. (2020). Supporting human autonomy in AI systems: A framework for ethical enquiry. In *Springer eBooks* (pp. 31–54). https://doi.org/10.17863/cam.45866

Carroll, B. J., Zhou, J., Burke, P. F., & Ammon, S. (2025). The user-first approach to AI ethics: Preferences for ethical principles in AI systems across cultures and contexts. *arXiv (Cornell University)*. https://doi.org/10.48550/arxiv.2508.11327

Caşcaval, A. (2024). The interaction between artificial intelligence, personality and technology addiction. *Conferința*, 131–137. https://doi.org/10.46727/c.v1.21-22-03-2024.p131-137

Castagna, P. J., & Hart, W. (2024). Light triad traits moderate the relationship between the dark tetrad and immoral character. *Personality and Individual Differences*, *222*, 112593. https://doi.org/10.1016/j.paid.2024.112593

Derish, F. V. (2021). The dark tetrad of personality: Review of recent research. *Вестник Пермского Университета Философия Психология Социология, 2*, 222–235. https://doi.org/10.17072/2078-7898/2021-2-222-235

Djakovic, N., & Rowlands, M. T. (2024). Differential association theory, the Dark Triad of personality and the prediction of antisocial behaviour. *Psychiatry Psychology and Law*, 1–17. https://doi.org/10.1080/13218719.2024.2404837

Duan, S. X., & Deng, H. (2023). Job performance in digital work: Do personality traits matter? *Journal of Computer Information Systems*, 1–13. https://doi.org/10.1080/08874417.2023.2255551

Durak, M., & Senol-Durak, E. (2014). Which personality traits are associated with cognitions related to problematic Internet use? *Asian Journal of Social Psychology*, *17*(3), 206–218. https://doi.org/10.1111/ajsp.12056

ElSayary, A. (2025). Navigating AI ethics through the lens of personality traits and well-being: policy recommendations for young people in the UAE. *Human Behavior and Emerging Technologies*. https://doi.org/10.1155/hbe2/5597545

Esmaeelinezhad, O., & Afrazeh, A. (2018). Linking personality traits and individuals' knowledge management behavior. *Aslib Journal of Information Management*, *70*(3), 234–251. https://doi.org/10.1108/ajim-01-2018-0019

Esther, T., Ahmed, A., Edward, T., Kolade, M., & Mayowa, A. (2023). A review of the ethics of artificial intelligence and its applications in the United States. *International Journal on Cybernetics & Informatics*, *12*(6), 122–137. https://doi.org/10.5121/ijci.2023.120610

Fowers, B. J., Novak, L. F., Kiknadze, N. C., & Selim, M. (2023). Is the concept of personality capacious enough to incorporate virtues? *Frontiers in Psychology*, *14*, 1232637. https://doi.org/10.3389/fpsyg.2023.1232637

Freyth, L., Batinic, B., & Jonason, P. K. (2022). Social media use and personality: Beyond self-reports and trait-level assessments. *Personality and Individual Differences*, *202*, 111960. https://doi.org/10.1016/j.paid.2022.111960

Gajda, A., Moroń, M., Królik, M., Małuch, M., & Mraczek, M. (2022). The dark tetrad, cybervictimization, and cyberbullying: The role of moral disengagement. *Current Psychology*, *42*(27), 23413–23421. https://doi.org/10.1007/s12144-022-03456-6

García-Carrera, P., Ortega-Ruiz, R., Camacho, A., Garandeau, C. F., Salmivalli, C., & Romera, E. M. (2025). Trajectories of Bystander Behaviors in Bullying during Secondary Education: the Role of Moral Disengagement and Conformity To Peer Pressure. *Journal of Youth and Adolescence*, *55*(1), 168–183. https://doi.org/10.1007/s10964-025-02276-8

Gazit, T. (2021). Exploring leadership in Facebook communities: Personality traits and activities. *Proceedings of the... Annual Hawaii International Conference on System Sciences/Proceedings of the Annual Hawaii International Conference on System Sciences*. https://doi.org/10.24251/hicss.2021.369

Giron, J., Sela, Y., Barenboim, L., Gilboa-Freedman, G., & Amichai-Hamburger, Y. (2024). Persona-physioSync AV: Personalized interaction through personality and physiology monitoring in autonomous vehicles. *Sensors*, *24*(6), 1977. https://doi.org/10.3390/s24061977

Gómez-Leal, R., Fernández-Berrocal, P., Gutiérrez-Cobo, M. J., Cabello, R., & Megías-Robles, A. (2024). The Dark Tetrad: analysis of profiles and relationship with the Big Five personality factors. *Scientific Reports*, *14*(1). https://doi.org/10.1038/s41598-024-55074-w

Gnisci, A., Mottola, F., Perugini, M., Senese, V. P., & Sergi, I. (2023). Development and validation of an instrument to measure personality in adolescence: The HEXACO Medium School Inventory Extended (MSI-E). *PLoS ONE*, *18*(1), e0280563. https://doi.org/10.1371/journal.pone.0280563

Greitemeyer, T., & Kastenmüller, A. (2023). HEXACO, the Dark Triad, and Chat GPT: Who is willing to commit academic cheating? *Heliyon*, *9*(9), e19909. https://doi.org/10.1016/j.heliyon.2023.e19909

Gupta, N. (2023). Artificial intelligence ethics and fairness: A study to address bias and fairness issues in AI systems, and the ethical implications of AI applications. *Revista Review Index Journal of Multidisciplinary*, *3*(2), 24–35. https://doi.org/10.31305/rrijm2023.v03.n02.004

Gylfason, H. F., Sveinsdottir, A. H., Vésteinsdóttir, V., & Sigurvinsdottir, R. (2021). Haters gonna hate, trolls gonna troll: The personality profile of a Facebook troll. *International Journal of Environmental Research and Public Health, 18*(11), 5722. https://doi.org/10.3390/ijerph18115722

Hammerschmidt, T. (2025). Navigating the Nexus of ethical standards and moral values. *Ethics and Information Technology, 27*(2). https://doi.org/10.1007/s10676-025-09826-5

Heck, D. W., Thielmann, I., Moshagen, M., & Hilbig, B. E. (2018). Who lies? A large-scale reanalysis linking basic personality traits to unethical decision making. *Judgment and Decision Making, 13*(4), 356–371. https://doi.org/10.1017/s1930297500009232

Hsieh, S. H., & Lee, C. T. (2024). The AI humanness: how perceived personality builds trust and continuous usage intention. *Journal of Product & Brand Management.* https://doi.org/10.1108/jpbm-10-2023-4797

Ienca, M. (2023). On artificial intelligence and manipulation. *Topoi, 42*(3), 833–842. https://doi.org/10.1007/s11245-023-09940-3

Jach, H. K., Bardach, L., & Murayama, K. (2023). How personality matters for education research. *Educational Psychology Review, 35*(3). https://doi.org/10.1007/s10648-023-09807-4

Jain, V., Wadhwani, K., & Eastman, J. K. (2023). Artificial intelligence consumer behavior: A hybrid review and research agenda. *Journal of Consumer Behaviour, 23*(2), 676–697. https://doi.org/10.1002/cb.2233

Johnson, L. K., Plouffe, R. A., & Saklofske, D. H. (2019). Subclinical sadism and the dark Triad. *Journal of Individual Differences, 40*(3), 127–133. https://doi.org/10.1027/1614-0001/a000284

Karlsson, A. M. C., & Kajonius, P. J. (2020). Not only trolls are trolling the internet: A study on dark personality traits, online environment, and commentary styles. *International Journal of Personality Psychology, 6*, 12–23. https://doi.org/10.21827/ijpp.6.37214

Kaya, F., Aydin, F., Schepman, A., Rodway, P., Yetişensoy, O., & Kaya, M. D. (2022). The roles of personality traits, AI anxiety, and demographic factors in attitudes toward artificial intelligence. *International Journal of Human-Computer Interaction, 40*(2), 497–514. https://doi.org/10.1080/10447318.2022.2151730

Kranenbarg, M. W., Van Gelder, J., Barends, A. J., & De Vries, R. E. (2022). Is there a cybercriminal personality? Comparing cyber offenders and offline offenders on HEXACO personality domains and their underlying facets. *Computers in Human Behavior, 140*, 107576. https://doi.org/10.1016/j.chb.2022.107576

Lee, K., Ashton, M. C., Griep, Y., & Edmonds, M. (2018). Personality, religion, and politics: An investigation in 33 countries. *European Journal of Personality, 32*(2), 100–115. https://doi.org/10.1002/per.2142

Lee, K., Ashton, M. C., Morrison, D. L., Cordery, J., & Dunlop, P. D. (2007). Predicting integrity with the HEXACO personality model: Use of self-and observer reports. *Journal of Occupational and Organizational Psychology, 81*(1), 147–167. https://doi.org/10.1348/096317907x195175

Leite, Â., Cardoso, S., & Monteiro, A. P. (2023). Dark personality traits and online behaviors: Portuguese versions of cyberstalking, online harassment, flaming and trolling scales. *International Journal of Environmental Research and Public Health, 20*(12), 6136. https://doi.org/10.3390/ijerph20126136

Leiva, V., & Castro, C. (2025). Artificial intelligence and blockchain in clinical trials: enhancing data governance efficiency, integrity, and transparency. *Bioanalysis, 17*(3), 161–176. https://doi.org/10.1080/17576180.2025.2452774

Leng, J., Guo, Q., Ma, B., Zhang, S., & Sun, P. (2020). Bridging personality and online prosocial behavior: The roles of empathy, moral identity, and Social Self-Efficacy. *Frontiers in Psychology, 11*. https://doi.org/10.3389/fpsyg.2020.575053

Li, M., Yang, G., Xu, X., Oh, I., & Xu, S. (2026). Relationships among perceived stress, anxiety, and well-being in Chinese hospital staff: the mediating role of self-efficacy and the moderating role of empathy. *Frontiers in Psychology, 17*, 1740682. https://doi.org/10.3389/fpsyg.2026.1740682

Masthoff, J., Grasso, F., & Ham, J. (2014). Preface to the special issue on personalization and behavior change. *User Modeling and User-Adapted Interaction, 24*(5), 345–350. https://doi.org/10.1007/s11257-014-9151-1

McArthur, J., Dunsworth, Z., & Ternes, M. (2023). World wide web of lies: Personality and online deception. *Telematics and Informatics Reports, 11*, 100075. https://doi.org/10.1016/j.teler.2023.100075

Međedović, J. (2024). Machiavellianism as a crucial Dark Tetrad trait for the prediction of life-course criminal behavior. *Current Psychology*. https://doi.org/10.1007/s12144-024-06500-9

Modgil, S., Singh, R. K., Mathiyazhagan, K., & Żywiołek, J. (2025). Role of generative AI towards sustainable procurement. *The International Journal of Logistics Management, 37*(2), 476–499. https://doi.org/10.1108/ijlm-01-2025-0062

Moreira, D., Azeredo, A., Ramião, E., Figueiredo, P., Barroso, R., & Barbosa, F. (2024). Systematic exploration of antisocial behavior. *European Psychologist, 29*(2), 108–122. https://doi.org/10.1027/1016-9040/a000527

Mumtaz, S., Carmichael, J., Weiss, M., & Nimon-Peters, A. (2024). Ethical use of artificial intelligence based tools in higher education: Are future business leaders ready? *Education and Information Technologies, 30*(6), 7293–7319. https://doi.org/10.1007/s10639-024-13099-8

Mustafa, S., & Zhang, W. (2023). Why do I share? participants' personality traits and online participation. *International Journal of Human-Computer Interaction, 40*(14), 3763–3781. https://doi.org/10.1080/10447318.2023.2201551

Nielsen, Y. A., Pfattheicher, S., & Thielmann, I. (2024). How much can personality predict prosocial behavior? *European Journal of Personality*. https://doi.org/10.1177/08902070241251516

Oksanen, A., Savela, N., Latikka, R., & Koivula, A. (2020). Trust toward robots and artificial intelligence: An experimental approach to human–technology interactions online. *Frontiers in Psychology, 11*. https://doi.org/10.3389/fpsyg.2020.568256

Oladimeji, K. E., Nyatela, A., Gumede, S., Dwarka, D., & Lalla-Edward, S. T. (2023). Impact of Artificial intelligence (AI) on psychological and mental health promotion: An opinion piece. *New Voices in Psychology*. https://doi.org/10.25159/2958-3918/14548

Otero-López, J. M., Santiago, M. J., & Castro, M. C. (2023). Big five personality traits and compulsive buying: The mediating role of Self-Esteem. *European Journal of Investigation in Health Psychology and Education, 14*(1), 103–116. https://doi.org/10.3390/ejihpe14010007

Panatik, S. A., Raof, N. N. A., Nordin, N. A., Yusof, J., & Shahrin, R. (2022). Effect of dark triad personality on cyberbullying behavior among Malaysian University students. *The Eurasia Proceedings of Educational and Social Sciences, 25*, 26–44. https://doi.org/10.55549/epess.1192356

Panno, A., De Cristofaro, V., Oliveti, C., Carrus, G., & Donati, M. A. (2021). Personality and environmental outcomes: The role of moral anger in channeling climate change action and pro-environmental behavior. *Analyses of Social Issues and Public Policy*, *21*(1), 853–873. https://doi.org/10.1111/asap.12254

Park, J., & Woo, S. E. (2022). Who likes artificial intelligence? Personality predictors of attitudes toward artificial intelligence. *The Journal of Psychology*, *156*(1), 68–94. https://doi.org/10.1080/00223980.2021.2012109

Pilch, I. (2023). Comparison of the Big Five and the HEXACO models of personality in the prediction of emotional wellbeing: An experience sampling study. *Trends in Psychology*. https://doi.org/10.1007/s43076-023-00311-w

Plaza-Del-Arco, F. M., Molina-González, M. D., Ureña-López, L. A., & Martín-Valdivia, M. T. (2020). Comparing pre-trained language models for Spanish hate speech detection. *Expert Systems With Applications, 166*, 114120. https://doi.org/10.1016/j.eswa.2020.114120

Radisavljević, D., Rzepka, R., & Araki, K. (2023). Personality types and traits—examining and leveraging the relationship between different personality models for mutual prediction. *Applied Sciences*, *13*(7), 4506. https://doi.org/10.3390/app13074506

Rauthmann, J. F. (2020). A (More) behavioural science of personality in the age of Multi–Modal sensing, big data, machine learning, and artificial intelligence. *European Journal of Personality*, *34*(5), 593–598. https://doi.org/10.1002/per.2310

Reinhardt, N., & Reinhard, M. (2023). Honesty–humility negatively correlates with dishonesty in romantic relationships. *Journal of Personality and Social Psychology*, *125*(4), 925–942. https://doi.org/10.1037/pspp0000456

Rivera, A., Abhari, K., & Xiao, B. (2025). Responsible AI design: The authenticity, control, transparency theory. *Journal of the Association for Information Systems*, *26*(5), 1337–1389. https://doi.org/10.17705/1jais.00948

Roberts, M. J. D., Connolly, R., Conley, J., & Miller, J. (2023). Digital citizenship and the big five personality traits. *Informatics*, *10*(3), 58. https://doi.org/10.3390/informatics10030058

Roos, J. M. (2023). The intersection of personality traits and social media usage: Large-Scale representative samples of internet users in Sweden. *Psych*, *5*(1), 70–79. https://doi.org/10.3390/psych5010008

Sims, C. M. (2016). Do the Big-Five personality traits predict empathic listening and assertive communication? *International Journal of Listening*, *31*(3), 163–188. https://doi.org/10.1080/10904018.2016.1202770

Sindermann, C., Yang, H., Elhai, J. D., Yang, S., Quan, L., Li, M., & Montag, C. (2022). Acceptance and fear of artificial intelligence: Associations with personality in a German and a Chinese sample. *Discover Psychology*, *2*(1). https://doi.org/10.1007/s44202-022-00020-y

Singh, J. P., Kumar, A., Rana, N. P., & Dwivedi, Y. K. (2020). Attention-Based LSTM network for Rumor Veracity Estimation of Tweets. *Information Systems Frontiers, 24*(2), 459–474. https://doi.org/10.1007/s10796-020-10040-5

Stachl, C., Pargent, F., Hilbert, S., Harari, G. M., Schoedel, R., Vaid, S., Gosling, S. D., & Bühner, M. (2020). Personality research and assessment in the era of machine learning. *European Journal of Personality*, *34*(5), 613–631. https://doi.org/10.1002/per.2257

Stein, J., Messingschlager, T., Gnambs, T., Hutmacher, F., & Appel, M. (2024). Attitudes towards AI: Measurement and associations with personality. *Scientific Reports*, *14*(1). https://doi.org/10.1038/s41598-024-53335-2

Sultan, H. (2025). Exploring EFL instructors' awareness of metacognitive strategy use in Saudi higher education institutions. *Journal of Research in Language & Translation, 5*(1). https://doi.org/10.33948/jrlt-ksu-5-1-4

Tian, Y., Zhao, Y., Lv, F., Qin, N., & Chen, P. (2021). Associations among the big five personality traits, maladaptive cognitions, and internet addiction across three time measurements in 3 months during the COVID-19 pandemic. *Frontiers in Psychology, 12*. https://doi.org/10.3389/fpsyg.2021.654825

Tsao, W. (2013). Big five personality traits as predictors of internet usage categories. *International Journal of Management, 30*(4), 374. https://www.questia.com/library/journal/1P3-3124287001/big-five-personality-traits-as-predictors-of-internet

Ubaradka, A., & Khanganba, S. P. (2024). The differential effect of psychopathy on active and bystander trolling behaviors: the role of dark tetrad traits and lower agreeableness. *Scientific Reports, 14*(1). https://doi.org/10.1038/s41598-024-60203-6

Upadhyaya, N., & Galizzi, M. M. (2023). In bot we trust? Personality traits and reciprocity in human-bot trust games. *Frontiers in Behavioral Economics, 2*. https://doi.org/10.3389/frbhe.2023.1164259

Verbeke, W., Ouwerkerk, C., & Peelen, E. (1996). Exploring the contextual and individual factors on ethical decision making of salespeople. *Journal of Business Ethics, 15*(11), 1175–1187. https://doi.org/10.1007/bf00412816

Völkel, S. T., Haeuslschmid, R., Werner, A., Hussmann, H., & Butz, A. (2020). How to trick AI: Users' strategies for protecting themselves from automatic personality assessment. In *Proceedings of the 2020 CHI Conference on Human Factors in Computing Systems* (pp. 1–15). https://doi.org/10.1145/3313831.3376877

Yang, Q., Farseev, A., Nikolenko, S., & Filchenkov, A. (2022). Do we behave differently on Twitter and Facebook: Multi-view social network user personality profiling for content recommendation. *Frontiers in Big Data, 5*. https://doi.org/10.3389/fdata.2022.931206

Yu, Y., Zhao, Y., Li, D., Zhang, J., & Li, J. (2021). The relationship between Big Five personality and social well-being of Chinese residents: The mediating effect of social support. *Frontiers in Psychology, 11*. https://doi.org/10.3389/fpsyg.2020.613659

Yu, F., Krägeloh, C., Bharatharaj, J., & Ding, X. (2024). Editorial: Moral psychology of AI. *Frontiers in Psychology, 15*, 1382743. https://doi.org/10.3389/fpsyg.2024.1382743

Zettler, I., Thielmann, I., Hilbig, B. E., & Moshagen, M. (2020). The nomological net of the HEXACO model of personality: A large-scale meta-analytic investigation. *Perspectives on Psychological Science, 15*(3), 723–760. https://doi.org/10.1177/1745691619895036

Zhang, Q., Liao, G., Ran, X., & Wang, F. (2025). The impact of AI usage on innovation behavior at work: The moderating role of openness and job complexity. *Behavioral Sciences, 15*(4), 491. https://doi.org/10.3390/bs15040491

Zhou, L., & Tang, L. (2022). Personality traits and user innovation engagement in open innovation platform: the moderating role of social network position. *Behaviour and Information Technology, 42*(14), 2428–2441. https://doi.org/10.1080/0144929x.2022.2126797

8

GENDER DIFFERENCES IN DIGITAL AND AI INTERACTIONS

Chapter Objectives

- To examine how gender influences cyber behaviors and engagement with AI systems.
- To explore how gendered online patterns impact mental health and ethical decision-making.
- To analyze the risks and benefits each gender may face in specific digital contexts (e.g., social networking vs. competitive gaming).
- To propose inclusive and gender-responsive strategies for safer, ethical digital and AI interactions.

Topics to Be Covered

- Introduction: Why Gender Matters in Digital and AI Contexts
- Gendered Patterns in Cyber Behavior
- Emotional and Relational Dynamics Among Female Users
- Competitive and Risk-Based Engagement Among Male Users
- Gendered Mental Health Outcomes and Ethical Implications
- Inclusive Digital and AI Design for Gender Equity
- Summary and Reflections

DOI: 10.4324/9781003657590-11

8.1 Introduction: Why Gender Matters in Digital and AI Contexts

Gender has become one of the most consistent predictors of variation in cyber behavior, mental health outcomes, and engagement with artificial intelligence (AI). From communication on social media to interactions with learning technologies or workplace automation, gendered patterns shape the way people experience technology. For instance, on one screen, a teenage girl scrolls through an endless feed of curated beauty tutorials and influencer posts, as the algorithm subtly reinforces her anxieties about her appearance. On another screen, a teenage boy is immersed in a competitive gaming environment where aggressive trash talk is the norm. These are not isolated incidents; they reflect a digital world deeply stratified by gender. These differences are not marginal; they influence access, attitudes, risks, and opportunities across almost every digital setting. Recognizing these distinctions provides a foundation for creating equitable and inclusive environments that serve the diverse needs of humans through technology. Research indicates that gendered experiences influence both confidence and trust in digital systems. For example, women often report higher levels of AI anxiety, paired with lower perceived knowledge and reduced willingness to experiment with emerging technologies compared to men (Russo et al., 2025). At the same time, women are more likely to utilize AI-based mental health resources, particularly chatbots, as these tools provide accessible forms of communication and emotional support (Russo et al., 2025). These contrasting findings highlight that gender does not act as a simple barrier or advantage but rather shapes distinct pathways of digital adoption and usage.

Public perceptions of AI also reflect variations in gender. Studies show that attitudes towards AI are influenced by social identity categories, such as gender, age, and cultural background, which collectively shape whether people perceive AI as a supportive resource or a potential threat (Grassini & Ree, 2023). These perceptions matter because they influence how individuals interact with systems ranging from automated hiring tools to healthcare platforms. Equally important are the ways in which AI technologies themselves adopt and reinforce gendered traits. Voice assistants, for example, are often feminized, reflecting broader social stereotypes and subtly reinforcing expectations about who provides care or service (Costa & Ribas, 2019).

Educational and workplace settings provide further evidence of the role of gender in digital engagement. Variations in digital literacy and confidence mean that women and men may not experience the same outcomes when using adaptive learning systems or AI-supported collaboration platforms. Lower self-efficacy in digital environments, even when actual performance is comparable, can discourage women from experimenting with advanced tools, which in turn limits the full benefits of AI integration in learning and professional contexts (Bentley et al., 2024; Yaseen et al., 2025).

The relationship between gender and digital engagement is not static. Cyberspaces can reinforce stereotypes through biased recommendation systems and targeted advertising, but they can also serve as spaces of empowerment, enabling identity exploration, community building, and new professional opportunities (Robinson et al., 2024). The challenge is that the risks, such as harassment, surveillance, or body image pressures, are often disproportionately borne by women and gender-diverse individuals, while the benefits are unevenly distributed. This duality illustrates why gender must be considered not only a demographic variable but also a structural factor embedded in both the design and use of technology. Understanding gender in digital contexts also requires attention to intersectionality. Gender rarely operates in isolation; it intersects with age, socioeconomic status, ethnicity, disability, nationality, education, religion, and digital access to create layered experiences. For example, virtual violence affects young women differently than older women, and digital divides are intensified when gender disparities combine with limited economic resources (Rajappan et al., 2025; Silva et al., 2025). These compounding effects underline the need for research and design practices that account for diversity across the full spectrum of gender identity.

This chapter introduces these complexities and considers their implications for digital well-being, ethical engagement, and the design of AI. It examines how gender shapes cyber behavior, how relational and emotional engagement differ from competitive and risk-based patterns, and how these differences translate into mental health outcomes and ethical challenges. It also proposes strategies for building digital systems that recognize gender differences without reinforcing stereotypes. By analyzing both risks and opportunities, the chapter highlights gender inclusivity as a central ethical priority for the future of digital and AI development.

> ***Takeaway:*** *Gender plays a central role in shaping how people experience, interact with, and are impacted by digital and AI systems.*
> ***Reflection:*** *In what ways have your digital experiences reflected or challenged traditional gender expectations?*

8.2 Gendered Patterns in Digital Engagement

Digital development has profoundly expanded the scope of human interaction, but these opportunities are not experienced in a gender-neutral manner. Distinct patterns of engagement emerge, shaped by social norms, cultural expectations, and the architecture of digital platforms themselves. Females often gravitate toward emotionally connected, socially supportive online environments, while males tend to engage in competitive, technical, and risk-oriented digital contexts (Li et al., 2026). These differences are not merely anecdotal but are consistently documented across multiple domains of digital activity, including communication styles, platform preferences, risk-taking behaviors, and political engagement (Harputlu & Güryay, 2024; Li et al., 2025).

One of the most consistent gendered distinctions lies in *communication styles and interaction goals*. Female users frequently adopt communication patterns that emphasize emotional depth, relationship-building, and supportive engagement. They rely on digital platforms to maintain and strengthen relationships, and in educational contexts, they report higher perceived support and engagement when platforms foster community and value their contributions (Korlat et al., 2021). This relational orientation makes platforms such as Instagram, WhatsApp, and Pinterest particularly appealing to female users, as these emphasize visual storytelling and close-knit community bonds (Lilleker et al., 2023; Rahayu et al., 2023). Male users, by contrast, tend to approach digital interactions through a competitive lens, seeking performance, status, and achievement (Aran-Ramspott et al., 2024a, 2024b; Oslé & Rosales, 2023). Gaming, debate forums, and technical communities attract higher male participation, reflecting a stronger affinity for spaces that reward competition and skill mastery (Carcelén-García et al., 2023; Gisbert-Pérez et al., 2024; Infanti et al., 2024). In educational settings, this manifests as greater enthusiasm for gamified learning and competitive simulations, aligning with risk-taking tendencies encouraged by socialization processes (Baker et al., 2024).

Beyond communication, gender differences extend to how individuals balance *social bonding with risk-oriented* digital activities. Women prioritize relational safety and social connectedness, often forming supportive communities online and exercising caution in disclosure and interaction (Aydın & Aydın, 2025; García et al., 2023; Tifferet, 2018). In contrast, men, particularly younger males, show higher engagement in risky digital behaviors such as participating in online challenges, gambling, or downloading potentially harmful content (Notten & Nikken, 2014). Older male users often continue this pattern through betting and other high-stakes online activities, which can generate cycles of both excitement and negative emotional consequences (Carcelén-García et al., 2023; Zarate et al., 2023). These divergent patterns create asymmetries in vulnerability: women are more exposed to harassment and relational stress, while men are more prone to the psychological costs of competitive and risky pursuits. In both cases, platform design often amplifies rather than mitigates these risks.

Gendered engagement also extends into *political and civic cyberspaces*. While overall levels of participation are relatively balanced, the style of engagement differs. Women are more likely to engage in lower-visibility activities, such as information sharing or private advocacy, that minimize exposure to harassment or conflict (Enock et al., 2024). Men, conversely, are more active in overt political debates, public discussions, and confrontational exchanges (Ahmed & Madrid-Morales, 2020; Enock et al., 2024; Lilleker et al., 2021). These differences suggest that women often strategize around digital risks, exercising caution in environments where political expression may lead to reputational or emotional harm.

The asymmetrical risks of digital participation highlight the persistence of *gender-specific vulnerabilities*. Young women report heightened insecurity, anxiety, and body-image pressures on visual and relational platforms, reflecting a disproportionate burden of social comparison and harassment (García et al., 2023; Vella et al., 2019). Men, meanwhile, experience risk in different forms: aggressive communication styles, normalization of toxic cyber behavior, and desensitization to ethical boundaries in competitive spaces (Enock et al., 2024; Enock et al., 2024; García et al., 2023). Both sets of vulnerabilities reveal that gender differences are not merely preference-based but are tied to systemic dynamics of digital culture, where platform affordances and community norms magnify underlying inequalities (Table 8.1).

Although these gendered patterns are well-documented, *cultural context* shapes how they are established. In developing regions, socio-cultural norms and restricted access worsen the gender digital divide, limiting women's participation in cyberspaces (Antonio & Tuffley, 2014; Çelik, 2025; Bhagat, 2025). Where women do participate, they often harness digital platforms for education and empowerment, reducing barriers to community development. In more egalitarian societies, gender gaps are narrower but remain visible in privacy attitudes, platform choices, and forms of expression (Hadfi et al., 2023; Shi, 2023; Yaman & Çakıroğlu, 2025). Thus, digital gender dynamics must be interpreted both as globally consistent tendencies and as contextually variable phenomena influenced by culture, economy, and infrastructure. Gendered patterns of digital engagement reveal the profound

TABLE 8.1 Comparative Gendered Patterns in Digital Engagement

Dimension	*Female Users*	*Male Users*
Communication Style	Emotionally expressive, supportive, relational focus	Direct, competitive, fact- and achievement-oriented
Platform Preferences	Social networking (Instagram, Pinterest, WhatsApp), community-based groups	Gaming, forums, technical platforms, sports content
Gaming Behavior	Cooperative, casual, narrative-focused, higher sensitivity to harassment	Competitive, achievement-driven, risk-tolerant, streaming-focused
Risk & Safety	Stronger privacy controls, risk aversion, safety-focused	Higher tolerance for risk, more prone to risky challenges
Political Engagement	Private advocacy, information sharing, low-visibility activism	Public debate, confrontational exchanges, opinion leadership
Digital Vulnerabilities	Body image pressures, relational stress, harassment	Aggression normalization, ethical desensitization, compulsive risk-taking

impact of socialization, cultural expectations, and platform design on cyber behavior. Female users frequently prioritize emotional connection, supportive interaction, and relational safety, while male users gravitate toward competitive, technical, and risk-oriented spaces (Aran-Ramspott et al., 2024; Li et al., 2025). These differences translate into distinct vulnerabilities and benefits: women's emotional investment exposes them to relational stress, while men's competitive drive can normalize aggression and risk-taking. Yet within these categories, variation remains high, and evolving technologies continue to blur traditional distinctions.

> ***Takeaway:*** *Females tend to favor emotionally connected, socially supportive digital platforms, while males often prefer competitive, technical, and risk-oriented online activities.*
> ***Reflection:*** *How do your preferred digital platforms reflect your own approach to communication, competition, or risk?*

8.3 Emotional Sensitivity and Relational Focus among Females

The digital development has reshaped how women experience relationships, emotions, and social connections. As mentioned earlier, female users often demonstrate heightened emotional sensitivity and relational focus in digital environments, which enables deep social bonds but also exposes them to unique vulnerabilities. Social networking platforms increase these dynamics: they provide avenues for support, self-expression, and empowerment, yet simultaneously increase pressures related to body image, harassment, and relational stress. Understanding this dual nature is crucial for developing platforms that foster connections while minimizing harm.

Evidence consistently shows that women express emotions more strongly and empathetically online compared to men. Studies demonstrate that female users employ more emotionally charged language, show higher levels of empathy in online exchanges, and are more susceptible to "emotional contagion" within communities (Li & Zhuo, 2023; Steinert & Dennis, 2022). This heightened responsiveness enriches digital interactions, but it also increases exposure to emotional manipulation and negative feedback loops. Relationship-focused communication, while vital for maintaining close digital bonds, can leave female users vulnerable to burnout when emotional reciprocity is imbalanced.

Women often shoulder disproportionate digital emotional labor. This includes mediating online conflicts, maintaining community well-being, and responding to harassment or discrimination (Li & Zhuo, 2023). Rodis (2023) highlights how women of color in particular navigate intersectional aggression, carefully balancing confrontation with self-preservation. Such "managed responses" illustrate the burden of sustaining supportive cyberspaces while simultaneously defending against harm (Clark et al., 2023; Stevens et al., 2021). Over time, this labor creates additional psychological strain, as women often engage in invisible work that sustains digital communities.

While social platforms offer women valuable social support, they also heighten risks for negative mental health outcomes. Research shows that young women experience elevated rates of depression, anxiety, self-harm, and sleep disturbances linked to intensive social media use (Barnea-Goraly et al., 2025; Kircaburun et al., 2018). Social comparison is a particularly harmful mechanism: carefully curated online portrayals by peers, influencers, and celebrities amplify feelings of inadequacy and distress. Yet, these same networks provide critical outlets for identity exploration, emotional expression, and professional development, revealing a paradox of risk and resilience in women's online lives (Le Blanc-Brillon et al., 2025; Chowdhury et al., 2025).

Body image concerns represent one of the most acute challenges for women in cyberspaces. The Elaborated Sociocultural Model illustrates how social media pressures contribute to the internalization of beauty ideals, body dissatisfaction, and disordered eating behaviors (Çınaroğlu & Yılmazer, 2025; Gibson et al., 2025; Rodgers et al., 2020). Delgado-Rodríguez et al. (2022) found that women with high symptoms of social network addiction report greater internalization of the thin ideal, while Vuković et al. (2017) and Dahlgren et al. (2024) link peer-based online comparisons to persistent body surveillance. These findings highlight the powerful role of algorithm-driven content curation, influencer marketing, and validation systems (e.g., likes, comments, and filters) in perpetuating unrealistic beauty standards. Platforms such as Instagram and TikTok, due to their visual intensity, exert a particularly strong influence on women's body image.

Cyber harassment remains a widespread and gendered phenomenon. Women face higher exposure to sexual harassment, appearance-based attacks, and intimate image abuse, with disproportionate psychological consequences including acute stress, PTSD, depression, and long-term trust issues (Geetha, 2024; Iroegbu et al., 2024). Female gamers and professionals often mask their gender identity to avoid targeted abuse (Nanclares et al., 2025; Vella et al., 2019; Zhou & Peterson, 2024). These risks create patterns of withdrawal and digital avoidance, limiting women's participation and silencing their voices in online communities. Addressing these harms requires multi-stakeholder collaboration: platforms must enforce stronger anti-harassment policies, governments must ensure accountability, and communities must cultivate cultures of intervention and support.

Age further shapes women's emotional experiences online. Adolescents, young adults (Rodgers et al., 2020), and adult women (aged 25–45) balance digital identity management with professional obligations and concerns about family privacy (Soria et al., 2024). Older women (45 and above) face digital literacy barriers and ageism but also benefit from online platforms to combat social isolation, pursue lifelong learning, and engage in advocacy (Borpujari, 2024; Soria et al., 2024). These trajectories highlight that female digital experiences evolve across the lifespan, but emotional sensitivity remains a central thread throughout.

FIGURE 8.1 The duality of relational digital engagement for females.

Evidence suggests that emotionally supportive platforms must be deliberately designed with women's experiences in mind (see Figure 8.1). Strategies include integrating wellness check-ins, algorithmic transparency, and body image protection features (Belenguer, 2022); developing robust reporting systems for harassment (Geetha, 2024); and embedding educational resources that foster digital literacy and emotional intelligence (Audrin & Audrin, 2023). Community-centered governance models can also empower users to shape safer digital cultures, while multi-stakeholder collaboration ensures accountability across industry, academia, and policy (Araghi et al., 2025) (Table 8.2).

> ***Takeaway:*** *Emotionally driven digital platforms enrich women's lives by offering support, identity exploration, and connection. However, they also expose female users to heightened risks, including body image pressures, harassment, and relational stress. Platform design and policy play a decisive role in whether these environments become empowering or harmful.*
>
> ***Reflection:*** *How can emotionally supportive platforms be reimagined to strengthen women's capacity for connection while minimizing risks such as body image pressures and online harassment?*

TABLE 8.2 Benefits and Risks of Emotionally Supportive Platforms for Female Users

Dimension	*Benefits*	*Risks*
Emotional Support & Connection	Access to peer support networks; opportunities for emotional expression and identity exploration; continuous availability of social connection (Barnea-Goraly et al., 2025)	Over-dependence on platforms for emotional regulation; exposure to manipulative or predatory behaviors exploiting emotional openness (Steinert & Dennis, 2022)
Mental Health	Destigmatization of mental health issues; access to resources, counseling, and crisis support communities (Audrin & Audrin, 2023)	Elevated rates of depression, anxiety, and self-harm linked to problematic social media use (Shannon et al., 2022)
Body Image & Identity	Opportunities for self-expression and body-positivity movements; access to diverse identity-based communities (Rodgers et al., 2020)	Appearance pressure, thin-ideal internalization, body dissatisfaction, and disordered eating (Delgado-Rodríguez et al., 2022; Digennaro & Tescione, 2024)
Social Capital & Empowerment	Professional networking, advocacy, and leadership opportunities; amplification of marginalized voices (Rodis, 2023)	Harassment, trolling, and silencing of female voices in professional and social spheres (Geetha, 2024)
Community & Belonging	Inclusion in affinity groups (e.g., motherhood, wellness, activism); collective action for social change (Boulianne, 2020)	Risk of echo chambers reinforcing negative thinking patterns; vulnerability to misinformation or harmful movements (Steinert & Dennis, 2022)

8.4 Competition, Risk, and Digital Ethics among Males

Male users' engagement in competitive gaming and high-risk online activities presents a complex environment where opportunities for growth coexist with significant ethical concerns. On one hand, these cyberspaces offer platforms for developing skills, fostering teamwork, and building social communities (Delello et al., 2025; Vansteenkiste et al., 2020). On the other hand, they frequently normalize aggression, erode ethical boundaries, and expose participants to manipulative systems that exploit psychological vulnerabilities (Jordan-Vallverdú et al., 2023; Oksanen et al., 2024).

Competitive gaming exemplifies this duality. Multiplayer platforms and esports offer opportunities for skill development and collaboration, with many gamers reporting improvements in teamwork, communication, and problem-solving skills (Huang, 2024). Studies highlight that these environments can help players strengthen resilience and adaptability, qualities that extend beyond the gaming context into academic and professional life (Freeman et al., 2022; Lobel et al., 2017). Yet, research also shows that competitive settings cultivate cultures where toxic behaviors are not only tolerated but often perceived as inherent to the gaming experience (Delello et al., 2025b; Overå & Talberg, 2025; McWhorter et al., 2025). Approximately 95% of male players report exposure to performance-based harassment, much of which is normalized as part of the competitive atmosphere (Gray et al., 2017; Sağ et al., 2026; Zach et al., 2024). Aggression, anger, and moral disengagement become embedded in the social fabric of these communities, reinforcing hostility as a default mode of interaction (Beres et al., 2023; Hannes & Parylo, 2014).

Masculinity further complicates this landscape. The concept of "geek masculinity" demonstrates how patriarchal dominance resurfaces in spaces that historically resisted mainstream male norms, transforming gaming into an arena where exclusion and control are reasserted (Bailey et al., 2020; Deng, 2024; Braithwaite, 2016). This reinforces the marginalization of women and minorities, who often face barriers to entry and sustained participation. At the same time, many men in these spaces experience heightened digital vulnerability. Research on the manosphere reveals that young men, particularly during periods of insecurity or social rejection, tend to gravitate toward toxic communities that reinforce narrow and often damaging notions of masculinity (Botto & Gottzén, 2023; Coufal & Wedel, 2025; Rodis, 2023). AI-powered systems intensify these vulnerabilities by tailoring interactions to exploit emotional needs (see Figure 8.2). For instance, studies on male users engaging with AI companions such as Replika illustrate how these technologies simultaneously provide comfort and perpetuate dependence, embedding problematic gender dynamics while offering temporary relief from feelings of isolation (Kim, 2024; Maples et al., 2024; Saracini et al., 2025). The erosion of ethical boundaries in competitive and risk-oriented contexts emerges through several mechanisms. Fairness in competition is undermined by monetization practices such as "pay-to-win" models, where financial expenditure rather than skill determines success, generating frustration and reinforcing inequality (Gibson et al., 2023; Freeman et al., 2022). Issues of data privacy and consent also arise, as platforms collect vast amounts of user behavior without providing a transparent explanation of how the data is utilized in training algorithms or monetization strategies (Facca et al., 2020; Gagrčin et al., 2024). Aggression becomes normalized through processes of moral disengagement, where harmful behavior is reframed as harmless or part of the game (Freeman et al., 2022). At the same time, exclusionary practices rooted in bias continue to marginalize underrepresented groups, reinforcing stereotypes and narrowing the inclusivity of these spaces (Bailey et al., 2020; Tang et al., 2025). These processes form a cycle in which exposure to toxic behaviors increases the likelihood of their reproduction, creating self-sustaining environments of hostility.

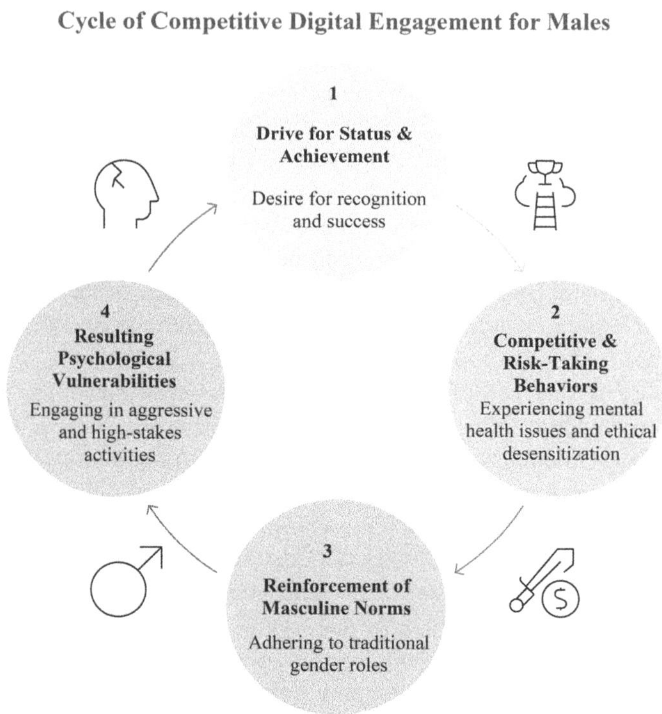

FIGURE 8.2 The cycle of feedback moves beyond a simple list of behaviors to show how they are interconnected in a self-reinforcing cycle.

The influence of digital manipulation is particularly notable. Personalized algorithms are often designed to maximize engagement, which means they exploit psychological vulnerabilities such as competitiveness, risk-taking, or emotional isolation. Loot boxes and similar mechanisms mirror gambling structures, disproportionately affecting young males and introducing risks of addiction and financial harm (Friehs et al., 2024). Beyond in-game monetization, algorithmic curation and targeted advertising direct male users toward hypermasculine influencers or extremist narratives, pushing them into echo chambers that reinforce risky or harmful behaviors (Agyare, 2025; Regehr et al., 2025). In this way, digital manipulation transforms competitive environments from spaces of skill-building into arenas of exploitation (Bentley et al., 2024). Despite these risks, competitive cyberspaces also hold meaningful potential for positive development. Gaming communities can provide a sense of connection and belonging, helping to alleviate symptoms of depression and loneliness by fostering supportive peer networks (Audrin & Audrin, 2023). Leadership and mentorship are cultivated through collaborative gameplay, where effective communication and shared responsibility are essential for success (Akgün et al., 2025; Lobel et al., 2017). Mindfulness and emotional regulation practices also show promise in reducing the impact of exclusion and hostility, equipping players with skills to manage stress and aggression more constructively (Beres et al., 2023). These protective factors highlight that competitive environments, if ethically designed and moderated, can foster not only technical and cognitive growth but also psychological well-being.

The ethical future of competitive gaming hinges on prioritizing player welfare over unchecked engagement. This involves transparency in game mechanics and monetization systems to prevent exploitation, the establishment of robust moderation strategies that actively counter toxic behavior, and the integration of well-being-oriented features such as break reminders and mental health resources (Audrin & Audrin, 2023; Facca et al., 2020). Narratives that challenge stereotypes and inclusive policies that support diverse identities are also essential in ensuring that these spaces encourage prosocial rather than harmful behaviors (Bailey et al., 2020).

Reflection on overlooked ethical boundaries reveals several pressing concerns. Monetization strategies raise questions about where engagement ends and manipulation begins, particularly when vulnerable players are targeted (Lee et al., 2025). Performance-based harassment, though sometimes perceived as less harmful than identity-based attacks, undermines the inclusivity and well-being of participants by entrenching cultures of aggression (Zsila et al., 2022). Emotional and financial insecurities among male players are often exploited by manipulative AI systems, leaving them vulnerable to dependency, scams, or extremist recruitment (Deng, 2024; Miller-Idriss, 2025). The cumulative psychological toll of these interactions gradually reshapes attitudes toward aggression, empathy, and masculinity itself, reinforcing problematic norms that extend far beyond cyberspace. Taken together, competitive and high-risk cyberspaces represent both promise and peril for male users. They can cultivate skills, foster community, and contribute to resilience, but they also risk normalizing harmful behavior and exploiting vulnerability (García et al., 2023; Waechter & Meschik, 2023). The challenge lies in striking a balance between the developmental potential of these spaces and the ethical safeguards necessary to prevent harm. By prioritizing fairness, inclusivity, and user well-being, digital environments can shift from reinforcing aggression to fostering healthier, more ethical forms of competition.

Beyond the normalization of aggression, these competitive, male-dominated spaces create their own distinct set of psychological vulnerabilities. The pressure to perform, to display dominance, and to suppress emotions in line with traditional masculine norms can lead to significant mental health strain (Mokhwelepa et al., 2025; Mogano et al., 2025). Failure to meet these expectations can result in social exclusion and intense feelings of inadequacy. Furthermore, some of these online subcultures can act as echo chambers for misogynistic ideologies, creating pathways to radicalization for disaffected young men (Connell & Messerschmidt, 2005; Coufal & Wedel, 2025). Therefore, the risks for male users are not limited to compulsive or aggressive behaviors but also include the psychological costs of conforming to rigid online masculinities and exposure to harmful belief systems.

Takeaway: *Competitive digital spaces can promote skill and community but may also normalize aggression, ethical transgressions, and exclusion.*
Reflection: *What ethical boundaries do you think are often overlooked in gaming or risk-oriented cyberspaces?*

8.5 Gendered Mental Health Outcomes and Ethical Implications

Gender-specific cyber behaviors translate into distinct mental health vulnerabilities, creating a complex landscape where biological differences, social expectations, and digital environments intersect to produce divergent psychological outcomes. These outcomes not only reveal different patterns of psychological risk between genders but also highlight profound ethical challenges in how digital platforms are designed, governed, and experienced. Addressing these disparities requires interventions that are not gender-neutral but gender-responsive, accounting for how women, men, and gender-diverse individuals navigate digital environments differently.

Large-scale studies have consistently demonstrated that digital engagement does not affect all users equally. Evidence from surveys of more than 221,000 adolescents across the United States and the United Kingdom found that the association between heavy digital media use and poor psychological well-being was significantly stronger among girls than boys (Barnea-Goraly et al., 2025). The outcomes are strikingly different: adolescent girls who are heavy social media users are nearly twice as likely to report symptoms of depression or suicidal ideation compared to low users, whereas boys show fewer direct associations between media use and clinical outcomes (Ahmed et al., 2020; Grund et al., 2025; Hilty et al., 2023; Weigle & Shafi, 2023). For adult women, digital environments also present disproportionate risks (Hilty et al., 2023; Weigle & Shafi, 2023). Research shows that 45% of women aged 18–29 report experiencing online harassment, with 21% reporting severe abuse such as stalking or physical threats (Korlat et al., 2021). This repeated exposure translates into heightened anxiety, chronic stress, and reduced feelings of safety in cyberspaces. Conversely, studies during the COVID-19 pandemic revealed that digital media use correlated positively with meaning in life for men but not for women, suggesting that men may experience greater psychological benefits from online engagement when compared with their female counterparts (Lilleker et al., 2021; So et al., 2023).

For women, digital mental health vulnerabilities often appear around themes of relational stress and body image. Cyberbullying and harassment remain a major concern, with evidence showing that cyber harassment often coexists with offline intimate partner violence, creating a continuum of trauma that increases mental health consequences (Stevens et al., 2020; Rajappan et al., 2025). Body image pressures are increased by social comparison mechanisms, where algorithmically curated content promotes unattainable beauty ideals, leading to lower self-esteem and higher rates of depressive symptoms among young women (Stevens et al., 2024; Steinert & Dennis, 2022). Even efforts to "curate" or "clean" feeds can unexpectedly increase depression for women, as selective exposure reinforces internalized social expectations (Huong, 2023; Vella et al., 2019).

Men, by contrast, face vulnerabilities shaped more by societal norms of emotional suppression and behavioral externalization. Studies suggest that men often channel emotional distress into anger, impulsivity, or substance use, with online gaming and digital platforms sometimes reinforcing these tendencies (Gray et al., 2017; Macdonald et al., 2020). Avoidant coping strategies, such as distraction through endless scrolling or immersive gaming, can worsen cycles of isolation and depression (Vella et al., 2019; Sinha et al., 2024). While gaming offers a sense of belonging, failure to meet competitive or performance-based expectations frequently leads to heightened aggression and social exclusion (Freeman et al., 2022; Lewinson et al., 2023).

The gendered nature of digital mental health raises pressing ethical challenges. Algorithmic bias is a significant concern: studies have shown that mobile-based mental health assessment algorithms often perform differently across genders, potentially leading to less accurate diagnoses and poorer treatment recommendations for women (Kasen et al., 2024; Rajappan et al., 2025). Similarly, design exclusion perpetuates disparities, as women, despite being 75% more likely than men to use digital health tools, remain severely underrepresented in health-tech investment, with only 3% of US venture capital funding directed toward women's health (Mechael, 2025; Perez, 2019). Privacy and safety issues further compound the problem, as women with mental health conditions express heightened fears that disclosure through digital platforms could lead to stigma, hostility, or threats to employment (Opozda et al., 2023; Kasen et al., 2024).

Addressing these inequities requires gender-responsive digital design and ethical practices that extend beyond dual assumptions. The personalization of mental health tools must account for the full gender spectrum, integrating intersectional perspectives on race, class, and culture (Opozda et al., 2023; Gautam et al., 2024). Effective design also requires prioritizing safety-first approaches, such as robust encryption, crisis response protocols, and participatory design processes that meaningfully involve males and females in development and evaluation (Denecke et al., 2025; Malloy et al., 2023; Meyerhoff et al., 2025; Wadley et al., 2013). Promising strategies include blended care models for women that combine digital tools with therapist oversight, anonymous disclosure platforms to mitigate stigma, and peer support networks that specifically address cyberbullying and relational trauma. For men, gamified or skill-oriented interventions can reframe emotional regulation as a performance-based strength rather than a stigma, thereby reducing barriers to help-seeking (Beres et al., 2023; Degenhard & Hatter-Fisher, 2025). The evidence is clear that gender-neutral frameworks in digital mental health are insufficient and often harmful. As shown in Figure 8.3, males and females face distinct risks and

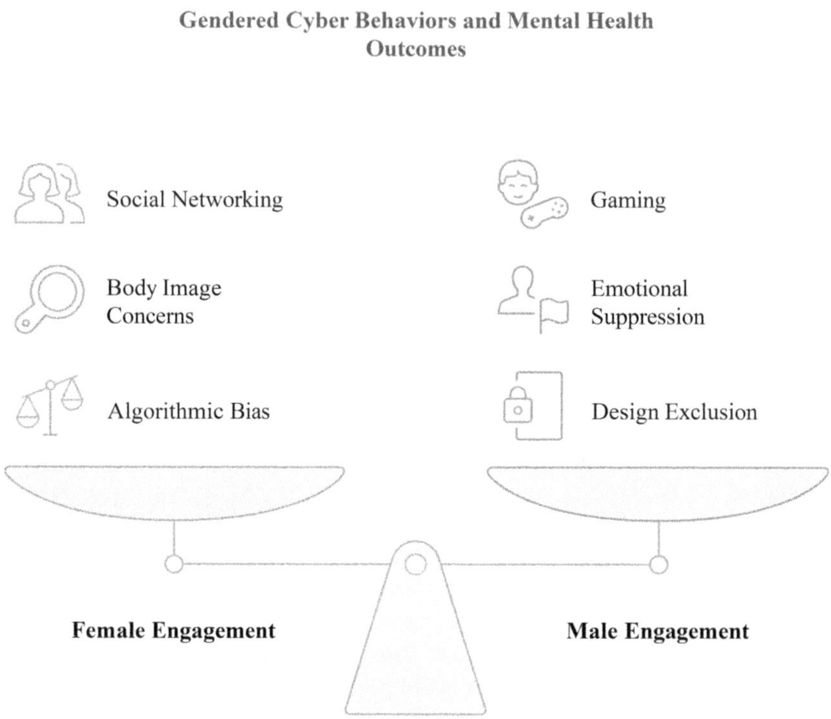

FIGURE 8.3 Gendered Cyber behaviors and their mental health outcomes, highlighting ethical implications across different populations.

opportunities shaped by their online engagement patterns, and interventions must be tailored accordingly. Developing effective, ethical strategies requires addressing algorithmic bias, ensuring equitable investment in the health needs of women and minorities, and embedding safety and inclusivity as core design principles. Most critically, it demands the direct participation of diverse gender groups in shaping digital mental health tools to ensure interventions are not only clinically effective but also socially just. These divergent outcomes highlight the urgent need for AI systems and digital platforms to be designed with a deep understanding of gendered risks. Without intentional, inclusive design, even well-intentioned technologies can inadvertently amplify historical biases and create new forms of harm. The following case study on Amazon's AI recruiting tool provides a stark example of this phenomenon.

Takeaway: *Gendered behaviors online result in distinct mental health outcomes and require targeted ethical strategies for prevention and support.*
Reflection: *What support systems or guidelines could help reduce the emotional risks tied to gendered online behavior?*

8.6 Inclusive Digital and AI Design for Gender Equity

Designing digital platforms and AI systems that are welcoming and ethical for all genders requires more than technical refinement. It requires a sustained commitment to ethics, inclusivity, safety, and fairness. Gender equity in digital design is not achieved through neutrality or "one-size-fits-all" approaches, but rather by actively addressing the specific vulnerabilities, risks, and aspirations of diverse user groups. As digital environments increasingly shape social, economic, and cultural life, the challenge lies in embedding equity principles into the foundations of technology, from conception through governance.

A central starting point is inclusive participation. Involving women, men, and gender-diverse individuals in every phase of development, conceptualization, design, and testing ensures that lived experiences shape the final product. Research highlights that a user-centered design framework incorporating diverse perspectives can mitigate biases and enhance the relevance and effectiveness of digital health interventions for diverse populations (Liu et al., 2023; Bucher et al., 2024).

Equally critical is the detection and mitigation of bias. AI systems are only as fair as the data and models on which they are trained. Transparent auditing of training datasets, regular bias testing, and the use of intersectional data approaches are essential steps in preventing discriminatory outcomes (Chen et al., 2021; Isabelle, 2012). Without such measures, digital systems risk reproducing offline inequalities in new, algorithmically reinforced forms (Chemnad & Othman, 2024). Fairness must also be dynamic: regular updates and corrections should be built into governance frameworks to ensure long-term accountability, rather than relying on one-time fixes.

Safety and privacy by design form another cornerstone of inclusive digital environments. Women and marginalized gender groups often face heightened risks of harassment, surveillance, and exploitation in cyberspaces. Digital platforms must therefore embed robust safety features such as real-time abuse detection, distress signaling, and intuitive reporting channels (Akpuokwe et al., 2024; Henry et al., 2020). Privacy protections are equally vital: customizable visibility settings, dynamic consent architectures, and strong encryption protocols empower users to control their own digital exposure (Bucher et al., 2024; Nebeker et al., 2019). These protections address both the individual need for security and the collective need for trust in digital systems.

Beyond core features, inclusive platforms should build education and capacity-building resources into their environments. Gender-sensitive onboarding that addresses online safety, privacy management, and respectful cyber behavior can cultivate healthier interactions (Agyare, 2025). Meanwhile, embedding digital literacy resources focused on AI ethics, bias awareness, and community norms helps empower users to navigate platforms critically and responsibly (Alon & Krtalić, 2024). Education in this sense functions not just as a user service but as a collective safeguard, shaping cultures of accountability within digital spaces.

Accessibility remains another critical pillar. Ethical design must adopt universal accessibility standards, ensuring that users with disabilities, including visual, auditory, and cognitive impairments, are supported through alt text, screen readers, and adaptive interfaces (Chemnad & Othman, 2024). At the same time, multilingual features enhance inclusivity for global users, allowing seamless participation across cultural and linguistic boundaries (Alon & Krtalić, 2024; Wang et al., 2024). Such features reflect the principle that inclusivity is not complete unless platforms remove barriers related to both identity and ability.

Finally, governance and accountability structures must anchor these efforts. Gender-diverse ethics boards that oversee content moderation, policy development, and AI auditing can ensure that equity commitments extend beyond symbolic gestures into enforceable action (Tripathi & Rajeev, 2023). Transparent reporting on how user concerns are addressed, combined with regular public audits, strengthens legitimacy and trust. At the same time, embedding financial inclusion features into platforms, such as equitable access to digital banking and financial tools, can advance gender equality beyond the digital space, empowering women and marginalized users with economic independence (Tripathi & Rajeev, 2023). Taken together, these strategies illustrate that ethical AI design is not a checklist but an evolving, participatory process. By embedding inclusivity into participation, bias mitigation, safety, representation, education, accessibility, and governance, digital systems can become environments where users of all genders feel represented, protected, and empowered. Furthermore, fostering digital literacy and critical thinking from a young age is one of the most effective long-term strategies for mitigating the impact of gender bias in AI (Long & Magerko, 2020; Ng et al., 2021). Education can empower users to recognize, question, and challenge the gendered narratives and stereotypes they encounter online. A hands-on, inquiry-based approach can be particularly effective in making the abstract concept of algorithmic bias tangible for young learners. Looking beyond the prevention of bias, the future of gender-inclusive design lies in using AI proactively to foster healthier and more equitable digital ecosystems. This involves moving towards a model of "value-sensitive design", where principles like empathy, collaboration, and mutual respect are embedded into the core architecture of a platform. For example, AI-powered tools could be developed to detect and flag misogynistic or harassing language in real-time, offering users immediate support and reporting options. Recommendation algorithms could be intentionally designed to amplify underrepresented voices and promote diverse content that challenges, rather than reinforces, gender stereotypes. The ultimate goal is to shift from a reactive stance of minimizing harm to a proactive one of actively cultivating digital spaces where all genders can thrive (Figure 8.4).

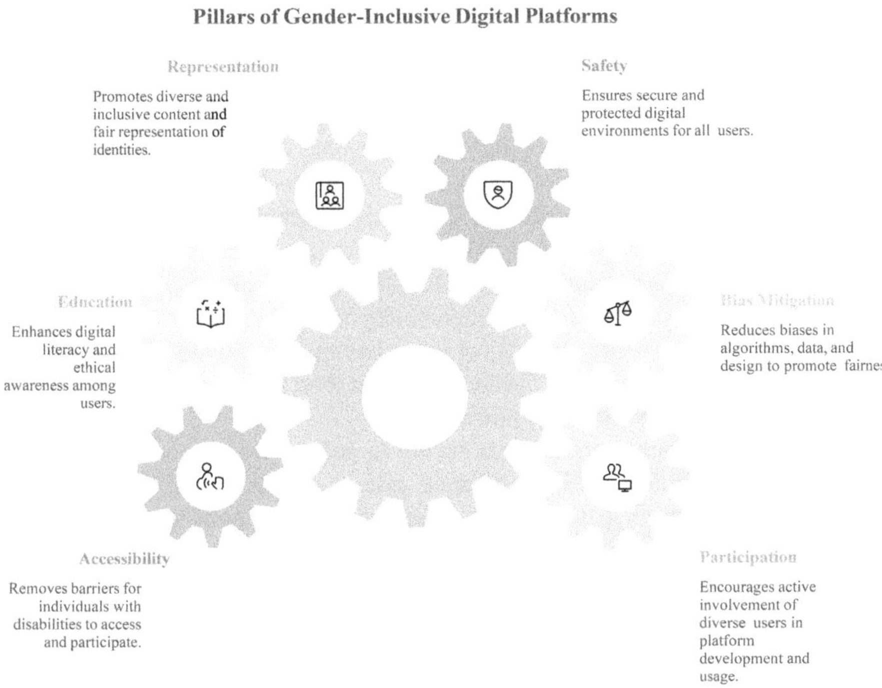

FIGURE 8.4 Key features for gender-inclusive, ethical digital and AI platforms.

> ***Takeaway:*** *Building ethical AI systems requires attention to gender differences. Designs must prioritize safety, fairness, and diverse engagement needs.*
> ***Reflection:*** *What features would you include in a digital platform to ensure it's welcoming and ethical for all genders?*

8.7 Summary and Reflections

This chapter has explored the various ways in which gender influences digital and AI-mediated experiences, demonstrating that online interactions are never neutral but are deeply intertwined with social expectations, cultural norms, and platform architectures. The discussion highlighted that female users often gravitate toward emotionally supportive and relationally oriented platforms, while male users are more frequently drawn to competitive and risk-based environments. These patterns are not trivial; they map onto distinct vulnerabilities, with women disproportionately affected by harassment, body image pressures, and relational stress, and men more often exposed to aggression, ethical desensitization, and risky behaviors in competitive spaces. At the same time, both groups find opportunities for connection, learning, and empowerment in digital environments, highlighting the duality of risks and benefits that gendered engagement entails.

The examination of mental health outcomes revealed that these gendered patterns have measurable psychological effects. Female users tend to report higher incidences of anxiety, depression, and body dissatisfaction linked to social media pressures, while male users face risks of aggression normalization, impulsivity, and addiction-like behaviors in gaming and high-risk contexts. Ethical challenges arise not only from these behavioral patterns but also from systemic biases within AI systems, where algorithms trained on incomplete or unbalanced datasets perpetuate existing inequalities. These insights collectively emphasize that ethical AI design must be responsive to gendered differences rather than assuming neutrality, which too often obscures or worsens inequities.

Crucially, the chapter argued that inclusive and gender-responsive design is not optional but foundational for creating safe and empowering digital spaces. Principles such as participatory design, bias auditing, safety-by-design, inclusive representation, and accessible governance were presented as key strategies to align technological innovation with equity goals. The challenge is not simply to recognize gendered differences but to respond to them in ways that prevent harm while fostering environments where all users, regardless of gender identity, can participate meaningfully and securely.

Looking ahead, gender inclusivity in digital and AI systems must be treated as a core ethical priority that intersects with broader issues of equity, justice, and human rights. Just as technology reshapes identity and interaction, it must also be reshaped to reflect the diversity of its users. The critical question that remains is how designers, policymakers, and educators will act upon these insights. If the future of AI is to be not only intelligent but also just, then attention to gender is essential.

References

Agyare, P. (2025). Gendered digital harms and youth Ideological Trajectories: Socioeconomic Challenges of Digital platforms. *SocioEconomic Challenges, 9*(3), 77–96. https://doi.org/10.61093/sec.9(3).77-96.2025

Ahmed, S., & Madrid-Morales, D. (2020). Is it still a man's world? Social media news use and gender inequality in online political engagement. *Information Communication & Society*, *24*(3), 381–399. https://doi.org/10.1080/1369118x.2020.1851387

Akgün, A. E., Keskin, H., Esen, E., & Aksoy, Z. (2025). Unveiling the nexus of the relationship between multiplayer digital game-playing experience and workplace loneliness: A moderated serial mediation analysis. *BMC Psychology, 13*(1), 1045. https://doi.org/10.1186/s40359-025-03408-2

Akpuokwe, N. C. U., Chikwe, N. C. F., & Eneh, N. N. E. (2024). Innovating business practices: The impact of social media on fostering gender equality and empowering women entrepreneurs. *Magna Scientia Advanced Research and Reviews*, *10*(2), 032–043. https://doi.org/10.30574/msarr.2024.10.2.0042

Alon, L., & Krtalić, M. (2024). "I wish I could use any language as it comes to mind": User experience in digital platforms in the context of multilingual personal information management. *Journal of the Association for Information Science and Technology*. https://doi.org/10.1002/asi.24964

Antonio, A., & Tuffley, D. (2014). The gender digital divide in developing countries. *Future Internet*, *6*(4), 673–687. https://doi.org/10.3390/fi6040673

Araghi, S., Birch, P., Heggart, K., Buchanan, J., & Wallace, H. (2025). Digital community management for crime prevention and public safety: Strategies for safer and more inclusive online communities. *Journal of Community Safety and Well-Being, 10*(3), 138–150. https://doi.org/10.35502/jcswb.478

Aran-Ramspott, S., Korres-Alonso, O., Elexpuru-Albizuri, I., Moro-Inchaurtieta, Á., & Bergillos-García, I. (2024a). Young users of social media: An analysis from a gender perspective. *Frontiers in Psychology, 15*, 1375983. https://doi.org/10.3389/fpsyg.2024.1375983

Aran-Ramspott, S., Korres-Alonso, O., Elexpuru-Albizuri, I., Moro-Inchaurtieta, Á., & Bergillos-García, I. (2024b). Young users of social media: An analysis from a gender perspective. *Frontiers in Psychology, 15*, 1375983. https://doi.org/10.3389/fpsyg.2024.1375983

Audrin, C., & Audrin, B. (2023). More than just emotional intelligence online: Introducing "digital emotional intelligence." *Frontiers in Psychology*, *14*. https://doi.org/10.3389/fpsyg.2023.1154355

Aydın, D. H., & Aydın, M. B. (2025). *The impact of digitalization on women's access to justice* (pp. 34–58). https://doi.org/10.1201/9781003507031-4

Bailey, E., Mühlmann, C., Rice, S., Nedeljkovic, M., Alvarez-Jimenez, M., Sander, L., Calear, A. L., Batterham, P. J., & Robinson, J. (2020). Ethical issues and practical barriers in internet-based suicide prevention research: A review and investigator survey. *BMC Medical Ethics*, *21*(1). https://doi.org/10.1186/s12910-020-00479-1

Barnea-Goraly, N., Richter, S. E., Katiyar, S., & Locane, J. (2025). Girltelligence: A safe and supportive social community app for teen girls and young women. *First Monday*. https://doi.org/10.5210/fm.v30i1.14114

Belenguer, L. (2022). AI bias: Exploring discriminatory algorithmic decision-making models and the application of possible machine-centric solutions. *AI and Ethics*, *2*(4), 771–787. https://doi.org/10.1007/s43681-022-00138-8

Bentley, S. V., Naughtin, C. K., McGrath, M. J., Irons, J. L., & Cooper, P. S. (2024). The digital divide in action: How experiences of digital technology shape future relationships with artificial intelligence. *AI and Ethics*, *4*(4), 901–915. https://doi.org/10.1007/s43681-024-00452-3

Beres, N. A., Klarkowski, M., & Mandryk, R. L. (2023). Playing with emotions: A systematic review examining emotions and emotion regulation in esports performance. *Proceedings of the ACM on Human-Computer Interaction*, *7*(CHI PLAY), 558–587. https://doi.org/10.1145/3611041

Bhagat, R. K. B. (2025). Women and the web: A comparative study of socio-cultural and digital infrastructural barriers. *International Journal on Research and Development – A Management Review, 14*(1), 273–280. https://doi.org/10.65521/ijrdmr.v14i1.686

Borpujari, P. (2024). "What shall i write tomorrow?" When older women reclaim new life course on Facebook. In *Linking Ages* (pp. 176–188). https://doi.org/10.4324/9781003429340-19

Botto, M., & Gottzén, L. (2023). Swallowing and spitting out the red pill: Young men, vulnerability, and radicalization pathways in the manosphere. *Journal of Gender Studies, 33*(5), 596–608. https://doi.org/10.1080/09589236.2023.2260318

Boulianne, S. (2020). Twenty years of digital media effects on civic and political participation. *Communication Research, 47*(7), 947–966. https://doi.org/10.1177/0093650218808186

Braithwaite, A. (2016). It's about ethics in games journalism? Gamergaters and geek masculinity. *Social Media + Society, 2*(4). https://doi.org/10.1177/2056305116672484

Bucher, A., Chaudhry, B. M., Davis, J. W., Lawrence, K., Panza, E., Baqer, M., Feinstein, R. T., Fields, S. A., Huberty, J., Kaplan, D. M., Kusters, I. S., Materia, F. T., Park, S. Y., & Kepper, M. (2024). How to design equitable digital health tools: A narrative review of design tactics, case studies, and opportunities. *PLOS Digital Health, 3*(8), e0000591. https://doi.org/10.1371/journal.pdig.0000591

Carcelén-García, S., Narros-González, M. J., & Galmes-Cerezo, M. (2023). Digital vulnerability in young people: gender, age and online participation patterns. *International Journal of Adolescence and Youth, 28*(1). https://doi.org/10.1080/02673843.2023.2287115

Çelik, N. (2025). WOMEN'S POSITION IN DIGITAL INEQUALITY: AN EVALUATION OF POLICIES AND PRACTICES IN TURKEY. *Marmara Universitesi Kadin Ve Toplumsal Cinsiyet Arastirmalari Dergisi, 9*(9), 1–22. https://doi.org/10.29228/mukatcad.45

Chemnad, K., & Othman, A. (2024). Digital accessibility in the era of artificial intelligence—Bibliometric analysis and systematic review. *Frontiers in Artificial Intelligence, 7*. https://doi.org/10.3389/frai.2024.1349668

Chen, I. Y., Pierson, E., Rose, S., Joshi, S., Ferryman, K., & Ghassemi, M. (2021). Ethical machine learning in healthcare. *Annual Review of Biomedical Data Science, 4*(1), 123–144. https://doi.org/10.1146/annurev-biodatasci-092820-114757

Chowdhury, S. Y., Banik, B., Hoque, M. T., & Uddin, M. S. (2025). A novel hybrid deep learning technique for speech emotion detection using feature engineering. *arXiv preprint*. https://doi.org/10.48550/arXiv.2507.07046

Çınaroğlu, M., & Yılmazer, E. (2025). Problematic social media use, self-objectification, and body image disturbance: The moderating roles of physical activity and diet intensity. *Psychology Research and Behavior Management, 18*, 931–952. https://doi.org/10.2147/PRBM.S517193

Clark, C. J., Graso, M., Redstone, I., & Tetlock, P. E. (2023). Harm hypervigilance in public reactions to scientific evidence. *Psychological Science, 34*(7), 834–848. https://doi.org/10.1177/09567976231168777

Connell, R. W., & Messerschmidt, J. W. (2005). Hegemonic masculinity. *Gender & Society, 19*(6), 829–859. https://doi.org/10.1177/0891243205278639

Costa, P., & Ribas, L. (2019). AI becomes her: Discussing gender and artificial intelligence. *Technoetic Arts, 17*(1), 171–193. https://doi.org/10.1386/tear_00014_1

Coufal, L., & Wedel, L. (2025). Radicalization within a network of misogynist extremists: A case study of an incel forum. *Humanities and Social Sciences Communications, 12*(1). https://doi.org/10.1057/s41599-025-05161-8

Dahlgren, C. L., Sundgot-Borgen, C., Kvalem, I. L., Wennersberg, A., & Wisting, L. (2024). Further evidence of the association between social media use, eating disorder pathology and appearance ideals and pressure: A cross-sectional study in Norwegian adolescents. *Journal of Eating Disorders, 12*(1), 34. https://doi.org/10.1186/s40337-024-00992-3

Degenhard, S. M., & Hatter-Fisher, D. (2025). Integrated online fantasy football platform promotes meditation activity among male-identifying undergraduate students. *Discover Psychology, 5*(1). https://doi.org/10.1007/s44202-025-00535-0

Delello, J., McWhorter, R., Yoo, S., Roberts, P., & Adele, B. (2025a). The impact of esports on the habits, health, and wellness of the collegiate player. *Journal of Intercollegiate Sport, 18*(1), 1–22. https://doi.org/10.17161/jis.v18i1.21714

Delello, J., McWhorter, R., Yoo, S., Roberts, P., & Adele, B. (2025b). The impact of esports on the habits, health, and wellness of the collegiate player. *Journal of Intercollegiate Sport, 18*(1), 1–22. https://doi.org/10.17161/jis.v18i1.21714

Delgado-Rodríguez, R., Linares, R., & Moreno-Padilla, M. (2022). Social network addiction symptoms and body dissatisfaction in young women: Exploring the mediating role of awareness of appearance pressure and internalization of the thin ideal. *Journal of Eating Disorders, 10*(1). https://doi.org/10.1186/s40337-022-00643-5

Denecke, K., Rivera-Romero, O., Giunti, G., Van Holten, K., & Gabarron, E. (2025). Key components of Participatory Design Workshops for Digital Health Solutions: Nominal group technique and feasibility study. *Journal of Healthcare Informatics Research, 9*(3), 359–379. https://doi.org/10.1007/s41666-025-00199-4

Deng, Z. (2024). "They don't mean to hurt": Female gamers' reluctance in recognizing and confronting sexism in gaming as an online-offline juxtaposition. *New Media & Society, 28*(1), 270–288. https://doi.org/10.1177/14614448241287831

Digennaro, S., & Tescione, A. (2024). Scrolls and self-perception, navigating the link between social networks and body dissatisfaction in preadolescents and adolescents: A systematic review. *Frontiers in Education, 9*, Article 1390583. https://doi.org/10.3389/feduc.2024.1390583

Facca, D., Smith, M. J., Shelley, J., Lizotte, D., & Donelle, L. (2020). Exploring the ethical issues in research using digital data collection strategies with minors: A scoping review. *PLoS ONE, 15*(8), e0237875. https://doi.org/10.1371/journal.pone.0237875

Freeman, G., Wu, K., Nower, N., & Wohn, D. Y. (2022). Pay to win or pay to cheat: How players of competitive online games perceive fairness of In-Game purchases. *Proceedings of the ACM on Human-Computer Interaction, 6*(CHI PLAY), 1–24. https://doi.org/10.1145/3549510

Friehs, M. A., Klarkowski, M., Frommel, J., Phillips, C., & Mandryk, R. L. (2024). Fighting fair: Community perspectives on the fairness of performance enhancement in esports. *Frontiers in Sports and Active Living, 6*. https://doi.org/10.3389/fspor.2024.1330755

Gagrčin, E., Naab, T. K., & Grub, M. F. (2024). Algorithmic media use and algorithm literacy: An integrative literature review. *New Media & Society, 28*(1), 423–447. https://doi.org/10.1177/14614448241291137

Gautam, K., Aguilar, C., Paudel, K., Dhakal, M., Wickersham, J. A., Acharya, B., Sapkota, S., Deuba, K., & Shrestha, R. (2024). "We know mental health problem is real, but it is somewhere invisible in the corner of the room": A qualitative study on preferences for mHealth intervention to address mental health challenges among men who have sex with men in Nepal (Preprint). *JMIR Human Factors, 11*, e56002. https://doi.org/10.2196/56002

Geetha, D. (2024). The impact of online harassment on women's societal development. *International Journal of English Literature and Social Sciences, 9*(6), 283–285. https://doi.org/10.22161/ijels.96.46

Gibson, E., Griffiths, M. D., Calado, F., & Harris, A. (2023). Videogame player experiences with micro-transactions: An interpretative phenomenological analysis. *Computers in Human Behavior, 145*, 107766. https://doi.org/10.1016/j.chb.2023.107766

Gibson, G., Liddelow, C., Burke, K. J., & Lee, M. F. (2025). Exploring the influence of social media 'Mumfluencers' on postpartum body image. *Journal of Health Psychology, 30*(14), 4268–4283. https://doi.org/10.1177/13591053251381895

Gisbert-Pérez, J., Martí-Vilar, M., Merino-Soto, C., Chans, G. M., & Badenes-Ribera, L. (2024). Gender differences in internet gaming among university students: A discriminant analysis. *Frontiers in Psychology, 15*, 1412739. https://doi.org/10.3389/fpsyg.2024.1412739

Grassini, S., & Ree, A. S. (2023). Hope or Doom AI-ttitude? Examining the Impact of Gender, Age, and Cultural Differences on the Envisioned Future Impact of Artificial Intelligence on Humankind (pp. 1–7). *ECCE '23: Proceedings of the European Conference on Cognitive Ergonomics 2023.* https://doi.org/10.1145/3605655.3605669

Gray, K. L., Buyukozturk, B., & Hill, Z. G. (2017). Blurring the boundaries: Using Gamergate to examine "real" and symbolic violence against women in contemporary gaming culture. *Sociology Compass, 11*(3). https://doi.org/10.1111/soc4.12458

Grund, T. U., Krüger, H., & Pascu, I. (2025). Social media use and adolescent depressive symptoms: The moderating roles of gender and parental monitoring. *International Journal of Mental Health and Addiction.* https://doi.org/10.1007/s11469-025-01566-3

Hadfi, R., Okuhara, S., Haqbeen, J., Sahab, S., Ohnuma, S., & Ito, T. (2023). Conversational agents enhance women's contribution in online debates. *Scientific Reports, 13*(1), 14534. https://doi.org/10.1038/s41598-023-41703-3

Harputlu, L., & Güryay, B. (2024). Gender Differences in Digital Literacy: An analysis. *Batı Anadolu Eğltim Bilimleri Dergisi, 15*(3), 3286–3300. https://doi.org/10.51460/baebd.1562102

Hannes, K., & Parylo, O. (2014). Let's play it safe: Ethical considerations from participants in a photovoice research project. *International Journal of Qualitative Methods, 13*(1), 255–274. https://doi.org/10.1177/160940691401300112

Hilty, D. M., Stubbe, D., McKean, A. J., Hoffman, P. E., Zalpuri, I., Myint, M. T., Joshi, S. V., Pakyurek, M., & Li, S. T. (2023). A scoping review of social media in child, adolescents and young adults: Research findings in depression, anxiety and other clinical challenges. *BJPsych Open, 9*(5), e152. https://doi.org/10.1192/bjo.2023.523

Huang, J. K. (2024). Building interpersonal skill profiles for players in competitive team-based online games [Master's thesis, Utrecht University]. Utrecht University Student Theses Repository. https://studenttheses.uu.nl/handle/20.500.12932/48016

Jordan-Vallverdú, V., Plaza-Navas, M., Raya, J. M., & Torres-Pruñonosa, J. (2023). The intellectual structure of esports research. *Entertainment Computing, 49*, 100628. https://doi.org/10.1016/j.entcom.2023.100628

Infanti, A., Valls-Serrano, C., Billieux, J., & Perales, J. C. (2024). Psychometric properties of the Spanish motives for online Gaming questionnaire in a sample of college students. *The Spanish Journal of Psychology, 27*, e16. https://doi.org/10.1017/sjp.2024.16

Iroegbu, M., O'Brien, F., Muñoz, L. C., & Parsons, G. (2024). Investigating the psychological impact of Cyber-Sexual Harassment. *Journal of Interpersonal Violence, 39*(15–16), 3424–3445. https://doi.org/10.1177/08862605241231615

Isabelle, L. (2012). La lithosphère et la tectonique des plaques. *Publications Docs-en-stock.com, 366*(6464), 447–453. https://doi.org/10.1126/science.aax2342

Kasen, P., Nguyen, J., Hildreth, C., Chapple, E., Donaldson, K., Eslami, N., & Garfield, S. (2024). Assessing whether women's unique needs and persistent disparities in mental health care are being addressed by emerging AI-Powered digital health solutions. *Medical Research Archives, 12*(11). https://doi.org/10.18103/mra.v12i11.5996

Kim, S. (2024). Research ethics and issues regarding the use of ChatGPT-like artificial intelligence platforms by authors and reviewers: A narrative review. *Science Editing, 11*(2), 96–106. https://doi.org/10.6087/kcse.343

Kircaburun, K., Alhabash, S., Tosuntaş, Ş. B., & Griffiths, M. D. (2018). Uses and gratifications of problematic social media use among university students: A simultaneous examination of the Big Five of personality traits, social media platforms, and social media use motives. *International Journal of Mental Health and Addiction, 18*(3), 525–547. https://doi.org/10.1007/s11469-018-9940-6

Korlat, S., Kollmayer, M., Holzer, J., Lüftenegger, M., Pelikan, E. R., Schober, B., & Spiel, C. (2021). Gender Differences in digital learning during COVID-19: Competence beliefs, intrinsic value, learning engagement, and perceived teacher support. *Frontiers in Psychology, 12*. https://doi.org/10.3389/fpsyg.2021.637776

Le Blanc-Brillon, J., Fortin, M., Lafrance, A., & Hétu, S. (2025). The associations between social comparison on social media and young adults' mental health. *Frontiers in Psychology, 16*, Article 1597241. https://doi.org/10.3389/fpsyg.2025.1597241

Lewinson, R., Wardell, J., Kronstein, N., Rapinda, K., Kempe, T., Katz, J., Kim, H., & Keough, M. (2023). Gaming as a coping strategy during the COVID-19 pandemic. *Cyberpsychology Journal of Psychosocial Research on Cyberspace, 17*(3). https://doi.org/10.5817/cp2023-3-3

Li, M., Yang, G., Xu, X., Oh, I., & Xu, S. (2026). Relationships among perceived stress, anxiety, and well-being in Chinese hospital staff: The mediating role of self-efficacy and the moderating role of empathy. *Frontiers in Psychology, 17*, 1740682. https://doi.org/10.3389/fpsyg.2026.1740682

Lilleker, D. G. C. 2. J., & Benetē, A. (2023). Research Handbook on Visual Politics. In *Edward Elgar Publishing eBooks*. https://doi.org/10.4337/9781800376939

Lilleker, D., Koc-Michalska, K., & Bimber, B. (2021). Women learn while men talk?: Revisiting gender differences in political engagement in online environments. *Information Communication & Society, 24*(14), 2037–2053. https://doi.org/10.1080/1369118x.2021.1961005

Liu, J., Pei, S., & Zhang, X. (2023). Online food delivery platforms and female labor force participation. *Information Systems Research, 35*(3), 1074–1091. https://doi.org/10.1287/isre.2021.0182

Lobel, A., Engels, R. C. M. E., Stone, L. L., & Granic, I. (2017). Gaining a competitive edge: Longitudinal associations between children's competitive video game playing, conduct problems, peer relations, and prosocial behavior. *Psychology of Popular Media Culture, 8*(1), 76–87. https://doi.org/10.1037/ppm0000159

Long, D., & Magerko, B. (2020). *What is AI literacy? Competencies and design considerations* (pp. 1–16). https://doi.org/10.1145/3313831.3376727

Macdonald, J. A., Greenwood, C. J., Francis, L. M., Harrison, T. R., Graeme, L. G., Youssef, G. J., DiManno, L., Skouteris, H., Fletcher, R., Knight, T., Williams, J., Milgrom, J., & Olsson, C. A. (2020). Profiles of depressive Symptoms and anger in Men: Associations with Postpartum family functioning. *Frontiers in Psychiatry, 11*, 578114. https://doi.org/10.3389/fpsyt.2020.578114

Malloy, J., Partridge, S. R., Kemper, J. A., Braakhuis, A., & Roy, R. (2023). Co-design of digital health interventions with young people: A scoping review. *Digital Health, 9*, 20552076231219117. https://doi.org/10.1177/20552076231219117

Maples, B., Cerit, M., Vishwanath, A., & Pea, R. (2024). Loneliness and suicide mitigation for students using GPT3-enabled chatbots. *Npj Mental Health Research, 3*(1), 4. https://doi.org/10.1038/s44184-023-00047-6

Mechael, P. N. (2025). State of gender in digital health: Where we are and what needs to happen to maximize benefits for all. *Women S Health Nursing, 31*(2), 81–87. https://doi.org/10.4069/whn.2025.06.25

Meyerhoff, J., Popowski, S. A., Lakhtakia, T., Tack, E., Kornfield, R., Kruzan, K. P., Krause, C. J., Nguyen, T., Rushton, K., Pisani, A. R., Reddy, M., Van Orden, K. A., & Mohr, D. C. (2025). Automated digital safety planning interventions for young adults: Qualitative study using online co-design methods. *JMIR Formative Research, 9*, e69602. https://doi.org/10.2196/69602

Miller-Idriss, C. (2025). Misogyny incubators: How gaming helps channel everyday sexism into violent extremism. *Frontiers in Psychology, 16*, 1537477. https://doi.org/10.3389/fpsyg.2025.1537477

Mogano, N. T. H., Letsoalo, D. L., & Oduaran, C. A. (2025). Effects of masculine culture on the mental health of Northern Sotho male youth. *BMC Psychology, 13*(1), 605. https://doi.org/10.1186/s40359-025-02934-3

Mokhwelepa, L. W., & Sumbane, G. O. (2025). Men's Mental Health Matters: The impact of traditional masculinity norms on men's willingness to seek mental health support; A systematic review of literature. *American Journal of Men S Health, 19*(3), 15579883251321670. https://doi.org/10.1177/15579883251321670

Nakandala, S., Ciampaglia, G., Su, N., & Ahn, Y. (2017). Gendered conversation in a social Game-Streaming platform. *Proceedings of the International AAAI Conference on Web and Social Media, 11*(1), 162–171. https://doi.org/10.1609/icwsm.v11i1.14885

Nanclares, E., Romero-Seseña, P., & Pereda, N. (2025). Unsafe Play: Understanding sexual victimization in digital gaming communities. *European Journal on Criminal Policy and Research*. https://doi.org/10.1007/s10610-025-09642-z

Nebeker, C., Ellis, R. J. B., & Torous, J. (2019). Development of a decision-making checklist tool to support technology selection in digital health research. *Translational Behavioral Medicine, 10*(4), 1004–1015. https://doi.org/10.1093/tbm/ibz074

Ng, D. T. K., Leung, J. K. L., Chu, S. K. W., & Qiao, M. S. (2021). Conceptualizing AI literacy: An exploratory review. *Computers and Education Artificial Intelligence, 2*, 100041. https://doi.org/10.1016/j.caeai.2021.100041

Notten, N., & Nikken, P. (2014). Boys and girls taking risks online: A gendered perspective on social context and adolescents' risky online behavior. *New Media & Society, 18*(6), 966–988. https://doi.org/10.1177/1461444814552379

Oksanen, A., Celuch, M., Oksa, R., & Savolainen, I. (2024). Online communities come with real-world consequences for individuals and societies. *Communications Psychology, 2*(1), 71. https://doi.org/10.1038/s44271-024-00112-6

Opozda, M. J., Galdas, P. M., Watkins, D. C., & Smith, J. A. (2023). Intersecting identities, diverse masculinities, and collaborative development: Considerations in creating online mental health interventions that work for men. *Comprehensive Psychiatry, 129*, 152443. https://doi.org/10.1016/j.comppsych.2023.152443

Overå, S., & Talberg, N. (2025). Not passive victims: A qualitative study of gendered understandings, experiences, and coping strategies of toxicity among Norwegian Esports students. *Performance Enhancement & Health, 13*(4), 100363. https://doi.org/10.1016/j.peh.2025.100363

Perez, C. (2019). *Invisible women: Exposing data bias in a world designed for men*. Abrams Press.

Rahayu, N. S., Masduki, & Ellyanawati, E. R. N. (2023). Women entrepreneurs' struggles during the COVID-19 pandemic and their use of social media. *Journal of Innovation and Entrepreneurship, 12*(1). https://doi.org/10.1186/s13731-023-00322-y

Rajappan, S. K., Ali, E. a. A., Hamad, A. a. F., Salman, Z. a. a. A., Alotaibi, S. M. M., & Riyadh, M. a. F. (2025). Relationship between cyberbullying and mental health of teenage victims in Saudi Arabia. *Journal of Family Medicine and Primary Care, 14*(6), 2237–2241. https://doi.org/10.4103/jfmpc.jfmpc_1592_24

Robinson, A., Flom, M., Forman-Hoffman, V. L., Histon, T., Levy, M., Darcy, A., Ajayi, T., Mohr, D. C., Wicks, P., Greene, C., & Montgomery, R. M. (2024). Equity in digital mental health interventions in the United States: Where to next? (Preprint). *Journal of Medical Internet Research, 26*, e59939. https://doi.org/10.2196/59939

Rodgers, R. F., Slater, A., Gordon, C. S., McLean, S. A., Jarman, H. K., & Paxton, S. J. (2020). A biopsychosocial model of social media use and body image concerns, disordered eating, and muscle-building behaviors among adolescent girls and boys. *Journal of Youth and Adolescence*, *49*(2), 399–409. https://doi.org/10.1007/s10964-019-01190-0

Rodis, P. D. C. I. (2023). The managed response: Digital emotional labor in navigating intersectional cyber aggression. *Social Psychology Quarterly*, *87*(1), 1–21. https://doi.org/10.1177/01902725231166377

Russo, C., Romano, L., Clemente, D., Iacovone, L., Gladwin, T. E., & Panno, A. (2025). Gender differences in artificial intelligence: The role of artificial intelligence anxiety. *Frontiers in Psychology, 16*. https://doi.org/10.3389/fpsyg.2025.1559457

Sağ, S., Engin, S. G., & Polat, E. (2026). Masculine behaviors in cyber dating abuse among athletes: the mediating role of dark personality traits and the moderating effect of digital habits. *BMC Psychology, 14*(1). https://doi.org/10.1186/s40359-026-04313-y

Saracini, C., Cornejo-Plaza, M. I., & Cippitani, R. (2025). Techno-emotional projection in human–GenAI relationships: A psychological and ethical conceptual perspective. *Frontiers in Psychology, 16*, 1662206. https://doi.org/10.3389/fpsyg.2025.1662206

Shannon, H., Bush, K., Villeneuve, P. J., Hellemans, K. G. C., & Guimond, S. (2022). Problematic social media use in adolescents and young adults: Systematic review and meta-analysis. *JMIR Mental Health, 9*(4), Article e33450. https://doi.org/10.2196/33450

So, W. W. Y., Woo, B. P. Y., Wong, C., & Yip, P. S. F. (2023). Gender differences in the relationships between meaning in life, mental health status and digital media use during Covid-19. *BMC Public Health, 23*(1), 1770. https://doi.org/10.1186/s12889-023-16672-x

Soria, M. S., Zakry, K. A., Hipiny, I., Ujir, H., Hassan, R., & Jerry, A. L. (2024). An instance segmentation method for nesting green sea Turtle's Carapace using Mask R-CNN. *International Journal of Computing and Digital Systems, 15*(1), 201–211. https://doi.org/10.12785/ijcds/160116

Stevens, F., Nurse, J. R. C., & Arief, B. (2021). Cyber stalking, cyber harassment, and adult mental health: A systematic review. *Cyberpsychology, Behavior, and Social Networking,* 24(6), 367–376. https://doi.org/10.1089/cyber.2020.0253

Regehr, K., Shaughnessy, C., Zhao, M., Cambazoglu, I., Turner, A., & Shaughnessy, N. (2025). Normalizing toxicity: The role of recommender algorithms for young people's mental health and social wellbeing. *Frontiers in Psychology, 16*, 1523649. https://doi.org/10.3389/fpsyg.2025.1523649

Shi, Y. (2023). Consumer behavior and cultural factors in social media: A cross-cultural comparative study. *Advances in Economics Management and Political Sciences*, *63*(1), 271–277. https://doi.org/10.54254/2754-1169/63/20231435

Silva, R., Dias Moura, H., Betetti, P., Santos, F., & Fortuna, C. (n.d.). Virtual violence as a contributing factor to the mental health of Young people: A scoping review. *The Canadian Journal of Nursing Research = Revue Canadienne De Recherche En Sciences Infirmieres*. https://doi.org/10.1177/08445621251364528

Steinert, S., & Dennis, M. J. (2022). Emotions and digital well-being: On social media's emotional affordances. *Philosophy & Technology*, *35*(2). https://doi.org/10.1007/s13347-022-00530-6

Tripathi, S., & Rajeev, M. (2023). Gender-inclusive development through fintech: Studying gender-based digital financial inclusion in a cross-country setting. *Sustainability*, *15*(13), 10253. https://doi.org/10.3390/su151310253

Vansteenkiste, M., Ryan, R. M., & Soenens, B. (2020). Basic psychological need theory: Advancements, critical themes, and future directions. *Motivation and Emotion, 44*(1), 1–31. https://doi.org/10.1007/s11031-019-09818-1

Vella, K., Klarkowski, M., Turkay, S., & Johnson, D. (2019). Making friends in online games: Gender differences and designing for greater social connectedness. *Behaviour and Information Technology, 39*(8), 917–934. https://doi.org/10.1080/0144929x.2019.1625442

Vuković, M. B., Lucić, M., & Štulhofer, A. (2017). Internet use associated body-surveillance among female adolescents: Assessing the role of peer networks. *Sexuality & Culture, 22*(2), 521–540. https://doi.org/10.1007/s12119-017-9480-4

Wadley, G., Lederman, R., Gleeson, J., & Alvarez-Jimenez, M. (2013). Participatory design of an online therapy for youth mental health (pp. 517–526). *OzCHI '13: Proceedings of the 25th Australian Computer-Human Interaction Conference: Augmentation, Application, Innovation, Collaboration.* https://doi.org/10.1145/2541016.2541030

Waechter, N., & Meschik, M. (2023). Peer socialization of male adolescents in digital games: Achievement, competition, and harassment. *Communications, 48*(4), 457–481. https://doi.org/10.1515/commun-2021-0079

Weigle, P. E., & Shafi, R. M. A. (2023). Social media and youth mental health. *Current Psychiatry Reports, 26*(1), 1–8. https://doi.org/10.1007/s11920-023-01478-w

Yaman, H., & Çakıroğlu, G. (2025). Empowering women in the digital age: A narrative review of technological opportunities and barriers. *İstanbul Gelişim Üniversitesi Sağlık Bilimleri Dergisi, 0*(26), 751–761. https://doi.org/10.38079/igusabder.1629806

Yaseen, H., Mohammad, A. S., Ashal, N., Abusaimeh, H., Ali, A., & Sharabati, A. A. (2025). The impact of adaptive learning technologies, personalized feedback, and interactive AI tools on student engagement: The moderating role of digital literacy. *Sustainability, 17*(3), 1133. https://doi.org/10.3390/su17031133

Zach, S., Davidovitz, M., & Cohen, R. (2024). Comparative perceptions of sexual harassment among athletes across different competitive levels. *Frontiers in Sports and Active Living, 6*, 1468534. https://doi.org/10.3389/fspor.2024.1468534

Zhou, Y., & Peterson, Z. D. (2024). Women's experiences of sexual harassment in online gaming. *Violence Against Women, 31*(8), 2037–2052. https://doi.org/10.1177/10778012241252021

Zsila, Á., Shabahang, R., Aruguete, M. S., & Orosz, G. (2022). Toxic behaviors in online multiplayer games: Prevalence, perception, risk factors of victimization, and psychological consequences. *Aggressive Behavior, 48*(3), 356–364. https://doi.org/10.1002/ab.22023

9

CULTURAL PERSPECTIVES ON CYBER BEHAVIOR AND AI ETHICS

Chapter Objectives

- To explore how cultural values shape cyber behavior and AI ethics.
- To compare digital and ethical norms between Gulf/Middle Eastern and Western societies.
- To analyze how cultural context influences attitudes toward privacy, AI use, and online engagement.
- To promote culturally sensitive approaches to AI development and ethical digital practices.

Topics to Be Covered

- Introduction: Why Culture Matters in Digital and AI Ethics
- Cultural Norms and Cyber Behavior in the Gulf and Middle East
- Individualism and Digital Openness in Western Cultures
- Cultural Perceptions of Privacy and Data Ethics
- AI Adoption and Cultural Alignment in the Gulf Region
- Cultural Challenges in Global AI Design and Ethics
- Moving Beyond Hofstede: A Detailed, Value-Based Approach
- Summary and Reflections

DOI: 10.4324/9781003657590-12

9.1 Introduction: Why Culture Matters in Digital and AI Ethics

Culture acts as a central framework through which individuals interpret, adopt, and regulate their interactions with digital technologies and artificial intelligence (AI). It influences not only patterns of technology adoption but also the ethical reasoning that shapes expectations of fairness, accountability, and privacy. Identical technologies can produce divergent user responses across societies, as cultural norms structure attitudes toward trust, risk, and responsibility in the digital domain (Jamalova, 2024). This perspective positions culture as a determining factor in how digital systems are integrated into everyday life and how ethical standards in AI are established and contested.

The role of cultural competence in AI education emphasizes this relationship. Research with Nigerian students highlights that embedding cultural relevance into AI curricula enhances understanding and acceptance, suggesting that educational outcomes improve when AI concepts are contextualized within local cultural frameworks (Sanusi & Olaleye, 2022). Similarly, in health-related AI applications, governance structures informed by cultural attitudes toward privacy, transparency, and accountability prove more capable of addressing ethical risks, as shown in studies of AI in population health (Couture et al., 2023). These findings demonstrate how culturally situated perspectives shape both grassroots engagement and institutional oversight of AI.

Cross-national studies further reveal how cultural context structures perceptions of accountability and ethics in AI. In Greece, students' ethical expectations of AI systems were intertwined with their cultural attitudes and digital literacy, influencing how they attributed responsibility for AI outcomes (Saklaki & Gardikiotis, 2024). Comparative research across Estonia, Germany, and Sweden identified recurring values such as efficiency and social diversity but also showed divergent national priorities, reflecting deep cultural variance in how AI ethics are conceptualized (Masso et al., 2023). This variance aligns with findings from Taiwan, where respondents emphasized nonmaleficence and expressed stronger support for the strict regulation of AI technologies (Chang et al., 2024). These examples confirm that ethical frameworks are not universally shared but emerge from culturally embedded moral traditions and social expectations.

Cultural perspectives are also central to how individuals perceive privacy and data governance. Intercultural information ethics (IIE) provides a conceptual lens for examining how localized understandings of privacy may conflict with standardized approaches to data management (Melo, 2023). Evidence shows that socio-cultural variables, including gender, income, and religion, influence acceptance of emotional data collection, particularly regarding the role of government versus private actors as data harvesters (Shukla, 2024). These findings illustrate that privacy expectations are shaped less by technological capability than by the ethical codes rooted in specific cultural contexts.

Another dimension is cultural proximity bias in AI acceptability. Individuals consistently demonstrate stronger trust in AI-generated content when it aligns with their cultural frame of reference while distancing themselves from outputs perceived as culturally distant (Tubadji et al., 2021). Such biases highlight the importance of cultural familiarity in the formation of trust and suggest that human–AI interaction cannot be separated from the cultural setting in which it occurs.

Despite the strengths of cross-cultural research, limitations persist. Heavy reliance on Hofstede's dimensions offers theoretical consistency but risks oversimplifying cultural complexity and ignoring variation within societies (Straub et al., 2002). Furthermore, the concentration of studies in developed regions leads to an underrepresentation of cultural influences in African, Latin American, and Middle Eastern contexts (Masso et al., 2023). Addressing these gaps is essential for building AI systems that are not only technologically advanced but also socially inclusive.

The implications of these findings are significant. For designers, cultural variation in accountability attribution suggests the need for AI explanation systems tailored to local expectations. For policymakers, the example of Nordic countries demonstrates how cultural values such as trust and transparency can structure national AI strategies (Robinson, 2020). For educators, embedding cultural context into digital literacy programs fosters more responsible engagement with AI systems (Suntharalingam, 2024). Across these domains, culture is not a peripheral consideration but a defining factor in ensuring that digital technologies and AI systems are ethically aligned with the societies in which they operate.

> ***Takeaway:*** *Cultural background plays a critical role in shaping how people engage with technology and perceive AI ethics.*
> ***Reflection:*** *How has your cultural background influenced your comfort with digital technologies or online sharing?*

9.2 Cultural Norms and Cyber Behavior in the Gulf and Middle East

Digital practices in the Gulf and Middle East are deeply rooted in cultural values such as collectivism, family honor, and modesty. These values shape online engagement, guide ethical boundaries, and influence how societies in the region approach AI. Collectivist orientations emphasize the primacy of family and community, which in turn generates more conservative cyber behaviors. This manifests in the careful management of personal information, avoidance of content that may undermine family reputation, and adherence to modest self-presentation online (Davidson & Martellozzo, 2012). These culturally grounded practices demonstrate that ethical engagement with technology in the region is inseparable from the preservation of family and social values.

Social media platforms complicate this picture. Despite the constraints imposed by modesty norms, channels such as Twitter have created spaces for public discourse that were previously limited in conservative societies. Studies show that Gulf users increasingly employ these platforms to engage in political and cultural discussions, demonstrating a careful negotiation between cultural values and the opportunities offered by digital tools (Al-Jenaibi, 2016). Such practices illustrate the dual role of cyberspaces in both reinforcing and subtly reshaping cultural norms.

Gender plays a decisive role in this digital ecosystem. Cultural expectations surrounding modesty and family honor impose stricter boundaries on women's digital engagement compared to men. Female users are often subject to greater scrutiny, which influences their willingness to share personal information, images, or opinions online (Davidson & Martellozzo, 2012). These restrictions reflect broader social frameworks in which technology use is mediated not only by individual choice but also by collective expectations of honor and respectability.

As AI systems expand into the region, technological adaptation becomes essential. Research indicates that technologies must reflect local values in order to be accepted as ethical and trustworthy. For instance, AI-driven systems in health, education, or social services require designs that respect privacy, modesty, and cultural restrictions on information sharing. Without such alignment, digital systems risk reproducing forms of technological colonialism that disregard local ethical traditions (Alrashdi et al., 2024; Melo, 2023).

The relationship between culture and cyber behavior in the Gulf also connects to broader cross-cultural research. Comparative studies demonstrate that cultural dimensions such as collectivism and uncertainty avoidance significantly predict patterns of digital adoption and ethical engagement (Sriwindono, 2022; Huang et al., 2021). However, the Gulf region represents a distinctive case: high respect for authority and family structures strengthens conservative practices, while rapid modernization and digital transformation increase exposure to globalized norms (Salehan et al., 2018). This tension results in cautious adoption of digital technologies, where the promise of innovation is balanced by ethical considerations anchored in family and community.

Privacy attitudes further illustrate this balance. Research shows that in Eastern majority contexts, acceptance of data collection depends strongly on whether the collector is a government body or a private company, with respondents often more tolerant of state-driven systems tied to collective welfare than commercial surveillance (Melo, 2023). Such findings demonstrate how local values recalibrate global debates about data ethics.

Critical analysis of existing research highlights both strengths and gaps. Evidence from the Gulf and the Middle East highlights the importance of collectivist and modesty-oriented frameworks, but the region remains underrepresented in comparative studies of AI ethics. Overreliance on Hofstede's dimensions risks flattening cultural complexity (Straub et al., 2002), while many models continue to treat culture as a fixed national attribute rather than a dynamic set of evolving practices (Fiske, 2002). To fully capture the Gulf experience, research must address intra-regional diversity and the rapid cultural change driven by technological modernization.

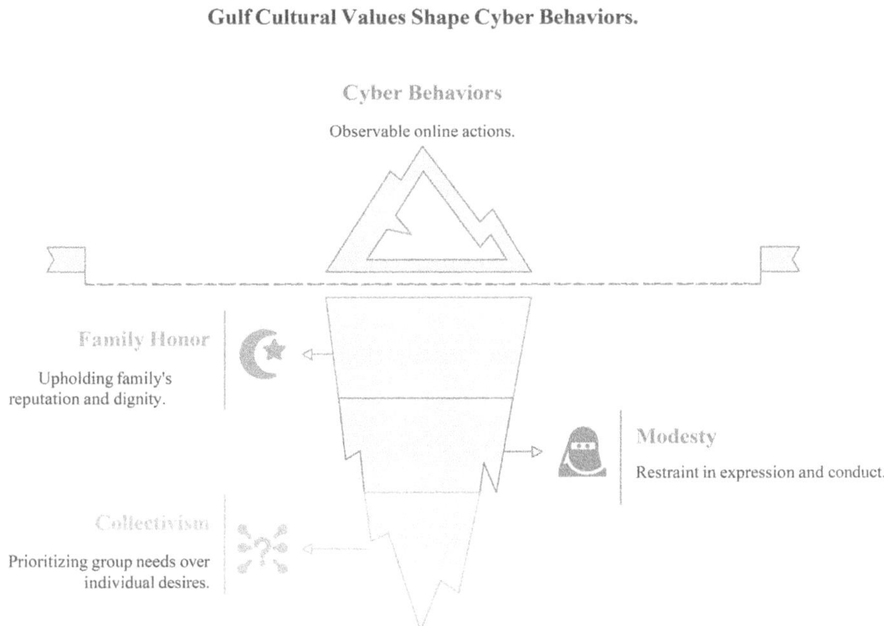

FIGURE 9.1 Cultural values and cyber behaviors in the Gulf region.

The implications are clear. For AI developers, systems designed for the Gulf must integrate respect for modesty and family reputation as part of ethical architecture. For policymakers, cultural values should inform the design of digital governance frameworks that protect privacy while enabling innovation. For educators, digital literacy initiatives must be tailored to the unique concerns of Gulf societies, equipping citizens to engage critically with AI technologies without compromising cultural integrity. Ultimately, the Gulf region illustrates how ethical cyber behavior cannot be divorced from cultural context and how technology must adapt to preserve social harmony while facilitating progress (Figure 9.1).

> ***Takeaway:*** *Collectivist cultures prioritize family, modesty, and privacy, which results in more cautious cyber behaviors and ethical boundaries.*
> ***Reflection:*** *How do cultural values around family or modesty shape your decisions about what you share or consume online?*

9.3 Individualism and Digital Openness in Western Cultures

Western societies, particularly those characterized by high individualism and liberal social norms, have developed a distinct orientation toward digital openness. Cultural values emphasizing autonomy, self-expression, and transparency often translate into cyber behaviors that favor greater information sharing, innovation, and experimentation on digital platforms. This orientation contrasts with that of collectivist cultures, where privacy, modesty, and family honor serve as boundaries for digital engagement. Understanding how individualism shapes digital practices is central to analyzing ethical frameworks and the design of AI systems in Western contexts.

One of the most significant outcomes of digital openness is increased transparency and accountability. For instance, e-government practices in European Union countries demonstrate how accessibility to digital data has expanded opportunities for civic participation and strengthened government accountability (Pina et al., 2007). Beyond governance, the ethos of openness extends to scientific research, where open data and open-access publishing are valued for their ability to increase credibility, equity, and efficiency in knowledge dissemination (Fleming et al., 2021). Similarly, research has shown that digital autonomy is positively associated with creative and innovative work behaviors, as individuals in open digital environments are more likely to experiment with new tools and approaches (Huu, 2023).

At the same time, the risks associated with prioritizing openness and autonomy are significant. Greater willingness to share personal data online often results in weaker privacy protections and limited awareness of how data is collected and used. This concern has been widely documented in studies of Western digital environments, where the erosion of privacy is frequently accepted in exchange for convenience or personalization (Robinson, 2020). Furthermore, while openness accelerates the dissemination of information, it also increases susceptibility to misinformation and data misuse, undermining trust in both platforms and institutions (Berch et al., 2024). Additional challenges emerge in balancing openness with broader ethical and strategic needs, such as security or macroeconomic stability, raising tensions between liberal norms and international standards (Kübek & Mancini, 2023; Nguyen et al., 2023).

Cross-cultural studies provide empirical evidence of how Western individualism shapes technology adoption and ethical perceptions. Cultures high in individualism and low in power distance tend to show higher technology adoption rates and stronger preferences for transparency and user control in AI systems (Jamalova, 2024; Salehan et al., 2018). Nordic countries provide a notable example, embedding cultural values of trust and openness into national AI strategies that prioritize fairness and accountability in policy design (Robinson, 2020). Comparative studies further demonstrate that Western populations are more likely to value personal autonomy and individual accountability in AI governance, whereas collectivist societies emphasize community benefit and harm prevention (Chang et al., 2024; Masso et al., 2023).

Privacy attitudes also reflect this divergence. Research in IIE highlights how Western digital practices often interpret informed consent and data sharing through the lens of personal choice, contrasting with societies where collective or religious norms define boundaries for data use (Melo, 2023). Experimental studies reveal that cultural proximity bias shapes the acceptability of AI-generated content, with individuals in individualistic contexts showing greater openness to machine-generated outputs provided transparency and choice are preserved (Tubadji et al., 2021). These findings reinforce the notion that Western approaches to digital ethics are anchored in personal agency, even when this entails increased exposure to risk.

While individualism fosters innovation and inclusivity in digital environments, it simultaneously raises new vulnerabilities. The paradox of Western digital openness lies in its capacity to strengthen democratic values while exposing individuals to privacy erosion and disinformation. Addressing this paradox requires careful policy design that preserves transparency and personal freedom without compromising ethical safeguards.

> ***Takeaway:*** *Western cultures often favor digital openness and innovation, placing a higher value on personal freedom even at the cost of privacy.*
> ***Reflection:*** *What are the potential benefits and risks of prioritizing openness and autonomy in online spaces?*

9.4 Cultural Perceptions of Privacy and Data Ethics

Cultural background strongly shapes how societies understand privacy, interpret surveillance, and respond to data ethics in the digital age. The expansion of AI technologies, particularly in domains such as facial recognition, online tracking, and algorithmic monitoring, has intensified cross-cultural debates about privacy and ethics. Although some cultures prioritize individual autonomy and strict protection of personal data, others emphasize collective benefit, social harmony, or national security, leading to diverse expectations for data ethics across regions.

Cultural Dimensions and Privacy Sensitivities: Hofstede's cultural framework provides a foundation for explaining how values such as individualism, power distance, and uncertainty avoidance mediate privacy perceptions. In highly individualistic societies, such as the United States and Western Europe, privacy is often equated with personal control over information, leading to skepticism about surveillance and strong demands for transparency in data use (Harris et al., 2003; Jamalova, 2024). Conversely, collectivist contexts, such as many Asian and Middle Eastern societies, may tolerate or even support certain forms of monitoring if they are framed as serving the public good, preserving order, or protecting community norms (Sriwindono, 2022; Rabayah, 2019).

Data Ethics and AI Systems: AI technologies intensify these cultural divergences. In Taiwan, national surveys show that nonmaleficence, avoiding harm, is the dominant ethical priority, with citizens strongly supporting regulation of AI systems to ensure they do not cause social damage (Chang et al., 2024). European contexts, by contrast, emphasize values such as *social diversity, accountability, and sustainability*, embedding these into AI governance and policy (Masso et al.,

2023; Robinson, 2020). Nordic countries exemplify how *trust, transparency, and openness* are integrated into privacy and AI policy frameworks, reflecting cultural expectations that governments act as stewards of both technology and citizens' rights (Robinson, 2020).

Surveillance, Tracking, and Facial Recognition: Different cultures assign varying levels of legitimacy to surveillance practices. Research shows that attitudes toward the harvesting of emotional data and biometric tracking are deeply influenced by religious affiliation, income level, and regional norms (Ho et al., 2022). In higher-context societies, trust in automated surveillance technologies increases when clear explanations and permission-seeking mechanisms are provided (Du et al., 2022). By contrast, in Western liberal contexts, transparency alone may not suffice: there is heightened anxiety about data misuse, especially when private companies rather than governments manage sensitive information (Pollach, 2005).

Technology Acceptance Models and Privacy Attitudes: Extensions of the technology acceptance model (TAM) demonstrate that cultural dimensions significantly affect how users evaluate privacy risks versus perceived benefits. For example, *long-term orientation* correlates with higher acceptance of surveillance if framed as enabling future security, while *low power distance cultures* demand strong mechanisms of user control and opt-out features (Salehan et al., 2018). These findings highlight that ethical expectations are not universal but instead mediated by cultural frames of reference.

Critical Evaluation: Although cross-cultural studies provide consistent evidence that cultural values shape privacy and data ethics, several limitations remain. Heavy reliance on Hofstede's framework risks oversimplification (McCoy et al., 2005). Treating nations as homogeneous units also neglects within-country differences, such as generational divides in privacy expectations. Furthermore, rapid changes in technology, from predictive algorithms to ubiquitous biometric systems, outpace the slow evolution of cultural measurement, raising concerns about the applicability of older cultural typologies to emerging ethical issues.

9.4.1 Implications for Companies and Policymakers

Companies that operate across borders must approach privacy and data ethics with sensitivity to cultural variation. One effective starting point is the recognition that privacy sensitivities are not uniform, even within Western contexts. Research comparing users in the United States and Belgium, for example, has shown significant differences in their tolerance of online data collection, shaped by distinct cultural understandings of privacy and acceptable surveillance (Harris et al., 2003). Such findings highlight the need to tailor corporate privacy policies to local values and expectations, rather than relying on standardized global frameworks.

Transparency and informed consent represent another critical area where cultural expectations diverge. While plain and accessible explanations of data practices may be considered a universal baseline, the way these explanations are framed matters greatly. In societies with high literacy and strong traditions of consumer rights, such as Northern Europe, transparency serves as a trust-building measure that allows users to give meaningful consent. In other cultural settings, however, where institutional trust may be lower or where questioning authority is socially discouraged, transparency must be paired with active efforts to empower individuals through education about data use (Pollach, 2005).

Local legal frameworks provide further guidance by embedding cultural attitudes into regulatory systems. The European Union's General Data Protection Regulation (GDPR) offers one of the clearest examples: its emphasis on autonomy, accountability, and individual rights reflects broader European cultural orientations toward personal privacy and state responsibility (Lin et al., 2024). For companies expanding into these markets, aligning with these regulations is not merely a matter of compliance but also a way of demonstrating respect for deeply rooted cultural expectations around data ethics.

Equally important is the adoption of privacy-by-design approaches, in which ethical safeguards and data protection measures are integrated into AI and big data projects from the earliest stages of development. This strategy signals a proactive commitment to protecting users' rights across regions, rather than retrofitting protections once concerns emerge. By embedding privacy into the design process, organizations can avoid accusations of neglect while ensuring greater adaptability to culturally specific ethical standards (Gilbert & Gilbert, 2024) (Figure 9.2).

Finally, promoting digital literacy remains essential for fostering informed user engagement in contexts where cultural norms or limited access to information may reduce individuals' ability to critically assess privacy risks. Programs that educate users on their data rights and on the implications of online surveillance can

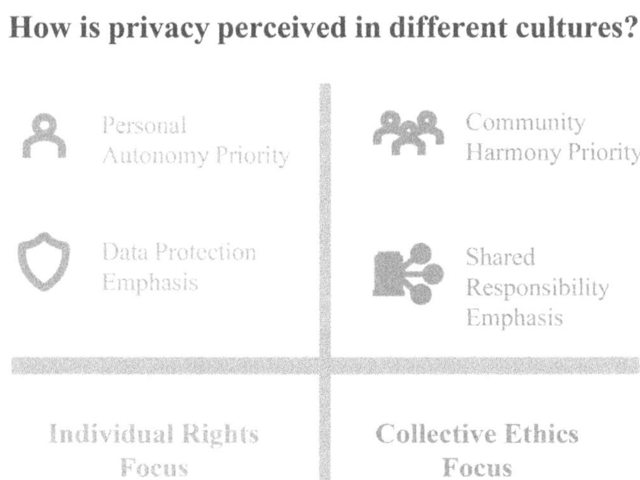

FIGURE 9.2 Two cultural models of privacy and data ethics.

empower communities to make decisions that align with their cultural and ethical priorities. In societies where questioning authority or institutions is discouraged, such educational efforts play an especially vital role in ensuring that informed consent is meaningful rather than superficial (Marín et al., 2022). Together, these measures underscore that respecting cultural diversity in privacy and data ethics is not optional for companies working in a globalized digital economy. Instead, it is a necessary strategy for building legitimacy, trust, and long-term engagement across varied cultural landscapes.

> ***Takeaway:*** *Cultural perspectives significantly affect how privacy is valued and how users respond to data tracking and algorithmic surveillance.*
> ***Reflection:*** *How should companies adapt their privacy policies to respect different cultural views?*

9.5 AI Adoption and Cultural Compatibility in the Gulf Region

The integration of AI in the Gulf region illustrates how technology is never culturally neutral but instead shaped by religious values, social traditions, and ethical norms. Gulf societies, deeply rooted in Islamic principles and collective cultural identities, approach AI adoption through a framework that prioritizes modesty, social harmony, and moral responsibility (Firnando & Wahyudi, 2024). Unlike purely utilitarian models of technology adoption observed in Western contexts, where efficiency and individual autonomy dominate, the Gulf approach emphasizes alignment with Shariah principles and cultural codes of conduct.

Religious values play a central role in shaping the boundaries of acceptable AI use. Applications that could challenge modesty norms, such as facial recognition in public spaces or AI-driven virtual assistants with anthropomorphic features, are examined to ensure compliance with Islamic ethics. Developers introducing AI in these contexts are expected to avoid content or design elements that could be perceived as intrusive, immodest, or incompatible with family-oriented values. This aligns with broader findings in technology adoption research, where cultural values such as collectivism and power distance strongly moderate acceptance models by shaping perceptions of appropriateness and trustworthiness (Huang et al., 2021; Sriwindono, 2022).

Ethical concerns are also reframed within cultural and religious contexts. Transparency, fairness, and accountability remain important, but they are interpreted through a moral lens grounded in Islamic teachings. For instance, fairness is understood not only in terms of algorithmic bias but also in terms of social justice, equity, and collective well-being (Huriye, 2023). Similarly, accountability is often seen as a shared responsibility among developers, regulators, and the broader community, resonating with the Gulf's communal ethics. Engagement with local religious scholars and cultural leaders becomes essential in this process, as they provide legitimacy and guidance on whether specific AI applications align with Islamic jurisprudence and cultural traditions (Sanusi & Olaleye, 2022).

Cultural competence, therefore, is not a peripheral consideration but a prerequisite for successful AI adoption in the region. Developers are expected to understand local customs, gender norms, and modes of interaction that define daily life in Gulf societies. For example, AI systems designed for education, healthcare, or public services must accommodate modesty practices, gender-segregated environments, and family-centered decision-making processes. This aligns with evidence that TAMs require cultural integration to fully explain adoption behaviors across diverse contexts (Nistor et al., 2014; Rose & Straub, 1998).

Practical measures for culturally aligned AI design include customization options that allow users to adapt interfaces according to modesty preferences, opt-in mechanisms for data collection that reflect communal trust, and language models sensitive to Arabic linguistic structures and religious expressions (Óhéigeartaigh et al., 2020). Such strategies also reinforce user trust by making AI systems feel locally grounded rather than externally imposed.

Education and awareness further strengthen compatibility between AI technologies and Gulf societies. Public initiatives that explain AI's potential in ways consistent with Islamic values, for example, its role in promoting efficiency in healthcare or fairness in public services, can increase acceptance and reduce misconceptions. This reflects findings that sociocultural factors, including religious identity, strongly influence comfort levels with digital tools and perceptions of data ethics (Ho et al., 2022).

Ultimately, AI adoption in the Gulf demonstrates how global technologies are localized through cultural negotiation. While universal ethical principles such as transparency and accountability remain relevant, their interpretation and prioritization vary across cultural and religious contexts. Developers seeking to introduce AI into conservative or religious societies must therefore adopt a pluralistic approach that respects local values while upholding broader ethical AI standards. By embedding cultural and religious considerations into design, policy, and practice, AI can become both a driver of innovation and a reinforcement of cultural identity in the Gulf region.

Takeaway: *AI technologies in the Gulf are shaped by religious and cultural standards, emphasizing ethical alignment with local values.*
Reflection: *What cultural considerations should developers keep in mind when introducing AI in conservative or religious communities?*

9.6 Cultural Challenges in Global AI Design and Ethics

As AI becomes a global phenomenon, one of the most pressing challenges is that AI systems are often designed within specific cultural frameworks yet deployed across vastly different societies. This creates tensions when the ethical assumptions and values embedded in AI reflect one region's worldview but are expected to govern behaviors worldwide. A one-size-fits-all approach to AI ethics rarely accounts for the diversity of moral reasoning, privacy expectations, and digital engagement norms that exist across cultures. Instead, culturally adaptive AI design is increasingly recognized as essential to ensure both inclusivity and ethical legitimacy (Pasupuleti, 2024; Tzachor et al., 2022).

Research consistently shows that cultural dimensions significantly shape cyber behavior and technology adoption. Hofstede's framework remains one of the most widely applied tools to explain these patterns, with power distance, individualism–collectivism, and uncertainty avoidance exerting strong influence on technology acceptance (Huang et al., 2021; Nistor et al., 2012; Sriwindono, 2022). For example, high power distance societies often display more hierarchical patterns of technology adoption, while collectivist societies prioritize social harmony and group influence in cyber behaviors (Rabayah, 2019; Rose & Straub, 1998). Uncertainty-avoidant cultures, such as those in parts of Southern Europe and Asia, require more reassurance and regulatory oversight before embracing novel AI applications (Cabinakova et al., 2013). These findings suggest that AI systems designed for individualistic, low power distance contexts, such as the United States or Northern Europe, may not align with the expectations of collectivist, high-context societies in Asia, Africa, or the Middle East (Straub et al., 2002).

Privacy and data ethics reveal another layer of cultural divergence. Western-centric approaches to privacy often emphasize individual consent and control, while many non-Western societies adopt collective or relational notions of information sharing (Schumacher et al., 2022). This tension gives rise to the concept of "digital dependency", which critiques how dominant cultural assumptions embedded in global AI systems impose foreign values on local populations, often clashing with existing ethical frameworks (Lucero & Martens, 2025; Sekalala & Chatikobo, 2024). This concept revealed how the West constructed a simplified, often derogatory, representation of the "Other" to justify its own dominance (Chowdhury, 2022). In the digital realm, this manifests as platforms designed with Western values of radical transparency and individual self-promotion being exported globally, often without regard for local norms of modesty, privacy, or community. We must now ask if non-Western users can truly express their authentic cultural identities on platforms whose very architecture reflects a different worldview (Lakshmi, 2025). For example, Nordic countries have built AI governance around values of trust and openness, while East Asian contexts emphasize harmony and collective welfare (Dang & Li, 2025). These examples illustrate that AI ethics are not universal but reflect the cultural logic of their origins (Figure 9.3).

The introduction of Western-designed social media platforms like Instagram and TikTok into the Gulf region provides a powerful illustration of digital colonialism in practice. These platforms are architected around values of individual self-promotion, visual self-disclosure, and the pursuit of public validation through

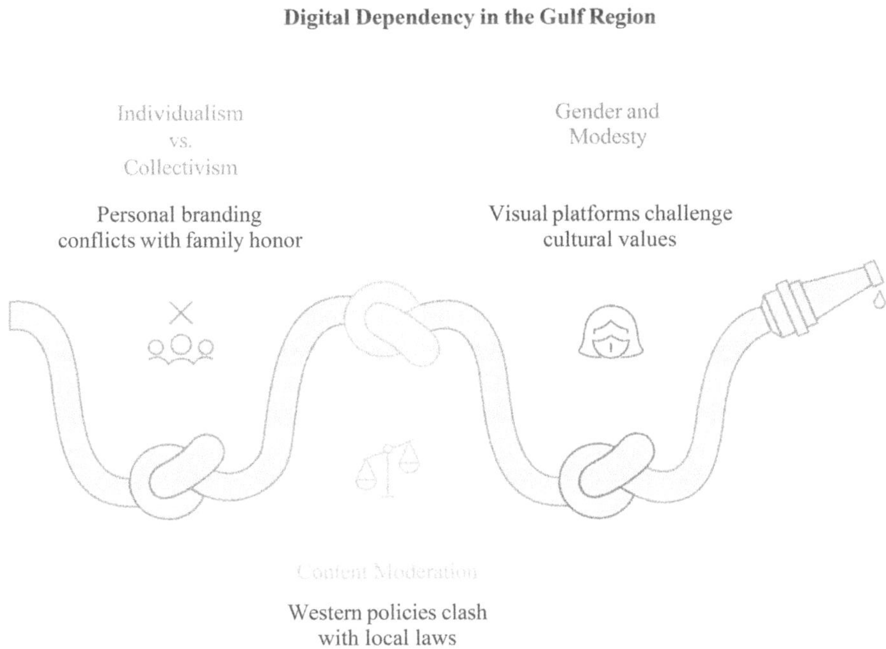

FIGURE 9.3 Digital dependency and social media in the Gulf region.

"likes" and "followers", values that often stand in direct tension with the region's deeply rooted cultural norms of modesty, family honor, and collective privacy.

Individualism vs. Collectivism: Features that encourage users to build a personal "brand" and share intimate details of their lives can conflict with collectivist values, where individual identity is secondary to family and community reputation. The pressure to perform a public self can create significant psychological stress for users navigating these competing expectations.

Content Moderation and 'Free Speech': Western-centric content moderation policies, often grounded in American First Amendment principles of free speech, frequently clash with local laws and cultural values regarding blasphemy, political dissent, and moral propriety. Content that is permissible in the West may be illegal or socially taboo in the Gulf, leading to situations where platforms are accused of either censorship (by Western observers) or moral laxity (by local communities).

Gender and Modesty: The visual-first nature of platforms like Instagram and the trend-driven, often provocative, content on TikTok can be particularly challenging for female users in a culture that values modesty. Women may face a difficult choice: either refrain from participating fully, participate under pseudonyms, or risk social sanction for behavior that would be considered normal in a Western context.

This case study demonstrates that digital dependency is not just about economic dominance but about the imposition of a cultural worldview through technological design. It forces non-Western users to adapt to a digital ecosystem built without their values in mind, creating a dynamic of cultural friction and reinforcing global power imbalances.

Cross-cultural research on AI further highlights divergent ethical priorities. In Taiwan, nonmaleficence, ensuring AI causes no harm, was the leading concern, resulting in support for stricter regulation (Chang et al., 2024). Meanwhile, studies in Estonia, Germany, and Sweden identified values around sustainability and social diversity as central to AI ethics, reflecting the cultural emphasis on welfare and inclusivity in Northern Europe (Masso et al., 2023). Accountability is also culturally relative: while some societies attribute responsibility to developers, others emphasize government or institutional oversight (Chang et al., 2024). This variability underscores that global AI governance cannot rely on uniform ethical principles but must instead adapt to local moral landscapes.

The evidence base demonstrates both strengths and limitations. Cross-cultural comparative studies provide robust insights into how cultural values influence technology adoption and AI ethics (Jamalova, 2024). However, reliance on national-level classifications risks oversimplification, ignoring subcultural or generational differences within societies (McCoy et al., 2005). Moreover, much of the existing research is concentrated in Western or developed contexts, leaving gaps in understanding how AI interacts with cultural frameworks in the Global South (Twati, 2007; Ebrahimi et al., 2010). Dynamic cultural shifts, driven by globalization, migration, and digital exposure, also complicate the assumption that cultures are fixed categories (Fiske, 2002).

For global technology companies, the implications are profound. Designing AI systems without cultural adaptation risks ethical conflicts, user rejection, or regulatory backlash. Instead, companies must pursue culturally adaptive AI that respects local traditions, engages with regional stakeholders, and incorporates flexible governance frameworks (Pasupuleti, 2024). Education and awareness are equally critical: fostering cultural competence among AI developers can mitigate blind spots and ensure more inclusive design (Sposato, 2025). Practical examples include tailoring AI explanations to align with local communication styles, adjusting privacy defaults to reflect collective or individualistic values, and embedding sustainability into AI policy frameworks in cultures that prioritize environmental stewardship (Ozor et al., 2025).

Ultimately, the challenge lies in balancing cultural respect with innovation. Universal principles such as transparency, accountability, and human dignity must anchor AI ethics, but their application must be flexible enough to accommodate regional diversity (Capurro, 2008; ÓhÉigeartaigh et al., 2020). Moving toward pluralistic, intercultural AI ethics offers a path forward: one that acknowledges cultural variation while ensuring that technology serves as a force for inclusive global progress rather than digital colonization.

Takeaway: *A one-size-fits-all approach to AI ethics may not work globally; cultural sensitivity is key to ethical and inclusive technology.*
Reflection: *How can global tech companies balance cultural respect with innovation when deploying AI across different regions?*

9.7 Moving beyond Hofstede: A Detailed, Value-Based Approach

Although Hofstede's cultural dimensions provide a useful starting point, the framework has been criticized for being dated and for oversimplifying complex cultural realities by treating nations as monolithic entities (Hassani et al., 2023). To develop a more detailed understanding of how culture influences AI ethics and cyber behavior, it is valuable to integrate more contemporary, psychologically grounded models. One of the most robust alternatives is Schwartz's Theory (Schwartz, 2006) of Basic Human Values. Schwartz's model identifies ten universal, motivationally distinct values that are recognized across cultures: Self-Direction, Stimulation, Hedonism, Achievement, Power, Security, Conformity, Tradition, Benevolence, and Universalism. Unlike Hofstede's binary dimensions (e.g., individualism vs. collectivism), Schwartz's values are arranged in a circular structure that represents the dynamic relationships of conflict and compatibility between them (Czupryna et al., 2024). For example, the value of "Self-Direction" (emphasizing independent thought and action) is in direct opposition to "Conformity" and "Tradition" (emphasizing restraint and respect for custom). This model offers a more granular lens for analyzing cultural friction in AI design (Gençoglu et al., 2021). For instance, an AI system designed in a culture that highly prizes "Self-Direction" and "Stimulation", such as a social media algorithm that rewards novel, provocative, and highly individualistic content, may directly conflict with the values of a culture that prioritizes "Security", "Conformity", and "Tradition". In such a context, the AI might be perceived not as a tool for self-expression but as a disruptive force that undermines social harmony and traditional norms. Similarly, an AI designed for workplace surveillance, optimized for "Security" and "Power", would likely face strong resistance in cultures that place a high premium on "Self-Direction" and personal autonomy (Barnes et al., 2024). By moving from broad cultural dimensions to a more fine-grained analysis of underlying human values, we can better predict, understand, and mitigate the ethical challenges that arise when AI systems cross cultural boundaries. This value-based approach allows for a more precise understanding of why a technology might be embraced in one context and rejected in another, providing a more robust foundation for the development of truly culturally sensitive AI (Clancy et al., 2025). Having explored the limitations of traditional cultural models and proposed a more nuanced, value-based alternative, we now turn to a summary of the chapter's key findings and a reflection on the path toward a more culturally inclusive digital future.

Takeaway: *Schwartz's value-based framework offers a more precise tool than Hofstede's cultural dimensions. Rather than broad labels like "individualism vs. collectivisim," it allows us to identify specific value conflicts, such as "Self-direction" (embedded in platform design) clashing with "Tradition" (prioritized by users). This precisision is essential for developing truly culturally sensitive AI sytems and moving beyond digital dependency toward value-aware design that respects diverse human values.*

Reflection: *As you comsider the AI systems and digital platforms you use daily, which of Scwartz's ten values do you believe they prioritize, and which values do they suppress or marginalize? How might your experinece of these platforms change if they were explicitly designed to support a broader spectrum of human values, including those you hold most?*

9.8 Summary and Reflections

This chapter has shown that culture is not a backdrop to cyber behavior and AI ethics but a determining force that actively shapes how technologies are understood, adopted, and governed. From the Gulf and Middle Eastern emphasis on collectivism, family honor, and modesty to the Western prioritization of autonomy, transparency, and openness, cultural values provide the moral architecture within which AI systems operate. These differences influence everything from privacy expectations and online engagement to the ethical interpretation of fairness, accountability, and harm prevention (Davidson & Martellozzo, 2012; Jamalova, 2024; Masso et al., 2023).

The comparisons highlight that while universal principles such as transparency and accountability are central to responsible AI, their application is mediated by local traditions, religious values, and social norms (Melo, 2023; Robinson, 2020; Chang et al., 2024). In the Gulf, for example, cultural compatibility requires AI to align with ethics and collective values, whereas Western societies often frame ethical AI in terms of individual rights and autonomy (Firnando & Wahyudi, 2024; Huang et al., 2021). This divergence demonstrates that one-size-fits-all models of AI governance risk creating ethical blind spots and even forms of "digital dependency" if they neglect the moral codes of local communities (Melo, 2023).

At the same time, cultural insights open opportunities for innovation. Culturally adaptive AI can enhance trust, inclusivity, and legitimacy by embedding local values into design and governance. Whether through privacy-by-design approaches tailored to different contexts, educational initiatives that foster cultural competence, or collaborative policymaking that respects diversity, the path forward lies in pluralism rather than uniformity (Óhéigeartaigh et al., 2020; Pasupuleti, 2024).

References

Al-Jenaibi, B. (2016). The Twitter revolution in the Gulf countries. *Journal of Creative Communications*, *11*(1), 61–83. https://doi.org/10.1177/0973258616630217

Alrashdi, D. H., Alyafei, A. H., Alanazi, S. A., Meyer, C., & Gould, R. L. (2024). Cultural adaptations of third-wave psychotherapies in Gulf Cooperation Council countries: A systematic review. *Transcultural Psychiatry*, *61*(2), 209–228. https://doi.org/10.1177/13634615241227691

Barnes, A. J., Zhang, Y., & Valenzuela, A. (2024). AI and culture: Culturally dependent responses to AI systems. *Current Opinion in Psychology*, *58*, 101838. https://doi.org/10.1016/j.copsyc.2024.101838

Berch, V., Lankevych, A., Naturkach, R., Bysaha, Y., & Prodan, V. (2024). The role of digital technologies in building an inclusive and transparent society: An analysis of the legal mechanisms of democratic governance. *Revista Amazonia Investiga*, *13*(79), 177–188. https://doi.org/10.34069/ai/2024.79.07.14

Cabinakova, J., Krönung, J., Eckhardt, A., & Bernius, S. (2013). The importance of culture, trust, and habitual patterns - determinants of Cross-Cultural egovernment adoption. *European Conference on Information Systems*, 182. https://aisel.aisnet.org/cgi/viewcontent.cgi?article=1405&context=ecis2013_cr

Capurro, R. (2008). Intercultural information ethics: Foundations and applications. *Journal of Information, Communication and Ethics in Society*, *6*(2), 116–126. https://doi.org/10.1108/14779960810888347

Chang, W. L., Liao, Y., Chao, E., Liu, S., & Lee, T. S. (2024). Ethical concerns about artificial intelligence: Evidence from a national survey in Taiwan. *Research Square (Research Square)*. https://doi.org/10.21203/rs.3.rs-3765278/v1

Chowdhury, R. (2022). Misrepresentation of marginalized groups: A critique of epistemic neocolonialism. *Journal of Business Ethics*, *186*(3), 553–570. https://doi.org/10.1007/s10551-022-05229-4

Clancy, R. F., Zhu, Q., & Majumdar, S. (2025). Exploring AI ethics in global contexts: A culturally responsive, psychologically realist approach. *AI And Ethics*, *5*(6), 6329–6338. https://doi.org/10.1007/s43681-025-00821-6

Couture, V., Roy, M., Dez, E., Laperle, S., & Bélisle-Pipon, J. (2023). Ethical implications of artificial intelligence in population health and the public's role in its governance: Perspectives from a citizen and expert panel. *Journal of Medical Internet Research*, *25*, e44357. https://doi.org/10.2196/44357

Czupryna, M., Growiec, K., Kamiński, B., & Oleksy, P. (2024). Schwartz human values and the economic performance. *Journal of Artificial Societies and Social Simulation*, *27*(1). https://doi.org/10.18564/jasss.5023

Dang, Q., & Li, G. (2025). Unveiling trust in AI: The interplay of antecedents, consequences, and cultural dynamics. *AI & Society*. https://doi.org/10.1007/s00146-025-02477-6

Davidson, J., & Martellozzo, E. (2012). Exploring young people's use of social networking sites and digital media in the internet safety context. *Information Communication & Society*, *16*(9), 1456–1476. https://doi.org/10.1080/1369118x.2012.701655

Du, N., Robert, L., & Yang, X. J. (2022). Cross-Cultural investigation of the effects of explanations on drivers' trust, preference, and anxiety in highly automated vehicles. *Transportation Research Record Journal of the Transportation Research Board*, *2677*(1), 554–561. https://doi.org/10.1177/03611981221100528

Ebrahimi, N., Singh, S. K. G., & Tabrizi, R. S. (2010). Cultural effect on using new technologies. *International Journal of Humanities and Social Sciences*, *4*(10), 2108–2112. https://doi.org/10.5281/zenodo.1056192

Firnando, H. G., & Wahyudi, M. (2024). The role of artificial intelligence in shaping the Islamic worldview of the digital economy. *Journal of Islamic Economics and Philanthropy*, *6*(3), 231–249. https://doi.org/10.21111/jiep.v6i3.11386

Fiske, A. P. (2002). Using individualism and collectivism to compare cultures–A critique of the validity and measurement of the constructs: Comment on Oyserman et al. (2002). *Psychological Bulletin*, *128*(1), 78–88. https://doi.org/10.1037/0033-2909.128.1.78

Fleming, J. I., Wilson, S. E., Hart, S. A., Therrien, W. J., & Cook, B. G. (2021). Open accessibility in education research: Enhancing the credibility, equity, impact, and efficiency of research. *Educational Psychologist*, *56*(2), 110–121. https://doi.org/10.1080/00461520.2021.1897593

Gencoglu, B., Helms-Lorenz, M., Maulana, R., & Jansen, E. P. W. A. (2021). A conceptual framework for understanding variability in student perceptions. *Frontiers in Psychology*, *12*, 725407. https://doi.org/10.3389/fpsyg.2021.725407

Gilbert, C., & Gilbert, M. A. (2024). The convergence of Artificial intelligence and privacy: Navigating innovation with ethical considerations. *International Journal of Scientific Research and Modern Technology.*, *3*(9), 9–17. https://doi.org/10.38124/ijsrmt.v3i9.45

Harris, M. M., Van Hoye, G., & Lievens, F. (2003). Privacy and attitudes towards internet-based selection systems: A cross-cultural comparison. *International Journal of Selection and Assessment*, *11*(2–3), 230–236. https://doi.org/10.1111/1468-2389.00246

Hassani, H. E., Tijani, O., Allaoui, B. E., & Salmoun, K. (2023). An assessment of ethics in a Cross-Cultural organizational context: A systematic Lliterature review. *International Journal of Organizational Leadership*, *12*(4), 512–535. https://doi.org/10.33844/ijol.2023.60393

Ho, T. M., Nguyen, M., Nguyen, H. T., & Vuong, Q. (2022). Sociocultural factors influence young people's attitude towards the harvesting of non-conscious emotional data. *OSF Preprints*. https://doi.org/10.31219/osf.io/df8zt

Huang, F., Sánchez-Prieto, J. C., Teo, T., García-Peñalvo, F. J., Olmos-Migueláñez, S., & Zhao, C. (2021). A cross-cultural study on the influence of cultural values and teacher beliefs on university teachers' information and communications technology acceptance. *Educational Technology Research and Development*, *69*(2), 1271–1297. https://doi.org/10.1007/s11423-021-09941-2

Huriye, A. Z. (2023). The ethics of Artificial intelligence: Examining the ethical considerations surrounding the development and use of AI. *American Journal of Technology*, *2*(1), 37–45. https://doi.org/10.58425/ajt.v2i1.142

Huu, P. T. (2023). Impact of employee digital competence on the relationship between digital autonomy and innovative work behavior: A systematic review. *Artificial Intelligence Review*, *56*(12), 14193–14222. https://doi.org/10.1007/s10462-023-10492-6

Jamalova, M. (2024). Cultural values and digital gap: Overview of behavioral patterns. *PLoS One*, *19*(10), e0311390. https://doi.org/10.1371/journal.pone.0311390

Kübek, G., & Mancini, I. (2023). EU trade policy between constitutional openness and strategic autonomy. *European Constitutional Law Review*, *19*(3), 518–547. https://doi.org/10.1017/s1574019623000226

Lakshmi, D. L. (2025). Rebranding empire in the age of generative AI. *Frontiers in Communication*, *10*. https://doi.org/10.3389/fcomm.2025.1604361

Lin, F., Brandimarte, L., Chen, H., Samtani, S., & Zhu, H. (2024). Automated analysis of changes in privacy policies: A structured Self-attentive sentence embedding approach. *MIS Quarterly*. https://doi.org/10.25300/misq/2024/17115

Lucero, H. C., & Martens, C. (2025). Colonial structures in AI: A Latin American decolonial literature review of structural implications for marginalised communities in the Global South. *AI & Society*. https://doi.org/10.1007/s00146-025-02547-9

Marín, V. I., Carpenter, J. P., Tur, G., & Williamson-Leadley, S. (2022). Social media and data privacy in education: An international comparative study of perceptions among pre-service teachers. *Journal of Computers in Education*, *10*(4), 769–795. https://doi.org/10.1007/s40692-022-00243-x

Masso, A., Kaun, A., & Van Noordt, C. (2023). Basic values in artificial intelligence: Comparative factor analysis in Estonia, Germany, and Sweden. *AI & Society*. https://doi.org/10.1007/s00146-023-01750-w

McCoy, S., Galletta, D. F., & King, W. R. (2005). Integrating national culture into IS research: The need for current individual level measures. *Communications of the Association for Information Systems*, *15*. https://doi.org/10.17705/1cais.01512

Melo, J. (Ed.). (2023). *Intercultural Information Ethics applied to the data Colonialism concept*. International Conference on Computer Ethics.

Nguyen, V. M. H., Ho, T. H., Nguyen, L. H., & Pham, A. T. H. (2023). The impact of trade openness on economic stability in Asian countries. *Sustainability*, *15*(15), 11736. https://doi.org/10.3390/su151511736

Nistor, N., Lerche, T., Weinberger, A., Ceobanu, C., & Heymann, O. (2012). Towards the integration of culture into the unified theory of acceptance and use of technology. *British Journal of Educational Technology*, *45*(1), 36–55. https://doi.org/10.1111/j.1467-8535.2012.01383.x

Óhéigeartaigh, S. S., Whittlestone, J., Liu, Y., Zeng, Y., & Liu, Z. (2020). Overcoming barriers to cross-cultural cooperation in AI ethics and governance. *Philosophy & Technology*, *33*(4), 571–593. https://doi.org/10.1007/s13347-020-00402-x

Ozor, N., Nwakaire, J., Nyambane, A., Muhatiah, W., & Nwobodo, C. (2025). Enhancing Africa's agriculture and food systems through responsible and gender inclusive AI innovation: Insights from AI4AFS network. *Frontiers in Artificial Intelligence*, *7*. https://doi.org/10.3389/frai.2024.1472236

Pasupuleti, M. K. (2024). Ethical AI governance: A global blueprint. *International Journal of Academic and Industrial Research Innovations(IJAIRI)*, *4*(3), 60–77. https://doi.org/10.62311/nesx/97832

Pina, V., Torres, L., & Royo, S. (2007). Are ICTs improving transparency and accountability in the eu regional and local governments? an empirical study. *Public Administration*, *85*(2), 449–472. https://doi.org/10.1111/j.1467-9299.2007.00654.x

Pollach, I. (2005). A typology of communicative strategies in online privacy policies: Ethics, power and informed consent. *Journal of Business Ethics*, *62*(3). https://doi.org/10.1007/s10551-005-7898-3

Rabayah, K. (2019). The impact of culture on acceptance of E-Learning: A palestinian case study using structural equation model. *2022 IEEE Global Engineering Education Conference (EDUCON)*. https://doi.org/10.1109/educon.2019.8725110

Robinson, S. C. (2020). Trust, transparency, and openness: How inclusion of cultural values shapes Nordic national public policy strategies for artificial intelligence (AI). *Technology in Society*, *63*, 101421. https://doi.org/10.1016/j.techsoc.2020.101421

Rose, G., & Straub, D. (1998). Predicting general IT use. *Journal of Global Information Management*, *6*(3), 39–46. https://doi.org/10.4018/jgim.1998070104

Saklaki, A., & Gardikiotis, A. (2024). Exploring Greek students' attitudes toward Artificial intelligence: Relationships with AI ethics, media, and digital literacy. *Societies*, *14*(12), 248. https://doi.org/10.3390/soc14120248

Salehan, M., Kim, D. J., & Lee, J. (2018). Are there any relationships between technology and cultural values? A country-level trend study of the association between information communication technology and cultural values. *Information & Management*, *55*(6), 725–745. https://doi.org/10.1016/j.im.2018.03.003

Sanusi, I. T., & Olaleye, S. A. (2022). An insight into cultural competence and ethics in K-12 Artificial intelligence education. *2022 IEEE Global Engineering Education Conference (EDUCON)*, 790–794. https://doi.org/10.1109/educon52537.2022.9766818

Schumacher, C., Eggers, F., Verhoef, P. C., & Maas, P. (2022). The effects of cultural differences on consumers' willingness to share personal information. *Journal of Interactive Marketing, 58*(1), 72–89. https://doi.org/10.1177/10949968221136555

Schwartz, S. (2006). A Theory of cultural value orientations: Explication and applications. *Comparative Sociology, 5*(2–3), 137–182. https://doi.org/10.1163/156913306778667357

Sekalala, S., & Chatikobo, T. (2024). Colonialism in the new digital health agenda. *BMJ Global Health, 9*(2), e014131. https://doi.org/10.1136/bmjgh-2023-014131

Shukla, S. (2024). Principles governing ethical development and deployment of AI. *International Journal of Engineering Business and Management, 8*(2), 26–46. https://doi.org/10.22161/ijebm.8.2.5

Sposato, M. (2025). Artificial intelligence in educational leadership: A comprehensive taxonomy and future directions. *International Journal of Educational Technology in Higher Education, 22*(1). https://doi.org/10.1186/s41239-025-00517-1

Sriwindono, H. (2022). EKSPLORASI EFEK MODERASI DIMENSI BUDAYA TERHADAP PENERIMAAN TEKNOLOGI INTERNET MASYARAKAT YOGYAKARTA. *SIBATIK JOURNAL Jurnal Ilmiah Bidang Sosial Ekonomi Budaya Teknologi Dan Pendidikan, 1*(9), 1909–1916. https://doi.org/10.54443/sibatik.v1i9.269

Straub, D., Loch, K., Evaristo, R., Karahanna, E., & Srite, M. (2002). Toward a theory-based measurement of culture. *Journal of Global Information Management, 10*(1), 13–23. https://doi.org/10.4018/jgim.2002010102

Suntharalingam, H. (2024). Enhancing digital learning Outcomes through the Application of Artificial Intelligence: A Comprehensive review. *International Journal of Innovative Science and Research Technology (IJISRT), 9*(4), 718–727. https://doi.org/10.38124/ijisrt/ijisrt24apr530

Tubadji, A., Huang, H., & Webber, D. J. (2021). Cultural proximity bias in AI-acceptability: The importance of being human. *Technological Forecasting and Social Change, 173*, 121100. https://doi.org/10.1016/j.techfore.2021.121100

Twati, J. M. (2007). *Societal and organisational culture and the adoption of management information systems in Arab countries*. https://doi.org/10.25904/1912/2274

Tzachor, A., Devare, M., King, B., Avin, S., & Héigeartaigh, S. Ó. (2022). Responsible artificial intelligence in agriculture requires systemic understanding of risks and externalities. *Nature Machine Intelligence, 4*(2), 104–109. https://doi.org/10.1038/s42256-022-00440-4

STREAM 4

Promoting and Sustaining Ethical Digital Well-Being

10

PROMOTING DIGITAL WELL-BEING AND ETHICAL AI USE

Strategies and Interventions

Chapter Objectives

- To provide practical strategies that support digital well-being and ethical AI use, especially for youth.
- To identify the roles of educators, parents, policymakers, and developers in creating ethical digital environments.
- To offer evidence-based interventions to reduce risks such as misinformation, cyberbullying, and screen overuse.
- To promote collaborative, multi-stakeholder approaches that prioritize ethical design and youth mental health.

Topics to Be Covered

- Introduction to Youth, Ethics, and Digital Well-being
- Digital Literacy and Ethics in School Curricula
- Parenting for Ethical Digital Balance and Responsibility
- Policy Measures for Ethical AI and Youth Protection
- Tackling Cyberbullying, Misinformation, and Harmful Content
- Designing Ethical AI Tools for Young Users
- Multi-Stakeholder Collaboration for a Safer Digital Future
- Summary and Reflections

DOI: 10.4324/9781003657590-14

10.1 Introduction: Youth at the Center of Digital Well-being and AI Ethics

Young people today are growing up in digital environments that offer both connection and risk. Their mental health, social development, and moral reasoning are constantly shaped by algorithms, online communities, and the design of digital platforms. Although these technologies provide opportunities for learning and support, they also introduce challenges that affect psychological resilience, ethical decision-making, and long-term well-being. Understanding these risks and developing strategies to support youth requires attention to the interplay of digital design, cultural background, and coping mechanisms.

Evidence highlights that one of the most pressing challenges is the relationship between social media content moderation and youth mental health. While intended to protect, restrictions on sensitive discussions can isolate young individuals from valuable support networks. Studies show that censorship of mental health content often prevents access to communities where youth might otherwise find understanding and shared coping strategies, leaving them vulnerable to worsening psychological outcomes (Zhang et al., 2023). At the family level, the role of parents is equally complex. Research demonstrates that high parental support, when paired with active coping strategies, can unintentionally increase anxiety in some adolescents, indicating that well-meaning interventions must be balanced with autonomy and context-specific guidance (Simpson et al., 2007).

Cultural and trauma-informed strategies offer further insight. For Indigenous youth and those living in conflict-affected regions, practices rooted in nature, cultural rituals, and faith-based resilience have proven protective for mental health (Cherewick et al., 2016; Katapally, 2020). These findings suggest that interventions must respect cultural worldviews rather than imposing uniform approaches. At the same time, digital health tools have yet to match young people's media preferences. Current mental health applications often lack interactive features, leading to poor engagement and low sustained use. Research recommends designing apps that are customizable and more closely aligned with youth digital practices to improve accessibility and impact (Wright et al., 2023).

An important direction lies in empowering young people to participate directly in shaping solutions. Studies in participatory action research reveal that when youth are included as active contributors to mental health initiatives, the resulting programs are more effective, community-driven, and sustainable (Smith et al., 2024). This principle of empowerment extends beyond research into digital literacy, ethics education, and platform design. By enabling youth voices to be heard in policy, technology, and community spaces, interventions can address risks while also fostering resilience. Cultural context adds another layer of complexity. Values, norms, and collective worldviews shape how digital technology is perceived, from comfort with online sharing to expectations of privacy and fairness in artificial intelligence (AI) systems. Collectivist contexts may encourage community-oriented engagement, while individualist contexts often emphasize autonomy and personal choice. These differences

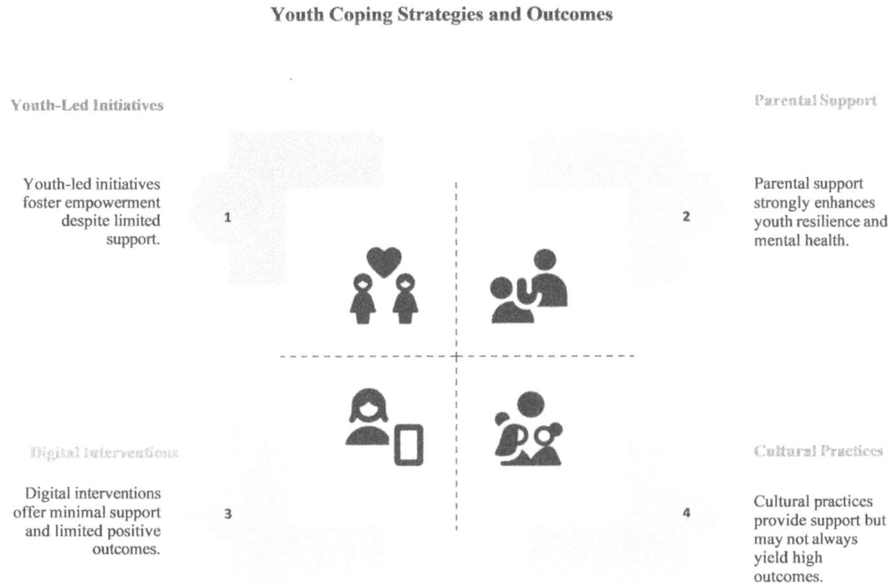

FIGURE 10.1 Youth coping strategies across contexts.

influence not only how young people experience digital technologies but also how they evaluate ethical challenges and respond to risks (see Figure 10.1).

This chapter situates youth at the center of digital well-being and AI ethics. It emphasizes that young people's challenges are not simply individual struggles but outcomes shaped by systemic design choices, family structures, cultural norms, and policy environments. By analyzing strategies that address misinformation, cyberbullying, and screen overuse, alongside ethical design and regulation, the chapter aims to provide a roadmap for supporting youth in digital spaces that are both safe and ethically grounded.

> ***Takeaway:*** *Young people face unique ethical and mental health challenges in cyberspaces, requiring focused, strategic interventions.*
> ***Reflection:*** *What are the most pressing digital issues young people around you are facing, and how are they coping?*

10.2 Digital Literacy and Ethics in School Curricula

The integration of digital literacy and ethics into school curricula has become essential in preparing young people for life in increasingly complex digital environments. Adolescents encounter a wide range of online challenges, from misinformation and cyberbullying to algorithmic bias and privacy concerns. Formal

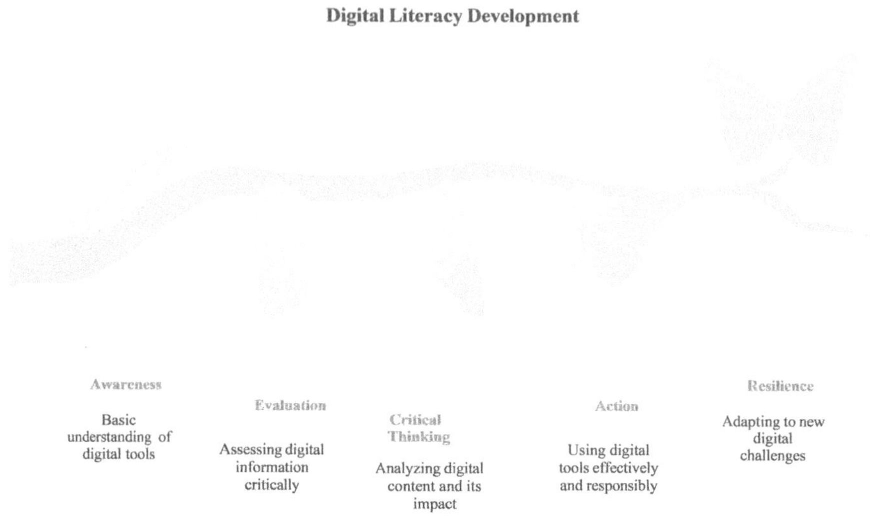

FIGURE 10.2 Digital literacy development pathway.

education plays a decisive role in equipping them not only with technical skills but also with the ethical reasoning and critical awareness needed to make thoughtful, responsible choices.

One effective approach is the use of experiential learning models, where students face simulated ethical dilemmas in controlled digital environments. High-fidelity simulations, such as case-based platforms that mirror real-world scenarios, allow learners to practice decision-making under conditions of ambiguity and pressure (see Figure 10.2). Research demonstrates that these immersive experiences build confidence in students' ability to act consistently with their values when confronted with actual dilemmas (Krautscheid, 2017).

Ethics education must also be sensitive to the sociocultural context in which it is delivered. Studies suggest that students respond more meaningfully to ethical scenarios that reflect the issues they encounter in their own communities, whether related to privacy, online speech, or cultural identity. Contextualized ethics education helps students connect abstract concepts with lived realities, enabling them to develop what has been termed an "authentic ethical voice" (Davies & Heyward, 2019; Ehrich et al., 2011). Table 10.1 compares contextualized versus generic ethics curricula.

Critical thinking and moral reasoning stand at the core of digital literacy education. Introducing structured ethical decision-making models in classrooms enables students to evaluate competing interests, anticipate potential harms, and articulate their reasoning with clarity. These skills extend beyond cyberspaces, preparing youth for ethical challenges in academic, professional, and civic life. Classroom discussions around ethical dilemmas foster a collaborative environment where students learn to listen, question, and construct arguments,

TABLE 10.1 Comparison of Contextualized vs. Generic Ethics Curricula

Dimension	*Generic Ethics Curriculum*	*Contextualized Ethics Curriculum*
Content Focus	Universal ethical principles (e.g., deontology, utilitarianism) applied to abstract, hypothetical dilemmas.	Ethical principles applied to specific, culturally relevant dilemmas that students are likely to encounter in their own communities (e.g., local privacy norms, online speech related to community issues).
Student Engagement	Moderate to low; students may perceive the content as abstract and disconnected from their lived experiences.	High; students see the direct relevance of the material to their daily lives, leading to more active participation and deeper discussion.
Relevance	Perceived as low by students who do not see how abstract principles apply to their specific social and digital contexts.	High; content directly addresses the ethical challenges and social norms of the students' own cultural and digital environments.
Transferability of Skills	Limited; students may struggle to apply abstract principles to novel, real-world situations that are not covered in the curriculum.	Strong; by learning to apply ethical reasoning to familiar contexts, students develop a more flexible and adaptable ethical framework that can be applied to new and unforeseen challenges.
Development of Ethical Voice	Encourages a detached, analytical voice that may not reflect the student's authentic values.	Nurtures an "authentic ethical voice" by empowering students to connect ethical principles to their own lived experiences, values, and community norms.
Cultural Sensitivity	Often reflects the values and assumptions of the dominant culture in which it was created, potentially marginalizing minority perspectives.	Explicitly designed to be culturally responsive, incorporating diverse perspectives and acknowledging that ethical priorities may differ across cultures.

deepening their understanding of how individual decisions affect wider communities (Ehrich et al., 2011).

Educators play a central role in this process, yet they often require targeted preparation. Professional development in ethics equips teachers with the tools to guide discussions, model ethical reasoning, and share their own decision-making experiences with authenticity. Evidence shows that when teachers receive structured training in ethics, their confidence in handling student dilemmas increases, and they provide stronger support in helping learners articulate and refine their moral reasoning (Cranston et al., 2006).

Collaborative approaches further strengthen digital literacy and ethics education. Encouraging students to share ethical dilemmas with peers and mentors broadens the range of perspectives they encounter and nurtures a sense of community. Shared problem-solving fosters resilience, as students learn that ethical challenges rarely have single solutions and that dialogue is often as valuable as resolution. This inclusivity also reflects broader principles of participatory education, where the collective wisdom of the group enhances individual decision-making capacities (Cranston et al., 2006).

Cultural factors shape how these curricula are perceived and implemented. Values such as individualism or collectivism, power distance, and uncertainty avoidance influence both classroom dynamics and student attitudes toward digital technologies. For example, studies indicate that collectivist cultures may prioritize social influence and communal responsibility in digital literacy education, whereas individualist cultures emphasize autonomy and self-directed ethical reasoning (Muhtaseb et al., 2023; Sriwindono, 2022). Designing curricula that acknowledge these differences ensures that digital ethics education is not only pedagogically sound but also culturally responsive.

By grounding ethics education in both universal principles and local realities, schools can ensure that students are prepared to manage dilemmas in ways that align with both global expectations and cultural norms.

Ultimately, embedding digital literacy and ethics into school curricula extends beyond teaching students how to use technology safely. It equips them with the intellectual tools to question, evaluate, and act with integrity in cyberspaces. This educational investment prepares youth not only to avoid harm but also to contribute positively to digital communities, ensuring that their participation reflects both competence and responsibility. Although formal education provides the foundational layer of digital literacy, these skills are most effective when reinforced within the family. The principles of critical thinking and ethical awareness learned in the classroom must be supported by parental guidance and a healthy home environment. The next section, therefore, shifts the focus from the school to the home, exploring the crucial role parents play in shaping their children's digital balance and responsibility.

Takeaway: *Teaching ethics and digital literacy in schools empowers youth to make thoughtful, informed, and responsible online decisions.*
Reflection: *How can schools better prepare students to face ethical dilemmas in digital environments?*

10.3 Parenting for Digital Balance and Responsibility

Parents occupy a central role in shaping the digital habits of children and adolescents. As technology becomes embedded in daily life, young people are exposed to both opportunities for learning and creativity as well as risks tied to privacy loss, excessive screen time, and exposure to harmful online content. The way parents frame conversations, model cyber behavior, and set boundaries significantly influences how children develop ethical awareness and self-regulation in digital environments.

One of the most effective strategies parents can adopt is engaging children in conversations about AI. By explaining how AI operates in familiar contexts, such as search engines, games, or virtual assistants, parents help demystify technology and reduce misconceptions. Research highlights that clear communication about AI's functions and its impact on everyday choices builds a foundation for informed usage and encourages critical reflection rather than passive consumption (Bajwa et al., 2024).

Privacy remains another pressing issue. Parents can emphasize the long-term implications of data sharing and the importance of protecting personal information online. While parental control systems may appear to provide safety, they can also raise privacy concerns if not applied transparently. Studies demonstrate that children and adolescents often feel constrained or mistrusted when controls are imposed without explanation,

TABLE 10.2 Comparison of Protective vs. Intrusive Parental Control Features

Dimension	*Intrusive Parental Controls*	*Protective Parental Controls*
Primary Goal	To monitor, restrict, and block child's activities without their input or awareness.	To guide, support, and empower the child to make safe and responsible choices.
Implementation	Secretive installation of monitoring software (spyware); non-consensual tracking of location and messages; rigid, unexplained blocking of websites and apps.	Collaborative setup of content filters; transparent discussion about location sharing for safety; joint agreement on time limits and app usage.
Impact on Trust	Erodes trust; child feels spied on, leading to secretive behavior and a reluctance to share problems with parents.	Builds trust; child feels respected and understood, fostering open communication and a willingness to seek parental guidance.
Development of Autonomy	Stifles autonomy; child does not learn self-regulation and may engage in risky behavior when controls are removed or circumvented.	Fosters autonomy; child learns to internalize safety principles and develop self-regulation skills in a supportive environment.
Long-Term Effectiveness	Low; children often find ways to bypass controls, and the lack of trust undermines long-term safety.	High; focuses on building lifelong skills of critical thinking, ethical awareness, and self-regulation that extend beyond any specific technology.
Focus	On preventing negative behaviors through external control.	On cultivating positive behaviors through internal motivation and shared values.

highlighting the need for balance between guidance and autonomy (Ali et al., 2020). Table 10.2 presents a comparative table contrasting protective versus intrusive parental control features that illustrate how intention and implementation shape outcomes.

Screen time management requires particular attention. Prolonged exposure to digital devices is linked to sleep disruption, sedentary behaviors, and decreased psychological well-being. Parents can encourage balance by focusing not only on the quantity of time spent online but also on the quality of digital engagement. Guiding children toward educational, creative, and socially enriching online activities while promoting offline hobbies creates healthier rhythms of use (Jago et al., 2012; Wolfers et al., 2024).

Equally important is reinforcing ethical behavior in cyberspaces. Conversations about cyberbullying, respect for others, and empathy in digital communication foster social responsibility. When children internalize principles of fairness and kindness, they are better equipped to resist harmful cyber behaviors and contribute positively to digital communities (Alfano et al., 2023). Parents who model respectful engagement themselves reinforce these lessons, showing that ethical behavior extends across both online and offline contexts.

AI also increasingly shapes children's play and learning environments, from intelligent toys to adaptive educational platforms. Parents should actively engage with these tools, discussing both their benefits and ethical implications. Research suggests that AI-driven educational technologies can foster creativity and inquiry-based learning, yet they also raise questions about dependency and data privacy (Kewalramani et al., 2021). Parental guidance ensures that children approach these technologies critically, balancing enthusiasm for innovation with awareness of responsibility.

Role modeling remains one of the strongest parental influences on children's digital practices. Studies confirm that children imitate parental behaviors, including patterns of screen use and online interaction (Jago et al., 2012). Parents who demonstrate balanced digital habits, respect for privacy, and open communication about digital dilemmas provide an implicit framework for their children to follow. This effect is amplified when parents maintain open dialogue, encouraging children to share their experiences, frustrations, and questions about the digital world without fear of judgment.

Cultural background further shapes parental strategies. In collectivist societies, family honor and communal responsibility often shape parental expectations, emphasizing cautious engagement and restricted sharing. In more individualist cultures, greater autonomy and self-directed exploration are often encouraged. These cultural orientations influence not only how parents communicate about digital ethics but also how children internalize values of privacy, responsibility, and technological trust (Chang et al., 2024; Lieberknecht, 2024; Imran et al., 2023).

By engaging in thoughtful conversations, modeling balanced behavior, and adapting approaches to cultural contexts, parents provide the foundation for responsible digital citizenship. Their guidance equips children with the skills and awareness needed to navigate digital environments confidently and ethically, ensuring that technology becomes a tool for development rather than a source of harm. Parental guidance, however, cannot operate in a vacuum. The effectiveness of family-level strategies is significantly influenced by the broader regulatory landscape. Without systemic safeguards, even the most diligent parents may find their efforts undermined by exploitative platform design and weak data protection laws. Recognizing this, we now turn our attention to the essential role of policy and regulation in creating a digital environment where ethical practices are not just encouraged, but required.

> ***Takeaway:*** *Parents play a critical role in shaping children's digital habits through boundaries, conversations, and role modeling.*
> ***Reflection:*** *What conversations should parents be having with their children about AI, privacy, or screen time?*

10.4 Policy Measures for Ethical AI and Youth Protection

Government policies play a decisive role in shaping how AI is deployed in contexts that affect young people. While schools, parents, and communities provide immediate guidance, systemic protections are necessary to safeguard against risks such as privacy violations, manipulative content, algorithmic bias, and exclusionary design. Effective policy frameworks set the standards for transparency, accountability, and fairness, ensuring that young users engage with technologies that support their growth rather than exploit their vulnerabilities.

Data privacy and security are among the most critical foundations of digital policy. Regulations inspired by international frameworks such as the General Data Protection Regulation (GDPR) and the California Consumer Privacy Act (CCPA) establish robust rules governing the collection, processing, and sharing of children's data. Research emphasizes that young people are particularly vulnerable to misuse of personal information, and policies must explicitly limit data harvesting, mandate safe storage practices, and enforce penalties for violations (Ijaiya, 2024). Figure 10.3 represents the data protection cycle, from collection to storage and deletion, which illustrates how policies safeguard youth at every stage.

Algorithmic transparency and accountability are equally necessary. Digital platforms increasingly rely on AI-driven recommendation systems that shape what young users see, consume, and believe. Without oversight, these algorithms can create echo chambers, normalize harmful content, or exacerbate biases. Policies requiring platforms to disclose how algorithms function, offer explanations for automated decisions, and provide mechanisms for user control are essential for trust-building (Jones, 2023).

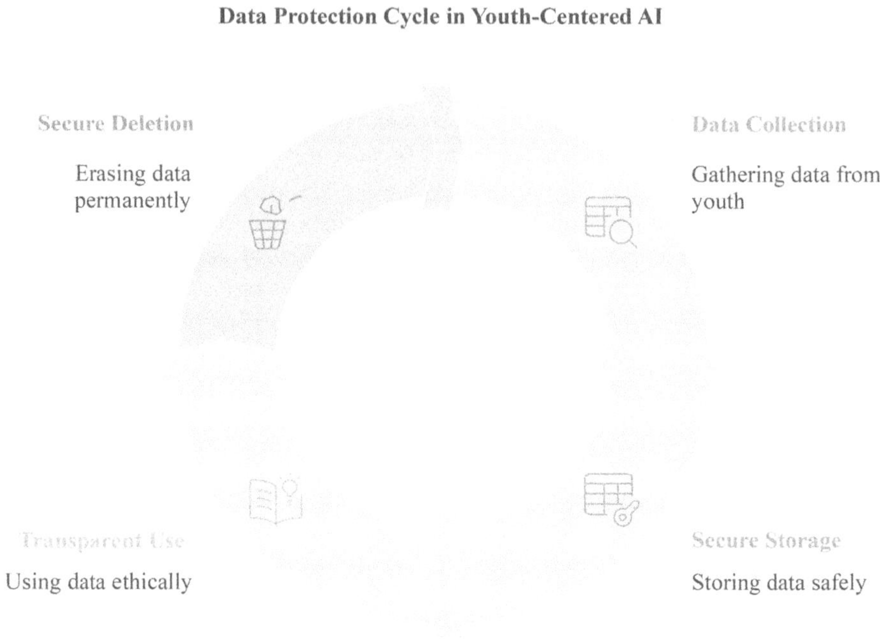

FIGURE 10.3 Data protection cycle in youth-centered AI.

Another pillar of youth protection is ensuring fairness in algorithmic outcomes. AI systems often perpetuate discrimination when trained on biased data, affecting young people's access to education, health resources, or digital opportunities. Policies mandating fairness audits and impact assessments create accountability structures that prevent these harms. In parallel, ethics-centered educational programs that teach children about bias and fairness in AI can empower them to critically interpret algorithmic outcomes, blending systemic safeguards with individual literacy (Grové, 2021).

Parental and youth education policies further extend these protections. Governments can invest in structured programs that provide parents and children with tools to understand privacy rights, safe digital behavior, and AI literacy. Evidence suggests that participatory methods, such as involving youth in the design of digital guidelines, create more effective and culturally relevant interventions (Grové, 2021).

Accessibility and inclusion must also be protected in legislation. Research indicates that digital inequities disproportionately affect users with disabilities, amplifying exclusion if accessibility standards are not enforced (Chemnad & Othman, 2024). Policies mandating universal design in AI-driven platforms, from captioning features to adaptive learning tools, ensure that protections are extended to all youth, regardless of ability.

Collaboration between governments, communities, and technology companies strengthens policy effectiveness. Evidence suggests that public-private partnerships can accelerate the development of youth-centered safeguards while ensuring local cultural and ethical values are respected (Folorunso et al., 2024). In practice, this means aligning global AI principles, such as transparency and accountability, with regional cultural frameworks, ensuring both consistency and contextual adaptability.

Finally, policies must address the problem of manipulative or harmful content. Regulation of cyberspaces requires monitoring systems that prevent exposure to harmful material while preserving freedom of expression. Strong content moderation policies, combined with legal consequences for platforms that fail to protect children, represent necessary safeguards (Chen, 2024). Ethical codes of conduct for AI in education are also recommended, ensuring that digital tools designed for learning reinforce equity, well-being, and psychological safety rather than exploiting attention or data (Chen, 2024). Together, these measures illustrate that youth protection requires a balance of regulatory enforcement, ethical design principles, and participatory education. When governments act decisively to regulate data, demand transparency, and enforce fairness, they create an ecosystem where young people can thrive in digital spaces with confidence and security. Robust policy frameworks provide the necessary foundation for accountability, but their true test lies in their application to the most persistent online harms. Regulations on data privacy and algorithmic transparency are only as effective as the mechanisms used to tackle cyberbullying, misinformation, and harmful content. This next section delves into the practical challenges of content moderation, examining the strategies and technologies required to make digital spaces safer on a day-to-day basis.

> ***Takeaway:*** *Strong policies can protect young users from unethical AI practices by enforcing data privacy, fairness, and transparency.*
> ***Reflection:*** *What rules or protections would you want in place if you were designing digital policy for youth?*

10.5 Tackling Cyberbullying, Misinformation, and Harmful Content

The online environments that young people inhabit provide vital spaces for learning, creativity, and connection, but they also expose them to risks that undermine mental health, ethical development, and civic trust. Among the most persistent threats are cyberbullying, misinformation, and exposure to harmful content. These challenges demand proactive responses from platforms, governments, educators, and communities alike, combining regulation, design innovation, and user empowerment.

Cyberbullying remains one of the most damaging forms of online harm for youth, often resulting in long-term psychological effects such as anxiety, depression, and diminished self-esteem. Platforms must ensure that reporting mechanisms are clear, accessible, and effective, while also embedding educational campaigns that teach empathy and respectful communication. Studies suggest that transparent moderation frameworks, combined with restorative practices, help foster accountability without silencing vulnerable voices (Franco et al., 2025).

Misinformation presents a parallel risk, distorting young people's perceptions of the world and weakening their trust in institutions. The speed at which false information circulates often surpasses the reach of corrective measures. Regulatory frameworks such as the European Union's Digital Services Act (DSA) demonstrate how governments can mandate greater accountability by requiring platforms to remove harmful misinformation promptly while preserving freedom of expression (Enarsson, 2024). At the same time, algorithmic transparency is essential: when youth understand how recommendation systems amplify content, they become more capable of questioning what they encounter online (Jones, 2023).

Content moderation technologies increasingly rely on AI. Although AI tools can detect harmful content at scale, they also risk amplifying bias if not carefully designed and monitored. Scholars argue that algorithmic systems must be subject to oversight mechanisms that apply fairness standards and include community input, particularly from marginalized groups disproportionately targeted by harmful content (Peterson-Salahuddin, 2024).

Cross-platform collaboration is equally necessary. Harmful content often migrates between platforms, moving from mainstream spaces to fringe communities and back again. Coordinated action between companies can prevent this diffusion and mitigate harm before it scales to a societal level (Gatta et al., 2023). This principle of collective responsibility highlights the need for digital ecosystems to operate with shared ethical commitments rather than competitive isolation. Equally important is the role of user education and empowerment. Youth digital literacy programs that explain how misinformation spreads, how to evaluate sources, and how to intervene in cases of cyberbullying can shift part of the responsibility to the community level. Evidence shows that young people who understand reporting mechanisms and misinformation patterns are more resilient to manipulation (Zhang et al., 2023). Governments and independent supervisors can further strengthen accountability by requiring regular audits of content moderation practices. Publicly available reports on the volume of harmful content removed, appeals upheld, and emerging risks increase trust in platforms while providing benchmarks for improvement (Cook et al., 2021). Transparency in these audits ensures that platforms are not only self-regulating but also externally monitored in ways that prioritize youth safety.

Addressing harmful digital content is not a matter of isolated technical fixes but requires a systemic approach. Transparent policies, robust regulation, algorithmic fairness, and digital literacy education must work together to mitigate risks. By aligning these strategies, societies can transform digital environments from spaces that normalize harm to spaces that prioritize safety, fairness, and the psychological well-being of young people. While content moderation addresses the symptoms of online harm, a more proactive approach requires embedding ethical principles directly into the design of AI systems themselves. Tackling harmful content after it has spread is a reactive measure; designing tools that promote well-being from the outset is a preventative one. The following section, therefore, explores how ethical AI design can create tools for young users that are not just less harmful but actively supportive of their mental health and development.

> ***Takeaway:*** *Proactive systems, content moderation, and user education are essential to prevent digital harms and promote safe engagement.*
> ***Reflection:*** *How can platforms be held more accountable for preventing the spread of harmful content among youth?*

10.6 Designing Ethical AI Tools for Young Users

The rapid growth of AI in everyday life has created new opportunities for supporting the mental health and digital well-being of young people. Yet these opportunities are accompanied by ethical risks if AI tools are not designed with the unique developmental, emotional, and cultural needs of adolescents in mind. Designing ethical AI systems for young users requires prioritizing psychological safety, empathetic engagement, inclusivity, and strong connections to human support networks.

A central design principle is personalization. AI tools that adapt to the needs, preferences, and emotional states of individual users can provide meaningful and relevant support. Personalization also fosters a sense of agency, helping young people feel understood rather than controlled by technology (Grové, 2021). Alongside personalization, the incorporation of empathetic interaction is essential. Conversational AI capable of recognizing emotions and responding with validation can create safe spaces where young people feel heard, while mood tracking and regular check-ins reinforce continuity of care (Mansoor et al., 2025). Figure 10.4 is a diagram mapping the cycle of interaction that illustrates how supportive engagement is sustained over time.

Psychoeducation strengthens this foundation by providing evidence-based strategies for managing stress, depression, and anxiety. Resources such as guided mindfulness, breathing exercises, and interactive learning modules help normalize conversations about mental health while equipping youth with coping tools (Grové, 2021). To maintain engagement, gamification elements, challenges, progress tracking, or reward systems can transform mental health practice into enjoyable, motivating activities (Gkintoni et al., 2024).

Privacy and data security represent non-negotiable design imperatives. Adolescents are particularly sensitive to privacy violations, and tools must guarantee that data is securely stored, never exploited, and always used transparently. Ensuring this confidence is essential to building trust and encouraging continued use

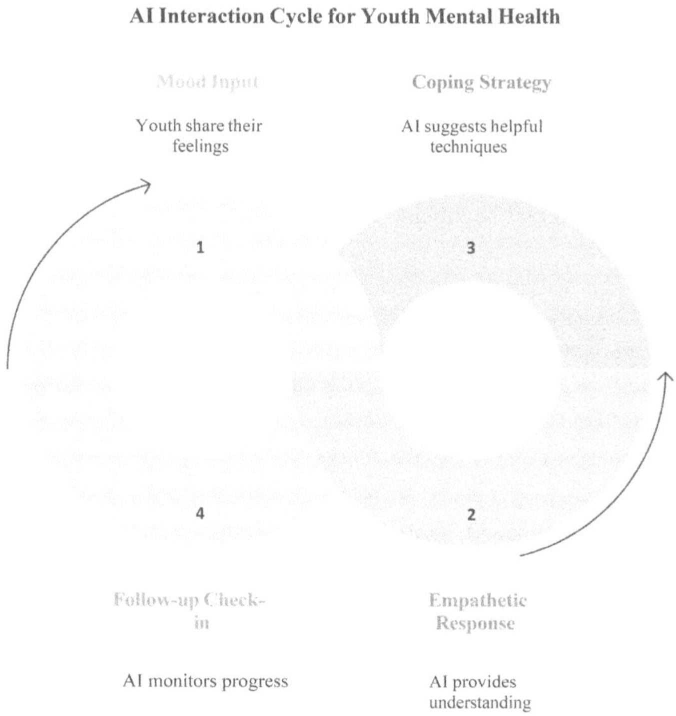

FIGURE 10.4 AI interaction cycle for youth mental health support.

(Alfano et al., 2023). In addition, parental and family support features can help strengthen offline safety nets. Carefully designed options that allow young people to involve parents or trusted mentors, when they choose to, extend the reach of support beyond the digital tool (Lai et al., 2023).

Ethical AI design also requires integrating pathways to professional mental health care. AI systems should act as bridges rather than replacements for professional support, providing referral mechanisms when critical risks such as suicidal ideation are detected (Mansoor et al., 2025). Cultural inclusivity is equally important, as youth come from diverse backgrounds that shape how they understand and interact with technology. Tools must include language options, culturally relevant psychoeducational materials, and features that respect different worldviews (Wani et al., 2024). Perhaps most importantly, youth should be active participants in the design process. Co-design initiatives in which young people directly shape AI tools ensure that technologies meet their actual needs while avoiding adult-centric assumptions. Evidence shows that when youth voices are included, outcomes are more engaging, credible, and impactful (Stiles-Shields et al., 2023).

In sum, ethical AI tools for young users must blend personalization, empathy, education, engagement, privacy, inclusivity, and collaborative design. When these principles are aligned, AI can become a constructive ally in promoting mental health and digital well-being, rather than another source of stress or vulnerability. Ethical design principles provide a powerful blueprint for individual tools, but their impact is limited if they are not adopted and supported across the entire digital ecosystem. The creation of a safer digital future cannot be the sole responsibility of developers. It requires a coordinated effort from all sectors of society. The final section of this chapter, therefore, broadens the lens to examine how multi-stakeholder collaboration between educators, parents, policymakers, developers, and youth themselves is the ultimate key to sustainable change.

> ***Takeaway:*** *Ethical AI tools must be tailored for younger audiences, prioritizing psychological safety, empathy, and positive reinforcement.*
> ***Reflection:*** *What features would you include in an AI tool designed to support mental health in teens?*

10.7 Multi-Stakeholder Collaboration for a Safer Digital Future

Protecting youth online requires coordinated action across multiple stakeholders. Educators, technology developers, policymakers, and youth themselves all have distinct roles to play in building safer, more ethical digital environments. Fragmented efforts are insufficient, as risks such as cyberbullying, misinformation, data misuse, and algorithmic manipulation operate across interconnected systems. Sustainable solutions depend on collaborative models that integrate expertise from education, governance, and technology while actively including the perspectives of young people.

One promising avenue is the use of co-design frameworks. When educators and developers work directly with youth in the design of interventions, the resulting tools reflect lived realities and better address the safety concerns most relevant to their users. Evidence shows that co-design not only strengthens the relevance of digital interventions but also improves uptake and sustainability by fostering a sense of ownership among young participants (Gonsalves et al., 2024). Figure 10.5 is a model of the co-design cycle that illustrates how collaboration generates more responsive tools.

Inclusive and collaborative learning environments provide another pathway for joint action. Educational settings that emphasize diversity and participation create opportunities for young people to develop collaboration skills while simultaneously contributing insights into digital safety challenges. Technology can act as a bridge in these contexts, enabling cross-cultural peer interaction and collective problem-solving (Mansoor et al., 2025). To sustain such initiatives, educators need structured training in collaboration strategies. Teacher preparation programs that

FIGURE 10.5 Co-design cycle for multi-stakeholder collaboration.

emphasize communication, negotiation, and problem-solving skills equip educators to work productively alongside developers and policymakers. Historical research highlights the importance of teaching collaboration as a deliberate skill, suggesting that equipping educators in this way enhances their ability to integrate technology meaningfully while safeguarding youth (Hudson & Glomb, 1997).

Frameworks and tools designed for structured collaboration also strengthen multi-stakeholder partnerships. Instructional methods such as scripted collaborative problem-solving or observational learning can be adapted to computer-mediated environments, providing systematic approaches for educators and developers to resolve challenges together (Rummel & Spada, 2005). In practice, these approaches ensure that expertise from different domains can be effectively integrated into joint solutions.

Engaging the youth themselves is equally important. Empowering young people as co-creators and leaders in digital safety initiatives enhances both the relevance and effectiveness of interventions. Research demonstrates that when youth are invited to design online communities or lead peer-awareness campaigns, they develop stronger commitments to safety while amplifying the impact of interventions (Ballard et al., 2023). Cultural context shapes these collaborative models in significant ways. Variations in power distance, individualism, and uncertainty

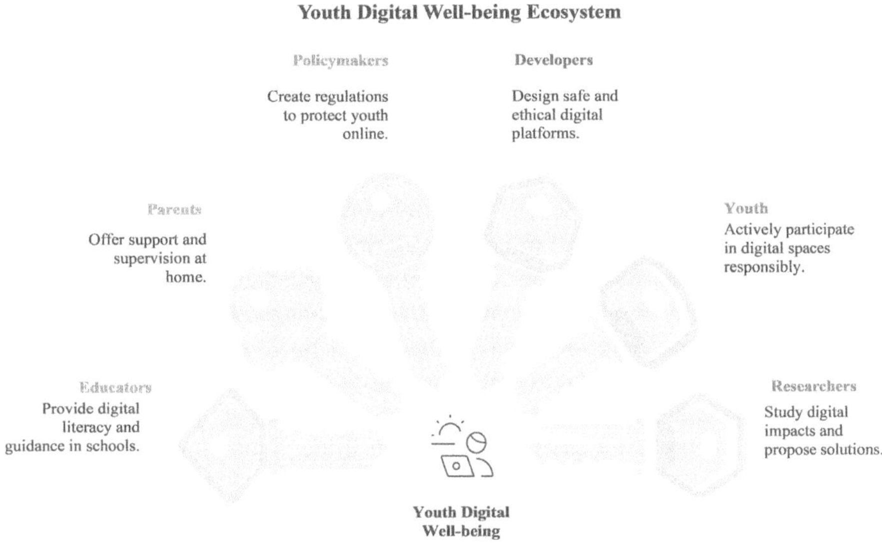

FIGURE 10.6 Multi-stakeholder ecosystem for youth digital well-being.

avoidance influence how stakeholders engage in joint projects and how responsibilities are shared. In collectivist contexts, collaboration may emphasize communal values and collective responsibility, whereas in individualist contexts, it often highlights autonomy and choice (see Figure 10.6). These cultural variations must be recognized to ensure that collaborative frameworks are not only effective but also respectful of local norms (Chang et al., 2024; Jamalova, 2024). Multi-stakeholder collaboration, therefore, represents more than shared responsibility; it is a process of aligning diverse expertise, perspectives, and cultural values toward the common goal of youth well-being. By institutionalizing collaboration through co-design, inclusive education, structured training, and youth empowerment, societies can create robust ecosystems that anticipate risks, respond to harms, and reinforce digital environments where young people can thrive.

> ***Takeaway:*** *Sustainable digital well-being requires collaboration between schools, governments, and developers to align ethical priorities.*
> ***Reflection:*** *How can educators and tech developers work together more effectively to protect youth online?*

10.8 Summary and Reflections

This chapter has emphasized the urgent need to prioritize digital well-being and ethical AI use in the lives of young people. Across the sections, it became clear that supporting youth requires not only equipping them with critical skills and resilience but also reshaping the environments, policies, and technologies that influence their daily experiences. The cyberspaces they inhabit are never neutral; they are shaped by design choices, regulatory frameworks, cultural values, and the quality of adult guidance available to them.

The first section highlighted how youth occupy the center of digital well-being and AI ethics. Their mental health, moral reasoning, and social relationships are deeply shaped by the design of online systems. Supporting them requires recognizing both the risks, such as isolation through misguided content moderation or exposure to harmful content, and the opportunities, including culturally rooted coping strategies and participatory forms of engagement. This foundation established the importance of addressing digital well-being not as an individual problem but as a systemic issue involving families, schools, platforms, and policymakers.

Education emerged as a powerful tool for instilling digital literacy and ethical awareness. Schools that integrate ethics into curricula help students develop moral reasoning, critical thinking, and decision-making confidence. The emphasis on experiential learning and contextualized curricula demonstrates how ethical education can be both practical and culturally responsive, preparing students for dilemmas that extend beyond the classroom into civic and professional life.

Parents also hold a decisive influence, shaping digital habits through conversations, boundaries, and role modeling. Their strategies must balance protection with autonomy, especially in contexts such as privacy, screen time, and online respect. Parenting that fosters trust and open dialogue, rather than control and surveillance, helps children internalize digital ethics and develop self-regulation.

Policy interventions further reinforce these supports. By enforcing data privacy protections, mandating algorithmic transparency, ensuring accessibility, and creating accountability structures, governments establish the systemic safeguards necessary for safe digital engagement. Policies also bridge gaps between parental and educational efforts, ensuring that protections are not left to families or schools alone but supported at institutional and societal levels.

Addressing cyberbullying, misinformation, and harmful content requires both technical and cultural interventions. Transparent moderation systems, oversight of algorithms, and educational initiatives that build digital literacy all work together to create safer online spaces. The evidence underscores that prevention is most effective when systems, communities, and individuals share responsibility for ethical digital engagement.

Designing ethical AI tools specifically for youth underscores the importance of aligning innovation with psychological safety and inclusivity. Personalization, empathy-driven interaction, privacy protections, and pathways to professional care ensure that these tools act as allies rather than risks. Involving youth as co-designers further strengthens both the relevance and trustworthiness of these interventions.

Finally, multi-stakeholder collaboration emerged as the cornerstone of sustainable digital well-being. Educators, developers, policymakers, and youth must work together, guided by frameworks that institutionalize collaboration and respect cultural diversity. No single actor can effectively address the complexity of risks youth face; it is only through joint, sustained efforts that safe and ethical digital ecosystems can be achieved.

Taken together, the chapter demonstrates that promoting digital well-being and ethical AI use is not a linear process but a collective project. Its success depends on aligning strategies across education, parenting, policy, design, and collaboration. By embedding empathy, fairness, transparency, and inclusivity into both practice and policy, societies can transform digital spaces into environments that support the psychological resilience, ethical awareness, and human flourishing of young people.

> ***Takeaway:*** *Digital well-being and ethical AI use require a systemic, collaborative approach that empowers youth, equips adults, and reshapes technologies toward safety and fairness.*
> ***Reflection:*** *Looking ahead, how might collective efforts across families, schools, governments, and industries redefine digital spaces so that they actively foster youth well-being rather than simply reduce harm?*

10.9 Future Research Directions and Open Questions

Although this chapter has outlined current best practices for supporting youth in the digital age, the rapid evolution of AI and digital environments leaves many critical questions unanswered. The following research agenda proposes key areas for future investigation to build a more robust evidence base for policy, education, and design.

First, longitudinal studies are urgently needed to understand the long-term developmental impacts of AI-mediated childhoods. Cross-sectional studies provide valuable snapshots, but they cannot capture the cumulative effects of growing up with algorithmic content curation, AI-driven social comparison, and immersive digital realities. Key questions include: *How does prolonged engagement with AI-driven platforms shape the development of identity, empathy, and critical thinking over time? What are the sleeper effects of early exposure to misinformation and algorithmic bias on adult civic engagement and trust in institutions?*

Second, more research is needed on the effectiveness of different intervention strategies across diverse cultural contexts. Although this book emphasizes cultural sensitivity, most existing research on digital literacy, parental mediation, and ethical AI is rooted in Western, Educated, Industrialized, Rich, and Democratic (WEIRD) societies. Future studies should prioritize co-designing and testing interventions in non-WEIRD contexts to identify culturally specific protective factors and risk moderators. For example, *how do collectivist values alter the effectiveness of privacy education, and what alternative frameworks might be more resonant?*

Third, the "black box" of algorithmic systems remains a significant barrier to research and accountability. Independent researchers need greater access to platform data and algorithmic models to audit for bias, assess the impact of content moderation policies, and understand how recommendation systems affect youth mental health. A critical area for investigation is the development of privacy-preserving research methodologies that allow for independent oversight without compromising user data. This includes exploring federated learning, differential privacy, and other advanced techniques to enable responsible data sharing.

Fourth, the psychological and ethical implications of generative AI represent a new frontier. As young people increasingly use AI to create text, images, and code, new questions emerge about authenticity, creativity, and skill development. Research should explore: *How does the use of generative AI affect the development of writing and critical thinking skills? What are the psychological impacts of forming relationships with highly personalized AI companions? How can we design these tools to augment human creativity rather than replace it?*

Finally, more work is needed to develop and validate metrics for "digital well-being" that go beyond simplistic measures like screen time. Well-being is a multidimensional construct that includes a sense of autonomy, competence, relatedness, and purpose. Future research should focus on creating validated scales and measurement tools that capture these richer dimensions of positive digital engagement, providing a more nuanced way to assess the true impact of technology on youth flourishing.

References

Alfano, L., Malcotti, I., & Ciliberti, R. (2023). Psychotherapy, artificial intelligence and adolescents: Ethical aspects. *PubMed, 64*(4), E438–E442. https://doi.org/10.15167/2421-4248/jpmh2023.64.4.3135

Ali, S., Elgharabawy, M., Duchaussoy, Q., Mannan, M., & Youssef, A. (2020). Betrayed by the guardian: Security and privacy risks of parental control solutions. *Annual Computer Security Applications Conference*, 69–83. https://doi.org/10.1145/3427228.3427287

Bajwa, R. S., Yunus, A., Saeed, H., & Zulfqar, A. (2024). Parenting in the age of artificial intelligence. In *Advances in human and social aspects of technology book series* (pp. 44–66). https://doi.org/10.4018/979-8-3693-3350-1.ch003

Ballard, P. J., Kennedy, H. K., Collura, J. J., Vidrascu, E., & Flewelling, R. L. (2023). Engaging youth as leaders and partners can improve substance use prevention: A call to action to support youth engagement practice and research. *Substance Abuse Treatment, Prevention, and Policy, 18*, Article 71. https://doi.org/10.1186/s13011-023-00582-7

Chang, I.-H., Hsu, P.-C., & Chen, R.-S. (2024). The effects of trust on user satisfaction with parenting apps for Taiwanese parents: The mediating roles of social ties and perceived value. *Education and Information Technologies, 29*, 15113–15131. https://doi.org/10.1007/s10639-024-12471-y

Chemnad, K., & Othman, A. (2024). Digital accessibility in the era of artificial intelligence—Bibliometric analysis and systematic review. *Frontiers in Artificial Intelligence, 7.* https://doi.org/10.3389/frai.2024.1349668

Chen, H. (2024). The ethical challenges of educational Artificial intelligence and coping Measures: A discussion in the context of the 2024 World digital education conference. *Science Insights Education Frontiers*, *20*(2), 3263–3281. https://doi.org/10.15354/sief.24.re339

Cherewick, M., Doocy, S., Tol, W., Burnham, G., & Glass, N. (2016). Potentially traumatic events, coping strategies and associations with mental health and well-being measures among conflict-affected youth in Eastern democratic republic of Congo. *Global Health Research and Policy*, *1*(1). https://doi.org/10.1186/s41256-016-0007-6

Cook, C. L., Patel, A., & Wohn, D. Y. (2021). Commercial versus volunteer: Comparing user perceptions of toxicity and transparency in content moderation across social media platforms. *Frontiers in Human Dynamics*, *3*. https://doi.org/10.3389/fhumd.2021.626409

Cranston, N., Ehrich, L. C., & Kimber, M. (2006). Ethical dilemmas: The "bread and butter" of educational leaders' lives. *Journal of Educational Administration*, *44*(2), 106–121. https://doi.org/10.1108/09578230610652015

Davies, M., & Heyward, P. (2019). Between a hard place and a hard place: A study of ethical dilemmas experienced by student teachers while on practicum. *British Educational Research Journal*, *45*(2), 372–387. https://doi.org/10.1002/berj.3505

Ehrich, L. C., Kimber, M., Millwater, J., & Cranston, N. (2011). Ethical dilemmas: A model to understand teacher practice. *Teachers and Teaching*, *17*(2), 173–185. https://doi.org/10.1080/13540602.2011.539794

Enarsson, T. (2024). Navigating hate speech and content moderation under the DSA: Insights from ECtHR case law. *Information & Communications Technology Law*, *33*(3), 1–18. https://doi.org/10.1080/13600834.2024.2395579

Folorunso, N. A., Olanipekun, N. K., Adewumi, N. T., & Samuel, N. B. (2024). A policy framework on AI usage in developing countries and its impact. *Global Journal of Engineering and Technology Advances*, *21*(1), 154–166. https://doi.org/10.30574/gjeta.2024.21.1.0192

Franco, M., Gaggi, O., & Palazzi, C. E. (2024). Integrating content moderation systems with large language models. *ACM Transactions on the Web*. https://doi.org/10.1145/3700789

Gkintoni, E., Vantaraki, F., Skoulidi, C., Anastassopoulos, P., & Vantarakis, A. (2024). Promoting physical and mental Hhealth among children and adolescents via gamification—A conceptual systematic review. *Behavioral Sciences*, *14*(2), 102. https://doi.org/10.3390/bs14020102

Gonsalves, P. P., Ansari, S., Berry, C., Gonsalves, F., Iyengar, S., Kashyap, P., Mittal, D., Pal, S., Razdan, E., & Michelson, D. (2024). Co-designing digital mental health interventions with young people: 10 recommendations from lessons learned in low-and-middle-income countries. *Health Education Journal*, *84*(4), 373–384. https://doi.org/10.1177/00178969241297821

Grové, C. (2021). Co-developing a mental health and wellbeing chatbot with and for young people. *Frontiers in Psychiatry*, *11*. https://doi.org/10.3389/fpsyt.2020.606041

Hudson, P., & Glomb, N. (1997). If it takes two to tango, then why not teach both partners to dance? Collaboration instruction for all educators. *Journal of Learning Disabilities*, *30*(4), 442–448. https://doi.org/10.1177/002221949703000411

Ijaiya, N. H. (2024). Harnessing AI for data privacy: Examining risks, opportunities and strategic future directions. *International Journal of Science and Research Archive*, *13*(2), 2878–2892. https://doi.org/10.30574/ijsra.2024.13.2.2510

Imran, A., Khanom, N., & Rahman, A. (2023). Parental perception of children's online behaviour: A study on ethnic communities in Australia. *International Journal of Environmental Research and Public Health*, *20*(7), Article 5342. https://doi.org/10.3390/ijerph20075342

Jago, R., Stamatakis, E., Gama, A., Carvalhal, I. M., Nogueira, H., Rosado, V., & Padez, C. (2012). Parent and child screen-viewing time and home media environment. *American Journal of Preventive Medicine*, *43*(2), 150–158. https://doi.org/10.1016/j.amepre.2012.04.012

Jones, E. (2023). Digital disruption: Artificial intelligence and international trade policy. *Oxford Review of Economic Policy*, *39*(1), 70–84. https://doi.org/10.1093/oxrep/grac049

Katapally, T. R. (2020). Smart indigenous youth: The smart platform policy solution for systems integration to address Indigenous youth mental health. *JMIR Pediatrics and Parenting*, *3*(2), e21155. https://doi.org/10.2196/21155

Kewalramani, S., Kidman, G., & Palaiologou, I. (2021). Using Artificial Intelligence (AI)-interfaced robotic toys in early childhood settings: A case for children's inquiry literacy. *European Early Childhood Education Research Journal*, *29*(5), 652–668. https://doi.org/10.1080/1350293x.2021.1968458

Krautscheid, L. C. (2017). Embedding microethical dilemmas in high-fidelity simulation scenarios: Preparing nursing students for ethical practice. *Journal of Nursing Education*, *56*(1), 55–58. https://doi.org/10.3928/01484834-20161219-11

La Gatta, V., Luceri, L., Fabbri, F., & Ferrara, E. (2023). *The Interconnected Nature of Online Harm and Moderation* (pp. 1–10). HT '23: Proceedings of the 34th ACM Conference on Hypertext and Social Media. https://doi.org/10.1145/3603163.3609058

Lai, T., Xie, C., Ruan, M., Wang, Z., Lu, H., & Fu, S. (2023). Influence of artificial intelligence in education on adolescents' social adaptability: The mediatory role of social support. *PLoS One*, *18*(3), e0283170. https://doi.org/10.1371/journal.pone.0283170

Lieberknecht, A.-K. (2024). Exploring determinants of parental engagement in online privacy protection: A qualitative approach. In *Proceedings of the 2024 European Symposium on Usable Security* (pp. 94–111). Association for Computing Machinery. https://doi.org/10.1145/3688459.3688476

Mansoor, M., Hamide, A., & Tran, T. (2025). Conversational AI in pediatric mental health: A narrative review. *Children*, *12*(3), 359. https://doi.org/10.3390/children12030359

Muhtaseb, R., Traxler, J., & Scott, H. (2023). Educators' perceptions of the influence of culture on social media use in education in Palestine. *Asian Journal of Distance Education*, *18*(1), 271–300. http://www.asianjde.com/ojs/index.php/AsianJDE/article/view/698

Peterson-Salahuddin, C. (2024). Repairing the harm: Toward an algorithmic reparations approach to hate speech content moderation. *Big Data & Society*, *11*(2). https://doi.org/10.1177/20539517241245333

Rummel, N., & Spada, H. (2005). Learning to collaborate: An instructional approach to promoting collaborative problem solving in computer-mediated settings. *Journal of the Learning Sciences*, *14*(2), 201–241. https://doi.org/10.1207/s15327809jls1402_2

Simpson, J. A., Winterheld, H. A., Rholes, W. S., & Oriña, M. M. (2007). Working models of attachment and reactions to different forms of caregiving from romantic partners. *Journal of Personality and Social Psychology*, *93*(3), 466–477. https://doi.org/10.1037/0022-3514.93.3.466

Smith, K. E., Acevedo-Duran, R., Lovell, J. L., Castillo, A. V., & Pacheco, V. C. (2024). Youth are the experts! Youth participatory action research to address the adolescent mental health crisis. *Healthcare*, *12*(5), 592. https://doi.org/10.3390/healthcare12050592

Sriwindono, H. (2022). Eksplorasi efek moderasi dimensi budaya terhadap penerimaan teknologi internet masyarakat Yogyakarta. *SIBATIK Journal: Jurnal Ilmiah Bidang Sosial, Ekonomi, Budaya, Teknologi, dan Pendidikan*, *1*(9), 1909–1916. https://doi.org/10.54443/sibatik.v1i9.269

Stiles-Shields, C., Ramos, G., Ortega, A., & Psihogios, A. M. (2023). Increasing digital mental health reach and uptake via youth partnerships. *Npj Mental Health Research*, *2*(1). https://doi.org/10.1038/s44184-023-00030-1

Wani, C., McCann, L., Lennon, M., & Radu, C. (2024). Digital mental health interventions for adolescents in low- and middle-income countries: A scoping review (Preprint). *Journal of Medical Internet Research*, *26*, e51376. https://doi.org/10.2196/51376

Wolfers, L. N., Nabi, R. L., & Walter, N. (2024). Too much screen time or too much guilt? How child screen time and parental screen guilt affect parental stress and relationship satisfaction. *Media Psychology*, *28*(1), 1–32. https://doi.org/10.1080/15213269.2024.2310839

Wright, M., Reitegger, F., Cela, H., Papst, A., & Gasteiger-Klicpera, B. (2023). Interventions with digital tools for mental health promotion among 11–18 Year olds: A systematic review and meta-analysis. *Journal of Youth and Adolescence*, *52*(4), 754–779. https://doi.org/10.1007/s10964-023-01735-4

Zhang, C. C., Zaleski, G., Kailley, J. N., Teng, K. A., English, M., Riminchan, A., & Robillard, J. M. (2023). Debate: Social media content moderation may do more harm than good for youth mental health. *Child and Adolescent Mental Health*, *29*(1), 104–106. https://doi.org/10.1111/camh.12689

11

EMERGING TRENDS IN CYBER BEHAVIOR AND DIGITAL RESILIENCE

Chapter Objectives

- To highlight key emerging trends in cyberpsychology and AI ethics that affect youth mental health.
- To examine the roles of personality traits and gender in shaping digital resilience and vulnerability.
- To evaluate the ethical responsibilities of AI systems in youth-centered digital platforms.
- To promote research and innovation aimed at fostering safer, more ethical digital experiences for young people.

Topics to Be Covered

- Introduction to Emerging Trends in Cyberpsychology
- Personality Traits and Digital Resilience
- Gender-Specific Vulnerabilities and Strengths
- Cultural Factors in Personality and Digital Resilience
- Ethical AI in Youth-Oriented Platforms
- Actionable Interventions for Youth Digital Well-being
- Practical Recommendations for Parents
- Research and Innovation for the Future of Digital Well-being
- Summary and Reflections

DOI: 10.4324/9781003657590-15

11.1 Introduction: Emerging Trends in Youth Cyber Behavior

The increasing intersection of cyberpsychology and artificial intelligence (AI) ethics is reshaping how young people experience mental health support, digital interaction, and ethical decision-making. Emerging developments reveal both opportunities for improved well-being and challenges that demand careful consideration. Four trends are particularly significant.

Digital mental health interventions are becoming a central component of youth care. Mobile applications, online platforms, and telehealth services now provide immediate access to mental health resources. These tools have shown promise in reducing symptoms of distress and building resilience (Hong et al., 2025; Leech et al., 2021; Zhou et al., 2021). At the same time, they introduce risks such as dependency on digital platforms and heightened privacy concerns when sensitive data is collected or stored without adequate safeguards (Liu et al., 2023; Opie et al., 2024).

The rapid integration of AI in mental health settings further extends these possibilities. AI-driven systems, including chatbots, are designed to deliver evidence-based support, coping strategies, and educational resources (Joseph & Babu, 2024; Pandya et al., 2024). Although these tools improve accessibility and consistency of care, their expansion raises important ethical issues. Protecting user privacy, ensuring responsible data management, and fostering trust are essential conditions for their effective adoption. Developing rigorous guidelines and ethical codes for AI in mental health remains a priority (Bhutani et al., 2024; Joerin et al., 2020).

Another influential development is the role of social media platforms powered by AI algorithms. These platforms not only enable self-expression and connectivity but also shape the formation of youth identity (Akintoye et al., 2023; Chang et al., 2025). The personalization of content and the continuous collection of personal data raise significant ethical concerns. Cyberbullying, surveillance, and the loss of autonomy emerge as risks when data practices are opaque or insufficiently regulated. Transparent policies and protective mechanisms are needed to preserve young people's agency in these digital spaces (Bhutani et al., 2024).

Finally, participatory approaches are gaining importance in the design of digital health solutions. Involving youth directly in the co-design of interventions ensures that tools reflect their needs and preferences (Lewis et al., 2024; Malloy et al., 2023). Such collaboration increases relevance and usability while empowering young people to contribute to decisions that affect their mental health. Interdisciplinary cooperation among technology developers, health professionals, and youth communities has proven critical to the development of sustainable digital interventions (Opie et al., 2024). These trends point to the transformative potential of digital and AI technologies in promoting youth mental health (see Table 11.1). At the same time, they highlight the need for continuous ethical vigilance and for young people to actively shape the systems designed for their care.

Emerging ethical frameworks seek to guide the safe and responsible integration of AI into youth mental health care. These frameworks do not merely highlight principles

TABLE 11.1 Emerging Trends in Youth Cyber Behavior

Emerging Trend	*Potential Benefits*	*Associated Risks*	*Key Ethical Issues*
Digital Interventions and Health Innovations	Timely access to resources; symptom reduction; resilience building	Privacy concerns; dependency on platforms; data misuse	Data protection; safeguarding sensitive information
AI-Powered Tools and AI Ethics	Accessible, consistent support; evidence-based coping strategies	Privacy violations; weak data protection; over-reliance on AI	Responsible AI use; establishing trust; ethical guidelines
Social Media and Youth Identity	Opportunities for self-expression; peer connection; identity exploration	Cyberbullying; surveillance; invasion of privacy	Transparency in data practices; protecting autonomy
Collaboration and Co-Design Approaches	Greater relevance of tools; youth empowerment; improved usability	Limited inclusivity; tokenistic participation; implementation challenges	Authenticity of participation; equitable collaboration

TABLE 11.2 Ethical Pillars for AI in Youth Mental Health

Ethical Pillar	*Core Principle*	*Example Practices*
Human-Centric and Transparent Design	Prioritize user needs; ensure clarity in AI decision-making	Co-design with youth and professionals; provide clear explanations of AI outputs
Privacy and Data Security	Protect sensitive information and give users control	Implement encryption, secure storage, and consent-based data access
Equity and Inclusivity	Address bias and ensure fair access for all groups	Use diverse datasets; test algorithms across cultural and social groups
Accountability and Professional Oversight	Distribute responsibility among developers, clinicians, and institutions	Require clinician oversight in AI-based care; publish accountability reports
Developmental Considerations	Adapt tools to youth cognitive, emotional, and linguistic levels	Design age-appropriate interfaces; tailor interventions to developmental stages

but offer structured approaches to design, deployment, and oversight (Figueroa et al., 2025; Marshall et al., 2025). Several key considerations stand out (see Table 11.2).

Human-centric and transparent design remains a primary focus. Ethical models emphasize the need for AI applications that prioritize users' well-being while maintaining clarity in how systems generate outputs (Sebastião & Dias, 2025).

Transparency requires that both young users and practitioners can understand the basis of recommendations or interventions. Co-design with stakeholders, including youth, mental health professionals, and technology developers, strengthens trust and ensures that applications respond to real needs rather than abstract ideals (Joerin et al., 2020; Olawade et al., 2024).

Privacy and data security are central to all ethical debates in this area. Sensitive health information demands strict safeguards, not only to comply with legal standards but also to preserve the confidence of young users (Figueroa et al., 2025). Ethical frameworks highlight the importance of data ownership, secure storage, and user control over personal information. Without these protections, the risks of misuse or exploitation increase substantially (Olorunfemi et al., 2024).

Equity and inclusivity are also prioritized. AI applications risk reinforcing existing inequalities if they are trained on narrow datasets or applied without sensitivity to diverse populations (Olorunfemi et al., 2024). Ethical guidelines stress the inclusion of varied cultural, linguistic, and socioeconomic groups in design and testing. Ensuring fairness is especially important for marginalized youth, who often face barriers in accessing traditional mental health services (Mansoor et al., 2025).

Accountability and professional oversight provide another safeguard. Frameworks underline that responsibility must be clearly distributed among developers, clinicians, and institutions. AI systems are intended to complement, not replace, human judgment (Anamika et al., 2024). Professional oversight in clinical contexts ensures that AI remains a supportive tool while final decisions continue to rest with trained practitioners (Fiske et al., 2019; Wahed et al., 2024).

Finally, developmental considerations are crucial. Youth differ from adults in cognitive, emotional, and linguistic development. AI applications must therefore be designed with age-appropriate features that engage without being overwhelming and that offer guidance suited to the user's developmental stage (Kurian, 2025). Tailoring interventions in this way ensures that tools are both accessible and effective (Mansoor et al., 2025). These frameworks aim to balance innovation with ethical responsibility. They provide pathways for creating AI systems that support mental health while avoiding harm, ensuring that young people benefit from technological advances without compromising their dignity, privacy, or agency. The discussion that follows builds upon these frameworks, examining how they can be adapted and applied specifically to AI in youth mental health. The chapter aims to propose ethical structures that ensure AI serves as a supportive partner in care, protecting young users while strengthening their opportunities for growth and resilience.

Takeaway: *As digital environments expand, young people face new psychological and ethical challenges that demand structured guidance and proactive safeguards.*
Reflection: *What changes have you noticed in how young people use and are affected by digital platforms in recent years?*

11.2 Personality Traits and Digital Resilience

11.2.1 *Big Five Personality Traits and Coping with Digital Threats*

Personality traits strongly influence how young people respond to online stressors such as cyberbullying, peer pressure, and exposure to risky behaviors (ElSayary et al., 2026; Evangelou et al., 2024). By identifying these patterns, it becomes possible to design support systems that are sensitive to individual differences and can strengthen resilience in digital contexts.

Neuroticism is often associated with vulnerability. Youth high in this trait report greater stress and anxiety when confronted with online harassment or exclusion (Wang, 2022). Their heightened sensitivity increases the likelihood of feeling victimized by cyberbullying or overwhelmed by peer demands. Interventions that focus on emotional regulation, resilience training, and guided stress management are particularly effective for this group (Chen et al., 2024; Romero & Alonso, 2019).

Extraversion provides both strengths and risks. Extraverted individuals frequently rely on broad social networks that can serve as protective buffers against negative online experiences (Favini et al., 2023; Gugushvili et al., 2022). However, their openness to social engagement also increases exposure to peer pressure and risky behaviors. For this group, digital literacy programs that emphasize maintaining constructive interactions and resisting harmful trends can reinforce resilience (Davey et al., 2003). Targeted programs in social media literacy can help extraverts maximize the benefits of their connections while avoiding unsafe practices, such as oversharing or succumbing to online group influence (Duan & Deng, 2023).

Conscientiousness generally offers a strong defense against digital threats. Conscientious youth adhere to responsible online practices, limit impulsive behaviors, and resist peer influence (Hylkilä et al., 2025; Joshi et al., 2023). Their responsible approach to online engagement equips them with strategies to counteract peer pressure and manage digital risks. Programs that reinforce self-regulation, time management, and awareness of online harms further strengthen this protective profile (Buchan et al., 2024; Galla & Wood, 2013). Additionally, raising awareness to encourage continued development of these qualities through structured self-management training reinforces resilience against cyberbullying and peer pressure (Chen et al., 2024; Srivastava et al., 2015).

Openness to Experience reflects adaptability and a willingness to experiment with new coping approaches. These individuals often seek diverse online content to enrich their perspectives, but they also encounter risks such as misinformation and exposure to disinhibited behaviors (Mayiwar et al., 2024). Youth high in openness benefit from programs that emphasize critical thinking, analytical reasoning, and media literacy, equipping them to navigate online risks while maintaining curiosity and innovation (Srivastava et al., 2015; Buchan et al., 2024; Davey et al., 2003).

Agreeableness supports positive social interactions but can create vulnerabilities. It is closely linked to cooperative and empathetic behavior. Young people high in agreeableness often seek harmony and may avoid confrontation, thereby increasing their susceptibility to cyberbullying or manipulative peer behavior (Congiu et al., 2024). Assertiveness training is valuable in this context, giving agreeable individuals the tools to maintain their prosocial orientation without compromising their ability to resist harmful influences (Davey et al., 2003; Duan & Deng, 2023).

Beyond specific traits, adaptive coping strategies are essential for all youth. Training programs that cultivate resilience, emotional toughness, and problem-solving skills provide universal benefits. The integration of digital tools, such as mental health chatbots, can complement these efforts by delivering personalized guidance aligned with personality profiles. Such approaches ensure that coping mechanisms remain both context-sensitive and scalable (Craig et al., 2019). Understanding these personality-based differences allows educators, clinicians, and policymakers to design interventions that reflect diverse psychological profiles. By aligning strategies with traits, support systems can help youth manage digital threats more effectively, reducing vulnerability while fostering stronger, more adaptive digital resilience.

11.2.2 HEXACO Traits, Vulnerabilities, and Interventions

HEXACO expands the Big Five by introducing the honesty-humility traits and modifies neuroticism into emotionality, which includes both negative and positive emotions. Similar to the previous section, each trait interacts with digital experiences in distinct ways, offering both protective factors and potential vulnerabilities (Evangelou et al., 2024).

Honesty-Humility plays a decisive role in ethical cyber behavior. Youth with lower levels of this trait are more likely to engage in behaviors associated with moral disengagement, rationalizing harmful actions such as cyberbullying (Sun et al., 2025). Online disinhibition becomes particularly pronounced in this group, as reduced concern for fairness or integrity weakens restraint against aggressive or manipulative behavior (Baiocco et al., 2017).

Emotionality reflects sensitivity to stress and negative affect in digital contexts. Young people scoring high on this trait are more vulnerable to distress caused by peer pressure, harassment, or cyberbullying (Molero et al., 2023). Their heightened emotional reactivity often amplifies the impact of online negativity. At the same time, they may benefit most from supportive interventions, such as AI-based chatbots or guided emotional regulation programs, which provide coping strategies for managing digital stressors (Gardner et al., 2012).

These patterns highlight that personality traits significantly shape digital resilience. Understanding how each trait dimension influences coping allows for targeted interventions (see Table 11.3). Personalized digital literacy programs, tailored mental health support, and resilience-building resources can be designed to align with individual personality profiles, equipping youth to better manage digital risks while benefiting from the opportunities of online engagement.

TABLE 11.3 Big Five and HEXACO Traits, Vulnerabilities, and Interventions

Big Five Trait	*Vulnerabilities in Digital Contexts*	*Recommended Coping Interventions*
Neuroticism	High stress and anxiety; heightened sensitivity to cyberbullying and peer pressure	Emotional regulation programs; resilience training; stress management support
Extraversion	Greater exposure to peer pressure due to frequent social interaction	Digital literacy programs on peer influence; focus on positive online interaction
Conscientiousness	Low susceptibility to risky online behavior, but may face overcommitment	Self-regulation and time management training; reinforcement of safe online habits
Openness to Experience	Exploration of diverse online content may increase exposure to harmful or misleading information	Critical thinking and media literacy education; analytical reasoning skills development
Agreeableness	Conflict avoidance increases vulnerability to cyberbullying and manipulative peer behavior	Assertiveness training; empowerment strategies; balanced empathy and conflict management skills
Honesty-Humility	Prone to online disinhibition; rationalizes harmful behaviors like cyberbullying	Ethics training; programs promoting fairness, integrity, and digital responsibility
Emotionality	Increased stress and negative emotions from cyberbullying and peer pressure	Emotional regulation training; AI chatbots for stress management; counseling tools

11.2.3 The Dark Tetrad and Digital Vulnerabilities

The Dark Tetrad of personality traits, narcissism, Machiavellianism, psychopathy, and sadism, captures dispositions associated with callousness, manipulation, and aggression (Gajda et al., 2022). These traits strongly influence how youth engage with digital platforms and cope with threats such as cyberbullying, moral disengagement, online disinhibition, and problematic internet use (Gholami et al., 2025). In contrast to the protective potential of other personality dimensions, the Dark Tetrad often intensifies risk and fosters harmful cyber behavior (Alavi et al., 2025).

Narcissism is characterized by an excessive need for admiration and recognition. Online environments provide fertile ground for narcissistic expression, where constant validation can be sought through posting, commenting, or aggressive attention-seeking behaviors (Balcerowska et al., 2024). This drive can escalate into problematic internet use and online disinhibition. Narcissism is also linked with moral disengagement, enabling individuals to rationalize unethical actions, such as cyberbullying, when these serve to protect self-esteem or enhance public image (Alavi et al., 2025; Brown et al., 2019).

Machiavellianism reflects a more calculated orientation. Youth high on this trait are strategic and manipulative, often exploiting digital anonymity to control or influence peers (Maftei et al., 2022). These behaviors exacerbate cyberbullying by masking manipulation through invisibility and reduced accountability. Moral disengagement becomes a tool for justification, allowing Machiavellian individuals to frame harmful acts as rational or necessary (Alavi et al., 2025; Gajda et al., 2022).

Psychopathy brings on impulsiveness and a lack of emotional connection. In cyberspace, these traits are strongly correlated with aggressive behavior and cyberaggression. The absence of empathy, combined with reduced inhibitions, increases the likelihood of online abuse and reckless engagement with harmful content (Martín-Martín & Bueno-Álvarez, 2023). Psychopathic youth are particularly prone to ignoring the long-term consequences of their actions, which amplifies the risks of problematic internet use and peer exploitation (Brown et al., 2019; Gajda et al., 2022).

Sadism presents perhaps the most overt form of harmful engagement. Youth with high sadistic tendencies derive satisfaction from others' suffering, making them especially likely to participate in or endorse cyberbullying (Gajda et al., 2022). Digital platforms amplify these behaviors by providing anonymity, a wide reach, and opportunities for escalation without direct consequences. Online environments that normalize aggression can further reinforce sadistic enjoyment of harm (Brown et al., 2019).

Given their tendency toward destructive cyber behavior, interventions for individuals displaying Dark Tetrad traits must be targeted and intensive. Educational strategies that emphasize empathy development, ethical reasoning, and accountability are essential. Programs designed to strengthen critical thinking and encourage perspective-taking may reduce rationalizations for harmful behavior. At the same time, monitoring and structured oversight are necessary to limit impulsive or manipulative activity, ensuring safer digital environments for peers (see Table 11.4). By addressing these traits directly, it becomes possible to mitigate their disruptive impact and promote more ethical engagement online.

Takeaway: *Personality traits shape how youth respond to digital threats. Although some traits support resilience, others, particularly those in the Dark Tetrad, can intensify vulnerability and drive harmful behaviors.*

Reflection: *How could schools or digital platforms design interventions that respond differently to youth with high-risk personality traits?*

TABLE 11.4 Dark Tetrad Traits Cyber Behaviors and Interventions

Dark Tetrad Trait	*Associated Online Behaviors*	*Recommended Interventions*
Narcissism	Attention-seeking; problematic internet use; online disinhibition; justification of cyberbullying to maintain self-image	Empathy training; digital responsibility programs; promoting authentic self-worth beyond online validation
Machiavellianism	Strategic manipulation; exploiting anonymity; calculated disinhibition; use of moral disengagement to justify harm	Critical thinking and ethics education; accountability structures; monitoring manipulative online activities
Psychopathy	Aggressive online behaviors; impulsivity; lack of empathy; disregard for consequences; high risk of cyberaggression	Emotional regulation and empathy development; strict moderation of harmful behaviors; guided support systems
Sadism	Derives pleasure from others' suffering; active participation in cyberbullying; reinforcement of harmful online communities	Targeted empathy-building; strict anti-harassment measures; close oversight of online participation

11.3 Gender-Specific Vulnerabilities and Strengths

Youth engagement with digital environments is shaped not only by personality but also by gendered patterns of interaction, preference, and response (Carcelén-García et al., 2023). These patterns reflect social conditioning, psychological tendencies, and platform design, resulting in different strengths and vulnerabilities for males and females (Li et al., 2025). Recognizing these differences allows for more targeted strategies that enhance engagement, safety, and mental health outcomes.

Interactive and competitive environments often attract male users. Evidence suggests that males perform well in digital contexts structured around competition, reflecting both early exposure to competitive activities and cultural norms that encourage assertiveness (Baker et al., 2024; Vázquez-Cano et al., 2022). Digital platforms can increase male engagement by integrating features such as leaderboards, ranking systems, or performance-based rewards. These elements align with the motivational drivers commonly observed in male users (Gneezy et al., 2003).

Social and collaborative engagement is more characteristic of female users. Platforms that encourage cooperation, social bonding, and empathetic interaction are particularly appealing to females, reflecting broader socialization patterns that emphasize relational strengths (Chi et al., 2022; Li et al., 2025). Strategies that integrate peer-support networks, collaborative tasks, and opportunities for social sharing can therefore foster more meaningful and sustained participation among female users (Theophilou et al., 2023).

Customization and personalization preferences also reveal differences. Female users often emphasize aesthetics, self-expression, and mood representation in avatar or profile design, while male users prioritize functional attributes that provide a competitive advantage (Ko & Kim, 2024; Zimmermann et al., 2022). Designing personalization toolkits that allow flexibility across both aesthetic and functional dimensions can ensure inclusivity, increasing user satisfaction while reflecting distinct preferences (Shen et al., 2016).

Anxiety and safety concerns disproportionately affect female users. Studies show that females frequently report higher anxiety in navigation-based tasks and express greater concern over safety and privacy (Su, 2023). These concerns may limit participation or confidence in digital contexts. Addressing this requires visible privacy protections, intuitive navigation systems, and the integration of clear security features that reassure users and build trust in the environment (Lawton & Kallai, 2002).

Learning and educational contexts further illustrate gender-based distinctions. Females tend to contribute more to communicative and cooperative activities within learning platforms, while males often respond positively to gamified elements that emphasize competition and challenge (Mellado et al., 2024). Designing blended educational systems that combine collaborative modules with gamified simulations can cater to both groups, improving learning outcomes across genders (Theophilou et al., 2023). Digital systems can be tailored to address gender-specific needs without reinforcing stereotypes. Effective customization requires balancing competition with cooperation, aesthetics with functionality, and safety with autonomy (see Figure 11.1). This approach supports equitable participation, strengthens mental health outcomes, and ensures that digital spaces serve as inclusive environments for both males and females.

> ***Takeaway:*** *Males and females face distinct challenges in cyberspaces, requiring gender-aware approaches that integrate competitive, collaborative, and safety-oriented strategies.*
> ***Reflection:*** *What types of support or guidance could better address the specific needs of girls and boys online?*

11.4 Cultural Factors in Personality and Digital Resilience

Cultural context profoundly shapes how personality traits contribute to digital resilience. Personality is not expressed in isolation but is filtered through cultural values, expectations, and social norms (Almulla et al., 2025; ElSayary et al., 2025). This interplay influences how youth respond to digital threats and how interventions should be tailored across societies.

Cultural dimensions such as individualism and collectivism strongly condition the expression of personality traits. In individualistic cultures, extraversion and openness are often linked to digital resilience because self-expression, independence, and innovation are culturally valued (Hamamoto et al., 2023). By contrast, in collectivist cultures,

FIGURE 11.1 Gendered cyber behavior patterns and design strategies.

conscientiousness and agreeableness may be more closely tied to resilience, reflecting cultural norms that emphasize group harmony, responsibility, and the maintenance of supportive social networks (Eley et al., 2013; Terracciano & McCrae, 2006).

The cross-cultural applicability of personality models such as the Five-Factor Model highlights both universality and variation. Local norms vary in their influence on resilience, despite the consistent presence of core traits across societies (Terrana & Al-Delaimy, 2023). For instance, the impact of neuroticism may be intensified in cultures where emotional expression is stigmatized but less so where open discussion of mental health is normalized (Terracciano & McCrae, 2006).

Cultural stereotypes and gender roles add another layer of complexity. In societies with rigid gender expectations, the interaction between traits and resilience may reinforce inequalities (Singh et al., 2025). Women, for example, may be expected to emphasize agreeableness and emotional expression, which can affect how they cope with digital challenges and how their resilience is perceived (Lippa & Tan, 2001).

Cultural influence also extends to the resilience strategies themselves. Interdependent societies often encourage coping through collective support, thereby reinforcing traits such as extraversion and agreeableness (Ciren et al., 2025). In contrast, more individualistic contexts prioritize self-reliance, aligning resilience more closely with traits such as openness and extraversion, which encourage initiative and adaptability (Athota et al., 2019; Ike et al., 2024).

This distinction between collective and individual approaches is particularly relevant in shaping digital coping. In collectivist contexts, cooperation and shared responsibility foster resilience, while in individualist cultures, digital strength is often built on personal initiative and independent problem-solving (Huang et al., 2021).

These cultural influences highlight the complexity of linking personality and resilience in digital environments. Effective interventions must account for cultural variation, ensuring that resilience-building strategies emphasize traits and practices most compatible with local values and worldviews. A culturally sensitive approach not only improves effectiveness but also avoids imposing one-size-fits-all solutions that fail to resonate with youth in diverse settings (Figure 11.2).

Takeaway: *The link between personality and digital resilience is not universal but is profoundly shaped by cultural context. Collectivist cultures may foster resilience through agreeableness and group harmony, while individualistic cultures prioritize extraversion and self-reliance. This means effective interventions must be culturally sensitive, not one-size-fits-all.*
Reflection: *If a "one-size-fits-all" approach to digital resilience is ineffective, what are the ethical responsibilities of global technology companies whose platforms are used across hundreds of cultural contexts?*

Cultural Contexts, Personality Traits, and Digital Resilience

Characteristic	Collectivist Cultures	Individualis t Cultures
Personality Traits	Conscientiousness, Agreeableness	Extraversion, Openness
Resilience Strategies	Community-based coping, Collaborative problem-solving, Reliance on social networks	Personal initiative, Self-reliance, Critical thinking and adaptability
Digital Resilience Outcomes	Stronger group support, Reduced isolation, Resilience reinforced by interdependence	Higher adaptability, Individual coping capacity, Resilience through personal agency

FIGURE 11.2 Cultural contexts, personality traits, and digital resilience.

11.5 Ethical AI in Youth Platforms

Developers of youth-centered technologies hold a significant ethical responsibility to ensure that systems are designed with safety, transparency, and privacy as core principles (Figueroa et al., 2025). Ethical AI development requires proactive measures that protect young users while fostering environments that promote trust and fairness. Three areas stand out as particularly critical: algorithmic transparency, content moderation, and privacy-first design.

Transparent algorithms are essential to accountability. When algorithms shape the information young people see, the decisions that guide these processes must be clear (Pellegrino & Stasi, 2024). Developers are expected to disclose how algorithms are trained, what data is being used, and how outcomes are generated. Providing documentation and explanations not only prevents misuse but also helps identify and correct hidden biases that may disadvantage certain groups of youth (Ajiga et al., 2024; Obie et al., 2023). Transparency builds trust by enabling both users and guardians to understand the logic behind automated systems, reducing the sense of hidden manipulation.

Safe content moderation is equally important. Digital platforms expose youth to a wide range of content, much of which poses risks if not managed effectively (Quintas-Froufe et al., 2024). Developers, therefore, have an ethical duty to establish robust moderation systems that combine AI-based detection with human oversight (Aydın & Battal, 2025). Effective moderation requires timely responses to user reports and proactive identification of harmful or inappropriate material. At the same time, moderation must balance protection with respect for user rights, ensuring that systems adhere to community standards and legal frameworks without overstepping into unnecessary surveillance (Aydin, 2024; Miao, 2019).

Privacy-first design represents a third ethical pillar. Systems that prioritize privacy at the earliest stages of development minimize risks of data exploitation and build safeguards around sensitive information (Ibitoye et al., 2025). For minors, this principle is especially critical. Privacy by design requires collecting only the data that is strictly necessary, offering users control over their information, and ensuring compliance with regulations such as the General Data Protection Regulation (Alhazmi & Arachchilage, 2021; Obie et al., 2023).

Beyond technical design, developers also carry a responsibility to foster a culture of ethical awareness. Ongoing education, ethical training, and integrating ethical reflection into software development practices help maintain youth well-being as a priority (Patón-Romero & Løvås, 2022). By embedding ethical wisdom into everyday practices, the technology sector can move beyond innovation alone to create digital platforms that are both effective and safe (Griffin et al., 2024).

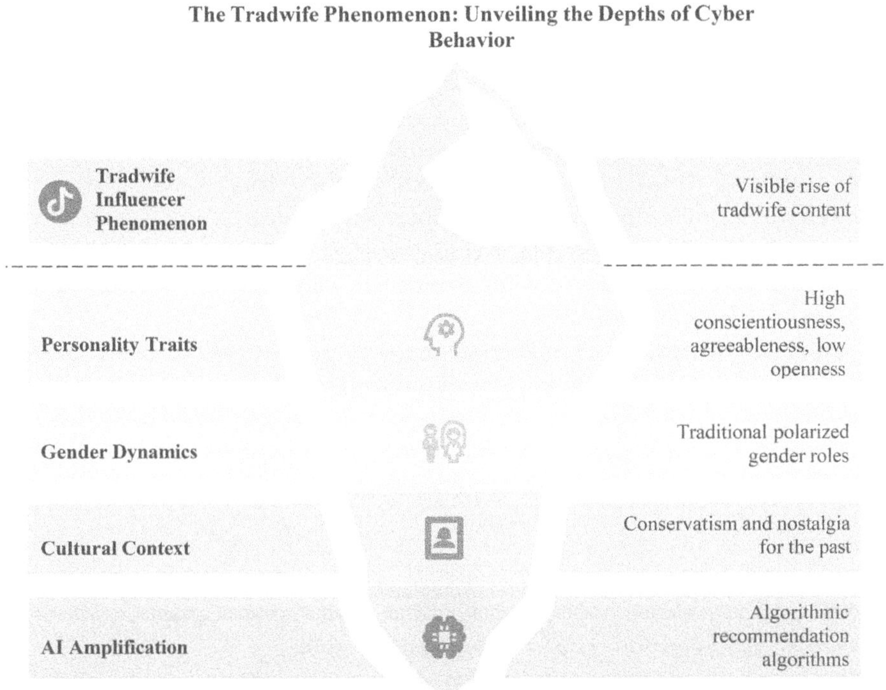

FIGURE 11.3 The tradwife phenomenon: Convergence of personality, gender, culture, and AI. This diagram illustrates how the tradwife influencer phenomenon emerges from the convergence of multiple factors. Individual personality traits (high conscientiousness and agreeableness, low openness) predispose individuals toward traditional lifestyles. These predispositions are then activated by cultural narratives emphasizing conservatism and nostalgia. Gender dynamics reinforce traditional roles and expectations. Finally, AI-driven algorithmic systems amplify this content through filter bubbles and recommendation algorithms, creating a powerful feedback loop that accelerates the movement's growth and reach.

SYNTHESIS CASE STUDY

The "Tradwife" Influencer Phenomenon

The rise of the "tradwife" (traditional wife) influencer phenomenon offers a compelling synthesis of the book's core themes (Figure 11.3). This movement, which promotes a return to traditional gender roles, illustrates the complex interplay of personality, gender, culture, and AI in shaping contemporary youth cyber behavior.

The phenomenon often attracts individuals with a personality profile characterized by high conscientiousness and agreeableness but low openness to experience, aligning with the structured and traditional lifestyle promoted. It is built on a foundation of highly polarized gender roles, resonating with young women seeking alternatives to modern feminism while also reinforcing rigid stereotypes. Culturally, the movement taps into a powerful undercurrent of conservatism and nostalgia, appealing to those with high uncertainty avoidance. Finally, AI-driven recommendation algorithms play a crucial role by creating powerful filter bubbles that amplify tradwife content, accelerating engagement, and creating a sense of widespread consensus.

Synthesis: The tradwife phenomenon is not simply a matter of individual choice; it is a complex ecosystem where psychological predispositions are activated by cultural narratives, reinforced by traditional gender roles, and amplified by AI-driven platforms. This case study demonstrates the urgent need for a multi-faceted approach to digital well-being that addresses not only individual psychology but also the cultural and technological systems that shape our online lives.

> ***Takeaway:*** *Developers must embed ethics into youth-facing AI systems, ensuring transparency, safety, and respect for young users' rights.*
> ***Reflection:*** *What ethical guardrails do you think are missing from the digital tools young people use today?*

11.6 Actionable Interventions for Youth Digital Well-being

Translating the insights from this book into practice requires developing targeted, evidence-based interventions. Although generic digital literacy programs are valuable, a more detailed approach is needed to address the specific vulnerabilities and opportunities related to personality, gender, and culture. Below are three examples of detailed, actionable interventions that can be implemented in educational and community settings.

11.6.1 An Empathy-Building Module for Young Men

Objective: To counter the normalization of aggression and emotional suppression in male-dominated cyberspaces by fostering empathetic communication and emotional intelligence.

Key Components

- *Scenario-Based Learning:* Participants engage with realistic, interactive scenarios depicting common online conflicts (e.g., toxic gaming chat, misogynistic memes, and cyberbullying). They are asked to consider the perspectives of all parties involved and to practice constructive, empathetic responses.

- *Emotional Vocabulary Building:* Many young men lack the vocabulary to articulate their own and others' emotions. This component involves exercises to identify and label a wider range of emotions beyond basic anger or frustration.
- *Peer-Led Dialogue:* Facilitated discussions with respected male role models (e.g., older students, community leaders) who can speak authentically about the pressures of online masculinity and the benefits of empathetic communication.
- *Focus on Action:* The module emphasizes concrete, prosocial actions, such as how to intervene as a bystander, how to report harmful content, and how to offer support to someone who is being targeted.

11.6.2 A Critical Digital Literacy Program for Young Women

Objective: To equip young women with the critical thinking skills needed to navigate the pressures of social comparison, body image, and online harassment.

Key Components

- *Algorithmic Awareness:* Participants learn how social media algorithms work, with a focus on how platforms like Instagram and TikTok create curated, unrealistic representations of beauty and success. This includes hands-on exercises to identify and analyze the algorithmic filtering in their own social media feeds.
- *Deconstructing Influencer Culture:* The program teaches participants to critically analyze the business models of influencer marketing, including the use of undisclosed ads, digital alterations, and parasocial relationships to build trust and drive consumption.
- *Digital Self-Defense:* This component provides practical strategies for dealing with online harassment, including privacy settings, blocking and reporting tools, and techniques for disengaging from toxic interactions.
- *Authentic Self-Expression:* The program encourages participants to develop their own authentic online voice, separate from the pressures of trends and social validation. This includes workshops on creating content that reflects their own values and interests, rather than simply replicating popular aesthetics.

11.6.3 A Culturally-Sensitive Resilience Program

Objective: To provide resilience-building strategies that are adapted to the specific cultural values and norms of the target community.

Key Components:

- *Collaborative Curriculum Design:* The program is co-designed with community leaders, parents, and youth to ensure that the content is culturally relevant and respectful.

- *Value-Aligned Strategies:* In collectivist cultures, the program might emphasize resilience through community support, shared responsibility, and seeking help from elders. In individualistic cultures, it might focus on self-reliance, personal goal-setting, and assertive communication.
- *Culturally-Relevant Scenarios:* The program uses scenarios and case studies that reflect the specific cultural challenges and opportunities faced by youth in that community.
- *Bilingual and Bicultural Facilitators:* The program is delivered by facilitators who can navigate the community's cultural nuances and create a safe, trusted space for dialogue.

Takeaway: *Effective Interventions move beyond generic digital literacy to address the specific needs of different groups. By tailoring programs to gender dynamics (empathy for males, critical literacy for females) and cultural context, we can build more targeted and effective digital resilience. This approach acknowledges that there is no one-size-fits-all solution to digital well-being.*
Reflection: *If these targeted interventions are more effective, what are schools' and educational institutions' responsibilities to move beyond generic programs and implement specialized, evidence-based digital literacy curricula?*

11.7 Practical Recommendations for Parents

Although schools and policymakers play a crucial role, parents remain on the front lines of guiding their children through the complexities of the digital world. The following recommendations provide practical, evidence-based strategies for fostering digital well-being at home.

First, rather than imposing top-down rules, parents should co-create a family media plan with their children. This collaborative process, which should cover not just screen time limits but also appropriate content, device usage rules, and consequences, fosters buy-in and teaches self-regulation (Zhang et al., 2025). Second, it is more effective to focus on a balanced "media diet" than to fixate solely on the quantity of screen time. A healthy media diet includes a mix of educational content, creative activities, social interaction, and entertainment; the goal is to help your child become a critical consumer of media, not just a passive one (Fitzpatrick et al., 2023; Ponti, 2023).

Furthermore, given the rapidly changing digital landscape, parents must have ongoing, open conversations about online life. Making these discussions a regular part of the family routine, with open-ended questions like, "What was the most interesting thing you saw online today?" can create a safe space for children to share their experiences (Mols et al., 2023; Νικολοπούλου, 2024). This approach is complemented by modeling healthy digital habits. Children learn more from what parents do than from what they say, and putting away phones during meals or limiting social media use serves as a powerful teaching tool (Ata-Aktürk & Akman, 2024).

Technology can also be used as a bridge, not a barrier. Playing a child's favorite video game or watching their favorite YouTuber not only builds the parent-child relationship but also provides a valuable window into their digital world (Νικολοπούλου, 2024). Throughout these interactions, it is essential to emphasize empathy and digital citizenship, regularly discussing the importance of kindness and respect online (Şimşek, 2025). Ultimately, while it is helpful to understand the technology, parents should focus on parenting. The core principles of communication, trust, empathy, and setting boundaries are just as important in the digital world as they are in the offline world (Sarwatay et al., 2021).

Takeaway: *The most effective parental guidance in the digital age is not about technological expertise but about applying timeless parenting principles to a new context. Co-creating media plans, having open conversations, and modeling healthy habits are more powerful than simply imposing rules. The goal is to foster self-regulation and critical thinking, not just compliance.*
Reflection: *How can parents shift their mindset from being a "digital police officer" focused on enforcement to a "digital mentor" focused on guidance and connection?*

11.8 Research and Innovation for the Future of Digital Well-being

Meeting the psychological and ethical challenges faced by young people in digital environments requires forward-looking research, adaptive frameworks, and innovative approaches. Future work must combine scientific rigor with creative collaboration to build systems that safeguard mental health while supporting ethical engagement.

Collaborative and interdisciplinary frameworks provide one path forward. Multidisciplinary teams that bring together psychologists, technologists, and ethicists can create solutions that no single discipline could achieve alone (Ogugua et al., 2024; Putica et al., 2025). Hackathons and similar collaborative platforms already demonstrate the potential of these models, fostering practical tools that anticipate risks and provide protection for youth in cyberspaces (Chernov et al., 2024).

Crowdsourcing and community participation represent another avenue for innovation. By involving wider communities, including youth themselves, research gains access to diverse perspectives and solutions (Davis et al., 2024; Magee et al., 2024). Approaches similar to those used in the Open Covid-19 initiative highlight how participatory design can empower young people to shape social media features, privacy protocols, and educational tools that reflect their lived needs (Kokshagina, 2021).

Citizen science and big data analytics hold promise for deepening the understanding of youth cyber behavior. Gathering large-scale behavioral data through participatory methods allows for the detection of patterns in psychological well-being, risk exposure, and coping strategies (Davis et al., 2024). Adaptive models informed by such data could improve the precision of interventions, making it possible to target support where it is most needed (Johnston et al., 2022).

Ethical AI integration is also a pressing research frontier. Developing collaborative governance models and embedding ethical design into AI systems ensures that digital platforms contribute positively to well-being while safeguarding privacy and fairness (Lee & Žarnic, 2024; Lubis et al., 2024). This work not only addresses immediate risks but also lays the foundation for trust between youth and technology (Lee & Žarnic, 2024).

Deep learning and other advanced AI techniques can further optimize support systems (Akintoye et al., 2023). Hybrid approaches, such as federated and transfer learning, offer dynamic adaptation to user interactions, enabling educational and psychological platforms to evolve alongside youth needs. These models have the potential to deliver personalized care and learning at scale (Talaei Khoei et al., 2023).

Digital sustainability initiatives highlight a broader perspective. Research linking technological innovation to sustainable development goals demonstrates how online platforms can promote mental health alongside wider social progress (Hameed et al., 2024; Ogugua et al., 2024). By aligning youth-focused digital

TABLE 11.5 Research Directions for Youth Digital Well-Being

Research Path	*Focus*	*Contribution to Youth Well-Being*
Collaborative and Interdisciplinary Frameworks	Multidisciplinary collaboration across psychology, technology, and ethics	Development of protective and proactive digital tools
Crowdsourcing and Community Participation	Engaging youth and communities in participatory design of platforms and tools	Inclusive solutions that reflect youth perspectives and needs
Citizen Science and Big Data Analytics	Large-scale behavioral data collection to predict risks and guide interventions	Targeted interventions informed by behavioral trends
Ethical AI and Technology Integration	Embedding ethical governance and privacy into AI system design	Trusted systems that safeguard privacy and fairness
Deep Learning and Artificial Intelligence	Personalized and adaptive learning or support through hybrid AI models	Dynamic platforms that adapt to user needs in real time
Digital Sustainability Initiatives	Aligning digital innovation with sustainable development and mental health goals	Digital environments that are safe, ethical, and socially responsible

environments with principles of sustainability, platforms can become not only safer but also socially responsible spaces (George et al., 2020). Through these approaches (see Table 11.5), research and innovation can continue to adapt to the shifting realities of youth engagement online. The goal is not simply to reduce risk but to create environments that actively contribute to resilience, inclusion, and ethical growth.

> ***Takeaway:*** *Continued research and innovation are key to protecting youth and enhancing their resilience in an AI-driven world.*
> ***Reflection:*** *What future innovations could improve how youth experience digital spaces in terms of mental health and ethics?*

11.9 Summary and Reflections

This chapter has examined the interplay between personality traits, gender, culture, and technology in shaping youth experiences online. The evidence shows that young people's resilience in digital environments is neither uniform nor accidental; it is mediated by psychological dispositions, cultural context, and the design of technological systems. Recognizing these factors is essential for promoting digital well-being and ensuring that youth engage with AI and online platforms in ways that are safe, ethical, and empowering.

Personality emerged as a critical lens for understanding digital resilience. Traits from both the HEXACO and Big Five frameworks illustrate how some dispositions, such as conscientiousness and agreeableness, provide protection, while others, including neuroticism or low honesty-humility, heighten vulnerability. The Dark Tetrad traits further highlight risks where tendencies toward manipulation, aggression, or cruelty can translate into harmful online behaviors. These findings underscore the value of tailoring interventions, such as resilience training, digital literacy, or empathy-building, to specific psychological profiles.

Gender-based patterns add another layer of complexity. Males often benefit from competitive and performance-driven environments, while females are more responsive to collaborative and socially supportive platforms. Yet these same tendencies expose youth to distinct vulnerabilities, such as safety concerns for females and the normalization of aggression among males. Gender-aware strategies, ranging from balanced gamification to stronger safety features, can enhance engagement while mitigating risks.

Cultural context also exerts a strong influence. Individualist societies tend to align resilience with traits like openness and extraversion, promoting independence and adaptability. Collectivist cultures, by contrast, emphasize conscientiousness and agreeableness, fostering resilience through interdependence and shared responsibility. These variations demonstrate that resilience-building interventions must be adapted to cultural frameworks rather than applied as universal models.

Alongside psychological and cultural factors, the design of youth-facing platforms carries ethical weight. Developers have clear obligations to build transparency into algorithms, enforce robust content moderation, and embed privacy-first design principles. These safeguards are not optional enhancements but foundational requirements for protecting young users' rights and ensuring safe participation in digital spaces.

Finally, the chapter highlighted the need for research and innovation to anticipate emerging challenges. Interdisciplinary collaboration, crowdsourcing, citizen science, ethical AI design, and sustainable digital practices offer pathways to create environments that evolve alongside youth needs. These initiatives demonstrate that ethical responsibility and technological progress can be pursued together, producing systems that are adaptive, inclusive, and trustworthy.

Takeaway: *Building ethical, resilient digital environments for youth requires ongoing effort, tailored strategies, and cultural sensitivity.*
Reflection: *What is one area where more attention or innovation is urgently needed to protect youth in digital spaces?*

References

Ajiga, D., Okeleke, P. A., Folorunsho, S. O., & Ezeigweneme, C. (2024). Enhancing software development practices with AI insights in high-tech companies. *Computer Science & IT Research Journal, 5*(8), 1897–1919. https://doi.org/10.51594/csitrj.v5i8.1450

Akintoye, O. S., Sanusi, H. M., Yusuf, R. A., & Odondi, A. A. (2023). Early detection of adolescent mental health risk using transformer models on social media datasets. *Journal of Frontiers in Multidisciplinary Research, 4*(1), 435–445. https://doi.org/10.54660/.jfmr.2023.4.1.435-445

Alavi, M., Garg, A., & Wanigatunga, N. (2025). The relationships between Dark Tetrad traits and adolescent cyberbullying and cybertrolling with online time and life satisfaction as moderators. *Discover Psychology, 5*(1). https://doi.org/10.1007/s44202-025-00351-6

Alhazmi, A., & Arachchilage, N. A. G. (2021). I'm all ears! Listening to software developers on putting GDPR principles into software development practice. *Personal and Ubiquitous Computing, 25*, 879–892. https://doi.org/10.1007/s00779-021-01544-1

Almulla, M. O., Alismail, A. M., Mahama, I., & Almulla, A. A. (2025). Resilience as a predictor of internet addictive behaviours: A study among Ghanaian and Saudi samples using structural equation modelling approach. *BMC Psychology, 13*(1), 77. https://doi.org/10.1186/s40359-025-02383-y

Anamika, Rabbani, S., & Perwej, Y. (2024). AI-Counsellor using emerging technique. *International Journal of Scientific Research in Science and Technology, 11*(3), 749–759. https://doi.org/10.32628/ijsrst24113237

Ata-Aktürk, A., & Akman, M. B. (2024). What happens beyond the Screen? Uncovering digital technology perception, usage, and parental mediation among 3–6-year-old Turkish children. *Journal of Child and Family Studies, 33*(10), 3191–3210. https://doi.org/10.1007/s10826-024-02888-x

Athota, V. S., Budhwar, P., & Malik, A. (2019). Influence of personality traits and moral values on employee well-being, resilience and performance: A cross-national study. *Applied Psychology*, *69*(3), 653–685. https://doi.org/10.1111/apps.12198

Aydin, İ. (2024). Ethical issues in educational technology. *Kastamonu Eğitim Dergisi*, 861–881. https://doi.org/10.24106/kefdergi.1426735

Aydın, K. E., & Battal, F. (2025). Can social media challenges determine life or death? Two adolescent cases from the pediatric intensive care unit. *Turkish Journal of Pediatric Emergency and Intensive Care Medicine*. https://doi.org/10.4274/cayd.galenos.2025.16768

Baiocco, R., Chirumbolo, A., Bianchi, D., Ioverno, S., Morelli, M., & Nappa, M. R. (2017). How HEXACO personality praits predict different selfie-posting behaviors among adolescents and young adults. *Frontiers in Psychology*, *7*. https://doi.org/10.3389/fpsyg.2016.02080

Baker, R. S., Richey, J. E., Zhang, J., Karumbaiah, S., Andres-Bray, J. M., Nguyen, H. A., Andres, J. M. a. L., & McLaren, B. M. (2024). Gaming the system mediates the relationship between gender and learning outcomes in a digital learning game. *Instructional Science*, *53*(2), 203–238. https://doi.org/10.1007/s11251-024-09679-3

Balcerowska, J. M., Sawicki, A., & Zajenkowski, M. (2024). A longitudinal study on the reciprocal relationship between narcissism and social Networking Sites addiction. *Journal of Research in Personality*, *114*, 104566. https://doi.org/10.1016/j.jrp.2024.104566

Bhutani, V., Bahadur, P. S., Sansaniwal, S. K., & Bais, P. (Eds.). (2024). Youth studes in the AI era. In *Advances in human and social aspects of technology book series* (pp. 393–413). https://doi.org/10.4018/979-8-3693-3350-1.ch022

Brown, W. M., Hazraty, S., & Palasinski, M. (2019). Examining the Dark Tetrad and its links to cyberbullying. *Cyberpsychology Behavior and Social Networking*, *22*(8), 552–557. https://doi.org/10.1089/cyber.2019.0172

Buchan, M. C., Bhawra, J., & Katapally, T. R. (2024). Navigating the digital world: Development of an evidence-based digital literacy program and assessment tool for youth. *Smart Learning Environments*, *11*(1). https://doi.org/10.1186/s40561-024-00293-x

Carcelén-García, S., Narros-González, M. J., & Galmes-Cerezo, M. (2023). Digital vulnerability in young people: Gender, age and online participation patterns. *International Journal of Adolescence and Youth*, *28*(1). https://doi.org/10.1080/02673843.2023.2287115

Chang, J. P., Cheng, S., Chang, S. M., & Su, K. (2025). Navigating the Digital Maze: A review of AI bias, social media, and mental health in Generation Z. *AI*, *6*(6), 118. https://doi.org/10.3390/ai6060118

Chen, W., Yuan, T., Pan, Y., Ma, Y., Sun, B., Yu, M., Lin, X., He, H., & Zhang, J. (2024). Borderline personality traits mediate the relationship between negative life events and nonsuicidal self-injury in a clinical sample with youth depression. *BMC Psychiatry*, *24*(1). https://doi.org/10.1186/s12888-024-05821-0

Chernov, I., Elsler, M., Maillart, T., Cacciatori, C., Tavazzi, S., Gawlik, B. M., Vystavna, Y., Anastasaki, A., DuBois, C., Warner, S., Neely, M. B., Muziasari, W., Christ, K., Abrate, T., Salyani, A., & Sullivan, T. (2024). Innovative solutions for global water quality challenges: Insights from a collaborative hackathon event. *Frontiers in Water*, *6*. https://doi.org/10.3389/frwa.2024.1363116

Chi, H., Liu, R., & Pan, J. (2022). Users' behaviour under the uneven gender ratio of social media platforms. *SHS Web of Conferences*, *148*, 03003. https://doi.org/10.1051/shsconf/202214803003

Ciren, Z., Tsui, H. K. H., & Chan, S. K. W. (2025). Effects of resilience interventions for adolescents and young adults without psychiatric diagnoses: A systematic review and network meta-analysis of randomized controlled trials. *Adolescent Research Review*. https://doi.org/10.1007/s40894-025-00270-6

Congiu, L., Moscati, I., & Scacchi, M. (2024). Digital nudging and cookie rejection: An experiment. *Italian Economic Journal*, *11*(1), 431–458. https://doi.org/10.1007/s40797-024-00268-4

Craig, S. L., Eaton, A. D., McInroy, L. B., D'Souza, S. A., Krishnan, S., Wells, G. A., Twum-Siaw, L., & Leung, V. W. Y. (2019). Navigating negativity: A grounded theory and integrative mixed methods investigation of how sexual and gender minority youth cope with negative comments online. *Psychology and Sexuality*, *11*(3), 161–179. https://doi.org/10.1080/19419899.2019.1665575

Davey, M., Eaker, D. G., & Walters, L. H. (2003). Resilience processes in adolescents: Personality profiles, Self-Worth, and coping. *Journal of Adolescent Research*, *18*(4), 347–362. https://doi.org/10.1177/0743558403018004002

Davis, K., Anderson, M., Yang, C., Choukas-Bradley, S., Bell, B. T., & Slovak, P. (2024). Cross-disciplinary perspectives on youth digital well-being research: Identifying notable developments, persistent gaps, and future directions. *Journal of Adolescent Research*, *40*(2), 259–295. https://doi.org/10.1177/07435584241291163

Duan, S. X., & Deng, H. (2023). Job performance in digital work: Do personality traits matter? *Journal of Computer Information Systems*, 1–13. https://doi.org/10.1080/08874417.2023.2255551

Eley, D. S., Cloninger, C. R., Walters, L., Laurence, C., Synnott, R., & Wilkinson, D. (2013). The relationship between resilience and personality traits in doctors: Implications for enhancing well being. *PeerJ*, *1*, e216. https://doi.org/10.7717/peerj.216

ElSayary, A., Calmaestra, J. & Gómez-López, M. (2026). The association between cyber behaviors and hedonic and eudaimonic well-being: the moderating role of personality traits. *BMC Psychology*. https://doi.org/10.1186/s40359-025-03812-8

Evangelou, S. M., Michanetzi, E. L., & Xenos, M. (2024). Exploring the impact of negative online feedback on well-being: A comprehensive analysis incorporating Big-Five personality traits and physiological responses. *Computers in Human Behavior Reports*, *15*, 100457. https://doi.org/10.1016/j.chbr.2024.100457

Favini, A., Gerbino, M., Pastorelli, C., Zuffianò, A., Lunetti, C., Remondi, C., Cirimele, F., Plata, M. G., & Giannini, A. M. (2023). Bullying and cyberbullying: Do personality profiles matter in adolescence? *Telematics and Informatics Reports*, *12*, 100108. https://doi.org/10.1016/j.teler.2023.100108

Figueroa, C. A., Ramos, G., Psihogios, A. M., Ekuban, E., Bansie, P., De Haas, M., Karnik, N. S., Ajilore, O., Anderson, E. E., & Stiles-Shields, C. (2025). Advancing youth co-design of ethical guidelines for AI-powered digital mental health tools. *Nature Mental Health*, *3*(8), 870–878. https://doi.org/10.1038/s44220-025-00467-7

Fiske, A., Henningsen, P., & Buyx, A. (2019). Your robot therapist will see you now: Ethical Implications of Embodied Artificial intelligence in Psychiatry, Psychology, and Psychotherapy. *Journal of Medical Internet Research*, *21*(5), e13216. https://doi.org/10.2196/13216

Fitzpatrick, C., Binet, M., Cristini, E., Almeida, M. L., Bégin, M., & Frizzo, G. B. (2023). Reducing harm and promoting positive media use strategies: New perspectives in understanding the impact of preschooler media use on health and development. *Psicologia Reflexão E Crítica*, *36*(1), 19. https://doi.org/10.1186/s41155-023-00262-2

Gajda, A., Moroń, M., Królik, M., Małuch, M., & Mraczek, M. (2022). The Dark Tetrad, cybervictimization, and cyberbullying: The role of moral disengagement. *Current Psychology*, *42*(27), 23413–23421. https://doi.org/10.1007/s12144-022-03456-6

Galla, B. M., & Wood, J. J. (2013). Trait Self-Control predicts adolescents' exposure and reactivity to daily stressful events. *Journal of Personality*, *83*(1), 69–83. https://doi.org/10.1111/jopy.12083

Gardner, K. J., Archer, J., & Jackson, S. (2012). Does maladaptive coping mediate the relationship between borderline personality traits and reactive and proactive aggression? *Aggressive Behavior*, *38*(5), 403–413. https://doi.org/10.1002/ab.21437

George, G., Merrill, R. K., & Schillebeeckx, S. J. D. (2020). Digital sustainability and entrepreneurship: How digital innovations are helping tackle climate change and sustainable development. *Entrepreneurship Theory and Practice*, *45*(5), 999–1027. https://doi.org/10.1177/1042258719899425

Gholami, M., Thornberg, R., Kabiri, S., & Yousefvand, S. (2025). From dark triad personality traits to digital harm: Mediating cyberbullying through online moral disengagement. *Deviant Behavior*, 1–19. https://doi.org/10.1080/01639625.2025.2453445

Gneezy, U., Niederle, M., & Rustichini, A. (2003). Performance in competitive environments: Gender differences. *The Quarterly Journal of Economics, 118*(3), 1049–1074. https://doi.org/10.1162/00335530360698496

Griffin, T. A., Green, B. P., & Welie, J. V. (2024). The ethical wisdom of AI developers. *AI And Ethics*. https://doi.org/10.1007/s43681-024-00458-x

Gugushvili, N., Täht, K., Ruiter, R. A. C., & Verduyn, P. (2022). Facebook use intensity and depressive symptoms: A moderated mediation model of problematic Facebook use, age, neuroticism, and extraversion. *BMC Psychology*, *10*(1), 279. https://doi.org/10.1186/s40359-022-00990-7

Hamamoto, Y., Honda, A., Miura, N., Tanabe-Ishibashi, A., Oba, K., Ishibashi, R., & Sugiura, M. (2023). Five major outcomes of digitalization: Relevance of a survival personality type during COVID-19 pandemic. *Frontiers in Psychology*, *14*, 1230192. https://doi.org/10.3389/fpsyg.2023.1230192

Hameed, K., Naha, R., & Hameed, F. (2024). Digital transformation for sustainable health and well-being: A review and future research directions. *Discover Sustainability*, *5*(1). https://doi.org/10.1007/s43621-024-00273-8

Hong, S. H., Chun, T. K., Nam, Y. J., Kim, T. W., Cho, Y. H., Son, S. J., Roh, H. W., & Hong, C. H. (2025). Digital mental health interventions for adolescents: An Integrative review based on the Behavior Change approach. *Children*, *12*(6), 770. https://doi.org/10.3390/children12060770

Huang, W., Cai, S., Zhou, Y., Huang, J., Sun, X., Su, Y., Dai, M., & Lan, Y. (2021). Personality profiles and personal factors associated with psychological distress in Chinese nurses. *Psychology Research and Behavior Management*, *14*, 1567–1579. https://doi.org/10.2147/prbm.s329036

Hylkilä, K., Kääriäinen, M., Peltonen, A., Castrén, S., Mustonen, T., Konttila, J., & Männikkö, N. (2025). Young adults' risk profiles and predictive factors of Problematic Social Media Use (PSMU): A cross-sectional study. *Current Psychology*, *44*(8), 6848–6862. https://doi.org/10.1007/s12144-025-07662-w

Ibitoye, A. O., Nkwo, M. S., & Orji, R. (2025). Rethinking responsible AI from ethical pillars to sociotechnical practice. *AI And Ethics*, *5*(6), 6207–6223. https://doi.org/10.1007/s43681-025-00809-2

Ike, O. O., Nwufo, I. J., & Adubi, P. C. (2024). The mental health of family caregivers: Do the complementary roles of personality trait, social support, and resilience matter? *Palliative Medicine in Practice*, *18*(4), 207–219. https://doi.org/10.5603/pmp.99443

Joerin, A., Rauws, M., Fulmer, R., & Black, V. (2020). Ethical artificial intelligence for digital health organizations. *Cureus*. https://doi.org/10.7759/cureus.7202
Johnston, A., Matechou, E., & Dennis, E. B. (2022). Outstanding challenges and future directions for biodiversity monitoring using citizen science data. *Methods in Ecology and Evolution*, *14*(1), 103–116. https://doi.org/10.1111/2041-210x.13834
Joseph, A. P., & Babu, A. (2024). The unseen dilemma of AI in mental healthcare. *AI & Society*, *40*(3), 1533–1535. https://doi.org/10.1007/s00146-024-01937-9
Joshi, A., Das, S., & Sekar, S. (2023). How big five personality traits affect information and communication technology use: A meta-analysis. *AJIS. Australasian Journal of Information Systems/AJIS. Australian Journal of Information Systems/Australian Journal of Information Systems*, *27*. https://doi.org/10.3127/ajis.v27i0.3985
Khoei, T. T., Slimane, H. O., & Kaabouch, N. (2023). Deep learning: Systematic review, models, challenges, and research directions. *Neural Computing and Applications*, *35*(31), 23103–23124. https://doi.org/10.1007/s00521-023-08957-4
Ko, C., & Kim, S. (2024). Adolescent female users' avatar creation in social virtual worlds: Opportunities and challenges. *Behavioral Sciences*, *14*(7), 539. https://doi.org/10.3390/bs14070539
Kokshagina, O. (2021). Open Covid-19: Organizing an extreme crowdsourcing campaign to tackle grand challenges. *R and D Management*, *52*(2), 206–219. https://doi.org/10.1111/radm.12470
Kurian, N. (2025). Developmentally aligned AI: A framework for translating the science of child development into AI design. *AI Brain and Child*, *1*(1). https://doi.org/10.1007/s44436-025-00009-z
Lawton, C. A., & Kallai, J. (2002). Gender differences in wayfinding strategies and anxiety about wayfinding: A cross-cultural comparison. *Sex Roles*, *47*(9/10), 389–401. https://doi.org/10.1023/a:1021668724970
Lee, J., & Žarnic, Ž. (2024). The impact of digital technologies on well-being. In *OECD Papers on Well-being and Inequalities*. https://doi.org/10.1787/cb173652-en
Leech, T., Dorstyn, D., Taylor, A., & Li, W. (2021). Mental health apps for adolescents and young adults: A systematic review of randomised controlled trials. *Children and Youth Services Review*, *127*, 106073. https://doi.org/10.1016/j.childyouth.2021.106073
Lewis, C. C., Taba, M., Allen, T. B., Caldwell, P. H., Skinner, S. R., Kang, M., Henderson, H., Bray, L., Borthwick, M., Collin, P., McCaffery, K., & Scott, K. M. (2024). Developing an educational resource aimed at improving adolescent digital health literacy: Using Co-Design as research methodology. *Journal of Medical Internet Research*, *26*, e49453. https://doi.org/10.2196/49453
Li, L., Yuan, X., Lin, L., Xiao, A., Chen, Y., Xia, Y., & Huang, X. (2025). A gender comparison based network analysis for social media addiction behaviors in cross-cultural contexts. *Scientific Reports*, *15*(1), 38925. https://doi.org/10.1038/s41598-025-22796-4
Lippa, R. A., & Tan, F. D. (2001). Does culture moderate the relationship between sexual orientation and Gender-Related personality traits? *Cross-Cultural Research*, *35*(1), 65–87. https://doi.org/10.1177/106939710103500104
Liu, Y., Wu, Y. C., Fu, H., Guo, W. Y., & Wang, X. (2023). Digital intervention in improving the outcomes of mental health among LGBTQ+ youth: A systematic review. *Frontiers in Psychology*, *14*. https://doi.org/10.3389/fpsyg.2023.1242928
Lubis, S., Purnomo, E. P., Lado, J. A., & Hung, C. (2024). Electronic governance in advancing sustainable development goals through systematic literature review. *Discover Global Society*, *2*(1). https://doi.org/10.1007/s44282-024-00102-3

Maftei, A., Holman, A., & Elenescu, A. (2022). The dark web of machiavellianism and psychopathy: Moral disengagement in IT organizations. *Europe's Journal of Psychology, 18*(2), 181–192. https://doi.org/10.5964/ejop.4011

Magee, R. M., Leman, A. M., & Balasubramaniam, G. (2024). Amplifying youth voices using digital technology: A case study in collaborative research with youth service organizations. *Journal of Participatory Research Methods, 5*(1). https://doi.org/10.35844/001c.92282

Malloy, J., Partridge, S. R., Kemper, J. A., Braakhuis, A., & Roy, R. (2023). Co-design of digital health interventions with young people: A scoping review. *Digital Health, 9*, 20552076231219117. https://doi.org/10.1177/20552076231219117

Mansoor, M., Hamide, A., & Tran, T. (2025). Conversational AI in pediatric mental health: A narrative review. *Children, 12*(3), 359. https://doi.org/10.3390/children12030359

Marshall, N. J., Loades, M. E., Jacobs, C., Biddle, L., & Lambert, J. D. (2025). Integrating Artificial intelligence in youth Mental health care: Advances, challenges, and future directions. *Current Treatment Options in Psychiatry, 12*(1). https://doi.org/10.1007/s40501-025-00348-x

Martín-Martín, M., & Bueno-Álvarez, J. A. (2023). Social networks and aggressive attitudes: Who is who. Scoping review of the scientific production on their relationships. *Frontiers in Psychology, 14*, 1249907. https://doi.org/10.3389/fpsyg.2023.1249907

Mayiwar, L., Asutay, E., Tinghög, G., Västfjäll, D., & Barrafrem, K. (2024). Determinants of digital well-being. *AI & Society, 40*(4), 3063–3073. https://doi.org/10.1007/s00146-024-02071-2

Mellado, R., Cubillos, C., Vicari, R. M., & Gasca-Hurtado, G. (2024). Leveraging gamification in ICT education: Examining gender differences and learning outcomes in programming courses. *Applied Sciences, 14*(17), 7933. https://doi.org/10.3390/app14177933

Miao, Z. (2019). Investigation on human rights ethics in artificial intelligence researches with library literature analysis method. *The Electronic Library, 37*(5), 914–926. https://doi.org/10.1108/el-04-2019-0089

Molero, M. M., Pérez-Fuentes, M. C., Martos, Á., Pino, R. M., & Gázquez, J. J. (2023). Network analysis of emotional symptoms and their relationship with different types of cybervictimization. *The European Journal of Psychology Applied to Legal Context, 15*(1), 23–32. https://doi.org/10.5093/ejpalc2023a3

Mols, A., Campos, J. P., & Pridmore, J. (2023). Family surveillance: Understanding parental monitoring, reciprocal practices, and digital resilience. *Surveillance & Society, 21*(4), 469–484. https://doi.org/10.24908/ss.v21i4.15645

Nikolopoulou, K. (2024). Children in the digital space: Issues researched and suggestions for future research. *Creative Education, 15*(05), 815–827. https://doi.org/10.4236/ce.2024.155049

Obie, H. O., Ukwella, J., Madampe, K., Grundy, J., & Shahin, M. (2023). *Towards an Understanding of Developers' Perceptions of Transparency in Software Development: A Preliminary Study* (pp. 40–45). 2023 38th IEEE/ACM International Conference on Automated Software Engineering Workshops (ASEW). https://doi.org/10.1109/asew60602.2023.00010

Ogugua, J. O., Okongwu, C. C., Akomolafe, O. O., Anyanwu, E. C., & Daraojimba, O. D. (2024). Mental health and digital technology: A public health review of current trends and responses. *International Medical Science Research Journal, 4*(2), 108–125. https://doi.org/10.51594/imsrj.v4i2.754

Olawade, D. B., Wada, O. Z., Odetayo, A., David-Olawade, A. C., Asaolu, F., & Eberhardt, J. (2024). Enhancing mental health with artificial intelligence: Current trends and future prospects. *Journal of Medicine, Surgery, and Public Health, 3*, Article 100099. https://doi.org/10.1016/j.glmedi.2024.100099

Olorunfemi, O. L., Amoo, O. O., Atadoga, A., Fayayola, O. A., Abrahams, T. O., & Shoetan, P. O. (2024). Towards a conceptual framework or ethical AI development in It systems. *Computer Science & IT Research Journal, 5*(3), 616–627. https://doi.org/10.51594/csitrj.v5i3.910

Opie, J. E., Vuong, A., Welsh, E. T., Esler, T. B., Khan, U. R., & Khalil, H. (2024). Outcomes of best-practice guided digital mental health interventions for youth and young adults with emerging symptoms: Part II. A systematic review of user experience outcomes. *Clinical Child and Family Psychology Review, 27*(2), 476–508. https://doi.org/10.1007/s10567-024-00468-5

Pandya, A., Lodha, P., & Ganatra, A. (2024). Is ChatGPT ready to change mental healthcare? Challenges and considerations: A reality-check. *Frontiers in Human Dynamics, 5*. https://doi.org/10.3389/fhumd.2023.1289255

Patón-Romero, J. D., & Løvås, I. V. (2022). A proposal to develop software to prevent young people to acquire extremist beliefs. *European Journal of Sustainable Development, 11*(4), 158. https://doi.org/10.14207/ejsd.2022.v11n4p158

Pellegrino, A., & Stasi, A. (2024). A bibliometric analysis of the impact of media manipulation on adolescent mental health: Policy recommendations for algorithmic transparency. *Online Journal of Communication and Media Technologies, 14*(4), e202453. https://doi.org/10.30935/ojcmt/15143

Ponti, M. (2023). Screen time and preschool children: Promoting health and development in a digital world. *Paediatrics & Child Health, 28*(3), 184–192. https://doi.org/10.1093/pch/pxac125

Putica, A., Khanna, R., Bosl, W., Saraf, S., & Edgcomb, J. (2025). Ethical decision-making for AI in mental health: The integrated ethical approach for computational psychiatry (IEACP) framework. *Psychological Medicine, 55*, e213. https://doi.org/10.1017/s0033291725101311

Quintas-Froufe, N., González-Neira, A., & Fiaño-Salinas, C. (2024). Corporate policies to protect against disinformation for young audiences: The case of TikTok. *Frontiers in Communication, 9*. https://doi.org/10.3389/fcomm.2024.1410100

Romero, E., & Alonso, C. (2019). Maladaptative personality traits in adolescence: Behavioural, emotional and motivational correlates of the PID-5-BF scales. *Psicothema, 3*(31), 263–270. https://doi.org/10.7334/psicothema2019.86

Sarwatay, D., Raman, U., & Ramasubramanian, S. (2021). Media literacy, social connectedness, and digital citizenship in India: Mapping stakeholders on how parents and young people navigate a social world. *Frontiers in Human Dynamics, 3*. https://doi.org/10.3389/fhumd.2021.601239

Sebastião, S. P., & Dias, D. F. (2025). AI Transparency: A conceptual, normative, and practical frame analysis. *Media and Communication, 13*. https://doi.org/10.17645/mac.9419

Shen, C., Ratan, R., Cai, Y. D., & Leavitt, A. (2016). Do men advance faster than women? debunking the gender performance gap in two massively multiplayer online games. *Journal of Computer-Mediated Communication, 21*(4), 312–329. https://doi.org/10.1111/jcc4.12159

Şimşek, E. E. (2025). The use of digital technology by parents from the perspective of children. *Turkish Academic Research Review - Türk Akademik Araştırmalar Dergisi [TARR], 10*(1), 54–69. https://doi.org/10.30622/tarr.1603562

Singh, R., Khanal, P., Tol, W. A., Jefferies, P., Jordans, M. J. D., & Lund, C. (2025). Exploring the role of resilience in selective prevention intervention for adolescents at risk of depression and anxiety in Nepal: Findings from a pilot cluster randomized controlled trial. *Child and Adolescent Psychiatry and Mental Health, 19*(1), 103. https://doi.org/10.1186/s13034-025-00964-8

Srivastava, S. C., Chandra, S., & Shirish, A. (2015). Technostress creators and job outcomes: Theorising the moderating influence of personality traits. *Information Systems Journal, 25*(4), 355–401. https://doi.org/10.1111/isj.12067

Su, P. (2023). Gender-Inclusive urban design: Insights from eye-tracking research. *Academic Journal of Humanities & Social Sciences, 6*(24). https://doi.org/10.25236/ajhss.2023.062419

Sun, Y., Cao, C., Tang, Z., Huang, F., Zhong, X., & Chen, I. (2025). Moral disengagement as mediator and guilt as moderator between cyber moral literacy and cyberbullying among late adolescents. *Scientific Reports, 15*(1), 43. https://doi.org/10.1038/s41598-024-83911-5

Terracciano, A., & McCrae, R. R. (2006). Cross-cultural studies of personality traits and their relevance to psychiatry. *Epidemiologia E Psichiatria Sociale, 15*(3), 176–184. https://doi.org/10.1017/s1121189x00004425

Terrana, A., & Al-Delaimy, W. (2023). A systematic review of cross-cultural measures of resilience and its promotive and protective factors. *Transcultural Psychiatry, 60*(4), 733–750. https://doi.org/10.1177/13634615231167661

Theophilou, E., Hernández-Leo, D., & Gómez, V. (2023). Gender-based learning and behavioural differences in an educational social media platform. *Journal of Computer Assisted Learning, 40*(6), 2544–2557. https://doi.org/10.1111/jcal.12927

Vázquez-Cano, E., Ramírez-Hurtado, J. M., Díez-Arcón, P., & Pascual-Moscoso, C. (2022). Academic and social behaviour profile of the primary school students who possess and play video games. *Child Indicators Research, 16*(1), 227–245. https://doi.org/10.1007/s12187-022-09975-9

Wang, L. (2022). The effects of cyberbullying victimization and personality characteristics on adolescent mental health: An application of the stress process model. *Youth & Society, 54*(6), 935–956. https://doi.org/10.1177/0044118X211008927

Wahed, M. A., Alqaraleh, M., Alzboon, M. S., & Al-Batah, M. S. (2024). AI RX: Revolutionizing healthcare through intelligence, innovation, and ethics. *Deleted Journal, 4*, 35. https://doi.org/10.56294/mw202535

Zhang, Y., Zhang, J., Yu, X., Zhang, J., Xu, Y., & Cui, H. (2025). The impact of electronic product use on children with tic disorders and ADHD, and management strategies: A review. *Frontiers in Psychiatry, 16*, 1665047. https://doi.org/10.3389/fpsyt.2025.1665047

Zhou, X., Edirippulige, S., Bai, X., & Bambling, M. (2021). Are online mental health interventions for youth effective? A systematic review. *Journal of Telemedicine and Telecare, 27*(10), 638–666. https://doi.org/10.1177/1357633x211047285

Zimmermann, D., Wehler, A., & Kaspar, K. (2022). Self-representation through avatars in digital environments. *Current Psychology, 42*(25), 21775–21789. https://doi.org/10.1007/s12144-022-03232-6

12

FUTURE DIRECTIONS IN CYBERPSYCHOLOGY, AI ETHICS, AND DIGITAL WELL-BEING

Chapter Objectives

- To explore upcoming trends in cyberpsychology and ethical AI development.
- To assess the future psychological impacts of AI in social media, education, and mental health tools.
- To emphasize the role of personality and gender in shaping youth responses to digital environments.
- To propose forward-thinking, ethical, and personalized strategies for enhancing digital well-being.

Topics to Be Covered

- Introduction: Where Are We Headed?
- AI in Social Media: Identity, Influence, and Engagement
- Reimagining AI in Education: Personalized Futures and Ethical Dilemmas
- Personality in 2035: Traits as Predictors of Adaptation and Risk
- Gendered Futures: Online Risk and Opportunity
- Designing the Future: Proactive Ethical Frameworks
- Two Futures: A Utopian and Dystopian Vision for 2035
- Summary and Reflections

DOI: 10.4324/9781003657590-16

12.1 Introduction: Where Are We Headed?

The pace of digital transformation has accelerated in recent years, with industries integrating advanced technologies such as industrial artificial intelligence (AI), edge computing, and the Internet of Things. A striking example is Industrie 4.0, which has reshaped the manufacturing sector by emphasizing human-centered, data-driven value creation, the development of innovative business models, and the adoption of agile organizational structures (Kagermann & Wahlster, 2022). Within this framework, connectivity between machines has become central, supported by developments such as team robotics and autonomous intralogistics systems (Franzè et al., 2023). These innovations are not only driving efficiency but are also contributing to the construction of resilient and sustainable systems (Kagermann & Wahlster, 2022).

Such progress inevitably raises the question of ethics in technological deployment. The development of AI requires careful attention to principles of safety, responsibility, and societal benefit (Konidena et al., 2024). Ethical AI is not an optional addition but a necessary condition for ensuring that emerging technologies are aligned with human welfare. In this regard, sovereignty and interoperability stand out as guiding principles, ensuring that AI systems function in ways that respect human autonomy and collective interests (Kagermann & Wahlster, 2022). Parallel to these developments is the growing need for trustworthy data infrastructures. By providing secure and transparent systems, these infrastructures support long-term adaptability in an economic and geopolitical environment marked by volatility.

At the same time, the field of cyberpsychology has gained prominence in understanding how these transformations intersect with psychological well-being, particularly among youth. With higher levels of exposure to digital technologies, young people face distinctive vulnerabilities that make research into their experiences essential (Davis et al., 2024; Frielingsdorf et al., 2025). This includes analyzing how online environments affect behavior, identity, and mental health and ensuring that digital tools are deployed in ways that promote rather than undermine personal growth and resilience (Kagermann & Wahlster, 2022). These developments indicate that digital transformation is not solely about technological innovation. It also requires ethical vigilance and a long-term vision that blends sustainability with human-centered outcomes (Omol, 2023; Pappas et al., 2023). The challenge is to develop digital ecosystems that adapt to rapid technological shifts while safeguarding individual well-being and societal cohesion.

Cyberpsychology plays a particularly important role in this landscape by offering insights that shape policy responses to digital youth engagement (Bhat et al., 2025; Davis et al., 2024). Its research highlights how young people interact with digital technologies, pointing to both opportunities and risks. These insights help policymakers design measures that maximize positive outcomes while addressing the challenges posed by online environments (Tsouparopoulou et al., 2025).

Several areas illustrate how cyberpsychology informs policy development. For instance, digital citizenship education has become a central theme. By studying cyber behavior and online ethics, cyberpsychology contributes to defining responsible practices of participation in cyberspace (Fortuna, 2023). Respectful interaction, civic responsibility, and accountability are emphasized as part of digital citizenship, providing the foundation for educational programs aimed at reducing harassment and encouraging constructive online engagement (Al-Ali et al., 2024; Meekaew & Jongnimitsataporn, 2023).

Privacy and security are equally critical. Digital literacy, as highlighted in cyberpsychological research, extends beyond technical know-how to include ethical awareness and the ability to safeguard personal information (Arora, 2025; Peraza-Balderrama et al., 2024). Insights in this area inform policies that stress the importance of privacy settings, secure data management, and responsible sharing practices, thereby offering protection against risks such as identity theft and cyberbullying (Mahmoudi-Dehaki & Nasr-Esfahani, 2025).

Responsible digital engagement represents another important dimension. By examining how online interactions influence behavior and well-being, cyberpsychology supports the creation of policies that encourage balanced technology use (Fortuna, 2023; Gulyamov & Rodionov, 2024). This includes raising awareness about the potential consequences of risky behaviors, such as sharing passwords or excessive reliance on social networking platforms, while promoting healthier and more sustainable forms of online engagement (Arora, 2025).

Cyberpsychology also contributes to addressing digital inequalities. Differences in access and usage patterns across socioeconomic or cultural groups influence how youth benefit from digital technologies (Davis et al., 2024; Hunter et al., 2023). Research in this area informs policy initiatives aimed at reducing the digital divide, promoting equitable access to resources, and strengthening social cohesion through inclusive technological practices (Afzal et al., 2023; Harris & Johns, 2020).

Mental health and well-being remain a final cornerstone of this discussion. Insights from cyberpsychology clarify the psychological consequences of digital interactions, pointing to risks such as anxiety, depression, or social withdrawal, but also to the potential for digital environments to offer support and community (Frielingsdorf et al., 2025; Uslu, 2025). These findings are crucial for designing policies that foster safe, supportive, and developmentally appropriate environments for young people (McCabe et al., 2022). The contribution of cyberpsychology lies in its ability to explain the complex interplay between technology and youth development (See Figure 12.1). By providing evidence-based insights into how digital engagement shapes behavior, identity, and mental health, it supports the creation of policies that balance empowerment with protection, aiming to secure ethical and sustainable digital futures (See Table 12.1).

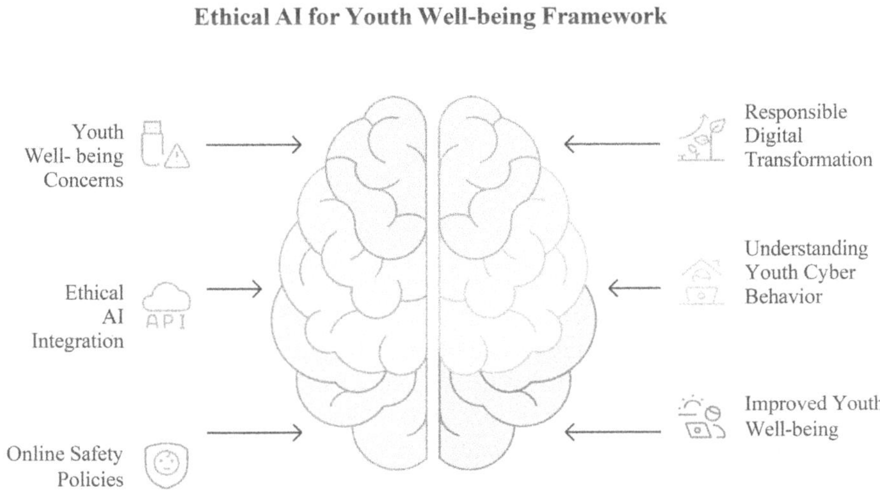

FIGURE 12.1 Linking digital transformation, ethical AI, and youth well-being.

TABLE 12.1 Cyberpsychology Contributions to Digital Youth Policy

Policy Area	*Cyberpsychology Insight*	*Policy Application*
Digital Citizenship Education	Research shows respectful and ethical cyber behavior reduces harassment and promotes civic engagement (Fortuna, 2023).	Integration of digital citizenship modules in school curricula to foster responsible online conduct.
Privacy and Security	Youth often lack awareness of privacy risks, making them vulnerable to cyberbullying and identity theft (Mahmoudi-Dehaki & Nasr-Esfahani, 2025).	Development of policies emphasizing strong privacy settings, secure data sharing practices, and awareness campaigns.
Responsible Digital Engagement	Excessive or risky online behaviors affect psychological well-being (Arora, 2025).	Guidelines for balanced screen use, youth education on consequences of risky behaviors, and parental/educator training.
Addressing Digital Inequalities	Disparities in digital access widen gaps in social participation and learning (Harris & Johns, 2020).	Policies aimed at reducing the digital divide through infrastructure development and equitable resource distribution.
Mental Health and Well-being	Online interactions can both support and harm youth psychological health (McCabe et al., 2022).	Creation of safe digital environments, provision of online counseling services, and supportive mental health policies.

Takeaway: *The rapid evolution of digital technologies demands forward-thinking strategies that prioritize ethics and mental health.*
Reflection: *What do you hope future digital platforms will do differently to better support mental well-being?*

12.2 AI in Social Media: Opportunities and Psychological Risks

AI systems embedded within social media platforms exert a strong influence on how young people perceive themselves and interact with peers. Algorithms that filter and prioritize content shape identity development, self-esteem, and social comparison, while at the same time raising pressing ethical questions concerning privacy, autonomy, and manipulation (Ahmmad et al., 2025; Elvira-Zorzo et al., 2025).

For instance, AI systems embedded in social media affect identity and Self-Esteem. The construction of online identity is increasingly mediated by AI tools that encourage selective self-presentation (Pflanzer et al., 2023; Plinio, 2025). Young users edit images and curate posts to present idealized versions of themselves, often guided by societal pressures surrounding beauty and appearance (Digennaro & Tescione, 2024; Zhang, 2025). This process not only frames how they wish to be seen but also generates cycles of comparison with others. Research shows that women in particular are more vulnerable to negative emotions when comparing their edited images with those of peers, reinforcing feelings of inadequacy and dissatisfaction (Li & Zhuo, 2023; Taylor & Armes, 2024).

Additionally, it creates an effect of social comparison. In other words, social media creates constant opportunities for both upward and downward comparison (Andrade et al., 2023; Opoku et al., 2025). Upward comparisons, directed at those perceived as more successful or attractive, tend to have the strongest psychological impact, often lowering self-esteem and amplifying feelings of inferiority (Blanc-Brillon et al., 2025; Ozimek et al., 2023). Although downward comparisons may provide temporary relief, they rarely counterbalance the cumulative effect of repeatedly seeing idealized portrayals of others (Layte et al., 2023; Lim & Tan, 2024). For many youths, the cycle of comparison becomes embedded in daily digital routines, influencing how they evaluate self-worth.

AI technologies can both create opportunities and raise ethical concerns. For instance, AI technologies provide clear benefits, such as enabling tailored recommendations that connect users with content aligned to their interests. These features foster engagement and support creative expression (Assad et al., 2025; Maiti et al., 2025). Yet, ethical concerns arise when personalization prioritizes attention and profit over well-being. Algorithms may amplify harmful or triggering content, reinforce unhealthy behaviors, or use personal data in ways that compromise user privacy. Concerns around surveillance and manipulation are heightened when AI systems are designed to maximize engagement at the cost of autonomy and psychological health (Bhutani et al., 2024; Polemi et al., 2024; Stevie & Ammara, 2023).

Another important aspect is the content curation and manipulation. The automated content selection further complicates the picture. By determining what users see and withholding alternative perspectives, algorithms construct personalized digital realities (Corella & Moreno, 2025; Sahebi & Formosa, 2022). This often leads to echo chambers, where existing views are continuously reinforced rather than challenged. For young people, whose worldviews and critical thinking skills are still developing, such algorithmic filtering raises concerns about bias, polarization, and the narrowing of perspectives (Sasahara et al., 2020).

As echo chambers form, several mechanisms explain how they take shape. First is the personalized content recommendations. AI analyzes user histories and continuously delivers similar content. The result is a feedback loop in which exposure narrows to align with existing beliefs, limiting opportunities for diverse thought (Mohamed et al., 2024). Second, there is homophily in interaction networks. Social media platforms cluster individuals with similar opinions, creating closed communities where ideas circulate within like-minded groups. This tendency, rooted in homophily, strengthens informational bubbles (Cinelli et al., 2021). Third is the social Influence and unfollowing mechanisms, where many users unfollow or block content that challenges their views. Algorithms amplify this tendency by steering them toward reinforcing content, further entrenching divisions (Sasahara et al., 2020). Finally, bias in information diffusion is another important aspect. Content that is emotionally charged or popular is often prioritized, even when it is biased or partisan. This amplifies certain narratives while silencing alternatives, shaping how youth construct their sense of social reality (Kitchens et al., 2020). Although these mechanisms are intended to optimize user engagement, they can intensify polarization and reduce openness to differing perspectives. For youth, this not only affects self-perception but also influences civic attitudes, tolerance, and social cohesion. Addressing these challenges requires a multi-level approach, involving algorithmic transparency, the integration of media literacy into education, and the design of systems that expose users to a wider range of content.

Takeaway: *AI-driven content shaping can affect youth self-esteem, peer interactions, and psychological well-being.*
Reflection: *How can we help youth stay in control of their digital identities in a world shaped by AI algorithms?*

12.3 Reimagining AI in Education: Personalized Futures and Ethical Dilemmas

The introduction of AI into education has created new possibilities for personalized learning, while also generating ethical challenges that must be carefully addressed. The tension between tailoring education to individual needs and safeguarding student rights is central to current debates. Several areas highlight both the opportunities and dilemmas of integrating AI in schools and universities.

Starting with personalization and predictive analytics, AI-driven systems can design educational pathways that reflect the needs, abilities, and pace of individual learners (Farhood et al., 2025). Adaptive learning technologies and intelligent tutoring systems can provide customized feedback, helping students to overcome difficulties and strengthen their understanding (Katiyar et al., 2024). Predictive analytics can further anticipate potential struggles and suggest interventions before learning gaps widen. However, these opportunities depend on extensive data collection, raising concerns about student privacy and the long-term implications of data storage and use (Ejjami, 2024).

Regarding ethical concerns and surveillance, the same data collection that enables personalization can also result in environments where students feel closely monitored. This sense of surveillance may restrict autonomy, discourage risk-taking, and reduce creativity in classrooms (Calderwood, 2025). The prospect of continuous tracking of performance, behavior, and even emotions has led to concerns about how far institutions should go in observing learners. Robust privacy safeguards and transparent communication about data use are essential in countering these risks (Huang et al., 2021).

Equity and algorithmic bias are other important aspects where AI is often presented as a tool for inclusion, yet biases embedded in datasets or system design may reproduce existing inequities (Ghanem et al., 2025). For example, predictive models that rely on incomplete or unrepresentative data may unfairly disadvantage certain student groups. Ensuring diverse datasets and regular fairness audits is critical to prevent such harms (Ejjami, 2024; Karpouzis, 2024). Without deliberate attention to equity, AI may widen rather than close educational gaps.

Accordingly, the role of educators became important, as AI should complement human teaching rather than replace it. Teachers remain essential as facilitators of student-centered learning, interpreters of data-driven feedback, and mentors who nurture curiosity and ethical reasoning (Yadav, 2024). The integration of AI requires educators to adapt their professional roles, learning how to use AI insights to refine strategies, support diverse learners, and promote initiative (Karpouzis, 2024; Walter, 2024).

Moving forward, collaboration between technology developers, educators, and policymakers will be key to ensuring responsible integration. Priorities include establishing ethical standards for AI in education, investing in teacher training to build digital competencies, and ensuring inclusivity across socio-economic backgrounds (Elam, 2024; Monika Singh et al., 2024). Policies must also encourage innovation while maintaining safeguards for fairness and accountability.

Furthermore, policymakers play a central role in shaping how AI is implemented in education, and their responsibilities span several interconnected domains. A primary task is to establish ethical frameworks that set clear guidelines for acceptable uses of AI (Ghimire & Edwards, 2024). These frameworks must address issues such as privacy, fairness, and accountability, ensuring that both institutions and developers adopt practices aligned with broader social values (Nguyen et al., 2022; Paschal & Melly, 2023).

Alongside ethical guidance, data privacy emerges as a major area of responsibility. Protecting student information requires strict regulation, with standards for how data is collected, stored, and shared (Noller & Thimesch, 2025). Without such safeguards, the risk of unauthorized access or misuse becomes significant, potentially undermining trust in educational technologies (Al-Zahrani, 2024; Sywelem & Mahklouf, 2024). Closely tied to this is the need for transparency and accountability. Policymakers can mandate that developers provide explanations of how algorithms operate and how decisions are made, enabling public scrutiny and helping maintain confidence among students, parents, and educators (Meduri et al., 2024).

Collaboration also plays a decisive role. Policies that encourage dialogue between educators, developers, and community stakeholders ensure that AI systems are not only technically effective but also culturally and contextually relevant (Bulut & Beiting-Parrish, 2024; mkaya, 2025). Furthermore, equity and inclusion must be central to policy agendas. By ensuring that access to AI-enhanced tools is distributed fairly across socio-economic backgrounds, policymakers can help prevent educational inequalities from widening due to technological adoption (Yadav, 2024).

Finally, there is a need for continuous monitoring and evaluation. Regular audits of AI systems in educational contexts enable the identification of biases, assessment of impact, and implementation of corrective measures where necessary (Paschal & Melly, 2023). Through this ongoing oversight, policymakers can ensure that the integration of AI remains responsive to emerging challenges. These responsibilities highlight the vital role of policymakers in building an ethical and inclusive digital future for education. By addressing these domains in concert, they help to ensure that AI supports learning while safeguarding the rights, dignity, and opportunities of all students.

> ***Takeaway:*** *AI has great potential to personalize education but must be implemented with transparency, fairness, and student protection in mind.*
> ***Reflection:*** *What ethical principles should guide the development of AI tools in classrooms?*

12.4 Personality in 2035: Traits as Predictors of Adaptation and Risk

As AI becomes increasingly embedded in environments such as the metaverse, emotion-recognition systems, and adaptive virtual spaces, personality traits emerge as critical predictors of resilience or vulnerability (Evangelou et al., 2024). Established psychological models, including the Big Five, HEXACO, and the Dark Tetrad, provide valuable frameworks for understanding how individuals may adapt to or struggle within these technologically mediated settings (Evangelou et al., 2024).

The Big Five model, with its five broad dimensions, has long demonstrated predictive value across multiple contexts, and it offers important insights into human adaptation to AI-driven environments. Individuals high in openness to experience tend to display greater adaptability to novel technologies and are more likely to hold positive attitudes toward AI (Stein et al., 2024). Research indicates that openness is associated with acceptance and reduced fear of AI across diverse cultural settings, suggesting that this trait may ease transitions into new virtual spaces such as the metaverse (Bartneck et al., 2023; Sindermann et al., 2022). It encourages individuals to embrace new ethical paradigms, supporting innovation while remaining receptive to diverse approaches to fairness and responsibility (Bian & Wang, 2024). Conscientiousness, while most often linked with structured cognition and goal-oriented behavior, may also enhance resilience by promoting organized engagement with AI systems (Ibrahim et al., 2025). Conscientious individuals often adopt cautious approaches that prioritize procedural justice, ensuring alignment between AI applications and established ethical codes (Aslam et al., 2024). Within educational applications, conscientious individuals are more likely to interact with learning technologies in ways that support persistence and achievement (Aslam et al., 2024). Extraversion contributes another layer of adaptability, as extraverted individuals typically report more positive perceptions of AI and may benefit from the increased opportunities for social interaction and teamwork offered by immersive virtual environments (Ozbey & Yasa, 2025). Additionally, extraverts may emphasize the ethical use of AI to strengthen social connectivity and community engagement in virtual settings (Azad & Kumar, 2024). Agreeableness is generally tied to cooperative and prosocial behavior, but its role in AI acceptance is less consistent. It supports decision-making that minimizes harm and promotes equitable outcomes in AI systems (Brendel et al., 2021). Findings suggest that in some contexts other factors, such as cultural orientation or prior exposure to technology, may overshadow the influence of agreeableness (Sindermann et al., 2022). Neuroticism, in contrast, is more consistently linked with fear and anxiety toward AI. Individuals with high levels of neuroticism are more vulnerable to AI-mediated stressors, which may heighten risk in virtual contexts that demand adaptability and confidence (Sindermann et al., 2022). Those individuals tend to favor strict safeguards and may demand stronger ethical protections against misuse, reflecting a cautious but protective stance (Gupta, 2023).

The HEXACO model expands upon the Big Five by adding honesty-humility, a trait concerned with sincerity, fairness, and modesty (Burro et al., 2023). While specific research into how honesty-humility shapes interactions with AI remains limited, its implications are notable. Individuals high on this trait are more likely to demonstrate ethical sensitivity and to approach AI systems with an orientation toward trust and fairness, potentially influencing how they evaluate the integrity of AI-mediated interactions (Yang et al., 2025). This dimension suggests that moral values embedded in personality may be a key factor in determining whether individuals use AI responsibly.

A very different set of implications arises from the Dark Tetrad traits: narcissism, Machiavellianism, psychopathy, and sadism. These traits, characterized by self-interest, manipulation, and callousness, can predict negative outcomes in AI-mediated environments (Calvillo et al., 2023; Sun et al., 2025). For example, narcissistic individuals may exploit AI to construct inflated self-presentations, while Machiavellian tendencies may encourage manipulative strategies in collaborative virtual spaces (Chakraborty, 2025). Psychopathy, with its impulsivity and lack of remorse, and sadism, with its enjoyment of others' suffering, pose particular risks for the misuse of AI tools in ways that may damage both individual well-being and collective trust (Yirmiya & Fonagy, 2025). The presence of these traits highlights the darker potential of personality–technology interactions, especially as digital environments become more immersive and socially complex.

These personality-based differences are also evident in responses to bias and fairness issues within AI systems. While some individuals emphasize transparency and accountability, others may focus more on outcomes related to equity or harm reduction (Gupta, 2023). This variability reinforces the importance of designing AI systems that can accommodate diverse perspectives on ethical practice. The literature suggests that personality traits play a central role in determining how individuals perceive, adapt to, and regulate their behavior in technologically mediated contexts. Traits not only shape acceptance and fear of AI but also guide the moral frameworks through which individuals make sense of ethical challenges. By integrating personality psychology into AI design and governance, systems can be developed that are sensitive to human diversity, fostering responsible use while mitigating risks. Future research should continue to examine how these traits interact with new digital environments, particularly as the metaverse and emotion-recognition technologies expand. Understanding these dynamics will be vital for ensuring that AI systems align with human values while supporting resilience and ethical decision-making (Matthews et al., 2024). As shown in Figure 12.2, a conceptual diagram illustrates how personality traits map to outcomes such as resilience, vulnerability, and ethical orientation (Table 12.2).

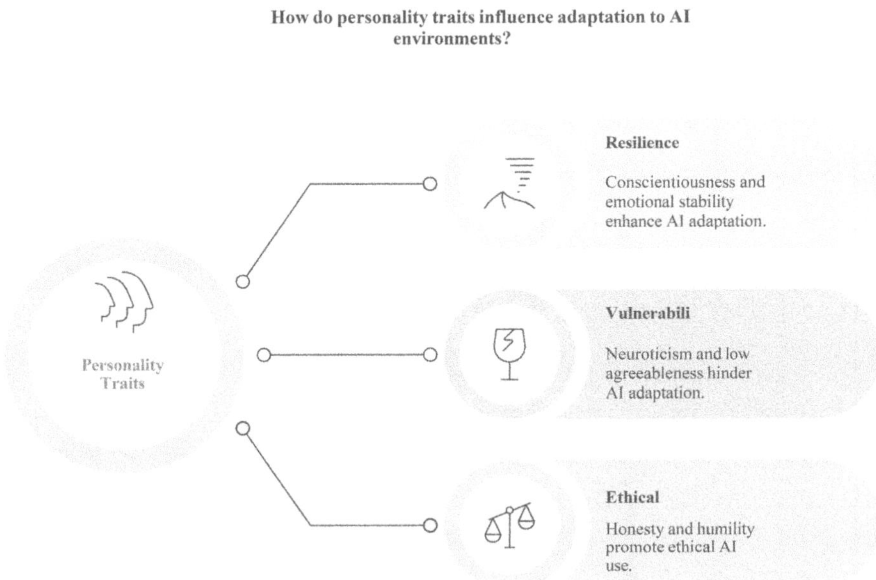

FIGURE 12.2 Personality traits and adaptation to AI environments.

TABLE 12.2 Personality Traits in AI-Mediated Environments

Personality Trait	*Adaptation Potential*	*Vulnerability/Risk*	*Ethical Orientation*
Openness to Experience	Strong adaptability to novel technologies such as the metaverse; positive attitude toward AI; acceptance across diverse cultural contexts (Sindermann et al., 2022).	May be overly willing to embrace untested technologies without caution.	Supports innovation and adaptability in ethical decision-making; open to new ethical paradigms (Bian & Wang, 2024).
Conscientiousness	Structured engagement with AI; persistence in educational applications; promotes organized and goal-driven use (Aslam et al., 2024).	Risk of rigidity and over-reliance on structured processes.	Emphasizes procedural justice, adherence to ethical codes, and alignment with standards (Aslam et al., 2024).
Extraversion	Facilitates positive perceptions of AI; supports teamwork and social interaction in virtual environments (Ozbey & Yasa, 2025).	Susceptible to peer influence and over-engagement in social platforms.	Advocates for ethical use of AI to strengthen community and collaboration (Azad & Kumar, 2024).
Agreeableness	Encourages cooperative, prosocial interactions; supports fairness in AI-mediated contexts.	May be vulnerable to exploitation or manipulation in virtual environments.	Prioritizes fairness, altruism, and minimizing harm in AI systems (Brendel et al., 2021).
Neuroticism	Limited adaptability; cautious stance may encourage protective safeguards.	Fear and anxiety toward AI; heightened susceptibility to stress in AI-mediated settings (Sindermann et al., 2022).	Supports stricter safeguards, emphasizing transparency and accountability in AI (Gupta, 2023).
Honesty-Humility (HEXACO)	Promotes trust in AI and fairness in collaborative use; orientation toward responsible adoption.	Research limited; may face challenges in contexts dominated by manipulation.	Aligns AI interaction with sincerity, modesty, and collective welfare.
Dark Tetrad Traits (Narcissism, Machiavellianism, Psychopathy, Sadism)	Low adaptability in terms of collective well-being; may adapt for manipulative gain.	High risk of unethical use; manipulative behavior; impulsivity; enjoyment of harm in digital spaces.	Ethical orientation is weak; traits predict exploitative or harmful behavior in AI-mediated environments.

Takeaway: *Individual personality traits will increasingly shape how youth respond to digital risks, requiring personalized support strategies.*
Reflection: *How might understanding your personality type help you navigate digital challenges more effectively?*

12.5 Gendered Futures: Online Risk and Opportunity

The evolution of digital platforms has created new opportunities for connection, work, and civic participation, but it has also amplified risks that are experienced differently by men and women. Gender-based disparities are deeply woven into cyberspaces, shaping how individuals engage, what challenges they face, and which forms of empowerment become available (Agyare, 2025). Understanding these distinctions is essential for building digital environments that are safe, inclusive, and equitable.

Gender-based experiences online often highlight asymmetries in exposure to harm and opportunity. For women, social media has become a frequent site of harassment and abuse. Gender-based violence is pervasive across platforms, sustained by the normalization of misogyny and discriminatory practices that mirror systemic inequalities offline (Agyare, 2025; Laffier & Rehman, 2023). Research highlights the need for platforms to align with human rights frameworks to confront and mitigate such harms effectively (Ahmed & Madrid-Morales, 2020; Vyas, 2020). These risks extend into the domain of digital labor, where women are frequently undervalued and subject to gendered occupational expectations (Stringhi, 2022). The concentration of market power within major digital platforms further exacerbates these biases, embedding structural inequities into emerging forms of online work (Munoz et al., 2024). A similar gendered divide can be observed in online political participation. While cyberspaces have expanded avenues for civic engagement, participation remains unequal, with disparities often linked to differences in educational access and confidence in navigating digital political forums (Ahmed & Madrid-Morales, 2020).

Yet, the digital sphere also offers women opportunities to reduce longstanding barriers. Social media networks, while reflective of gender imbalances, can serve as pathways to information and resources that narrow gaps in areas such as education and economic advancement (Osei-Appiah et al., 2023). Empirical work suggests that access to these resources may help close gender divides in professional and civic domains (Schneider, 2022). The gig economy is a notable example of this dual dynamic. Although digital labor platforms offer flexibility and access to income-generating opportunities, they also expose women to challenges stemming from algorithmic bias and precarious employment arrangements (Vyas, 2020). These contradictions reveal how digital environments can simultaneously empower and disadvantage female users, depending on how systems are designed and regulated.

Addressing these imbalances requires intentional and sustained strategies. Scholars argue that platforms must adopt governance models and design principles that explicitly confront online gender-based violence while embedding protections against broader inequalities (Schneider, 2022). Policy measures that target equity within the gig economy and social networking sites can help reduce digital biases, ensuring that women are not disproportionately excluded from the benefits of technological advancement (Ahmed & Madrid-Morales, 2020; Vyas, 2020). Such measures are crucial in transforming digital platforms from sites of risk into spaces of empowerment.

A deeper examination of gender-based violence online reveals the scope of reforms needed at the platform level. Integrating human rights by design is one important step, requiring companies to adopt international human rights instruments as guiding standards (Agyare, 2025; Fuente, 2023). This approach ensures that digital systems do not reproduce or amplify inequalities and instead operate within frameworks that prioritize dignity, fairness, and justice (Wernick & Artyushina, 2023). Complementing these commitments, enhanced content moderation is essential. A hybrid model combining advanced AI tools with human oversight allows platforms to detect abusive content more effectively, while efficient reporting mechanisms empower victims by offering timely support and escalation (Afrouz, 2021).

Beyond moderation, platforms can also contribute to cultural change through awareness and education campaigns. Social media's reach provides an avenue to challenge norms that perpetuate gender-based violence. Campaigns that teach users how to identify, prevent, and report abuse encourage active community engagement and build cultures of zero tolerance (Miller & Demirbilek, 2023). Alongside education, data-driven insights are critical. The collection and transparent reporting of information on online violence allow companies to build accountability while providing researchers and policymakers with evidence to inform broader strategies against both digital and offline gender violence (Faith, 2022).

Finally, building networks of support is indispensable. Partnerships with organizations specializing in counseling, legal assistance, and advocacy can connect victims with resources beyond the platform itself (Basit et al., 2025). By embedding links to external services and offering educational materials on digital safety and privacy, platforms can empower women and other vulnerable groups to navigate digital spaces more safely (Miller & Demirbilek, 2023). These strategies point toward a comprehensive model for addressing gender-based challenges online. By embedding human rights into design, strengthening moderation systems, raising awareness, committing to transparency, and developing support networks, digital platforms can reduce the risks women face and foster spaces that encourage empowerment and equity (Table 12.3).

Takeaway: *Males and females may face distinct challenges online; strategies should reflect their differing experiences and vulnerabilities.*
Reflection: *What gender-related risks or strengths do you notice in how people use digital platforms?*

TABLE 12.3 Risks, Opportunities, and Interventions in Gendered Digital Spaces

Area of Engagement	*Risks*	*Opportunities*	*Recommended Strategies*
Online Safety	High exposure of women to harassment, gender-based violence, and normalized misogyny on platforms.	Platforms can reduce barriers by creating safer spaces for participation and expression.	Adopt human rights by design, strengthen AI–human hybrid content moderation, and improve reporting mechanisms (Afrouz, 2021).
Digital Labor	Women undervalued in digital work; biases reinforced through platform power and algorithmic systems (Munoz et al., 2024).	Flexible work arrangements in the gig economy create access to income-generating opportunities.	Establish equitable policies in digital labor markets; address algorithmic bias and ensure fair pay structures (Vyas, 2020).
Political Engagement	Gender gap in online political participation, linked to educational disparities and exposure to harassment (Ahmed & Madrid-Morales, 2020).	Digital spaces offer increased access to civic information and avenues for advocacy.	Encourage gender-inclusive civic participation, protect women against online abuse in political forums.
Civic and Economic Participation	Persistent inequalities in access to resources; women more vulnerable to exclusion.	Social media and digital platforms reduce barriers to information, training, and economic opportunities.	Foster awareness campaigns, create partnerships with NGOs, and expand equitable access initiatives (Miller & Demirbilek, 2023; Faith, 2022).

12.6 Designing the Future: Proactive Ethical Frameworks

Building proactive ethical frameworks for AI in cyberspaces requires the collective involvement of developers, educators, policymakers, and the wider community. Such frameworks are essential for ensuring that technological progress aligns with ethical principles, safeguards human dignity, and promotes inclusivity.

A first consideration lies in ethical design and transparency. Developers must embed fairness, accountability, and explainability into AI systems from the outset (Cheong, 2024). Establishing clear ethical guidelines reduces algorithmic biases and ensures that AI decision-making processes remain transparent to end users, thereby reinforcing both accountability and trust (Azad & Kumar, 2024). Equally important is collaborative policy development. Policymakers should work closely with educators and technology communities to create comprehensive regulatory structures that uphold ethical standards (Kasztelnik, 2024). Such policies should directly address pressing issues, including data privacy, misuse of AI systems, and inequitable access to emerging technologies (Saheb & Saheb, 2024).

Education forms another critical component of these frameworks. By integrating AI literacy into curricula, educators can equip students with the tools to critically assess technologies and understand their wider implications (Daher, 2025). Topics such as AI ethics, data protection, and societal impacts must be part of this educational process, preparing future generations to make informed decisions about how AI is used in different sectors (Alali & Wardat, 2024).

Regular ethical audits and reviews provide the necessary oversight for these initiatives. By implementing structured monitoring systems, organizations can evaluate whether AI deployments are consistent with agreed ethical standards and make adjustments to address new challenges or risks (Yan & Liu, 2024). Alongside these technical and institutional measures, empowerment through training and resources is essential. Providing educators and policymakers with appropriate training not only increases their confidence in using AI tools but also deepens their ability to recognize ethical implications, allowing them to design systems that contribute to inclusive educational and societal outcomes (Mariyono & Nur Alif Hd, 2025). These collaborative guidelines outline a pathway for AI that is not only technologically advanced but also ethically grounded and socially responsive (Figure 12.3).

User feedback and community engagement represent a second pillar of proactive ethical frameworks. Their inclusion ensures that policies remain holistic, contextually relevant, and reflective of societal values (Gros et al., 2025; Kumar, 2025). Promoting inclusivity and public trust begins with engaging diverse communities in conversations about AI. When policymakers incorporate feedback from those who are most affected by technological systems, trust increases, and the resulting frameworks are more likely to address the needs of marginalized groups (Abhulimen & Ejike, 2024). Contextual relevance is equally critical. Local challenges and socio-cultural dynamics vary, and user engagement allows policymakers to tailor AI policies so that they remain practically applicable in different contexts rather than remaining abstract principles (Huriye, 2023).

Transparency and accountability are also strengthened when community engagement becomes an ongoing process rather than a one-time consultation (Fayemi, 2025; Stix, 2021). Continuous dialogue allows stakeholders to observe how AI policies are crafted and applied, ensuring that institutions remain accountable for both their actions and their omissions (Pasupuleti, 2024). Engagement also contributes to ethical norm-setting. Users and communities play a direct role in shaping the values that guide AI design and deployment. This participatory model prevents "ethics dumping", in which developers shift ethical responsibilities onto end users who lack the resources or knowledge to manage them effectively (BéLisle-Pipon & Victor, 2024).

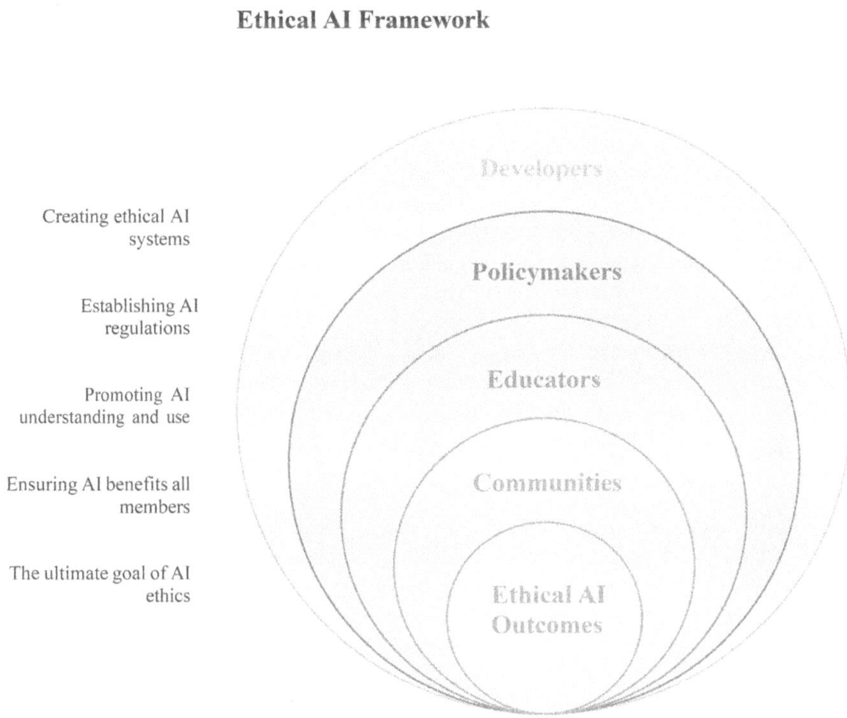

FIGURE 12.3 Multi-stakeholder ethical AI framework.

Finally, community engagement provides valuable input for innovation and adaptation. Because technology develops rapidly, policies that incorporate real-time user feedback can adjust to emerging risks while maintaining ethical consistency. Such adaptability ensures that policies remain robust even as AI introduces new complexities (Stix, 2021).

Incorporating user feedback and sustaining community participation, therefore, strengthens ethical frameworks by making them responsive, equitable, and trusted. By combining top-down oversight with bottom-up engagement, stakeholders can create AI systems that protect privacy, promote fairness, and support the well-being of young people and society as a whole (Table 12.4).

> ***Takeaway:*** *The future of ethical AI requires inclusive, collaborative efforts that protect youth privacy, equity, and mental well-being.*
> ***Reflection:*** *Who should be responsible for ensuring ethical AI use among young people—and how?*

TABLE 12.4 Guidelines for Ethical AI Development

Dimension	*Key Actions*	*Responsible Stakeholders*	*Expected Outcome*
Ethical Design and Transparency	Incorporate fairness, accountability, and explainability in AI systems; establish clear ethical guidelines (Azad & Kumar, 2024).	AI Developers, Regulators	Minimized bias, transparent decision-making, greater user trust.
Collaborative Policy Development	Create comprehensive regulatory frameworks addressing privacy, misuse, and equitable access (Azman & Tümkaya, 2025).	Policymakers, Educators, Tech Communities	Stronger protections for users; alignment of AI with social values.
Ethical AI Education	Integrate AI literacy into curricula, including ethics, privacy, and social impacts (Ng et al., 2023).	Educators, Education Authorities	Informed students capable of critical assessment and responsible use of AI.
Interdisciplinary Collaboration	Promote ongoing dialogue between developers, educators, policymakers, and communities (Alali & Wardat, 2024).	Cross-sector Stakeholders	Shared responsibility, inclusive frameworks, culturally relevant AI applications.
Regular Ethical Audits and Reviews	Monitor AI deployments and adjust to emerging risks (Yan & Liu, 2024).	Regulators, Independent Review Boards	Continuous compliance, adaptability to new challenges, long-term accountability.
Empowerment through Training and Resources	Provide training for educators and policymakers on AI tools and ethical implications (Mariyono & Nur Alif Hd, 2025).	Governments, Universities, Professional Bodies	Improved capacity to apply AI responsibly in education and policy.
User Feedback and Community Engagement	Incorporate community input into policy formation and norm-setting (Angela Omozele Abhulimen & Onyinye Gift Ejike, 2024; Huriye, 2023; Pasupuleti, 2024).	Policymakers, Developers, Civil Society	Greater inclusivity, contextual relevance, transparency, and accountability.

12.7 Two Futures: A Utopian and Dystopian Vision for 2035

This section explores two divergent future scenarios for the year 2035. These are not predictions but rather imaginative explorations of the potential consequences of the choices we make today.

A Utopian Vision: The Age of Digital Flourishing. In this future, AI has been successfully harnessed to promote human well-being, guided by a strong ethical framework (Csernatoni et al., 2025). Social media platforms have evolved from attention merchants to "digital public squares", with algorithms optimized for viewpoint diversity and constructive dialogue, mitigating the worst effects of polarization (Kieslich et al., 2024). AI-driven educational tools provide deeply personalized learning pathways that adapt to individual students' needs, fostering creativity and critical thinking rather than rote memorization (Costello et al., 2024). Mental health chatbots, now seamlessly integrated into primary care, offer empathetic, evidence-based support to millions, reducing stigma and improving access to care, with demonstrated efficacy in randomized controlled trials (Heinz et al., 2025). The digital world is not without its challenges, but a strong foundation of ethical AI, robust data privacy laws, and a digitally literate populace has created an environment where technology serves, rather than subverts, human values.

A Dystopian Vision: The Age of Algorithmic Control. In this future, the unchecked pursuit of profit and control has led to a digital world that is deeply damaging to human well-being, a reality often described as "surveillance capitalism" (Zuboff, 2022). Social media platforms have become powerful engines of social control, with algorithms that amplify outrage and create isolating "filter bubbles" to maximize engagement (Weigle & Shafi, 2023). AI-driven educational tools have created a system of constant surveillance and standardized testing, stifling creativity and exacerbating inequality through biased algorithmic governance (Sarin & Hill-Bonnet, 2025; Zainuddin, 2024). Mental health chatbots, now owned by large tech corporations, use sensitive personal data to manipulate users and sell them products, a form of "hypernudging" that erodes autonomy (Coghlan et al., 2023). The digital world is a place of constant anxiety, social comparison, and manipulation, where human autonomy has been sacrificed at the altar of algorithmic efficiency.

12.7.1 The Choice Ahead

These two scenarios are not predetermined; the future of our digital world will be shaped by the institutional and societal choices we make today (Schlund & Zitek, 2024). By prioritizing ethical AI, promoting digital literacy, and demanding accountability from tech companies through collective action and regulation, we can steer our digital future toward the age of digital flourishing, rather than the age of algorithmic control (Gill, 2023; Xavier, 2024).

12.8 Summary and Reflections

This chapter has provided a forward-looking synthesis of the book's central themes, exploring the future trajectories of cyberpsychology, AI ethics, and digital well-being. It began by examining the dual-edged nature of AI in social media, where algorithmic personalization can foster connection but also risks creating manipulative echo chambers and exacerbating social comparison. A similar tension was identified in the realm of AI in education, which promises tailored learning pathways but also raises significant ethical concerns regarding surveillance and the standardization of creativity.

Throughout this exploration, the chapter has reiterated a core argument of this book: that the impacts of these future technologies are not uniform. They are profoundly mediated by individual differences in personality, which shape digital resilience and vulnerability, as well as by societal constructs of gender, which influence the risks and opportunities users encounter in evolving digital spaces.

In response to these complex challenges, the chapter has underscored the urgent need for proactive ethical frameworks. Rather than reacting to harm after it occurs, a human-centered approach to AI development is essential to ensure that technological advancement serves human values. This critical choice was illustrated through the exploration of two divergent future scenarios for 2035: a utopian vision of digital flourishing, where technology enhances human connection and creativity, and a dystopian vision of algorithmic control, where it is used for manipulation and surveillance.

Ultimately, the chapter concludes not with a prediction but with a call to action. The future is not something that happens to us; it is something we build. The path we take toward flourishing or control will be determined by the collective commitment of all stakeholders to prioritize ethical foresight, human dignity, and psychological well-being in the design and governance of our digital world. Accordingly, this book proposes an integrated framework that provides a comprehensive overview of the book's core argument. It illustrates how individual-level factors (personality), sociocultural factors (gender and culture), technological factors (AI and platform design), and ethical frameworks converge to shape youth digital engagement. This engagement, in turn, leads to a range of digital well-being outcomes (mental health,

FIGURE 12.4 Integrated framework: Youth digital well-being in the age of AI.

identity development, social resilience, and ethical engagement). The model also highlights the critical role of interventions at the individual, systemic, and ethical governance levels, which create a feedback loop that can positively influence digital well-being outcomes. This holistic perspective highlights the need for a multifaceted approach to creating a more ethical and human-centered digital future for young people (See Figure 12.4).

References

Abhulimen, A. O., & Ejike, O. G. (2024). Ethical considerations in AI use for SMEs and supply chains: Current challenges and future directions. *International Journal of Applied Research in Social Sciences*, *6*(8), 1653–1679. https://doi.org/10.51594/ijarss.v6i8.1391

Afrouz, R. (2021). The nature, patterns and consequences of technology-facilitated domestic abuse: A scoping review. *Trauma Violence & Abuse*, *24*(2), 913–927. https://doi.org/10.1177/15248380211046752

Afzal, A., Khan, S., Daud, S., Ahmad, Z., & Butt, A. (2023). Addressing the digital divide: Access and use of technology in education. *Journal of Social Sciences Review*, *3*(2), 883–895. https://doi.org/10.54183/jssr.v3i2.326

Agyare, P. (2025). Gendered digital harms and youth ideological trajectories: Socioconomic challenges of digital platforms. *SocioEconomic Challenges*, *9*(3), 77–96. https://doi.org/10.61093/sec.9(3).77-96.2025

Ahmed, S., & Madrid-Morales, D. (2020). Is it still a man's world? Social media news use and gender inequality in online political engagement. *Information Communication & Society*, *24*(3), 381–399. https://doi.org/10.1080/1369118x.2020.1851387

Ahmmad, M., Shahzad, K., Iqbal, A., & Latif, M. (2025). Trap of social media algorithms: A systematic review of research on filter bubbles, echo chambers, and their impact on youth. *Societies*, *15*(11), 301. https://doi.org/10.3390/soc15110301

Al-Ali, A., Alsmairat, M. A., Qawasmeh, R., Mahrakani, N. J., & Alhazzani, N. S. (2024). Exploring the role of digital citizenship and digital empowerment to enhance academic performance of business students. *International Journal of Data and Network Science*, *8*(2), 1275–1284. https://doi.org/10.5267/j.ijdns.2023.11.007

AlAli, R., & Wardat, Y. (2024). Opportunities and challenges of integrating generative artificial intelligence in education. *International Journal of Religion*, *5*(7), 784–793. https://doi.org/10.61707/8y29gv34

Al-Zahrani, A. M. (2024). Unveiling the shadows: Beyond the hype of AI in education. *Heliyon, 10*(9), Article e30696. https://doi.org/10.1016/j.heliyon.2024.e30696

Andrade, F. C., Erwin, S., Burnell, K., Jackson, J., Storch, M., Nicholas, J., & Zucker, N. (2023). Intervening on social comparisons on social media: Electronic daily diary pilot study. *JMIR Mental Health, 10*, e42024. https://doi.org/10.2196/42024

Arora, R. (2025). Privacy and personal space in context of social media interactions. *International Journal of Advanced Research, 13*(07), 136–142. https://doi.org/10.21474/ijar01/21319

Aslam, M. A., Murtaza, F., Haq, M. E. U., Yasin, A., & Azam, M. A. (2024). A Human-Centered approach to academic performance prediction using personality factors in educational AI. *Information, 15*(12), 777. https://doi.org/10.3390/info15120777

Assad, A., Fyadh, M., Kaleel, A., & Gabr, M. (2025). Artificial intelligence in media studies in Arab countries: A systematic review. *Discover Education, 4*(1). https://doi.org/10.1007/s44217-025-00520-8

Azad, Y., & Kumar, A. (2024). Ethics and artificial intelligence. In *Advances in web technologies and engineering book series* (pp. 228–268). https://doi.org/10.4018/979-8-3693-1762-4.ch012

Azman, Ö., & Tümkaya, S. (2025). Navigating the ethical landscape of AI integration in education: Balancing innovation and responsibility. *F1000Research*, *14*, 299. https://doi.org/10.12688/f1000research.160011.1

Bartneck, C., Yogeeswaran, K., & Sibley, C. G. (2023). Personality and demographic correlates of support for regulating artificial intelligence. *AI And Ethics*, *4*(2), 419–426. https://doi.org/10.1007/s43681-023-00279-4

Basit, L., Santoso, P., & Rizky, F. (2025). Multi-platform analysis of sexual harassment networks: Gender dynamics and digital amplification. *Social Network Analysis and Mining*, *16*(1). https://doi.org/10.1007/s13278-025-01563-3

Bélisle-Pipon, J., & Victor, G. (2024). Ethics dumping in artificial intelligence. *Frontiers in Artificial Intelligence*, *7*, 1426761. https://doi.org/10.3389/frai.2024.1426761

Bhat, R., Kowshik, S., Suresh, S., Alamelu, G., Gite, S., & Albattat, A. (2025). Digital companionship or psychological risk? The role of AI characters in shaping youth mental health. *Asian Journal of Psychiatry*, *104*, 104356. https://doi.org/10.1016/j.ajp.2024.104356

Bhutani, V., Bahadur, P. S., Sansaniwal, S. K., & Bais, P. (2024). Youth studes in the AI era. In *Advances in human and social aspects of technology book series* (pp. 407–428). https://doi.org/10.4018/979-8-3693-3350-1.ch022

Bian, X., & Wang, B. (2024). Exploring the influence of artificial intelligence usage on ethical decision making among public sector employees: Insights into moral identity and service motivation. *Business Ethics and Leadership*, *8*(3), 133–150. https://doi.org/10.61093/bel.8(3).133-150.2024

Blanc-Brillon, J. L., Fortin, J., Lafrance, L., & Hétu, S. (2025). The associations between social comparison on social media and young adults' mental health. *Frontiers in Psychology*, *16*, 1597241. https://doi.org/10.3389/fpsyg.2025.1597241

Brendel, A. B., Mirbabaie, M., Lembcke, T., & Hofeditz, L. (2021). Ethical management of artificial intelligence. *Sustainability*, *13*(4), 1974. https://doi.org/10.3390/su13041974

Bulut, O., & Beiting-Parrish, M. (2024). The rise of artificial intelligence in educational measurement: Opportunities and ethical challenges. *Chinese/English Journal of Educational Measurement and Evaluation*, *5*(3). https://doi.org/10.59863/miql7785

Burro, R., Vicentini, G., & Raccanello, D. (2023). Big Five personality traits and coping strategies of italian university students during the COVID-19 pandemic first wave. *Frontiers in Psychology*, *14*, 1150674. https://doi.org/10.3389/fpsyg.2023.1150674

Calderwood, S. J. (2025). Surveillance digitisation, performativity, and Teacher-Student relationships in a blended learning setting. *Postdigital Science and Education*. https://doi.org/10.1007/s42438-024-00537-6

Calvillo, D. P., León, A., & Rutchick, A. M. (2023). Personality and misinformation. *Current Opinion in Psychology*, *55*, 101752. https://doi.org/10.1016/j.copsyc.2023.101752

Chakraborty, D. (2025). Psychological Dispositions and AI utilization: Unpacking narcissism, machiavellianism, and psychopathy in e-commerce. *Journal of Promotion Management*, *31*(4), 549–577. https://doi.org/10.1080/10496491.2025.2484714

Cheong, B. C. (2024). Transparency and accountability in AI systems: Safeguarding wellbeing in the age of algorithmic decision-making. *Frontiers in Human Dynamics*, *6*, 1–11. https://doi.org/10.3389/fhumd.2024.1421273

Cinelli, M., De Francisci Morales, G., Galeazzi, A., Quattrociocchi, W., & Starnini, M. (2021). The echo chamber effect on social media. *Proceedings of the National Academy of Sciences*, *118*(9). https://doi.org/10.1073/pnas.2023301118

Coghlan, S., Leins, K., Sheldrick, S., Cheong, M., Gooding, P., & D'Alfonso, S. (2023). To chat or bot to chat: Ethical issues with using chatbots in mental health. *Digital Health*, *9*, 20552076231183542. https://doi.org/10.1177/20552076231183542

Corella, Á. S., & Moreno, N. H. (2025). Racism in the digital Age: The impact of social media algorithms on public discourse. *The Age of Human Rights Journal*, *25*, e9603. https://doi.org/10.17561/tahrj.v25.9603

Costello, E., Tlili, A., Adarkwah, M. A., Lo, C. K., Bozkurt, A., Burgos, D., Bonk, C. J., Mishra, S., Stracke, C. M., & Huang, R. (2024). Taming the monster: How can open education promote the effective and safe use of generative AI in education? *Journal of Learning for Development, 11*(3), 398–413. https://jl4d.org/index.php/ejl4d/article/view/1657

Csernatoni, R., Broeders, D., Andersen, L. H., Hoijtink, M., Bode, I., Lindsay, J. R., & Schwarz, E. (2025). Myth, Power, and Agency: Rethinking artificial intelligence, Geopolitics and war. *Minds and Machines*, *35*(3). https://doi.org/10.1007/s11023-025-09741-0

Daher, R. (2025). Integrating AI literacy into teacher education: A critical perspective paper. *Discover Artificial Intelligence*, *5*(1). https://doi.org/10.1007/s44163-025-00475-7

Davis, K., Anderson, M., Yang, C., Choukas-Bradley, S., Bell, B. T., & Slovak, P. (2024). Cross-disciplinary perspectives on youth digital well-being research: Identifying notable developments, persistent gaps, and future directions. *Journal of Adolescent Research*, *40*(2), 259–295. https://doi.org/10.1177/07435584241291163

De La Fuente, O. P. (2023). Online misogyny and the law: Are human rights protected on the net? *The Age of Human Rights Journal*, *21*. https://doi.org/10.17561/tahrj.v21.8270

Di Plinio, S. (2025). Panta Rh-AI: Assessing multifaceted AI threats on human agency and identity. *Social Sciences & Humanities Open*, *11*, 101434. https://doi.org/10.1016/j.ssaho.2025.101434

Digennaro, S., & Tescione, A. (2024). Scrolls and self-perception, navigating the link between social networks and body dissatisfaction in preadolescents and adolescents: A systematic review. *Frontiers in Education*, *9*. https://doi.org/10.3389/feduc.2024.1390583

Ejjami, R. (2024). The adaptive personalization theory of learning: Revolutionizing education with AI. *Journal of Next-Generation Research 5 0*. https://doi.org/10.70792/jngr5.0.v1i1.8

Elam, K. M. (2024). Exploring the challenges and future directions of big data and AI in education. *Journal of Artificial Intelligence General Science (JAIGS)* ISSN 3006–4023, *1*(1), 81–93. https://doi.org/10.60087/jaigs.v1i1.173

Elvira-Zorzo, M. N., & Gómez, P. B. (2025). Identity construction and digital vulnerability in adolescents: Psychosocial implications and implications for social work. *Youth*, *5*(4), 119. https://doi.org/10.3390/youth5040119

Evangelou, S. M., Michanetzi, E. L., & Xenos, M. (2024). Exploring the impact of negative online feedback on well-being: A comprehensive analysis incorporating Big-Five personality traits and physiological responses. *Computers in Human Behavior Reports*, *15*, 100457. https://doi.org/10.1016/j.chbr.2024.100457

Faith, B. (2022). Tackling online gender-based violence; understanding gender, development, and the power relations of digital spaces. *Gender Technology and Development*, *26*(3), 325–340. https://doi.org/10.1080/09718524.2022.2124600

Farhood, H., Nyden, M., Beheshti, A., & Muller, S. (2025). Artificial intelligence-based personalised learning in education: A systematic literature review. *Discover Artificial Intelligence*, *5*(1). https://doi.org/10.1007/s44163-025-00598-x

Fayemi, K. A. (2025). Leveraging artificial intelligence for smarter climate policy and strategic government planning. *Journal of Sustainable Development*, *18*(6), 77. https://doi.org/10.5539/jsd.v18n6p77

Fortuna, P. (2023). Positive cyberpsychology as a field of study of the well-being of people interacting with and via technology. *Frontiers in Psychology*, *14*, 1053482. https://doi.org/10.3389/fpsyg.2023.1053482

Franzè, C., Paolucci, E., & Pessot, E. (2023). Sustained value creation driven by digital connectivity: A multiple case study in the mechanical components industry. *Technovation*, *129*, 102918. https://doi.org/10.1016/j.technovation.2023.102918

Frielingsdorf, H., Fomichov, V., Rystedt, I., Lindstrand, S., Korhonen, L., & Henriksson, H. (2025). Associations of time spent on different types of digital media with self-rated general and mental health in Swedish adolescents. *Scientific Reports*, *15*(1), 993. https://doi.org/10.1038/s41598-024-83951-x

Ghanem, S., Moraleja, M., Gravesande, D., & Rooney, J. (2025). Integrating health equity in artificial intelligence for public health in Canada: A rapid narrative review. *Frontiers in Public Health*, *13*, 1524616. https://doi.org/10.3389/fpubh.2025.1524616

Ghimire, A., & Edwards, J. (2024). From guidelines to governance: A study of AI policies in education. In *Communications in computer and information science* (pp. 299–307). https://doi.org/10.1007/978-3-031-64312-5_36

Gill, K. S. (2023). Moving the AI needle: From chaos to engagement. *AI & Society*, *38*(1), 1–4. https://doi.org/10.1007/s00146-023-01627-y

Gros, C., Martens, M., Aliman, N., Kester, L., & Werkhoven, P. (2025). Ethical frameworks for automated vehicles: A systematic analysis and design. *AI And Ethics*, *5*(6), 6041–6062. https://doi.org/10.1007/s43681-025-00803-8

Gulyamov, S., & Rodionov, A. (2024). Cyber hygiene as an effective psychological measure in the prevention of cyber addictions. *Psychology and Law*, *14*(2), 77–91. https://doi.org/10.17759/psylaw.2024140206

Gupta, N. (2023). Artificial intelligence ethics and fairness: A study to address bias and fairness issues in AI systems, and the ethical implications of AI applications. *Revista Review Index Journal of Multidisciplinary*, *3*(2), 24–35. https://doi.org/10.31305/rrijm2023.v03.n02.004

Harris, A., & Johns, A. (2020). Youth, social cohesion and digital life: From risk and resilience to a global digital citizenship approach. *Journal of Sociology*, *57*(2), 394–411. https://doi.org/10.1177/1440783320919173

Heinz, M. V., Mackin, D. M., Trudeau, B. M., Bhattacharya, S., Wang, Y., Banta, H. A., Jewett, A. D., Salzhauer, A. J., Griffin, T. Z., & Jacobson, N. C. (2025). Randomized trial of a generative AI chatbot for mental health treatment. *NEJM AI*, *2*(4). https://doi.org/10.1056/aioa2400802

Huang, C., Samek, T., & Shiri, A. (2021). AI and ethics: Ethical and educational perspectives for LIS. *Journal of Education for Library and Information Science*, *62*(4), 351–365. https://doi.org/10.3138/jelis-62-4-2020-0106

Hunter, J. F., Walsh, L. C., Chan, C., & Schueller, S. M. (2023). Editorial: The good side of technology: How we can harness the positive potential of digital technology to maximize well-being. *Frontiers in Psychology*, *14*, 1304592. https://doi.org/10.3389/fpsyg.2023.1304592

Huriye, A. Z. (2023). The ethics of artificial intelligence: Examining the ethical considerations surrounding the development and use of AI. *American Journal of Technology*, *2*(1), 37–45. https://doi.org/10.58425/ajt.v2i1.142

Ibrahim, F., Münscher, J., Daseking, M., & Telle, N. (2025). The technology acceptance model and adopter type analysis in the context of artificial intelligence. *Frontiers in Artificial Intelligence*, *7*, 1496518. https://doi.org/10.3389/frai.2024.1496518

Kagermann, H., & Wahlster, W. (2022). Ten years of industrie 4.0. *Sci*, *4*(3), 26. https://doi.org/10.3390/sci4030026

Karpouzis, K. (2024). *Artificial Intelligence in Education: Ethical Considerations and Insights from Ancient Greek Philosophy* (pp. 1–7). https://doi.org/10.1145/3688671.3688772
Kasztelnik, K. (2024). Artificial intelligence-assisted curriculum development: Innovations in designing educational content for the 21st century learner. *Journal of Higher Education Theory and Practice*, *24*(11). https://doi.org/10.33423/jhetp.v24i11.7367
Katiyar, N., Awasthi, V. K., Pratap, R., Mishra, K., Shukla, N., Singh, R., & Tiwari, M. (2024). Ai-driven personalized learning systems: Enhancing educational effectiveness. *Educational Administration: Theory and Practice*. https://doi.org/10.53555/kuey.v30i5.4961
Kieslich, K., Diakopoulos, N., & Helberger, N. (2024). Anticipating impacts: Using large-scale scenario-writing to explore diverse implications of generative AI in the news environment. *AI And Ethics*, *5*(5), 4555–4577. https://doi.org/10.1007/s43681-024-00497-4
Kitchens, B., Johnson, S. L., & Gray, P. (2020). Understanding echo chambers and filter bubbles: The impact of social media on diversification and partisan shifts in news consumption. *MIS Quarterly*, *44*(4), 1619–1649. https://doi.org/10.25300/misq/2020/16371
Konidena, B. K., Malaiyappan, J. N. A., & Tadimarri, A. (2024). Ethical considerations in the development and deployment of AI systems. *European Journal of Technology*, *8*(2), 41–53. https://doi.org/10.47672/ejt.1890
Kumar, S. N. P. (2025). Ethical frameworks for AI-driven decision systems: A comprehensive analysis. *Global Journal of Computer Science and Technology*, 53–60. https://doi.org/10.34257/gjcstdvol25is1pg53
Laffier, J., & Rehman, A. (2023). Deepfakes and harm to women. *Journal of Digital Life and Learning*, *3*(1), 1–21. https://doi.org/10.51357/jdll.v3i1.218
Layte, R., Brannigan, R., & Stanistreet, D. (2023). Digital engagement and adolescent depression: A longitudinal mediation analysis adjusting for selection. *Computers in Human Behavior Reports*, *10*, 100293. https://doi.org/10.1016/j.chbr.2023.100293
Li, P., & Zhuo, Q. (2023). Emotional straying: Flux and management of women's emotions in social media. *PLoS ONE*, *18*(12), e0295835. https://doi.org/10.1371/journal.pone.0295835
Lim, A. J., & Tan, E. (2024). Social media ills and evolutionary mismatches: A conceptual framework. *Evolutionary Psychological Science*, *10*(3), 212–235. https://doi.org/10.1007/s40806-024-00398-z
Mahmoudi-Dehaki, M., & Nasr-Esfahani, N. (2025). Nurturing responsible digital citizens in the online world. In *IGI global eBooks* (pp. 99–122). https://doi.org/10.4018/979-8-3693-6675-2.ch004
Maiti, M., Kayal, P., & Vujko, A. (2025). A study on ethical implications of artificial intelligence adoption in business: Challenges and best practices. *Future Business Journal*, *11*(1). https://doi.org/10.1186/s43093-025-00462-5
Mariyono, D., & Hd, A. N. A. (2025). AI's role in transforming learning environments: A review of collaborative approaches and innovations. *Quality Education for All*, *2*(1), 267–290. https://doi.org/10.1108/qea-08-2024-0071
Matthews, G., Hancock, P. A., Szalma, J. L., Lin, J., & Panganiban, A. R. (2024). Individual differences in teaming with artificial intelligence, Robots, and virtual agents in the workplace. In *Oxford university press eBooks* (pp. 345–367). https://doi.org/10.1093/oxfordhb/9780192897114.013.25
McCabe, E., Amarbayan, M., Rabi, S., Mendoza, J., Naqvi, S. F., Bajgain, K. T., Zwicker, J. D., & Santana, M. (2022). Youth engagement in mental health research: A systematic review. *Health Expectations*, *26*(1), 30–50. https://doi.org/10.1111/hex.13650
Meduri, K., Podicheti, S., Satish, S., & Whig, P. (2024). Accountability and transparency ensuring responsible AI development. In *Advances in human and social aspects of technology book series* (pp. 83–102). https://doi.org/10.4018/979-8-3693-4147-6.ch004

Meekaew, N., & Jongnimitsataporn, P. (2023). How capable are they of becoming a digital teacher? Correlation analysis of individual characteristics, digital self-efficacy, and digital xitizenship among pre-service teachers in northeast Thailand. *Higher Education Studies*, *13*(2), 63. https://doi.org/10.5539/hes.v13n2p63

Miller, K., & Demirbilek, M. (2023). The role of social media in the fight against gender violence. In *Advances in human and social aspects of technology book series* (pp. 90–99). https://doi.org/10.4018/978-1-6684-8893-5.ch006

Mohamed, E. a. S., Osman, M. E., & Mohamed, B. A. (2024). The impact of artificial intelligence on social media content. *Journal of Social Sciences*, *20*(1), 12–16. https://doi.org/10.3844/jssp.2024.12.16

Munoz, I., Kim, P., O'Neil, C., Dunn, M., & Sawyer, S. (2024). Platformization of Inequality: Gender and race in digital labor platforms. *Proceedings of the ACM on Human-Computer Interaction*, *8*(CSCW1), 1–22. https://doi.org/10.1145/3637385

Ng, D. T. K., Su, J., Leung, J. K. L., & Chu, S. K. W. (2023). Artificial intelligence (AI) literacy education in secondary schools: A review. *Interactive Learning Environments*, *32*(10), 6204–6224. https://doi.org/10.1080/10494820.2023.2255228

Nguyen, A., Ngo, H. N., Hong, Y., Dang, B., & Nguyen, B. T. (2022). Ethical principles for artificial intelligence in education. *Education and Information Technologies*, *28*(4), 4221–4241. https://doi.org/10.1007/s10639-022-11316-w

Noller, D. T., & Thimesch, A. E. (2025). Artificial intelligence in higher education: Legal accountability and best practices for upholding student privacy and nondiscrimination rights. *The Journal of Physician Assistant Education*, *36*(3), e308–e311. https://doi.org/10.1097/jpa.0000000000000688

Omol, E. J. (2023). Organizational digital transformation: From evolution to future trends. *Digital Transformation and Society*, *3*(3), 240–256. https://doi.org/10.1108/dts-08-2023-0061

Opoku, D., Donkor, C., Yeboah, J. N. O., & Quagraine, L. (2025). Navigating the relationship between social media use and mental health in the digital age. *Discover Mental Health*, *5*(1), 149. https://doi.org/10.1007/s44192-025-00285-4

Osei-Appiah, S., Mutsvairo, B., & Orgeret, K. S. (2023). Women and digital political communication in non-western societies. *Information Communication & Society*, *26*(13), 2507–2517. https://doi.org/10.1080/1369118x.2023.2257995

Ozbey, F., & Yasa, Y. (2025). The relationships of personality traits on perceptions and attitudes of dentistry students towards AI. *BMC Medical Education*, *25*(1), 26. https://doi.org/10.1186/s12909-024-06630-5

Ozimek, P., Brandenberg, G., Rohmann, E., & Bierhoff, H. (2023). The impact of social comparisons more related to ability vs. More Related to Opinion on Well-Being: An Instagram Study. *Behavioral Sciences*, *13*(10), 850. https://doi.org/10.3390/bs13100850

Pappas, I. O., Mikalef, P., Dwivedi, Y. K., Jaccheri, L., & Krogstie, J. (2023). Responsible digital transformation for a sustainable society. *Information Systems Frontiers*, *25*(3), 945–953. https://doi.org/10.1007/s10796-023-10406-5

Paschal, M. J., & Melly, I. K. (2023). Ethical guidelines on the use of AI in education. In *Advances in educational technologies and instructional design book series* (pp. 230–245). https://doi.org/10.4018/979-8-3693-0205-7.ch013

Pasupuleti, M. K. (2024). Ethical AI governance: A global blueprint. *International Journal of Academic and Industrial Research Innovations*, *4*(3), 60–77. https://doi.org/10.62311/nesx/97832

Peraza-Balderrama, J. N., Valdés-Cuervo, Á. A., Parra-Pérez, L. G., & Urías-Murrieta, M. (2024). Multidimensional scale to assess digital security in adolescents. *Revista Electrónica De Investigación Educativa*, *26*, 1–19. https://doi.org/10.24320/redie.2024.26.e06.5992

Pflanzer, M., Dubljević, V., Bauer, W. A., Orcutt, D., List, G., & Singh, M. P. (2023). Embedding AI in society: Ethics, policy, governance, and impacts. *AI & Society*, *38*(4), 1267–1271. https://doi.org/10.1007/s00146-023-01704-2

Polemi, N., Praça, I., Kioskli, K., & Bécue, A. (2024). Challenges and efforts in managing AI trustworthiness risks: A state of knowledge. *Frontiers in Big Data*, *7*, 1381163. https://doi.org/10.3389/fdata.2024.1381163

Saheb, T., & Saheb, T. (2024). Mapping ethical artificial intelligence policy landscape: A mixed method analysis. *Science and Engineering Ethics*, *30*(2), 9. https://doi.org/10.1007/s11948-024-00472-6

Sahebi, S., & Formosa, P. (2022). Social media and its negative impacts on autonomy. *Philosophy & Technology*, *35*(3). https://doi.org/10.1007/s13347-022-00567-7

Sarin, P., & Hill-Bonnet, L. (2025). Suspending disbelief: The algorithmic theater of student computer tracking software. *Surveillance & Society*, *23*(2), 182–198. https://doi.org/10.24908/ss.v23i2.17764

Sasahara, K., Chen, W., Peng, H., Ciampaglia, G. L., Flammini, A., & Menczer, F. (2020). Social influence and unfollowing accelerate the emergence of echo chambers. *Journal of Computational Social Science*, *4*(1), 381–402. https://doi.org/10.1007/s42001-020-00084-7

Schlund, R., & Zitek, E. M. (2024). Algorithmic versus human surveillance leads to lower perceptions of autonomy and increased resistance. *Communications Psychology*, *2*(1). https://doi.org/10.1038/s44271-024-00102-8

Schneider, N. (2022). Governable spaces: A feminist agenda for platform policy. *Internet Policy Review*, *11*(1). https://doi.org/10.14763/2022.1.1628

Sindermann, C., Yang, H., Elhai, J. D., Yang, S., Quan, L., Li, M., & Montag, C. (2022). Acceptance and fear of artificial intelligence: Associations with personality in a german and a chinese sample. *Discover Psychology*, *2*(1). https://doi.org/10.1007/s44202-022-00020-y

Stein, J., Messingschlager, T., Gnambs, T., Hutmacher, F., & Appel, M. (2024). Attitudes towards AI: Measurement and associations with personality. *Scientific Reports*, *14*(1), 2909. https://doi.org/10.1038/s41598-024-53335-2

Stevie, A. B., & Ammara, A. (2023). The shortcomings of artificial intelligence: A comprehensive study. *International Journal of Library and Information Science*, *15*(2), 8–13. https://doi.org/10.5897/ijlis2023.1068

Stix, C. (2021). Actionable principles for artificial intelligence policy: Three pathways. *Science and Engineering Ethics*, *27*(1), 15. https://doi.org/10.1007/s11948-020-00277-3

Stringhi, E. (2022). Addressing gendered affordances of the platform economy: The case of UpWork. *Internet Policy Review*, *11*(1). https://doi.org/10.14763/2022.1.1634

Sun, R., Tang, M., Zhou, J., Loan, N. T. T., & Wang, C. (2025). The dark tetrad as associated factors in generative AI academic misconduct: Insights beyond personal attribute variables. *Frontiers in Education*, *10*. https://doi.org/10.3389/feduc.2025.1551721

Sywelem, M. M. G., & Mahklouf, A. M. E. (2024). Ethical considerations in the integration of artificial intelligence in education: An overview. *Computer Science & Information Technology*, 01–15. https://doi.org/10.5121/csit.2024.141201

Taylor, J., & Armes, G. (2024). Social comparison on Instagram, and its relationship with self-esteem and body-esteem. *Discover Psychology*, *4*(1). https://doi.org/10.1007/s44202-024-00241-3

Tsouparopoulou, E., Symeonaki, M., Parsanoglou, D., & Kazani, A. (2025). European youth and digital engagement: Attitudes, skills, and civic participation. *Journal of Applied Youth Studies*, *8*(2), 219–247. https://doi.org/10.1007/s43151-025-00168-z

Uslu, O. (2025). Understanding digital wellbeing: Impacts, strategies, and the path to healthier technology practices. *Discover Social Science and Health*, *5*(1). https://doi.org/10.1007/s44155-025-00259-5

Vyas, N. (2020). 'Gender inequality- now available on digital platform': An interplay between gender equality and the gig economy in the European Union. *European Labour Law Journal*, *12*(1), 37–51. https://doi.org/10.1177/2031952520953856

Walter, Y. (2024). Embracing the future of artificial intelligence in the classroom: The relevance of AI literacy, prompt engineering, and critical thinking in modern education. *International Journal of Educational Technology in Higher Education, 21*, Article 15. https://doi.org/10.1186/s41239-024-00448-3

Weigle, P. E., & Shafi, R. M. A. (2023). Social media and youth mental health. *Current Psychiatry Reports*, *26*(1), 1–8. https://doi.org/10.1007/s11920-023-01478-w

Wernick, A., & Artyushina, A. (2023). Future-proofing the city: A human rights-based approach to governing algorithmic, biometric and smart city technologies. *Internet Policy Review*, *12*(1). https://doi.org/10.14763/2023.1.1695

Xavier, B. (2024). Biases within AI: Challenging the illusion of neutrality. *AI & Society*, *40*(3), 1545–1546. https://doi.org/10.1007/s00146-024-01985-1

Yadav, S. (2024). Navigating the landscape of AI integration in education: Opportunities, challenges, and ethical considerations for harnessing the potential of artificial intelligence (AI) for teaching and learning. *BSSS Journal of Computer, 15*(1), 38–48. https://doi.org/10.51767/jc1503

Yan, Y., & Liu, H. (2024). Ethical framework for AI education based on large language models. *Education and Information Technologies*, *30*(8), 10891–10909. https://doi.org/10.1007/s10639-024-13241-6

Yang, J., Xie, W., & Ni, J. (2025). A framework for AI ethics literacy: Development, validation, and its role in fostering students' self-rated learning competence. *Scientific Reports*, *15*(1), 38030. https://doi.org/10.1038/s41598-025-21977-5

Yirmiya, K., & Fonagy, P. (2025). Mentalizing without a mind: Psychotherapeutic potential of generative AI. *Journal of Medical Internet Research*, *27*, e79156. https://doi.org/10.2196/79156

Zainuddin, N. (2024). Does artificial intelligence cause more harm than good in schools? *International Journal of Language Education and Applied Linguistics*, *14*(1), 1–3. https://doi.org/10.15282/ijleal.v14i1.10432

Zhang, L. (2025). A study on cyborgized body presentation in social media and the identity anxiety of young women. *Humanities and Social Science Research*, *8*(4), p223. https://doi.org/10.30560/hssr.v8n4p223

Zuboff, S. (2022). Surveillance capitalism or democracy? the death match of institutional orders and the politics of knowledge in our information civilization. *Organization Theory*, *3*(3). https://doi.org/10.1177/26317877221129290

GLOSSARY OF KEY TERMS

A

Adaptive learning technologies Educational systems that personalize learning experiences to individual student needs, providing customized feedback, pacing, and content recommendations based on learner performance and preferences. These technologies use algorithms to adjust difficulty levels and instructional strategies in real-time.

Addictive design elements Features intentionally incorporated into digital platforms to maximize user engagement and time spent on the platform, often exploiting psychological vulnerabilities. Examples include infinite scroll, variable reward schedules, notifications, and gamification elements that trigger dopamine responses.

Adversarial attacks Deliberate attempts to manipulate or exploit artificial intelligence systems by providing misleading input data or feedback to cause the system to make errors or behave in unintended ways.

Affective computing The field of artificial intelligence focused on recognizing, interpreting, processing, and simulating human emotions through computational systems. Applications include emotion recognition software and AI-driven mental health support tools.

Agile ethics An approach to ethical AI development that emphasizes iterative design, continuous feedback loops, stakeholder engagement, and adaptive refinement of ethical principles based on real-world implementation experiences.

Algorithmic bias Systematic errors or discrimination in artificial intelligence systems that result from biased training data, flawed algorithm design, or unexamined assumptions. Algorithmic bias can perpetuate and amplify existing social inequalities based on race, gender, socioeconomic status, and other characteristics.

Algorithmic discrimination The practice or outcome of artificial intelligence systems treating individuals or groups unfairly or unequally based on protected characteristics or correlated proxies, resulting in disparate impact on opportunities, resources, or treatment.

Algorithmic transparency The degree to which the decision-making processes of artificial intelligence systems are understandable to users and stakeholders. Transparent algorithms provide explanations for their outputs and allow users to understand how their data is being used.

Anonymity The state of being unknown or unidentified online. Digital anonymity can enable freedom of expression but also facilitate harmful behaviors such as cyberbullying and harassment without accountability.

Artificial intelligence (AI) Computer systems designed to perform tasks that typically require human intelligence, including learning from experience, recognizing patterns, understanding language, and making decisions. In the context of this book, AI refers to machine learning systems, recommendation algorithms, and automated decision-making systems used in digital platforms and applications.

Attachment styles Patterns of emotional bonding and interpersonal relating developed in early relationships that influence how individuals form connections and manage intimacy in adulthood. Attachment styles (secure, anxious, avoidant, disorganized) affect how young people engage in digital relationships.

Attention economy An economic system in which the scarcity of human attention is the primary resource. Digital platforms compete for user attention through engaging content, notifications, and algorithmic curation, often prioritizing engagement over user well-being.

Autonomy The capacity and right of individuals to make informed decisions about their own lives, including decisions about digital engagement, data sharing, and use of technology. Ethical AI design respects user autonomy by providing meaningful choice and control.

B

Behavioral addiction Compulsive engagement with a behavior (such as social media use or gaming) despite negative consequences, characterized by loss of control, tolerance, withdrawal symptoms, and continued engagement despite harm. Distinguished from substance addiction but shares similar neurobiological mechanisms.

Behavioral curation The process through which artificial intelligence systems shape user behavior by selectively presenting content, opportunities, and interactions based on algorithms designed to maximize engagement or achieve specific outcomes.

Bias testing Systematic evaluation of artificial intelligence systems to identify and measure discriminatory outcomes across different demographic groups. Bias testing involves testing algorithms on diverse datasets and user populations to detect disparate impacts.

Big five personality model A widely-used psychological framework describing five major dimensions of personality: Openness (curiosity and creativity), Conscientiousness (organization and discipline), Extraversion (sociability and assertiveness), Agreeableness (cooperation and compassion), and Neuroticism (emotional sensitivity and anxiety). Also known as the Five-Factor Model (FFM).

Biometric data Physiological or behavioral measurements that can be used to identify individuals, including fingerprints, facial recognition, voice patterns, and eye movements. Biometric data collected through devices and apps raises significant privacy concerns.

Boundary dissolution The blurring or disappearance of distinctions between previously separate domains, such as the merging of online and offline identities, or the integration of work and personal life through digital platforms.

C

Catfishing Deceptive cyber behavior in which an individual creates a false identity to lure another person into an emotional or romantic relationship. Common on social media and dating platforms.

Civic engagement Participation in democratic processes and community activities, including voting, volunteering, activism, and community organizing. Digital platforms can facilitate or hinder civic engagement depending on how they are designed and used.

Clinical safety review Systematic evaluation of artificial intelligence systems designed for mental health applications to ensure they meet clinical standards, do not cause harm, and provide appropriate care. Includes assessment of diagnostic accuracy, treatment recommendations, and crisis response protocols.

Co-design A participatory design approach in which end-users, stakeholders, and designers collaborate throughout the development process to create solutions that meet actual needs and values. Youth co-design involves young people in developing digital platforms and policies that affect them.

Cognitive biases Systematic patterns of deviation from rational judgment that occur when processing and interpreting information. Examples include confirmation bias, availability bias, and social comparison bias, which are often amplified by algorithmic curation.

Cognitive distortions Inaccurate or irrational thought patterns that can contribute to mental health problems such as depression and anxiety. Digital environments can amplify cognitive distortions through social comparison, cyberbullying, and exposure to misinformation.

Cognitive load The amount of mental effort required to process information and complete tasks. Digital environments with excessive notifications, competing stimuli, and complex interfaces can increase cognitive load and reduce well-being.

Collective intelligence The aggregated knowledge, skills, and insights of a group that exceeds what any individual member could achieve alone. Digital platforms can facilitate collective intelligence through collaboration and knowledge sharing.

Commercial surveillance The systematic collection and analysis of user data by corporations for marketing, behavioral prediction, and profit. Commercial surveillance raises concerns about privacy, manipulation, and exploitation.

Community moderation The process of managing user-generated content and interactions within online communities to maintain safety, civility, and alignment with community standards. Can be human-moderated, AI-moderated, or hybrid.

Computer-mediated communication (CMC) Communication that occurs through digital channels and platforms rather than face-to-face. CMC has distinctive characteristics including asynchronicity, reduced nonverbal cues, and permanence of messages.

Confirmation bias The tendency to seek, interpret, and remember information that confirms pre-existing beliefs while dismissing contradictory evidence. Algorithmic curation can amplify confirmation bias by showing users content aligned with their existing views.

Consent Voluntary, informed agreement to participate in an activity or share information. Meaningful consent requires clear information about what is being consented to, genuine choice, and the ability to withdraw consent.

Cyber behavior Patterns of human action and interaction that occur in digital environments. Cyber behaviors include social-commercial behaviors (social media engagement, online shopping), aggressive behaviors (cyberbullying, harassment), and addictive behaviors (compulsive platform use).

Cyberbullying Deliberate, repeated harassment, humiliation, or aggression directed at an individual through digital channels. Cyberbullying can include insults, threats, exclusion, impersonation, and the sharing of embarrassing content.

Cybernetic self A theoretical concept describing identity as continuously constructed and reconstructed through feedback loops in digital environments. The cybernetic self emphasizes the dynamic, relational nature of digital identity formation.

Cyberpsychology The scientific, interdisciplinary study of the psychological phenomena emerging from human interaction with digital technology, particularly the internet. Cyberpsychology examines how individuals perceive themselves and others online, form digital identities and relationships, and are affected by technological design.

Cybersecurity Measures and practices designed to protect digital systems, networks, and data from unauthorized access, theft, and damage. Cybersecurity is essential for protecting youth privacy and preventing identity theft.

D

Dark patterns User interface design choices that manipulate users into taking actions that benefit the platform or company rather than the user. Dark patterns exploit psychological vulnerabilities and cognitive biases to increase engagement or data collection.

Dark tetrad A group of four personality traits associated with antisocial and harmful behavior: narcissism, psychopathy, Machiavellianism, and sadism. Individuals high in Dark Tetrad traits may engage in cyberbullying, online manipulation, and exploitation.

Data governance Organizational policies, procedures, and practices for managing data collection, storage, use, and deletion. Ethical data governance ensures data is used responsibly, securely, and in alignment with user rights and values.

Data minimization An ethical principle and regulatory requirement that organizations collect only the minimum amount of personal data necessary to accomplish specific, legitimate purposes. Data minimization reduces privacy risks and user vulnerability.

Data retention Policies determining how long personal data is stored before being deleted or anonymized. Appropriate data retention limits reduce privacy risks and comply with data protection regulations.

Deepfakes Synthetic media (images, videos, or audio) created using artificial intelligence to depict individuals saying or doing things they did not actually say or do. Deepfakes can be used for misinformation, harassment, or exploitation.

Developmental vulnerability Characteristics of adolescent development that create susceptibility to harm from digital engagement, including incomplete prefrontal cortex development, heightened peer sensitivity, identity formation processes, and developing emotional regulation skills.

Disinhibition effect The tendency for individuals to behave with less restraint and more aggression online compared to face-to-face interactions, attributed to anonymity, psychological distance, and reduced social cues in digital environments.

Digital citizenship The knowledge, skills, attitudes, and values necessary to participate safely, ethically, and responsibly in digital environments. Digital citizenship includes digital literacy, ethical behavior, privacy awareness, and critical thinking about technology.

Digital divide Inequalities in access to digital technology and the internet based on socioeconomic status, geography, disability status, and other factors. The digital divide creates disparities in educational and economic opportunities.

Digital footprint The trail of data and information left behind by individuals as they interact with digital platforms and services. Digital footprints include browsing history, social media posts, location data, and transaction records.

Digital identity The representation of self in digital environments, including social media profiles, online personas, and digital artifacts. Digital identity is constructed through self-presentation, feedback from others, and algorithmic curation.

Digital literacy The knowledge, skills, and competencies necessary to effectively and safely use digital technology and the internet. Digital literacy includes technical skills, critical evaluation of online information, privacy awareness, and ethical digital behavior.

Digital native An individual who has grown up with digital technology and the internet as a normal part of their environment. Digital natives have different patterns of technology use and expectations compared to digital immigrants.

Digital well-being A state of physical, mental, social, and emotional health supported by responsible and balanced use of digital technology. Digital well-being encompasses mental health, social relationships, privacy, autonomy, and ethical engagement with technology.

Disinformation Deliberately false or misleading information created and spread with the intent to deceive or manipulate. Disinformation differs from misinformation, which is false information spread without malicious intent.

Dopamine A neurotransmitter associated with reward, motivation, and pleasure. Digital platforms are often designed to trigger dopamine release through variable reward schedules, creating reinforcement loops that encourage continued engagement.

Dark web The portion of the internet that is intentionally hidden and requires specific software to access. The dark web can facilitate both privacy-protective activities and illegal behaviors.

E

Emotional contagion The tendency for emotions to spread through groups, including through digital channels. Social media can facilitate the rapid spread of both positive and negative emotions through networks.

Emotional dependency Reliance on digital platforms or AI systems to meet emotional needs, characterized by compulsive checking, anxiety when separated from the platform, and difficulty managing emotions without digital support.

Emotional intelligence The capacity to recognize, understand, and manage emotions in oneself and others. Emotional intelligence is important for healthy digital relationships and for resisting manipulation through emotional appeals.

Emotional sensitivity Individual differences in responsiveness to emotional stimuli and experiences. Individuals high in emotional sensitivity may be more vulnerable to cyberbullying, social comparison, and emotional manipulation on digital platforms.

Empathy The capacity to understand and share the feelings of others. Reduced nonverbal cues in digital communication can impair empathy and increase misunderstandings and conflict.

Engagement optimization The process of designing digital platforms and content to maximize user engagement, often through exploiting psychological vulnerabilities and attention mechanisms. Engagement optimization prioritizes platform metrics over user well-being.

Ethical AI Artificial intelligence systems developed, deployed, and governed in ways that align with human values, protect human rights, and promote human flourishing. Ethical AI incorporates principles of fairness, transparency, accountability, and respect for autonomy.

Ethical by design An approach to technology development that integrates ethical principles and safeguards throughout the design and development process rather than as an afterthought. Ethical by design requires ongoing stakeholder engagement and iterative refinement.

Ethical framework A set of principles, values, and guidelines for making decisions about right and wrong conduct. Ethical frameworks provide structure for addressing complex ethical dilemmas in AI development and digital platform design.

Ethical vigilance Ongoing, systematic attention to ethical issues and potential harms in technology development and deployment. Ethical vigilance requires continuous monitoring, stakeholder feedback, and willingness to modify systems when harms are identified.

Exploitation Taking unfair advantage of someone's vulnerability, labor, or resources for personal gain. Digital exploitation includes data exploitation, labor exploitation, and sexual exploitation of minors.

F

Feedback loop A cycle in which the output of a system becomes input that influences subsequent outputs. In digital platforms, feedback loops can reinforce engagement (positive feedback) or create echo chambers (reinforcing feedback).

Filter bubble A personalized universe of information created by algorithmic curation that shows users content aligned with their existing preferences and beliefs while filtering out contradictory information. Filter bubbles can limit exposure to diverse perspectives.

Five-factor model (FFM) See Big Five Personality Model.

Flourishing A state of optimal human functioning characterized by engagement in meaningful activities, positive relationships, personal growth, and a sense of purpose. Digital well-being supports flourishing by enabling positive engagement while minimizing harm.

Fomo (fear of missing out) Anxiety or apprehension about missing out on social experiences, events, or information shared on social media. FOMO can drive compulsive checking of social media and contribute to anxiety and depression.

Fortnite phenomenon The widespread adoption of online gaming platforms as primary social spaces for youth, particularly during periods of social isolation. Represents a shift in how youth form peer relationships and spend leisure time.

G

Gamification The application of game design elements (points, badges, leaderboards, challenges) to non-game contexts to increase engagement and motivation. Gamification can be beneficial for learning but can also exploit psychological vulnerabilities.

Gender The socially constructed roles, behaviors, and attributes associated with being male, female, or non-binary. Gender influences digital engagement patterns, mental health outcomes, and vulnerability to online harms.

Generational differences Variations in values, behaviors, and technology use across age cohorts (e.g., Gen Z, Millennials). Generational differences in digital engagement reflect different formative experiences with technology.

Global connectivity The ability to form relationships and access information across geographic and cultural boundaries through digital platforms. Global connectivity creates opportunities for learning and connection but also risks of exposure to harmful content.

Granular consent A consent model that allows users to make specific choices about different types of data sharing and platform features rather than requiring all-or-nothing consent. Granular consent provides greater user control and autonomy.

Grooming A process of building trust with a minor for the purpose of sexual exploitation. Online grooming occurs through digital platforms and can involve deception, manipulation, and gradually escalating inappropriate contact.

H

Harassment Repeated, unwanted contact or behavior intended to intimidate, threaten, or harm another person. Online harassment can include insults, threats, doxxing, and coordinated attacks.

HEXACO model A personality model describing six dimensions: Honesty-Humility, Emotionality, eXtraversion, Agreeableness, Conscientiousness, and Openness to Experience. The HEXACO model includes Honesty-Humility, which is particularly relevant for predicting ethical behavior.

Human oversight The requirement that important decisions affecting individuals are reviewed and approved by qualified human professionals rather than being made entirely by automated systems. Human oversight is essential for protecting vulnerable populations.

Human-AI collaboration Partnership between human judgment and artificial intelligence systems in decision-making and problem-solving. Effective human-AI collaboration leverages the strengths of each while mitigating their individual limitations.

I

Identity exploration The process through which adolescents experiment with different aspects of self-presentation and values to develop a coherent sense of identity. Digital platforms provide spaces for identity exploration but also risks of identity confusion and distress.

Implicit bias Unconscious attitudes or stereotypes that influence behavior and decision-making. Implicit biases in training data and algorithm design can lead to algorithmic discrimination.

Impression management The process of controlling how others perceive you through selective self-presentation. Digital platforms enable sophisticated impression management through the curation of content and the careful construction of profiles.

Incident response plan Organizational procedures for identifying, responding to, and learning from adverse events or harms caused by AI systems. Incident response plans include reporting mechanisms, investigation procedures, and remediation strategies.

Inclusivity The practice of ensuring that systems, policies, and services are accessible and welcoming to people of diverse backgrounds, abilities, and identities. Inclusive design considers the needs of marginalized and vulnerable populations.

Individualism A cultural orientation emphasizing individual autonomy, personal achievement, and self-expression. Individualistic cultures exhibit different patterns of digital engagement than collectivist cultures.

Industrie 4.0 The fourth industrial revolution is characterized by the integration of digital, physical, and biological systems. Industrie 4.0 includes widespread adoption of AI, IoT, and automation in manufacturing and services.

Infinite scroll A design feature that automatically loads new content as users scroll, eliminating the need to click to load more content. Infinite scroll increases engagement but can encourage compulsive use.

Information overload Exposure to excessive amounts of information that exceed cognitive capacity to process effectively. Digital environments can create information overload through constant notifications and content streams.

Informed consent Voluntary agreement to participate in an activity or research based on clear, accurate information about what is being consented to, potential risks and benefits, and alternatives. Informed consent requires understanding and genuine choice.

Intersectionality The interconnected nature of social categories (race, gender, class, sexuality, disability, etc.) and how they interact to create overlapping systems of advantage and disadvantage. Intersectional analysis recognizes that individuals have multiple, intersecting identities.

Internet of things (IoT) A Network of physical devices, vehicles, appliances, and other objects embedded with sensors and software that collect and share data. IoT devices raise privacy and security concerns, particularly when used to monitor youth.

J

Just-in-time intervention Delivery of support or intervention at the moment when it is most needed and likely to be effective. AI systems can enable just-in-time mental health interventions by detecting distress and providing immediate support.

K

Key performance indicators (KPIs) Measurable values that indicate how effectively an organization is achieving its objectives. In digital platforms, KPIs often emphasize engagement metrics rather than user well-being.

L

Latent Dirichlet allocation (LDA) A machine learning technique for discovering abstract topics in large collections of documents. LDA can be used to analyze patterns in user-generated content and identify emerging trends.

Learning analytics The collection and analysis of data about learner behavior and performance to understand and optimize learning. Learning analytics can personalize education, but also raise privacy concerns.

Longitudinal study Research that follows the same individuals over an extended period to track changes and outcomes. Longitudinal studies are valuable for understanding the long-term effects of digital engagement on youth development.

M

Machiavellianism A personality trait characterized by strategic manipulation, self-interest, and willingness to deceive others to achieve goals. Individuals high in Machiavellianism may engage in online manipulation and exploitation.

Machine learning A subset of artificial intelligence focused on developing systems that can learn from data and improve performance without explicit programming. Machine learning powers recommendation algorithms and other AI applications in digital platforms.

Marginalized communities Groups that face systemic disadvantage and exclusion based on characteristics such as race, ethnicity, socioeconomic status, disability, or sexual orientation. Digital platforms can provide opportunities for marginalized communities, but also expose them to harassment and discrimination.

Media literacy The ability to critically evaluate and create media messages. Media literacy is essential for navigating digital environments and resisting manipulation through misinformation and persuasive content.

Mental health A state of psychological well-being characterized by emotional regulation, positive relationships, a sense of purpose, and the ability to cope with stress. Digital engagement can support or undermine mental health depending on how platforms are designed and used.

Meta-analysis A Statistical technique for combining results from multiple studies to draw overall conclusions about a research question. Meta-analyses can provide comprehensive evidence about the effects of digital engagement on youth outcomes.

Microaggressions Brief, everyday slights, insults, or invalidations directed at individuals from marginalized groups. Microaggressions can occur online and contribute to cumulative stress and psychological harm.

Misinformation False or misleading information spread without malicious intent. Misinformation differs from disinformation, which is deliberately false information created to deceive.

Mobile-first design Design approach that prioritizes the mobile experience, recognizing that many users access digital platforms primarily through smartphones. Mobile-first design has implications for how content is presented and how engagement is optimized.

Moderation Management of user-generated content and community interactions to maintain safety and civility. Moderation can be human-moderated, AI-moderated, or hybrid.

Moral development The process through which individuals develop an understanding of right and wrong and the capacity for ethical reasoning. Moral development continues through adolescence and is influenced by social relationships and experiences.

Moral disengagement Psychological mechanisms through which individuals justify harmful behavior and reduce self-censure. Digital anonymity can facilitate moral disengagement and increase the likelihood of harmful online behavior.

N

Narcissism A personality trait characterized by excessive self-focus, need for admiration, and lack of empathy. Individuals high in narcissism may use social media for self-promotion and may engage in cyberbullying.

Neuroscience The scientific study of the nervous system and brain. Neuroscience research reveals how digital engagement affects brain development, particularly in adolescence.

Neuroticism A Big Five personality trait characterized by a tendency toward negative emotions such as anxiety, sadness, and irritability. Individuals high in neuroticism may be more vulnerable to the mental health impacts of cyberbullying and social comparison.

Nomophobia Fear of being without one's mobile phone or being unable to use it. Nomophobia reflects dependence on mobile devices and can interfere with offline activities and relationships.

Non-binary gender Gender identity that does not fit exclusively into male or female categories. Non-binary individuals may face unique challenges and opportunities in cyberspaces.

O

Offline self The identity and behaviors expressed in face-to-face interactions and physical spaces. The distinction between offline and online self is becoming increasingly blurred as digital and physical worlds integrate.

Online disinhibition effect See Disinhibition Effect.

Online harassment See Harassment.

Online identity See Digital Identity.

Openness to experience A Big Five personality trait characterized by curiosity, creativity, and openness to new ideas and experiences. Individuals high in openness may be more likely to explore diverse online communities and perspectives.

Opt-in vs. opt-out Different approaches to consent and data collection. Opt-in requires users to explicitly agree to data collection, while opt-out allows collection unless users explicitly refuse. Opt-in provides stronger privacy protection.

P

Parasocial relationships One-sided relationships in which an individual develops feelings of connection and intimacy with a media figure or online persona who does not know them. Parasocial relationships are common in social media and can affect mental health.

Parental monitoring Supervision and oversight of children's digital activities by parents. Parental monitoring can protect youth from harm, but can also invade privacy and undermine autonomy if overly intrusive.

Peer influence The impact of peers on individual attitudes, values, and behaviors. Digital platforms amplify peer influence through social comparison, social proof, and conformity pressures.

Personality traits Stable patterns of thoughts, feelings, and behaviors that characterize individuals. Personality traits moderate how individuals experience digital environments and respond to risks.

Personalization Customization of digital experiences based on individual user data and preferences. Personalization can enhance user experience, but can also create filter bubbles and enable manipulation.

Phishing Deceptive attempts to obtain sensitive information (passwords, financial data) by impersonating trusted sources. Phishing is a common cybersecurity threat, particularly for youth who may be less aware of risks.

Phubbing The practice of snubbing someone by ignoring them in favor of a mobile phone. Phubbing can damage relationships and degrade the quality of face-to-face interaction.

Policymakers Government officials and administrators responsible for developing policies and regulations affecting digital technology, education, and youth protection.

Post-deployment audit Systematic evaluation of AI systems after they have been deployed to assess real-world performance, identify unintended consequences, and ensure continued alignment with ethical principles.

Practitioners Professionals who work directly with youth, including educators, mental health professionals, social workers, and counselors. Practitioners implement interventions and support youth digital well-being.

Privacy The right to control information about oneself and limit access to personal data. Privacy is essential for autonomy and protection from exploitation and discrimination.

Privacy by design An approach to technology development that integrates privacy protections throughout the design and development process rather than as an afterthought. Privacy by design includes data minimization, purpose limitation, and user control.

Privilege Unearned advantages and benefits granted to individuals based on membership in dominant social groups. Understanding privilege is important for recognizing how digital platforms and algorithms may advantage some groups while disadvantaging others.

Psychological dependency Reliance on digital platforms or substances to manage emotions or cope with stress. Psychological dependency can develop through reinforcement loops in digital platforms.

Psychological distance The subjective sense of remoteness or separation from others in digital communication. Psychological distance can reduce empathy and increase disinhibition.

Psychometric testing Standardized assessment of psychological characteristics such as personality traits, intelligence, and mental health. Psychometric tests are used in research to measure individual differences.

Psychopathy A personality trait characterized by a lack of empathy, callousness, and a tendency toward manipulative and harmful behavior. Individuals high in psychopathy may engage in cyberbullying and online exploitation.

Public health approach Framework for addressing health issues at the population level through prevention, early intervention, and treatment. A public health approach to digital well-being emphasizes prevention and systemic change rather than individual responsibility alone.

Q

Qualitative research Research methods focused on understanding meaning, experience, and context through in-depth exploration. Qualitative research provides a rich understanding of how youth experience digital engagement.

Quantitative research Research methods focused on the measurement and statistical analysis of numerical data. Quantitative research provides evidence about the prevalence and magnitude of effects.

R

Recommendation algorithm An Artificial intelligence system that predicts user preferences and suggests content, products, or connections. Recommendation algorithms are central to how digital platforms curate experiences and shape behavior.

Reflection questions Prompts designed to encourage critical thinking and self-examination. Reflection questions are used throughout this book to promote engagement and application of concepts.

Regulation Government rules and requirements that govern how organizations develop, deploy, and use technology. Regulation can protect youth privacy and safety, but can also stifle innovation if poorly designed.

Reinforcement learning A Machine learning approach in which an AI system learns through trial and error, receiving rewards or penalties for different actions. Reinforcement learning is used to optimize recommendation algorithms and engagement metrics.

Relational aggression Harm inflicted through damage to relationships or social status, including exclusion, rumor-spreading, and public humiliation. Relational aggression is common in cyberbullying and particularly affects females.

Resilience The capacity to adapt and recover from adversity. Digital resilience includes the ability to cope with cyberbullying, misinformation, and other online risks.

Revenue model The way an organization generates income. Many digital platforms use advertising-based revenue models that incentivize maximizing user engagement rather than user well-being.

Risk assessment Systematic evaluation of potential harms and their likelihood. Risk assessment is important for identifying vulnerable populations and designing appropriate safeguards.

S

Sadism A personality trait characterized by the enjoyment of causing suffering to others. Individuals high in sadism may engage in cyberbullying and online harassment.

Safeguarding Measures and practices designed to protect vulnerable individuals from harm. Safeguarding for youth includes protecting them from exploitation, abuse, and other harms.

Safety by design An approach to technology development that integrates safety protections throughout the design and development process. Safety by design includes identifying risks, implementing safeguards, and testing for unintended consequences.

Sampling bias Systematic error in research resulting from non-random or unrepresentative sampling. Sampling bias can limit the generalizability of research findings.

Screening Initial assessment to identify individuals who may have a mental health condition or be at risk. AI-assisted screening can increase access but requires human follow-up for confirmation and treatment.

Self-efficacy Belief in one's capacity to successfully complete tasks and achieve goals. Digital platforms can support or undermine self-efficacy depending on the feedback and opportunities for success they provide.

Self-esteem Overall evaluation of one's worth and value. Social media can affect self-esteem through social comparison, feedback from others, and algorithmic curation of opportunities for self-presentation.

Self-harm Deliberate injury to oneself, typically as a way of coping with emotional distress. Cyberbullying and other online harms can increase the risk of self-harm among vulnerable youth.

Self-presentation The process of controlling how others perceive you through selective disclosure and impression management. Digital platforms enable sophisticated self-presentation through profile curation.

Sentiment analysis A Computational technique for identifying and categorizing emotional tone in text. Sentiment analysis can be used to detect cyberbullying, misinformation, and mental health concerns in user-generated content.

Sexting Exchange of sexually explicit messages or images, typically between peers. While sexting between consenting adults is legal, it raises concerns about youth who may be coerced or exploited.

Sextortion Extortion through the threat of distributing intimate images or information. Sextortion is a form of cybercrime that particularly affects youth.

Sexual exploitation Abuse of power or trust to coerce or manipulate someone into sexual activity. Online sexual exploitation of minors includes grooming, sextortion, and distribution of sexual images.

Shame Painful emotion resulting from the perception that one has violated social norms or failed to meet expectations. Cyberbullying and public humiliation online can trigger intense shame.

Silos Isolated groups or communities with limited interaction with others. Digital filter bubbles create information silos that limit exposure to diverse perspectives.

Sleep disruption Interference with sleep quality and quantity. Excessive screen time, notifications, and blue light exposure can disrupt sleep, which is essential for adolescent development and mental health.

Social cognitive theory Psychological theory proposing that behavior is influenced by personal factors, environmental factors, and reciprocal interactions between them. Social Cognitive Theory explains how digital environments shape behavior through modeling and reinforcement.

Social comparison Tendency to evaluate oneself by comparing to others. Social media amplifies social comparison through curated presentations of others' lives, contributing to anxiety and depression.

Social contagion Spread of behaviors, emotions, or ideas through social networks. Social contagion can be positive (the spread of prosocial behaviors) or negative (the spread of harmful behaviors).

Social influence The process through which individuals' attitudes and behaviors are shaped by others. Digital platforms amplify social influence through likes, shares, and algorithmic amplification.

Social media Digital platforms that enable users to create, share, and interact with content and other users. Social media is central to how many youth form identities and relationships.

Social proof Tendency to assume that if many people are doing something, it must be correct or appropriate. Digital platforms exploit social proof through likes, shares, and user counts.

Social withdrawal Reduction in social interaction and engagement with others. Excessive digital engagement or cyberbullying can lead to social withdrawal and isolation.

Socioeconomic status (SES) Position in social hierarchy based on income, education, and occupation. SES influences access to technology, digital skills, and vulnerability to online harms.

Stakeholder engagement Involvement of individuals and groups affected by technology in its design and governance. Stakeholder engagement, including youth voices, is essential for ethical technology development.

Stigma Negative attitudes and discrimination directed at individuals with certain characteristics or conditions. Mental health stigma can prevent youth from seeking help, particularly online.

Suicidal ideation Thoughts about suicide or self-harm. Cyberbullying and other online harms increase the risk of suicidal ideation among vulnerable youth.

Surveillance Systematic monitoring of individuals' activities, communications, and location. Commercial surveillance and government surveillance raise concerns about privacy and freedom.

Sustainable development goals (SDGs) United Nations goals for global development, including quality education, good health and well-being, and reduced inequalities. This book connects digital well-being to SDGs 4 and 3.

Symbolic interactionism Sociological perspective proposing that meaning is created through social interaction and the interpretation of symbols. Symbolic interactionism helps explain how digital identity is constructed through interaction.

T

Takeaway Summary of key points from a section or chapter. Takeaways throughout this book highlight essential concepts for the reader's understanding.

Targeted advertising Advertising tailored to individuals based on their data, behavior, and predicted preferences. Targeted advertising enables the manipulation and exploitation of psychological vulnerabilities.

Theory of planned behavior Psychological theory proposing that behavior is determined by intention, which is influenced by attitudes, subjective norms, and perceived behavioral control. The Theory of Planned Behavior explains how people make digital engagement decisions.

Therapeutic alliance Collaborative relationship between therapist and client characterized by trust, mutual respect, and shared goals. Therapeutic alliance is important for treatment effectiveness and may be compromised by AI-mediated interactions.

Tradwife phenomenon Trend among some young women, particularly on social media, of promoting traditional gender roles, domesticity, and submission to male authority. The Tradwife phenomenon represents the convergence of personality, gender, culture, and algorithmic amplification.

Transparency Openness about how systems work, what data is collected, and how decisions are made. Transparency is essential for user understanding and trust in AI systems.

Trauma Psychological injury resulting from exposure to overwhelming stress or adverse events. Cyberbullying and online harassment can cause trauma, particularly in vulnerable individuals.

Trust Confidence in the reliability, honesty, and competence of others or systems. Trust is essential for healthy relationships and effective use of technology.

Trustworthiness Quality of being reliable, honest, and worthy of confidence. Trustworthiness in AI systems requires transparency, accountability, and demonstrated commitment to user well-being.

U

Unmet needs Healthcare or social needs that are not being met by existing services. AI-assisted mental health tools can help address unmet needs for mental health support.

Usability testing Evaluation of how easily users can understand and use a system. Usability testing is important for ensuring AI systems are understandable and accessible to diverse users.

User autonomy The capacity and right of users to make informed decisions about their digital engagement and data use. User autonomy is a core principle of ethical AI.

User experience (UX) Overall experience of users when interacting with a system, including ease of use, satisfaction, and achievement of goals. User experience design should prioritize user well-being, not just engagement.

User feedback loop A Mechanism for collecting and responding to user input about system performance and satisfaction. User feedback loops are essential for identifying problems and improving systems.

V

Variable reward schedule An Unpredictable pattern of rewards that increases engagement and persistence. Variable reward schedules are used in digital platforms to create addictive engagement patterns.

Vulnerability Susceptibility to harm or exploitation. Vulnerability to online harms is influenced by individual characteristics, developmental stage, and environmental factors.

Vulnerable populations Groups at increased risk of harm due to characteristics such as age, disability, mental health condition, or marginalized identity. Vulnerable populations require special safeguards in digital environments.

W

Well-being State of physical, mental, social, and emotional health and flourishing. Digital well-being is a key focus of this book.

Wellness Proactive approach to health emphasizing prevention and positive health practices. Digital wellness includes healthy technology habits and balance.

Y

Youth Individuals in the developmental period of adolescence and young adulthood, typically ages 10–24. Youth are the focus of this book due to their unique developmental characteristics and digital engagement patterns.

Youth co-design A Participatory design approach in which young people collaborate with designers and policymakers to develop digital platforms and policies that affect them. Youth co-design ensures that youth voices are heard and their needs are addressed.

Youth-centered AI Artificial intelligence systems designed with youth needs, values, and well-being as central considerations. Youth-centered AI includes safeguards for developmental vulnerabilities and opportunities for youth agency.

Z

Zero-knowledge proof A Cryptographic technique that allows verification of information without revealing the information itself. Zero-knowledge proofs can enhance privacy in digital systems.

INDEX

Note: **Bold** page numbers refer to tables and *italic* page numbers refer to figures.

www.ingramcontent.com/pod-product-compliance
Ingram Content Group UK Ltd.
Pitfield, Milton Keynes, MK11 3LW, UK
UKHW020156200926
475702UK00016B/2728
* 9 7 8 1 0 4 1 1 0 9 6 0 0 *